258

To Faith,
Some day I'll
see one of your
pictures in
this book.
Love
from,

Rogier van der Weyden. The Annunciation. c. 1460. Metropolitan Museum of Art, New York City. (Metropolitan Museum)

ART
THROUGH THE AGES

Helen Gardner

THIRD EDITION

NEW YORK

HARCOURT, BRACE AND COMPANY

CONTENTS

Mediterranean Art

Far Eastern Art

American Art

PART TWO: MEDIEVAL ART

European and Near Eastern Art

Far Eastern Art

African and Oceanian Art

American Art

PART THREE: RENAISSANCE ART

Renaissance Art in Italy

Renaissance Art in Northern, Western, and Eastern Europe

Renaissance Art in the Americas

PART FOUR: MODERN ART

Nineteenth-Century Art

Twentieth-Century Art

Appendix

PREFACE

B ECAUSE today and only today, the concept of one total world inescapably thrusts itself forward, I have been motivated, in preparing this third edition of *Art Through the Ages*, both in the incorporation of new material and in the reorganization of the old, by a desire to present a world panorama of art; to look at the world horizontally; to present a view of Ancient, Medieval, Renaissance, and Modern Art, each as a whole the world over; to show where contacts did or did not exist, and how the world of the relatively isolated cultures of antiquity has gradually become one world, with national barriers so breached that we are now talking of international styles in art.

History of art thus viewed does not organize with neat precision into the four chronological cross sections mentioned above. All cultures are not at the same stage of evolution at the same time; some are long-lived, while others are short; some are in the archaic stage, while others are at a climax. Yet whatever their relative state of evolution, the contacts which they make are highly important. Even though every scheme of organization contains inconsistencies and disadvantages, the panorama becomes particularly valuable at a time when the world has shrunk to its present size; it helps to break down our Europocentric attitude toward art, to reorient our thinking, and to enlarge our horizons.

The *Introduction* I have enlarged along the same lines as in the second edition, that is, I have isolated the problem of form, as a necessary preliminary for any discussion of the arts, historical or critical.

Part One presents a panorama of the arts in ancient times and shows how great cultures arose and evolved on all the continents, largely in isolation yet with some vital contacts that affected the forms of art expression.

Part Two continues the panorama through the Middle Ages when the contacts between Asia, Northern Africa, and Europe became more pronounced and a lively intercourse brought about mutual exchanges of ideas, motifs, and forms.

Part Three shows the Renaissance as the period when the world began to shrink at an ever accelerating rate. This was the age of discovery, exploration, and colonization. It witnessed the transplanting of European arts to large sections of the world, most important of which was the hitherto unknown western hemisphere, where the conflict or assimilation of European arts with the indigenous American arts transformed them into American-European styles.

Part Four reveals the world, through unbelievable advances in transportation and communication, as one world in which the nations are becoming acquainted with each other, are learning from each other, and are to a considerable extent producing works of art which, despite national divergencies, come within an international framework.

After years of experience and experimentation in teaching history of art in the School of the Art Institute of Chicago, I am still of the opinion that the most effective presentation of the large amount of material involved is the chronological survey. In the first place, each culture takes its position in historical sequence. In the second place, the influences of one culture on another within an era can be clearly discerned. In the third place, the influence of earlier periods on later ones can be seen; for example, the influences which classical art exerted on the Renaissance and post-Renaissance periods, or the influences of the ancient Far East, of Egypt, and of the primitive peoples on modern art. Finally, each culture is analyzed for the characteristic art forms which give substance to its own individual essence in a manner known as its style.

I hardly need mention that in covering so wide a field in one volume, it has been necessary both to limit the material to the visual arts and to stress the significant movements. In general the objective has been to focus attention upon works of art as art and to omit biographical and anecdotal matter, not because such material has no legitimate place, for it is frequently illuminating, but because it is secondary and can be found easily in almost any library. Controversial questions of attribution and influence have been omitted as belonging properly to specialized books. The space thus gained has been used for analysis of the few works discussed, in the conviction that thorough study of a few works is more helpful than the recital of names and dates.

An indispensable part of the study of art is the illustration. Few works, therefore, are discussed for which there is no illustration for reference. The new system of numbering the illustrations according to the numbers of the pages on which they occur is expected to facilitate greatly ease of reference.

The bibliographies have been compiled with a well-equipped but not specialized art library in mind. Hence, rare and costly books have usually been omitted, and among the works in foreign languages only a few which are particularly desirable for their illustrations have been included.

The writing of so comprehensive a book as well as the assembling and sifting of so large a mass of details make necessary the advice and coöperation of many individuals. Such coöperation has been given cordially and generously on the part of individuals, museums, and publishers. For criticism on the manuscript of the first edition the author was indebted to Professors T. G. Allen, J. H. Breasted, W. E. Clark, Edith Rickert, Walter Sargent, and E. H. Wilkins of the University of Chicago; to Professor Grant Showerman of the University of Wisconsin; and to Mr. R. B. Harshe and Mr. C. F. Kelley of the Art Institute of Chicago; for criticism of the second edition to Miss Kathleen Blackshear of the Art Institute of Chicago, Mr. James C.

Boudreau of Pratt Institute, Professor B. M. Donaldson of the University of Michigan, and Professor F. J. Roos, Jr. of the University of Illinois; for criticism of the third edition to Mr. C. F. Kelley of the Art Institute of Chicago, Professors G. G. Cameron and K. C. Seele of the University of Chicago, Professor Ralph Fanning of Ohio State University, and Professor James C. Boudreau of Pratt Institute.

The task of securing illustrations was largely the work of Harold Allen. This task was lightened appreciably by the generous assistance of individuals, libraries, museums, and publishers, acknowledgment of which is made with each cut. Especial help on the illustrations as well as in details of research was generously given by Miss Etheldred Abbot, Librarian Emeritus, and Miss Ruth E. Schoneman, Librarian, and their assistants of the Reference and Photograph Departments of the Ryerson and Burnham Libraries of the Art Institute of Chicago.

For the new analytical drawings of paintings and sculpture the author is indebted to Miss Kathleen Blackshear, Michaill Waskowsky, and Harold Allen; for other new drawings and maps to Harold Allen; for bibliographical research to Miss Edith Prior of the Ryerson Library and Harold Allen; for proof to Miss Kathleen Blackshear and Harold Allen.

H. G.

Publishers' Note

The text of *Art Through the Ages:* Third Edition was in galley proof at the time of Miss Gardner's death. Thus the text in this edition, including the foregoing preface, is as Miss Gardner wrote it. Fortunately, her close co-workers, Miss Kathleen Blackshear and Harold Allen, were in a position to carry on and see the work through the press.

INTRODUCTION: THE FORMS OF ART

The Nature of Art

WHAT is art? We do not know. The essential nature of that mysterious, intangible, indefinable something that we call art baffles us. On the other hand, we do know definitely that from the earliest times until today human beings the world over have given expression to human experience in concrete tangible forms which we call works of art. And we know that art is essential to man's well-being. Take away the finest of our buildings, our pottery, pictures, music, poetry, drama, and the dance. What kind of life would result?

Thus works of art exist and always have existed, and have been essential to man's well-being. They are human experiences translated into forms that we apprehend through our senses. We see pictures and dances; we see and hear literature; we hear music; we feel the surfaces of a carving or a jar, and the texture of a piece of satin or velvet. But that is not all. Our sensory impressions and our perceptions lead to emotional reactions, and intelligence enters to rationalize. Sensation, emotion, and intelligence all enter into the process of understanding.

How, then, shall we go about understanding? There can be no cut-and-dried formula. The very complexity of the art object requires many approaches, no one of which has priority. Some people approach a painting from one angle, some from another, each according to his temperament and habit of mind. All that matters is that a person shall eventually approach it from all angles, so that his understanding of it can be full and intelligent.

Hence in approaching a work of art, it is well to keep in mind its chief facets: that it is a form created by some artist; that it has a cultural or time context; a content or subject matter; and usually a function or use.

Let us examine these a little more closely. Every work of art is a form, a living structure possessed of an organic oneness that sets it apart from other objects and marks it as a work of art. Who created this form? It was some artist. That is, a work of art is the objectification of a human experience. The artist is one who "selects and rearranges details from life experience into concrete form." (Thomas Munro) Thus his creative activity is synthic — that is, it consists of selecting parts and welding them into an integrated whole. The intangible quality of this oneness — that is, whether it has an inner vitality or not — determines whether the artist has succeeded: "only that which is utterly intangible matters." (D. H. Lawrence) A work of art may be above adverse criticism technically and at the same time be devoid of life. That statement is aptly illustrated by the Chinese saying that to paint a tiger successfully, the artist must have within himself the potentiality to be one.

The observer, the critic, on the other hand, approaches the work of art from the opposite direction, the analytical. He sees the completed work of art, the integrated form, and in trying to understand it he attempts to see how the artist put the parts together to attain the observable results. While it is impossible for one person to relive another's experience, the intelligent critic comes as close to that experience as is humanly possible, and by training he is able to feel the quality of its inner intangible essence.

A work of art, then, is a form created by the artist out of human experience. At the same time it has a cultural context. It exists in time, and its form reflects the forces of that time — social, economic, political, and religious. From this angle the form reveals a style — a mode of the time of its creation, a mode that colors all works of art of the time so that together they express the essence of the time. Buildings, paintings, sculpture, pottery, literature, music, drama — all the arts reflect the mode of their age. Each elucidates the others. A mode or style, however, like time, is never static. It evolves, attains its maturity, and declines. So a work of art may conform to the prevailing style; it may revert to a previous style; or it may be revolutionary in that it looks forward, experiments, and embodies new elements which foretell the approach of a new style.

Again, works of art have content. Even such objects as masks, pottery, and textile designs that are abstract or geometric and seem merely decorative may actually contain profound human meaning. This content bears a direct relation to the time of their creation. It was not by accident that Renaissance painters painted Madonnas, that modern painters produce still life, abstract, or nonobjective paintings, and that the Chinese developed the landscape scroll. It was not by accident that the design on early Chinese bronzes

and on some American Indian pottery relates to clouds and rain, or that Mayan carvings so frequently repeat the motif of the plumed serpent and the jaguar.

Another approach to a work of art is to consider its function or purpose. Probably a large majority of works of art were created to serve a definite purpose in a definite place. This statement hardly seems valid to one walking through a museum. A museum, however, is at best an artificial, though necessary, storehouse of objects taken away from their original place and time; but when each object is traced back to its origin, the reasons for its creation and for its form become clearer. Paintings and statues belonged to certain buildings, and rugs to certain palaces; Indian jars were made to hold water carried to the top of the mesa, and the tall slender Chinese vase was used to pour the wine at the rites of ancestor worship. The function of buildings we usually take for granted. But equally functional are many pictures, statues, and textiles, as well as much pottery and metalwork.

The Nature of Form

OF these essential approaches to a work of art, we shall isolate for discussion the first — that of form and the ability to see form. "Form" has many meanings. Here — in fact all through this book — it is used in its widest sense: that of a total organic structure, a synthesis of all the elements of which that structure is constructed, and the manner in which these elements are related and united to create its distinctive character. "Organic," according to Webster, means "Possessed of a complete structure comparable to that of a human being; forming a totality, in which the relation of the parts involves relation to the whole." "Structure," according to the same authority, means "Something constructed or built; the arrangement of the parts . . . in a substance or body." This is the meaning of the broadly inclusive term "form." The Chinese have a saying that we see with our ears. "Chesterton once observed shrewdly," says J. B. Priestley, "that there was a great difference between an eager man who wanted to read a book and a tired man who wanted a book to read." Reading a book, listening to music, or seeing a picture requires concentrated activity of both the emotions and the intelligence. Listen to a piece of music. You hear a succession of sounds, at times harmonious, at times discordant, which may produce a certain mood, somber or gay. But so far you have penetrated the music's minimum significance only. It is so little in relation to what is there. You may be too incapable, or perhaps too lazy, to penetrate farther. If, on the other hand, you listen attentively enough to catch a melody, perhaps just a few bars, to hear it again in another key and again in its original form; or if you have noticed a second melody with which the first interweaves, and if you have discovered that the quality of each varies according to the instrument on which it is played — if you have heard all this and realize that these interweavings, repetitions, and variations cohere into a pattern of rhythmic movement, then you are on your way to understanding music.

So with a piece of literature. A writer uses words; he combines them into phrases, phrases into sentences, and sentences into paragraphs or verses; and by repetition, variation, and movement toward a climax he creates a pattern which not only conveys the content but, because of its inherent capacity to arouse emotional response, vivifies the content, gives it a dynamic quality that is not inherent in the mere meaning of the words and the sentences. Thus music is not a mere succession of sounds, nor literature one of words alone, but a *related* and integrated succession.

Try looking at a picture. If you see it only for its subject matter, as an illustration or as a historical document, or for its associational ideas or its general mood, then you have not grasped its maximum significance. Look again. Your curiosity might ask *why* it creates a certain mood, a certain reaction in you. Now you may see that a certain color — blue for example — dominates; that it appears in a large area and is repeated in several small areas; that it is now light in tone, now darker. You also notice areas of yellow; and you observe that the blues and the yellows seem to play over against each other, and that each seems to enhance the brilliance of the other. Or you may notice a brightly lighted area, perhaps triangular in shape, and your eye moves from one part of the picture to another under the guidance of repeated triangular areas. Each color and each light area appears and reappears in repetition and variation, like the themes in music, so related and interwoven that together they form the same kind of coherent whole that a musical composition does. Watch an artist who begins his picture by organizing his canvas into color areas with no visible representational content. Then see how a light area becomes a house; a blue spot, a figure; and a dark-green mass, trees. But the basic color organization remains to vivify the content, to give it a life not secured by a mere imitation of nature. That is the difference between art and nature.

In these three arts — and it is equally true in all the arts — we find a basic structure that not only conveys and vitalizes the content, but of itself delights the eye or the ear. And if one is to understand art, he must be able to *see* this structure, to see it with the artist's vision.[1] "In truth I have painted by opening my eyes day and night on the perceptible world, and also by closing them from time to time that I might better see the vision blossom and submit itself to orderly arrangement."[2]

The Elements of Form

WHEN an artist creates a work of art, he gives substance to his concept in tangible visible material. For this purpose the world offers him innumerable possibilities. His choice, however, is not left to chance. Each material has its own potentialities and limitations, and it is part of the artist's creative activity to determine whether a certain material is suitable for the expression of his concept and whether he has technical proficiency in handling this material. The character of the material, and the processes and tools with which it is worked, are vital determinants in the character of the form: the way in which hammer and chisel slowly carve a figure from unyielding stone, or the fingers swiftly build a form from yielding clay. Nor are materials interchangeable. A theme suitable for

[1] From this point, because of lack of space, we shall discuss visual form only. But we suggest that the reader apply the method outlined to the arts of music, literature, drama, and the dance.

[2] A statement by Rouault quoted by Monroe Wheeler in *Painters and Sculptors of Modern America*, Thomas Y. Crowell, 1942, p. viii. On the artist's vision see Roger Fry, *Vision and Design*, "The Artist's Vision"; Leo Stein, *The A-B-C of Æsthetics*, "Pictorial Seeing" and "To Make Pictures by Seeing Them"; Thomas Munro, *Scientific Method in Æsthetics*, "The Analysis of Form"; Ralph Pearson, *Experiencing Pictures*.

pigment could hardly be successful if carried out in stone. To see materials as a contributing element in the total form is a prime prerequisite for understanding.

Other elements or components that artists use to create forms and which one must train one's eye to see are line, light and dark, color, texture, areas, mass and volume, space and movement (Fig. 5A). If an artist is working in two dimensions — width and height — and observing surface continuity, as in painting or tiles or textiles, he will chiefly use line, light and dark color, texture, and areas. Except as an illusion, actual depth does not occur. If he is working in three dimensions — width, height, and depth — as in building, sculpture, pottery, or basketry, he works basically with mass, volume, and space in addition to the elements of two-dimensional art. The fourth dimension — movement in space — so fundamental in music, literature, the drama, and the dance, is only suggested in the visual arts, though it may actually exist in sculpture.

These components provide the artist with his means for creating forms which have coherence, unity with variety, balance, and emphasis. Each element, however, has an inherent character with its own potentialities and limitations; and the artist chooses for his use according to the nature of the project in hand, his own individuality, and the controlling forces of his environment.

LINE

This is an elastic term. A line may be an edge, a meeting of areas. In a building, the edge where planes or surfaces meet is, for practical esthetic purposes, a line. Line may be a contour, in which case it delineates an object. It may be sculptural; that is, of such a quality that it suggests mass. Or it may be calligraphic, an element of enrichment of surface (Fig. 488A)[1]; if it is, though it may serve also as an edge or a contour, its main emphasis is upon itself for its own sake, for movement or pattern. The character of line is dependent partly upon the implement with which it is made (brush, burin, chalk, silver-point) and partly upon the personality and the skill of the artist. It may be broad or thin, sharp or blurred, firm or wavering, tight or loose, delicate or bold, energetic or weak (Figs. 737A, 748A, 749A).

Whatever its function and character, line suggests movement in some direction: vertical, horizontal, diagonal, or curved, each of which produces a certain emotional reaction. We all know the uplift of the vertical (Fig. 713A), the tranquillity of the horizontal (Fig. 711A), the dynamism of the diagonal (Fig. 760A), and the suavity of the curve (Fig. 674A). It is not only the effect of line direction of which the artist makes use, but also the relationships that he sets up among the various lines. They may repeat or parallel one another for a harmonious effect (Fig. 730A), or oppose one another for needed contrast (Fig. 736A); they may radiate from a certain spot or converge upon it for emphasis (Fig. 407A). A diagonal may give the needed verve to a tranquil balance of vertical and horizontal (Fig. 612A); a succession of diagonals constituting a zigzag may create a highly dramatic effect (Fig. 423A). Lines may be continuous or broken, and when they are broken one may still feel the continuity of the movement even though the actual line is invisible. It is seldom that only one kind of line is used in a design. More likely two or more interplay, with varying degrees of harmony and contrast, like themes in a musical composition.

[1] The arabic number of a figure is that of the page on which it occurs.

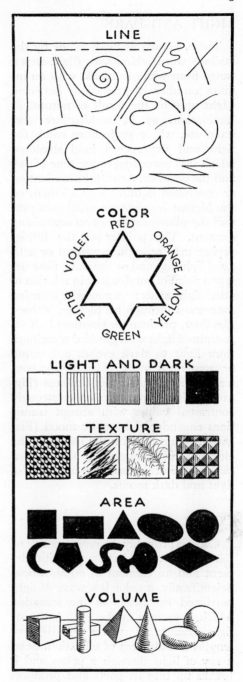

[A] *The Elements of Form. All visual design consists of combinations of these fundamental components.*

LIGHT AND DARK

These, known as "values" or by the Italian word *chiaroscuro* (light-dark), range from white to black, with an infinite number of gradations between. Light may be the result of natural illumination, as in architecture and sculpture, where projections catch the light and depressions hold shadows, which shift according to the time of day and the weather. Artificial illumination or controlled lighting is an element of the highest importance to the sculptor and the photographer as an organizing element. The painter or the lithographer may reproduce natural or artificial lighting, and at the same time use it as a point of emphasis or in relation to other light areas as a means of securing movement through his picture. Values, like lines, produce an emotional effect. A diffused light with gradual transitions from light to dark evokes a tranquil or mysterious mood (Fig. 687A); contrasted values suggest restlessness (Fig. 512A); highly concentrated or strongly contrasted values with abrupt transitions engender a dramatic mood (Fig. 566A). Again, as with the use of all the elements, what matters is the *relationships* of the areas, and the interplay of light and dark motifs.

COLOR

Color is probably the most emotive of the elements. It is both a scientific element and an element of organization. Scientifically, a color is a wave of light perceived by means of the sensation which it arouses in the eye. A ray of light consists of waves of different lengths and degrees of vibration. Send a ray of light through a prism and it breaks up into its parts and produces the spectrum. When light strikes a surface, that surface may reflect all the waves, or colors, equally, and the eye registers a white surface. It may absorb all the waves except the green, which it reflects. Then the eye sees that surface as green. It may absorb all the rays except the blue and the red. The surface is then violet. Individuals vary widely in their sensory reaction to light, from hypersensitivity, which at times causes violent reactions, all the way to complete lack of sensation. A person may be blind to one color alone, or he may be totally blind to all colors and consequently see the world in terms of white, black, and the intermediate grays. Thus the nature of light and the sense of sight are both involved in the science of color.

As an element for the artist's use, a knowledge — intuitive, if not scientific — of the spectrum, its composition, and the interrelationship of its components is essential. It is convenient to arrange the colors of the spectrum in a wheel (Fig. 7A). Of these colors, three are indivisible and so are known as the primaries: blue, red, and yellow. If the primaries are mixed, they produce the secondaries or binaries: blue plus yellow equals green; red plus yellow, orange; red plus blue, violet. Further mixture makes possible an infinite number of colors, depending upon the proportion of each component.

Notice on the color wheel that red is opposite green, and orange opposite blue. Opposites are called complements. If they are mixed, they soften each other; if mixed in equal proportions, they produce a gray, a neutral which can be vibrating and elusive, as a gray compounded of black and white is not. If complementaries are juxtaposed, each intensifies the other and produces brilliance and sharp contrast. On the other hand, colors near each other on the wheel, called adjacents, (blue, blue-green, and green, for example) produce a harmonious effect. However, it is not only the relationships of the colors that concern the artist. Each color has three qualities: hue, value, and intensity. Hue is the name of the color: blue, red, blue-green, orange-red. Value is the amount of light in a hue according to a scale range varying from white to black: light greens, middle greens, dark greens. Intensity, also called chroma or saturation, is the color strength or brilliance: a brilliant yellow or a dull yellow.

Another attribute of color which concerns the artist is its warmth or coolness. Orange and its adjacents are warm; blue and its adjacents are cool; green is warm as it approaches yellow and cool as it approaches blue. Furthermore, colors appear to advance or retreat according as they are warm or cool. Red lettering on a poster looks as if it were in relief; the blue around Cézanne's apples draws the eye back into space and gives the apple depth and solidity. Thus color in itself has the capacity to express depth — a capacity that is now being used in interior architecture to increase spaciousness and height; for example, by the use of a retreating color on walls and ceiling.

An additional attribute is the psychic effect of colors. We recall the cheer of yellow, if not too intense; the quieting effect of blue, the excitingness of red. Thus a dominant color alone can set the emotional quality, the mood, of a work of art.

But, as with line and with light and dark, what matters most is the relationships among the colors. A design composed of adjacents will have a tranquil harmonious effect; it may, in fact, seem weak unless a certain quality of the complementary hues contributes enough contrast to give the design virility. On the other hand, a design composed of complementaries frequently needs some areas of adjacents to soften the tension which results from the use of complementaries alone. Thus most color schemes present major and

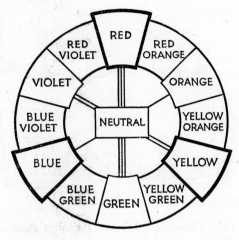

[A] *Color Wheel.*

minor themes, which interplay, like major and minor themes of volumes, lines, and lights and darks. The color scheme which an artist selects depends upon the idea to be expressed. For a tranquil theme he is not likely to use a dynamic color contrast, nor for a dramatic subject, a quiet color harmony.

TEXTURE

Every material has a texture, or structural quality, that determines the character of its surface, which is apprehended by our sense of touch. It may be hard or soft, rough or smooth, warm or cold, grained or pebbly. But the eye too seems to share in apprehending these qualities. A fabric *looks*, as well as feels, rough or smooth. A rough surface creates light and shadow; a smooth surface means the absence of shadow and often the presence of reflected light, as in satin. Color also varies according to the texture of the surface upon which it falls. Compare three pieces of cloth of exactly the same hue: a satin, a velvet, and a wool. The hue will vary both in quality and in value because the different textures have different degrees of reflective power. Thus we have a

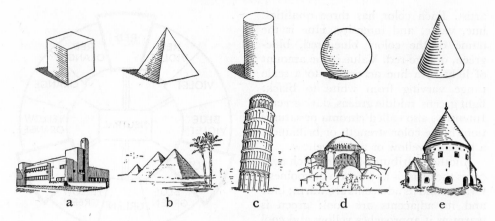

[A] *Geometric Solids and Buildings Based upon Them.* a. *cube.* b. *pyramid.* c. *cylinder.*
d. *sphere.* e. *cone.*

visual equivalent of the tactile sensation, and with it an enlargement of the potentiality of line and color. A painter or an engraver may use lines or motifs to create a textural effect whose purpose is to enrich the surface (Figs. 211A and B) or to carry movement. Another way in which texture is used is in such imitations of actual textures as are found in some realistic paintings. Such illusionistic reproduction of texture often serves the same esthetic functions as the nonnaturalistic textures just mentioned. Again, the important factor is the *relationships* of the areas. The builder, the sculptor, the potter, the painter, in fact all artists, make effective use of texture in playing off contrasting smooth and rough surfaces (Fig. 718A). In interior architecture texture is a highly essential element where several materials are combined for their textural effects as well as for their functions.

AREA, MASS, AND VOLUME

These we associate primarily with geometry. Areas are two-dimensional and in shape are most often square, circular, elliptical, triangular, or amoeboid. At times the shapes are precise, at times only suggestive. By means of line, light and dark, and color, the artist creates areas which serve as thematic material. For example, he may base his design upon the interplay of triangles, or of triangles and amoeboid areas. Mass, with its weight and solidity, exists in space. Volume is mass given definite shape, which may be solid or hollow. Volumes are rectangular, spherical, cylindrical, conoid, or pyramidal, and serve as thematic material for the three-dimensional arts. A building, for example, may consist basically of a group of rectangular volumes (Fig. 96A), or a piece of pottery, of a combination of cylinders and a sphere (Fig. 241A). In using volumes the architect is dealing with actual space — not with the illusion of space found in painting — so that space itself becomes a primary organizing element. It may be interior space created by the surfaces of the volume; or it may be external space — that is, how the volume is related to surrounding space, as a building to its environment. It may be the space determined by a rectangular block of stone or by a cylindrical block of wood, each of which will affect differently the sculptor's organization of a sculptural figure.

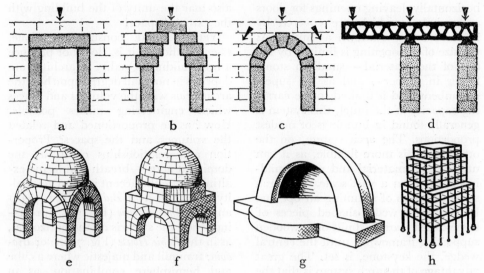

[A] *Architectural Construction.* a. *Lintel* (*Fig. 118A*); b. *Corbeling* (*Fig. 110A*); c. *Round Arch* (*Fig. 174D*); d. *Cantilever* (*Fig. 705A*); e. *Dome on Pendentives* (*Fig. 261A*); f. *Dome on Squinches* (*Fig. 290A*); g. *Concrete* (*Fig. 714A*); h. *Steel* (*Fig. 712A*).

Form in the Visual Arts

ARCHITECTURAL FORM

A building is a mass existing in space. This mass consists of one or more volumes which, being hollow, create interior space, a space for human activity. With the rarest exceptions, no building exists for its own sake. On the contrary, the human activity for which it was constructed is not only its reason for being, but a determinant of its plan and form. If, for example, it is to house large crowds — a temple, a transportation terminal, a factory — it will provide large unbroken spaces for these purposes. If it is to be a house, or a building filled with small business offices, it will divide the interior space into many small units.

Another determinant is its material, which prescribes the mode of its construction. Building materials are various: stone, brick, adobe, tile, wood, glass, steel, concrete, plywood, plastics, to mention only the most important. Each of these has its own inherent qualities of strength, durability, elasticity, size, color, and texture.

A further determinant of architectural form is the site. It makes a great difference whether a building stands in a crowded city or in the open country; whether on flat land or in the hills; whether in a warm climate or a cool one.

Given the function, the material, and the site, how is a building constructed? Its creation begins with a plan, evolved from function, material, and site, and is the result of two activities: mechanical and esthetic. The mechanical activity is engineering, and its function is to give the structure stability by controlling and balancing the physical forces of weight, pressure, and resistance. From this mechanical angle, there are four kinds of construction: lintel, arch, concrete, and steel (Fig. 9A).

In the lintel system courses are laid

horizontally, leaving openings for doors and windows which are covered by horizontal blocks known as lintels. As the size of the opening is limited by the size of the material — small in stone, larger in timber — and as the super-incumbent load is limited to the carry-ing capacity of the lintel, this system is generally found in buildings of modest proportions. The arch system, on the other hand, is more flexible, as it can utilize small material and make build-ing possible on a vast scale. The arch system consists of spanning an opening by means of wedge-shaped pieces of stone called *voussoirs*, built on a wooden supporting framework until the central wedge, the keystone, is set. The great advantage of the arch system is that the load or thrust of the superstructure does not bear down vertically only, but out-ward also, so that a much greater load can be carried than in the lintel sys-tem, provided the outward thrust is sufficiently balanced by buttressing.

In concrete construction a hollow framework is built, into which concrete in a semiliquid state is poured. When this has hardened, the framework is removed and the result is a solid, homo-geneous structure of great strength and durability.

Steel construction means erecting a framework of steel beams; this, because of the tensile strength of the material, is sufficient to hold floors, partitions, and roof, and thus has no need of supporting walls, but only of a protective sheathing. Steel is generally used with reinforced concrete — concrete into which steel or iron bars have been imbedded in order to make strong foundations. An important extension of steel construc-tion is the cantilever — a horizontal beam supported at one end only, yet sufficient in strength to support floors and walls. This method eliminates a multiplicity of supporting members which not only obstruct the view but also mar the unity of the building with the external space.

Yet adequate construction alone, essential though it is, does not produce a fine building. Quality in architecture depends in no small degree upon how the artist deals with the volumes and spaces which engineering makes possible. How has he proportioned and related the volumes and the spaces? Propor-tion and relationships constitute the dominant note — breath-taking and ex-alting where the accent is upon vertical-ity, as in the *RCA Building* (Fig. 713A) and the *Amiens Nave* (Fig. 345A); relax-ing when the stress is on the horizontal, as in the *Robie House* (Fig. 706A) or *Byo-doin;* tranquil and majestic where a cube and hemisphere combination, as in *Santa Sophia* (Fig. 259A). The surfaces of these volumes, however, are not un-broken. For practical purposes a build-ing must have doors and windows; and as light envelops a building and pene-trates its interior, the light and shadow created by these openings play an im-portant role in breaking up surfaces into effective designs. Are these open-ings — collectively known as fenestra-tion — statically regular, or dynamically varied with arresting accents? Are they vertical or horizontal in pro-portion, and do they contain thematic material for repetition, such as a curve or a pointed arch? Is there any sculp-ture on the building to produce move-ment by its broken light and shade, and to inject additional line direction, such as the curve or the diagonal, into an otherwise rectilinear composition? Be-sides line direction, and light and dark, the color and the texture of the ma-terials contribute to the ensemble. A certain unity and solidity may result from the use of one material alone, and vivifying contrasts may result from such combinations as stone and brick, wood and stucco, marble and bronze, or steel, glass, and concrete.

SCULPTURAL FORM

Sculpture, like architecture, is an art of volume and space; but, unlike architecture, it aims at arrangements of volumes in space to be seen externally only, like the exterior of a building. In this respect a building may be sculptural. Most statues, on the other hand, notably those of stone or wood, are solid. Genetically, they are masses of material organized. Their organization, however, is subject to the space occupied by the original mass. A sculptor confronted by a block of stone or a piece of timber may retain much of the mass, and his statue will then be solid and weighty; or he may lighten the mass by taking away a considerable amount of material, even to the point of perforating the mass and thus securing more movement through space. The bronze-worker, on the other hand, starting with no mass at all, constructs a mass out of clay, and in the process creates both the space and the volumes organized within it.

All sculpture, whether of the stone or the clay type, is an art of mass, volume, contour, and surface treatment. It is likewise an art that gains in power in proportion to its simplification, clarity, and monumentality. But in contrast to architecture, it is usually representational, and strikingly limited to the human and animal figure, which afford the sculptor possibilities for complex arrangements.

The complexity of sculptural form admits many approaches. Its general forms, its materials and the processes of working them, its function, and its site are some of the more important. In general, sculpture falls into three classes: in the round, relief, and intaglio. "In the round" means a three-dimensional figure which you can walk around and see from numerous angles. Relief is sculpture in which the figures or shapes are attached to a background from which they project. It is called high relief if they project boldly; low relief, or bas-relief, if they project slightly. The third, and less common, class is intaglio, in which the figures are sunk into the background.

Depending upon materials and processes, sculpture can be carved out of hard material, or it can be modeled in soft material and then fired, glazed, or cast in metal. As for function, a vast mass of sculpture has been created as a coherent part of a building, often of the same material — a fact that is determinant of its form. Again, much sculpture consists of isolated statues, though probably the majority of statues and reliefs have been made for some specific site — this again, whether outside or inside, was a vital element in the total form. These classifications and approaches should not be taken too rigidly, for they tend to impede a comprehensive grasp.

Let us look at sculpture in the round from various viewpoints — first, carving and its materials. Stone is and always has been universal. It is a hard, weighty, unyielding material, and though breakable has strength and durability. It comes in many shapes of various proportions, which limit the final form. Its texture is variable: fine, coarse, crystalline, striated. The tools with which stone is worked suit an obdurate medium: a wooden mallet, different steel chisels and drills, and abrasives for smoothing and polishing. Carving stone is a slow, laborious process that taxes physical strength as well as judgment. A false step may ruin a work. The character of both the material and the process inevitably influences the sculptor toward simplification of mass and elimination of detail. Carving is a process of subtraction. "I mean by sculpture," said Michelangelo, "that which is done by taking off. . . . The finest artist has no concept which the marble alone does not contain within itself."

To penetrate the block, and to extricate the figure as it were, the sculptor draws an outline on the block and with a point cuts away large chunks of stone. He thus lays bare the main masses of the figure. Then, with chisels and drills, he defines the form more in detail; and finally he may smooth or even polish it, or certain parts of it only. Frequently he leaves the chisel marks on some of the surfaces, to secure contrast of texture. In carving a figure the sculptor may work in from the sides as if he were carving a relief on each side of the block. By this procedure he creates a figure definitely rectangular in form, quiet, static, and monumental in effect (Fig. 13A). Or, disregarding the surfaces of the block, he may compose a figure whose parts move backward and forward or spirally through the mass of the material, and which create movement in space and a dynamic or restless effect (Fig. 13B).

Wood-carving corresponds to stone-carving, except that the material is softer and has a grain, which the carver must follow if he is to avoid splitting the wood, and which he can utilize effectively in his design. His chisels are sharper, though lighter, than those used in stone-carving. Because of the cylindrical nature of wood, many wood carvings are basically cylindrical in form (Fig. 778B).

Modeling, in distinction from the subtractive process of carving, is a process of addition, a building-up technique. Clay, the usual material, is one of the most yielding mediums, is responsive to a light touch, lends itself to improvisation, and invites fantasy as the fingers — the chief tool — are stimulated by its pliability. If the figure is of any considerable size, it must be built up on an armature. Otherwise the soft material would collapse. A certain amount of subtractive activity is possible when a sculptor, starting with a mass of clay, scoops out hollows and builds up projections, in this way producing movement inward and outward through the mass. Often one feels, if one does not actually see, traces of finger marks indicative of the process by which the artist attained a certain effect and without which he could not have attained this effect — an illustration of the significance of the technical process in the total expression.

The sculptor in clay is confronted with the problem of how to make the soft clay permanent. If the figure is small, he can hollow it out enough for firing, like pottery. If it is too large for this process, he can cast it in plaster or metal, of which bronze is the most common. An almost universal method is the *cire-perdue*, or wax-lost, process, in which a core of clay or some crude material approximates the ultimate form. Over this a coating of wax is laid, in which the sculptor completes the form with all its details. The wax is then covered with a coat of fine pipe clay of the consistency of cream, laid on with a brush very carefully so as to reproduce, when hardened, every minute detail of the wax. Successive coats are added, and then layers of coarse plaster until a thick firm shell is formed. Vent holes are left so that the wax can be drawn off when the mass is heated. Thus a thin space is left between the core and the pipe-clay mold, into which molten bronze is poured — a process requiring expert skill, for the metal must run into every tiny detail of the mold. When the metal has cooled and hardened, the shell is broken away, the core is dug out, the surface is finished and polished, and sometimes details are added by chasing. Bronze is a rigid, tough material which enables the artist to compose open designs not practicable

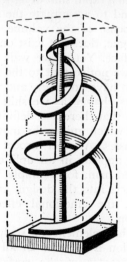

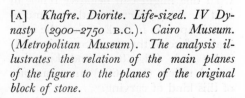

[A] *Khafre. Diorite. Life-sized. IV Dynasty (2900–2750 B.C.). Cairo Museum. (Metropolitan Museum). The analysis illustrates the relation of the main planes of the figure to the planes of the original block of stone.*

[B] *Michelangelo. Moses. Marble. Height c. 100 in. 1513–16. Church of San Pietro in Vincoli, Rome. The analysis illustrates an organization of backward and forward spiraling movements confined but not dominated by the planes of the original block.*

in stone. Its somber color produces strong contours, and strong contrasts of light and dark result from its reflective quality. It requires sharp edges in its details if they are to carry.

In creating a sculptural figure in any material, the artist is not imitating natural appearance, though nature is his starting-point. He is extracting from the figure certain arrangements of its parts — its head, torso, arms, and legs — using sometimes only one or two of these parts, sometimes all. Like the architect, he is dealing first with related volumes, chiefly cylindrical or spherical. In establishing relationships he makes use of light and dark, and line. Hollows hold shadow, like windows in a building; projections catch the light, and their alternation creates movement. If the surfaces are treated simply with but slight nuances, they accentuate the volume. If they are treated with naturalistic detail which results in a rapid shift of light and dark, they tend to accentuate the surface at the expense of the volume. Line, we may argue, does not exist on a rounding surface. Yet as we walk around a statue we notice that to the eye it appears to have contours, and that these contours change as we shift our position, so that there is a definitely linear quality which guides the movement of the masses. Another aspect of linear quality appears in an uplifted or outstretched arm, for example, in that it introduces into the design, as in architecture, the emotional effect of line direction.

Another element of sculptural organization is texture. In all sculpture the character of the surface of the material contributes to the effect: rough granular granite, translucent striated alabaster, grained wood, rough irregular clay, reflecting bronze. An infinite number of effects are inherent in the nature of the material and in the manner in which the surfaces are treated. Enlivening contrasts result from a combination of surface treatments, such as the juxtaposition of rough and smooth areas.

Thus sculpture is an organic structure — not however, as an end in itself, but to convey some aspect of life experience. Michelangelo's statement, "Life seems to move within the stone," has perhaps a more profound meaning than is at first apparent. For great sculpture, far from trying to imitate visual perception, impregnates material with vitality, with a living quality which no words can define but which is emotionally appealing. It may be the living quality of representation which is heightened and vivified by the quality of the organic structure.

In relief, the third dimension of sculpture in the round is suggested, but not actual. Starting with the plane, or surface, of the material, the sculptor's problem is to cut away enough of the mass to leave the figures projecting in such a way that they give an illusion of depth. Having drawn his design on the stone, the carver begins cutting into the material, sometimes sharply at right angles, leaving clean-cut edges; sometimes with a rounding-off of the edges which softens the contours; or perhaps undercutting considerably to secure deeper shadow. The depressions made by the subtraction of material tend to hold shadow; the remaining projections catch the light. Thus line, and light and shade, are important organizing elements in relief. Movement tends to be lateral and the planes, which indicate depth, to be parallel.

Intaglio is the opposite of relief. It is what one might call negative relief, in that the design is cut into the ground so that it appears in dark against the original surface of the stone. Sumerian cylinder seals (Fig. 87A) and Egyptian mural reliefs (Fig. 68A) are examples of this kind of carving.

[A] *Building a Ceramic Piece by the Coil Method. From the flat base the sides are built up of successive, ropelike coils of clay, which are then joined by the fingers. (Harold Allen)*

[B] *Throwing a Clay Piece on the Potter's Wheel. As the wheel turns the lump of wedged clay is centered, hollowed, and shaped by pressure of the hands. (Harold Allen)*

CERAMIC FORM

Pottery (ceramics), exclusive of tiles, is akin to sculpture in the round in that it is an art of three dimensions, and to sculpture in clay in that it consists of a building-up process in the same plastic material. Being a nonrepresentational art (except for ceramic sculpture), it is close to architecture as an almost purely geometric art. Ceramic sculpture is a border-line art between ceramics and sculpture, for it uses the materials and the processes of the one, and partakes of the representational character of the other.

Pottery is clay shaped and hardened by heat. It is one of the oldest and most universal of the arts because of its utilitarian character: that of a container. Much pottery is utilitarian only, but much of it has also an esthetic quality so high that it sometimes constitutes one of the major art expressions of a culture — as with the Chinese, the Iranians, and the American Indians.

According to the character of the clay and the degree of firing, pottery is earthenware, porcelain, or stoneware. Earthenware, the most common, has a relatively coarse base, and is fired at low heat. Being porous, it requires treatment to render it impervious. Sometimes porosity is an advantage, as when evaporation is desired for cooling purposes. Porcelain is made of a fine clay, kaolin, to which feldspathic rock is added. Fired at a high temperature, it becomes vitreous throughout and thus is impermeable. Porcelain can be shaped thin enough to be translucent, and when struck it produces a musical tone. Stoneware is of the same nature as porcelain, but of a coarser texture, partially vitrified, and with relatively thick walls.

Whatever the character of the base, a general four-step process is applicable to all: the preparation of the clay, the shaping, the decorating, and the firing. First the potter washes and wedges the clay to give it a smooth texture and to free it of air particles, after which he adds any other ingredient, such as the feldspar in porcelain. He is then ready to shape it. Several methods are possible. If the piece is small, he may shape it with his fingers; or he may build the walls of ropelike coils of clay (Fig. 15A), which he can smooth with his fingers or some implement, or leave unsmoothed. Another method is to throw the clay on a wheel, shaping it with the hands as the mass revolves (Fig. 15B). Still another method is to press or pour the clay into a mold — the process suitable for mass production. One needs to remember, however, that the original piece from which the mold is made was built up by hand-shaping, coiling, or throwing. The third step is drying to a leather-hard condition — hard enough to handle without injuring the shape — and decorating, usually with glaze. Polishing produces a texture which has a decorative quality of its own.

Glazing is one of the most universal methods for securing color, other decorative effects, and imperviousness. Glaze is melted glass, which may be transparent or opaque, glossy or mat; and it may be colored by the addition of metallic oxide. The glaze can be poured over the surface of the vessel, painted or sprayed on; or if the vessel is small, it can be dipped into the glaze. If the base is coarse, it is sometimes necessary to cover it with slip (clay thinned to a fluid consistency), to furnish a base for a transparent glaze. Painting is another common method of decoration. The design may be painted on the slip and covered with the transparent glaze; or it may be painted over a glaze or done by the wax-painting process. In the latter method the design is painted in wax, and the object is then entirely covered with pigment and heated. As the wax melts off it leaves the parts it covered in the orig-

inal white against the color. Other decorative methods consist of relief, incising, stamping, or sgraffito — that is, covering the vessel with two coatings of slip or glaze of different colors and then, by cutting a design through the outer coat, producing a two-color pattern.

The final step in pottery-making is the firing. Sometimes an extra firing is necessary at the decorative stage; often only one firing is sufficient. Much of the world's finest pottery has been fired out of doors by primitive methods which entailed great skill in controlling the heat. Today most firing is a matter of mechanical control. A further means of decoration added after firing is luster — a thin, transparent, metallic film, which requires another firing at low temperature, and which produces an evanescent, iridescent effect.

Ceramic form must take into consideration three factors: first, the volumes of which it is composed; second, the materials and the manner of their use; and third, the function. The nature of the ceramic process — coiling or throwing — predicates a form based upon sphere, egg, cylinder, or cone; and such additions as handles, covers, or spouts are subordinate to the basic shape (Fig. 17A). The majority of vessels are based not upon one shape, but on a combination of two or more shapes (Fig. 17B); and the quality of any ceramic product is a matter of the proportions of these basic shapes and the interrelations of part to part — of the neck to the body, for example, or of the lip to the body and the base. Contour, as in sculpture, and color and texture also, whether uniform or in contrasting areas, are important elements in stressing the relationships of parts.

The use of materials is a source of pleasure in the enjoyment of pottery: evidence of fingers and tools shaping yielding clay, and leaving contrasting

[A] *Basic Geometric Volumes Most Suitable to the Ceramic Processes: cylinder, ovoid, sphere, cone. (Harold Allen)*

[B] *Combinations of the Basic Geometric Volumes in Ceramic Design. (Harold Allen)*

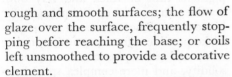

rough and smooth surfaces; the flow of glaze over the surface, frequently stopping before reaching the base; or coils left unsmoothed to provide a decorative element.

Pure form alone frequently is the sole source of our pleasure in pottery. In the majority of cases, however, function and the relation of function to forms — as in a building — is a determinant of quality. In general, the function of pottery is to transport, store, prepare, and serve food and drink. Thus a storage jar must have a large opening; a water bottle needs a long neck to facilitate the flow of the liquid; a shallow bowl or plate is suitable for serving, and a vessel with a handle and a spout for pouring. Size and weight also are related to function. A Chinese ceremonial tea bowl of porcelain should be small and of eggshell thinness to be satisfactory, whereas a storage jar for grain needs large size and thick walls to hold the heavy weight and to withstand rough usage. Vessels intended to hold liquids must acquire imperviousness, and this quality, which usually implies the use of glaze, has a direct effect upon the texture and color of the ceramic piece.

PICTORIAL FORM: Painting

In contrast to architecture, sculpture in the round, and pottery — which employ the third dimension — painting is constructed as a flat surface with no actual depth. Though it frequently expresses depth and space, it does so only through illusion. A painting always remains one continuous surface. The materials of the painter are this surface and pigment. The surface may be almost any material, though plaster or stone, wood, canvas, paper, and silk are the most common. Pigment is coloring matter secured from earth, mineral, and vegetable matter; or it can be made synthetically. Ground into a powder, it is mixed with some vehicle to reduce it to a liquid or pliant state suitable for use with brush, palette knife, finger, or spray. According to the kind of surface and vehicle, most painting falls into four classes: fresco, tempera, oil, and water color. Encaustic, casein, and duco paintings are also met not infrequently. Each of these mediums, with its individual brush strokes, texture, and quality of color, produces an effect peculiar to itself, so that the medium and the process by which it is worked constitute a vital element in the construction, and also in the understanding, of a picture.

Fresco is painting on damp plaster with water color. This becomes chemically incorporated with the surface, and thus a part of its actual texture. The wall requires special preparation, usually several coats of plaster, before the final thin coat, about one to two inches thick, is laid on. A preliminary drawing, known as a cartoon, is worked up in detail and is then transferred to the moist surface. The colors which a fresco painter can use are limited to those not affected by the lime in the plaster — chiefly the earth colors. The technique requires clear thinking and unfaltering workmanship, for once the color is laid on, it cannot be altered except by changes or additions made after the painting is dry. Alteration of this sort, called "dry" painting, is subject to the danger of subsequent peeling. Fresco is the most architectural of the painting techniques. Far from being an enlarged easel picture, it is subject to severe architectural requirements. It is part of an interior space and hence controlled by location in the building, by scale, and by the fact that it must be seen — at both long and short range — from many angles. All this requires simplification and clarity of composition carried out in bold brush strokes (Figs. 189A and B, 473A–477A, 757A–761A).

Tempera is painting on an especially prepared wooden panel in pigment mixed with egg. The panel is first covered with linen, on which are laid layers of gesso (plaster of paris) which are smoothed and polished to an ivory-like finish. On this surface the painter draws his design in detail; he then puts on an underpainting, usually of green for the figures and red for any areas to be covered with gold; finally he adds the local colors in pigments mixed with egg yolk. As this pigment dries

quickly, he works with small brushes in fine strokes, a painstaking technique. The result is a smooth hard surface with luminous depth and a linear decorative quality (Fig. 484A).

Oil as a vehicle for pigment is slow in drying and allows the painter to use broader, looser strokes than tempera and to make subtler transitions from light to dark. Some painters have begun with a tempera panel as a base (tempera-oil; Fig. 536A). The majority have used a canvas surface, which they cover with a ground as in tempera (indirect oil; Fig. 510A); or they brush the pigment directly on the canvas (direct oil; Fig. 727A). A painter may use his pigment thin or thick and rely both on the canvas and on the pigment for his textures. The various oil techniques make possible a freer expression, richer color and atmospheric effects, greater solidity, and more complex spatial organization. Direct oil is peculiarly adaptable, like clay in the hands of the sculptor, to spontaneous expression and improvisation.

Water color is painting on paper or silk with pigment mixed with water and some binding medium, such as gum. There are several kinds of water-color painting, of which transparent, gouache, and Chinese-ink are perhaps the most important. Transparent water color is a most evanescent medium, adaptable for spontaneous expression. The pigment is applied in thin washes, and areas of the paper — usually white or of a light tint — are left to provide the lightest areas, a method which produces a luminous or sparkling effect. The character or grain of the paper also plays no little part in the general effect.

Gouache is water color rendered opaque by the addition of some filler, such as zinc white. It has more body than the transparent water color and lends itself to richer color effects and to meticulous detail, as in Persian mini-

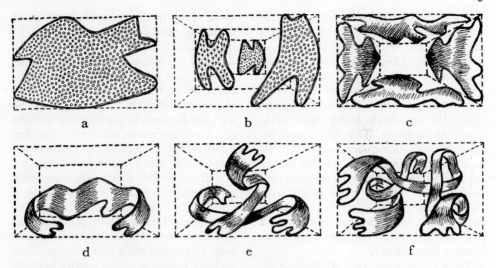

a   b   c

d   e   f

[A] *Some Spatial Arrangements Possible in Painting.* a. *Flat plane with no depth (Fig. 150A);* b. *Depth in three parallel planes (Fig. 489A);* c. *Planes receding at an angle to the picture plane (Fig. 527A);* d. *Planes receding on a curved diagonal (Fig. 499A);* e. *Intersecting S-curve planes (Fig. 513A);* f. *Complex backward and forward movement of planes (Fig. 761A).*

atures. The painters of these miniatures prepared the paper by rubbing it with a crystal egg until it was smooth and glossy — a process reminiscent of tempera painting. Interesting effects can be obtained by a combination of the transparent and the gouache methods.

Chinese ink is a medium peculiar to the Far East. The water-color materials are Chinese ink and sized silk or paper (that made of bamboo pulp is preferable) sized or unsized. Chinese ink is not the ink with which we are familiar, but a solid made of carbon and glue and molded into a cake. If a particular kind of texture is desired, other ingredients are added — pulverized oyster shells, for example, to obtain a dead finish. The cake of ink is rubbed in water on a slab to secure a semifluid — a process requiring great skill. It is then applied to silk or paper with a brush. Like fresco, when once applied Chinese ink admits no alteration. Hence the artist must be very sure of what he wants to do and of his technical ability to do

it. Extraordinarily various effects can be secured in this medium, from bold richly black strokes, through varied tones, to a hairline of the utmost delicacy (Fig. 380A).

The medium and the process by which it is used, it is clear, are vital elements in making a picture. Some painters limit themselves to perfecting one technique alone, some use several. Tradition, training, and the whole cultural background may determine which process a painter shall use. This is illustrated by the almost universal use of fresco and tempera in fifteenth-century Florence; of Chinese ink in Sung China; of gouache in medieval Persia; and of indirect oil in recent times, as well as of a whole galaxy of revivals and experimentations today.

Whatever the vehicle for his pigment, whatever the surface on which he works, and whatever his subject matter, the painter composes his material — that is, he builds an organic structure — out of line, color, light and dark, and texture. Some compose in a two-dimensional style; that is, with lines and areas of color, with light and dark, and with texture. Thus they retain the two-dimensional character of the surface. Others organize in spots of color with blurred edges and with gradual transitions, the emphasis being upon relationships in space. This space may be shallow, with movement largely lateral, as in relief, and with the receding planes parallel to the plane of the original surface. Or it may be deep space with planes receding at an angle to the original surface, with movement backward and forward, often complex and interlocking (Fig. 543A).

Thus painting is potentially one of the richest of the arts, in that it offers the artist the broadest scope in the use of elements. He may use them all if he chooses, and with infinite variety, even though his use of volume, space, and movement is illusory only, not actual. To *see* how he builds an organic structure out of certain materials by means of certain elements and how he relates the structure to the subject matter is fundamental to understanding painting.

PICTORIAL FORM:
Drawings and Prints

In no one of the pictorial arts is the Chinese conception of expression so true as in drawing. Expression, according to the Chinese "is the result of the action of the mind traveling unhesitatingly through the brush." (Tomita) So direct and spontaneous is the connection between the concept in the artist's mind and his hand that a drawing reveals more of his personality than a so-called finished work. The fact that so many drawings are made as preliminary sketches and not meant for exhibition makes them even more revealing.

A drawing can be made on any surface, though paper is most frequently used. The medium varies, just as in painting, and each medium has its own capacities and limitations. Pencils, crayons of various kinds, and pen-and-ink are perhaps the most usual; silver-point, though rare, has a unique character. Pencils (graphite) are of varying degrees of hardness or softness and for this reason are versatile; they are adaptable for modeling the figure or for meticulous detail. Charcoal (carbon), a soft material which perishes with wear, lends itself to broad, bold, general effects. Red crayon, also soft, has the advantage of color. These two mediums are often used for drawings by sculptors, to express mass and volume. Pen-and-ink is also versatile, partly because of the element of color provided by the ink, and partly because of the varying effects due to the material out of which the pens are made: quill, reed, or steel. Quill pens tend to make a soft, often very delicate, line, reed pens, a somewhat harder line. Steel pens can create a multitude of effects, from a hard steely line to one of the utmost delicacy and subtlety.

Prints are impressions made from plates, and vary in kind according to the process by which the plate is made. Though the finished print is usually on paper (and the selection of the paper is important), the work of the artist is concentrated chiefly on making the plate — always, however, with the effect of the print in mind. His materials are a plate of metal, or a block of wood, or a slab of stone; tools suitable for each material; paper and ink; and a press or hand tools for printing. The great advantage of prints is that since many impressions can be made from one plate, they lend themselves to mass production. There are three important ways of making the plate: relief, intaglio, and planography.

The woodcut is the best example of relief. On a block of wood the artist draws his design and then with knives and gouges cuts the wood away, leaving in relief the lines and surfaces he wishes to have take the ink. The block is then inked and covered with a sheet of moist paper which, subjected to pressure, takes the ink from the parts of the plate it ˙ touches — the areas in relief — leaving the untouched parts — the areas cut back — in white. In cutting the wood the carver is restricted, because of the grain, to a simple direct expression in which the lines and areas are strong and bold, and transitions from black to white are abrupt. Prints in several colors can be made by cutting a block for each color.

In intaglio, the second important method, the design is sunk into a plate, usually copper. Engraving, etching, and dry point are the chief examples. In engraving, the artist works with a steel graver, the burin, set in a wooden handle. Holding the tool so that its handle rests in the palm of his hand, he pushes it into the plate with enough force to cut the metal; and according to the pressure and the angle at which he holds the tool, he can make his furrow narrow or broad, deep or shallow. In cutting the metal his burin raises ridges of metal, called burr, along the sides of the furrow; this he usually scrapes away so as to make his line clean-cut. The hardness of the metal and its resistance to the tool tend to produce a precise, crisp line, somewhat inflexible. Graduations of line can be secured by manipulation of the burin, graduations of tone by hatchings — that is, by engraving lines across those already engraved.

In etching, the copper plate is covered with a protective ground of wax or varnish. In this the design is drawn with an etching needle, or any pointed tool which moves easily and lightly through the ground, exposing the metal below but not cutting into its surface.

The plate is then immersed in an acid which etches, or bites, the exposed parts of the metal, acting in the same capacity as the burin in engraving. But the fact that the artist can make his design in a soft material frees him from the restrictions forced on the woodcutter and the engraver by their mediums and thus makes etching the most facile of the graphic arts in its process and the most capable of subtleties of line and tone.   '

In both engraving and etching the printing process is the same. The ink is thoroughly worked into the engraved or bitten furrows and the surface is cleaned. A sheet of moist paper is passed over the plate, and together the two are put through a press, where the ink is absorbed from the furrows and thus transferred to the paper.

Dry point is a process that lies between etching and engraving. It is similar to engraving in that the design is cut upon a metal plate by a steel needle; but it differs from engraving in that the burr is left on the plate. The rough surfaces, holding the ink, produce soft, furry lines, richly black. As the needle cuts but lightly into the plate, it can produce a much more delicate and flexible line than the burin in engraving.

The planographic process differs from relief and intaglio in that the printing surface is not cut or bitten, but retains its original surface or plane; a chemical action is utilized to make the plate. Lithography is such a process. On a special kind of stone (hence the name), which has been cut and polished, the design is drawn with a greasy crayon, or with a brush and specially prepared ink. The stone is then given a chemical treatment which does not affect the drawing but which prepares the rest of the surface to take up moisture. This surface is then moistened. An inked roller is now passed over the stone. The moistened surface repels the greasy ink, which only the lines of the drawing retain, just as the relief lines retain the ink in the process of printing woodcuts. Then paper is pressed against the inked stone. Linear and tonal values of great range and subtlety characterize lithographs, because of the freedom possible in making the original drawing and the nature of the materials used.

TEXTILE FORM

A textile is anything woven. Like pottery, textiles are ancient and universal because of their function — that of a covering. The materials of the weaver are fibers: vegetable (cotton, linen, jute, and hemp); animal (wool, hair, silk); mineral (gold, silver, asbestos); glass; synthetic (nylon, rayon, celanese). These fibers differ greatly. Linen fibers are long, cotton fibers are short; hemp fibers are coarse and tough; silk fibers are fine and lustrous. The first step in processing fibers is spinning them into threads. Here again they vary in capacity, from those, such as linen and silk, that can be spun into the finest threads through the cottons and wools to the coarsest, such as hemp. Now the fiber is ready for the weaver. His tool is the loom. A loom may be vertical or horizontal, and consists fundamentally of two parallel beams, held firmly apart. On these is strung the warp, through which is interlaced the weft (woof, filling). This weaving process involves three fundamental steps: (1) shedding — raising the warp threads to make a shed, through which (2) the weft is thrown or shot, and (3) battening — beating down the weft threads against the woven fabric. A great variety of weaves results from the manner in which the weft is inserted; for example, plain cloth, tapestry, twill, satin, and damask. Any weave can be enriched with additional weft, as is found in embroidery, brocades, and pile fabrics.

Textiles are primarily functional, and function determines what fibers shall be used and how. One kind of fiber and process of weaving will be used when a fabric, such as a blanket or a carpet, is to provide warmth or is to have hard usage — to be walked on, for example. Another kind of fiber and another weave will be used to make a light delicate fabric for coolness, or for hanging in soft folds.

Textile form is two-dimensional. In the weaving process, the artist makes and organizes his surface at the same time; and in doing this he uses the organizing elements that are two-dimensional: line, areas of color and texture, and light and dark. Texture is one of the most important elements — the actual "feel" of a fabric as well as its visual quality. The smooth lustrous character of satin or linen, for example, appeals equally to the senses of touch and of sight. Even color, as we have seen, is somewhat dependent upon texture, for one hue will have different values in different weaves. Intricate patterns, sensed by both the touch and the eye, can be woven in one color alone; and richly complex designs result from combining several weaves and colors. The artist can also produce patterns by painting or stamping a design upon a piece already woven, a process used largely today in machine-made fabrics.

Batik is a painting process in which the artist draws his design on cloth — usually white cotton cloth — and covers with wax the areas that he wishes to have remain white. He then dips the cloth into a pigment, which the unpainted areas absorb. Then the wax is melted off, leaving the areas it covered white. A similar process has already been noted in the decoration of ceramics.

FORM IN METALWORK

Metalwork consists of a very large group of objects made of gold, silver, copper, bronze, brass, pewter, iron or steel, aluminum, chromium — to mention the more important metals. All metals share, each to a varying degree, hardness, tenacity, and thus durability; elasticity for manipulation; opaque and reflecting surfaces. They also share, in varying degrees, capacities upon which depends their use as materials for the artist: capacities for fusibility, ductility, and malleability. Being fusible, a metal can be molded, and cast. Being ductile, it can be drawn into wires or threads. Being malleable, it can be beaten or hammered into sheets, at times of incredible thinness — gold, for example. These sheets can be beaten into shape over molds; or can be cut into flat patterns and shaped; or can be perforated into patterns. The malleability and ductility when heated, especially of iron, give the artist a very plastic material, which he can hammer, weld, turn and twist into innumerable shapes, and thus provide a light, open design, such as a gate or a grille, which affords visibility and at the same time protection because of its strength. For ornamentation, chasing or engraving is perhaps the simplest method; repoussé is also common. Repoussé consists of beating a sheet of metal into a mold of resistant material in such a way as not to break the metal, and thus leave a pattern in relief on one side and in intaglio on the other (Fig. 117A). Another decorative process is damascening — inlaying in a metal base shapes or figures of other metals of different color and texture (Fig. 306A). Another is plating — covering one metal wholly or in part with another metal. Still another is enameling, for the purpose of introducing a wider range of hue and texture.

Two important enameling processes are cloisonné and champlevé. In cloisonné enamels the design is outlined by soldering strips of thin gold about a thirtieth of an inch wide, called *cloisons*, to a metal base, usually gold. The cells formed by the cloisons are then filled with enamel, a vitreous compound, colored or uncolored, translucent or opaque, which when subjected to heat fuses with the metal base. A second coat of enamel is sometimes added to fill any concavities, frequently covering the cloisons. This must be ground away until the surface becomes perfectly smooth, showing all the cloisons and polished to a glasslike finish — a laborious process, yet one upon which depends much of the rich effect (Fig. 271A). In champlevé enamels the design is drawn on a metal plate in a fine line and the metal is cut away to a depth of from one-sixteenth to one-thirty-second of an inch, leaving a narrow raised metal ridge to indicate the outline of the design. The depressions are usually roughened (to hold the enamel more securely) and then filled with enamel, usually opaque, which is fused and polished as in the cloisonné method (Fig. 359A). In general, there is more boldness and vigor in the champlevé process, more delicacy and elegance in the cloisonné, for greater facility is possible when working with cloisons than with the more rigid lines left by cutting away the metal field.

Metalwork, because of the nature of the medium, is adaptable both for irregular hand-wrought shapes and also for the meticulously precise shapes made by the machine. In both, the visual evidence of the manner of working the raw material is a part of the pleasure derived — the strokes of the hammer in wrought silver, the slight irregularities of the tractable iron, and the machinelike precision of the steel implement. With its rigid form and hard, precise edges, whether hand-wrought or machine-made, metalwork stands in direct opposition to ceramic objects made of the most pliant of mediums and shaped, even on the wheel, by the slightest pressure of hands or fingers. As in ceramics, texture is an important visual element in all metalwork, and frequently a maximum of effect is due to an opposition of a smooth, highly reflective surface to one worked in repoussé or chased. In addition, the strong contrasts of light and dark due to this reflective quality, and emphatic lines and edges, are visual elements used by the artist for the expression of proportion and relationships of parts, and of the movement of repeated and contrasted shapes. Color too is an important element, as one can see in a gold object, which, by its power to reflect, shows many other hues besides the orange-yellow that we ordinarily associate with it.

SUMMARY

If in this Introduction we have isolated and stressed the observation of form as an organic structure, it is because most of us are prone to disregard actual seeing. "We understand and believe what we are told in print, but we see very little directly with our eyes."[1] Yet seeing form is a sine qua non of understanding. Form may be simple, easily observable, or it may be subtly complex. As Alfred H. Barr says of painting (though his statement is applicable to all the arts): "Some of them [pictures] may take a good deal of study, for although we have seen a million pictures in our lives we may never have learned to look at painting as an art. For the art of painting, though it has little to do with words, is like a language which you have to learn to read. Some pictures are easy, like a primer, and some are hard with long words and complex ideas; and some are prose, others are poetry, and others still are like algebra or geometry. But one thing is easy, there are no foreign languages in painting as there are in speech; there are only local dialects which can be understood internationally, for painting is a kind of visual Esperanto."[2] Although understanding involves the use of the artist's vision, it is well to recall again what was said at the beginning of this Introduction: that a work of art is more than an observable form. For form rises out of its environment. Every age has its attitudes and modes of thinking which, together with the contemporary social, economic, political, and religious forces, are factors which determine to a large degree both subject matter and style. Every artist belongs to a social unit. How the members of that unit live and work, how they are governed, how they think, what they believe, and how they give outward expression to that belief — in all this the artist, like every other individual of the group, is rooted; and even though he be a rebel against it, he cannot entirely escape it. Both the content and the form of his expression are largely determined by it. This environment, however, is not static. Every age, in fact every work of art, exists in time, takes its place in a sequence that is always growing, changing, evolving. Furthermore, most works of art were and are created with a definite function to perform, often in a definite location. Hence if we are to grasp the total, the maximum, significance of a work of art, it is necessary to relate and synthesize all approaches. But we must always realize that in the last analysis it is that intangible, un-

[1] W. R. Lethaby, *Form in Civilization*, Oxford University Press, 1922, p. 17.

[2] Alfred H. Barr, *What is Modern Painting?* Museum of Modern Art, 1943, p. 3.

provable, but felt element of quality as a living force that is the final basis for judgment.

BIBLIOGRAPHY

Abell, Walter, *Representation and Form*, Scribner, 1936

Barnes, Albert C., *The Art in Painting*, 3rd ed. rev., Harcourt, Brace, 1937

Blossfeldt, Karl, *Art Forms in Nature*, Weyhe, 1929

Brooklyn Museum, *The Art and Technique of Ceramics*, Museum, 1937

Casson, Stanley, *The Technique of Early Greek Sculpture*, Oxford University Press, 1933

Doerner, Max, *The Materials of the Artist*, trans. by Eugen Neuhaus, Harcourt, Brace, 1934

Durst, Alan L., *Wood Carving*, Studio, 1938

Focillon, Henri, *The Life of Forms in Art*, Yale University Press, 1942

Franklin, Christine Ladd, *Colour and Colour Theories*, Harcourt, Brace, 1929

Fry, Roger Eliot, *Vision and Design*, Brentano's, 1924

Gardner, Helen, *Understanding the Arts*, Harcourt, Brace, 1932

Gill, Eric, *Sculpture*, Saint Dominic's Press, Ditchling, Sussex, Eng., 1924

Guillaume, Paul, and Munro, Thomas, *Primitive Negro Sculpture*, Harcourt, Brace, 1926

Hildebrand, Adolf, *The Problem of Form in Painting and Sculpture*, Stechert, 1945

Hooper, Luther, *Hand-Loom Weaving*, Pitman, 1920

Kepes, Gyorgy, *Language of Vision*, Theobald, Chicago, 1944

Kronquist, Emil, and Pelikan, A. G., *Simple Metalwork*, Studio, 1940

Laurie, A. P., *The Painter's Methods and Materials*, Lippincott, 1926

Le Corbusier, Charles (pseud. of Charles E. Jeanneret-Gris), *Towards a New Architecture*, Harcourt, Brace, 1927

McMahon, Ames P., *The Art of Enjoying Art*, McGraw-Hill, 1938

Moreau-Vauthier, Charles, *The Technique of Painting*, Putnam, 1912

Munro, Thomas, *Scientific Method in Æsthetics*, Norton, 1928

Opdyke, George H., *Art and Nature Appreciation*, Macmillan, 1932

Pearson, Ralph M., *Experiencing Pictures*, Harcourt, Brace, 1932

———— How to See Modern Pictures, Dial Press, 1925

Read, Herbert E., *The Anatomy of Art*, Dodd, Mead, 1932

———— *Art and Industry*, Harcourt, Brace, 1935

Reath, Nancy A., *The Weaves of Hand-Loom Fabrics*, Pennsylvania Museum, Philadelphia, 1927

Rindge, Agnes M., *Sculpture*, Harcourt, Brace, 1929

Robins, William P., *Etching Craft*, Dodd, Mead, 1923

Sargent, Walter, *The Enjoyment and Use of Color*, Scribner, 1923

Stein, Leo, *The A-B-C of Æsthetics*, Liveright, 1927

Thurston, Carl H. P., *The Structure of Art*, University of Chicago Press, 1940

Venturi, Lionello, *Painting and Painters*, Scribner, 1945

Weitenkampf, Frank, *How to Appreciate Prints*, rev. ed., Scribner, 1932

Wengenroth, Stow, *Making a Lithograph*, Studio, 1936

Youtz, Philip N., *Sounding Stones of Architecture*, Norton, 1929

Part One

[A]   *The Acropolis. Athens. This rocky hill stands about 200 feet above the plain. In the background are the slopes of Mt. Hymettus. (E. L. Highbarger, Evanston, Illinois)*

ANCIENT ART

WORLD PANORAMA

O UT of an apparently world-wide, prehistoric, Neolithic base arose the
great civilizations of ancient times. These we see in the Near East
(in Egypt, the valley of the Tigris-Euphrates, and Persia); around
the Mediterranean (in Crete, Greece, and westward to the Pillars of Her-
cules); in the Far East (in India, China, and Japan); and in the Americas
(in Middle, South, and North America).

Within each area there were many regional contacts and exchanges of ideas,
motifs, and modes of expression. In the Near East and Mediterranean areas,
Egyptian motifs and forms appear in the Tigris-Euphrates Valley and in
Persia; and among the cultures of this valley and Persia forms were inter-
changed in toto. Egypt reached out to Crete and vice versa. Cretan art is
basic in Greek art, and motifs from the Tigris-Euphrates Valley appear in
Greek ornament. Greek art, in turn, spread both east and west; and the
Romans carried the Greco-Roman forms all the way around the Mediterranean and northwest into Spain and France. In the Far Eastern area, the
independent civilizations which arose in India and China were brought together by the rise and spread of Buddhism, which was later transmitted to
Japan. In Middle America, the Maya and the Toltecs exerted mutual influences on each other and on their neighbors; in South America, the coastal
Chimu and Nazca and the highland Tiahuanaco compromised their differing
art forms.

Over and above these regional interactions were injected those from afar,
the most notable of which were those between the Near and the Far East.
A direct contact appeared in Sumeria and India; bronze and glazed-tile
techniques in China quite clearly derive from Persia; the silk trade flourished
between China and the Roman Empire; Hellenic forms spread, in the wake
of the conquests of Alexander the Great, into India and influenced Buddhist
sculpture; and the nomads of central Eurasia spread the so-called animal
style from China to western Europe. In the Americas, habits of mind and
visualization, not to mention definite motifs, similar to those of the Far East
point at least to a common ancestry in prehistoric times. But because there
was relatively little exchange of goods, the assimilation of outside influences
played only a minor role in the development of these great civilizations of
antiquity. For the most part they evolved indigenously — each dependent on
the materials at hand, each expressing its own culture in its own idiom.

Prehistoric Art

1

PALEOLITHIC ART

(EARLIEST TIMES TO ABOUT 20,000 B.C.)

WHEN in the long development of human life did art first appear, and why? What was its character? Was it childishly crude, or was it in any way comparable to those accomplishments which the world has looked upon as its greatest? Did it reveal any grasp of those fundamentals which underlie all great art expression?

Until recently the life story of man was thought to have been brief, perhaps a few thousand years at most. The researches of the past half-century, however, have shown that, instead of a few thousand years, vastly remote ages — a million years or more — and an amazingly slow evolution lie behind man of today. This growth we can read only in human remains and in extant objects made by man until we reach the invention of writing, only four or five thousand years ago. From that point we are guided by the written document as well.

In 1879 a Spaniard who was interested in the problem of the antiquity of man was exploring a cave on his estate at Altamira in northern Spain, search-

ing for further examples of flint and carved bone, for he had already found such relics in this cavern. With him was his little daughter. Since the cave was dark, he was working by the light of a lamp. The child was scrambling over the rough rocks. Suddenly she called out, "Bulls! Bulls!" pointing to the ceiling, so low that he could touch it with his hand. To satisfy the child, he lifted his lamp and there saw on the uneven surface numbers of bison and other animals naturalistically painted in bright colors. When the discovery was published and the painting declared to be the work of men who lived long ages before, people shook their heads. And, for a time, the skeptics had their way. "Impossible," they said. "The work is too good and the color too fresh; some erratic person of recent years has done this for some unknown purpose." Slowly, however, the belief began to grow among a few that all these things were revealing ages of far greater antiquity than man had ever dreamed of. Slowly skepticism broke down, and further great discoveries

have yielded enough evidence for us to
catch a glimpse of man and his activities
in this remote age.

When, then, in this long evolution
of human activities did art first appear?
And under what phase of art expression?

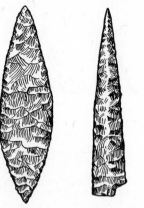

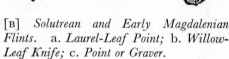

[A] *Flint Fist Hatchet. L. 7½ in. British
Museum, London.*

[B] *Solutrean and Early Magdalenian
Flints. a. Laurel-Leaf Point; b. Willow-
Leaf Knife; c. Point or Graver.*

FLINTS, CARVINGS,
ENGRAVINGS

Europe at the time of earliest man[1]
offered a physical environment greatly
different from that today. Already three
glacial epochs had passed, and the
warm moist climate of the third inter-
glacial age provided man a comfortable
habitation. We see him, a hairy, rugged,
strong-jawed man, without clothing,
possessing a small stone hand ax and
fire, living a life of self-defense against
the wild elephant, the hippopotamus,
the wolf, and the rhinoceros.[2] His predecessors during long millenniums had
made two vital discoveries: the control
of fire and the use of stone for tools.
The former, man had first observed,

perhaps, as lightning cleft a tree and
started flames in the dry leaves or as red-
hot lava burst from the crater of a volcano; the latter, he gradually adopted
to replace his wooden implements so
that he could protect himself better,
obtain his food more easily, and com-
bat animals larger than hare and rabbit. The early stone implements, such
as the scraper and the hand ax, or fist
hatchet (Fig. 30A), which evolved after
ages of experiment in chipping stone,
seem purely utilitarian. They are not
hafted, but are grasped by the hand
for clubbing or for crude cutting. Gradually there appears in these tools something more than a capacity for better
striking and a sharper cutting edge — a
feeling for proportion and symmetry.
Here we can recognize that of two
flints which cut equally well one is more
pleasing than the other because of a
quality in the form that has nothing to
do with the utility of the tool yet un-
mistakably enhances the object to the
eye. Such a feeling for form, for a
balance between the *what* and the *how*,
we recognize as a fundamental art impulse.

[1] For the earliest human remains, see G. G.
MacCurdy, *The Coming of Man*, University
Society, 1932, Chaps. V–VI.

[2] Eight vivid life-sized dioramas of prehistoric men and their environment are on exhibition in the Chicago Natural History
Museum. For reproductions and descriptions
see the pamphlet *Prehistoric Man* by Henry
Field, Chicago Natural History Museum,
Chicago, 1933. See also Henry F. Osborn, *Men
of the Old Stone Age*, 3d ed., Scribner, 1924, for
reconstructions of both human and animal types.

This sensitivity to form reveals itself increasingly in the late Chellean and the Mousterian ages,[1] the ages of the Neandertal hunter. The climate was becoming cool as the fourth glacial age approached. The animals migrated or adapted themselves to the changing conditions. Now the mammoth and the woolly rhinoceros, the reindeer and the arctic fox, became abundant. Man sought shelter in overhanging cliffs, and while contending with the beasts for cave shelters discovered that fire at the mouth of his cavern protected him not only from marauding animals but

[1] By "prehistory" is meant human history before the invention of writing. It includes the Stone Age and in some localities the Bronze and Iron ages, for the discovery or introduction of metals and the invention of writing vary widely in different localities. The following table outlines the main epochs:

A. Eolithic (Dawn of the Stone Age)
   1,000,000–500,000 B.C.
   Java and Peking men

B. Paleolithic (Old Stone Age)
   500,000–20,000 B.C.
   1. Chellean (Chelles, a town near Paris)   *Warm, third inter-glacial*
      Piltdown and Heidelberg men
   2. Mousterian (Le Moustier, a site in the Dordogne Valley)
      Neandertal man
   3. Aurignacian (Aurignac, a small village in the French Pyrenees)   *Cold, fourth glacial*
      Cro-Magnon man (a small cave in the Dordogne Valley)
   4. Solutrean (Solutré, a site in east-central France)
   5. Magdalenian (La Madeleine, near Les Eyzies in the Dordogne)

C. Mesolithic (Middle or Transitional Stone Age) 20,000–12,000 B.C.   *Temperate of today*

D. Neolithic (New or Late Stone Age) 12,000–3000 B.C.

E. Bronze 3000–1000 B.C.

F. Iron 1000 B.C.–A.D.

from the damp cold as well. The increasing variety and quality of his implements — axes, knives, scrapers, points — aided him not only in procuring and preparing food but also in skinning and dressing pelts for clothing for himself and, with the appearance of family life, for his family.

In addition to his growing sensitiveness to the form of his tools is a response to the quality of his material, evidence for which Dr. MacCurdy finds in tools made from rock crystal and topaz.[2] Color has made its appeal, and our hunter appears to have decked his body and his skin clothing with ornament. Even in the face of an energy-consuming climate, then, latent impulses that are fundamental in the arts were finding expression.

In the meantime a great migration, probably from Asia, brought a new race, the Cro-Magnon,[3] up the Danube, or along the northern coast of Africa into the habitable parts of Europe, for Africa and Europe were still land-connected. Though the glaciers were relatively small in extent, the climate was extremely cold, yet dry and not so taxing as the damp cold of the Mousterian times. Game was abundant and extraordinarily varied — mammoth, reindeer, bison and wild cattle, horse, ibex, bear and rabbit, ducks, geese, and ptarmigan. The newcomers were hunters, and lived, like their predecessors, under shelving rocks and in the entrances to caves. They clothed themselves with skins, which they had learned to sew together with bone needles. To the comfort thus secured they added the note of embellishment, as we infer from a necklace (Fig. 32D) made by some

[2] See MacCurdy, *op. cit.*, p. 108 and Frontispiece.
[3] The cultures known as Aurignacian, Solutrean, and Magdalenian belong to the larger unit known as Cro-Magnon, whose people stand in marked contrast to Neandertal man and close to the modern human type.

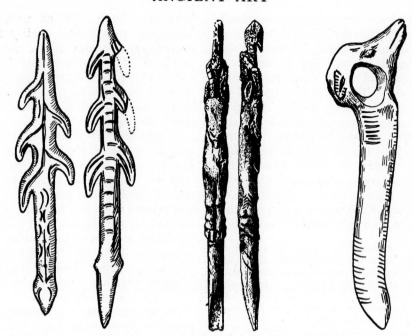

[A] *Harpoons. Of reindeer horn. L. c. 6 in. Magdalenian.* [B] *Dart-Thrower. Of rein-deer horn. L. 10½ in. (Piette)* [C] *Baton with Fox's Head. Of staghorn. L. c. 14 in. Magdalenian.*

hunter who had a decided feeling for the relationship of the parts. With ameliorated climatic conditions and a better physical and mental endowment than Neandertal man, Cro-Magnon man made rapid and marked advances culturally, and particularly in the arts — reaching in the Magdalenian culture a climax of prehistoric art.

The old tools carried on, but were far in advance of the Mousterian in quality of form and in precision and beauty of cutting. In the thin, sharp

[D] *Necklace of Stag Teeth, Fish Verte-brae, and Shells. Paleolithic.*

laurel-leaf points and willow-leaf knives of the Solutreans (Fig. 30B), most skillful of the Cro-Magnon stoneworkers, we find a refinement in shape, proportion, and character of the curve, and a rhyth-mic movement over the surface made by the flakings. A new process in stone-working, pressure against the flint with a small piece of bone, enabled the craftsman to produce a tool that was as effective for use as it was pleasing to the eye. New materials were derived from the hunt — bone, ivory, reindeer, or staghorn. From these, with his sharp stone points, the craftsman not only fashioned bone javelin points, needles, harpoons (Fig. 32A), arrow-straight-eners, batons, and dart-throwers or throw sticks but decorated them, some-times with lines and conventional pat-terns, sometimes with the animal form (Fig. 32B). Around a reindeer horn

[A] *Bison with Turned Head. Carved in reindeer horn. From the rock shelter La Madeleine, Dordogne. Magdalenian. As the figure is broken, its function is uncertain.*

[B] *Charging Mammoth. Engraved on a piece of ivory tusk. (De Mortillet)*

an ibex has been carved in such a way that the figure is not "applied" to the surface but is an integral part of a cylindrical object and in no way interferes with the javelin resting firmly against the crotch. Note, for example, how the horns snugly encircling the stick emphasize this cylindrical shape. To feel such a relationship between the cylindrical core and the animal form requires no mean intelligence and sensitivity. Likewise the baton in Figure 32c reveals a highly imaginative quality in the relationship between the piece of horn and the head of a fox, while the cross markings not only enable the hand to hold the baton more securely but furnish a rhythmic movement over the surface.

On stone, ivory, and horn, on both flat and curving surfaces the hunter-

artist engraved many figures — some, linear or geometric ornament; a great many, animals.[1] In the *Bison with Turned Head* (Fig. 33A), one is impressed partly by its striking vitality and partly by the formal beauty expressed by the simplest means. The head is so turned that it is entirely framed by the massive bulk of the body, and its pattern involves a vivid play of curve and countercurve and a surface contrast obtained by the use of incised lines as a decorative convention to indicate the mane. Figure 33B shows an infuriated mammoth charging forward. There is a largeness, a strikingly direct statement of a few essentials, expressed by a line so sure that it is convincing and so economical that it incorporates all details without specifically stating them. The animal is in profile, with only two

[1] Many of these engraved pieces are fragments and thus their purpose is unknown.

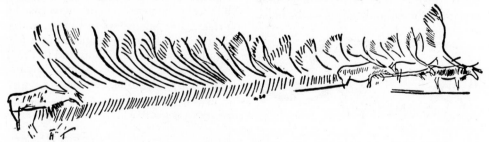

[C] *Herd of Reindeer. Engraved on the wing bone of an eagle. L. 8 in. (Capitan and Breuil)*

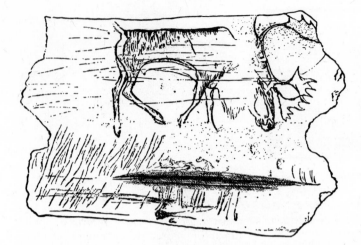

[A] *Grazing Reindeer.
Engraved around a piece
of reindeer antler. L. 5 in.
(Heim)*

legs showing, and there is no shading, no background. The whole figure is sensitively adjusted to the space which it fills. In the *Grazing Reindeer* (Fig. 34A) a momentary pose is expressed with great naturalism. This keen-visioned hunter had observed the action of every part of the animal as it bent its head to browse, and with phenomenal memory he transferred the vision, with a sharp flint point, to the piece of horn. If the scratches beneath the reindeer are intended to suggest landscape, it is a unique example of such representation. In the *Deer and Salmon* (Fig. 35A) we have what is rare: a conscious grouping of several figures. The movements of each animal and the forward movement of the group are portrayed with a few essential lines. Even the backward turn of one head, which may represent the animal calling to the herd,

helps the artist to integrate the head and the antlers with the other figures without overlapping — which seems definitely to have been avoided, as one notes in the placing of the salmon. These fish may symbolize a stream, and the two lozenges above the stag may be the engraver's signature. In the *Herd of Reindeer* (Fig. 33C), a visual impression is forcibly expressed by emphasizing, through distortion and repetition, the most characteristic feature, the antlers.

PAINTING

So far the manifestations of the art impulse in early man appear in his tools, weapons, and small personal belongings. To see his more monumental expression in painting and sculpture let us penetrate several caverns of France and Spain, subterranean water channels varying in length from a few hundred to some four thousand feet and now choked, at places almost impassably,[1] by deposits, stalactites, and

[B] *Woolly Rhinoceros. Drawing at Font-de-Gaume. L. c. 25 in. Aurignacian.*

[1] For an interesting account of a recent discovery of sculpture and also a vivid picture of the perils incident to the exploration of subterranean caves, see Norbert Casteret, "Discovering the Oldest Statues in the World," *National Geographic Magazine*, August, 1924, p. 123.

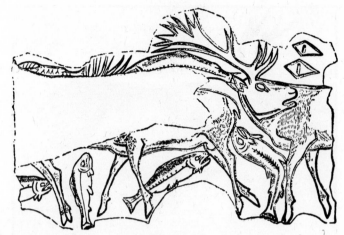

[A] *Deer and Salmon. Engraved reindeer antler. L. 5½ in. Magdalenian.*

stalagmites. Far inside these caverns, far beyond the sheltering entrance where the Cro-Magnon hunter lived, the hunter-artist, in utter quiet and darkness, with the help of artificial light engraved and painted on the walls many pictures, chiefly of animals.[1] For light he used a tiny stone lamp, filled with marrow or fat and supplied with a wick, perhaps of moss. For drawing he used chunks of red and yellow ocher, and for painting he ground these same ochers into powder and mixed them with some medium, perhaps animal fat. With a large flat bone for a palette, with brushes which he could make from reeds or bristles, and with scrapers for smoothing the wall and sharp flint points for engraving, his tools were complete. The chalk drawing of a *Bison* (Fig. 35B) is a simple complete statement based upon a keen vision of the peculiar characteristics of the specific animal, the essentials of which are expressed by a bold continuous line. The horns are in front view, perhaps because the memory picture triumphed over the visual illusion, or perhaps because of the formal relationship thus made possible between

the horns and the hump — that same feeling for shapes and their interrelations which we have been noting in flints, dart-throwers, and engravings.

In the *Woolly Rhinoceros* (Fig. 34B) is the same visual grasp of the animal form, equally convincing and monumental. Here the contour is broken and more varied, and is accented at points as if to suggest the mass of the figure, while short lines indicate hair and serve as rudimentary shading.

The *Reindeer* of Figure 36A has been completely painted and modeled naturalistically in light and dark. It

[1] For a picture of the Cro-Magnon artist at work see Charles Knight's reconstruction in Osborn, *op. cit.*, PL. VII.

[B] *Bison. Incised and drawn on a cave wall. Aurignacian. (After a drawing by Breuil)*

was first incised on the wall, which had been somewhat smoothed by the scraper, and outlined in paint; then the details were added, and the figure was modeled in various tones. It seems natural, almost realistic. Yet note the character of the line of the back, and the beauty of line as line in the horns. Through the painted figure, as through the chalk drawings, there runs an inexplicable something, whether the figure is at rest or in movement, a life rhythm (for lack of a more precise term), which makes it not a stuffed animal but a vitally living creature. In the *Bellowing Bison* (Fig. 37A), for instance, how the painting makes one realize that single measured movement which controls every part of the body! Noteworthy also is a rudimentary attempt, in the hind legs, at three-dimensional drawing.

There is great variety in these primeval paintings, variety both of kind and of pose — mammoth, bison, reindeer, horse, boar, wolf; standing, walking, browsing, running, crouching. The majority are isolated figures, often superimposed, inexplicably, one on another, and with no relationship to each other or to the wall space, such as was

evident in the engravings and carvings. A notable exception is the *Procession of Mammoth* at Font-de-Gaume. Each painting reflects the keen observation of the hunter-artist, and especially an extraordinary memory for instantaneous poses, whose accuracy has been proved and hardly surpassed by the motion-picture camera of today. Yet this observation was of the selective type. It saw and recorded only those essential aspects which interpret the appearance and the character of the animal, its grace or awkwardness, its cunning or dignity.

But why were these paintings hidden in dark caverns in the heart of the mountain? And why do they represent almost entirely the game animals? Some scholars explain them as expression only, an outlet of the art impulse for its own sake in terms of the artist's own environment as a hunter. Others, with more probability and by analogy with practices of primitive peoples of today, see in them a magic purpose. These obscure isolated caverns may have been sacred places, and the bison painted on the wall may have been intended to bring success in the hunt, as the ibex carved on the dart-

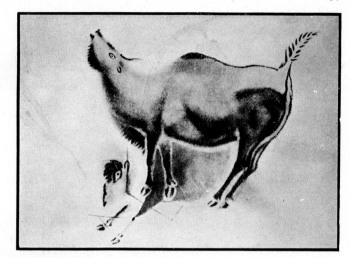

[A] *Bellowing Bison.*
Cave of Altamira, Spain.
c. 15,000 B.C.

thrower may have been believed to make the arm more sure and powerful in bringing down the game. At the same time, admitting the magic purpose, has not the art impulse found its outlet? Is there not combined in these paintings the same dual attainment of effective function and satisfying form that we noted even in the early flints?

In southeastern Spain Paleolithic paintings of an entirely different, and not yet entirely explicable, nature have been discovered. They are but a few inches in size and consist of a whole group of figures, both human and animal. Hunting, fighting, and dancing scenes are expressed with great vigor and with an exaggeration of movement that is in distinct contrast to the imposing dignity and serenity of the paintings at which we have been looking. They give evidence of an entirely opposite point of view toward form, for now it is not the visual perception of the object that the hand records, but a mental concept of it. These painters put together, quite unnaturalistically, symbols for the different parts of the body, symbols which convey the artist's idea with great conviction; for example, the contrasts of dynamic movement in Figure 38A.

SCULPTURE

The animal carvings on the throw sticks (Figs. 32B and C) foreshadow the capacity of the Paleolithic artist as a true sculptor. In the Cap-Blanc *Frieze of Animals* life-sized horses in procession, carved in relief ten or twelve inches deep, testify to the same sureness of vision as the paintings, and present the same naturalistic rendering. So also do the *Clay Bisons* modeled on the floor of the cavern of Tuc d'Audoubert. In the few extant examples of the human figure, however, a different approach appears. The Willendorf *Statuette* (so called from the cave in Austria where it was found) shows a concentration upon the repetition of bulbous shapes, with which the arms are integrated. In the small *Head of a Woman*, carved from bone, details are subordinated to the basic oval. Thus in sculpture, as well as painting, two divergent views[1] of representation are presented. Both of these basic but paradoxical concepts have occurred with varying degrees of dominance in the art expressions of all peoples.

[1] See Roger E. Fry, *Vision and Design*, Coward-McCann, 1924, "The Art of the Bushmen," for a discussion of these two contrasting attitudes.

[A]   *Hunters. H. c. 4 in. Caves of Eastern Spain. (Obermaier and Wernert)*

SUMMARY

The art of the hunter-artists is the art of a roaming hunter culture in which men first gave expression to their emotions as artists by infusing proportion, symmetry, quality of line, and decorative fitness into their objects of the hunt, of daily life, and of personal adornment. In their cave paintings of animals they proved themselves men of sure eye, able to grasp essentials and express them with an economical and forceful naturalism. In some of the paintings and carvings, however, especially those of the human figure (which, as far as we can tell, had no magical significance), the artist's feeling tends away from the visual impression toward a mental conception and thus toward a more abstract kind of representation.

2

MESOLITHIC AND NEOLITHIC ART

(ABOUT 20,000–2000 B.C.)

AS the ice of the Paleolithic Age melted in the increasing warmth, the reindeer migrated north, the mammoth and the woolly rhinoceros disappeared, and the hunter-artists vanished. Why and where? These are still unanswered questions. What we do know is that the ice age gave way to a transition period known as the Mesolithic. Europe became geographically, climatically, and biologically the Europe of today. Man still roamed as a hunter but seemed entirely devoid of the art impulse that manifested itself so vigorously in the Paleolithic Age. His tools were crude. The only art ob-

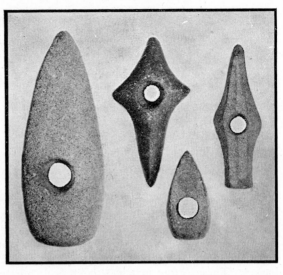

[A] *Scandinavian Daggers. Of stone flaked by pressure. L. 11½ in. Neolithic. (After Müller)*

[B] *Ground and Polished Stone Axe Heads. American Museum of Natural History, New York City. (American Museum of Natural History)*

jects to warrant attention in a brief survey are the painted pebbles of the Azilians, which are of interest chiefly, perhaps, as possible examples of an early form of writing.

Cultural evolution seemed to mark time. Then, about 10,000 B.C., there appeared changes which profoundly affected life — the domestication of animals and the cultivation of grain; the appearance of pottery and textiles and, late in the period, of metal. With grain, and the appearance of the farmer, permanent homes and village life replaced the nomad and his cave dwelling, and abodes developed into the comfortable homes of the Swiss lake villages.

STONEWARE, POTTERY, TEXTILES

New industries required new tools, which continued to be made chiefly of stone. Some of these, fashioned by the old method of chipping and flak-

ing by pressure, attained a climax of stonecutting in their beauty of shape and proportions, in the precision and rhythm of their flaking (Fig. 39A). But a new method of toolmaking, that of grinding and polishing, appeared, by means of which man could obtain a smooth surface and a fine cutting edge, and by attaching a wooden handle supply himself with a tool comparable to those of modern times (Fig. 39B).

Some of the demands made by permanent, more secure, and better-equipped homes were met by pottery and textiles. The idea of clay fashioned into a shape and hardened by fire may have been suggested by the attempt to protect a basket from fire by smearing clay on it before placing it over the flames. Neolithic pottery was made by hand, for the potter's wheel was apparently unknown. It was simple and rugged, sometimes pleasing in shape and proportion, with decoration — concentric lines, spirals, zigzags, dots, chevrons, the basic universal motifs —

[A]   *Neolithic Pottery*

well adapted to the shape and often strengthening the structural lines and surfaces (Fig. 40A). Only a few pieces of textiles have survived, but many objects, such as spinning whorls, loom weights, and bundles of fibers, are evidence of the weaving of cloth and of baskets. These latter articles, together with tools and implements, not only supplied the home but constituted objects of trade. For commerce had arisen, and with the interchange of goods came interchange of ideas, more definite social groupings, and a great acceleration in man's development in comparison with the long eons of time consumed in his early advances.

BUILDING

With the growth of communities, social organization, and trade and industry, monumental stone structures appear. *Dolmens* (*dol*, table, and *men*, stone), tombs or monuments to the dead, consisted of several stones set on end with a covering slab, hence the name. Single megaliths, *menhirs* (*men*, stone, *hir*, long), at times seventy feet high, were set up on end individually, or were arranged in long rows, as at Carnac in Brittany. Their purpose, though not clear, may have had to do with a cult of the dead or the worship of the sun. Sometimes they were arranged in a circle known as a *cromlech*, the most imposing of which is *Stonehenge* (Fig. 41A). This circle consists of

an outer ring of huge monoliths capped with lintels roughly cut just as they came from the quarry and laid without mortar. Inside this is a line of smaller stones; then a broken ring of five pairs of huge monoliths, each pair with its lintel; and again an inner broken circle of smaller stones, inside of which is a large slab that may have served as an altar. In the arrangement there is a feeling for order and symmetry, and a rhythm that is varied by alternating the large and small concentric circles. Such a structure is not properly speaking architecture. But it is the nearest approach to it that we find in western Europe until Roman times.[1]

GENERAL

Europe gives us the best picture of prehistoric art because it is there that excavation and research have been most intensively pursued. In other geographical areas, however, evidences of Paleolithic and especially of Neolithic culture are coming to light, as in China, Africa, and America. And though these studies are too recent and too incomplete to warrant conclusive findings, it seems fairly certain that we can see spread over large areas of the world in prehistoric times a culture in which are evident many of the charac-

[1] For recent studies and excavations of *Stonehenge*, based upon air photography, see "Stonehenge" article, Encyclopædia Britannica, 14th ed.

teristics seen in Europe. Neolithic culture, varying widely in extent of time in different areas, seems, as has been said, to have been a world-wide base from which evolved the great cultures of antiquity, each conditioned by all the varying geographical, social, economic, and religious forces peculiar to itself.

SUMMARY

Neolithic life was the result of great changes. Though man still hunted, he adopted a more settled kind of life because of the development of agriculture. He began to build a home, to make pottery and textiles, and to erect monumental structures of stone. He learned new methods of making stone tools, so efficient that they have been used down to the present time. His esthetic impulse seems feeble, in contrast to the brilliant, vital expressions of his Paleolithic predecessors, though his pottery shows interesting adaptations of simple motifs to ceramic decoration, and his stone structures give evidence of a feeling for orderly relationships. He perhaps was marking time, slowly assimilating and evolving ideas and methods that were to produce great art in succeeding ages.

[A] *Stonehenge. Trilithons, pairs of upright monoliths carrying stone lintels. Salisbury Plain, England. (Harold Allen)*

BIBLIOGRAPHY

Avebury, John Lubbock, Baron, *Pre-Historic Times*, 7th ed., Holt, 1914

Boyle, Mary E., *In Search of Our Ancestors*, Little, Brown, 1928

Breasted, James H , *Ancient Times*, 2d ed. rev., Ginn, 1935

Brown, Gerard B., *The Art of the Cave Dweller*, R. V. Coleman, 1928

Burkitt, Miles C., *Our Early Ancestors*, Macmillan, 1929

Childe, Vere G., *The Dawn of European Civilization*, Knopf, 1925

—————— *The Most Ancient East*, Knopf, 1929

Frobenius, Leo, and Fox, D. C., *Prehistoric Rock Pictures in Europe and Africa*, Museum of Modern Art, New York City, c. 1937

Kuhn, Herbert, *Die Malerei der Eiszeit*, Munich, 1922 (Particularly valuable for the illustrations)

MacCurdy, George G., *Human Origins*, 2 vols., Appleton, 1924

Osborn, Henry Fairfield, *Men of the Old Stone Age*, 3d ed., Scribner, 1918

Parkyn, Ernest A., *An Introduction to the Study of Prehistoric Art*, Longmans, Green, 1915

Peake, Harold J. E., and Fleure, H. J., *Hunters and Artists*, Yale University Press, 1927 (The Corridors of Time, Vol. II)

Piette, Edouard, *L'art pendant l'âge du renne*, Paris, 1907

Raphael, Max, *Prehistoric Cave Paintings*, tr. by Norbert Guterman, Pantheon Books, 1945

Sawtell, Ruth O., and Treat, Ida, *Primitive Hearths in the Pyrenees*, Appleton, 1927

Sollas, William J., *Ancient Hunters and Their Modern Representatives*, 3d ed. rev., Macmillan, 1924

Spearing, Herbert G., *The Childhood of Art; or, The Ascent of Man*, rev. ed., Holt, 1930

Swindler, Mary H., *Ancient Painting*, Yale University Press, 1929

Near Eastern Art

3

EGYPTIAN ART

Early Egypt and the Old Kingdom

(ABOUT 4500–2475 B.C.[1])

FROM the top of the Great Pyramid we look out over the undulating floor of a vast desert plateau through which cuts a narrow valley of luxuriant green, of fields and palms fringing a winding river. Above blazes a glorious sun in a cloudless sky. This is Egypt (Figs. 43A, 44A, 49A).

Of this environment several facts persistently confronted the Egyptian: the brilliant sun, the Nile River, and the great geographical contrasts of his land — the barrenness and stern majesty of illimitable deserts; the rich fertility and delights of the valley with its trees, grains, flowers, and birds, all gifts of the sun and the river. So insistently did these facts of environment impress themselves on his mind that

[1] There is considerable difference of opinion among scholars on the question of Egyptian chronology and of the spelling of Egyptian names. In Chapter 3 of this book, the chronology is that of J. H. Breasted; the spelling follows that of the Oriental Institute of the University of Chicago

they early became dominating forces in his attempt to account for his inexplicable world. Evil and beneficent spirits animated all things. In the daily spectacle of the sun he envisaged a mighty god Re (Ra), or Amun-Re, sailing across the sky each day in his bark, and back to the east by night along a river of the nether world. In the annual rise of the Nile he saw the resurrection of Osiris, who after a tragic earthly life and death became god of the dead. Just as Osiris entered upon a new existence in another world and just as nature with the rise of the Nile burst into new life, so to every Egyptian lay open the opportunity for a similar experience of revived life after death. This hope constituted one of the most powerful influences in Egyptian civilization and Egyptian art.

While Paleolithic man of western Europe was coping with the rigors of a glacial age his relative in North Africa was enjoying a more leisurely life in a land of abundant rain and luxuriant vegetation. Then, with a change of climate in northern Africa which brought about desert conditions, Stone Age man with his animals gathered about the oases or migrated to the abundant waters of the Nile Valley.

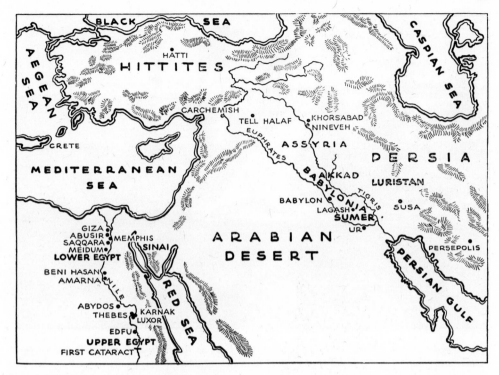

[A] *Egypt and the Ancient Near East*

Along the river he built his hamlets, tamed the animals, and began to plant grain. Before 3000 B.C. he had evolved a system of picture writing, invented a calendar, worked out a system of irrigation, and had discovered metal — perhaps accidentally as the molten drops of copper separated from the rock in his campfire in Sinai.

Tiny states began to emerge along the river and slowly coalesced into two kingdoms, Upper and Lower Egypt, which were finally united about 3400 B.C. by a king called Menes. At the head of the political and social system we see a supreme pharaoh, who probably owned all the land; a group of suppressed nobles received their appointments from him. The mass of the people were (with possible exceptions) slaves. The chief economic basis was agriculture, though commerce was carried on with the Beduins of Sinai and with the Aegean lands. Toward the end of the Old Kingdom the highly efficient government of the pharaoh weakened. The landed nobles, who were gaining power, began to lay the foundations of a feudal state.

A vivid picture of Egyptian life comes from the tombs, for the provision for life hereafter was one of the chief concerns of existence in this world. The Egyptian believed that there was a force called the *ka* which was the counterpart of the body. It came into being with the body, continued through life with it, was in all features like it, though invisible, and at death accompanied it into the next world. As the *ka* and the body were coexistent, the body must be carefully preserved through mummification, and the *ka* through offerings of all kinds. Thus to

[A]   *Egypt at Low Nile. At the top of the steep bank is the cultivated area with palm trees; in the background rise the cliffs of the desert plateau. (Author)*

secure necessities and luxuries for the spirit land, which was but a reflection of this world, it was necessary to paint or carve them upon the tomb walls, or to place in the burial chambers small models, each of which, with the proper incantation, would function normally in the hereafter. It is these beliefs that motivate most of Egyptian art — its pyramids, sculpture, painting, and fine goldwork.

ARCHITECTURE AND SCULPTURE

Recall for a moment the Egyptian landscape: stern, vast, and of generally horizontal lines, both in the valley floor and in the strata and crests of the cliffs. No gently curving hills or jagged picturesque mountains relieve the monotony. A contrastingly luxuriant valley, a thread of an oasis, twists through the rocky desert plateau. Considering this setting, the social organization within it, the importance to himself of the Egyptian's religious ideas, and the abundant supply of stone, what forms and purposes would one expect his architecture to embody? Apart from the palaces and houses, temporary and flimsy though comfortable enough in the warm climate, it is not surprising to find massive enduring tombs and temples of stone as the dominant architectural expression.

In the Old Kingdom, the desire to create a permanent safe abiding-place for the dead led to the erection of tombs, of which the pyramids,[1] or royal tombs,

[1] The pyramid field extends for about 50 miles on the western bank of the Nile south from the Delta, in the vicinity of the Old Kingdom capital, Memphis (Fig. 43A); for Lower Egypt was the center of civilization in the Old Kingdom.

[A] *Pyramids of Khafre and Khufu. Giza. IV Dynasty (2900–2750 B.C.). (Hoyningen-Huene from Steindorff's* Egypt, *J. J. Augustin, Publishers)*

are the climax. A distant view of the *Pyramids of Giza* (Fig. 49A) reveals their position on the desert plateau safe above the highest level of the Nile. They rise with unbroken line and surface from the plateau base to an apex, comprising a form of great simplicity and dignity. Contrast for a moment the façade of a Gothic cathedral (Fig. 349B) with its multiplicity of vertical lines, each pointed arch, statue, pinnacle, buttress, and tower contributing to the soaring quality and to the broken light and shade. Notice how different is the feeling of unrest and exaltation there experienced from the quiet repose that comes from the unity of the unbroken line and surface of the pyramid.

Such a structure, simple geometric form though it is, was not conceived in a moment, but was the result of a long evolution. As far back as we can trace the Egyptian, he buried his dead in a pit over which he heaped up the sand, holding it in place with stones and twigs. By slow process this pit and sand heap grew; the actual chamber below the ground became rectangular and was faced with wood, brick, and finally stone. At the same time the mound above was covered with brick or stone, which followed in a general way the lines of a sand heap and thus attained a shape that looks like a low truncated pyramid, called a *mastaba* (Fig. 46A). Finally, some king who was ambitious to erect a still mightier tomb began to

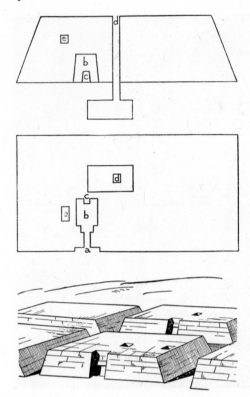

[A] *Typical Mastaba.* a. *entrance;* b. *chapel;* c. *false door;* d. *shaft down which the sarcophagus was let into the burial chamber below;* e. *serdab for the statue. L. 40–50 ft. Mastaba is an Arabic word meaning a bench or terrace.*

pile mastaba upon mastaba, forming a step pyramid; and then, by filling in the steps, attained the pure pyramidal form.[1]

The mastaba was a solid mass except for the chapel, a reception room for the *ka* where offerings were made, and the *serdab* or cellar, a tiny secret chamber built in the heart of the structure to contain a statue of the deceased that could represent him in the spirit world if anything should happen to the actual

[1] For a graphic illustration of this development, see James H. Breasted, *Ancient Times,* new ed., Ginn, 1935, p. 74.

body. The chapel became complex, as time went on, with additional rooms and corridors which were covered with reliefs that vividly picture the everyday life of the Egyptian, for the benefit, as has been said, of the *ka.*

These reliefs represent the production of grain; the raising of cattle; the making of jewelry, vases, and pottery; hunting on the desert or in the papyrus swamp; processions of offering-bearers; and banquet scenes. Thus they provide the dead with both the necessities and the pleasures of life. The scenes are arranged in horizontal zones and the figures are carved in very low relief and painted in flat colors which are partly naturalistic and partly governed by a color scheme that creates a pleasing wall decoration apart from the subject interest.

Figure 47A represents a harvesting scene. In the upper rows the harvesters are cutting the grain, leaving a high stubble just as they do in Egypt today; below, men with staves are driving the donkeys back and forth over the threshing-floor, tying the grain in great bags, and loading it on the donkeys' backs or tossing the bundles into the granaries. The figures are drawn with very little overlapping except in the case of the animals, where depth is suggested by repeating the silhouette. The figures of the men, so full of life and movement, are drawn according to an Egyptian formula — the head and legs in profile, the torso and the eye in front view.

This conventional method of treating the figure, which persists in both reliefs and painting throughout the entire course of Egyptian art, we can see more clearly in a rare wooden panel from a mastaba, that of *Hesire* (Fig. 48A). Though a single figure is represented, it is not placed in the center of the panel; yet the balance is maintained by the staff and the writing

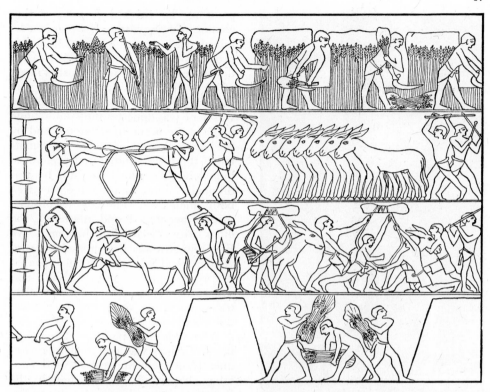

[A]   *Work in the Fields. Reaping, threshing, and stacking. From the mastaba of Ti, Saqqara.*

utensils — which Hesire holds in his left hand; the horizontals of feet, baton, girdle, and shoulders happily balance the otherwise insistent verticals. Look more closely at the figure itself. To appreciate its high quality we must frankly accept the conventional way in which different parts of the body are drawn from different points of view. This was not because the Egyptian could not execute a profile, as we shall see, but simply because this conventional method of drawing the figure, established early in Egypt, held a more powerful grip upon the artist than did a naturalistic rendering. Possibly, actual rather than visual truth appealed more strongly. The artist knew that a man had two arms, although in a profile he could see but one, and his instinct bade him indicate the fact rather than record the visual image. In the case of *Hesire*, the feeling of distortion is not disconcerting, so skillfully has the artist united the parts and so decoratively compelling is the entire panel. In this relief we feel the proud bearing of a noble and also the strength of a man of determination. Note the individualized face with its high cheekbones and firm mouth, the careful modeling about neck, shoulders, and knees; the firmness and strength of the carving, especially in the kilt and the wig, which produce a broken texture to contrast with the relatively smooth surfaces of the rest of the figure.

How the artist went about his work we have learned from some of the tombs where the walls have been left

[A]   *Panel of Hesire. Wood. H. c. 4 ft.
c. 2800* B.C. *Cairo Museum.*

painting, he covered it with a thin coating of fine plaster. His pigment he mixed with some binding medium, probably a gum, and applied it to the dry stone or plaster, with brushes made of reeds, in flat even tones, using no light and shade. Whatever modeling was done was done by the contour line made in the preliminary sketch and by the chisel. Proportions were not a matter of the artist's individual preference but were determined for him by traditional canons, as were the forms of both men and animals. Sculptors' models he copied and mastered, too often with mechanical hardness. All Egyptian art was determined by convention; and when great art appeared it was because the artist's ability and personality were so superior that they transcended the restrictive traditional influences.

We wonder that painting rather than painted reliefs was not used more frequently in these finely decorated mastaba chapels. It is as though the Egyptian scorned the brush as inferior to the chisel. What he could do in the field of painting is illustrated by one rare example, the *Geese of Meidum* (Fig. 50A). On a border are painted two pairs of waddling ducks and feeding geese. The birds fill the panel with a symmetrically balanced composition that is both naturalistic and abstract: naturalistic in that the painter has observed the birds and their characteristic movements keenly; abstract in that he has filtered these observations into a decorative pattern without loss of the essentials of the form and movements of the birds. There is no background, except for some sparse herbage, and no natural illumination which would give rise to the use of light and shadow to indicate volume in the figures. On the contrary, the painter has seen in the fowl flat areas of light and dark color which he has marked off

unfinished. He planned his decoration with the help of guide lines to proportion both the spaces and the figures; then he sketched the latter in, made an incision along the lines of the preliminary sketch with a chisel, and cut away the background, leaving his design in relief. If the stone was too uneven to offer a good foundation for

[A] *Pyramids of Khufu and Khafre. Restored. Giza. (Hoelscher)*

with firm lines and repeated with effective variation — all of which contributes to the decorative quality of the panel.

However, the pyramid and not the mastaba is the most characteristic structure of the Old Kingdom. Most important are the great *Pyramids of Giza*, of which that of *Khufu*, or *Cheops* (Fig. 45A), is the largest. With the exception of the galleries and burial chamber (Fig. 52B) it is solid masonry of limestone which was roughly cut in the quarries in the eastern Nile cliffs directly across the river and floated over at high Nile to the base of the plateau where the tomb was to be built. There the masons finished cutting the stones and marked them with red ink to indicate the place of each in the structure. Then they were laid course upon course by great gangs of slaves who dragged them by sheer human labor up the temporary ramps.[1] The angles

left by the decreasing courses were filled with casing stones of a pearly-white limestone, cut with such nicety that the eye can scarcely detect the joinings. Thus the pyramid presented a perfectly smooth surface from foundation to tip.[2]

Nicety of engineering is also apparent in the fact that — without modern surveying instruments and machinery, and with only a knotted rope for laying out the huge base and only human labor to drag stones of two-and-one-half tons into place — so accurate is the work that the most delicate modern instrument can detect only about one-half inch of error in the measurement of one side. Yet it is not alone huge size, successful mechanical engineering, and skill in stonecutting that constitute the art of such a structure, but its formal engineering as well — the proportions, and the simple dignity of the form, so

[1] An unfinished pyramid in the foreground of Figure 49A shows these ramps.

[2] A few of these casing stones can still be seen at the base. The ragged condition of the pyramid is due to the depredations of the Muslim builders of Cairo.

[A]   *Geese of Meidum. So called because the panel was found in a tomb*

consistent with its function and so adapted to its geographical setting.[1]

On the east side of the Great Pyramid are three small pyramids belonging to members of the royal family, while clustered about are rows of mastabas of the great nobles who, having been associated with the pharaoh in life, wished to continue in this place of honor even in the tomb. The pyramid of the pharaoh, however, is the dominating structure of the whole cemetery (Fig. 49A), just as he himself had been the dominating power of Egyptian life.

The middle pyramid of the triple group at Giza, the *Pyramid of Khafre*, is somewhat smaller than that of Khufu, indicating an economic and political waning in the power of the pharaoh. This pyramid is important, however, because from the remains surrounding it we can study all the additional structures, which, together with the pyramid itself, comprise the pyramid complex. To do this let us look first at the

---

[1] The massiveness, solidity, and weight of the *Pyramid of Khufu* is better realized when one recalls some dimensions (in round numbers): base, 775 ft., covering 13 acres; height, 450 ft. (originally 480 ft.); the flat space now on the top, 30 ft. square. According to Petrie the structure contains about 2,300,000 blocks of stone, each of which averages in weight 2½ tons. These stones are chiefly limestone except about the burial chambers, where very finely cut granite is used.

mastaba-shaped structure in the right foreground of Figure 49A. This building is near the town in the valley, at the base of the plateau on which the pyramid stands. In order to provide for the spirit of the dead, offerings must be placed at the tomb frequently. The hot climb up over the sandy hill led to the erection of a covered causeway from the valley up to the little chapel adjoining the eastern side of the pyramid. For as the spirit land lay in the west, the spirit must come toward the east to receive the offerings. Hence tombs were built on the western bank, and the chapel was on the eastern side of the pyramid. The beginning of the causeway presupposed some kind of entrance or vestibule. To provide that is the function of the building in the valley.

Thus we have seen that a pyramid complex consists of (1) the pyramid itself, within or below which was the burial chamber; (2) the chapel adjoining the pyramid on the eastern side, where the offerings were made and ceremonies performed, and where were kept in store chambers the linen, grain, honey, oil, and other offerings of food and drink, together with the rich ceremonial vessels (Fig. 55B) for use in the daily rites; (3) the covered causeway leading over the cliffs; and (4) the valley temple, or vestibule of the causeway, down in the valley.

chapel near Meidum. IV Dynasty (2900–2750 B.C.). Cairo Museum.

The valley temple of the *Pyramid of Khafre* is built on the lintel system; that is, the upright supports are bridged over with horizontal beams, or lintels. Here supports and lintels are huge red-granite monoliths, finely proportioned, skillfully cut and polished, and entirely devoid of decoration. Alabaster slabs cover the floor, and seated statues, the only embellishment, are ranged alongside. This interior, protected from the hot sun by the great blocks, must have been cool and dim. It is lighted by a few rays filtering in from above, slantwise. This is because the pillars of the central aisle are higher than the side walls, and the roof over the central part is therefore at a higher level than that over the sides. In the vertical space left between these two levels are slits in the stone, through which the light comes, forming an embryonic clerestory (Fig. 52C), a structural feature that became characteristic of early Christian churches. With its plain, simple dignity, it is a remarkably impressive room, harmonizing with the simple massive tomb to which it led.

Leaving Giza and traveling up the river to Abusir, let us look at the chapel and valley temple of the *Pyramid of Sahure* (Figs. 52A, 53A), much smaller in size and built about a hundred years after that of Khafre. Here we see something not found at Giza — columns,

in place of rectangular pillars, and wall paintings. From the natural forms of his environment the Egyptian found in the palm tree, with its tall trunk and spreading leaves, an inspiration for the design of his columns. The elegance of this design, in no way hampering the column's function of support, together with the bright colors on the walls, lends an air of splendor which contrasts sharply with the austere simplicity of the *Valley Temple of Khafre.*

As we have seen in the case of the latter and of the mastabas, sculpture in the round also played its part in the tomb architecture of the Old Kingdom. Its function was bound up with the desire either to perpetuate or to serve the dead. Should a carefully mummified body by any chance perish, then a statue as nearly like the original as possible could represent the body in the world to come. Hence we are not surprised to find portraiture early developed.[1] As for its form, both material and style are in complete harmony with the simple, geometric, grandly monumental structures of which it is an integral part. Though wood, clay, and bronze were used, stone was the primary material — the

[1] As with the pyramids, a long evolution in carving must be presupposed for the high accomplishment of the Old Kingdom sculpture, though we have only incomplete evidence of it.

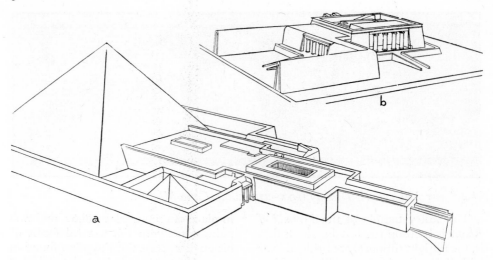

[A]   *Pyramid of Sahure. Restored. Abusir. c. 2735* B.C.   a. *pyramid, chapel, and upper end of causeway;* b. *valley-temple.*

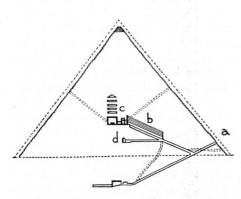

[B]   *Section of the Pyramid of Khufu.* a. *entrance;* b. *grand gallery;* c. *King's chamber;* d. *Queen's chamber.*

[C]   *Valley-Temple of Khafre. Section showing the clerestory. (After Hoelscher)*

limestone and sandstone of the Nile cliffs, the granite from the dikes at the cataracts, and diorite from the desert.

The statue of *Khafre* (Fig. 13A) illustrates the style. Located in the valley temple of the pyramid, it is one of the row of statues which served as hostages for the real body. The rectangular masses of the statues, in complete harmony with the surrounding rectangular space, served to break the severe simplicity of unadorned surfaces. We see the pharaoh seated on his throne, on which is the intertwined lotus and papyrus, symbol of united Egypt. He faces directly forward, with no turn in any part of the figure. About his head are the protecting wings of the hawk, symbol of his semidivine station as son of the sun god. He wears the simple kilt of the Old Kingdom and a linen headdress which covers his forehead smoothly and falls in plaited folds over the breast. The false ceremonial beard is partly broken off.

As a portrait the statue is characterized by aliveness, yet it is permeated with a feeling of imperturbable calm

[A] *Pyramid of Sahure. Restored. Abusir. Colonnaded hall of the chapel. c. 2735* B.C.
(*Borchardt*)

that conveys the impression not of an individual but of something greater — the enduring power of the pharaoh, the abstract conception of the dignity of kingship. This impression derives from several contributing factors: the character of the form, the summary nature of its carving, and the distinctive quality of its material. The figure is carved from diorite, a stone so hard that it will turn a steel tool. The large planes are cut generally parallel to the planes of the block of stone, and there is no movement from side to side. Furthermore, the figure, the bird, and the throne compose, with a feeling of inevitability, into a unity of architectural quality.

Standing figures present the same formal qualities, even in a group such as the *Menkaure* (*Mycerinus*) *and His Queen* in the Boston Museum. In *Ranofer* (Fig. 54A) we see a figure facing directly forward with left foot advanced and arms held close to the side. By simplifying the contour, the wig adds to the compactness of the figure, which is massive and rather angular. The firmly placed erect head, in fact the whole figure, is permeated with an intense vitality. As in the *Khafre*, the individual traits of the man are submerged in the generalized features. The erect head and the whole bearing denote a person of the noble classes.

The vivacity of many of the Old Kingdom statues is enhanced by the use of rock crystal for the eyes, and of color, which not only covers the entire surface but adds details not carved in the stone, such as hair, brows, and jewelry. In the case of female figures the flesh is of a yellowish tone because the Egyptian woman led a more secluded life than the man, whose tanned skin is usually painted a dark reddish color. Thus while the color is partly naturalistic it is, even more, decorative, for it is laid on flat and strongly differentiates the parts of the figure.

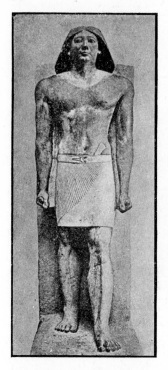

[A]   *Ranofer. H. c. 62 in. Of limestone, painted. V Dynasty (2750–2625 B.C.) Cairo Museum.*

[B]   *Seated Scribe. H. c. 2 ft. Of limestone, painted, with eyes of inlaid rock crystal. Found in a tomb at Saqqara. V Dynasty (2750–2625 B.C.) Louvre, Paris.*

In the *Sheikh el-Beled* and the *Seated Scribe* (Fig. 54B) we find lively expressions of the lower classes whose function was to serve the king in the spirit world. Both are more highly individualized than the kings and nobles. The *Sheikh* is a self-satisfied fellow, perhaps a middle-class overseer. He stands erect and in frontal pose, but lifts one arm to hold his staff. Here the sculptor is working in wood and by making the arms of separate pieces, which he apparently did not dare to do in stone, he could use a freer pose. Again, because of the cylindrical character of wood, we note a basic cylindrical form in the figure. Originally, the wood was covered with linen tightly glued on, to furnish a surface for painting.

As we turn to the *Scribe*, which is carved from stone, we see the same four-sided organization as in *Khafre*. Here is a keen alert servant with a spare face, square jaw, and thin lips — a shrewd man with a sense of humor. He sits cross-legged, Eastern fashion, with his pen in his hand (as is indicated by the position of the fingers) ready to take down what his master will dictate. Legs, back, and arms are blocked out in large masses only; chest, shoulders, and head alone are individualized. Yet the expression of momentary expectancy — an abstract idea — which fills the entire figure has been caught and transformed into the permanency of stone in a manner that is large, and truly sculptural.

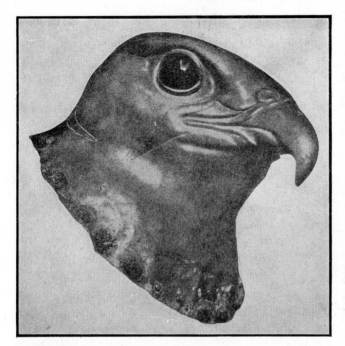

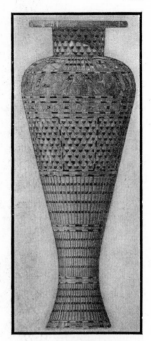

[A] *Head of a Hawk. Gold. H. 4 in. Cairo Museum.*
(Fechheimer)

[B] *Ceremonial Vase. Restored. Of gold and lapis lazuli. H. c. 2 ft. c. 2750 B.C. (Stoedtner)*

STONEWORK AND GOLDWORK

The dignity and the vitality of Old Kingdom building, carving, and painting repeats itself in the creations of the various craftsmen. This was particularly true in the work of the stonecutters, who furnished vessels for household use, in the products of the goldsmiths, who provided the jewelry so necessary in Egyptian costume, and in the fine ceremonial objects for the tomb ritual.

The stonecutter had inherited a tradition dating far back into prehistoric times. With the invention, before 3000 B.C., of the stone-pointed drill with shaft, fly wheel, and crank for turning and, somewhat after 3000 B.C., of the tubular drill of metal, he was enabled to produce vessels of astonishing quality. Such hard stones as porphyry, diorite, and hematite were used where the variegated color of the stone adds a decorative quality. Among the softer stones alabaster was widely used, not only for its attractive ivory color but also because its veining could be utilized as a decorative element, and the stone could be worked to a transparent thinness. The vessels are generally simple and rugged in shape, and they vary in size from a tiny jar for unguent to great storage jars, bowls, and plates a foot in diameter. Ornament is rarely found, for the craftsman depended for his effects upon shape and proportions, and upon the material for its own intrinsic weight, color, and texture. It is an indication of the craftsman's sensitivity that we find a small unguent jar made from delicate alabaster and a large storage jar from heavy porphyry.

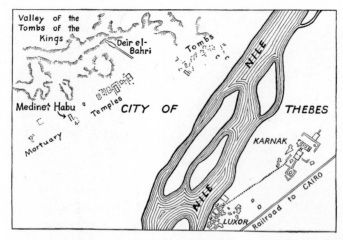

[A] *Map of Thebes, showing the most important temples and tombs. The dwellings have disappeared.*

The goldsmith, with an abundant supply of material, developed many ways of working it. He could cast, chase, solder, hammer, or plait it with amazing technical skill. A hawk's head (Fig. 55A) was originally attached to a bronze body by rivets still left just below the neck. Here the goldsmith has hammered the metal into shape, probably over a mold, soldered the parts together, and inserted eyes cut from red jasper. Like the painter of the *Geese of Meidum* (Fig. 50A), he had observed his bird form well, and with an amazing economy of modeling has given expression to the essential form and character of the hawk.

SUMMARY

By the beginning of the Old Kingdom those conventions had been established which controlled, with but one important break at the time of the Empire, the long course of Egyptian art. The builders of the Old Kingdom were primarily tomb-builders, and their stone mastabas and pyramids are still massive, static, and enduring, thoroughly in harmony with their site and function. Into them fitted the imposing portrait sculpture that was required by religious belief, conventional in form and conception, but filled with an intense vitality. Paintings and painted reliefs, chiefly in the chapels of the tombs, were based upon conventions which evolved from mental rather than visual concepts of the world. They were finely chiseled, gaily decorative, and teeming with eager life. The stone-cutter and the goldsmith provided additional evidence of sensitivity to material and effective design in creating objects of daily use and personal adornment, objects which partake of the sobriety and dignity of the pyramids and the statue of Khafre.

The Middle Kingdom and the Empire

(2160–1090 B.C.)

THE tendency toward the decline of the pharaoh's power, with the corresponding gain in the power of the nobles, had plunged the country into a period of struggle and disorder. Out of this eventually arose a feudal state, at the head of which still stood the pharaoh; but he maintained his power by balancing the nobles one against another. Economically it was a period of great prosperity. Agriculture was developed by building canals and reclaiming the land; commerce was carried on not only in the south but also with Asia and the Aegean Islands. And now Egypt became a military power. Athirst for conquests, it extended its boundaries not only far south into Nubia but east to the Euphrates. Thus on the monuments we see military subjects: weapons, chariots, and the horse, which, coming with the pre-Indo-Europeans from the grasslands of central Asia, finally reached the Nile Valley about 1700 B.C. The wealth that came from the booty taken in these wars made possible the development of the capital city, Thebes, into a great metropolis with magnificent palaces, tombs, and temples ranged along both banks of the river (Figs. 43A, 56A).

A considerable change had taken place in thought and religion. The Egyptian could now look back over his own history for centuries. In the light of the futility of man's greatest efforts the fresh and vital faith of the Pyramid age gave way to pessimism, which is reflected in the portraits of the age (Fig. 70A) and in its literature.

"Follow thy desire while thou livest,

.   .   .   .

Celebrate the glad day!
Rest not therein!
For lo, none taketh his goods with him,
Yea, no man returneth again, that is gone thither."[1]

A broadening horizon of thought and the growth of the idea of world empire fired the imagination of a young king (1375–1358 B.C.), who, applying the

principle of political power to the realm of religion, conceived the idea of one god and creator, whom he called Aton, an old name of the sun god Re. He then broke both politically and religiously with the powerful though corrupt priesthood at Thebes, took for himself the name Akhnaton, which means "spirit of Aton," and set up a new capital at a place that he called Akhetaton, meaning "Horizon of Aton" (now known as Amarna). Something of the spirit of the new faith we feel in the hymns that Akhnaton wrote:

The Splendor of Aton

"Thy dawning is beautiful in the horizon of heaven,
O living Aton, Beginning of life!
When thou risest in the eastern horizon of heaven,
Thou fillest every land with thy beauty;
For thou art beautiful, great, glittering, high over the earth;
Thy rays, they encompass the lands, even all thou hast made.

.   .   .   .

How manifold are all thy works!
They are hidden from before us,
O thou sole god, whose powers no other possesseth.
Thou didst create the earth according to thy desire,
While thou wast alone:
Men, all cattle large and small,
All that are upon the earth,
That fly with their wings,
The countries of Syria and Nubia,
The land of Egypt.
Thou settest every man in his place,
Thou suppliest their necessities."[1]

Egypt by this time, however, was too crystallized by the traditions of thou-

[1] James H. Breasted, *A History of Egypt from the Earliest Times to the Persian Conquest,* Scribner, 1909, p. 206.

[1] *Ibid.,* pp. 371 ff., where a complete translation is given in parallel arrangement with one of the Hebrew Psalms, which it approximates to an amazing degree.

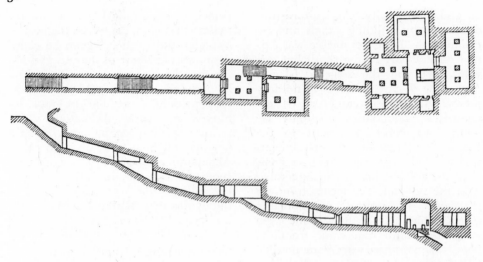

[A] *Tomb of Seti I. Section and Plan. Thebes, Valley of the Tombs of the Kings. XIX Dynasty (1350–1205 B.C.). (Benoit)*

sands of years, too enthralled by its nobles, military leaders, and particularly by the powerful priesthood of Amun, to accept an idea so contrary to tradition. Akhnaton, by nature not a practical man of affairs, became entirely absorbed in the religion of Aton. The result was that, through upheavals at home and invasions from without, the Empire dwindled while its ruler pursued his monotheistic ideals. At his death the power at Thebes was restored and after a period of decline the Empire was reorganized by Seti I ⟨1313–1292 B.C.) and Ramesses II, the Great (1292–1225 B.C.), but it was never firmly re-established.

Life in "Hundred-Gated Thebes" and at Amarna, too, was luxurious and magnificent. The enormous wealth of the pharaoh enabled him to erect a palace with decorations that reproduced for him the outdoor world in which he delighted. On the floors and walls, which were painted or decorated in glazed tiles, were represented ducks swimming in the water and the animal life of the marshes (Fig. 75A); across

the deep-blue background of the ceiling flew flocks of birds, and butterflies. The furniture was superbly designed and skillfully constructed (Fig. 76B). Magnificent gold and silver vessels, blue faïence lotus cups, glass vases of various colors, rich jewelry (Figs. 76A, 78A and B, 79A) — all these tell of a magnificence quite in contrast to the sterner dignity of the Pyramid age.

ARCHITECTURE
AND SCULPTURE

As the Old Kingdom was preeminently the period of the pyramid-builder, so the Middle Kingdom and the Empire were that of the temple-builder. This was not because burial no longer demanded the elaborate care shown earlier. An even more scrupulous attention was given to the protection of the body, but in a different way. Robberies and neglect had shown the futility of the pyramid for perfect preservation; and while pyramids continued to be built by the earlier pharaohs of the period, they were small, and made of

[A]   *Temple of Queen Hatshepsut. Deir el-Bahri. XVIII Dynasty (1580–1350 B.C.) (Hoy-ningen-Huene from Steindorff's* Egypt, *J. J. Augustin, Publishers)*

brick. Today they are little more than mounds, though their substructures have yielded rich finds of jewelry and other mortuary equipment.

The nobles no longer sought a locality for burial near that of the king, but hollowed out their tombs and chapels in the cliffs bordering the Nile. The pharaohs themselves, perhaps following the example of their retainers, chose for their burial site a wild, desolate valley west of the cliffs at Thebes now known as the Valley of the Tombs of the Kings (Fig. 56A), where deep in the rocky hills they carved burial chambers which were reached by long corridors, sometimes extending five hundred feet into the hillside[1] (Fig. 58A). The entrances were carefully concealed; and because of the impracticability of making offerings at the actual tombs, the mortuary

temples, which correspond to the chapel abutting the eastern side of the pyramid, were separated from the tombs and built on the eastern side of the cliffs along the bank of the river. In each case the temple was on the axis of the tomb, and hence in the same relative position as the pyramid chapel. These temples were dedicated to the gods, and each provided the king who built it with a place for worshiping his patron god during his lifetime, and then served as his mortuary chapel after death. Hence they became elaborate and sumptuous, befitting both the kings and the gods of a mighty empire.

The noblest of these royal mortuary temples is *Deir el-Bahri*,[2] the temple of Queen Hatshepsut (Fig. 59A). The site

---

[1] The *Tomb of Tutankhamun*, discovered in the valley in 1922, is a rock-cut tomb of this type.

[2] *Deir el-Bahri*, meaning "The North Monastery," is the modern Arab name of the locality, from a monastery, now destroyed, that was built on the site.

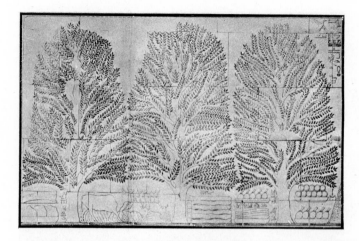

[A] *Frankincense Trees. Deir el-Bahri. (Naville)*

is a sloping bay in the western cliffs (Fig. 56A), above which tower rocks weathered into columnar shapes, the vertical lines of which contrast happily with the long horizontals of the plateau edge; the rough surfaces afford deep shadows and a more broken mass of light and shade than is usual in Egypt. The temple rises from the valley floor in a series of colonnaded terraces connected by ramps to the cliffs in which were cut the sanctuary and the shrines. Notice in the distant view how effec-

tively the long horizontals and verticals of the colonnades and their rhythm of light and dark repeat the pattern of the cliffs above — an intentional relationship between the architectural design and its natural setting.

Consistency and a reserved taste, both in the general plan and in every part, give this temple striking unity and quiet dignity. In the colonnades, for example, the pillars are either simply rectangular or chamfered off into sixteen sides rather than of the more

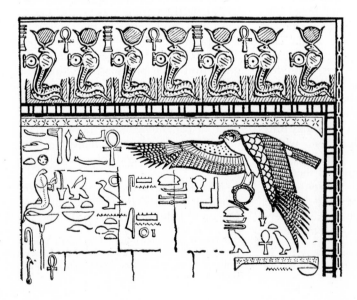

[B] *Polychrome Design. Showing the hawk of lower Egypt that hovers protectingly about the pharaoh. The motif of the border is the* uræus *combined with the sun disk. The figures are painted in bright colors, chiefly red and blue, with a little green and yellow. Deir el-Bahri. (Naville)*

elaborate lotus or papyrus form, and are sensitively proportioned and spaced. The great amount of sculpture that adorned the temple is very definitely an integral part of the entire design. The statues in the round, perhaps two hundred in number — sphinxes guarding the approach, statues of the queen flanking the doorways and the pillars or kneeling along the procession path — are purely architectural in their simple masses, as are the painted low reliefs (Figs. 60A and B) which cover all the walls. The bright color and the gardens, however, added a vivacious note for in Hatshepsut's day the terraces were not the barren places they now are, but luxuriant gardens filled with frankincense trees and strange rare plants brought here from the faraway land of Punt. "It was a gorgeous way up which the procession of Amūn passed. . . . In its brilliancy of color under the Egyptian skies the long vista must have been a magnificent reiteration of a claim to almost superhuman power."[1]

[1] "The Egyptian Expedition 1930–1931," *Metropolitan Museum of Art Bulletin*, March, 1932, Sec. II, p. 14.

[A]   *Temple of Amun. Karnak. Central aisle of the hypostyle hall. The columns are 66 ft. high, and the capitals 22 ft. wide at the top. XIX Dynasty (1350–1205 B.C.). See Figs. 64A and B for an idea of the original appearance and the plan.*

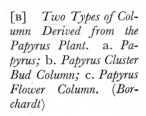

[B]   *Two Types of Column Derived from the Papyrus Plant. a. Papyrus; b. Papyrus Cluster Bud Column; c. Papyrus Flower Column. (Borchardt)*

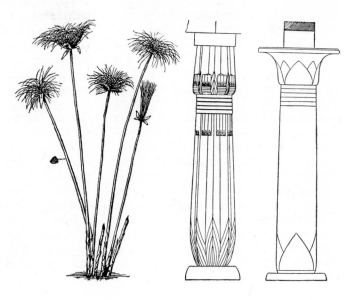

[A]   *Temple of Horus. Edfu. View from the side showing the pylon and the open court. Though later in date, it preserves all the characteristics of the typical pylon temple. (Gaddis and Seif)*

The Egyptian temple to the gods we shall illustrate by a small temple at *Edfu* (Figs. 62A, 63A), because it is in an excellent state of preservation and, though later in date than the Theban age, illustrates clearly the fundamental plan of a pylon temple, which did not change essentially over many centuries. To one approaching, the dominating feature is the great façade, or pylon, which is simple, massive, with sloping walls and generally unbroken lines. The broad surface too is unbroken, except for the doorway with its overshadowing cornice, the four grooves to hold the great flagstaffs, and the low reliefs. A round molding finishes both the top and the sides. Passing through the doorway, we enter an open court surrounded on three sides by a colonnade. Beyond rises a roofed hall, the hypostyle hall, where the cool dimness contrasting with the bright sunshine of the open court, together with the rhythm of the

massive shafts, inspires a feeling of solemnity. Still farther on lies the sanctuary, low, dark, mysterious, and secluded. A girdle wall, beginning at the pylon, surrounds the structure. This temple at *Edfu* shows us the general arrangement of a typical pylon temple (Fig. 63B), which always includes a pylon, an open colonnaded court, a hypostyle hall, a sanctuary — sometimes surrounded by smaller chambers for the storage of the temple treasures and for the use of the priests — and a girdle wall.

This plan clearly evolved from ritualistic requirements. Egyptian religious practices were not congregational, as were the Greek, the Buddhist, and the Christian. Only the pharaoh and the priest could enter or view the sanctuary; a chosen few were admitted to the hypostyle hall; the masses, only into the open court; and the girdle wall shut off the entire site from the outside

[A]   *Temple of Horus. Edfu. View from the top of the pylon showing part of the open court, the hypostyle hall, the sanctuary, and the girdle wall. (Gaddis and Seif)*

world. The passage, which became progressively mysterious, from the large sunlit court to the small secret unseen sanctuary, naturally inspired a feeling of solemnity and awe. From this essential plan, once evolved, the conservative Egyptian did not deviate for hundreds of years, even after the Greeks

and the Romans brought other ideas into the Nile Valley.

It is not surprising to find that the Egyptian temple, like the pyramid, is simple and massive when we recall again the geographical conditions of the country — that narrow strip of luxuriant river valley bordered on both

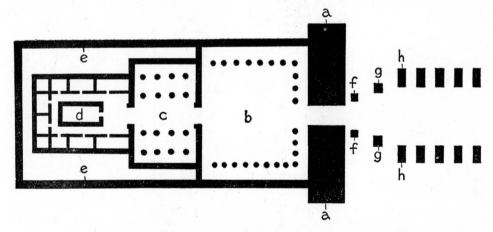

[B]   *Plan of a Typical Pylon Temple. a. pylon; b. court; c. hypostyle hall; d. sanctuary; e. girdle wall; f. colossal statues of the pharaoh; g. obelisks; h. avenue of recumbent animals.*

[A] *Temple of Amun. Karnak. Section of the hypostyle hall, central part. From a model in the Metropolitan Museum of Art, New York City. (Metropolitan Museum)*

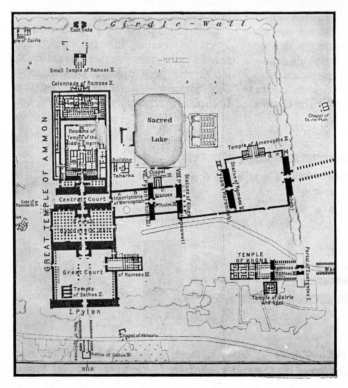

[B] *Temple of Amun. Karnak. In process of building for c. 2000 years to the 1st cent. B.C. Ramesses I, Seti I, and Ramesses II, all of the XIX Dynasty (1350–1205 B.C.), built the great hypostyle hall. (Baedeker)*

[A] *Temple of Amun. Luxor. Right: central colonnade of an unfinished hypostyle hall.
Center and left: double colonnaded court. XVIII Dynasty (1580–1350 B.C.). (Gaddis and Seif)*

sides by vast sterile deserts; a landscape of predominantly horizontal lines; and over all a continuously clear sky and overwhelming sunshine. Protection from the heat demanded thick walls with few apertures, and covered colonnades. Thus the temple in its outline presents a group of simple geometric volumes — pyramidal and rectangular — with great areas of unbroken wall space. The approach is along a broad avenue bordered on both sides by statues of recumbent animals with metal disks between their horns. In front of the massive pylon stand two obelisks (Fig. 63B) nearly a hundred feet high, covered with hieroglyphs, their glittering metal tips catching and reflecting the sunshine. On each side of the doorway stands a colossal statue of the pharaoh, harmonizing in its simple

massiveness with the massive pylon; in the grooves rest the huge wooden staffs that carry the flags floating above the cornice. The walls are covered with low reliefs, painted in bright colors, enriching the surface but not destroying the solidity of the walls. The great door of cedar of Lebanon is inlaid with shining metal. Surrounding and framing the whole structure are the rich green masses of palms and the brilliant sky. A magnificent and awe-inspiring sight.

The two most famous temples of the Empire are *Luxor* and *Karnak* (Fig. 64B). If we look at these closely, we shall see that they are merely complex arrangements of the simple plan of *Edfu;* for it became the custom for each succeeding pharaoh to add to his glory by building on an additional hypostyle hall or pylon to what was already a

[A] *Temple of Amun. Luxor. Colossal statues of Ramesses II in the great court. H. c. 23 ft.
c. 1250* B.C. *(Steindorff and Seele)*

complete temple. One fact only, which
Edfu does not illustrate, needs to be
mentioned. In the hypostyle hall of
Karnak (Fig. 64A) the central rows of
columns are higher than the side rows,
which means that the roof over the
center is higher than that on the sides.
The wall space connecting these two
levels is filled with perforated stone
windows. Here is a fully developed
clerestory, the beginning of which we
saw in the valley temple of the *Pyramid
of Khafre* (Fig. 52C).

The decorative motifs that the Egyptian used in the embellishment of his
temples were taken chiefly from the
lotus, the papyrus, and the palm. The
palm we saw used in the colonnade of
the *Pyramid of Sahure* (Fig. 53A). The
lotus was popular with the Egyptians,
who used it as a decorative motif in all
their arts — not so successfully, however, in the capitals, for its spreading

petals militate against the needed feeling of solidity in an architectural supporting member.

The papyrus plant (Fig. 61B), now
extinct in Egypt but in early days plentiful, produced a flower whose feathery
petals formed a bell-shaped mass. The
columns forming the central row of
the hypostyle hall of *Luxor* (Fig. 65A)
have capitals the shape of which has
been suggested by the papyrus flower,
and the columns of the colonnade in
the background are based on a cluster
of papyrus buds. The stems of this
cluster are tied tightly below the buds,
whose swelling contours form the capital. Were it not for this broad band to
hold the stems firmly together, the
shaft would give one a feeling of inse-
curity by seeming incapable of performing its function of support. The
shafts of both the flower and the bud
type contract at the base, as does the

[A] *Rock-cut Temple of Ramesses II. Abu Simbel. Seated statues of Ramesses 66 ft. high.*
(*Oriental Institute of the University of Chicago*)

stem of the plant; for when conventionalizing his plant forms, the Egyptian closely observed nature. In design, proportions, and workmanship, these colonnades at *Luxor* are among the noblest to be found in the pylon temples.

This becomes more apparent when we turn to the hypostyle hall of *Karnak* (Fig. 61A). Here, according to the usual convention, the columns of the central aisle are of the papyrus-flower type; those of the side aisles are of the papyrus-bud type. But compare the latter with the bud type at *Luxor*. At *Karnak*, only the general contour of the cluster has been retained, producing a heavy, ungainly shaft. It is as if the architects, in haste to complete this mighty hall, were depending upon bulk and scale to create an effect. And indeed they were partly successful in their attempt, for notwithstanding the shabby workmanship, a certain overwhelming impressiveness results from the mere number and size of these mighty shafts.[1]

Equally impressive, and architecturally fitting, is the colossal sculpture used at the entrance and in various parts of the temple — masses of stone as simply geometric as the pylon itself but at the same time portraits, impersonal to be sure, of the pharaoh (Figs. 66A, 67A).

The tombs of the nobles as well as the temples were decorated with reliefs which related to the life of the deceased. The zonal arrangement, characteristic of the Old Kingdom, continued; but the grouping became more

[1] It is interesting to note that the Egyptian did not use cement in these gigantic structures, but depended upon the huge weight of the stones to hold them in place. For the technical methods of lifting these stones to such heights, see Somers Clarke and Reginald Engelbach, *Ancient Egyptian Masonry*, Oxford University Press, 1920.

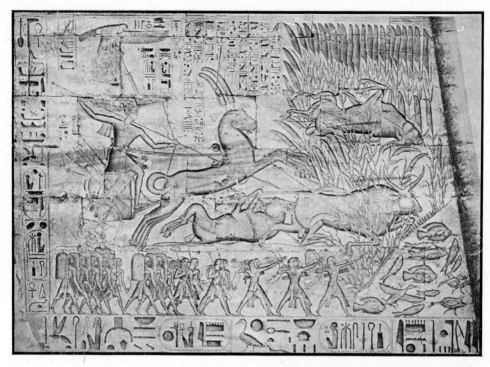

[A]   *Wild Bull Hunt. On the pylon of the Temple of Ramesses III at Medinet Habu, Thebes. XX Dynasty (1198–1167 B.C.). (Oriental Institute of the University of Chicago)*

complex, with more overlapping. The figures not only are expressive of emotion but are more curvilinear, in contrast to the angularity of the Old Kingdom reliefs. This is partly due to the elaborate pleated linen garments which supplanted the simple kilt and straight garment of earlier ages. All these changes are indicative of a turn toward nature on the part of the sculptors, instead of implicit following of traditional modes of representation.

The naturalistic tendency seen in these reliefs received powerful impetus from Akhnaton's revolution. The new faith, with its conception of a sole creator of all life, turned men's attention to nature and lifted art expression above traditional convention. But reaction in art as well as in religion set in after the failure of the revolution.

The priests of Amun had triumphed. Not only did they attempt to eradicate the heresy by destroying the works of art created by the Amarna artists, or at least by removing from them all references to the hated Aton, they also shackled the artists even more securely than before. For it was the priests who controlled both subjects and methods of representation. Even under these restrictions, a brief period of high attainment was reached by the Egyptians before their art was strangled by crystallizing conventions, as we see in the *Wild Bull Hunt* (Fig. 68A), in which the king is spearing bulls in the swamps along the river (indicated by fish in the corner). Above a base of spearmen and archers moving with vigorous rhythmic swing, the zonal arrangement gives way to the large panel of the

[A]   *Osiris and Goddesses. XIX Dynasty (1350–1205 B.C.). Temple of Seti, Abydos.*

pharaoh in his chariot and three animals carved with bold vigor, the chariot group in terms of the old convention, the animals with extraordinary visual reality, and all tied together in a compositional unity. Note here that the ground is not cut away, leaving the figures in relief, but a deep groove is chiseled along the contours, giving the effect of a heavy line.

The wall decorations in the *Temple of Seti I* at Abydos (Fig. 69A), on the other hand, illustrate the crystallized convention. The figures are highly conventional in form, but the carving is very sure, with graceful sweep of contour and softly rounded relief which casts delicate shadows. With no in-terior modeling and no feeling for structure (note that both hands are the right one), the figure has become a highly stylized convention — affected, stilted, entirely lacking in the vivacity of the Old Kingdom reliefs. Yet the entire wall space, with the sensitively related panels, the beauty of the carving, and the color laid on flat in large areas, stands as a superb piece of mural decoration.

The portraits of the pharaohs and the nobles reveal a naturalizing tendency; the individual, with his idiosyncrasies and emotions, is emerging from the Old Kingdom generalizations and abstractions. In *Amenemhet III* (Fig. 70A) we see not only the warrior

[A] *Amenemhet III. Obsidian. H. c. 5 in. XII Dynasty (2000–1788 B.C.). MacGregor Collection, Tamworth.* (Journal of Egyptian Archaeology)

[B] *Akhnaton. Painted sandstone. H. c. 8 in. 1375–1358 B.C. Staatliche Museum, Berlin. (Grantz)*

and the ruler, but the individual man who lived and thought intensely. In the strong mouth, the drooping lines about the nose and the eyes, and the shadowing brows, we discern a man who, though still powerful, has lost faith. The head is carved in obsidian (note its reflective quality), a stone so obdurate that it must have put to the test the most accomplished skill in cutting, grinding, and polishing, yet so large and powerful is the characterization that the diminutive size becomes colossal in its impressiveness.

This trend toward naturalism was accelerated by the Amarna sculptors, as one sees in the numerous portraits and reliefs of king, queen, and princesses. In the portraits of *Akhnaton* (Fig. 70B) we do not feel primarily the ruler or even the official class to which this man belongs. What is significant is a thoroughly human characterization which emphasizes, in the pose of the head, the

long neck, the drooping mouth and lids, and in the air of almost effeminate delicacy, the essential elements of his character, which was primarily that of the dreamer and idealist.

For the expression of individual charm, the head of *Nofretete* (Staatliche Museum, Berlin), wife of Akhnaton, stands pre-eminent. In the long slender neck, the sensitive mouth, and the delicate modeling one feels an aristocratic, queenly bearing combined with a simple, unaffected grace. A use of color that is more conventional than naturalistic differentiates and relates the parts, and places emphasis upon the recurrent themes of cylindrical masses and curves.

When we compare these heads with those of *Khafre* (Fig. 13A) and *Ranofer* (Fig. 54A), we observe a striking difference. We miss the vivacity, the alertness, and the serene grandeur of the earlier work, in which individuality is

[A] *Reconstructed Town Houses at Amarna. The conical objects in front of the houses are corncribs with steps for filling from the top.* (Journal of Egyptian Archaeology)

subordinated to generalization. In its place we find that the chief aim of the artist has been to express the significant characteristics of the individual, his emotions, and his inner life.

The domestic architecture of the Empire,[1] though but scantily preserved because of the perishable materials of which most of it was constructed, appears to have presented to the eye as simple geometric masses and unbroken lines as the temples (Fig. 71A). Because the windows were few and small, a central hall rising above the other rooms afforded a clerestory for lighting. The flat roof was utilized for an open loggia,

¹ For domestic architecture see "The Town House in Ancient Egypt" by N. de G. Davies, *Metropolitan Museum Studies*, Vol. I, Pt. II, 1928–29; Henri Frankfort on private houses in Amarna, *Journal of Egyptian Archaeology*, November, 1922, pp. 144–49; and the *Medinet Habu* publications of the Oriental Institute of the University of Chicago relating to the palace of Ramesses III.

or for a garden when the houses were packed close together in the crowded city. In a royal palace such as that at *Medinet Habu* there was every comfort and luxury, including a private bath with each room, as well as a grandly impressive audience hall reminiscent of the temple hypostyle hall. In this audience hall an important note is the roof, which is vaulted rather than made of lintels as in the temple hall.[2] The walls, largely unbroken because of few windows, the ceilings, and the floors were elaborately painted and must have been very gay.

PAINTING

The wall paintings of the palaces and the tombs were the chief field of the painter, and in this respect his work was tied up with that of the builder and the

² The Egyptian understood the arch, but used it chiefly in substructures.

[A] *Wall Decoration in the Tomb of the Noble Khnumhotep. Beni Hasan. Detail of the right side showing the noble harpooning fish in the papyrus swamps. c. 1900* B.C.

[B] *Tomb of Nakht. Thebes. XVIII Dynasty (1580–1350* B.C.*). (Metropolitan Museum, New York City)*

sculptor. In the Old Kingdom painting functioned more as an accessory to relief than as an independent art. In the Middle Kingdom and the Empire, however, the painters began to omit the relief and to paint directly on the wall, partly because the walls of the tombs excavated in the cliffs were too coarse and rough for carving and partly because of the greater ease and freedom of the brush in comparison with the chisel. The rough walls were covered with stucco and plaster, on which the figures were drawn in firm outline with the help of squaring for proportioning, and the enclosed space was filled in with flat color. This was not true fresco, for the pigments were mixed with some binding medium, such as gum, and applied to a dry surface. The purpose of this painting was tomb and palace decoration, and in the tomb it served a magic purpose also.

There were many stock subjects, such as hunting and banqueting scenes. In Figure 72A, for instance, the nobleman is out in the papyrus marsh in his reed boat, harpooning fish. His figure is expressed in the conventional way, as was proper for one of his station. In the river scene below, however, there is a freedom of action that reveals the capacity of a conventional figure to express all kinds of movement. Notice the wave line, a convention to express water, and the oval-topped area in which are shown the two speared fish. This represents a side channel of the main stream flowing into the distance through papyrus plants. To express distance or depth, the painter places the distant part above the near, as if he were laying out a ground plan.

This combination of several aspects of a figure or a scene without regard to visual appearance is an early example of the same attitude toward visual appearance found in the work of many other peoples: the Maya, the North-

[A] *Group of Offerings. From the tomb of Nakht (Fig. 72B). (Metropolitan Museum, New York City)*

west Coast Indians, the Chinese bronze-workers, and some modern painters, notably Picasso.

Figure 72B gives us a glimpse into a tomb[1] the decorative scheme of which is based on a system of a dado, four zones, and a border, with a zigzag ceiling pattern which copies the ceiling decoration of an Egyptian house (see also Figure 77A). The zonal arrangement is ordered into a symmetrical balance about the false door, which was provided for the spirit to pass through in order to receive the offerings presented by the kneeling figures and heaped up in the lower zone (Fig. 73A). Like that of the human figure, the drawing of the objects is not based upon visual perception from a consistent point of view but upon traditional conventions. Of these objects — loaves of bread, onions, grapes, fowl, quarters of meat, lotus,

[1] For fine color reproductions of this tomb, see N. de G. Davies, *The Tomb of Nakht at Thebes*, Metropolitan Museum of Art, 1917.

papyrus — some are seen in profile, some in front view, some from above; but all are combined into a pattern of subtly varied symmetry and great esthetic power through the repetition with variation of shape, motif, color, value, and texture.

On one of the side walls the zonal arrangement is broken by the large figures of the noble and his wife and by the vivacious scenes of agriculture and stock-raising. On the opposite wall (not seen in the illustration) is a *Banquet Scene* (Fig. 74B), where six guests are seated upon mats near a blind harper. They wear long thin garments, wigs held by fillets, and on the crown of the head a conical object containing perfumed unguent; they have wreathed lotus flowers about their heads or hold the flowers in their hands; all wear elaborate collar-necklaces and large disk earrings, one of which a little serving-maid is adjusting. There is greater freedom of pose and variety of

[A] *Fowling Scene. From a Theban tomb. XVIII Dynasty (1580–1350 B.C.). British Museum, London. (Oriental Institute of the University of Chicago)*

[B] *Banquet Scene. From the tomb of Nakht, Thebes. XVIII Dynasty (1580–1350 B.C.).*

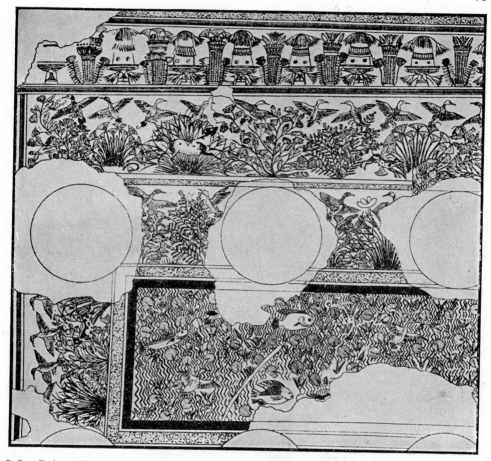

[A]   *Painted Floor Decoration. Detail. From the palace of Akhnaton. Amarna. (Petrie)*

movement here than in Old Kingdom work, and a suavely flowing line that has a beauty of its own. The figures overlap and are related compositionally — line, shape, and color repeating, varying, and contrasting. This is also true in a *Fowling Scene* (Fig. 74A) in which the noble is standing in his boat and driving the birds from a papyrus swamp with his boomerang. In his right hand he holds three birds he has caught; his hunting cat, on a papyrus stem just in front of him, has caught two more in her claws and is holding the wings of a third with her teeth. His two companions, perhaps his wife and little daughter, are enjoying the lotus they have gathered. The water and the figures are represented by the usual conventions, but cat, fish, and birds show a trend toward a naturalism based upon visual perception.

As in sculpture, this tendency toward naturalism received great impetus from Akhnaton. In his own palace at Amarna the floor decoration of one room represented a pool of water surrounded by the appropriate zones of life and vegetation (Fig. 75A). In the center was the pool, with birds, fish, and aquatic plants; bordering this was the marshland, with birds flying about; beyond,

[A]   *"Perfume Spoon." Wood. Louvre, Paris.*

[B]   *Cedarwood Chair. Decorated in embossed gold, claws of ivory. Cairo Museum. (Howard Carter)*

the meadowland with tall grasses through which calves were running. All the forms, both plant and animal, were painted with a new freedom. An illusion of nature, however, did not dominate; for the Egyptian's never-failing sense of design grouped the scenes into an orderly arrangement by enclosing

them with firm lines and a conventional outer border, so that representation and decoration were happily blended. Here at Amarna we see the painter, like the sculptor, reaching out spontaneously into a new field of visual exploration, but he was still too deeply imbedded in traditional forms to break the shackles permanently.

WOODWORK, METALWORK, GLASS, CERAMICS

The magnificence and ostentation of the Empire was bound to be reflected in the furnishings of the palace and in the adornment of the king and the nobles, and all of it is seen in the mortuary equipment from which the extant examples have come. Magnificent furniture, which probably had been used in the palace before it served the tomb, was found in the tomb of Tutankhamun.[1] A relatively simple chair (Fig. 76B) illustrates particularly well the functional, structural, and esthetic excellence of the design. It is made of cedarwood with carvings and ornaments of gold which combine such in-

[1] The discovery of this tomb in 1922, one of the most startling archaeological discoveries of modern times, revealed for the first time the almost unbelievable magnificence of royal burial equipment in the Empire. For the history of the discovery, and illustrations and descriptions of the equipment, see Howard Carter and A. C. Mace, *The Tomb of Tut-ankh-amen,* London, 1927–33, Vols. I–III.

[A] *Painted Decoration of a Tomb Ceiling, which probably copies that of some palace.*

scriptions and symbols as the sun disk, the uraeus, royal birds with the two crowns, the symbol of millions of years, the life sign, and the names of the pharaoh into a design of architectural quality.

In addition to furniture, there was a demand for great quantities of smaller articles for household equipment and personal use which employed many craftsmen working in various materials — stone, wood, ivory, glazed terra cotta, glass, metal, and semiprecious stones. The stoneworker brought the Old Kingdom traditions of his craft to a point of technical virtuosity, as is seen in the elegant alabaster vases from Tutankhamun's tomb. The design incorporates elaborate seminaturalistic handles, though the object is all cut from one piece of stone. The body of the vase is worked to a translucent thinness. Wood was particularly de-

sirable for carving such small toilet articles as the cosmetic receptacles of a cosmetic-loving people. In these receptacles one sees how the Egyptian relied for his designs upon the human, plant, and animal life with which he was familiar. The *"Perfume Spoon"* of Figure 76A combines into a functional and esthetic unity a duck and a girl swimming. The duck forms the receptacle, with the opening between the wings, and the girl, the handle, both forms being united by the girl's arms and by the repetition of the heads.

Glazing had been known by the Egyptian from prehistoric times and had early been used to cover tiles for wall decoration. It had then been applied to various objects, but in the Empire period it reached a climax both in its technical development and in the variety of its uses — beads, pendants, scarabs, amulets, vases, figurines, and

[A] *Glass Vase. Dark blue with dragged pattern in light blue, yellow, and white. H. 3¼ in. Metropolitan Museum of Art, New York City.* (*Metropolitan Museum*)

architectural decorations. The blue color, particularly deep and pure, the craftsmen obtained from copper by a long process that required great skill in the preparation of the material and patience in tending the furnaces during the long even roasting, for no mechanical devices were known to regulate the heat.

Glass was not the common, inexpensive medium among the Egyptians that it is at present, for the blowpipe was not invented until about the first century B.C. It was therefore necessary to mold the hot glass over a copper and paste core that could later be removed — a slow, laborious process. Such a vase as that illustrated in Figure 78A was made in this way. It is deep-blue in color. For decoration, threads of light-blue, yellow, and white glass were wound about the still hot neck and

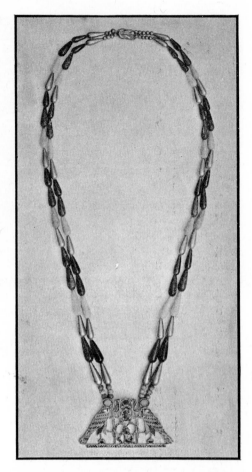

[B] *Necklace with Pectoral. XII Dynasty (2000–1788 B.C.). Metropolitan Museum of Art, New York City.* (*Metropolitan Museum*)

body and dragged back and forth by a hooked instrument, forming the zigzag that is known as the "dragged pattern."

Metalworkers and lapidaries were in demand because of the great amount of gold used in furniture and in many small articles, and particularly because of the importance of jewelry in the Egyptian costume — crowns, collar-necklaces, necklaces with pendants, armlets, bracelets, ornaments and clasps for all parts of the clothing. The lavish use of gold became especially evident upon the discovery of the Tutankhamun

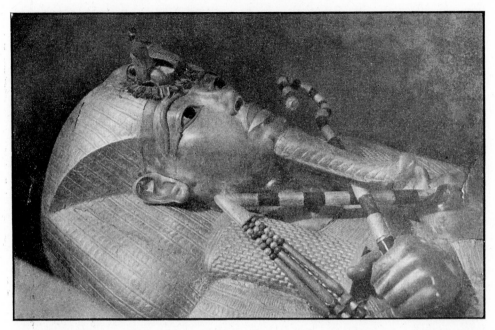

[A]   *Effigy of Tutankhamun upon the First Coffin. Gold over wood inlaid with glass, faïence, and lapis lazuli. Cairo Museum. (Howard Carter)*

tomb, notably in the concentric gold coffins (Fig. 79A), which are magnificent examples of the goldsmith's craft. Such too are the diadem found on the head of the king, and the collar-necklaces. The latter are elaborate examples of a popular form of jewelry. The chain and pectoral, or pendant, was also popular. The chain in Figure 78B consists of drop beads arranged in pairs in a fourfold unit of blue-green feldspar, lapis lazuli, carnelian, and gold, with a gold clasp ingeniously designed with a dovetail groove and a tongue. The pectoral is an openwork gold plate engraved on the underside and inlaid on the upper side with turquoise, lapis lazuli, and carnelian. In the center the kneeling figure of a man is holding palm branches on which rests the royal cartouche, flanked on each side by a royal falcon; the intermediate space is filled with the uraeus and the sun disk, from which hangs the sign of life. The birds are united skillfully to the central design by the uraeus, the life sign, and the claws braced against the palm branches, and all parts are held together by the firm base. The blues of lapis and turquoise are well balanced, and the whole design is unified by the careful distribution of the red carnelian.

SUMMARY

The Egyptian Middle Kingdom and the Empire were ages of great productivity and accomplishment in all the arts. Wealth fostered magnificence and display on a colossal scale. Great temples were the symbols of the age, in particular the pylon temple, grandly simple in mass and contour, gigantic in size, a solid and enduring mass of stone decorated with sculpture which, whether as colossal statue or low painted relief, was supremely architectural. This impressive manifestation, in its plan, its elevation — in fact in every respect — was a form determined by ritualistic requirements and royal pride, by stone, and by the local setting. Portrait sculpture, still important, became more individualistic than in the Old Kingdom, and less freshly vivacious. Painting continued to function as decoration for tombs and palaces.

The wider outlook upon life that characterized the Empire, and notably the influence of Akhnaton's religious revolution, led the artists along a path that a few had already begun to discover — the path of nature. For a brief time visual perception gained on mental concepts, and the fresh point of view inspired artists with new creative power. Freedom of pose, variety of movement, and freely flowing curves supplanted stiffness and angularity.

But the Egyptian, by nature conservative, soon fell back upon the conventions, which now had become empty forms — highly decorative, but artificial rather than vital. Craftsmen in wood and stone, gold, glass, and ceramics contributed to the magnificence of tomb, temple, and palace furnishings and to personal adornment. When not flamboyantly elaborate, the furniture, jewelry, and alabaster and ceramic objects reveal great technical skill, fertile imagination, and an innate sense of design that adapted the forms of nature admirably to utilitarian or decorative ends.

BIBLIOGRAPHY

Baikie, James, *The Life of the Ancient East*, Macmillan, 1923

Breasted, James H., *Ancient Times*, 2d ed. rev., Ginn, 1935

———— *Development of Religion and Thought in Ancient Egypt*, Scribner, 1912

———— *A History of Egypt from the Earliest Times to the Persian Conquest*, 2d ed. rev., Scribner, 1909

Capart, Jean, *Egyptian Art*, tr. by W. R. Dawson, Stokes, 1923

———— *Lectures on Egyptian Art*, University of North Carolina Press, 1928

———— *Primitive Art in Egypt*, tr. by A. S. Griffith, Lippincott, 1905

Childe, Vere G., *The Most Ancient East*, Knopf, 1929

Clarke, Somers, and Engelbach, Reginald, *Ancient Egyptian Masonry*, Oxford University Press, 1930

Cossío, Manuel Bartolomé, and Pijoán, José, *Summa Artis*, Vols. I–X, Madrid, 1931–46, Vol. III

Davies, Nina M. Cummings, *Ancient Egyptian Paintings*, University of Chicago Press, 1936

Davies, Norman de G., *The Tomb of Nakht at Thebes*, Metropolitan Museum of Art, New York City, 1917

Frankfort, Henri, ed., *The Mural Painting of El-'Amarneh*, London, 1929

Laurie, Arthur P., *The Materials of the Painter's Craft in Europe and Egypt*, Lippincott, 1911

Maspero, Sir Gaston C. C., *Art in Egypt*, Scribner, 1912

———— *Manual of Egyptian Archæology*, tr. by A. S. Johns, 6th ed., Putnam, 1926

———— *Popular Stories of Ancient Egypt*, tr. by Mrs. C. H. W. Johns, Putnam, 1914

Murray, Margaret A., *Egyptian Sculpture*, Scribner, 1930

Petrie, Sir William M. Flinders, *Arts and Crafts of Ancient Egypt*, McClurg, 1910

———— *Decorative Patterns of the Ancient World*, London, 1931

———— *Social Life in Ancient Egypt*, London, 1932

Ranke, Hermann, *The Art of Ancient Egypt*, Vienna, 1936

Ross, Sir Edward Denison, ed., *The Art of Egypt through the Ages*, Studio, 1931

Schäfer, Heinrich, and Andrae, Walter, *Die Kunst des alten Orients*, Berlin, 1925

Smith, Earl B., *Egyptian Architecture as Cultural Expression*, Appleton-Century, 1938

Steindorff, George, and Hoyningen-Huene, George, *Egypt*, 2d ed. rev., Augustin, 1945

Swindler, Mary H. *Ancient Painting*, Yale University Press, 1929

Weigall, Arthur E. P. B., *The Life and Times of Akhnaton, Pharaoh of Egypt*, rev. ed., Putnam, 1923

Winlock, Herbert E., *The Treasure of El-Lāhūn*, Metropolitan Museum of Art, New York City, 1934

Worringer, Wilhelm, *Egyptian Art*, tr. by Bernard Rackham, Putnam, 1928

[A] *Copper Relief from the Temple of Ninkhursag. British Museum, London. (British Museum)*

4

ART IN THE TIGRIS–EUPHRATES VALLEY AND PERSIA

Sumerian Art

(ABOUT 4000–1925 B.C.)

AS we leave the Nile Valley and travel eastward into Asia to the Valley of the Two Rivers (Fig. 43A), in which arose another civilization contemporary with the Egyptian, we look in vain for tombs, temples, or palaces. "Standing on the summit of this mound one can distinguish along the eastern skyline the dark tasselled fringe of the palm-gardens on the river's bank, but to north and west and south as far as the eye can see stretches a waste of unprofitable sand. To the south-west the flat line of the horizon is broken by a gray upstanding pinnacle, the ruins of the staged tower of the sacred city of Eridu . . . and to the north-west a shadow thrown by the low sun may tell the whereabouts of the low mound of al 'Ubaid; but otherwise nothing relieves the monotony of the vast plain over which the shimmering heat-waves dance and the mirage spreads its mockery of placid waters. It seems incredible that such a wilderness should ever have been habitable for man, and yet the weathered hillocks at one's feet cover the temples and houses of a very great city."[1]

[1] C. L. Woolley, *Ur of the Chaldees*, Scribner, 1930, p. 13.

Why this condition of complete ruin? Of the two rivers that form this valley, the western, the Euphrates, is quiet and majestic, but it is almost unnavigable because of cataracts in the north and sandbars in the south. The eastern river, the Tigris, rising in the mountains to the northeast, is more rapid, and forms the highway of commerce for the valley. Like the Nile in Egypt, both rivers, flooded during the season of heavy rains, bring down vast quantities of rich alluvium, forming an amazingly productive soil. But these floods prove equally destructive, for they not only change the courses of the rivers but soon reduce buildings made of nonresisting material, such as the Babylonians used, to heaps which the sands blowing in from the desert convert into rather natural-looking mounds.

The valley divides naturally into two parts, the lower of which is generally called Babylonia.[1] It is an extraordinarily fertile region of flat river bottoms. The upper part, Assyria, is more barren, and stretches up into the plateau country along the higher reaches of the Tigris. Taken as a whole, this valley, in contrast to Egypt with its secure isolation and its peaceful and strangely uniform civilization, is open on the west to the Arabian Desert and on the east, north, and northwest to highland plateaus, and is thus exposed alike to peaceful wanderers and warring invaders. The story of the valley is one of conflicting groups, racially differentiated; of infiltration, conquest, absorption. Out of this shifting complexity arose four[2] outstanding cultures:

the Sumerian (with Semite elements), the Assyrian, the Chaldean, and the Achaemenian Persian.

Our earliest glimpses of the peoples of the Valley of the Two Rivers take us into the Neolithic age, perhaps into the same cultural stratum that we find in Egypt. In that age metal was discovered and a system of writing devised, at a time roughly contemporary with the same developments in the Nile Valley. By what people or peoples these advances were made, we do not know. At the dawn of historical times we find in the lower Tigris-Euphrates Valley the Sumerians, who may have migrated into the valley from the eastern plateaus. They were an agricultural people, and eventually built strong walled towns, such as Ur and Lagash. Then in from the western deserts drifted Semite nomads, who turned from grazing to agriculture, absorbed much of the Sumerian culture, and built their own cities farther north — Kish, Akkad, Babylon. Though the Sumerian culture largely prevailed, the ruling power swung back and forth between the two peoples, the Semites producing two of the mightiest kings, Sargon (active 2750 B.C.) and Hammurabi (2123–2081 B.C.), under whom Babylon became the capital of the first Babylonian Empire.

Owing to control of the floods by irrigation, this lower part of the Valley of the Two Rivers was now a rich agricultural land. Next to adventure, trading was the major activity of the community. Religious beliefs and practices centered about great nature gods: Anu, god of the sky; Enlil, creator and ruler of the earth and "lord of the storm," who sent both beneficent and destructive floods; Ea, lord of the depths and as lord of waters a healing, benevolent god; Nannar or Sin, the moon god; Shamash, the sun god; and Ishtar (Venus), goddess of love and fertility. In contrast to the Egyptian, the Su-

---

Strictly speaking, "Babylonia" is not applicable until Babylon became the capital under Hammurabi about 2100 B.C.

[2] Probably also the Hittite (at its climax about 1500 B.C.), at present obscure though emerging through the work of archaeological expeditions in Anatolia and through the recent partial decipherment of the Hittite writing.

[A] *Ziggurat at Ur. Reconstructed. H. 92 ft. 2300–2180* B.C. *(Joint Expedition of the British Museum and the University Museum, University of Pennsylvania)*

merian took too gloomy a view of a future world, "the place whence none return," to give elaborate attention to burial. Though personal burial equipment, especially that of royalty, was sumptuous, the tomb and its decoration provide neither monumental architecture nor an intimate picture of life. It was the present life that mattered — the palace for its enjoyment, and the temple to propitiate the gods for material prosperity. The god was an earthly ruler and a great landowner; Nannar, for example, was king of Ur and as such had a court with a huge organization covering every activity from that of high priest and minister of war to that of director of donkey transport. Thus the temple and its adjuncts were a huge mundane establishment, and the priesthood became an important factor in the business life of the country, the priests rented land and bartered in wool, cattle, herds, fruits, perfumes, and the products of the craftsmen.

ARCHITECTURE AND SCULPTURE

Poverty in building materials faced the Sumerian. His country provided him with little wood and no stone — only the mud of the river bottoms. Brick, both baked and unbaked, had to supply his need, except for a small amount of imported stone. Thus when building on a large scale with this small material — too small to span any considerable distance as could the stone lintels of the Egyptian — the Sumerian was compelled to adopt the arch as his basic structural principle.

An early example of building is a small temple to the mother goddess (Ninkursag, near Ur). It stood on a spacious platform and was gaily colorful. It was built of brick with wood lintels sheathed in copper. Stone steps led to the doorway, which was guarded by lions to ward off malevolent spirits, and was flanked by friezes of animals, birds, and men carved in white shell or

[A] *Standard. Detail. 3500–3200* B.C. *Baghdad Museum. (Joint Expedition of the British Museum and the University Museum, University of Pennsylvania)*

stone set in black. The platform, the guardian figures, the friezes, the vivid color — these we shall meet constantly in Babylonia, Assyria, and Persia.

Above the doorway of this temple was a large copper panel decorated with a design composed of a lion-headed eagle with outstretched wings clutching the backs of two stags (Fig. 81A). The significance of this design, found frequently in the valley, is not known. The heads of the animals are in the round, the bodies in high relief, the wings in low relief. The stags are treated naturalistically, in contrast to the conventional treatment of the wings; thus a variation in texture is added. Copper was a material in the use of which the Sumerians showed great skill.

The use of figures of engraved shell set in a dark ground is well illustrated by a *Standard* (Fig. 84A), a triangular box on a pole, probably used ceremonially. Here the figures are laid in

lapis lazuli with an occasional dash of red, and vividly picture Peace and War. In the upper zone the king and his chariots are seen; in the middle and lower zones, his attendants and captives. In general, the design forecasts the great series of narrative reliefs of Assyria and Persia.

The most characteristic structure of the Valley of the Two Rivers is the *ziggurat*, a tower of several stories belonging to a temple, and undoubtedly the dominating feature of every Sumerian city of any consequence. The *Ziggurat at Ur* (Fig. 83A) may be taken to illustrate the type. It consists of four stages decreasing in size and height upward, the lowest, fifty feet high, forming a massive base. This stage is broken on one side by a triple stairway of one hundred steps each branch of which converges upon an entrance leading directly to the shrine, thus centering interest upon the focal point, both architectural and religious, and

[A] *Stele of Urnammu. 2300* B.C. *University Museum, Philadelphia. (Joint Expedition of the British Museum and the University Museum, University of Pennsylvania)*

also providing a fine setting for the elaborate pageantry connected with the ceremonial rites. The structure is a solid mass of earth and crude brick with a thick facing of baked brick laid in bitumen, with pitch-dipped reed mats laid between every few courses.[1] The walls have a decided batter (an inward slope) and all the surfaces and lines are slightly curved, giving the mass compactness and relieving it of the illusion of sag found in long unbroken lines.[2] The stages were differentiated not only in size and propor-

tion but also in color, which seems to have been used symbolically. Above the white court rose the black lower stage suggesting the underworld; a red middle story, the earth; and the blue shrine with gilded dome, the heavens and the sun.[3] Added to these large, strongly contrasted areas of color was the greenery of the trees and gardens, which seem to have been planted on all the terraces.[4] Thus a ziggurat must have been colorful and imposing.

[1] The mound made by the ruin of this ziggurat is known locally as Al Mughair, "Mound of Pitch."

[2] See remarks on the *Parthenon* (pages 126–27), in which these variations from regularity were first scientifically studied.

[3] The color is very problematical. That color was used is not questioned. But the actual hue found may have been ancient restoration, and the symbolism is uncertain. The statements above follow Mr. Woolley's suggestions.

[4] Such were the famous Hanging Gardens of Babylon; the Tower of Babel at Babylon was a ziggurat similar to that at Ur, only larger.

[A]   *Gudea. Diorite. H. 3½ ft. c. 2450* B.C. *Louvre, Paris.*

The *Ziggurat at Ur* belonged to the *Temple of Nannar*, the moon god, god and king of Ur. The temple occupied one side of the Sacred Area and about it were grouped, rather irregularly, temples of Ningal, the moon goddess, and those of minor related deities, together with various secular structures belonging to the court of the god.[1] A large court, on a terrace ten feet above the Sacred Area level, surrounded by storerooms and chambers, leads to a spacious upper terrace, where rises the massive ziggurat. Platforms and terraces, so characteristic of buildings in this valley, are easily explained as pro-

[1] For an air view see Frontispiece to C. J. Gadd, *History and Monuments of Ur*, Dutton, 1929, and the *National Geographic Magazine*, August, 1928.

tection from recurring floods. Not so evident is the origin of the ziggurat. If the Sumerians migrated from the hill country, the tower with an altar on its summit may well be the "Mountain of God," or the "High Places" where they were wont to worship, created artificially in their new homes on the plains.

With a few exceptions, the sculpture of the Sumerians consists of reliefs which served a decorative and narrative purpose in a building, or of reliefs on monuments, such as the *Stele of Urnammu*, one zone of which (Fig. 85A) shows a group of figures crisply cut in fairly high relief and simply organized into a balanced group. The scene represents King Urnammu pouring a libation into a vase containing date-palm leaves. The god Nannar, seated on the right, holds a pickax, a measuring rod, and a builder's line, symbolizing his order to the king to build him a temple. In the fragmentary zone below, the king is seen with the builder's tools carrying out the divine orders. The figures are clothed in the heavy woolen garments characteristic of the costume of the valley. Although there appear here some of the conventions noted in Egypt, as in the shoulders, there is an extraordinary vitality in these figures — vigor and largeness in the modeling, and technical excellence in the stonecutting. The fact that the objects and the seated and standing figures just fill the space adds to the decorative effect.

Sculpture in the round, which is comparatively rare — probably because of the lack of stone — is best illustrated by the statues from Tello (Lagash). Figure 86A, carved from diorite which must have been imported from a considerable distance, represents *Gudea*, priest-king of Lagash. He is seated in frontal position, with hands tightly clasped in the attitude of devotion. He wears a woolen cap, the fleece kilt of the priest-king, here covered with inscriptions, and a

[A]   *A Cylinder Seal and the Impression Made When It Is Rolled over Soft Clay. H. c. 1 in. The impression shows a hero fighting a bull, and a being, half man half bull, fighting a lion. The inscription names the owner, the scribe Lugal-Lam. Reign of Sargon of Akkad. 2341–2300 B.C. Oriental Institute of the University of Chicago. (Oriental Institute)*

long woolen mantle which falls away from the right shoulder, leaving the arm exposed. The squat proportions, possibly due to the proportions of the block of stone, add to the compact massiveness of the figure. The parts are like reliefs carved on the four-sided matrix, and so closely knit together that one is always aware of its control. Details are cut with sharp precision, as in cap, eyebrows, eyes and mouth, and fingers, and thus introduce a broken texture to contrast with the subtly modeled surfaces in the face and the exposed arm. An intermediate texture motif is seen in the folds of the drapery, the fingers, and the feet. Taken as a whole, the statue is permeated with a tense vitality, like the statues of the Old Kingdom in Egypt. Like them, it reveals a capacity to infuse stone with a living quality and at the same time retain the intrinsic qualities of stone.

Great skill in stone carving in miniature size we see in the cylinder seals. The seal consisted of a cylindrical piece of stone, usually about an inch and a half high, pierced for the attachment of a cord (Fig. 87A). They were made of various colored stones, both hard and soft, such as obsidian, agate, carnelian and jasper, lapis lazuli, and alabaster,

and were decorated with a design in intaglio, so that when the seal was rolled over the soft clay a raised impression was made, as in the use of sealing wax today. With this impression the Sumerian sealed, signed, and identified his letters and documents, which were written on clay tablets. In a *Seal of King Sargon* (Fig. 88A), on each side of the central group is a mythological figure, perhaps Gilgamesh, one knee bent upon the ground, holding a vase from which issue two streams of water. In the center, back to back, are two bulls that lift up their heads to drink and with their horns ingeniously hold the inscription containing the name of Sargon; below is the conventional wavelike representation of a stream. The scene refers to water as the gift of the gods. In this seal we perceive the organization of the figures into a carefully related balanced group, tied firmly together by the wave lines of the river, with pleasing contrasts of texture in both smooth and rough areas. The modeling, particularly in the bulls, shows a powerful naturalism and at the same time no hesitation on the part of the engraver to use conventional forms in horns, hair, and water. Upon recalling the very small curved surface upon

[A]   *Seal of King Sargon I. 2750 B.C. Red jasper. H. 1½ in. Collection de Clercq, Paris.*

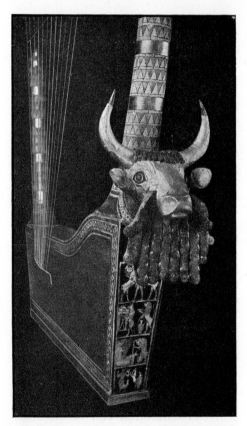

[B]   *Harp. Reconstructed. Bull's head of gold foil and lapis lazuli with inlaid eyes. 3500–3200 B.C. University Museum, Philadelphia.*

which the design is engraved in intaglio, we realize the extraordinary skill in carving, every line of which, strong and unfaltering, was graved by hand. Later importation of the drill brought deterioration in the quality of seal-cutting.

METALWORK

This amazing technical skill is also apparent in the products of the metalworkers and other craftsmen. Thanks to sumptuous royal burial equipment, although it involves the ghastly rite of human sacrifice, we glimpse the gorgeousness of personal adornment, the richness and at times impeccable taste in furniture, implements, and utensils.

Among the metals, copper seems to have been especially prized, and the craftsmen reveal an understanding of various processes of working it: casting, repoussé, and engraving. Such figures as those in Figure 81A were made by building up a wooden core, covering it with bitumen, in which the modeling was done, and then hammering thin plates of copper over it.

With gold the Sumerians were lavish, if we are to judge from the equipment of the *Royal Tombs* at Ur. Here is a *Cup* (Fig. 89A) of masterly proportions and

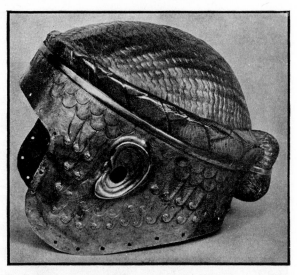

[A] *Gold Cup. 3500–3200 B.C. University Museum, Philadelphia.*

[B] *Gold Helmet. 3500–3200 B.C. Baghdad Museum. (Figs. 88B–89B, Joint Expedition of British Museum and University Museum, University of Pennsylvania)*

strong contour, its surface hammered into flutings which emphasize both the surface direction and the contour; a delicately engraved herringbone pattern and double zigzag finish both the lip and the base. In a gold helmet (Fig. 89B) are found repoussé and engraving of a quality hardly to be surpassed either in technical excellence or in design. The hair is treated conventionally, making a beautifully varied pattern of wave lines, spiraling, and sharply angular braiding which covers the entire surface.

The combination of gold with other materials is illustrated in a harp (Fig. 88B) of wood inlaid with a geometric pattern of shell, lapis lazuli, and red stone. The sounding box terminates in a bull's head of gold, the eyes, beard, and horn tips of which are of lapis, giving a dashingly bold effect. The sloping end of the box is filled with four zones containing figures of engraved shell set in a dark ground, which represent animals playing human roles.

SUMMARY

The Sumerian-Semite age, culminating in the first Babylonian Empire,[1] was a heroic age that is summed up in the Babylonian Gilgamesh epic. The people were farmers and traders, interested in the here and now, and they worshiped great nature gods who dwelt in their cities as god-kings. With only one plentiful material — brick — they built gay colorful palaces and temples, with the monumental ziggurat towering over all. Their sculpture, not abundant because of lack of stone, has great vitality. Both their statues in the round and their carved cylinder seals show a combination of naturalism and convention. They were lavish in their use of gold and were expert technically in using gold, copper, lapis lazuli, and shell. Vitality permeates all their products, whatever the material used.

[1] There is a great dearth of works of art from Babylon of the first empire, the *Stele of Hammurabi* (Louvre) being the chief monument.

[A]   *Palace of Sargon II. Restored. Dur-Sharrukin (Khorsabad). 722–705* B.C. *(Place)*

Assyrian Art

(ABOUT 1000–612 B.C.)

TURNING to the upper Tigris-Euphrates Valley (Fig. 43A), we find the Semite settlements of Ashur dominated by the kings of Sumer and Akkad and harassed by the tribes of the surrounding highlands, especially by the Kassites, a pre-Indo-European people from the northeastern plateaus who were drifting into the valley, bringing with them the horse (about 2000 B.C.); and by the Hittites of Anatolia, who invaded the valley about 1925 B.C. This latter people, but little known until recent times, comprised a loosely united federation of mountaineers who worshiped the great mother goddess. At their capital Hatti (the modern Boghaz Keui), at Carchemish, Tell Halaf, and other sites, they built massive fortress-palaces with bold architectural sculp-

ture at the entrances.[1] We see gigantic ponderous basalt statues of deities standing on the backs of animals; the "Great Mother" seated on a pedestal adorned with monsters as elemental as the rock itself; reliefs of ceremonial processions and hunting scenes filled with movement; and over the surfaces of some of the figures, though entirely subservient to the dominating planes, plays a wealth of decorative detail.[2]

At the hands of these invaders the Babylonian Empire of Hammurabi declined and fell. But the people of Ashur, toughened by the buffetings, gradually pushed outward to subdue, incorporate, and organize into a powerful empire,

[1] See the Frontispiece to Max, Freiherr von Oppenheim, *Der Tell Halaf*, Leipzig, 1931, for a reconstruction of the palace entrance.

[2] There seems to be a definite and important influence of Hittite art upon the Assyrian, in its vitality, its uses of architectural sculpture, and its composition and subject matter, the details of which are still to be worked out.

[A]   *Palace of Sargon II. Façade (detail of Fig. 90A). (Place)*

centered at Nineveh, not only western Asia to the Mediterranean Sea but Babylonia and Egypt as well. Very quickly this empire flowered (885–612 B.C.), and with equal rapidity it fell in turn to new invaders, the Semitic Chaldeans from the western desert and the Iranians from the northeastern plateau.

The Assyrian state was essentially military. Its ferocity is reflected in the purely Assyrian sun god from whom it took its name, Ashur, a savage, aloof deity rather than a royal city dweller like the nature gods of Sumeria. There is a tingling energy about the Assyrian and a grim cruelty, whether he is fighting, hunting, or indulging in luxurious indolence. Tense, forceful movement, in marked constrast with the calm, refined monumentality of Egyptian art, characterizes the expression of the alert and warlike Assyrian.

ARCHITECTURE AND SCULPTURE

Sumerian forms are basic in Assyria, but are adapted to meet the demands of a different type of civilization. This is clear in the buildings and their sculptural decorations. As for materials, stone, though near at hand, was not easily procured and hence was limited in its constructional use to foundations and substructures, but it was lavishly employed for reliefs; brick served for the superstructure. The temples follow the Sumerian type seen at Ur, with platform, open courts, and dominating ziggurat. The palace is more characteristically Assyrian — the here and now on a grand scale.

Sargon's palace at Dur-Sharrukin (Khorsabad), for example, is a vast rambling structure of stone and brick

[A] *A Guardian of the Gate. From the palace of Ashurnasirpal II. Metropolitan Museum of Art, New York City. (Metropolitan Museum)*

covering about twenty-five acres of ground, palace and temple combined (Fig. 90A). There are two entrances to the platform, one by a ramp for vehicles, the other by a monumental double stairway leading directly to the main entrance. A great many small rooms are grouped about two open courts: one, reached by the main entrance, a center for the affairs of state and the royal living-quarters; the other, toward the rear, for the domestic service. At the left is the temple, at the back of which rises the ziggurat.

The palace façade (Fig. 91A) shows a massive crenelated wall broken by huge rectangular towers flanking an arched doorway, about which stand, like guardian sentinels, colossal winged bulls with human heads. Around the arch and on the towers are friezes of brilliantly colored glazed tiles. The whole effect is sumptuous and grandly impressive. Dazzling brilliance seems to have been an objective, to judge from the words of an Assyrian king: "The splendid temple, a brilliant and magnificent dwelling . . . I made its interior brilliant like the dome of the heavens; decorated its walls, like the splendour of the rising stars, and made it grand with resplendent brilliancy." [1]

The colossal bulls, or lions, at the entrance (Fig. 92A) serve both to ward off enemies, visible and invisible, and to provide an impressive and fitting architectural decoration. They are partly in the round and partly in high relief, and combine the front view at rest with the

[1] Inscription of Tiglath-Pileser I (1100 B.C.) quoted in P. S. P. Handcock, *Mesopotamian Archaeology*, Putnam, 1912, p. 142.

[A] *A Winged Being and the King's Armsbearer. From the palace of Ashurnasirpal II, Nimrud (Kalhu). 9th cent.* B.C. *Metropolitan Museum of Art, New York City. (Metropolitan Museum)*

[B] *A Median Bringing Horses to King Sargon II. 722–705* B.C. *Metropolitan Museum of Art, New York City. (Metropolitan Museum)*

side view in movement, contriving the latter by the addition of a fifth leg. The gigantic size, the bold vigorous carving, the fine sweep of wings, and the patterning of the surface by the conventional treatment of details — all these contribute to their impressiveness and architectural fitness.

On the interior these palaces were paved with stone slabs (Fig. 94A) carved with lotus motifs (an influence from Egypt) and with the more characteristically Mesopotamian rosette and palmette. The brick walls were sheathed below with limestone and alabaster reliefs — literally miles of ceremonial, military, and hunting scenes arranged in zones. Above were brightly colored paintings. The reliefs of Ashurnasirpal (Fig. 93A) contain large firmly planted

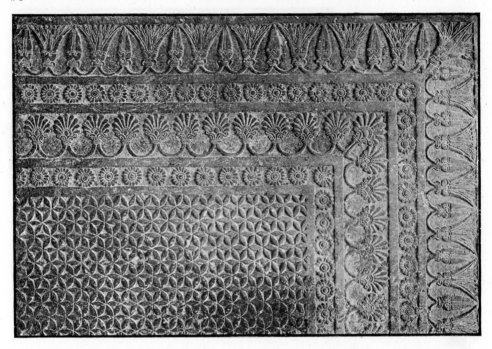

[A]   *Paving Slab from the Palace at Nineveh. Alabaster. c. 700* B.C. *British Museum, London. (Mansell)*

figures which just fill the space, single figures endlessly repeated, often without defined relationships, though at times they are balanced about a tree of life. The thickset figures with carefully curled hair and beard are sheathed in heavy fringed robes and bedecked with jewelry. They stand in profile, though both shoulders are seen and the eye is front view. They are cut clearly and firmly in parallel planes with little modeling except in the exposed limbs, where the exaggerated muscles form a vigorous pattern. Details are engraved rather than modeled, and inscriptions are cut across both background and figure. Something clear, definite, and majestic imbues these quiet colossal figures.

In the age of Sargon II and Sennacherib the relief is higher (Fig. 93B), more rounding, with a tendency toward naturalism. (Contrast the servant's hand with those in Fig. 93A.) In this design the

figures overlap, are composed into a unit, become pictorial with landscape setting and movement, and reveal a greater interest in narration than in decoration. There is more modeling, especially in the horses' heads, and a beautifully varied patterning of the surface through differing conventions used for mane, trappings, hair, and cloak.

In Ashurbanipal's palace are many banquet and hunting scenes, and though the wall as a whole suggests episodes rather than decorations, there are some magnificent expressions of animal life. Hunting was one of the chief pastimes of the Assyrian. On horseback, in chariot, and with hunting dogs, he sought the wild asses on the plateau, or — the most-prized prey — the lion. In Figure 95B the king, mounted, is spearing one lion; another lion, wounded, fiercely attacks a riderless horse. These friezes express movement and intense vitality.

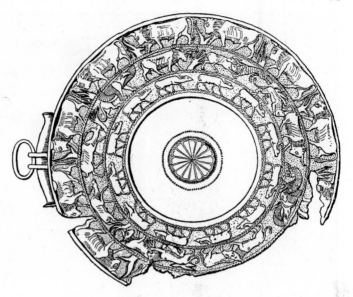

[A] *Bronze Bowl. 8th cent. B.C. British Museum, London.*

METALWORK

Among the craftsmen of Nineveh, the metalworker had skill in handling and designing his material, if we are to judge from a shallow bronze bowl decorated in repoussé with concentric rows of animals about a central rosette (Fig. 95A). One notes here a pleasing gradation in scale in the three borders. The inner-most contains gazelles moving to the right; the middle, various animals with the direction of movement uncertain; the outer, bulls moving toward the left. The figures are naturalistically conceived, and have conventional details such as manes and wings. The effect is highly decorative, and in no small measure reminiscent of the Sumerian animal friezes.

[B] *King Ashurbanipal Hunting Lions. 668–626* B.C. *British Museum, London. (Metropolitan Museum, New York City)*

[A]   *Ishtar Gate. Restored. Babylon. 606–539* B.C. *(Koldewey)*

SUMMARY

In Assyria we find an architecture of worldly magnificence — huge palaces of innumerable rooms around open courts. They are built of stone and brick with flashing surfaces of brilliantly colored tile, and have colossal, grandly impressive sculpture at the doorways. On the interior walls are seen an endless succession of reliefs picturing incidents of war, the hunt, and a luxurious life — a grandiloquent repetition of scenes to satisfy the vanity of the monarch. It is a grimly realistic, though stylized, art, teeming with movement and vitality, as forceful as its creators were energetic, especially in the depiction of animal life. Here are not the static elegance, the abstractions, the sensitivity to relationships, found in Egyptian art, but a brusque power in expressing everyday events, many of them violent, lived and perceived intensely; and often in a form that is architecturally fitting.

Chaldean or Neo-Babylonian Art

(612–539 B.C.)

AT the fall of Nineveh, two kingdoms were established, the Chaldean in the south, and the Medo-Persian on the eastern plateaus. Nebuchadnezzar, the Chaldean, built Babylon anew so that it surpassed Nineveh in the splendor of its palaces, temples, and Hanging Gardens. This is the Babylon of which the Greek traveler Herodotus wrote, and the city of the Hebrew captivity. Commerce and business flourished. The science of astronomy made advances. The Chaldeans divided the circle into 360 degrees, laid out the signs of the zodiac, and knew at least five planets. But the power and magnificence of Chaldean Babylon was short-lived, for in 539 B.C. it opened its gates to Cyrus the Persian.

[A]   *Lion of Procession Street. Restored. Glazed tile. Babylon. L. 7 ft. 606–539* B.C. (*Stoedtner*)

ARCHITECTURE

Until recently nothing but a mound marked the traditional site of Babylon. Among the buildings since excavated the *Ishtar Gate* (Fig. 96A) illustrates best the chief contribution of the Chaldean builder — ceramic architectural decoration. The general design of the gate, which is double, conforms to the types we have found in Sumeria and Assyria. Glazed tile we found in the shrine on the summit of the ziggurat at Ur. At Khorsabad its use had been extended widely, but the surface of the bricks, even when figure work was used, was flat. The Chaldean builders added relief. On the *Ishtar Gate*, for example, rose, forty feet above the pavement, tier after tier of animals in relief in brilliant enameled tile. From the *Ishtar Gate* to the *Temple of Marduk* led the Procession Street, along which processions passed on festal days. The walls bordering this street were decorated with sixty huge

lions (sacred to Ishtar) molded in relief and glazed in white and yellow or yellow and red against a ground of turquoise or dark-blue, with the usual rosette motif in the border (Fig. 97A).

Near the *Ishtar Gate* rose the huge *Palace of Nebuchadnezzar* with its terraced gardens, and at no great distance the great ziggurat of the *Temple of Marduk* (the "Tower of Babel") with its Hanging Gardens. Indeed this main gateway of Chaldean Babylon, together with the adjacent palaces and temples with their brilliant gleaming surfaces flashing in the sunshine of rich tropical gardens, must have impressed those who saw it with their gorgeous magnificence.[1]

[1] The process of making enameled reliefs is not known. The enamels used by the Chaldeans are opaque and hard, and indicate great ability on the part of the craftsmen to keep the colors from flowing into each other. Probably each brick was molded and enameled separately according to its place in the design. See Koldewey and Andrae on this (bibliography at the end of this chapter).

[A]   *Stairway to the Royal Audience Hall. Persepolis. (Oriental Institute of the University of Chicago)*

Achaemenian Persian Art

(539–331 B.C.)

THE end of the Assyrian power and the establishment of the Chaldean had been brought about by the combined efforts of the Semitic Chaldeans and the Medo-Persians — Iranian (a branch of the Indo-European) peoples who had migrated from the northern grasslands and gradually built up an empire on the mountainous plateaus[1]

[1] We know almost nothing of the peoples of this plateau before the Persian flowering in the sixth and fifth centuries B.C. From the time of the Stone Age village of about 4000 B.C., with its remarkable painted pottery, recently discovered by the Oriental Institute of the University of Chicago, to the time of the Achaemenidae there is almost a complete gap, which current expeditions hope to fill.

east of the Tigris-Euphrates Valley. The Medo-Persians appear to have brought with them a conception of religion formulated by their great prophet Zoroaster (Zarathustra), which recognized the conflict of Good (Ahuramazda, Ormazd) and Evil (Ahriman), the ethical value of right conduct, and the final triumph of good.

About 550 B.C. Cyrus, a Persian vassal of the Median Empire, threw off the yoke and with his powerful archers and daring horsemen swept over western Asia, swiftly conquering from the Persian Gulf to the Mediterranean Sea. Before his armies Babylon fell in 539 B.C. Still further conquest added Egypt to the Persian Empire, which was thoroughly organized and enjoyed a remarkable period of prosperity under Darius. It was a humane, intelligent rule, though no rights of citizenship

[A] *Subjects Bringing Gifts of Animals, Spears, and Vessels to the King. Detail from the stairway to the royal Audience Hall, Persepolis. (Oriental Institute of the University of Chicago)*

were extended to the people. The king's word was the one law. Though the earlier emperors were rulers with a conscience and a feeling of responsibility for their rule, their followers became luxurious Oriental despots. Decline set in, and the decadent state fell before the armies of Alexander the Great in 331 B.C.

ARCHITECTURE AND SCULPTURE

The present chief source of our knowledge of Achaemenian building is Persepolis [1] (Fig. 43A), apparently a royal

[1] Persepolis is now being excavated and restored by the Oriental Institute of the University of Chicago. See *Asia*, September–October, 1933 and *National Geographic Magazine*, October, 1933, for excellent illustrations.

suburb of the Persian capital, built chiefly by Darius and Xerxes. Upon a huge platform stood a group of palaces and audience halls approached by a great double stairway, with an entrance flanked by colossal human-headed bulls. Stone was plentiful in this mountainous country. Hence the platform, the great monumental stairways with their thousands of feet of carvings, the gateways, and the columns of the great audience halls were of stone, though brick was used in walls and wooden lintels for roofing. The most noticeable thing — not found in the architecture of the valley and sharply differentiating Persepolis from Khorsabad — is the use of the column on a grand scale. The audience hall (*apadana*) is a characteristic building, a vast hall filled with columns to hold the roof, built on a terrace, and

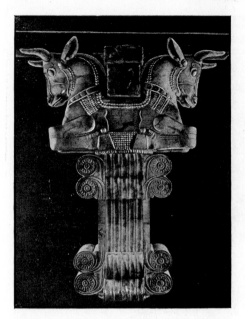

[A]   *Capital from the Palace of Artaxerxes at Susa. H. of column c. 67 ft. Louvre, Paris. (Oriental Institute of the University of Chicago)*

approached, as was the entire Persepolis group, by a broad monumental stairway (Fig. 98A). In the hall the king held audience, surrounded by his bodyguard and court, receiving both local subjects and representatives from the vast Persian Empire, who are pictured in the reliefs on the stairway (Figs. 98A, 99A). The total impression is one of magnificent, stately ceremonial. The slender fluted columns are peculiarly Achaemenian; the Iranian love of the animal figure, in whole or in part, as a decorative motif, is illustrated in the capitals, which are composed of the foreparts of two bulls placed back to back above a group of volutes (Fig. 100A). The wooden lintels were covered with brilliant color and gold, and the walls sheathed with enameled tiles.

How many of these forms the Persian possessed before the building of Persepolis we do not now know. He seems to have appropriated motifs and forms from the various peoples with whom his conquests brought him in contact: from Babylonia and Assyria, from Ionia and Egypt. Yet so thoroughly adapted are these forms that the *Hall of One Hundred Columns* of Xerxes, for example, is an entirely different entity from the *Hypostyle Hall* at Karnak.

Sculptured friezes play an important part at Persepolis for both decorative and narrative purposes. The spacious double stairways which formed so impressive an approach to the audience halls were decorated with friezes and panels in low relief, separated by moldings and finished with crenelations. Figure 99A shows a detail of the great procession of royal guards and representatives of various parts of the empire bringing tribute and gifts to the king. The evenly spaced single figures, broken into groups by conventionalized trees and varied by the occasional use of animal forms, have the decorative quality of the Sumerian (Fig. 84A) and the early Assyrian (Fig. 93A). The accomplished cutting of the stone, both in the suavely rounding surfaces and in the crisply chiseled details, is in itself an element of beauty. About all these sculptures, aside from their decorative and narrative elements, there is a serenity, a something apart from reality, quite distinct in feeling from the dynamic naturalism of the Assyrian, which may be, as M. Grousset has suggested, a reflection of the "abstract spiritualism" of the Iranian faith.

METALWORK

The Iranians, like other members of this group of civilizations, were skilled metalworkers. They excelled in gold, to judge from an armlet (Fig. 102A) whose decoration consists of two winged monsters, the bodies and hind legs of which are indicated in relief; the wings,

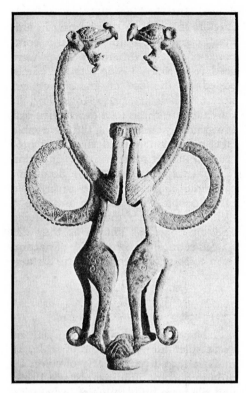

[A]   Bronze Rod-holder. From Luristan. L.
$6\frac{5}{16}$ in. 7th to 5th cent. B.C. Museum of Fine
Arts, Boston. (Boston Museum)

[B]   Winged Ibex Vase Handle. Silver.
Achaemenid Persian. H. c. 10 in. Berlin.
(Iranian Institute, New York City)

breasts, and necks are covered with
cloisons that were once filled with colored stones cut to fit the depressions.
The animal forms are highly conventionalized, so that their simplified outline forms a bold, vigorous design
peculiarly fitted to the medium.

In some of the Luristan bronzes[1] also
we find a vivid grasp of the essentials
of an object expressed by means of con-

[1] A great number of small objects made of
several kinds of bronze have been excavated
recently in the mountains of Luristan, a province
of western Persia near Kermanshah. Though
they include objects of personal adornment
such as long pins, weapons, and ceremonial
objects, a great number are from harnesses
and chariots. Scholars differ widely as to their
dates.

ventions that are extraordinarily decorative. In Figure 101A notice how a
rhythmic movement is carried by the
circle motif. The small circles in the
terminals of the tails expand into those
formed by the wings, and then into the
slightly elliptical shape made by the
long necks, which terminate in serpent
heads. Other examples of Iranian metalwork display a vivid naturalism, as in
the Winged Ibex Handle (Fig. 101B).

At this point it may be well at least
to mention the highly important metalwork of such nomadic peoples as the
Sarmatians and the Scythians, who
roamed the steppes of central Eurasia.
It shows an affinity with Sumerian and
Persian art, and may have a common

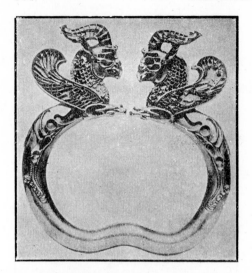

[A] *Armlet. Gold. H. 5 in. c. 400* B.C.
British Museum, London. (Dalton)

[B] *Sarmatian Gold Ornament, Lion-griffin killing a horse. From Siberia. Hermitage, Leningrad. (M. I. Rostovtzeff, The Animal Style in South Russia and China, Princeton University Press)*

origin with them. Over this vast area extended, after Neolithic times, a culture whose great vitality found expression in a style of equal vitality and of extraordinary esthetic excellence. It was an art confined to the making and embellishing of objects of everyday life among nomadic hunters, and its chief theme was the animal figure. The materials were mostly bronze and gold, which local mines provided in abundance. Interlocking fighting animals (Fig. 102B), objects terminating in animal heads, and fantastic figures composed of parts of different animals were used repeatedly. Color was sometimes added by the use of enamel or cut stones. "Their art," says Roger Fry, "is the exact antithesis to a descriptive art. It was not by cataloguing the observable facts about an animal that they proceeded, but by some intimate intuition of what might be called the dominant rhythmic character of the beast." No other people "has had so intimate a feeling for the rhythms of the living animal; none has known as they did how to reduce the complexity of natural form to so simple and yet vital a statement."[1]

SUMMARY

Achaemenian art was a kingly art of great splendor — splendor of scale, of materials, and particularly of color. Its most important buildings of stone, brick, and tile were built to house in befitting magnificence a thoroughly human — though absolute — monarch. Spacious stone stairways with elaborate carvings and forests of decorative stone columns combined to give this regal impression. The sculptured friezes of Persepolis reveal accomplished stonecutting and great decorative beauty and are permeated with a feeling of serenity in contrast to the greater intensity of the Assyrian. The Iranians were also skillful in gold, silver, and bronze metalwork, in which they made great use of the animal form, at times rendering it

[1] *The Arts of Painting and Sculpture,* London, 1932, p. 66. This art — its origin and its relationship with Sumerian, Persian, Greek, Far Eastern, and west-European art — has recently been the subject of much scholarly research, and the term *Urasian animal art* is now being applied to it. See Michael Ivanovich Rostovtzeff, *The Animal Style in South Russia and China,* Princeton University Press, 1929, pp. 100–06.

quite naturalistically and at times, especially in the Luristan bronzes, giving it a highly conventional form.

BIBLIOGRAPHY

Andrae, Walter, *Coloured Ceramics from Ashur, and Earlier Ancient Assyrian Wall-Paintings*, London, 1925

Baikie, James, *The Glamour of Near East Excavation*, Lippincott, 1928

———— *The Life of the Ancient East*, Macmillan, 1923

Breasted, James H., *Ancient Times*, 2d ed. rev., Ginn, 1935

Childe, Vere G., *The Most Ancient East*, Knopf, 1929

Cossío, Manuel Bartolomé, and Pijoán, José, *Summa Artis*, Vols. I–X, Madrid, 1931–46, Vol. II

Encyclopédie photographique de l'art, Vols. I–III, Paris, Edition "Tel," 1935–38: Vols. I–II

Gadd, Cyril J., *History and Monuments of Ur*, Dutton, 1929

Garstang, John, *The Hittite Empire*, Long & Smith, 1929

Grousset, René, *The Civilizations of the East*, tr. by C. A. Phillips, 4 vols., Knopf, 1931–34: Vol. I

Hall, Harry R. H., *The Ancient History of the Near East*, 8th ed. rev., Macmillan, 1932

———— *La sculpture babylonienne et assyrienne au British museum*, Paris, 1928

Handcock, Perry S. P., *Mesopotamian Archaeology*, Putnam, 1912

Harcourt-Smith, Simon, *Babylonian Art*, London, 1928

Jastrow, Morris, *The Civilization of Babylonia and Assyria*, Lippincott, 1915

Koldewey, Robert, *The Excavations at Babylon*, Macmillan, 1914

Martin, Richard A., *Ancient Seals of the Near East*, Chicago Natural History Museum, 1940

Pottier, Edmond, *L'art hittite*, 2 pts. in 1 vol., Paris, 1926–31

Rostovtzeff, Michael Ivanovich, *The Animal Style in South Russia and China*, Princeton University Press, 1929

Sarre, Friedrich P. T., *Die Kunst des alten Persien*, Berlin, 1922

Schäfer, Heinrich, and Andrae, Walter, *Die Kunst des alten Orients*, Berlin, 1925

Woolley, Sir Charles Leonard, *Dead Towns and Living Men*, rev. ed., Oxford University Press, 1929

———— *The Development of Sumerian Art*, Scribner, 1935

———— *The Sumerians*, Oxford University Press, 1928

———— *Ur of the Chaldees*, Scribner, 1930

Zervos, Christian, *L'art de la Mésopotamie*, Weyhe, 1935

See also the General Bibliography, pp. 791–92

Mediterranean Art

5

AEGEAN ART

(ABOUT 3000–1100 B.C.)

ONE of the important legends of the Greek peoples was that of King Minos. So important was it that, like many legends, it seems to be based on a kernel of historical truth. Before the year 1900, however, nothing had been found to substantiate the story. Already Heinrich Schliemann had proved that the Homeric tales of Troy were based on historical fact. As a child Schliemann had been told the story of the Trojan War and of the great walls that protected the ancient city; and in spite of opposition he strongly maintained his belief that those walls must still be standing. Not until middle life, however, when he had finally amassed a fortune, was he free to follow his dream. He then went to the locality which his knowledge of the *Iliad* led him to believe was the site of Troy, and there found nine cities built one on the remains of another. There were ancient walls and signs of a great conflagration, and Schliemann proclaimed that he had found the actual city. Subsequent excavations proved that the site was correct. He continued his excavating at Mycenae, whence sailed the proud chieftains to avenge the capture of Helen, and his success was even more startling. Massive fortress-palaces, elaborate tombs, great quantities of gold jewelry and ornaments, cups, and inlaid weapons — all revealed a pre-Hellenic civilization of high culture and wide extent that is now called Mycenaean.

But Mycenae, after all, did not prove to have been its center. Sir Arthur Evans had long considered Crete a potentially fertile field for investigation. Under Turkish rule excavation was impossible, but when in 1898 Crete was free from the Turkish regime the opportunity came, and about 1900 work began. In a short time, Evans's faith was rewarded far beyond his expectations. His spade did not dig very deep before it uncovered the palaces of the old kings. Sea kings they were. No fortified walls protected their palaces, for the broad reaches of water around their island served in the place of walls. Their ships plied to the three continents to which their island was gateway (Figs. 43A, 121A). Of these sea kings, whose power extended over the islands of the Aegean and over parts of the mainland, the greatest was Minos.

It was a proud people who ruled from these luxurious palaces, to judge from

[A] *Palace of Minos. Knossos. Colonnaded hall. Restored. c. 1500 B.C. (Evans)*

The Prince (Fig. 107B), an alertly alive athletic figure. It was also a gay people, fond of festivals and the circus (Fig. 109A). All their art is permeated with an aliveness quite distinct from the grave sobriety of Egyptian art — except for the work of the Amarna artists, with which it has an affinity of style.

Who were the people who developed this civilization,[1] the first on the northern side of the Mediterranean Sea? We do not know their origin. In Neolithic times they were there. Early they had

bronze and a system of writing, not yet deciphered. The climate of Crete is mild and sunny but, though the winter rains make production easy in the fertile places, the land is not primarily agricultural. Its location in the Mediterranean makes it the gateway to three continents. Thus the Cretans became a seafaring people, traders and colonizers, bartering their own wares, notably their pottery and metalwork, around the Aegean, in Asia, and in Egypt, where — to judge from the number of representations of it in Egyptian tomb paintings — their pottery seems to have been popular. Their religion consisted of nature worship with rites performed not in great temples but, though sometimes before little shrines in the palaces, chiefly in caves, gorges, and groves. "Spiritual devotion in such surroundings," Mr. Forsdyke suggests, "must have led . . .

[1] Several names are used for this civilization, "Aegean" being the most inclusive. It is frequently called "Minoan," after its most famous king and most brilliant age, though strictly speaking the term is anachronistic if used before 1500 B.C. At present there seems to be a tendency to apply "Cretan" or "Minoan" to that aspect of the civilization which definitely belongs to the island of Crete, "Helladic" to that of the mainland, and "Cycladic" to that of the islands.

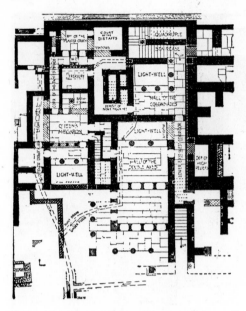

[A]   *Palace of Minos. Knossos. Plan of the domestic quarter, with dotted lines to indicate the drainage system. (British School Annual)*

to an intimate and emotional understanding of life and beauty in all the works of nature."[1]

At the time of its climax, under King Minos, the Cretan civilization had spread to neighboring islands and to the mainland, to Mycenae, Tiryns, and Troy, where, however, conditions were somewhat different from those on the island. Warlike Achaean Greek nomads were beginning to filter in, which necessitated fortifications. As the invaders became more numerous and more powerful, there was a restless shifting about, with frequent conflicts between the barbarian invaders and the inhabitants. Such a conflict we see in the Homeric tale of the siege of Troy. Finally, the last great wave of invaders, known as the Doric Greeks, swept across to Crete, burned Minos's palace at Knossos, and

[1] E. J. Forsdyke, *Minoan Art*, Oxford University Press, 1931, p. 29.

by 1100 B.C. had taken possession of the Aegean world. The Cretan culture, already giving evidence of decay, continued for some time, and made definite and valuable contributions to the second civilization to arise in historical times in Europe — the Hellenic.[2]

ARCHITECTURE AND PAINTING

The demands for building were simple and limited. There was no demand in Crete for tombs, temples, halls of justice, nor even for fortresses. Only a palace for the king and his retainers was necessary — one that was large, comfortable, gay, with ample staircases and courtyards for pageants and shows. Such was the *Palace at Knossos* (Fig. 106A), a large rambling structure built around open courts. There were gaily decorated living-rooms of all kinds; bathrooms, and a drainage system; audience halls with finely paved floors; workshops and long corridors which led to magazines where, in huge jars, were stored wine, oil, grain, and honey. Everything spoke of luxury, wealth, and splendor: gold cups and ornaments; pottery cups of eggshell thinness; a gaming-board glittering with gold, silver, ivory, and blue enamel.

At several points in the palace fine broad stairways led to upper stories; for the building was set on a hillside and in some places was several stories high. In the colonnaded hall (Fig. 105A) we see one of these stairways. The foundation and the lower parts of the building were

[2] The history of Crete falls into three divisions: Early Minoan (about 3500 to 2200 B.C.), Middle Minoan (2200–1600 B.C.), and Late Minoan (1600–1100 B.C.). In the early part of the Late Minoan occurred the reign of King Minos (about 1500 B.C.). The Homeric age, so called because it is described in the Homeric poems, which were written much later, includes the period of the great migrations and conflicts from about 1350 to 1100 B.C.

[A] *Cupbearer. Fresco from Knossos. H. c. 5 ft. c. 1500 B.C. Candia Museum.*

[B] *A Prince or Priest-King. Painted relief. Restored. From Palace at Knossos. c. 1500 B.C. Candia Museum. (Figs. 107A and B, Metropolitan Museum, New York)*

built of huge, finely cut blocks of stone, but the columns were of wood. Each column has a small circular base, carries a cushionlike capital with a square block to support the lintel, and tapers toward the base — a curious fact, not yet satisfactorily explained, but characteristic of Aegean column construction (Figs. 108A, 112B). Both columns and walls were painted brightly.

Painting was mural decoration, and the chief decorative element of the pal-

aces. Its subject matter was Cretan life: bullfights, processionals and ceremonials, many scenes from nature, birds, animals, flowers, fish and sea life. Technically these paintings are fresco. A tall slender *Cupbearer* (Fig. 107A), one of a procession of youths, is holding a gold-mounted silver vase. He has long curly hair, wears an elaborately embroidered loincloth with a silver-mounted girdle, and has silver ornaments on his arms, neck, and ankles; on his wrist is an

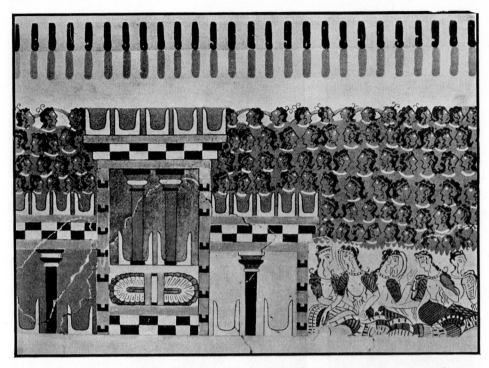

[A]   *Temple Fresco. Restored. From a small sanctuary in the Palace at Knossos. c. 1600 B.C.*

agate seal. The pinched waist, the reason for which we do not know, is characteristic of both the men and the
women of Crete. The effect of the procession must have been highly decorative, as the dark figures[1] moved
rhythmically against the flat ground
broken into wavy bands. Although, as
in Egyptian painting, the flat tones
serve the purpose of decoration, still
the youth standing so erect, with shoulders thrown far back, is not cold, formal,
and conventional, but full of life and
keenly conscious of the pride of his race
and the nobility of the ceremony that he
is performing. In *The Prince* (Fig. 107B)
there is more movement, and the ground
is broken by areas with lilies, now dark
against light, now light against dark.
This figure is partly modeled in relief,

and the drawing, while resembling the
Egyptian, is filled with elasticity and
individuality, which one sees also in the
Head of a Young Girl, jaunty and piquant
with her large eye, individual profile,
rouged lips, and gay, beribboned dress.
    This vivacity and spontaneity are
seen also in the *Temple Frescoes*[2] (Fig.
108A), in which crowds are massed about
a shrine as if attending some ceremonial
or show. Over large washes of red, indicating men, heads are outlined in
black with white collars and white eyes,
producing a very convincing impression
of a crowd. In contrast to the crowd represented by this "shorthand" method,
on each side of the shrine are groups of

[1] As in Egypt, male figures are painted red
and female figures yellow.

[2] Also called *Miniature Frescoes* because of
their small scale, which was necessitated by the
size of the room, about 6 by 15 feet. A dado fills
the lower part of the wall, with the frescoes
above on the eye level.

[A]   *Toreador Scene. Fresco. c. 1500 B.C. Candia Museum. (Metropolitan Museum, New York City)*

ladies, with the entire figure painted in detail. Their elaborate dresses with flounced skirts and tight bodices are painted in bright colors, and the effect of their holding a spirited conversation is heightened by gestures.

The *Toreador Scene* (Fig. 109A) shows how well these painters could represent a dramatic moment, fill it with spirit, with instantaneous poses, and still, as it were, keep it on the wall. Here the remarkable vivacity and the decorative quality are both made effective by the long sweeping curves in the body of

the bull combined with the S-curves in the horns and tail and in the vaulting youth, and by the vivid patterning of the surface.

In the nature scenes one finds not only understanding but a profound love of nature and a high degree of imagination and spontaneity in representing it. In the *Flying Fish Fresco* (Fig. 109B) the impression is of an easy swinging movement and countermovement combined with a short quick rhythm in the rocks and the edges of the fins, like surging waves which break in light crests: an

[B]   *Flying Fish Fresco. Candia Museum. (Metropolitan Museum, New York City)*

impression of blues, yellows, browns, definitely and happily distributed over a flat surface.

As we pass from Crete to the mainland, we notice that the gay, open palace has given way to a more somber, compact, massive fortress-palace, often built on a hilltop. At *Tiryns*, for example, the walls are twenty feet thick, built of unhewn or roughly dressed stone, called "Cyclopean walls" by the later Greeks. Through them, at intervals, run corbeled galleries (Fig. 110A). The nucleus of the palace, a hall of state

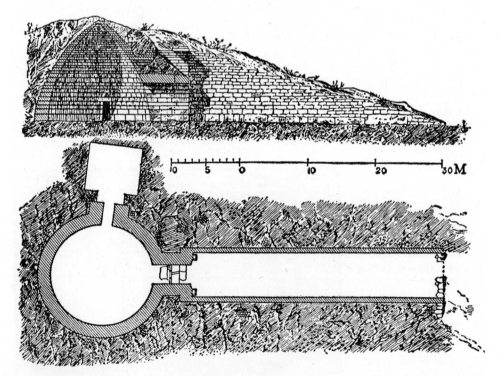

[B]   *Tomb Called the "Treasury of Atreus." Mycenae.* (*Perrot and Chipiez*)

[A] *Frieze. Of alabaster with blue glass inlay. Tiryns. Thought to be a prototype of the Doric frieze of triglyphs and metopes (Fig. 125Aa). (See note 1, page 126.)*

known as a *megaron*, was a rectangular room with a hearth in the center, around which were four columns to support the roof; at the entrance were a vestibule and a porch. In all these changes from the Cretan palace are reflected a colder climate and another race, the invaders from the North.

The sternness of these fortress-palaces is relieved by frescoes similar to the Cretan, by carvings (Figs. 111A and B), and, at Mycenae at least, by monumental architectural sculpture. At this fortress-palace the stone in the walls about the entrance is more finely cut than elsewhere in the structure. The door itself is formed of two great pillars capped with a huge lintel, above which the layers of stone are not solid, but by forming a corbeled arch leave a triangular opening to relieve the weight on the lintel. This space is filled with a slab on which are carved in high relief the two lions from which the gate is named (Fig. 112B). The lions stand in a balanced position on either side of a shaft on the base of which they rest their forepaws. Holes near the top indicate that the heads, now lost, were made of separate pieces of stone or metal. Groups similar to this are seen on Cretan seals and probably constitute a heraldic device. The lions are carved with breadth and vigor, and the whole design admirably fills the triangular space in which it is placed, harmonizing

in dignity, strength, and scale with the massive stones that form the walls and the gate. In its visual as well as its functional effectiveness it seems to partake of the spirit of the warring Agamemnon and Menelaus.

Another type of building found on the mainland was the so-called beehive tomb. When first discovered, it was thought these structures were store-

[B] *Fragment of a Tomb Ceiling. Carved green schist. Orchomenos. (Journal Hellenic Studies) Compare, for decorative motifs, Figs. 77A and 94A.*

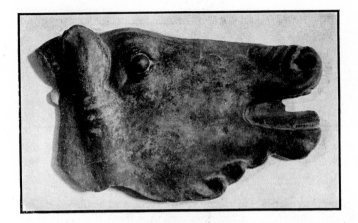

[A] *Head of a Bull. Painted clay relief. L. 26 in. Candia Museum. (Metropolitan Museum, New York City)*

houses for treasure; hence the most important is known as the *Treasury of Atreus* (Fig. 110B). Probably for the sake of protection, it was built into the hill and approached by a long passage cut through the side. Its beehive shape is formed by corbeling courses of stone laid on a circular base. The small rectangular chamber at the side is hewn from the rock. Frequent holes in the in-

terior seem to indicate that decorations, such as bronze rosettes, were affixed. In the monumental entrance we find the same combination of lintel and corbeled-arch construction as in the *Lion Gate*. Among the motifs of decoration, we see on the column the chevron; on the bands above, the spiral, rosette, and palmette. The columns here, as at Knossos, taper toward the base.

[B] *Lion Gate. Mycenae. Probably late Minoan.*

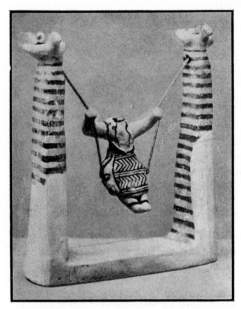

[A] *Girl in a Swing. Clay painted. H. 5½ in. c. 1600 B.C. Metropolitan Museum of Art, New York City. (Metropolitan Museum)*

SCULPTURE

Sculpture in the round, judging from the small amount extant, seems not to have interested the Aegean peoples. Perhaps the chief examples are the figurines of ivory, usually combined with gold, best illustrated by the *Snake Goddess*[1] (Fig. 113B). On her head is an elaborate coronet, the holes in which indicate gold attachments — probably ornaments and the usual curls. The flounces of her skirt are banded with gold and her outstretched hands hold two gold snakes that coil about her arms. Like the *Cupbearer*, she stands proudly erect with shoulders thrown back, firmly grasping the snakes, a forceful figure based upon

[1] A possible companion figure, the *Divine Boy*, has many parallel characteristics, and may indicate that both figures belonged to a shrine group. For this see Sir A. J. Evans, *The Palace of Minos*, Vols. I–IV, Macmillan, 1921–35, Vol. III, pp. 436 ff.

[B] *Snake Goddess. Gold and ivory. H. 6½ in. c. 1500 B.C. Museum of Fine Arts, Boston. (Boston Museum)*

a strong curve in the back and the vigorous diagonals in the arms. Mention should be made of the clay figurines of Cretan ladies, simply and sketchily molded and gaily glazed, which show such an intelligent feeling for material; and of the *Girl in a Swing* (Fig. 113A), in which one discerns a peculiar sensitivity for clay as the medium for a summary momentary expression.

Sculpture in relief appears frequently in stone, clay, and various metals. The *Head of a Bull* (Fig. 112A), probably a fragment from a bullfighting scene,

[A] *Kamares Vase. From Knossos. H.
c. 9 in. 2000–1800 B.C. Candia Museum.
(Metropolitan Museum, New York City)*

[B] *Octopus Jar. H. c. 8 in. 1600–1500
B.C. Candia Museum. (Metropolitan Museum, New York City)*

gives one a vital impression of an enraged animal; a small steatite vase, the *Harvester Vase* (Fig. 116A), furnishes an equally vital impression of a riotous crowd and one perfectly in unison with a curving surface of stone. A crowd of harvesters singing and shouting follow a figure carrying a rattle. Their forward movement and lusty exuberance are expressed with direct forcefulness. Pitchforks — long, straight, and carved in low relief — fill the upper part of the band; the figures, in higher relief, fill the lower. Thus is created a variation in texture and in design that is pleasing to the touch as well as to the eye, and the entire design hugs the surface so tightly that it seems to be an integral part of the wall of the vase.

The same kind of virtuoso miniature carving is found in the Cretan seals, which are not of the cylinder type like the Babylonian, but are settings in rings and bracelets with the design cut in intaglio. A variety of hard stones of various colors were used and a variety of subject matter — often with heraldic significance. The animal subjects are noteworthy for their vivacious life and beauty of composition and carving.

POTTERY, METALWORK

Among the craftsmen of Crete the potter was of special consequence, and his wares were important articles of commerce. In the early *Kamares Ware*[1] (Fig. 114A) we find a robust shape with a lustrous black ground on which is a quasi-geometric pattern of creamy white interspersed with yellow and red, forming a brilliant and harmonious piece of decoration. As time went on, the tendency of the potters was away from geometric and conventional design toward the naturalistic, with decorative motifs taken from their own immediate world of nature. Sea life, for example, furnished decorative motifs: dolphins and seaweed, fish nets, or the octopus. On a jar decorated with an octopus (Fig. 114B), the tentacles reaching out over the curving surfaces make one particularly aware of the volume of the vase. From the land, crocuses, irises, lilies, reeds, and grasses present to the artist's seeing eye patterns which have all the reality of nature and

[1] So called from the cave on Mt. Ida where a large number of examples have been found.

[A] *Palace Style Vase. H. c. 30 in. 1500–1350 B.C. National Museum, Athens. (Metropolitan Museum, New York City)*

[B] *Palace Style Vase. 1600–1500 B.C. (Seager)*

at the same time maintain the surface continuity of the wall of a jar.

Among the large jars called *Palace Style*, because many have been found at Knossos and appear to belong to the period of its most splendid development, that represented in Figure 115A has an interesting design of skillfully interlaced birds combined with concentric bands and spirals, painted with a bold sweep of line. Areas of light and dark are broken here and there by a patterning of dots and wave lines, every part moving in unison with the curving surface. In Figure 115B, the double-ax motive plays through the design — in the shape of the handles, in the spaces between the handles and between the horns of the ox, on the rim, and on the foot. It probably has some religious significance, and the vase may have been used for ceremonial purposes. Notice the nat-

uralistic sprays of olive in the midst of an otherwise conventional design.

Another craftsman of great importance was the goldsmith, who fashioned jewelry of gold leaf which exhibits the charming naturalness of all Minoan work. Among his creations were ornamental disks with sensitively fitted spirals and with patterns derived from the butterfly and the octopus; masks, whose function is uncertain; and, particularly, a variety of cups decorated in repoussé with designs of sea plants, octopuses, and human and animal figures.

The *Vaphio Cups*[1] (Fig. 117A) are notable examples of this type of cup. They are a pair of teacup shape, each made of two plates of gold, one of which was worked in repoussé to decorate the outside, the

[1] So called because they were found in a grave at Vaphio in Laconia.

[A] *Harvester Vase. Restored. Black steatite. W. c. 4 in. c. 1500 B.C. Candia Museum. (Metropolitan Museum, New York
City)*

other left plain to make a smooth finish
on the inside. The plates were then fastened together and the handles riveted
on; some of the details were engraved.
On one cup is a bull-hunting scene filled
with the greatest movement. In the
center is a bull caught in the meshes
of a net. A second bull, charging furi-
ously, impales with his horns a hunter
whose companion falls to one side. A
third bull dashes madly from the fracas.
On the other cup is a quiet. scene,
possibly representing bull-hunting by
means of a decoy cow. At the right a
peaceful bull has been attracted, and
moves toward the cow; in the center
he stands beside her; at the left the
same bull, captured and hobbled by
the trapper, is bellowing in anger. The

three seenes are well united by the trees
and the trapper, and the whole design
is admirably composed to fit the space.
In both cups, the spaces not filled by
the animal and human figures contain
landscape details of trees and rocks in
the same style as is seen in the paintings. Depth is indicated by placing the
farther object above the nearer, as in
the trees holding the net. The lowness
of the relief and the conventional treatment of the trees produce a rich play
of light and shade, together with varying areas of smooth and rough textures.

Skill in a different kind of metalworking is seen in Cretan damascened dagger
blades, in which the figures are inlaid on
the bronze in gold, electrum, and some
black substance. On one blade is represented a lion hunt, in which the bodies
of the fleeing animals, elongated as if to
accentuate their rapid movement, fit
marvelously into the tapering shape.

SUMMARY

In Aegean art, notably in that of
Crete, we find nothing of the quiet,
somber dignity found in Egyptian art
or of the dim mysteriousness of the
Egyptian temple, but a style directly
expressive of a democratic people intimate with nature. It is a refreshing,
sprightly art, imaginative and naturalistic rather than abstract. Its restlessness
and movement reflect an exuberance of
body and mind. The adventures of the
Cretans on the sea were equaled by the
love of pleasure at home to which their
palaces bear witness. These palaces with
their equipment and articles of personal
adornment constitute practically the entire Cretan art expression, except for
similar articles made for trading. They
were equipped comfortably, even luxuriously, and their walls were gay with
frescoes which picture life on land and
on sea, and decorate as well. The unceasing variety in Aegean pottery and

[A] *Vaphio Cups. Gold. H. 3½ in. 1600–1500* B.C. *(National Museum, Athens)*

paintings (contrast the unceasing repetitions in Egypt and Assyria), the vivacity and oddity of their color relations, reflect the eagerness, restlessness, and adventuresomeness of the Cretan sea kings; and the magnificence of their metalwork is witness that the descriptions in Homer of the shield of Achilles and the house of Alcinoüs were based not upon imagination, but upon the actual appearance of the civilization which they reflect.

BIBLIOGRAPHY

Baikie, James, *The Sea-Kings of Crete*, 3d ed., Macmillan, 1920

Bell, Edward, *Prehellenic Architecture in the Aegean*, London, 1926

Bossert, Helmuth T., *Altkreta*, 3d ed. enl., Berlin, 1937

Breasted, James H., *Ancient Times*, 2d ed. rev., Ginn, 1935

Burrows, Ronald M., *The Discoveries in Crete*, 2d ed., Dutton, 1908

Buschor, Ernst, *Greek Vase-Painting*, tr. by G. C. Richards, Dutton, 1922

Evans, Sir Arthur John, *The Palace of Minos*, 4 vols. in 6, Macmillan, 1921–35

Forsdyke, Edgar J. *Minoan Art*, Oxford University Press, 1932

Fowler, Harold N., Wheeler, J. R., and Stevens, G. P., *A Handbook of Greek Archaeology*, American Book Company, 1909

Glasgow, George, *The Minoans*, London, 1923

Hall, Harry R. H., *Ægean Archaeology*, London, 1913

———— *The Ancient History of the Near East*, 8th ed. rev., Macmillan, 1932

———— *The Civilization of Greece in the Bronze Age*, London, 1928

Hawes, Charles H., and Hawes, Harriet A. B., *Crete, the Forerunner of Greece*, Harper, 1909

Mackenzie, Donald A., *Myths of Crete and Pre-Hellenic Europe*, London, 1917

Mosso, Angelo, *The Palaces of Crete and Their Builders*, Putnam, 1907

Pendlebury, John S., *Archaeology of Crete*, London, 1939

———— *A Handbook to the Palace of Minos at Knossos*, Macmillan, 1933

Rodenwaldt, Gerhart, *Die Kunst der Antike*, 2d ed., Berlin, 1927

Sheppard, John T., *The Pattern of the Iliad*, London, 1922

Swindler, Mary H., *Ancient Painting*, Yale University Press, 1929

Tsountas, Chrestos, and Manatt, J. I., *The Mycenaean Age*, Houghton Mifflin, 1897

See also the General Bibliography, pp. 791–92.

[A]   *Parthenon. Athens. Of Pentelic marble. Ictinus and Callicrates, architects. 447–432* B.C.

6

GREEK ART

Geometric, Archaic,
and Fifth-Century Art

(ABOUT 1100–400 B.C.)

IN marked contrast to Egypt, a land monotonous with the long horizontals of alluvial plain between desert plateaus and under invariable sunshine, Greece is a country of diversified geography and climate (Fig. 121A). The deeply indented bays of its rugged coast line make the country half land and half sea; mountain ridges divide it into many small units. The semitropical climate, though marked by alternations of wet and dry seasons, is free from extremes of heat and cold. The unusually crystalline atmosphere is softened by a haze. Both sky and sea are brilliant in color. Little wonder is it that the Greeks, who were by nature sensitive to beauty and gifted with imagination, in their joy in nature should people mountains, woods, streams, sky, and sea with divinities; that they should picture Zeus, the king of this realm of gods, as reigning from their loftiest peak, Olympus; the Muses, as dwelling in the deep, cool groves on the long slopes of Parnassus and Cithaeron; and Apollo, the god of wisdom, as speaking from the awe-inspiring clefts of Delphi. These geographical and climatic conditions probably had something to do with the eager individualistic strain in the race.

Who were the Greeks?[1] They appear to be the product of a racial and cultural intermingling, with at least three components: the Mediterranean race, the Cretan culture, the Indo-European invaders. About 2000 B.C. these nomads began drifting in and mingling with the native inhabitants. About 1500 B.C. the Dorians, cruder, more militant Indo-Europeans, began to penetrate the Aegean lands. To this period belongs the siege of Troy, which is typical of the numerous conflicts between the Aegean strongholds, such as Troy or Mycenae, and the invaders. Those of the conquered peoples who had the means fled; the remainder mingled with the conquerors. Slowly they amalgamated, the invaders taking over certain elements of the gifted Cretan civilization. It was the Indo-European, however, whose religion, language, and fresh energizing power triumphed.

The enterprising Hellenes early became a trading and colonizing people, and thus not only enlarged the geographic and cultural boundaries of Hellas but made contacts with the older civilizations — Egypt, Babylonia-Assyria, Phoenicia — from which they acquired ideas, motifs, conventions, processes. Tribal organizations evolved into city-states, each an individual unit,

[1] In using the word "Greek" one needs to remember that the Greeks called themselves "Hellenes" and their country "Hellas."

ruled first by kings, then by nobles, then by tyrants or benevolent despots; and finally came the extraordinary experiment of democracy. To govern, however, was not an accomplishment of the Greeks.

In religion, nature worship evolved into nature personification. The gods assumed human forms of grandeur and nobility, though not free from human frailty. Man, in other words, became "the measure of all things"; to create the perfect individual became an ideal. Hence the interest in athletics and the characteristic Olympic games, athletic, literary, and musical contests celebrated every four years in honor of Zeus.

Athens, in many ways, stands as the symbol of Greek culture, though one must not forget the contributions in science, philosophy, and the arts of Asia Minor and Magna Graecia. Should one have visited Athens at the time of its brief flowering after the Persian wars, what would one see? An enterprising business city of about a hundred thousand people, situated on a fertile plain about a lone hill some five miles inland from a bustling harbor. In appearance the city was rather mean, an unplanned mass of small sun-dried-brick houses along winding lanelike streets with no sidewalks and no drainage system. The chief open place was the agora, or market place, with its plane trees for shade; it was surrounded by public offices and covered colonnades called stoas. Though the market always served its primary purpose as a central place for the sale of vegetables, cheese, honey, and flowers, its use was much wider; for here the citizens congregated to lounge in the cool of the stoa, to discuss the latest political development or a new philosophical idea. Outside the walls were olive groves, and the gymnasiums where the men went daily, primarily for the bodily exercise that played so large a part in the education and the daily life of the Athenian, but also, again, for discussion. And above both the olive groves and the roof tops towered the Acropolis, or higher city, formerly a fortress but in this age crowned with temples rising in bright colors against an intensely blue sky.

Since an important part of the conduct of business, at times even the entire responsibility, was assumed by slaves, the Athenian had a great deal of leisure to spend in the open and to devote largely to the commonwealth — the world's first important experiment in democracy. This democracy manifested itself in the great religious festivals, such as the Panathenaic procession, in which all the citizens, men and women, old and young, were represented; or at the dramatic performances of Aeschylus and Sophocles, where the audience of citizens approved with silence or applause, or condemned with a shower of figs and olives. The comedies of Aristophanes were enjoyed to the utmost when they satirized the great figures of the day with a daring that would be tolerated in no city not truly democratic. Quality was demanded in these plays by an audience that was composed of a people who were not art critics or theorizing esthetes but who could be depended upon, more often than not, to judge between good drama and bad.

Among the Greeks, then, we see a humanistic culture, with individual freedom for the members of the free classes. Neither theocracy nor absolutism dominated this democratic spirit — a spirit already evidenced in the Cretan civilization and possibly a gift of the Cretan to the Greek. Compared to the life spans of some of the other ancient cultures its duration was short. It was homogeneous and relatively unimpeded by outside influences.

The remains of the Greek civilization are abundant enough for us to discern clearly in them the normal evolution of the art of a culture, the cycle of its style. Such an evolution exists in every style and consists of three stages observable in all animate life: youth, maturity, decline. The first stage, usually called the archaic, is one of energetic growth, in which the artist, striving to give substance to his concepts, is daring in his experimentation with his material. In this struggle for expression he uses simple abstract or geometric forms, usually massive and monumental, with each part a conventional device, a concept of the mind rather than of visual perception. These parts are built into an organic structure, to which the constantly repeated conventions lend a decorative quality and in which is never lost either a recognition of the material or a fine craftsmanship in the handling of it. As time passes, a trend toward visual perception becomes discernible, and a more naturalistic outlook. This brings the style to its maturity. In this period, known as the classic stage, the artist has mastered the early problems, and is soberly confident and vigorous. While retaining something of the ruggedness and monumentality of the archaic age, he has refined its proportions, has tempered conventional forms with naturalism of a broadly generalized type, and has produced an art of restraint and placid rhythms.

But the very forces that brought the style to its classic stage now operate to lead it into excesses. At first its classic sturdiness and tranquillity evolve into elegance, delicacy, and emotionalism. Then naturalism degenerates into realistic imitation, and tranquillity into exaggerated movement and grandiose scale. Individual freedom delimits space, disregarding the limitations of material. Such is the last stage of a style, the flamboyant, or baroque. And the artist, faced by its excesses, often reveals in his work an archaistic tendency — that is, a nostalgia for earlier times.

[A]   *Crete and Greece*

ARCHITECTURE

With no use for the home except as an unpretentious place in which to eat and sleep, with no monarch to house royally, with religious rites performed in the open, what reason did the Greek have to build greatly? Far earlier than we can trace the practice by monuments, the Greek carved statues of his gods, statues that were very sacred. To carve the statue and to protect it, then, was a motivation for both sculpture and architecture. The idea of simple protection, however, soon developed into that of beautiful protection, with additional sculpture, partly to embellish the protective building, partly to tell something of the deity symbolized within, and partly as votive offerings. In addition to those purely religious in purpose, statues were erected to commemorate impor-

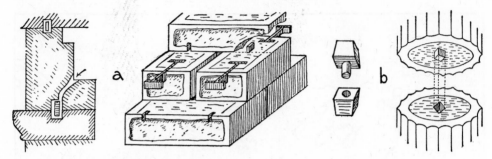

[A] *Construction Techniques.* a. *Cramps and Dowels. Iron or bronze cramps hold the stones of the same course; iron dowels, packed with lead poured in through channels left for that purpose, hold the stones of different courses;* b. *Two Drums, showing the cuttings left in the center for the bronze or wooden pivot which held the stones in place, correctly centered, and about which they were ground to secure a perfect joining.*

tant events, and particularly the victors at the great national games. It was a very simple and limited range of pur- pose, but a key to Greek art.

Materials in abundance were at hand. Plenty of timber, and literally moun- tains of marble: Hymettus, just east of Athens, with its bluish-white stone; Pen- telicus, north of the city, with its glit- tering white, peculiarly adapted for carving. The islands of the Aegean, Paros in particular, supplied varying quantities and qualities. Ivory and met- als, especially bronze, of which great quantities were used, it was necessary to import. In building, cement was not used; the stones were held firmly by a series of cramps and dowels (Fig. 122Aa).

There is a great gap between Aegean art and the emergence of the truly Greek expression about 600 B.C. Cretan culture was already in decadence when the Dorians arrested all cultural growth until they had assimilated the vastly superior civilization with which they had come in contact, and had evolved along individual lines. Probably very early they carved statues and built wooden structures to protect them, which by 600 B.C. they had translated into less-perishable stone. The temple discloses in its plan a close affinity with

the Mycenaean megaron, and even in its most elaborate form retains the ut- most simplicity: a single or double room (the cella) with no windows and one door (or two for a double cella), and with either (1) a portico with two col- umns, between the extended walls, or (2) a colonnade across the entire front, or (3) a colonnade across both front and back; or (4) any of these plans sur- rounded by a single or a double colon- nade (Fig. 123A).

In elevation the temple consists of three parts: a base, columnar supports, and a superstructure of lintels and slop- ing roof with gable ends. Such an eleva- tion is known as an order. Three orders evolved in the course of the Greek style and are differentiated, partly by details but chiefly by the relative proportions of the parts.

The earliest of the Greek architec- tural orders to be formulated was the Doric. We might expect that as time went on an adventurous people would develop a new style. Not so the Greek. His adventurousness was of an intellec- tual kind: though all the elements of the style were present in definite rela- tionships early, there remained the re- fining of these relationships. The process covered about two centuries (Fig. 124A).

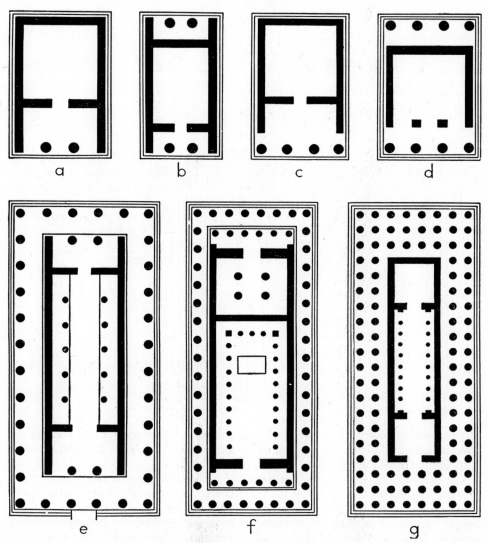

[A] *Plans of Greek Temples.* a. Treasury of the Athenians *at Delphi, a temple* in antis, *so called because the portico is formed by the projecting side walls,* antae, *and two columns set between them;* b. Temple of Artemis *at Eleusis, a temple* in antis *at both ends;* c. Temple B *at Selinus, Sicily, a* prostyle *temple, so called because the columns stand in front of the cella and extend the width of it. Sometimes an additional colonnade is placed at the back of the temple, and it is then called* amphiprostyle *as in* d; d. Temple of Nike Apteros (Wingless Victory) *on the Acropolis at Athens;* e. Temple of Aphaia *at Aegina, a* peripteral *temple, so called because a colonnade completely surrounds the cella, which in this case is in antis at both ends;* f. Parthenon *(Fig. 1184), a* peripteral *temple; to the* prostyle *cella an additional room for treasure has been added. Sometimes the* peripteral *plan is embellished by doubling the surrounding colonnade, and it is then called* dipteral *as in* g; g. Temple of the Olympian Zeus *at Athens (Fig. 1594).*

a   b   c   d

[A] *The Evolution of Proportion in the Doric Order.* d *is the Parthenon, which appears to have attained the subtlest proportions.*

In this habit of mind lies the key to an understanding of Greek art as well as of its extraordinary limitations.

The early Doric temples, such as the *Heraeum* at Olympia (about 620 B.C.), the *Basilica* (540 B.C.) and the *Temple of Demeter* (520 B.C.) at Paestum in Italy, and the *Temple of Apollo* (540 B.C.) at Corinth, show a clear distribution of parts: a base; fluted columns, with cushionlike capitals which support an entablature consisting of an architrave and a frieze composed of alternating triglyphs and metopes[1]; and a crowning pediment, which is the natural gable end formed by a sloping roof. Such a temple is a simple type of lintel con-

[1] *Triglyph:* a rectangular stone with three groovings (two whole and two halves); *metope:* the space between (the triglyphs).

struction, on a scale small enough for stone lintels to bridge the span between the columns.

Ornament plays a large part in the design, and is concentrated on the upper part of the building — in the metopes and the pediments. This ornament is basically sculpture, but it is not sculpture in the natural color of the stone but gaily painted in red and blue, with touches of green, yellow, black, and perhaps a little gold. The unpainted parts may have been rubbed with wax. By the use of color the artist could bring out more clearly the relationships of the parts, could soften the glitter of the stone, and could provide a background to set off the figures.

Unlike Egyptian temples, Greek temples faced outward. Rites were performed in the open, and the building itself served only to house the cult statue. Mass, volume, and interior space did not concern the Greek. It was on the exterior, on the outside surfaces, that he concentrated his attention, in order to make the temple a suitable monument, like a piece of sculpture, to the deity. The deeply broken light and shade, the quiet movement in the colonnade, and the lighter, more rapid movement in the gay superstructure result from a relief concept — as if reliefs were carved on an inner rectangular volume whose mass and solidity are not felt, as they are in the Egyptian temple with its solid walls and clearly defined volumes (Fig. 62A).

The culmination of the Doric order is the *Parthenon* (Fig. 118A).[1] It stands on the crest of the Acropolis, harmonizing with the contours of the hill; its broken light and shade play into the varying tones of the mountain landscape (Fig. 27A). The general impression is one of repose, of a sensitive balance between the supporting members and the load between the vertical line and the horizontal line, both largely unbroken. Everything contributes to calm. Contrast for a moment the restless movement of a Gothic cathedral (Figs. 348B, 349A and B) and the serenity of the *Parthenon* becomes even more apparent.

The plan of the temple (Fig. 123Af) shows a double cella, one room serving to house the cult statue, the other, the temple treasure. In elevation the *Par-*

<hr>

[1] The *Parthenon* was the temple of Athena Parthenos, meaning "Athena the Maiden," who was the patron goddess of Athens. Its ruined condition is due to the fact that at the time of the war between the Turks and the Venetians in 1687, the building was used as a powder magazine and exploded when hit by a well-aimed shot. A large part of the remaining sculpture was obtained by Lord Elgin, with the permission of the Turkish Government, in 1801–03, and became the property of the British Museum in 1816.

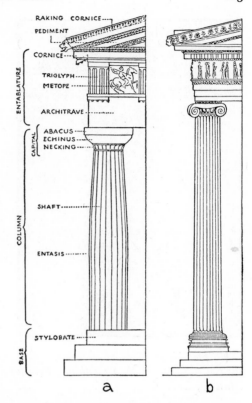

[A]   *A Comparison of Greek Orders*. a. *The Doric Order;* b. *The Ionic Order.*

thenon reveals the highest refinements of the Doric order. From the stylobate, the upper member of the triple base, the columns rise directly without individual bases, like trees from the ground. The shaft diminishes in diameter as it rises, and its contour is a very subtle curve, barely perceptible and known as the *entasis*. The grooves, or flutings, of the shafts with their soft shadows and repeated vertical lines both strengthen the rhythm and emphasize the feeling of support in the shaft, and finally individualize the columns by contrasting them with the plain wall of the cella against which they are seen. The shafts are not monoliths but consist of separate drums bonded together by dowels of wood and metal (Fig. 122Ab) with such

[A] *The Upper Part of a Column from the Eastern Porch of the Erechtheum. British Museum, London.*

nicety that the joinings were originally scarcely visible.

The capital consists of three parts — the necking, the echinus, and the abacus. The purpose of a capital is to form the transition from the shaft to the lintel; that is, from the vertical member, the load-carrying element, to the horizontal member, the load. An esthetically successful capital will not make this transition too abruptly. In the Doric capital we get our first suggestion of the horizontal in the necking; yet the vertical flutings continue up into the capital to the point at which we feel more insistently the horizontal; that is, at the row of concentric ridges that separate the necking and the echinus. The simple vigorous curve of the echinus then carries the line up to the square abacus — not directly, however, for it turns inward as it meets the block, thus

avoiding abruptness. The strength of this curve, rising so vigorously and then turning inward so gracefully, was not worked out by the Greek in a short time, but only after a long series of experiments dealing with the angle and the proportions. In the rectangular abacus we are carried easily into the horizontal architrave. Thus by a carefully thought-out design based upon skillful interplay of direction, we pass gradually from vertical to horizontal, from supporting elements to supported (Fig. 125Aa).

The architrave is severely plain and the frieze is composed of alternating triglyphs and metopes. If the wood-construction theory of the origin of the Doric temple is valid, out of a discarded function the Greek has made an esthetic asset.[1] For the triglyphs repeat the verticals of the columns in a more rapid tempo. The architrave and the frieze are separated by a simple stringcourse and united by the molding with bead-like ornaments beneath each triglyph. The deeply projecting cornice finishes the design and protects the frieze from rain. Unity of design between the frieze and the cornice is obtained by undercutting the cornice to correspond with the triglyphs and the metopes, and by the use of color. A second cornice, known as the raking cornice, finishes the pediment.

The curve, or entasis, found in the column has been noted. This variation from the straight line is characteristic of all parts of the building. The stylobate has a slight upward curve (a rise of three and three-fifths inches for a length of two hundred and twenty-eight feet); the columns incline inward, and are placed not at equal intervals, but closer together toward the corners, lend-

[1] According to the wood-construction theory triglyphs and metopes originated in the beam ends and the spaces between; and the undercuttings of the cornice, in the ends of the roof rafters.

[A]   *Erechtheum. Athens. c. 420–409 B.C. (Clarence Kennedy)*

ing a feeling of stability at those points. In fact, there is not a straight line in the building. While the purpose of the Greek in avoiding straight lines and complete regularity was undoubtedly to correct optical illusions, it also seems probable "that the builders of the Parthenon (whether by intelligent imitation or by intuitive artistic taste) had applied to architecture the same secret of beauty which governs natural forms — the tempering of geometric accuracy by minute deviations."[1]

In the Ionic *Erechtheum*[2] (Figs. 125Ab,

[1] Rhys Carpenter, *The Esthetic Basis of Greek Art*, Longmans, 1921, p. 195. For a sensitive analysis of the *Parthenon* by a modern architect, see C. E. Le Corbusier, *Towards a New Architecture*, Harcourt, Brace, 1927.
[2] The *Erechtheum*, so named after Erechtheus, to whom it was dedicated in part, conforms in plan (Fig. 127B) to Figure 123Ac, but has several unusual features, which may have been due partly to the irregular character of the ground on which the temple stands and partly to the number of shrines that it contained. For it was said to mark the site of the contest between Poseidon and Athena for the possession of Athens, and to shelter within its area the mark made by the trident and the salt spring of the former and the olive tree of the latter.

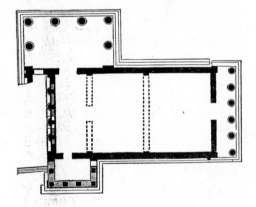

[B]   *The Erechtheum Plan. The temple probably contained more than one shrine.*

127A and B) we note, in comparison with the *Parthenon*, more slender proportions, greater elegance and grace, richer embellishment. In detail, the columns have individual bases, one member of which is delicately carved; on the necking is a honeysuckle band; the echinus is decorated with bead and reel, egg and dart, and the double guilloche (Fig. 126A). Perhaps the most conspicuous part of the Ionic capital is the double scroll or volute inserted between the

[A]   *Carving from the Erechtheum, with Honeysuckle, Bead and Reel, Egg and Dart, and Leaf and Dart Motifs. Acropolis Museum, Athens. (Alincri)*

narrow echinus and the abacus. The architrave is divided into three horizontal faces and the frieze was originally covered by a continuous band of low relief, in place of the Doric triglyphs and metopes. Stringcourses and cornices, doorway, and wall bands are delicately carved with dentils, egg and dart, bead and reel, honeysuckle, and braid patterns (Figs. 128A, 129A). This ornament, though rich, is confined to certain places and is strictly subordinated to the design of the whole. The Greek marble was particularly adaptable to the carving of moldings, which show not only beauty of chisel work but of profile, and reveal a sensitive and intelligent choice of the particular decorative motif that is adapted to a concave, convex, or angular type of molding. The value of these moldings to the Greek may be judged from the fact that he paid, according to the building inscriptions of the *Erechtheum*, the same price for carving one foot of egg and dart as for one human figure.

The *Temple of Nike Apteros* (the Wingless Victory, Fig. 123Ad), a small amphiprostyle Ionic temple set precipitously on the top of the cliff at the side

cf the *Propylaea* or *Gateway to the Acropolis*, is an example cf the bold placement for effective clarity often found in the location of Greek temples.

SCULPTURE

Architectural decoration, both in relief and in the round, was the purpose of much of Hellenic sculpture, though many independent statues were made for cult, votive, and commemorative purposes. Much of it was carved from the same material as the building and was painted not naturalistically but conventionally, to harmonize with a polychrome structure. If this use of color appears strange, one needs only to recall the tradition of color in architecture and sculpture in the eastern Mediterranean and western Asiatic countries — Egypt, Babylonia, Assyria, Persia, Asia Minor, Crete.

As for technical processes,[1] the sculp-

[1] For technical processes and tools see Stanley Casson, *The Technique of Early Greek Sculpture*, Oxford University Press, 1933; G. M. A. Richter, *The Sculpture and Sculptors of the Greeks*, Yale University Press, 1930; and Rhys Carpenter, *The Sculpture of the Nike Temple Parapet*, Harvard University Press, 1929.

[A] *Fragment of a Cornice from the Siphnian Treasury. Delphi. Delphi Museum. (Clarence Kennedy)*

tor carved the stone directly and used clay only when his conception required the use of clay as a medium. Bronze was popular, worked by solid casting, by hammering over a wooden core, or by the cire-perdue process.

Geometric and archaic sculpture is the expression of a vigorously growing people. The artist in his struggle for expression uses simple forms tending to the geometric, with each part a conventional device, a symbol created by mind and memory[1] rather than a naturalistic rendering based directly upon visual experience. These parts are combined architecturally; that is, are built into a perfectly articulated entity.

These qualities we recognize in the *Hera of Samos* (Fig. 130A).[2] The *Hera* is basically a cylinder, possibly reflecting a wooden prototype translated into

[1] For this explanation see Emanuel Loewy, *The Rendering of Nature in Early Greek Art*, London, 1907.

[2] One should at least mention among the earliest expressions in the Greek cycle the polychrome wood statues which have inevitably disappeared and the early stone statues, such as the *Artemis* found at Delos (Athens, National Museum), in which is a timid approach to a rectangular block of stone and an overshadowing of the representation by the material.

stone. The goddess stands in frontal pose, feet together, the right arm held tightly to the side, the left bent to the breast, probably holding some attribute.

[B] *Head of the Statue of the "Apollo" type (Fig. 131A). Metropolitan Museum of Art, New York City. (Metropolitan Museum)*

[A]   *Hera of Samos. Marble.*
H. 6 ft. c. 550 B.C. Louvre,
Paris.

[B]   *Seated Man. From the Sacred Way of the Temple*
of Apollo near Miletus. 550–530 B.C. British Museum,
London. (British Museum)

The statue is compact, with fine strong
contours, particularly as it sweeps out
to join the base. There is an indication
of the simple planes of the figure in the
upper part. Linear conventions carved
on the stone indicate linen in the long
undergarment and wool in the mantle;
and the two are united by a strong
curve that repeats the contour curve.
The simple quiet harmony of all parts,
the long unbroken lines and quiet surfaces, imbue the *Hera* with a reposeful
majesty. This feeling permeates the
seated figures from a temple near Miletus (Fig. 130B). An impression of power
derives from the sheer massiveness and
weight of the stone, and one of dignity
from the simple four-sided organization, as in the *Khafre* (Fig. 13A). Conventional devices, breaking up the surfaces,
not only represent different kinds of
cloth but set up movement over the surfaces and create varying textures.

Again we are vaguely reminded of
Egyptian statues by one of the so-called
Apollo figures — in the pose with left
foot advanced, in the broad square
shoulders, and in the four-sided organi-

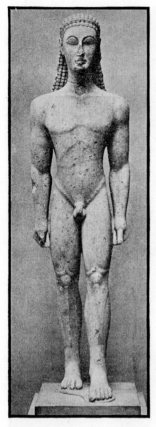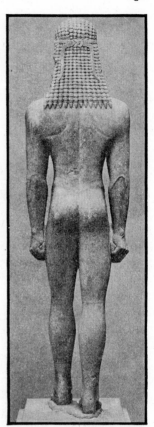

[A] *Statue of the "Apollo" type. H. 6 ft. 4 in. c. 600 B.C. Metropolitan Museum of Art, New York City. (Metropolitan Museum)*

zation (Fig. 131A). Here is a solid figure constructed of a few broad planes definitely related to the block of stone. On these planes anatomical details are indicated by shallow groovings or ridges, not obvious, but clearly enough seen to show that each is related to the other in a pattern. The boldly conceived device for the hair,[1] which falls on the back in an angular mass (repeated in the angular fingers), with the half angular, half curved knot of the fillet, furnishes a decorative note which complements the patternings of the torso

and limbs. Notice how the conventional ear (Fig. 129B), in line a continuation of the line of the jaw and in grooving a repetition of the eyelid, is the unifying element of the hair and the face. Almost any archaic head shows protruding eyes; abrupt transitions between the planes of the face, giving the impression of prominent cheekbones; mouth with upturned corners[2]; and stylized hair. All the conventions of this statue are cut firmly, and with their repeating

[1] This is to be distinguished from the Egyptian wig. Greek men wore the hair long until sometime in the fifth century B.C.

[2] Causing the "archaic smile," which appears to result from the difficulty in making the transition between the lips and the cheeks. For archaic heads of other civilizations see Figs. 225A and B, 227A, 234A.

[A] *Votive Figure Found on the Acropolis. Marble, painted. H. c. 4 ft. Early 5th cent. B.C. Acropolis Museum, Athens. (Alinari)*

[B] *Figure Found on the Acropolis. Marble, painted. H. c. 3 ft. Early 5th cent. B.C. Acropolis Museum, Athens. (Alinari)*

lines and motifs create a formal pattern of great esthetic power.

In time the trend sets in the direction of naturalism, both in pose and in details. The protruding eyes are taking their natural place within the eye socket; the "archaic smile" is disappearing; the hair hints at the thickness of its mass; and the drapery at actual deep folds. All this we see in the female figures, probably votive, found on the Acropolis at Athens (Figs. 132A and

B). All of them stand in the same frontal position, left foot advanced, right hand holding up the mantle, left arm bent at the elbow and extended as if holding something. The ladies here represented wear linen chitons, indicated by ripple marks, and woolen mantles that fall in broad conventional folds from the right shoulder. The marble is undercut along the edge of the folds, giving a feeling of depth, and is painted to represent the decorative

[A] *Archer. From the Temple of Aphaia at Aegina (Fig. 133B). (Clarence Kennedy)*

border and the allover pattern of the goods. The elaborately dressed hair falls down behind in conventional waves, and a few locks, separating, fall over the breast. Notwithstanding the vigorous, half-abstract, decorative beauty in these statues, one feels, possibly, an overelaboration and a lack of

that perfect unity of all details found in the *Apollo.*

The early reliefs have the same stylistic character as the early sculpture in the round, and in addition solve the problem peculiar to relief: the suggestion of a greater depth than is measurably present.

[B] *Temple of Aphaia at Aegina, Eastern Pediment. Incident from the Trojan War. Conjectural restoration by Furtwängler. c. 500 B.C. Glyptothek, Munich.*

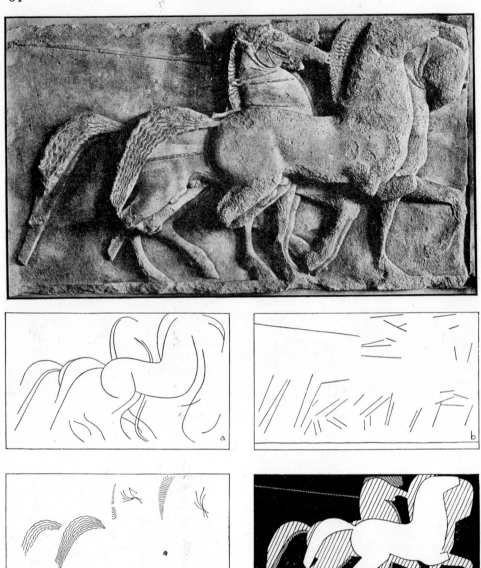

[A]   *Horses from a Frieze on the Treasury of the Siphnians, Delphi. c. 525 B.C. (Clarence Kennedy) The analyses show: a, the dominating organization of rhythmically related curves: b, a subordinate and more rapid rhythm of straight lines: c, repeated line patterns: d, the arrangement of the figures in depth on planes parallel with the plane of the background, an organization especially appropriate for a decorative relief. Compare the strong but controlled rhythms in this and in the Parthenon frieze (Figs. 142A, 144A) with the more violent rhythms found in the reliefs of the Hellenistic period (Figs. 160A, 162A).*

[A] *Temple of Zeus at Olympia, Western Pediment. Battle of Centaurs and Lapiths. Restored by Treu. c. 460 B.C.*

A solution of this problem we find in the friezes on the *Siphnian Treasury* (Fig. 134A), where the horses give a sense of vivid life, a feeling of the figure in space, and a decorative effectiveness. Space is indicated by a series of shallow parallel planes, with sharp edges which give emphasis to the contours of the horses' necks, bodies, and tails. The broad carving of the bodies seems to insist upon the chief planes, while the conventions for the manes and the tails break these planes in certain areas to add movement and texture to the design.

We have already begun to see the path of evolution which the cycle is taking. Starting with simple, almost geometric forms, with conventional devices for details, all of which are brought into a harmonious unit possessing decorative beauty, the sculptor begins to temper these forms by observing nature and making his statue represent a little more of what the eye actually sees.

The pedimental figures of the *Temple of Aegina* (Fig. 133B) illustrate this change. The scene probably represents some episode from the Trojan War. Athena, with aegis and spear, stands in the center, with fighting groups arranged in a balanced position on either side. In each group a warrior with helmet, shield, and drawn sword attacks his falling opponent, to whose help a friend rushes with outstretched arms. Behind him an archer, with bent knee, takes aim at the warrior; a fallen

wounded soldier occupies the corner. The most noticeable thing in the group is the freedom of movement and variety of pose. The figures are modeled with a vigor and an understanding of the human physique that reflect a careful observation of nature. The *Archer* (Fig. 133A), for example, is complicated in pose in comparison with the statues that we have studied; but the form is so compact and so simple in outline as to be almost geometrical. It is the contrasting direction of line seen in the vertical of the back, the horizontal of the arm, and the diagonal of the firmly braced leg that gives one so strong an impression of the powerful draw upon the bow, and at the same time a feeling of the perfect equilibrium of the whole figure. Many of the conventions are still present; the angular motifs in the cuirass, for example, strike a harmonious note in the total angularity of the figure.

The use of figures in the round to decorate the pediment of the temple posed the Greek a problem with which he struggled from the earliest temples of which we have evidence to the *Parthenon*. A gable is a space difficult to fill without being too obvious in treating the central axis and the narrow corners. On the old *Temple of Athena* at Athens the *Three-bodied Monster* (Acropolis Museum), with coiling tail and bold conventional coloring, in its simple directness must have been peculiarly deco-

[A]   *Three-sided Relief. Sometimes called the "Ludovisi Throne." Subject unknown. Marble. H. 40 in. c. 480 B.C. Terme (National) Museum, Rome. (Alinari)*

[B]   *Figure from the Eastern Pediment of the Temple of Zeus, Olympia. Marble. H. c. 3 ft. c. 460 B.C.*

rative. At *Aegina,* while any judgment is hazardous because of the uncertainty in the arrangement of the fragments, the figures seem somewhat forced in pose and unrelated. At Olympia, however, in the *Temple of Zeus,* despite the fragmentary remains, unity is discernible, together with unobtrusive movement from corner to apex.

On the western pediment is represented the *Battle of the Centaurs and Lapiths* (Fig. 135A). In the center stands Apollo, calmly majestic as if witnessing the scene but not of it. On each side are the combatants, in balanced groupings of twos and threes, with reclining figures in the corners. In comparison with the pediment of *Aegina* the design is complicated, and the unity among the figures and their relation to the space are more subtle. *Apollo* (Fig. 137A) stands austerely erect, the outstretched arm and turn of the head balancing the vertical of the body, and producing an

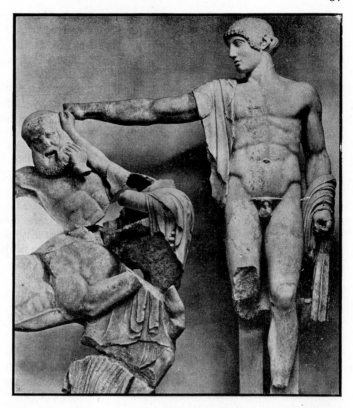

[A] *Apollo. From the Western Pediment of the Temple of Zeus, Olympia (Fig. 135A). c. 460 B.C.*

effect that is architecturally fitting and monumental. There is simple modeling without detail in both the figure and the drapery, which is arranged in broad folds that enhance the majestic effect. The figure has great vitality and at the same time poise and restraint, so that both the conception and the expression harmonize in their forceful directness. In a detail from the eastern pediment (Fig. 136B), the clear, definite relationship of parts is evident. This sculpture at Olympia, simple, direct, of monumental breadth and animating power, constitutes for many the climax of Greek sculpture, and has served as a stimulation to and a point of affinity with some modern sculptors — Maillol, for example (Fig. 776A). The same qualities are equally apparent in the metopes of this temple.

This balance between the ideal of thought form (conventions, symbols) and the ideal of seen form (visual appearance), which manifests itself in a restrained naturalism and in a feeling for material, we see again in the so-called *Ludovisi Throne* (Fig. 136A), neither the purpose nor the subject of which is definitely known. As decorative design we have a composition of single curves and S-curves about the central head, with stabilizing verticals in the folds of drapery. The beautiful texture of the stone, the feeling of order and logic in the inseparable unity of stone and figure, the skilled, sensitive cutting of the varied conventions for hair and textiles, conventions which are quite under the control of the firm organization yet lend to it a living quality through their unobtrusive variations — these attributes

[A]   *Myron. Discobolus. Reconstructed copy of the bronze original. Terme (National) Museum, Rome.*

make this relief of outstanding value.[1]

As an example of the bronze work of the late archaic age, the *Charioteer of Delphi* (Fig. 139A) will serve. The dark color with reflections and sharp contours, the crisp edges of the details necessitated by the darkness of the material, are characteristic of work in bronze. The statue belonged to a group with chariot and horses, and was probably erected to commemorate a victory at the races. It represents a youthful aristocrat who stands firmly on both feet, holding the reins in his outstretched

hand. He is dressed in the customary garment of a driver, girdled high and held in at the shoulders and the back to keep it from flapping. The hair is confined by a band tied behind. The eyes, which are made of glass paste and shaded by lashes of hairlike strips of bronze (a curiously inconsistent detail, an example of virtuosity in attempted naturalism but fortunately inconspicuous), and the slightly parted lips add vivacity to the face. We feel the austerity of archaic work in the figure, especially in the lower part, where the folds of the dress have almost the architectural quality of a fluted column; in the sharp lines of the brow; and in the conventional way in which the hair is worked above the band. But we notice also the naturalistic curls below the band; the masterly modeling in the hand and in the feet, the toes of which are clutching the floor of the chariot; the slight twist of the torso that gives one the feeling of an organic structure beneath the dress. The statue is a portrait, yet there are but few individualistic traits about it. Broad generalization characterizes it so far as representation is concerned. As in the sculptures at Olympia, monumental conception combines with directness and dignity of expression.

Another bronze of this age, the *Discobolus* (Discus-thrower) of Myron[2] (Fig. 138A), contrasts with the *Charioteer* in its movement, unusual for the fifth century B.C. Here an instantaneous pose has been caught between the backward and the forward thrust of the arm in hurling the quoit, and out of it, by means of formal qualities, has been made an abstract expression of concentrated force. For although the human figure has been used to convey the idea, we are primar-

[1] This late archaic art from about 480 to 450 B.C. is usually known as the transitional age. It is well to recall that this is the generation following the Persian Wars.

[2] The original of this statue is lost. A considerable number of copies exist, from which Figure 138A is constructed. For the question of copies in Greek sculpture see Richter, *op. cit.*

[A]   *Charioteer of Delphi. Bronze. H. 6 ft.
Part of a chariot group. Delphi Museum.
(Alinari)*

ily aware of the great sweep of an arc beginning with the quoit, moving along the right arm, the curve of the shoulders, down the left arm, taken up in the right leg, and so strongly felt that its very momentum easily carries the eye over the space back to the quoit. Cutting across and finally uniting with this arc is a great S-curve, and a stabilizing vertical, the axis, from shoulder to weight-holding leg. The face, contrary to what we should expect at such an intense moment, is impassive and broadly generalized. Such a free, noncompact pose, suitable for bronze, again shows the artist's complete understanding of the capacity of his material. This sensitivity to bronze is seen in two horses (Figs. 140A and B) which show

the same feeling for material and also, by comparison, the same trend toward naturalism in the animal as in the human figure. This new naturalism, however, is used with great discretion, and the impression of energetic spirit results largely from the use of archaic conventions, moderately tempered.

A statue that brings us to the end of the transitional age is the *Athena Lemnia* of Phidias[1] (Fig. 141A), which stood on the Acropolis at the left side of the

[1] While it cannot be proved conclusively that this statue is a copy of the original bronze by Phidias, it is generally thought to be so. The body is now in Dresden, the head in Bologna — a fact easily explained, since Greek statues were often made of several pieces of marble, a finer quality being used for the head.

[A]   *Statuette of a Horse. Bronze. H.*
c. 7 in. 8th cent. B.C. *Metropolitan*
Museum of Art, New York City. (Metro-
politan Museum)

[B]   *Statuette of a Horse. Bronze. H. c. 14 in.*
c. 470 B.C. *Metropolitan Museum of Art, New*
York City. (Metropolitan Museum)

road that leads from the great gateway to the *Parthenon*. She stands erect,
though with more freedom of pose than
the *Charioteer*. She wears the woolen
Doric chiton, which falls in rich folds,
somewhat severe, and over this the
aegis. The head is turned to the right
and slightly lowered. Contrary to the
usual representations, she does not wear
her helmet, but carries it in her hand.
Thus Phidias has emphasized her more
gracious aspect — "the thoughtful
Athena with the delicate cheeks," according to a Latin writer. One here discerns a sculptor governed by what his
eye sees, yet by no means absolutely.
The figure is an organic structure with
capacity for movement; the drapery,
undercut to suggest depth, begins to
look like cloth and falls in more casual
folds; the mass of hair has volume,
though the details are conventionally
treated; the features, though generalized and broadly carved, take their
natural places as part of the structure
of the head.

Some, as has been said, see in the
sculpture of the late archaic age the
climax of the Greek cycle. Others see
it in the *Parthenon* sculpture. It is a moot
point whether the sculpture of the *Parthenon*, even in parts, is the work of
Phidias. His most famous statues, the
Athena of the *Parthenon* and the *Zeus* of
the temple at *Olympia*, were made of
gold and ivory, and hence have long
since disappeared, and our knowledge
of his art can best be gained through the
sculptural decorations of the *Parthenon*,
which we know were made under his
supervision, and which may be, in parts,
actually by his hand.

The sculptural decorations of the *Parthenon* are found at three points: the
pediments, the metopes, and an additional continuous frieze[1] which ran
around the top of the cella wall and
thus inside the colonnade. The metopes
provide movement by compositions of

[1] Not to be confused with the regular Doric
frieze of triglyphs and metopes. This continuous
frieze, an Ionic feature, is unusual.

[A]   *Phidias (?). Athena Lemnia. (See note 1, p. 139)*

two struggling interlocking figures in high relief — Centaurs and Lapiths, gods and giants, Greeks and Amazons.

The subject of the eastern pediment (Fig. 144C), the ancient writers tell us, was the birth of Athena, who sprang full-armed from the head of Zeus. Again, the remains are fragmentary, but from a drawing made by a Frenchman traveling in Athens in 1674 we can get a glimpse of part of the composition. In the left corner, the sun god Helios in his chariot is rising out of the sea. Only the head, the shoulders, and the arms of Helios and the heads of the horses are shown. The horses approach a seated male figure turned toward them, which may personify Mt. Olympus, though it is usually identified as Dionysus. Closely connected are two seated figures, probably Demeter and Persephone, approached by a standing figure. The center is entirely gone. On the right are three seated female figures closely grouped, one turned toward the center. In the corner projecting over the cornice is seen the head of one of the horses of Selene, the moon goddess, who is sinking into the west as Helios rises in the east. In the *Three Fates*, as the group of three seated female figures is called (Fig. 143B), there is a quiet majesty, a highly generalized form with all the elements of the human structure expressed in their essential aspects only, and a balance between the material and

[A]   *Parthenon Frieze, Northern Side. Cavalcade of Mounted Youths.*
metal and affixed by rivets, the holes for which are seen in the horses'

the subject matter. The single figure at the left is in the frontal position, is four-sided, and quite one with the block of marble, although there is considerable movement in the limbs and head. The drapery, though by comparison with the archaic it is decidedly naturalistic, upon close observation is seen to create a definite undulating pattern. So, notwithstanding the advance of naturalism, we find sculpture that still recognizes the integrity of the material and which is monumental in its breadth and serene majesty.

The frieze along the top of the cella wall, in very low relief, was seen in half-light against a colored ground between the columns, enriching the plain wall and bringing movement into a static composition. It represents the Panathenaic procession, which took place every four years when the citizens of Athens gathered in the market place and carried to the *Parthenon* the peplos or robe for the statue of Athena. In the part of the frieze that decorated the western side of the building the procession is forming — youths are lacing their sandals, holding their horses or mounting, guided by marshals who stand at intervals, and particularly at the corners, to slow down the movement and guide the horsemen at the turn. In the friezes of the two long sides the procession moves in parallel lines, a cavalcade of spirited youths, chariots, elders, jar-carriers, and animals for sacrifice. The movement becomes slower and more solemn as it nears the eastern side, when after turning the corner it approaches the seated divinities, who appear to be guests of Athena at her great festival.[1] The cavalcade of mounted youths (Fig. 142A) is filled with rhythmic movement and spirited action. The backward glance of some of the youths gives a balance to the general forward movement of the procession; and the infinite variety in the poses of the youths and the horses frees it from any feeling of monotony. There is a flat background with no distance and no unnecessary details. We have, in fact, all the essential elements of a procession of spirited youths expressed with a naturalism tempered by decorative fitness. Notice how the figures just fill the space; how the heads,

[1] A convenient and inexpensive reproduction of the entire frieze, which is necessary for a realization of the unity of composition and the rhythmic flow of line, is published by the University Prints, Newton, Massachusetts.

Accessories, such as the bridles and reins, were painted on or made of heads. Marble. H. 40 in. British Museum, London. (Mansell)

whether the figures are standing or mounted, are on a level[1]; how the flanks of the horses form a central band of largely unbroken surface, and their legs beat a rapid rhythm in the lower third of the panel. Originally details and ac-

cents were stressed by color and even by bronze reins added — a disconcertingly realistic detail. In the slab representing the jar-carriers (Fig. 144A) the insistent motif of a youth carrying a jar upon his right shoulder is repeated, making a design of decorative quality, ease, and grace of rhythm that is readily felt but only understood when one observes the subtle variations that occur in the pose of the head, the arms, and

[1] This particular practice of distorting natural proportions for decorative purpose is known as *isocephaly* (heads equal, or on a level). It is a practice by no means limited to Greece. Indeed it is universal.

[B]   *Parthenon, Eastern Pediment. Three Female Figures, called the "Three Fates." British Museum, London. (British Museum)*

[A] *Parthenon Frieze, Northern Side. Jar-Carriers. Acropolis Museum, Athens. (Mansell)*

[B] *School of Polyclitus. Maiden. Bronze. H. 10 in. 5th cent.* B.C. *Antiquarium, Munich. (Clarence Kennedy)*

[C] *Birth of Athena. Parthenon, Eastern Pediment. c. 438* B.C. *Drawing by Jacques Carrey,* A.D. *1674. Bibliothèque Nationale, Paris.*

the hands, and in the arrangement of the drapery.

A contemporary of Phidias was Polyclitus, whose well-known interest in working out an ideal set of proportions for the human figure[1] is illuminating

[1] Illustrated in his *Doryphorus*, the statue of an athlete called the *Canon*. It exists only in hard dry Roman copies found in the museum at Naples and elsewhere.

because it enables us to co-ordinate the interests of sculptor and of builder and to realize that they are identical; namely, the refinement of proportions. Something of the Polyclitan style we see in a bronze statuette of a *Maiden* with turbanlike headdress (Fig. 144B). The weight rests on the right foot; the left foot is slightly raised, so that the figure is thrown into an easy pose. The little statue is simply constructed, with suavely flowing planes causing high lights on the reflecting surfaces to set up a quiet rhythm — a design well suited to the bronze medium.

The style of Phidias and of Polyclitus dominated Greek sculpture during the late fifth century B.C. when the Greek's objective became, more definitely, natural appearance. A fragment from the balustrade of the *Temple of Athena Nike* (Fig. 145A) has a little flavor, perhaps, of virtuosity in the extraordinary skill shown in revealing the figure beneath the drapery, and in the slight turning-away from a perfect balance between stone and cloth to a slight overbalance on the side of an illusion of cloth. At the same time there is a masterly expression of movement, quite abstract, in the folds which hang between the arm and the leg, a rhythmic flow of concentric curves, to secure which seems to have been the reason for the uplifted leg — an excellent example of the use of pose or gesture to obtain an effect of lyric charm.

PAINTING

That schools of painting existed, and paralleled sculpture in an evolution from geometric and conventional to naturalistic, we know from literary evidence, from the powerful influence they exerted on pottery decoration, and from Roman copies. But the actual paintings are entirely gone, the mural paintings in the stoas and other public build-

[A] *Nike Fixing Her Sandal. From the Temple of Athena Nike. 421–415* B.C. *Acropolis Museum, Athens.*

ings as well as the panel pictures. As shadowy to us as ghosts are these famous painters so far as our visual knowledge of their work is concerned. There was Polygnotus, contemporary of Phidias, who was a painter as well as a sculptor. Polygnotus attempted, by placing figures one above another, to suggest depth. He used a very limited range of color, and appears to have created, with others, as grandly monumental a style in painting as the sculptors attained in the temple at *Olympia* and in the *Parthenon*. Then there was Apollodorus the "Shadow-Maker" (fifth century), who seems to have experimented with the use of shadow to make his figures appear round, in conformity with the general naturalistic trend of the day.

A   B   C

[A]   *The* Amphora (*meaning to carry on both sides, referring to the two handles*) *was a vessel for storing provisions — wine, corn, oil, honey. It had an opening large enough to admit a ladle and usually a cover to protect the contents.*   [B]   *The* Cylix (*from the Greek root "to roll," referring to the vases being turned on the wheel*) *was the chief form of the drinking cup.*   [C]   *The* Oinochoë (*from the Greek verb "to pour out wine"*) *was the wine jug. The lip is pinched into a trefoil shape, which facilitates pouring. Vase painting showing a youth pouring wine from a slender, high-handled oinochoë into a cylix held by his companion while another youth approaches carrying an amphora.*

POTTERY, METALWORK, INTAGLIO, ENGRAVING

Among the elements of the Aegean culture that the Greek appears to have taken over and expanded was the pottery trade. In the course of time, as increasing exports created a demand for containers for such substances as oil and honey in addition to articles for general household use, the potters' quarters at Athens, known as the Ceramicus,[1] came to be no inconsiderable part of the city.

While the Mycenaean was fashioning his stately *Palace Style* jars (Figs. 115A and B), among the Greeks a new kind of pottery was appearing, of simple, rugged shape, with geometric decoration and occasional abstract natural forms.

[1] Situated both inside and outside the Dipylon Gate. The name is derived from the Greek word for "potter," whence our "ceramics."

[A]   *The* Hydria (*from the Greek word for* "*water*") *was the water jar, used chiefly to bring water from the spring. It has three handles, two for lifting and one for carrying. Vase painting showing two youths filling their hydriae at a fountain.*   [B]   *The* Lecythos (*oil flask*) *has a long, narrow neck adapted to pouring oil slowly. It was used chiefly in funeral rites. Vase painting showing two men at a tomb; on the plinth are lecythi, oinochoë, a crater, a lyre, and a wreath.* [C]   *The* Crater (*from the Greek verb* "*to mix*") *was the bowl for mixing the wine and water, the usual beverage of the Greek; hence it had a wide mouth. Vase painting showing a youth filling his cylix from a crater.*

In comparison with the Cretan, the decorative scheme and its relation to the shape seem to have been intellectually considered rather than spontaneously felt. This *Geometric* pottery, made from about 1100 to 800 B.C., culminated in the *Dipylon* ware,[1] of which a large funerary amphora (Figs. 148A, 146A) is

[1] So called because these vases have been found in great numbers in the cemetery near the Dipylon Gate of Athens.

an example. Its vigorous shape and small handles, none too sensitively proportioned, are decorated in a rich brown glaze on light clay, with bands containing geometric motifs and human figures. The latter occur with extreme rarity in Aegean pottery. Here we see the Greek concentrating upon his chief concern, man. The subject is a funeral procession. Though the drawing is primitive and the figures are symbolical, **the** deco-

[A] *Detail from a Dipylon Vase.*

[B] *Geometric Amphora. Dipylon Style. Colossal size. 8th cent. B.C. National Museum, Athens. Such vases were erected as monuments over tombs. The scene in the band between the handles represents a funeral with the deceased lying on a bier surrounded by mourners.*

rative quality is far more effective than in later, more naturalistic drawing (Fig. 164A). As we stand by these huge *Dipylon* jars we feel something of the majesty of the *Hera of Samos* (Fig. 130A), whose prototypes were probably being carved in wood when the Dipylon period was at its height.

Considering the extent of his pottery-making, the number of shapes which the Greek used is surprisingly small. Having worked out a few, each according to its functional requirements, he devoted himself to refining proportions, contours, placement of the handles, and decoration. Here again is the same interest in refinements within narrow limitations that we saw was a dominant interest in architecture and sculpture. Of these shapes those most frequently found are: the *amphora*, the general storage jar (Fig. 146A); the *hydria*, the water jar (Fig. 147A); the *crater*, the bowl for mixing wine (Fig. 147C); the *cylix*, the drinking-cup (Fig. 146B); the *oinochoë*, the wine pitcher (Fig. 146C); and the *lecythos*, the oil flask (Fig. 147B). In determining the uses of these vases[1] we are guided by the paintings on the pottery; for in these paintings the Greeks have given us an amazing revelation of their everyday life (Fig. 153A).

[1] The common, though misleading, term generally used in speaking of Greek pottery. One needs to remember that these "vases" were largely the pots and pans of everyday life and the containers used by the trader, though some were used for religious and funereal purposes.

[A] *Corinthian Oinochoë. Black and purple figures on a yellowish-brown clay base. H. 8⅝ in. First quarter 6th cent. B.C. Metropolitan Museum of Art, New York City. (Metropolitan Museum)*

[B] *François Crater. H. c. 2 ft. First half 6th cent. B.C. Named after the man who found it in a grave in Italy. Archeological Museum, Florence. (Furtwängler-Reichhold)*

As the Greek expanded his trade and colonization, we see evidences in his pottery of closer contact with the older civilizations of the Near East. Rows of animals (Fig. 149A); winged beasts, and rosettes recall Assyria (Fig. 95A); the lotus, Egypt. With the passing of the seventh century B.C. the Greek drew in upon his chief concern — himself and his immediate interests, secular and religious. The animal friezes and geometric motifs, often so decorative and suitable as motifs on a curving surface, disappeared before the frankly humanistic attitude. Probably no other people have used the human figure so preponderantly in ceramic decoration as did the Greeks.

The *François Vase* (Fig. 149B) is a crater with volute handles, of extraordinary vigor both in its shape and in its proportion, and decorated with concentric bands filled with human and animal figures. These are painted in a brownish-black glaze with touches of white or purple on the natural reddish clay, which is left as a background. On the foot, in the battle of the cranes and pigmies, is animated movement and decorative patterning. The rays above happily suggest the spreading movement of the surface of the crater, but this is halted abruptly by the horizontal bands, in some of which one feels the preponderance of the narrative interest over the decorative. Here are pictured various mythological scenes, the Calydonian hunt, the funeral games of Patroclus, the procession of the gods to the wedding of Peleus and Thetis.

Soon the touches of white and purple tended to disappear, leaving the figure in black alone against the reddish clay (known as the black-figured style). The glaze had now, after centuries of experiment, become a velvety jet-black color. In this glaze the figures were painted on the natural red clay and the details

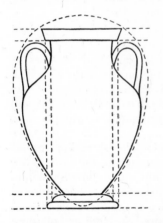

[A] *Amphora, Painted by Exekias. Ajax and Achilles Playing Draughts. Black-figured. 550–525* B.C. *Vatican, Rome. (Furtwängler-Reichhold) The analysis reveals a basic egg shape and a subtle relationship of part to part. The jar probably had a cover which contributed to the shape and proportions.*

incised with some hard pointed instrument, exposing the red beneath. Occasionally a little white and purple were added. The zonal arrangement disappeared and in its place a few larger figures furnished the decoration, sometimes grouped in a reserved panel, as in an amphora of Exekias (Fig. 150A). This is a strong compact shape in which the handles not only harmonize with the curve as an integral part of the design, but are attached in such a way that they appear to fulfill their function of supporting the weight. The surface is painted solid black, except for the band with rays just above the base, the decorated panel on the body, and the handles. In the large panel we see Ajax and Achilles seated on stools, bending intently over their game of draughts. Ajax, on the right, as the inscription tells us, calls out "Three"; Achilles, on the left, "Four." It is a close game. All the elements make for a design that is

[A] *Cylix Painted by Euphronios. Cattle of Geryon. Red-figured. D. 17 in. c. 500 B.C. Munich.*
(Furtwängler-Reichhold)

balanced, yet subtly varied: one hero is helmeted, the other not; slight differences occur in the position of the limbs and the spears and the decoration of the shields. There is much greater naturalism than formerly in the pose and the proportion of the figures, and greater freedom in drawing. The skill and surehandedness seen in the profusion and the delicacy of the incised lines of the hair, and in the very elaborate cloaks, are a delight in themselves. We recognize a kinship, stylistically but without infringement of medium, between this work and archaic sculpture in the formal and decorative beauty of the figures and of the schematic devices used for details. A cylix of Exekias (Fig. 154A), with a representation of Dionysus sailing over the sea carrying his gifts to mankind, is even more decorative in its adaptation of the figures to the circular shape.

In Figure 151A, we notice a change from black figures on red to red figures on black (known as the red-figured style). The natural reddish clay was covered with a red slip and polished. The decorator then incised his design on the clay, next painted it, frequently in a slightly raised line, and finally filled in the background with black glaze. The advantage of the red-figured process over the black-figured was that a line painted by a brush was more free and facile than one incised by a metal tool. The school of painting that was rapidly developing at this time in Athens was probably a primary influence on the style of pottery decoration. And the popularity of the cylix at this time may be due to the fact that its broad flattish surfaces offered a large enough area for groups of figures. Yet, paradoxically, the potter was concentrating, as were the builders and the carvers, upon the niceties of form — proportion, thinness of walls, character of profile, integration of handle with body. Nor did he enlarge his limited color scheme: the polished coppery red against a velvety black that creates such an effect of reserved elegance. Yet one feels creeping into the craft a conflict between ceramics — the art of clay shapes with suitable decoration — and painting; between clinging to the limitation of the medium and vying with the painter. In fact, some of the inscriptions on the pottery say that So-and-So "made me," So-and-So "painted me." This shows an attempt to combine the two arts — to the advantage of neither. And yet another art seems to have influenced the craft, that of the metalworker. Greek pottery was thrown on the wheel and turned until it was highly refined. As a result, in its rigidly perfect walls and contours and in the exceptional thinness of its walls, it participates in qualities peculiar to metalwork.

In the cylix of Euphronios (Fig. 151A) are represented scenes from one of the labors of Heracles, the cattle of Geryon — on one side the fight over the cattle, on the other side the animals being driven away by four youths. Though the narrative element is lively, the effect is still primarily decorative. In the herd of cattle the flat silhouettes of the bodies are shaped to the space, and in the central disk the figures of the youth and the horse form a compact pattern that seems to partake of the rotary motion of the circle and at the same time to restrain that movement by the severely angular lines of the cloak. To compose the figures pictorially also concerned the decorator. All the figures are drawn with fine firm lines that have a decorative quality of their own.

From the point of view of drawing the human figure, as a problem isolated from ceramics, it is interesting to note a gradual progression toward visual appearance, a problem which occupied the Greek from the time of the Dipylon ware. In proportion as he neared his objective he seemed to lose his feeling for ceramic decoration, to allow the painter's objectives to triumph over ceramic requirements, even though he kept the figure flat, drew and modeled with line alone, and included no details of background except a few hints in abstract form. This is true on some of the amphoras, in which the human figure is bent over the shoulder of the jar, thus marring the effect of figure drawing and adding nothing to decorative fitness.

The metalworker occupied a position as important as the potter's, and his

[A]   *Scene in a School. From a cylix painted by* Duris. *Red-figured. On the left the Athenian boy is taking a lesson on the lyre; in the center he is reciting before a master who is following with his scroll; at the right sits the boy's slave, who accompanies him to school; on the wall hang cylixes and lyres.* (*Furtwängler-Reichhold*)

wares reflect the general style of his day. Bronze was always a favorite medium with the Greeks, who used it widely, not only for sculpture but also for various kinds of utensils — pots and pans, dishes for the table, sacrificial vessels, tools, weapons.

Another art, involving both metalwork and intaglio engraving, is seen in the coins. Strange though it may seem, the finest Greek coins were struck not at Athens nor even anywhere in continental Greece, but in Magna Graecia, particularly at Syracuse in Sicily. In the *Demareteion*[1] (Fig. 154Ba), on the obverse is a four-horse chariot, with a Victory flying above; in the segment below, a running lion; and about the edge, a row of dots. On the reverse a profile head, perhaps of the nymph Arethusa,

in a faint circle, is surrounded by four dolphins with a Greek inscription which reads in translation "of the Syracusans." The coin is thicker and less even in shape than modern coins, and the metal runs up around the edge on one side of the reverse. This is because Greek coins were struck by hand on an anvil that held the die,[2] without a circular frame to keep the metal from running over the edge. The relief, too, is higher than in modern coins, for the Greek was not hampered by the modern necessity for "stacking." Though the object is small, there is a quiet orderliness and a feeling of amplitude. The circle of the disk is repeated by the dolphins and the inner ring, until the eye inevitably reaches the head in the center. The design is clear and effective, particularly when it is compared with that of later coins decorated with the same motif, in which the naturalistic tendency has entailed decorative loss. Fig-

[1] These coins are named after Demarete, wife of the tyrant Gelon. According to one story, after their defeat at Himera the Carthaginians obtained very favorable terms from Gelon through the influence of Demarete, to whom they gave a large amount of silver from which these coins were struck.

[2] Of course the skill of the engraver lay in the cutting of the die in intaglio, of which the finished coin is an impression.

[A] *Inside of a Cylix Painted by Exekias. Dionysus Sailing over the Sea. Black-figured. D. 14½ in. 550–525* B.C. *Munich. (Furtwängler-Reichhold)*

[B] *Silver Coins of Syracuse.* a. *Demareteion.* c. *479* B.C. b. *"Medallion" signed by Euaenetus. Late 5th cent.* B.C. *British Museum, London.*

[A] *Gem. Stag. Intaglio. Rock Crystal.*
W. $\frac{15}{16}$ in. 5th cent. B.C. Museum of Fine
Arts, Boston. (Boston Museum)

[B] *Gem. Flying Heron. Engraved by*
Dexamenos. Bluish chalcedony. L. 2 in.
450–440 B.C. Hermitage, Leningrad.

ure 154Bb is an example. Here the relief
is still higher, casting considerable
shadow; the hair is arranged naturalistically, with ringlets to soften the
contours; the dolphins are subordinate
because of the larger size of the head; a
circle of dots encloses the design. On
the reverse is the victorious four-horse
chariot, seen three-quarters view, dashing forward under the lash of the driver,
toward whom a Victory is flying with
the crown; in the segment below is a
suit of armor, the prize of the race.[1]

Another activity of the engraver lay in
the carving of gems that were mounted
in rings and used as seals. Perhaps an
inheritance from the Cretan was the
love of animal and bird forms and their
frequent use on the seals (Fig. 155A).
In the *Flying Heron* (Fig. 155B) we see a
sympathetic observation of nature in
the erect head, the legs thrust back, and
the position of the wings. The oval shape
of the body, repeating the oval shape
of the seal, combines with the sharp
angles of the beak and the wings, cut
with firm crisp lines, to create a design
admirably adapted to the shape of the
gem. Like the coins, the gems are relief
sculpture in miniature. In carving them

[1] This coin type is indicative of the popularity of chariot-racing in Syracuse.

the craftsman probably used a metal
drill with powdered emery and oil, so
that the process required not only keen
eyesight but a very sensitively trained
touch and a patience that considered
neither time nor money.

SUMMARY

Greek art from its earliest days to the
late fifth century passed through two
stages of the evolution of the Greek
style: the archaic, and the climax or
classic. In all its manifestations it displayed niceties of relationship within
extraordinary limitations.

The temple was the chief type of
building. It was small in size and simple
in plan, and during these centuries admitted little variation. But its proportions and the interrelationships of its
details were increasingly refined, until
it reached a climax in the Doric *Parthenon* and the Ionic *Erechtheum.*

Sculpture served two functions: to
add color, movement, and enrichment
to the exterior surfaces of the temple,
and to supply votive and commemorative statues. Bronze and polychromed
stone were the chief materials. The style,
by a series of experiments and by tempering conventional devices with natu-

[A]   *Demeter. From the temple of Demeter at Cnidus. Marble. c. 350 B.C. British Museum, London. (Clarence Kennedy)*

ralism, evolved from the geometric and early archaic to the climax stage of its cycle either in the late archaic, as at Olympia, or in the work of the Periclean age. All this sculpture shows a broadly generalized, impersonal aspect of the figure, with attention upon proportions and increasing movement.

Pottery and metalwork followed the same trend. Shapes remained the same but submitted to refinement of proportions and precision of contour. And though probably in the fifth century decorators were too much under the influence of the contemporary school of painting, still they revealed ability in composing figures within areas difficult to fill.

Fourth-Century and Hellenistic Art

(400 B.C. TO THE FIRST CENTURY B.C.)

THE disastrous Peloponnesian War left Greece drained of its strength and reduced Athens politically to a secondary place. Sparta and then Thebes took the leadership, both unsuccessfully, until Philip of Macedon, shrewdly playing upon mutual jealousies, brought the country into subjection and a semblance of unity. The work of his son Alexander was to spread Hellenic culture over large areas of the East by his conquests. Athens was no longer the center of this civilization, but only a provincial city-state in comparison with the magnificent cosmopolitan metropolises of Asia Minor and Egypt — Ephesus, Rhodes, Pergamon, Alexandria (Fig. 121A).

Another result of the Peloponnesian War was to turn the Greek from his ideal of the state to that of the individual. "Know thyself," Socrates had taught as he went about daily among the people in the streets, the agora, and the gymnasium and by questioning endeavored to help them to gain "wisdom" empirically, to weigh and judge out of their own experience rather than to consult an oracle. The serene idealism of the fifth century that was born of a simple robust faith and had produced the *Parthenon* and Sophocles gave way to the unrest of skepticism, to realism, and to the intellectual independence of Plato and Aristotle. The spirit of eager inquiry, inherited from the earlier Ionian philosophers and mathematicians, became a truly scientific mentality in such thinkers as Aristotle and Archimedes, and made valuable contributions to science, measuring with fair accuracy the circumference and the

[A] *Corinthian Capital. From the Temple of the Olympian Zeus, Athens. W. 8½ ft. National Museum, Athens.*

diameter of the earth, long since known to be spherical, and discovering many facts about astronomy, geometry, the natural sciences, and medicine.

While Greece had been passing through the cycle of growth, flowering, and decay, Rome, in the Italian peninsula, had been slowly developing. Gradually it had conquered Italy, Sicily, and Carthage, and then, partly through circumstance and partly through desire for expansion, it came eastward, defeated the Macedonian power, and made Greece a Roman province. While this was a political victory, it was not a cultural one. Hellenic ideas continued to dominate both in the East and in the West, though deeply modified by the taste of the victors, and under new conditions even furnished many of the fundamentals of medieval culture.

ARCHITECTURE

The result of the Peloponnesian War was a cessation of building in the countries immediately affected. But in Asia Minor there was great activity, and the Ionic temple reached a climax of grandeur, if not of refinement, in the *Temple*

of *Artemis* (*Diana*) at Ephesus, a peripteral temple with a double colonnade and elaborately sculptured bases for many of the columns[1] — an illustration of the emphasis upon ornament for its own sake at the expense of the clarity, unity, and proportion of the fifth-century temples.

The more varied, complex, and cosmopolitan culture, especially of the Hellenistic age, created a demand for a greater variety of buildings — choragic and sepulchral monuments (*Monument of Lysicrates* and *Mausoleum of Halicarnassus*), sumptuous open-air altars (*Pergamon*), theaters (at *Epidaurus*, of *Dionysus* at Athens), civic structures (stoas), and even for towns and cities as a whole (*Priene* and *Ephesus*). For the conception of town-planning in the modern sense had been heretofore largely lacking. Athens, Delphi, Olympia, were groups of buildings set down hit or miss, whereas *Priene* was laid out on a plan definitely related to the topography of the site and to the activities of the community.

[1] For a restoration of this temple see W. J. Anderson and R. P. Spiers, *The Architecture of Ancient Greece*, Scribner, 1927, Pl. L.

[A] *Praxiteles. Hermes with the Infant Dionysus. Marble. H. 7 ft. c. 350 B. C. Olympia.*

The Doric order practically disappeared with the ascendancy of the Ionic and its variant, the Corinthian. It is chiefly the capital (Fig. 157A) that differentiates the latter two. The Corinthian capital has a bell-shaped core decorated with two rows of conventionalized acanthus leaves from which rise volutes, the longer ones reaching out to support the corners of the abacus, the shorter uniting with a floral orna-

ment to decorate the core, the whole design successfully effecting the transition from the circular column to the rectangular abacus. The Corinthian order was a favorite with the Romans and appears in the Greco-Roman buildings erected after the Romans appeared in the East, such as the *Temple of the Olympian Zeus* (Figs. 159A, 123Ag), which, though built by Greeks on the plan of the *Parthenon* (except for the double colonnade), in scale at least and hence in grandiose impressiveness represents a different age and a different ideal from those of the *Parthenon* on the Acropolis near by.

SCULPTURE

Changing ideals also made themselves manifest in sculpture, though its function remained much the same as in the sixth and fifth centuries. Skepticism as to the old faith, the enhancement of the individual, reliance upon reason — changes such as these foretokened that the generalization and the impersonality of the fifth century would give way to something individual and personal, to an expression of personal emotions and idiosyncrasies. In the *Hermes* of Praxiteles (Fig. 158A), for example, one is inclined to feel a definite personal charm more insistently than one feels marble. The god is represented standing, resting his weight on the left arm, a pose that gives an easy curve to the body. On this arm he holds the infant Dionysus, who reaches for something (probably a bunch of grapes) that the god is holding in his right hand. There is a languid ease and grace throughout the figure. Hermes is looking not at the child, but off into space, with a dreamy expression in his eyes and a half-smile playing about his mouth; the whole figure, particularly the head, is deep in the mood of reverie. The modeling is exquisite. Soft shadows follow the planes

[A] *Temple of the Olympian Zeus. Athens. 174* B.C.–A.D. *131. Columns: H. 56 ft., D. 6 ft. 4 in. For plan see Fig. 123Ag. (Dmitri Kessel,* Life Magazine)

[B] *Aphrodite. Found at Cyrene in North Africa. Marble. c. 100* B.C. *after 4th cent. type. Terme (National) Museum, Rome.*

as they flow imperceptibly one into another. The marble is finished with the utmost delicacy, so that over the features a fleeting expression seems to glide; and the delicacy is enhanced by the contrastingly rough way in which the hair is indicated, and by the deep folds of the realistic drapery, whose broken masses, again by contrast, stress the flowing surfaces of the figure. Aphrodites were popular. Something of their style we may see in the *Aphrodite of Cyrene* (Fig. 159B), and in a *Head from Chios* (Boston Museum) in which the features seem veiled, so imperceptibly do the planes merge. Such effects as these can be obtained only by brilliant technical skill in stone-carving. The work of Scopas — to judge from a few rather battered heads — shows intensity of feeling, conveyed especially by means of the upturned head and the deep-set eyes shadowed by heavy brows.

These fourth-century sculptors, however, did not entirely abandon the traditions of the fifth century, as we see in the *Demeter of Cnidus* (Fig. 156A), in which the generalized majesty of Phidias is combined with the individual humanness of Scopas and Praxiteles. The goddess is heavily draped in her cloak, one corner of which is drawn up over the back of the head, throwing into relief the quietly tragic face. But compare the drapery of the Demeter with that of the

[A]   *Frieze of the Mausoleum of Halicarnassus. c. 350* B.C. *British Museum, London. (British Museum)*

single *Fate* (Fig. 143B). In the former, the casualness of the folds of actual cloth, copying the accidents of natural appearance, has taken the place of a carefully considered design based upon natural appearance. Therein lies one difference between the fourth century and the fifth: The fourth-century (and later) sculptors were motivated by a desire to present in their statues an illusion of natural appearance; the fifth-century sculptors were motivated by a desire to control their presentations by the limitations imposed by the nature of stone; that is, to reconcile content and medium. This is again illustrated in one of the friezes on the *Mausoleum* (Fig. 160A) depicting a fight between Greeks and Amazons. The figures are thin and lithe, somewhat strained in pose; their faces have the same expression of human passion as their bodies; and the restless drapery intensifies the impetuosity that sweeps through the group — all at the expense of those precise formal relationships which made for the decorative beauty of fifth-century friezes.

An important sculptor of the generation following Praxiteles and Scopas was Lysippus, court sculptor of Alexander the Great. No work of his is known to be extant, but two important innovations of this time may possibly be credited to him. One was the change in taste, noticeable in all the arts, in the matter of proportions. The new canon of taste required a more slender, supple figure. This may, indeed, have been influenced by the second innovation (foreshadowed to be sure in earlier work), the realization of the figure in space, truly three-dimensional carving (Fig. 161A). Volume always exists in a statue in the round, but by no means is there always a visual grasp of space. The earliest figures were in a stiff frontal position, with the planes closely related to the four sides of the stone block, and could be seen best from only one or two positions. Even when the figure was loosened up, especially in the limbs, and then was thrown into a curve, it was still more or less four-sided and seen satisfactorily only from some one or two points of view. In this respect the *Apollo* (Fig. 131A) and the *Hermes* (Fig. 158A) are more closely related than the *Hermes* and the *Apoxyomenos* (Fig. 161A). This statue is still limited by the ideal space

[A] *Lysippus (?). Copy of the Apoxyome-*
nos. Marble. Late 4th cent. B.C. Vatican,
Rome.

[B] *Nike of Samothrace. To commemorate*
a naval victory in 306 B.C. Louvre, Paris.

determined by the block of stone, but
within it the planes swing backward and
forward, and from any point of view
the eye is carried easily and inevitably
through this space.[1]

Such a movement of planes is found
in the *Nike of Samothrace* (Fig. 161B), as is
clearly seen if the statue is compared
with the *Nike of Paeonius*, or the *Nike*

[1] Comparisons for three-dimensional quality
can be made intelligently only by seeing the
figures from several points of view. Series to
illustrate this evolution can be found in Richter,
op. cit.

on the east pediment of the *Parthenon*.
The turn in the torso not only guides
into depth but produces a feeling of
movement that is strongly supplemented
by the clinging wind-swept drapery,
whose restless curves and minute folds
are so complicated that they almost become a tour de force. As it is, the sculptor just saved himself by bringing their
main lines into harmony with the planes
of the figure.

The tendency toward restlessness and
the expression of intense feeling reached
a climax in the *Altar at Pergamon*, on the

[A]   *Frieze from the Altar of Zeus at Pergamon. c. 175* B.C. *Pergamon Museum, Berlin.*

frieze of which is represented the battle between the gods and the giants (Fig. 162A). Athena, moving rapidly toward the right, clutches one of the winged giants by the hair, forcing him to the ground; on the right Earth, mother of the giants, a half-length figure, looks to Athena appealingly; above her, Victory approaches to crown the goddess. Force is there, powerfully displayed. The artist obtained it by using violent contrasts, such as those in the lines of direction in the bodies of Athena and the giant; by extravagant modeling; and by the agonized expression of the faces. The restless base reflects the baroque taste of Hellenistic culture, just as the austere Olympian and Phidian sculptures reflect that of the fifth century. If one wishes violent movement with realistic details, one finds it at *Pergamon;* if one wishes quiet movement with conventional details clearly related, one finds it on the *Siphnian Treasury,* at Olym-

pia, and on the *Parthenon.* It is a matter of taste.

Realism reached a climax in such statues as the *Aphrodite of Syracuse,* in which the feeling for stone as stone has quite surrendered to the ambition of making stone look like soft warm flesh. It again reveals itself in the modeling of the *Pergamon* figures; in the *Laocoön* (Vatican), in which intensity of emotion and of movement is seen not only in the modeling but in the faces and in the writhing serpents, which however tie the three figures into a compact group; and in the Hellenistic pictorial reliefs such as the *Peasant Going to Market* (Vienna). The subject matter became more varied and included genre (Fig. 163A), now trivial or frivolous, now charming, now repulsive — the work frequently of high technical excellence, but hardly of significance.

In the midst of unconvincing, insignificant expressions, however brilliant

[A] *Old Market Woman. Marble. 2d cent.*
B.C. *Metropolitan Museum of Art, New York
City. (Metropolitan Museum)*

[B] *Lady with a Fan. Tanagra
figurine. Terra cotta, painted. H. 8 in.
Museum of Fine Arts, Boston.*

they may be technically, one usually
finds archaistic tendencies, as has been
noted. For in an age of decline, as the
seeds of a new era are being sown, the
most sensitive artists are likely to turn
for stimulation to more robust works, to
primitive and archaic art. This probably explains the simple dignity and
calm of the *Aphrodite (Venus) of Melos*
(Louvre), which seems to share the fifth-
century largeness of expression without
sharing its vitality. Other examples ac-

tually copy the earlier forms, especially
the conventions for the drapery and the
hair.

One group in the field of late sculpture stands alone, the *Tanagra Figurines*,
perhaps the most charming examples of
Greek genre (Fig. 163B). Thousands have
been found, chiefly in graves, and their
purpose is unknown. They represent all
kinds of everyday scenes, trivial in subject but dainty in execution and bright
in color. The robes are usually rose or

[A] *Vase Painting. British Museum, London.* (*Gardner,* The Principles of Greek Art, *Macmillan*)

blue, the hair a reddish brown, the shoes red; and the fans or other accessories have touches of gilding. In all of them there is a natural grace and charm. These figurines frequently reveal a spontaneous momentary pose suitable for expression in clay, and in them we see true clay technique. Great quantities of these figurines were made in molds, a single subject often being constructed out of several parts, so that by changing the head or the arms a considerable amount of variety could be obtained.

PAINTING

In the fourth century and the Hellenistic age we find the same situation as in the fifth century. While we know that a flourishing school of painting existed, no paintings are extant. Zeuxis and Parrhasius (fifth and fourth centuries), Apelles and Protogenes (of the time of Alexander the Great) are characters in famous stories which stress technical skill and realism, the same characteristics that we find in sculpture. A basis for actual knowledge or judgment of their painting is quite lacking.

While the Greek painters experimented in perspective, light and shade, and color, line seems to have been their pre-eminent means of expression, used both to model and express volume and also calligraphically (Fig. 164A). In the *Alexander Mosaic* (Fig. 165A), which is probably a Roman copy based on a Greek painting, we perhaps catch a glimpse of a Greek composition on a large scale, though allowance should be made for the mosaic technique. It is a battle scene, usually thought to represent the Battle of the Issus. The center of interest is the wounded horseman in the foreground falling from his steed. Darius is fleeing in his chariot, but he looks back at the wounded man with anguish in his face and arm outstretched as if in helpless appeal. Another horseman in the foreground has dismounted, and while attempting to hold his horse

[A] *Battle Scene between Alexander and Darius. Mosaic. From the floor of the House of the Faun, Pompeii. L. 17 ft. c. 100 B.C. Naples Museum.*

looks toward his wounded companion as if to offer his mount. Here, then, is a well-defined center of interest toward which all the main lines of the composition lead. The group occupies a shallow space terminated by the flat background toward which the eye is led by the foreshortened horses. Thus there is movement in space as well as laterally. The background is flat, with no indication of landscape except a gnarled tree. The upper part of the panel is unbroken except for the tree and the spears, which unite the upper and lower parts of the picture and provide an interesting contrast to the vigor and movement of the lower part as well as a contrast of diagonal to curvilinear line direction.

METALWORK

In the fifth century B.C. the ceramic industry was already declining, for unknown reasons, and by the fourth had almost disappeared. But the work of the goldsmith was much in demand, not only about the Aegean but among the Scythians and the Sarmatians of southern Russia.[1] From the earliest days jewelry — necklaces, earrings, pins, bracelets, rings — was important in the costume of Greek women (though not of the men, as it was in Egypt, Assyria, and Crete), and the art of the goldsmith may have been an inheritance from the Aegean. Before the Hellenistic age gold was used chiefly for its own sake, for its color and texture, and for the shimmer of surface which resulted from the various processes of working it — casting, repoussé, engraving, soldering, granulation, filigree — in which high quality of workmanship continued through the fourth century. Variations of color were achieved through a sparing use of enamel. In the Hellenistic age the quality of craftsmanship declined and the introduction of semiprecious stones added a more obvious richness.

[1] See pages 101–02. Note particularly the mutual interactions of racial art traditions, the Iranian tending toward conventional treatment, the Greek toward naturalistic.

SUMMARY

After the fifth century, Greek building activity centered outside the Greek
mainland, particularly in Asia Minor,
and because of the more cosmopolitan
character of late Greek civilization,
broadened its scope to include secular
structures. Buildings became grandiose
in scale, with elaborated Ionic or Corinthian orders predominating.

In sculpture, easy grace and human
emotions replaced the more rugged and
impersonal sculpture of the fifth century, with a concentration on delicate
surface treatment. As sculptural form
became truly three-dimensional — organized in space with movement
through the space — details became
realistic, and technical virtuosity led
to giving the stone the appearance of
flesh, in complete disregard of the limitations of the material. Thus much late
Greek sculpture lacked truly sculptural
quality.

Painting, all examples of which are
now lost, appears to have functioned as
mural decoration in public buildings
and as panels; and to have sought to
express volume in the figures and to
place them in space, a spatial concept
analogous to that seen in sculpture.
Thus its trend was in the direction of
an imitation of visual perception.

In its spread over the Near East, Hellenistic art mingled with Eastern forces,
and the fusion was to result in the flowering, centuries later, of Byzantine art.

BIBLIOGRAPHY

Alexander, Christine, *Jewelry, the Art of the
Goldsmith in Classical Times*, Metropolitan
Museum of Art, New York City, 1928
Anderson, William J., and Spiers, R. P., *The
Architecture of Ancient Greece*, rev. by W. B.
Dinsmoor, Vol. I of *The Architecture of Greece
and Rome*, 2 vols., London, 1927

Beazley, John D., *Attic Black-Figure*, Oxford
University Press, 1928
———— and Ashmole, Bernard, *Greek
Sculpture and Painting to the End of the Hellen-
istic Period*, Macmillan, 1932
Bell, Edward, *Hellenic Architecture*, Harcourt,
Brace, 1920
Boas, George, ed., *The Greek Tradition*, Johns
Hopkins Press, 1939
Borovka, Gregory, *Scythian Art*, tr. by V. G.
Childe, Stokes, 1928
British Museum, *A Catalogue of Sculpture in the
Department of Greek and Roman Antiquities*,
Pts. I–II, Museum, London, 1928–31
———— *A Guide to the Principal Coins of
the Greeks from about 700 B.C. to A.D. 270*,
Museum, London, 1932
Budde, Erich G., *Helladic Greece*, Rhode Island
School of Design, *Bulletin of the Museum of
Art*, December 1939, pp. 1–17
Buschor, Ernst, *Greek Vase-Painting*, tr. by G. C.
Richards, Dutton, 1922
Carpenter, Rhys, *The Esthetic Basis of Greek Art
of the Fifth and Fourth Centuries B.C.*, Long-
mans, Green, 1921
Casson, Stanley, *The Technique of Early Greek
Sculpture*, Oxford University Press, 1933
Charbonneaux, Jean, *La sculpture grecque ar-
chaïque*, Paris, 1938
———— *La sculpture grecque classique*, Paris,
1943
Collignon, Maxime, ed., *Le Parthénon*, 8 pts.,
Paris, 1910–12
Cossío, Manuel Bartolomé, and Pijoán, José,
Summa Artis, Vols. I–X, Madrid, 1931–46:
Vol. IV
Encyclopédie photographique de l'art, Vols. I–III,
Paris, Edition "Tel," 1935–38: Vols. II–III
Fowler, Harold N., Wheeler, J. R., and Stevens,
G. P., *A Handbook of Greek Archaeology*,
American Book Company, 1909
Fyfe, David Theodore, *Hellenistic Architecture*,
Macmillan, 1936
Gardiner, Edward N., *Olympia: Its History &
Remains*, Oxford University Press, 1925
Gardner, Ernest A., *Ancient Athens*, new ed.,
Macmillan, 1907
———— *The Art of Greece*, Studio, 1925
———— *Greece and the Ægean*, McBride,
1934
———— *A Handbook of Greek Sculpture*,
2d ed., Macmillan, 1929
Gardner, Percy, *The Principles of Greek Art*,
Macmillan, 1914
———— and Blomfield, Sir Reginald,
Greek Art and Architecture, Oxford Uni-
versity Press, 1922
Goodyear, William H., *Greek Refinements, Studies
in Temperamental Architecture*, Yale Univer-
sity Press, 1912

Grinnell, Isabel H., *Greek Temples*, Metropolitan Museum of Art, New York City, 1943

Hege, Walter, and Rodenwaldt, Gerhart, *Olympia*, Berlin, 1936

Hoyningen-Huené, George, and Davis, George, and others, eds., *Hellas*, 2d rev. ed., Augustin, 1944

Johansen, Peter, *Phidias and the Parthenon Sculptures*, tr. by Ingeborg Andersen, Copenhagen, 1925

Lamb, Winifred, *Greek and Roman Bronzes*, Dial Press, 1929

Laurie, Arthur P., *Greek and Roman Methods of Painting*, Putnam, 1910

Lawrence, Arnold W., *Classical Sculpture*, Peter Smith, 1929

———————— *Later Greek Sculpture*, Harcourt, Brace, 1927

Livingstone, Sir Richard Winn, *The Greek Genius and Its Meaning to Us*, 2d ed., Oxford University Press, 1915

———————— ed., *The Legacy of Greece*, Oxford University Press, 1921

Loewy, Emanuel, *The Rendering of Nature in Early Greek Art*, tr. by John Fothergill, London, 1907

Marquand, Allan, *Greek Architecture*, Macmillan, 1909

Metropolitan Museum, *Greek Painting*, Museum, New York City, 1944

Minns, Ellis H., *Scythians and Greeks*, Putnam, 1914

Paton, James M., ed., *The Erechtheum*, restored by G. P. Stevens, text by L. D. Caskey and others, Harvard University Press, 1927

Payne, Humfry, and Young, G. M., *Archaic Marble Sculpture from the Acropolis*, London, 1936

Pfuhl, Ernst, *Masterpieces of Greek Drawing and Painting*, tr. by J. D. Beazley, Macmillan, 1926

Pottier, Edmond, *Douris and the Painters of Greek Vases*, tr. by Bettina Kahnweiler, 2d ed., Dutton, 1917

Poulsen, Frederik, *Delphi*, tr. by G. C. Richards, Bonnier, 1922

Richter, Gisela M. A., *Ancient Furniture; A History of Greek, Etruscan and Roman Furniture*, Oxford University Press, 1926

———————— *Animals in Greek Sculpture*, Oxford University Press, 1930

———————— *The Craft of Athenian Pottery*, Yale University Press, 1923

———————— *Handbook of the Classical Collection*, 6th ed., Metropolitan Museum of Art, New York City, 1930

———————— *The Sculpture and Sculptors of the Greeks*, 2d ed., Yale University Press, 1930

Ridder, André H. P. de, and Deonna, Waldemar, *Art in Greece*, tr. by V. C. C. Collum, Knopf, 1927

Robertson, Donald S., *A Handbook of Greek and Roman Architecture*, Macmillan, 1929

Rodenwaldt, Gerhart, *Die Kunst der Antike*, Berlin, 1927

———————— and Hege, Walter, *Die Akropolis*, 2d ed., Berlin, 1930

Roes, Anna, *Greek Geometric Art: Its Symbolism and Its Origin*, Oxford University Press, 1933

Rostovtzeff, Michael Ivanovich, *The Animal Style in South Russia and China*, Princeton University Press, 1929

———————— *Iranians and Greeks in South Russia*, Oxford University Press, 1922

———————— *Out of the Past of Greece and Rome*, Yale University Press, 1932

Schrader, Hans, *Die Archäischen Marmorbildwerke der Akropolis*, Frankfurt-am-Main, 1939

Smith, A. H., *The Sculptures of the Parthenon*, British Museum, London, 1910

Solon, Léon V., *Polychromy*, Architectural Record, 1924

Swindler, Mary H., *Ancient Painting*, Yale University Press, 1929

Warren, Herbert L., *The Foundations of Classic Architecture*, Macmillan, 1919

Zervos, Christian, *L'art en Grèce*, Paris, 1934

[A]   *Sarcophagus from Cervetri. Terra cotta, painted. 6th–5th cent.* B.C. *Villa Papa Giulio, Rome. (Anderson)*

7

ETRUSCAN AND ROMAN ART

(ABOUT 1000 B.C.–A.D. 500)

ALTHOUGH the early histories of Greece and Italy run nearly parallel chronologically, the former reached a climax in the fifth and fourth centuries B.C., a period during which the latter was still slowly developing. The story of early Rome is a story of struggle for existence, particularly against the Etruscans, who came to Italy probably from Asia Minor and were closely allied culturally to the Greeks. In the sixth century B.C. they were in control of all Italy from their heavily fortified cities — Corneto, Cervetri, Veii, Perugia, Orvieto, Praeneste, and other sites in what is now Tuscany. They were farmers, traders on sea as well as on land, cruel warriors, and pirates. At home they lived luxuriously in gaily decorated houses, feasted and danced unrestrain-

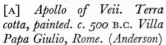

[A] *Apollo of Veii. Terra cotta, painted. c. 500* B.C. *Villa Papa Giulio, Rome.* (*Anderson*)

[B] *Archer. Bronze. c. 7th cent.* B.C. *British Museum, London.*

edly. They were adept in working metal and clay. They constructed their fortifications, city gates, bridges, aqueducts, and sewers of heavy stone masonry on the arch principle; small buildings they made of wood gaily painted or faced with colored terra-cotta tiles. Their temple was based upon the Greek prostyle plan (Fig. 123AC), rested on a high base with a flight of steps, and was probably made of brick with wooden columns and a heavy wooden superstructure brightly painted.[1] With an emphasis upon a future life not unlike that of the Egyp-

tian, they paid much attention to burial, so that the tombs, which were built or carved in the hillside, and which imitated the interior of Etruscan houses, furnish us in their wall paintings a picture of Etruscan life. The sarcophagi, with their recumbent figures, supply some of the best examples of sculpture.

The Etruscans showed a peculiar preference for clay — a local material both excellent in quality and abundant. For architectural decoration they made terra-cotta tiles which are highly decorative in their pattern and gay colors, notably so the masklike roof tiles. Likewise their sculpture in the round, the *Apollo of Veii* (Fig. 169A), for example, is clay rather than stone, though one feels the archaic Greek stone prototype. But in the awkward vigor of the stride,

[1] There is no even fairly well preserved Etruscan temple extant. For a reconstruction see Anderson and Spiers, *The Architecture of Ancient Rome*, Pl. VIII; or S. F. Kimball and G. H. Edgell, *A History of Architecture*, Harper, 1918, Fig. 37.

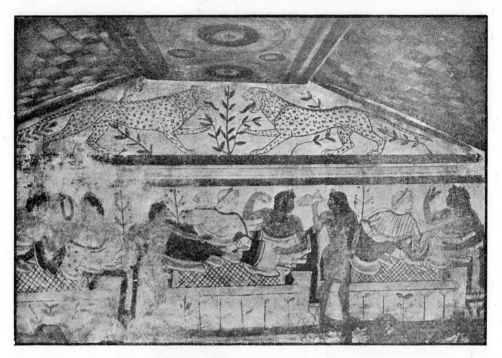

[A]   *Tomb of the Leopards. Corneto. 5th cent.* B.C.

in the boldly conceived form, and in the striking, conventional use of color there is the crude vigor of the Etruscan. In the recumbent figures of the sarcophagi is a similar eager vitality. Even if the later clumsy cinerary urns show lack of sensitiveness, the early life-sized mortuary figures, such as the examples in the British Museum, the Louvre, and in Rome (Fig. 168A), reveal a definite relationship between the figures and the sarcophagus. With the flowing surfaces painted in conventional color, with the patternlike archaic features and expressive hands, they are direct and convincing both in form and in the expression of an inner vitality and significance.

Another favorite medium was bronze (Fig. 169B). In the head of the so-called *Orator* (Fig. 173A) is a forceful personality, realistically portrayed; in the *Chimera* (Florence) a more conventional treatment, very vital and decorative; in both, a fine technical command of the material. Bronze was used also for many smaller objects — cinerary urns, toilet boxes, and mirrors, which were engraved with mythological and genre scenes imitative of the Greek products which were imported in great quantity by wealthy Etruscans. We feel in them a provincial Greek art with a stamp of verve and boldness and with an unusual decorative beauty — qualities that are repeated in Etruscan jewelry.

The same qualities impress one looking at an Etruscan tomb (Fig. 170A) fashioned after an actual Etruscan room with sloping roof. Both the roof and the walls are gaily painted, the roof chiefly with conventional, geometric designs, the walls with scenes of funeral banquets, dancing, athletic contests, hunting. These paintings, thoroughly decorative, are usually in fresco, though

[A] *Flute-Player. Tomb of the Triclinium, Corneto. Early 5th cent.* B.C.

at times painted directly on the stone. The bright color is used conventionally in flat tones within outlines, with no regard for the hues of nature, for one horse may have a red and a yellow leg or a blue coat and a red mane. In this *Tomb of the Leopards* (so called from the two hunting leopards in the gable) is a banquet scene perhaps too conventionally imitative to be interesting except for the truly decorative quality of the lines and the lights and darks that fill the wall area. On the side wall, however, are dancing figures filled with action and rhythmic movement that make charming decorative motifs. In like manner the *Flute-Player* (Fig. 171A) of the *Tomb of the Triclinium* expresses the feeling of joyous movement, of the rhythm of inner vitality translated into objective form by simple direct conventions.

What the art of Rome would have been had Roman civilization remained within the boundaries of Italy it is futile to ask. In its early days Rome employed

Etruscan builders and ceramic workers; and later it did not forget the high temple platform nor, eventually, Etruscan realistic portraiture. But the fact is that its conquest of Etruria was followed by the subjugation of the entire peninsula; and thence, with an imperial policy well defined, Rome was forced to enlarge its boundaries until they included the entire Mediterranean basin and most of western Europe. Rome early came in contact with Greece and became aware of Greek art. But only in the late republican and Augustan ages came the terrific impact of Hellenism. "Conquered Greece led the conqueror captive," conceded Horace, a poet of the Augustan age. Shiploads of Greek marbles and bronzes were brought to Rome by generals and provincial governors to adorn their palaces, and when the supply was exhausted, copies were made or Greek artists were employed to create new ones. Art became to a large extent mere copying of Greek

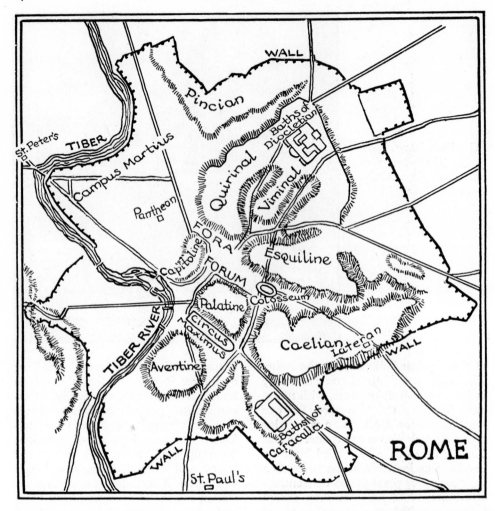

[A]   *Rome. A map to indicate the general location of important classical and medieval sites.*

works. Finally assimilation took place, and imperial Rome emerged as a product of Etruscan, Roman, and Greek elements. Possibly it was still strongly enough Greek for its art to be called a continuation of the Hellenic tradition working according to Roman tastes and ideals. In portrait sculpture and in architecture especially, however, Rome made definite, individual contributions.

In the main, the energy of Rome was utilized in conquest and administration, and its conquests opened the way for the spread of its civilization. Roman cities sprang up especially in what is now Spain, France, and England, each a center for the propagation of Roman government, language, and customs, and closely connected with Rome by a well-planned system of roads and harbors. Both by force of circumstance and by temperament the Roman was warlike, practical, fond of pleasure. His life, in comparison with the simplicity of the Athenian, was complex, for the demands of life were much greater. Rome

[A]   *Orator. Bronze. 4th or 3d cent.* B.C. *Archaeological Museum, Florence.*

about A.D. 200 was the magnificent capital of the greatest empire the world had yet known, an empire that was efficiently organized, with fifty thousand miles of magnificent highways and sea routes safe for travel and commerce. The city itself (Fig. 172A), of more than a million people, was both cosmopolitan and magnificent. The scale, power, and complexity of the Empire called for impressive scale in the structure and appearance of its capital. And while the practical demands arising from the administration of a great empire required the building of roads, bridges, sewers, and aqueducts, the imperial ideal called for public buildings that would express adequately the dignity, power, and diversified interests of the state. To build practically and grandly required skill in engineering. Thus arose Rome's contribution to architecture, though its

chief gift to world civilization lay in the field of law and organization.

With the wealth that came with conquest, there crept in pleasure-loving ideals, luxuriousness, and decay. In time the great Roman Empire became a hollow shell, and the frontiers gave way on all sides. By A.D. 500 Rome itself had fallen before the Northern tribes that had been harassing its boundaries ever since Julius Caesar had driven them back in the first century B.C.

ARCHITECTURE

In Greek architecture we discerned a concentration upon the temple. In Rome, on the contrary, as the capital of a complex world empire, practical as well as esthetic needs led to the erection of many kinds of buildings, secular as well as religious, and frequently on

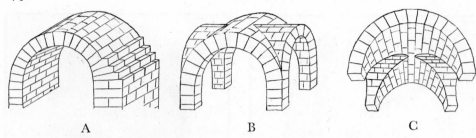

A   B   C

[A] *Barrel Vault.* [B] *Groin Vault seen from above.*   [C] *Groin Vault seen from below.*

a scale hitherto untried. Ample material was at hand — abundant wood, stone (marble, travertine, tufa), good clays for brick, lava and pozzolana (sandy earth) for concrete. Those materials not at hand could be imported easily by the Roman fleets — rare colored marbles, nearly fifty varieties of which were used for their color and texture. But ample as this material was, the quantity and scale of Roman building precluded extensive use of solid stone masonry and of the lintel system. Brick and concrete covered with stucco or faced with stone or marble veneer supplanted solid stone construction,

with the arch rather than the lintel system as the structural principle.

The chief engineering problem involved in Roman architecture was how to enclose and roof over a vast space, to give it proper illumination and still keep the space open and free of the columns that would be necessary were a flat roof used, as in the hypostyle halls of Egypt (Fig. 64A). Given the problem of roofing over a rectangular room by the simplest arch system, the result will be a barrel vault (Fig. 174A), which is, in essence, a succession of arches joined together, resting directly upon the side walls, which must either be thick enough

[D] *Pont du Gard. Nîmes. Augustan Age.*

[A] *Temple of Fortuna Virilis. Rome. c. 100 B.C. (Anderson)*

to support the weight or be reinforced by buttresses. This vault can be made of stone or brick masonry, or it can be made of concrete by building up a temporary wooden framework (known as centering) the exact size and shape of the finished vault, to hold the mass until it is set. The vaulting that we see in Figure 174B and c and Figure 179A has been made by cutting the barrel vault at right angles at regular intervals by other barrel vaults, securing what is known as the cross or groin vault, because the line of intersection is called the groin. A barrel vault over so large an area not only would have been heavy in appearance but would have allowed no space for windows. The advantage of the groin vault is not only that it is lighter in appearance because of its broken surface but also that it admits of clerestory windows. The use of the groin vault secures another advantage. In the barrel vault the thrust — that is, the downward and outward forces exerted by the vault — is felt along the entire length of the wall; in the groin

vault it is felt only at the points at which the groins converge. Hence it is at these points only that heavy buttressing is needed, and the interior is thus kept free of load-carrying walls. Proper support is secured by heavy walls built at right angles, which are pierced by arches and thus form side aisles to the main hall (Fig. 178A).

Their public-service structures — roads, bridges, aqueducts, sewers — the Romans, like the Etruscans, built solidly and well. Their stone bridges combine utilitarian requirements and fine sweep of line. The aqueducts, which still swing across the Campagna to bring the mountain water to Rome or span streams in several tiers as in the *Pont du Gard* (Fig. 174D), have a stark beauty of adequate function united to the rhythmic movement of well-spaced arches.

Among religious buildings, the *Temple of Fortuna Virilis* (Fig. 175A) illustrates one type of temple derived obviously from the Greek peripteral style, but differing in the high base with projecting moldings and a flight of steps ex-

[A]   *Pantheon. D. and H. 142 ft. From an engraving by Piranesi.*

tending across the front. Its cella is larger than the Greek and becomes incorporated with the colonnade part way along the sides and across the back.[1]

The circular temple was also a popular type. Sometimes it was peripteral, as in the temple near the Tiber in Rome and in that at Tivoli. Of all circular temples the most imposing is the *Pantheon* (Fig. 177A), which consists of a circular wall with but one opening, the doorway. On this wall rests a dome, low and rather inconspicuous on the exterior; at the entrance is a colonnaded portico of Greek design. As one steps within (Fig. 176A) one is surprised. For the dull unpromising exterior gives little hint of the wonderful spaciousness and light within. This impression results from a very simple space-design carried out on a large scale — a dome set on a circular wall and lighted by an aperture in the crown. The builder's purpose seems to have been to make his dome impressive from the interior. The walls are covered with rich marble facing; the dome is deeply coffered and was originally decorated with bronze

rosettes. Domes had been constructed before, but never on such a scale. The Roman's ideal of great scale made him daring, while his practical nature and his engineering skill kept him within the bounds of structural possibilities. The walls, twenty feet thick, are made of brick and concrete and are solid except for the niches, about which are imbedded in the masonry relieving arches of brick that extend the entire thickness of the wall and carry the thrust of the dome to the solid masonry.[2] The dome is constructed of horizontal layers of brick laid in thick cement, the load of which is carried by a series of ribs converging on the crown. Between these ribs are the typical Roman coffers, which both diminish the weight and ornament the dome.

Civic buildings were important in an imperial capital, and together with important temples were grouped about the forums. The *Roman Forum* was originally the market place where the peasants brought their produce for sale; booths and shops ran along the sides. But religious and civic activities be-

[1] A column thus incorporated with the wall is known as an *engaged column.*

[2] For illustration see Anderson and Spiers, *op. cit.*, p. 78, Fig. 19.

[A] *Pantheon. Originally the walls were faced with marble and stucco and the dome was covered with bronze plates.* A.D. *120–124.*

gan to encroach early; the shops were crowded out to the side streets and the *Forum* became primarily the center of the city's civic life. In the open space were commemorative statues of emperors and generals, and the great platform from which public speeches were made; entirely surrounding it and crowning the surrounding hills were imposing buildings. The *Imperial Forums*, built by various emperors from Augustus on, reach a culmination in the *Forum of Trajan* (Fig. 177B), where all the units of the vast group are definitely related to one another and to a unified design, instead of being merely set down wherever there was space and the topography permitted, as in the old *Roman Forum*. It is perhaps illuminating to recall that the *Forum of Trajan* was designed by an architect from the East, Apollodorus of Damascus. Hills were leveled to make space for this enormous forum, which in plan strikingly resembles, as scholars have pointed out, the Egyptian temple. Through a monumental archway one passed into an open court with colonnades on three sides and great circular wings with shops, thence into the basilica with its many

columns, and beyond into the temple of the deified emperor.

An important civic building was the basilica, a covered hall used for various purposes, particularly for a law court. It was an oblong structure with a semi-

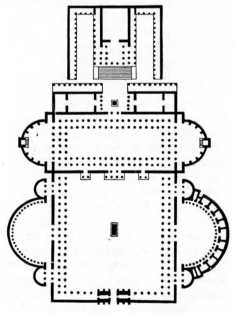

[B]   *Plan of the Forum of Trajan.*

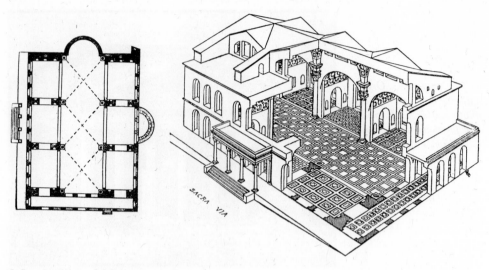

[A]   *Basilica of Maxentius or Constantine. Rome.* A.D. *306–312. Plan and section of reconstruction.*

circular tribunal (or apse) at one end, where the judge sat, and was divided by rows of columns or piers into a central and side aisles. The roof of the central aisle was higher than that of the side aisles, thus permitting a clerestory. The structural principle was not the lintel system of the *Fortuna Virilis* (Fig. 175A) but the arcade; that is, a series of arches. Between the arches, however, are engaged columns that support an entablature running the entire length of the building. In this arrangement we find one of the most characteristic features of Roman architecture: a combination of the arch and lintel systems. Structurally, it is the arch that is the vital part of the construction; the column and the entablature serve only as decoration. The *Colosseum* (Fig. 180A) and the *Arch of Titus* (Fig. 181A) illustrate the principle. In the early basilicas, the arcades supported a wooden roof. In a late example, the *Basilica of Maxentius* (Fig. 178A), fully developed vaulting was used, barrel over the aisles and groin over the nave, thus enabling the builder to make use of isolated supports and huge arches, overpowering even in the ruins today.

The places of amusement — the circus, the theater, and the amphitheater — and the great baths (*thermae*) so essential to imperial Rome challenged the engineering ability of the builders. Here huge crowds must be accommodated, sometimes out of doors, sometimes within, with an appearance of luxury and display commensurate with the taste of the day. The *Colosseum* (Fig. 180A) was one of these places of amusement. The vast size of the structure prevented extensive use of stone and led to the use of concrete faced with brick on the interior, with hard stone at points of stress, and an exterior of travertine masonry set with no mortar but clamped by iron dowels. The design consists of a system of arches both parallel with and at right angles to the outer circumference. The exterior consists of three stories of arches and a solid attic. Between the arches of each story are engaged columns that support a continuous entablature. The engaged columns add to the rhythm, and the entablature not only unifies the arched openings and binds them into a firmly felt unity but also forms a fine single sweep of curve which, repeated on each story, accents the basic cylindrical form. The effect of the building without this decoration can be seen on the right side of the illustration, where a bare monotony results from the loss of the rhythm and the accent of the vigorous curves. The combination of structural solidity and effective decoration has created a building imposing in dignity and magnificence. On the ground story the columns are of the Doric order; on the second, of the Ionic; and on the third, of the Corinthian — an arrangement known as superimposed orders. The fourth story is ornamented by flat Corinthian pilasters. The *Colosseum* is a conspicuous example and a possible justification of the Roman practice of using a structural member for a nonstructural and purely esthetic purpose.[1] For, constructionally, the columns do not carry the load.

The impression of material power, at times grandiose, is felt in high degree in the thermae that provided the Roman not only with his daily bath, hot, warm, or cold, but with his library and lounging-place, for the numerous recreation rooms had the same function as the modern athletic club. A ground plan (Fig. 179B) gives us some conception of the great extent of these baths and also of the orderly planning that characterizes the organization of multitudinous parts into a single whole. Figure 179A reconstructs one hall of the *Baths of Caracalla*. The impression is of vast spaciousness and, in the rich marble facings, carvings, and coffered ceilings, of magnificence and splendor. Here, as in the *Pantheon*, the Roman builder conquered space; that is, he so enclosed a great volume of unbroken space as to

[1] A point which leads to infinite debate and no absolute conclusion. "*De gustibus non est disputandum.*"

[A]   *Baths of Caracalla. Central Hall, restored by Spiers.* A.D. *211–217. Rome. (Anderson and Spiers)*

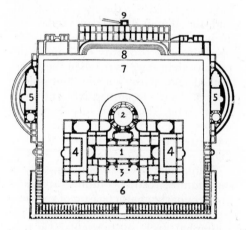

[B]   *Baths of Caracalla. Rome.* A.D. *211–217. The central building is 750 by 380 ft.* 1. *tepidarium, or warm lounge;* 2. *calidarium, or hot room;* 3. *frigidarium, or cooling room with a swimming pool open to the air;* 4. *open peristyles;* 5. *lecture rooms and libraries;* 6. *promenade;* 7. *garden;* 8. *stadium;* 9. *aqueduct and reservoirs.*

[A] *Colosseum or Flavian Amphitheater. Rome.* A.D. *70–82.* (*Anderson*)

make one standing within it conscious of it. And this he accomplished, as we have described, by the use of the vault and the dome. Impressive today are even the ruins of these huge vaults; indeed they are probably even more impressive than they were when they were decked out with marble and gilded coffers. As in the aqueducts, the sheer engineering, the great simple moving masses and surfaces, are some of the most powerful expressions of the Romans.

Commemorative monuments — altars, tombs, rostra, columns, arches — are peculiarly characteristic of the realistic Roman, who established, in the triumphal arch in particular, a type that has survived for centuries. In the *Arch of Titus* (Fig. 181A) the great central opening is flanked by solid masses of masonry with engaged columns that rise from a plain base to support the entablature, which has a sculptured frieze uniting the three parts. The decoration is restrained, and confined chiefly

to the arch. The *Arch of Constantine* illustrates the more elaborate triple arch with more sumptuous sculptural decorations.

Ornament the Roman used lavishly; frequently, in the attempt to obtain magnificence, he overloaded his buildings and concealed the structure. The restraint of the Greek in the use of moldings and decoration was too severe to suit the Roman taste, which loved display, and preferred the Corinthian capital to the more austere Doric and Ionic. In his best work, however, the Roman proved himself a master of a certain kind of decoration. This we can see best in a section of the *Ara Pacis* (Fig. 182B). From a central group of acanthus rises a vertical foliate form and curving stems that branch off so as to cover the surface with spiral forms that terminate now in a leaf, now in a flower or rosette; near the top a swan with outspread wings has alighted. While naturalistic representation has formed the basis of the decoration, the

[A] *Arch of Titus. Restored on the sides. A bronze four-horse chariot surmounted the arch. Rome.* A.D. *81.* (*Alinari*)

ultimate effect is dependent partly upon the delicacy and the precision of the carving and partly upon the carver's restraint in keeping his design a clear decorative pattern.

The motif of the foliate spiral rising from a bed of acanthus, known as the *rinceau* (Fig. 182A), became one of the most popular in Roman decorative art, especially as applied to pilasters and borders, and later formed the basis of much Renaissance ornament. With the Flavian emperors, this naturalistic ornament sacrificed decorative quality to a greater illusion of actual appearance. Details of plant and bird forms were copied from nature, and the cutting of the marble followed the irregularities of nature instead of retaining definite planes of stone; an almost atmospheric

effect was produced, as in the rose columns on the *Tomb of the Haterii* (Lateran).

The same tendency is discernible in figure reliefs. In the procession of men, women, and children on the *Ara Pacis* (Fig. 183A) the relief is higher in the foreground figures and lower in the background, giving one a distinct sense of depth and atmosphere. Details are worked out to a greater extent, and there is a considerable amount of portraiture in the faces; in fact, we feel the individual figures here quite forcibly. The purpose has been to give an illusion rather than an organized expression of a procession, as in the *Parthenon Frieze* (Fig. 144A). This realistic tendency is carried still further in the reliefs on the inner side of the *Arch of Titus*, in which

[A]   *Roman Rinceau. Lateran Museum, Rome.*

architectural details contribute a pictorial quality. And the tendency reaches a climax in the *Column of Trajan*, in which a detailed pictorial record of military campaigns spirals around the shaft from the base to the summit.

The ornamentation discussed so far was carved in stone. Another medium used most effectively by the Romans

[B]   *Ara Pacis (Altar of Peace). Erected in 13 B.C. to commemorate the victories of Augustus in Spain and Gaul. Detail of decoration. Terme (National) Museum, Rome.*

was stucco applied as a finish to the rough concrete vaults and walls. The surface was divided by moldings into geometric patterns that frequently enclosed figures, or was filled with naturalistic spirals or other motifs and dainty figures. The addition of marble dust made the stucco both durable and fine in texture. The moldings and the figures were worked in the wet stucco partly by stamps, noticeably in the moldings, and partly freehand. As in the fresco technique, the rapidity with which plaster dries requires rapid workmanship; and the figures depend for their effect not so much upon careful modeling as upon spontaneity, ease of workmanship, and freely flowing line.

An additional note of magnificence as well as comfort in imperial Rome was supplied by the system of parks and gardens, including perhaps thirty great parks around the city, with lawns, trees, gardens, and fountains, made possible by the unparalleled water supply. Every Roman of sufficient means had a villa set in a park, perhaps on the outskirts of the city or in the Alban or Sabine hills near by.

Domestic architecture figured prominently. The palaces and villas of the emperors, now in fragmentary ruins, rivaled the thermae in size and sumptuousness: huge groups of rooms about

[A] *Ara Pacis. Detail of Procession. Uffizi, Florence.*

courts, rooms of state and private apartments, gardens and baths. Sometimes, as in the *Palace of Domitian*, the units of the establishment were related to a central axis — a plan we have seen used in the thermae and the *Forum of Trajan*. Sometimes, as in the *Villa of Hadrian*, the units were irregularly placed because of the character of the topography.[1]

Probably the average person lived, in the crowded city, in an apartment house (*insula*), which was several stories high, a habitation to each story, with windows and loggias on the street and on the courtyard, about which several insulae were sometimes grouped.[2] As the Roman lived largely in the open, about the public buildings, in the places of amusement, and in the porticoes and parks, he may have been content with his crowded living-quarters if only they provided him a corner for sleeping and a protection for his lares and penates.

The homes of the well-to-do away from the congested metropolitan areas

[1] The *Palace of Domitian* on the Palatine in Rome, the *Villa of Hadrian* near Tivoli, and the *Palace of Diocletian* at Spalato are examples of Roman imperial palaces. See Anderson and Spiers, *op. cit.*, Chap. VIII, for descriptions and reconstructions.

[2] On the analogy of houses found at Ostia, Rome's seaport. The *Casa di Diana* is a typical insula. For a reconstruction see Anderson and Spiers, *op. cit.*, Pl. XC; D. S. Robertson, *A Handbook of Greek and Roman Architecture*, Macmillan, 1929, pp. 308–09.

[A]　*Vista of a Pompeian House from the Atrium.*

are of the atrium type found at Pompeii and Herculaneum. Many of these, protected by the volcanic ash and lava in which they were buried, are extraordinarily well preserved, with their mural decorations still fresh and sometimes with their equipment and household utensils undisturbed. Such a house stood flush with the sidewalk. Through a narrow entrance, one entered a vestibule (Fig. 185A) that led to a court known as the (1) *atrium*, roofed over along the four sides so as to leave an opening in the center, with a corresponding sunken place in the floor to collect rain water; along the sides were small rooms, except at the end, where the atrium extended the full width of the building, forming two wings, (2) *alae*. Behind the atrium was the (3) *tablinum*, in which the family archives and statues were kept, and which could be shut off or could afford a passage to the (4) *peristyle*, a large colonnaded court with fountains and garden, about which

were grouped the private apartments of the family, the atrium serving more as a reception room or a room of state. At the back there was sometimes a (5) garden; the (6) small rooms along the outer sides opening on the street were shops. It is clear that the house faced inward, depending upon its courts for light and air, and when opened its entire length (Fig. 184A) afforded a charming vista of open court with colored marbles, gardens, fountains and statues, and brightly painted walls.

This type of house, with its small number of doors and windows, offered considerable stretches of wall space for decoration. The type of decoration commonly used was a realistic representation of architectural openings and resulted in an originally plain, almost cell-like room not only becoming gaily brilliant in color but appearing to open on vistas of garden, architecture, or landscape, thus lending an air of spaciousness to the room (Figs. 188A, 189B).

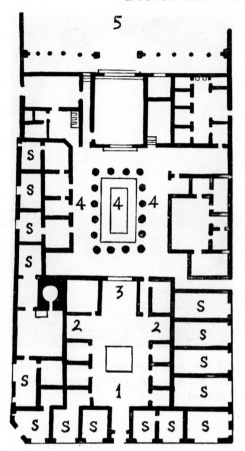

[B]   *The Emperor Augustus Addressing His Army. Marble, originally painted. Found in the Villa of Livia, wife of Augustus, at Prima Porta. Vatican, Rome.*

[A]   *House of Pansa. Pompeii.   1. atrium; 2. alae; 3. tablinum; 4. peristyle; 5. garden; S. shops.*

SCULPTURE

Statues in great profusion stood in the forums, and in both public and private buildings. Villas and huge baths were perfect museums of Greek sculpture, originals,[1] copies, or adaptations to suit Roman taste. Such, however, are not Roman art. Authentic Roman sculpture is best represented in the portraits.

[1] We read of 285 bronze and 30 marble statues brought from Corinth in 145 B.C.; of 500 bronzes brought from Delphi by Nero — two illustrations only of the ransacking of Greece to deck Rome.

In the late Greek period, the generalization that distinguished the earlier portraits had given way to some surprisingly individualistic work. The Roman's desire for literal facts, together with his custom of keeping in his house, always before his eye, the *imagines* (wax masks) of his ancestors, influenced the sculptor still further to accentuate this individuality. In addition, one must not disregard the Etruscan influence. In the head of an *Unknown Roman* (Fig. 186A), for example, one is struck by the intensely alive quality. The bony structure of the head, the keen eye, the sparse hair, the sagging skin beneath the chin, all the lines and wrinkles that designate the peculiar characteristics of an individual — all these qualities combine to

[A]   *Unknown Roman. Terra cotta with traces of color. 1st cent.* B.C. *Museum of Fine Arts, Boston. (Boston Museum)*

[B]   *Portrait of a Child. Marble. 1st cent.* A.D. *Museum of Fine Arts, Boston. (Boston Museum)*

give us a realistic portrait of one of those rugged men of dominant will who helped, in the days of the Republic, to lay the foundations of Rome's greatness.

But when we turn to the statue of *Augustus* (Fig. 185B), the feeling is different. The emperor stands easily. He wears an elaborately decorated metal cuirass with leather fringe over his linen tunic and carries his military cloak thrown over his left arm. In every part of the costume is seen skill in the rendering of texture: the soft and heavy quality of the cloths, the rigidity of the metal, and the tough nature of the leather. In his left hand he holds the scepter; his right is lifted in the direction of his glance as if he were addressing his troops; for Augustus himself had led the army on his conquests. But the face does not characterize Augustus in de-

tail, as does the head of the *Unknown Roman.* There are no individual lines to indicate personal idiosyncrasies. It is rather a generalized type distinctly reminiscent of Greek work. If we recall that the Augustan age was a period when the acquisition of Greek statues and the influence of Greek art was at its height, we can easily see why Roman realism had given way.

The sympathetic understanding of youth and childhood is frequently to be seen in Roman sculpture. In many portraits of children the soft flesh and the rounding features that distinguish the child are well indicated; but even more remarkable is the artist's ability to understand the workings of the child mind and to depict that characteristic moment of hesitation between laughter and tears that reveals itself so clearly in the

[A] *Vespasian.   Marble* A.D.   [B] *Caracalla. Marble.* A.D. *211–217. Berlin. (Berlin*
69–79. Terme (National) Mu-   *Museum)*
seum, Rome

quiver about the mouth. In these portraits of the youthful aristocrats of Rome
we discern the real feeling of the child,
now bashful, now eager and alert (Fig.
186B).

The generalizing tendency of the
Augustan age did not maintain itself
long against the Roman love for literal
fact. Thus the spirited portrait of *Vespasian* (Fig. 187A) is an individualistic
expression of the rugged soldier that we
know Vespasian to have been, an expression not so detailed as the Republican portraits, nor so trenchant. The incisiveness and the linear quality of the
latter have softened to a gradual blending of detail, producing the same atmospheric quality that is to be found
in the Flavian reliefs. When we come
to such a portrait as that of *Caracalla*
(Fig. 187B), certain elements have been
added to achieve a greater illusion of

life. The large bust that includes shoulders and arms, the turn in the head that
greatly heightens the vivacity, the rough
mass of hair that contrasts with the
smoothly finished face, the naturalistic
treatment of the eyes, deep-set in the
shadow of heavy brows — all these
means have combined to create an illusion of natural appearance in conjunction with convincing characterization.

PAINTING

Painting functioned chiefly in collaboration with building — as wall decoration. These murals are now to be
found, as has already been said, chiefly
at Pompeii and Herculaneum. They are
executed in fresco. The plaster at Pompeii was laid very thick, and keeping it
moist for a considerable length of time
enabled the painter to work leisurely.

[A]   *Frescoes from the Villa of Livia. Prima Porta. (Stoedtner)*

The colors were bright — red and black to throw the panels or figures into relief, with rich creamy white in the borders. A certain brilliance of surface that enlivened the effect the Roman obtained by a careful preparation of the wall surface; the plaster, which was specially compounded with a mixture of marble dust and laid on layer after layer, was beaten with a smooth trowel until it became very dense, and then was polished until it assumed an almost marblelike finish.

Sometimes the wall space assumed an architectural appearance (Fig. 189B). Columns and windows were painted on the surface in perspective, to give them an appearance of relief. This framework often enclosed a large painting in the center. On the sides, architectural details were so portrayed that they produced an illusion of depth and distant landscape.

In the frescoes of the *Villa Item* (*Villa of the Mysteries*) near Pompeii (Fig. 189A)

the feeling of the wall is much more definitely retained and the figures move within a very shallow space, as in a relief. The figures are constructed in light against a darker ground, and with an extraordinary grasp of the structure of the figure and of its place within the shallow space in relation to the adjoining figures. Expressive drawing and a slight use of shadow suggest both volume and structure, with much the same result as that accomplished by line alone in Figure 164A. In the *Villa of Livia*, on the other hand, the surface of the wall has been composed to create the illusion of a garden, as if the side of the room opened out upon the garden represented (Fig. 188A). A low fence separates the spectator from the scene and also gives solidity and unity to the composition, where trees, plants, and vines in cool green-grays stand out against a blue sky, with bits of bright color in the flowers, fruits, and brightly plumaged birds flying about or enjoying the fresh

[A]   *Frescoes in the Villa Item (Villa of the Mysteries) near Pompeii. Augustan Age.*

[B]   *Wall Decoration of a Pompeian House. Architectural style, creating an illusion of depth. (Anderson)*

water of the fountains. It is a charming bit of nature brought in from the out-of-doors to delight the life lived inside; in spirit it is closely akin to the naturalistic carvings of which the Roman was so fond.

Besides these mural paintings, independent or panel painting was practiced for a variety of purposes — votive pictures for temples, portraits for libraries and for private houses — and great quantities of Greek paintings as well as statues were taken to Rome from Greece. Yet practically nothing remains except the mural paintings, a few in Rome, the great majority in Pompeii and Herculaneum. Probably many of the panel pictures in these murals were copies of famous Greek works. Even when not copying, the painters, many of whom were Greeks, were working in the Hellenic tradition. In the best of these we see, besides their largeness of design and a certain measured reposefulness, a knowledge of perspective, a consistent use of light and

shade and of the cast shadow, and a unity of the figure with the landscape or architecture — all fundamental principles that had been worked out by the Greek.

METALWORK, POTTERY, GLASS

The skill of the Romans in the use of metal we see not only in the casting of large sculpture but also in such small bronzes as the candelabra stands, furniture supports, and household utensils in great variety that have been found at Pompeii. But the wealth and splendor of life made demands upon the goldsmith and the silversmith as well, to furnish fine plate for luxurious tables. Much of this was looted by thieves at

[A] *Silver Crater from the Hildesheim Treasure.*
Probably Augustan Age. Berlin. (Giraudon)

[B] *Portland Vase. Blue and white*
glass. H. c. 10 in. 1st cent. A.D.
British Museum, London. (Mansell)

the time of the destruction of Pompeii or by the barbarians in later ages, but a few finds of such treasure, hidden away, have come to light to give us a glimpse of the lavishness displayed at the famous Roman feasts.[1] The silver crater from Hildesheim (Fig. 190A) for mixing wine is finely shaped, with handles so adjusted that one feels their unity with the structural lines of the vase. Low reliefs, done in repoussé, give a play of delicate light and shade over the surface, adding richness without overloading. At the base the relief is higher, more elaborate, and more compact, thus strengthening the support. The design here consists of two griffins back to back in balanced position, from which rises a conventional plant form;

from this and from the sweeping wings of the griffins delicate spirals rise and spread over the surface, terminating in naturalistic forms. Clinging to the stems and tendrils are tiny children attacking with tridents the sea animals that twine among the spirals. In a two-handled silver cup from Boscoreale we see the Roman love of realism; for here sprays of fruiting olive have been wreathed about the cup, a charming idea and one conveying an illusion of natural appearance, since the fruit is molded in the round. This ornamentation, however, not only obscures the structural lines of the cup but by attracting interest to itself destroys the harmony that results when decoration is kept subordinate.

In surviving Roman pottery the most conspicuous accomplishment is the *Arretine* bowl, made of a fine reddish clay, with the decoration stamped in relief on the outside by means of molds in which the design was cut in intaglio.

[1] One of the rich finds of silverware was at Hildesheim, Germany; this is now in the museum at Berlin and is known as the *Hildesheim Treasure.* Another, the *Boscoreale Treasure,* most of which is in the Louvre, was discovered at Boscoreale near Pompeii.

Then a reddish glaze was added. A sacrificial scene is represented in Figure 191A; winged figures are decorating an altar to which women clad in diaphanous drapery are bringing offerings. These figures remind one of the stucco reliefs in their dainty charm and, being in very low relief, are unobtrusively decorative.

The Roman lapidaries of the Augustan age were skilled in cameo-cutting, which consists of carving a design in relief from a striated stone, such as sardonyx, in such a way that each layer — the layers usually are alternately light and dark, and number from two to nine — will be utilized in working out the design.

The cameo technique was carried by the Roman into the craft of the glassworker, as we see in the *Portland Vase* (Fig. 190B). Up to the second or first century B.C. glass had been molded, a laborious process. About that time the blowpipe was invented, causing a rapid growth of the glass industry, and glass supplanted, to a large extent, the more usual pottery for everyday use. In making such a vase as the *Portland*, the glassworker shaped the deep-blue vase with his blowpipe and then dipped it into opaque white liquid glass. The handles were molded separately and added. When thoroughly hard, the white layer was cut away, leaving the raised white figures in relief against the deep-blue ground. The subject is not understood. At the left a young woman is reclining on some rocks beneath a fig tree, in the usual attitude of sleep; at the right another young woman is seated on a pile of rocks, holding a scepter. The figures are carved with characteristic naturalism. The mask beneath the handle is more decorative.

A very effective use of glass we find in the *Millefiori* or "thousand-flower" bowls, which when held up to the light give an impression of rich mosaic and

[A] *Arretine Bowl. Red clay. 40* B.C.–A.D. *60. Metropolitan Museum of Art, New York City. (Metropolitan Museum)*

hence are sometimes called mosaic glass. The process was as follows: Threads of different-colored glass were fused together into a larger thread, drawn out, and then cut into small pieces that were fitted into a mold and fused into a solid mass. By carefully regulating his color and pattern, the glassworker could create a color harmony of surpassing richness.

SUMMARY

The tonic effect of the vital Etruscan art persisted in Rome notwithstanding its Hellenization. The bold vigor of Etruscan stone construction on the arch principle in the hands of Roman engineers in urban, cosmopolitan Rome, and under the stimulation of an imperial ideal, produced structures of large conception and daring engineering — bridges, temples, palaces, theaters, baths, basilicas, triumphal arches. Engineering in fact was only another manifestation of that Roman impulse toward order which found expression also in law and governmental organization. By means of vaulting the Romans solved the problem of enclosing great space without intermediate support, though they usually concealed the construction with lavish ornament to suit the taste of the day. Thus the great baths are characteristically Roman in their combination of mechanical and esthetic engineering with glittering sumptuousness.

Again it may have been the Etruscan inheritance, combined with the Roman passion for literal fact rather than for abstractions, that led to a realistic portraiture of great vitality. In the wall paintings, too, the practical Roman sought his objective directly: if the room is small and stuffy, enliven it and open it to the outside in imagination if not in actuality! If these wall paintings are debatable as mural decoration, they at least have a clear raison d'être.

BIBLIOGRAPHY

Alexander, Christine, *Jewelry, the Art of the Goldsmith in Classical Times*, Metropolitan Museum of Art, New York City, 1928

Anderson, William J., and Spiers, R. P., *The Architecture of Ancient Rome*, rev. by Thomas Ashby, Vol. II of *The Architecture of Greece and Rome*, 2 vols., Scribner, 1927

Bailey, Cyril, ed., *The Legacy of Rome*, Oxford University Press, 1923

Breasted, James H., *Ancient Times*, 2d ed. rev., Ginn, 1935

Chase, George H., *Greek and Roman Sculpture in American Collections*, Harvard University Press, 1924

Goldscheider, Ludwig, *Etruscan Sculpture*, Oxford University Press (Phaidon Edition), 1941

———— *Roman Portraits*, Oxford University Press (Phaidon Edition), 1940

Grenier, Albert, *The Roman Spirit in Religion, Thought, and Art*, tr. by M. R. Dobie, Knopf, 1926

Gusman, Pierre, *L'art décoratif de Rome*, 3 vols., Paris, 1908–14

Hanfmann, George M. A., *The Etruscans and Their Art* (Reprint of the *Bulletin of the Museum of Art*, Rhode Island School of Design, July, 1940), Rhode Island Museum Press, Providence, 1940

Lamb, Winifred, *Greek and Roman Bronzes*, Dial Press, 1929

Lanciani, Rodolfo Amadeo, *Ancient Rome in the Light of Recent Discoveries*, Houghton Mifflin, 1888

Laurie, Arthur P., *Greek and Roman Methods of Painting*, Putnam, 1910

Lukomskii, Georgii Kreskentevich, *L'art étrusque*, Paris, 1930

McClees, Helen, *The Daily Life of the Greeks and Romans*, 6th ed., Metropolitan Museum of Art, New York City, 1941

Mau, August, *Pompeii: Its Life and Art*, tr. by F. W. Kelsey, new ed. rev., Macmillan, 1902

Platner, Samuel B., *A Topographical Dictionary of Ancient Rome*, completed and rev. by Thomas Ashby, Oxford University Press, 1929

Poulsen, Fredrik, *Etruscan Tomb Paintings: Their Subjects and Significance*, tr. by Ingeborg Andersen, Oxford University Press, 1922

Richter, Gisela M. A., *Handbook of the Classical Collection*, 6th ed., Metropolitan Museum of Art, New York City, 1930

Rivoira, Giovanni Teresio, *Roman Architecture*, Oxford University Press, 1925

Robertson, Donald S., *A Handbook of Greek and Roman Architecture*, Macmillan, 1929

Rodenwaldt, Gerhart, *Die Kunst der Antike*, Berlin, 1927

Showerman, Grant, *Eternal Rome*, new ed., Yale University Press, 1925

———— *Rome and the Romans*, Macmillan, 1931

Strong, Eugénie Sellers, *Art in Ancient Rome*, 2 vols., Scribner, 1928

———— *Roman Sculpture from Augustus to Constantine*, Scribner, 1907

Swindler, Mary H., *Ancient Painting*, Yale University Press, 1929

Weege, Fritz, *Etruskische Malerei*, Halle, 1921

Wickhoff, Franz, *Roman Art*, tr. by Mrs. S. A. Strong, Macmillan, 1900

See also the General Bibliography, pp. 791–92

Far Eastern Art

8

HINDU ART: INDUS, VEDIC, AND BUDDHIST

(ABOUT 3300 B.C.–A.D. 600)

CONTEMPORARY with the great cultures of the Near East and the Mediterranean (the Egyptian, the Sumerian-Assyrian-Chaldean-Persian, and the Classical), and actually in direct contact with them at certain points, were the equally great cultures of the Far East and of the Americas (see Fig. 195A). First we shall look at those of the Far East: the Hindu, the Chinese, and the Japanese.

India comprises the substance of a continent within itself. It is surrounded by water except on the northern boundaries, the only gateway for invaders until recent times. The country divides geographically into three units: first, the wall of the Himalayas, a barrier and also a source of vital river systems, and the traditional home of the gods; second, the northern river valleys, generally known as Hindustan, including the basins of the Ganges and the Indus, very fertile, densely populated, the home of the Aryan invaders and the seat of the strongest political powers; third, peninsular India, comprising the Deccan and the Tamil states, tropical tablelands south of the northern river basins and naturally separated from

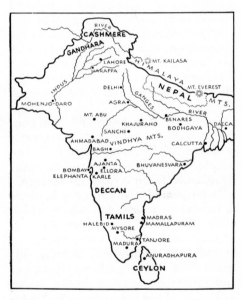

[A]   *India.*

them by mountains and forests, the home of the Dravidian races (Fig. 193A).

Among these divisions are great extremes of climate and of geography, from tropical heat to perpetual snow and glaciers; from desert conditions to the heaviest rainfall in the world. The northern river basins have a wonderfully productive soil and the mountainous regions are rich in stone, woods, ivory, gold, and precious stones. Economically, greatest poverty stands opposed to greatest wealth — wealth still kept in the form of the family treasure, gold and jewels.

Likewise, among the people, numbering over three hundred million, there is great diversity of race, language, and custom. Politically, India has always been divided into many minor principalities and only rarely in its long history has any considerable area been unified for more than a brief time.

Unity is not lacking, however; that is, a deeper and more fundamental unity than that manifested in political co-operation and in uniformity of dialect and custom. This is evident in the religious and cultural life of India — in the Brahman faith, the national sacred literature, the caste system, and the Hindu attitude toward fundamental spiritual truths. For perhaps no other people have felt so profoundly and pondered so deeply over the fundamental problems of life; and with no other people have spirituality and spiritual significance taken greater precedence.

India shared the common heritage of Eurasia — a Neolithic culture which gradually evolved into an age of metal. In the fourth or third millennium B.C. a distinctive civilization, recently discovered at Mohenjo-daro, Harappa, and other sites, existed in the Indus valley.[1] This has been known as "Indo-Sumerian" or more recently as "Indus." Mohenjo-daro appears to have been a wealthy city, the center of an agricultural and commercial people with a high level of craftsmanship and design. To judge from the similarity of their stone and clay figures of men and animals, and of their animal-figured seals, to those produced in Sumeria, their city seems to have maintained commercial relations with the Near East.

In the meantime the Dravidians, a dark-skinned people who may have descended from the Neolithic peoples, spread over the peninsula. They seem already to have reached a highly developed state when nomad Aryans began to penetrate the valley of the Ganges. Driving the Dravidians to the highlands south of the Ganges, the Aryans settled down as an agricultural people. They lived in villages, possessed domesticated horses, rode in chariots, and knew the use of metal. They were organized into a tribal state, with the family as a unit. They worshiped and gradually personified the powers of nature. The sky became Varuna, god of right and justice; the rain, Indra, in addition assumed the role of war god. This we see in the most ancient Hindu hymns, contained in the *Vedas*, which are lyrical expressions of nature worship. The ritual connected with this worship was first performed by the father as head of the family; but soon it became the prerogative of the priests, called the Brahmans, who crystallized it into a system with elaborate rites and sacrifices and infused into it philosophical speculations about the meaning of existence and the nature of the world soul. "The 'troubled intensity' of man's search after the soul and its moral earnestness"[2] constitutes the theme of the treatises known as the *Upanishads*, which are considered, even today, the Bible of the Hindu.

[1] For an account of these discoveries, see Sir John G. Cumming, *Revealing India's Past*, India Society, London, 1939. They have been too recent and too incomplete to admit of more than tentative conclusions as to the origin and the nature of the culture and its relation to others in the peninsula.

[2] Lin Yutang, *The Wisdom of China and India*, Random House, 1942, p. 33. This volume gives translations of much from the *Vedas* and the *Upanishads*. See also Sir Monier Monier-Williams, *Indian Wisdom*, 4th ed., London, 1893.

[A]   *The Ancient Cultures.*

While religious conceptions were crystallizing into a theological system, social and economic conditions were evolving into a social order, the caste system, which divides the Hindu people into four main classes: (1) the priests, who conduct the ritual and preserve the sacred texts; (2) the warriors, who are rulers and public administrators; (3) the agriculturalists, who till the soil and produce the wealth; and (4) the sudras, the laborers. The first three comprise the Aryans, the fourth probably originated in conquered peoples. These main divisions have become subdivided into more than twenty-five hundred groups. A Hindu belongs to a caste by birth, and to change from it is practically impossible, though he is permitted individual freedom within its limits. According to him, this system, which seems to have evolved naturally in ancient times, is a part of the order of nature.

The world soul concept of the *Upanishads*, the universal spiritual principle — the impersonal absolute from which all individual souls emanate and to which, theoretically, they return — postulates a concept of an endless succession of lives (known as the transmigration of souls) in which the acts of each life determine the status of the next — higher for the good or lower for the wicked. Few attain the goal: absorption into Nirvana. Though the Hindu believes that everyone, each according to his ability, might catch some gleam of this ultimate, yet for most men both the lofty conceptions of the *Upanishads* and the mystic insight required for their realization were too difficult. Hence we see the love and worship of the old gods bringing about a compromise with the metaphysical speculations of the Brahmans in the form of the Trimurti, a triple aspect of the one supreme reality: Brahma, the creative aspect, cognition, wisdom; Vishnu, the sustaining aspect, love, emotion; Shiva, the destructive aspect, will, power. Of the three, Vishnu and Shiva were the more popular, and their worship developed into powerful cults.

As religious ideas were evolving, the great epics were also taking shape. The *Ramayana* tells of the deeds of the prince Rama during his exile, brought about by court intrigue, and the recovery of his lost bride Sita. The *Mahabharata*, like the *Iliad*, deals with a war between two clans, here the Kurus and the Bharatas. But inserted, frequently at a later date than the first collecting of the legends, are such religious treatises as the *Bhagavad-gita*, the *Lord's Song*, which is probably the highest expression of Hindu faith.[1]

[1] For translations of the *Ramayana* and *Mahabharata*, see Frederika Macdonald, *Iliad of the East*, Lane, 1908; Sister Nivedita (M. E. Noble) and A. K. Coomaraswamy, *Myths of the Hindus and Buddhists*, Holt, 1914; and Lin Yutang, *The Wisdom of China and India*. For the *Bhagavad-gita*, see the translations by A. W. Rider, University of Chicago Press, 1929; L. D. Barnett, Macmillan, 1905; and Lin Yutang, *op. cit.*

The concept of one universal reality permeating the cosmos the writer of the *Bhagavad-gita* expresses when he says:

"There is naught higher than I, O Wealth-Winner; all this universe is strung upon Me, as rows of gems upon a thread.

"I am the taste in water, O son of Kunti; I am the light in moon and sun, the *Om* in all the Vedas, sound in the ether, manhood in men.

"The pure scent in earth am I, and the light in fire; the life in all born beings am I, and the mortification of them that mortify the flesh.

"Know Me to be the ancient Seed of all born beings, O son of Pritha; I am the understanding of them that understand, the splendor of the splendid."[2]

The young Prince Siddhartha (died about 543 B.C.), brought up in this traditional Brahman faith, looking about him, became impressed with the suffering that he saw everywhere. To attain Nirvana one must pass through an almost endless succession of reincarnations, each with its own suffering. So he applied himself to the problem of seeking relief from this distress. Leaving his family and his luxurious surroundings, he gave himself up to the life of an ascetic and through meditation obtained the knowledge that enabled him to bring a means of salvation to his people. Hence he became a Buddha, that is, an enlightened one. His solution was to recognize that the individual was an illusion only and that suffering was due to self-interest — to the assertion of the interests of the individual rather than the submersion of the individual in the larger universal life that embraces all nature in its fellowship and is the only reality. The means of escape from the

[2] *Bhagavad-gita*, tr. by L. D. Barnett, p. 119, by permission of the publishers, The Macmillan Company.

fetters of the individual into this supreme universal life lay not in the elaborate sacrifices prescribed by the Brahman priests, but partly in meditation, in order to bring the soul through retirement and concentration into union with the divine, and partly through moral actions done in a spirit of complete selflessness. This was the path that led to the conquest of self, to peace of mind, to wisdom, and to release from bondage.

For forty-five years Gautama (Siddhartha's name as a Buddha) taught the Eightfold Path, the Wheel of the Law, as he wandered, a mendicant, through the Ganges Valley winning disciples and building up a society of the faith which was not only to dominate India for centuries but to reach out into large areas of eastern Asia as a powerfully energizing influence.

In a culture based upon these concepts of religion, sociology, and economics, how does the artist function? What are his aims? Hindu art, whether Brahmanical or Buddhist — and one must remember that Buddhism retained many of the fundamental tenets of Brahmanism — is primarily a religious art. Even secular objects are imbued with religious significance. As the Hindu always tended to be speculative, the artist was motivated by the need to objectify the ultimate reality that lay behind visible appearance. His was "the sacred task of rendering explicit the implications of the Cosmic life"[1] — which closely approximates the early-Christian ideal, "to render visible the mysteries of the supra-natural world.[2]"

The Hindu artist considered himself a pious craftsman, a servant in the temple or the palace, and, as a descendant of Visvakarma, lord of the arts, the heir of an ideal above the idiosyncrasies of individual expression. He must have the capacity to learn his craft. "One who knows amiss his craft, after his death will fall into hell and suffer. . . . Vision without technique is as unfortunate as skill without vision."[3] To attain vision, the artist practiced *yoga* — that is, through meditation he attuned his mind to and identified himself with that which he was to objectify.[4] He visualized the concept in every detail before the work of his hands began. His visualization, however, was not dictated by his individual preferences, but in terms of a canon which stipulated proportion, pose of body, and gestures of limbs and hands, and which constituted for the artist a kind of language, as words do for the writer, or mathematical formulas for the engineer. The positions of the hands known as *mudras* (lives of the hands) are vibrant symbols of characteristic activities — teaching, meditating, not-fearing — and epitomize the essential significance of the painting, statue, or dance. No image can be beautiful, according to Hindu theory, which is not created according to the canon. Thus the artist's visualization derived from what the canon prescribed, not from what his eye saw. Whether carving or drawing a figure, he never worked from a living model. His work is based on conception, not perception; and it reflects an attitude toward nature and a habit of mind that are in strong contrast to the freer, more individualistic viewpoint of the Occident, yet which have nevertheless produced some of the most profound art of the world.

---

[1] Mulk Raj Anand, *The Hindu View of Art*, London, 1933, p. 172. For the close relationship of Hindu and early Christian ideals, see A. K. Coomaraswamy, *The Transformation of Nature in Art*, Harvard University Press, 1934.

[2] See note 1, p. 250.

[3] Mulk Raj Anand, *op. cit.*, p. 177.

[4] Dr. Coomaraswamy refers to a similar point of view in Dante: "Who paints a figure, if he cannot be it, cannot paint it." The Chinese and Japanese also possess this habit of mind.

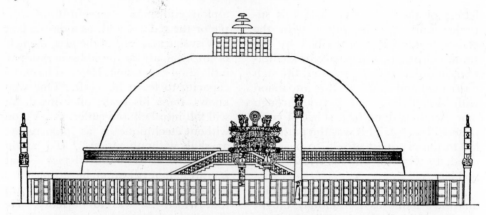

[A]   *Sanchi Stupa. Restored. D. 121 ft. 3d cent.* B.C. *(Archaeological Survey of India)*

During the evolution of this civiliza-tion foreign influences from the West penetrated India several times; for the Greeks under Alexander had reached northwestern India and later came in-vasions of the Sassanian Persians. Evi-dences of these influences are somewhat apparent in Indian art. But in A.D. 320 a native dynasty was restored and this, the Gupta period, forms the Golden Age of Hindu culture (about A.D. 300–600.) A Chinese pilgrim (Fa-heen or Fa-hsien) in writing of his travels in India in the fifth century describes the rich and prosperous condition of the country. He tells of charitable institu-tions and hospitals, institutions of learn-ing, great monasteries, rich palaces with carved and painted ornamentation; of a mild, adequate government, and re-ligious toleration. Fine buildings were erected, only to be destroyed later by the Muhammadans. Sculpture and painting reached a climax of attain-ment, as did music, science, and San-skrit literature. For this was the period of the most famous poets, of whom Kalidasa was the greatest. Europe was being plunged into chaos by the fall of the Roman Empire and the inroads of the barbarians; and although the By-zantine Empire was flourishing under

Justinian at Constantinople and the Sassanian power was at a climax under Chosroes I and Chosroes II at Ctesi-phon, at this time India in the sum total of its broad culture was probably the most enlightened nation in the world.[1]

ARCHITECTURE
AND SCULPTURE

Of the early cities of India of which we read in Hindu literature nothing is left. The earliest type of structure that has survived is the Buddhist *stupa*, a mound of solid brick or stone to mark some sacred place or to hold some relic. Most representative is the great *Sanchi Stupa* (Fig. 198A). It is hemispherical, with a flattened top, and rests upon a high circular terrace; a massive balus-trade surrounds the mounds, the usual method in India of protecting a sacred

[1] The broad divisions of Hindu history are:

3300–2000 B.C.	Indus Age
2000–700 B.C.	Vedic Age
500 B.C.–A.D. 300	Age of Buddhism
A.D. 300–600	Gupta dynasty, Hinduism; Buddhism absorbed by renascent Brahmanism
A.D. 600–800	Classic Age; Rajputs
A.D. 800–1818	Medieval Age; Muham-madan invasion; Mughal Empire

[A]   *Gate at Sanchi. Upper part. (India Office)*

place; at the four cardinal points are ornamental gateways, lavishly carved (Fig. 199A). Originally a balustrade surrounded the terrace, and served to guide the pilgrims in their procession, or circumambulation, about the shrine, an early practice common in Hindu religious ceremony. A double stairway with balustrades afforded an entrance to the terrace. On the flattened top of the mound was another balustrade surrounding the reliquary, which was surmounted by an umbrella, the symbol of royalty. Both the balustrades and the gateways appear from the construction to be stone copies of wooden rail fences and gates. They are, in fact, the work of the carpenter executed in stone. This

[A] *Dryad. Pier of Sanchi Gate (Fig. 199A). (India Office)*

gives us a clue to why earlier examples of architecture have not survived: they were of wooden construction and could not withstand the destructive climate of India. The richly carved gates are strong accents against the unbroken surface of the stupa, and illustrate the exuberance and never-ending rhythmic movement found in Hindu ornament. Piers, crossbars, and brackets are filled to overflowing with carvings which in content combine Buddhist symbols, such as the stupa, the sacred tree, or the wheel, with narrations of the former incarnations of Gautama Buddha when he was a bird or an elephant.[1] For in early Buddhism the Buddha was repre-

sented only by symbol or by reference to these earlier lives. In the upper bar of the gate illustrated, for example, people are worshiping stupas and sacred trees. Whatever is represented in the *Sanchi* reliefs — man, animal, or plant — tends to be of the same height, expressive of the unity and the equality of all animate life; and all are surcharged with vitality. The figures are placed one above another to fill the space, and are carved in high enough relief to enable their simplified planes to be seen clearly against the dark ground. As decoration, the carving fills every inch of the surface with ceaseless movement brought to a halt by firm edges and spiraling terminals. One lower bracket is filled with a *Dryad* (Fig. 200A) clinging to a tree, and their association is expressed by their formal relationship. For the figure and the tree interpenetrate inseparably by a flow of movement. The limbs of the figure and the branches of the tree are sinuous interweaving cylinders; the masses of the body rise and fall in the full breasts, the slim waist, and the bulbous hips. The tree is highly conventional, and the figure follows the canon in its proportions: broad shoulders, narrow waist, large breasts and hips. The carving on the *Sanchi Gates* is not primitive but, like the architecture, seems to be a translation into stone of an earlier, fully developed art of perishable material, perhaps wood, and an expression of the Vedic animistic faith — an art which the Buddhists took over as part of their tradition but molded to new purposes.

Another important type of Buddhist building was the assembly hall for congregational worship.[2] Probably many of these halls were of wooden construction; those that are now extant are rock-cut — hollowed out from the side

---

[1] These stories, a constantly recurring theme in Buddhist art, are known as the Jataka tales. For these tales see the edition by H. T. Francis and E. J. Thomas, Cambridge University Press, 1916; and E. W. Burlingame, tr., *Buddhist Parables*, Yale University Press, 1922.

[2] Sometimes called a *chaitya hall;* that is, a temple or hall containing a *chaitya* (a monument).

[A] *Buddhist Assembly Hall. Karle. c. 1st cent. B.C. (India Office)*

of a cliff. Rock-cut churches, monasteries, and temples were popular in India, as they afforded excellent shelter both from the heavy rain and from the glaring heat. Though chiseled from the solid rock, they imitated the form of the wood or masonry structures. Such a hall we find in *Karle* (Fig. 201A). The hall consists of a nave with a semicircular end, and aisles from which the nave is separated by a row of columns. At the circular end within the nave stands the shrine in the form of a stupa, which was the symbol of the faith in the early days of Buddhism before statues of Buddha were made. The roof is in the form of a great barrel vault with ribs which reproduce the bamboo construction of its prototype. Originally there were fresco mural decorations, and painted banners hung from the roof. One large leaf-shaped window was placed above the entrance in such a way that the light fell directly upon the stupa and brought out the rich colors of the

decorations before it was lost in the dim shadows of the high vaulting.

It was not until several hundred years after the death of Gautama that statues of the Buddha began to supplant the symbolic stupa.[1] Frequently he is represented in meditation — a yoga practice — as one sees in the *Great Buddha of Anuradhapura* (Fig. 202A). The Buddha is seated with legs crossed, one hand

[1] Owing partly to the influence of Greece that had penetrated to northwestern India through the conquests of Alexander the Great and had strongly influenced the sculptors of Gandhara, who combined the Indian conception with the Greek method of expression. The result is interesting historically, for it penetrated to China also. But it is curiously exotic, and typical neither of Greece nor of India. In the sculpture of India, China, and Japan, the attributes of Buddha are the protuberance of wisdom on the top of the head; the split and elongated ear lobes (symbolizing the renunciation of riches, in the form of jewelry so heavy that it lengthened the lobes); and the mark on the forehead, often a jewel, that symbolizes the third eye of spiritual vision.

[A]   *The Great Buddha of Anuradhapura, Ceylon. Of domolite. Colossal size. 5th or 6th cent.* A.D.

resting on the other in his lap in the mudra of meditation; the back is erect, but the eyelids are lowered as if to turn the mind and the sense organs inward. A thin drapery falls from the left shoulder, indicated by a diagonal line across the breast. The figure rises from its broad base to a height equal to that of the base (a proportion of quietude) and is carved with geometric simplicity — simple, massive, rounding forms that flow into each other, producing a monumental effect. For the aim of the sculptor was not to tell what the Buddha looked like physically, but to make the observer realize the spiritual realm which he attained — inner serenity. "As a lamp in a windless spot flickers not, such is the likeness that is told of the strict-minded man . . . when the mind, held in check, comes to stillness . . . and when he knows the boundless happiness that lies beyond sense-instruments and

is grasped by understanding, and in steadfastness swerves not from Verity, than which, once gotten, he deems no other boon better."[1] This stillness is not the negation of power, but denotes the acquisition of the greatest spiritual values; and the "moral grandeur" of the concept equals the esthetic grandeur of the form.

Thus Buddhist art in its early stages, as illustrated by the *Sanchi Stupa*, was "popular, sensuous, and animistic Indian art adapted to the purposes of the illustration of Buddhist anecdote and the decoration of Buddhist monuments."[2] Later it produced the Buddhas of southern India and Ceylon — the *Buddha of Anuradhapura* (Fig. 202A) for example — which constitute a truly Buddhist art of great vitality and monumentality, significant in content for its expression of spiritual values, and in style for its austere massiveness and conventional treatment of details.

As we enter the Gupta age, however, when Buddhism was waning under the impact of a renascent Brahmanism, the trend was toward ease, grace, and humanism. A popular subject was the Bodhisattva *Avalokiteshvara*.[3] A bronze statuette of this divinity represents the Bodhisattva seated in an easy pose, the weight borne by the left arm, and the right hand, supported by the raised leg, held in the traditional mudra of teaching. The shoulders are broad and strong, the waist narrow, the limbs rounded,

[1] *Bhagavad-gita*, tr. by Barnett, p. 114, by permission of the publishers, The Macmillan Company.

[2] A. K. Coomaraswamy, *The Dance of Siva*, Sunwise Turn, 1924, p. 54.

[3] A Bodhisattva is a being who is destined at some time to become a Buddha; even at present he is an active force for salvation and his worship is the center of a cult. Avalokiteshvara, "the lord who looketh down in great compassion," is one of the most important Bodhisattvas not only in India but, under a different form, in China and Japan also.

[A] *Buddha Expounding the Law to His Mother, Maya. Borobudur. c. 9th cent.* A.D.

and the skin smooth; on the head is the protuberance of wisdom, here covered by a crown, and the ears are elongated — all traditional characteristics and conventions. Through the figure flows a suave rhythm which emphasizes serene youthfulness and tender compassion. Its material, bronze, is highly suitable for both the character and the small size of the figure.

Buddhism was a strongly missionary religion. An important point to which it penetrated was Java, where the Buddhist priests erected the great *Stupa of Borobudur* (Fig. 204A). This shrine was an elaborated stupa. About it wound five procession paths, along which were sculptured, in relief in the coarse native stone of which the stupa was built, stories of the Buddhist faith, for the instruction and stimulation of pilgrims. In Figure 203A the Buddha, seated in a temple, with hand uplifted in the mudra of teaching, is expounding the law to his mother, Maya, and her attendants.

The conventional trees, which fill the space above the seated figures, and the elaborate costumes contribute to the richly decorative character of the relief.

PAINTING

The early painting of India, of which we read in the ancient literature, is lost. The earliest extant work reveals a highly developed art serving the same function as sculpture — a didactic and decorative purpose in religious places. Noteworthy among early works are the paintings in the *Ajanta Caves*. These cave temples formed a Buddhist monastic retreat in an isolated ravine in central India. Here the artists covered walls and ceilings with paintings usually referred to as frescoes but which are closer to a tempera technique. The pigments are mineral, not the earth colors characteristic of fresco. The walls were first coated with rough plaster (often mixed with some binding material, such as

[A] *Stupa of Borobudur. Java. c. 9th cent.* A.D.

rice husks) and then covered with a coat of smooth white plaster, on which the figures were drawn in red and covered with a transparent underpainting, usually green. The local colors were then added, and finally the contours were repainted in brown or black. In the earlier examples — the *Ajanta Frescoes* cover several centuries — the figures are large and imposing, as in the scenes which tell of the life of the Buddha when he was a great white elephant in the Himalayas; or in the *Adoration,* in which a woman and child, perhaps the wife and child of Gautama, stand in fervid devotion before the majestic figure of the Buddha with his begging bowl, clad in a yellow robe, his feet on a lotus — all against a deep-blue ground. In the later paintings, in Cave I, a vast drama is spread on the walls with all the exuberance and overflowing quality of the *Sanchi Gates.* Scene crowds upon scene in a panorama of aristocratic life used in the service of religious themes. The figures are smaller than in the earlier paintings, are more consciously grouped, and are more closely related to an architectural setting. In Figure 205A, for example, a *Rajah,* a former incarnation of the Buddha, is represented with his hands in the mudra of exposi-

tion, explaining the doctrines to his wife and a group of court attendants. Perhaps the first impression is that of a scene lived intensely. How has the painter been able to produce this effect? Very little by facial expression, but largely by the highly expressive pose of body and gesture of hands, and by the dynamic use of line, light, and color. The drawing is according to the canon (compare the *Dryad,* Fig. 200A). The line itself is full of vitality. At times it models the figure as in sculptural drawing; or it may combine with a slight shadow to give an effect of roundness and solidity. This shadow is not the result of natural or artificial illumination, but is an abstract means of expressing roundness by using a high light on the parts nearest the observer. Notwithstanding, the strong contours, combined with the sharply linear quality in the details, tend to flatten the scene as a whole. To this effect the broad bands of the saris contribute, with their slow wavelike movement above the dark almost unbroken base. Despite this flat decorative quality, there is a sinuous movement back and forth in the shallow depth between the foreground and the angular framework of the pavilion.

A superb example of Buddhist paint-

[A]   *Rajah in the Mudra of Exposition. Ajanta. 5th–6th cent.* A.D. *(Art Institute of Chicago)*

ing is the great figure of a *Bodhisattva* (or so it is thought to be), which stands out with particular force against a wavering background of smaller figures and contrasting color. The saint is richly garbed and adorned with a rope of pearls and other jewels, and he wears a high headdress ornamented with sapphires; in his right hand he holds a blue lotus. The pose, it has been suggested, may derive from a dancing pose. For dancing was an important element in Hindu ritual. Whatever the interpretation, the figure is filled with a feeling of intense compassion, expressed by the same means that are employed in the *Rajah* group.

These paintings at *Ajanta* are more than accomplished drawings and paintings per se. To the Hindu they are above all a vehicle for the expression of an inner life. They are saturated with an intense vitality which reflects an equally intense feeling on the part of the painter. "The theme is all in all." This inner significance of the subject so motivates the artist and permeates his being that, using the language of the canon merely as a means to an end, he never loses sight of the end.

SUMMARY

The art of India was primarily religious and symbolic. The earliest surviving buildings are the Buddhist stupas, with elaborately carved gates; the cave assembly halls, in which a stupa symbolized the Buddha; and the monastic caves, which contained both carvings and paintings. Sculpture and painting functioned both decoratively and didactically: to ornament entrances, to decorate walls, and at the same time to narrate incidents in the life of the Buddha and his worshipers.

In form the art of India was strictly obedient to accepted canons of technique and representation. The artist was a pious craftsman highly trained in these canons and motivated by a need for expressing, within or by means of the canons, inner significance. Thus he was not concerned with visible appearances; nor was he an individual free to follow his own idiosyncrasies, but an instrument of something behind and greater than the individual — the consciousness of his race. Thus in both painting and sculpture the figure was not an imitation of natural appearance, but an expression, in terms of an understood language of form, of spiritual values.

See the Bibliography on page 377.

9

CHINESE ART

(ABOUT 3000 B.C.–A.D. 907)

IN studying Chinese art we are dealing with a people whose native conservatism has preserved their fundamental traditions for more than four thousand years — a unique instance in the history of civilizations. To be sure, foreign influences have entered China and become powerful, but eventually they have been absorbed or assimilated by truly Chinese thought and action.

China is vast both in population and in geographical extent, a land of more than four hundred million people, with an area, including Tibet, Chinese Turkestan (Sinkiang), Mongolia, and Manchuria, of more than twice the size of the United States, though China proper includes a little less than half this area (Fig. 207A). The fertile eastern plains are traversed by two great river systems that have their rise in the mountains of the west. The Hwang Ho, or Yellow River, with swift current brings down great quantities of silt that is still building up the alluvial plains — now providing rich agricultural lands, now destroying farms and people with its floods and erratic changes of course. The Yangtze Kiang, or Blue River, through its navigability serves as a great artery of commerce. As one would expect in so large a country, there is great variety of climate, vegetation, language, and custom. North China, centering about Peiping, has a cool, dry climate and many stretches of plain; South China, centering about Canton, is moist and tropical, with mountains near by to afford a summer refuge from the enervating heat. To west and north are vast

[A]   *The Far East, Showing the Principal Trade Routes to the West.*

areas of desert plateau. Agriculture forms the economic basis of life; even in the mountainous regions small patches of tillable land are intensively cultivated. The natural resources are great — mines of gold and other metals, quarries, "jade mountains." Formerly there were great forests, now destroyed.

The earliest beginnings of Chinese culture appeared in Paleolithic times with the Peking man, who lived in the valley of the Yellow River somewhat earlier than Neandertal man lived in Europe, and who had weapons similar to those found in Paleolithic Europe. Then followed a great gap in time — probably it will be filled by further excavations — until a Neolithic culture appeared in the same valley, an agricultural people who cultivated rice and made textiles and a fine painted pottery. The earliest historical culture was the Shang, centered in the Honan province and comprising perhaps one-fifth of present China.[1] The people, when not at war, were primarily agricultural, and for this reason interested in the powers of nature — sky, stars, wind, and rain. About these powers their religion centered. The dragon — in varying forms one of the most important motifs in Chinese art, and the emblem of the emperor — possibly had its origin in the great alligators that infested the rivers and early became objects of worship, symbolizing the coming of spring and rain. Likewise the phoenix, because of its fabulous renewal of life from its own ashes, symbolized the sun and the warmth that brings about the ever recurrent life in nature.

Two other fundamentals of this early civilization have persisted as basic elements of Chinese culture. First, the social basis, the unit of which was the family and not the individual. The customs of one's ancestors constituted the established law, and the perpetuation of the family was the vital necessity. To these the rights and freedom of the individual were sacrificed. He was but one link in the social chain, and the chain unbroken was paramount. Such an attitude fostered the second fundamental, which was a pious reverence for the dead, a continual looking to the past rather than to the future, and an

[1] Chinese civilization may be traced back to about 3000 B.C. The important periods are:

Shang dynasty	1766–1122 B.C.
Chou dynasty	1122–255
Ts'in dynasty	255–206
Han dynasty	206 B.C.–A.D. 221
Wei and the Six dynasties	A.D. 221–618
T'ang dynasty	618–907
Sung dynasty	960–1280
Yüan or Mongol dynasty	1280–1368
Ming dynasty	1368–1644
Ts'ing or Manchu dynasty	1644–1911

The spelling and the dates used in this chapter are those of H. A. Giles. For maps illustrating the geographic extent of China in the various dynasties, and the old trade routes, see E. H. Parker, *China*, 2d ed. rev., Dutton, 1924.

acceptance of the past as the ultimate authority. The result of such a culture was unity and harmony, and in art an expression that was racial rather than individual.

These peculiarly Chinese ideas and institutions, which have continued with little fundamental change to the present time, were established by the Shang and formulated by the Chou, a people of great vitality. This formulation was largely the work of Confucius (551–479 B.C.), philosopher, historian, and statesman. The early climax of Chinese culture reached in the Chou dynasty, it is interesting to note, was roughly contemporary with cultural climaxes in Persia, Greece, and India. While Confucianism is frequently classed as a religion, it is neither a religion nor a philosophy, but a social and ethical system that aims to secure a stable society by regulating human relationships. "Chinese Humanism," says Lin Yutang, "in its essence is the study of human relations through a correct appreciation of human values by the psychology of human motives to the end that we may behave as reasonable human beings." [2]

Meanwhile, in the valley of the Yangtze Kiang, the "land of thorns," lived the "jungle barbarians," of a different race and a different conception of life. Among them grew up a sect known as the Taoists — followers of the Tao, the impersonal force or principle identified with nature. These dwellers by the Blue River had an intense love of nature — of the mountains, rivers, mists, and clouds that are characteristic of that part of China. They claimed as their founder Lao-tzu (Lao-tse) (570?–490 B.C.), a contemporary of Confucius but a teacher who recognized the individual to a far greater extent, for he taught that the self must be recognized in order to be brought into harmony with the

[2] *The Wisdom of India and China*, p. 571.

great impersonal force permeating the universe that was the ultimate good.

Toward the end of the Chou dynasty the Ts'in, a Tatar people who were living on the western boundaries and serving the Chou as horseherds and charioteers, finally became the dominating power, and the king of Ts'in became the first emperor of China (246 B.C.). The Ts'in consolidated the empire, set up a strongly centralized government, built the Great Wall as a protection against the Mongolian nomads, and in order to abolish local patriotism burned the written books. They also gave to the country the name by which we know it: China — Ts'in, or Chin, land. They, in turn, were overcome by the Han, who by dividing the land set up a feudal state. The Han were the great supporters of Confucian ideals, and established Confucian writings as the exclusive classical literature of China. Under the Han, China expanded westward to protect itself against the barbarous tribes of central Asia and also to keep open the great trade routes over which its silks and other products were carried west even to the Roman Empire.

These highways were most important in the history of Chinese civilization. Along them traders, pilgrims, and armies traveled between eastern and western Asia. While in China proper the native culture had been developing until it had formed established traditions, over these highways the Buddhist faith was slowly making its way as the Buddhist monks and missionaries established their monasteries farther and farther eastward, especially in eastern Turkestan, which had become a Chinese protectorate. Here in the oases that formed a chain of cities across the desert plateaus the religion of India met the culture of China, and the fusion of the two formed the basis of the later great art of China.

Buddhism, during the thousand years since its founding, had developed into something much more comprehensive than the simple teaching of Prince Siddhartha. As a strongly missionary religion, its conception of salvation included the whole universe; and in this aspect perhaps even more important than the Buddha were the Bodhisattvas. Avalokiteshvara, the lord of pity, under the name Kuan-yin was to become (in female form) one of the most important of the Chinese and Japanese Buddhist deities. With well-established traditions, China was ready for the stimulation that the emotionalism and the mysticism of Buddhism could give it. The ground had been prepared by the Taoists, whose ideas were somewhat akin to those of the Buddhists. We read of pilgrims such as Fa-heen (or Fa-hsien)[1] traveling through India (A.D. 399–414) visiting sacred places, learning of the faith, and collecting literature about it. The translation of the Indian idea into a Chinese mode of expression we see developing in Turkestan. But its full assimilation and ultimate expression took place in China proper in the T'ang dynasty (618–907), a golden age in all the arts — painting, sculpture, metalwork, poetry, music. Toward the end of the T'ang period, a conservative reaction set in against Buddhism and other religions that had secured a foothold; it soon developed into a revolution that demanded a return to the Confucian system. The success of the revolutionists (845) brought about the destruction of temples and monasteries with their great series of frescoes, and a general ruin of all works of art. This is why so little real T'ang art has survived. Another reaction in favor of Buddhism restored many of the temples and monasteries in the tenth century, but by that time most of the paintings were irretrievably lost.

[1] See page 198.

[A] *Wine Vessel, Ku. Bronze. H. 12¼ in. Shang Dynasty. Buckingham Collection, Art Institute of Chicago. (Art Institute)*

METALWORK

In the writings of the Chou period — and they are plentiful — we read of temples, palaces, sculpture, and paintings, almost all of which have been lost because of the perishable materials of which they were made and the devastating character of the climate. One of the greatest expressions of the age, however, and one that is peculiarly Chinese, has survived — the bronzes. Their full significance is seen only in relation to their users, a people organized socially on the unit of the family, whose reverence for ancestors was equal to

that which they felt for winds, rains, and clouds, those manifestations of nature about which centers the worship of an agricultural people. These basic cultural factors suggest the origins of the uses, shapes, and decorative motifs of the vessels and throw light upon the impression of deep significance and hieratic character that we feel in them. [1]

Something of this spirit we discern in the frequent inscriptions found on the bronzes, as on one of the bells that were used to summon the spirits of the departed, or the guests to the banquet, or to serve as one of the instruments of the orchestra: "I, Kuo-Shu Lü, say: Grandly distinguished was my illustrious father Hui Shu, with profound reverence he maintained a surpassingly bright virtue. He excelled alike in the rule of his own domain and in his liberal treatment of strangers from afar. When I, Lü, presumed to assume the leadership of the people and to take as my model the dignified demeanor of my illustrious father, a memorial of the event was presented at the Court of the Son of Heaven, and the Son of Heaven graciously honoured me with abundant gifts. I, Lü, humbly acknowledge the timely gifts of the Son of Heaven and proclaim their use in the fabrication for my illustrious father Hui Shu of this great sacrificial tuneful bell. Oh, illustrious father seated in majesty above, protect with sheltering wings us who are left here below. Peaceful and glorious, extend to me, Lü, abundant happiness! I, Lü, and my sons and grandsons for ten thousand years to come, will everlastingly prize this bell and use it in our ritual worship." [2]

[1] There is but little accurate knowledge concerning these bronzes, for though the Chinese themselves have great reverence for them, and early began to collect them, compile catalogues of them, and write treatises about them, these studies are lacking in scientific accuracy.

[2] S. W. Bushell, *Chinese Art*, 2 vols., Brentano, 1924, Vol. I, p. 73.

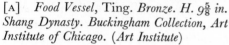

[A] *Food Vessel*, Ting. *Bronze. H. 9⅝ in. Shang Dynasty. Buckingham Collection, Art Institute of Chicago. (Art Institute)*

[B] *Wine Vessel*, Tsun. *Bronze. H. 6¼ in. Shang Dynasty. Buckingham Collection, Art Institute of Chicago. (Art Institute)*

The purpose of these vessels seems to have been in some instances ritual (to be used in the sacrificial rites of ancestor worship), in some, to record important events or favors from the king; and in others, for eating and drinking on especial occasions. Whatever their purpose, they were considered one of the greatest family possessions, and by invaders, most desirable loot. Their shapes seem to be dictated by function. Figure 210A shows a tall slender drinking vessel holding about a pint and probably used in religious ceremonies; Figure 211A, a food vessel; and Figure 211B, a wine vessel of a shape derived from an owl. The decorative motifs are similar on all the bronzes: highly conventionalized representations of dragons, cicadas, snakes, birds, or animals connected with an agricultural people and undoubtedly symbolic in their formative period. A common motif is the so-called ogre mask, which consists of a highly conventionalized animal head that has been cleft into two halves and spread out laterally on each side of the nose. Another motif almost always found, especially as a ground pattern, is the fret which is usually interpreted as the cloud or thunder pattern. The Chinese adapted these motifs, with great ingenuity and variation, to the surfaces to be decorated, and displayed particular sensitivity for the relation of the motif in scale to its function in the total design. In Figure 210A the lanceolate pattern accents the slender proportions of the cup. In Figure 211A the bold ogre mask occupies the heaviest part of the jar and is set off by the wavering pattern of the more delicate fret of the background. In Figure 211B the decorative scheme is built upon a bold curve with a strong pattern and upon the interplay of countercurves in the feet and the tail; by this framework the minor allover pattern is controlled.

[A] *Stone Relief. From a tomb. L. c. 5 ft. Han Dynasty. (Chavannes) Under a tree full of nesting birds before a two-story house stand an unhitched horse and an empty chariot. Inside the house four men, two of whom are kneeling, bow before a personage whose importance is indicated by both his size and his position under a canopy. On the upper floor servants attend a lady seated in the middle. The tiled roofs are covered with monkeys and peacocks. On the left at a distance an archer shoots at the birds. Beyond him a scribe writes down the names of four kneeling men. In the lower zone on the right the principal chariot of a procession is preceded by two men on foot carrying batons, two horsemen carrying banners, and two other chariots.*

Technically, these bronzes illustrate a pinnacle in bronze-working. The casting, by the cire-perdue process, shows a perfection of skill not only in molding and casting tiny details so that very little if any finishing was necessary, but in the ability to cast a piece with handles and even with the base in one piece — a skill not surpassed by modern mechanical methods. One element of charm in these bronzes today is accidental, for the beautiful blue, green, and iridescent color was not intentional on the part of the artist but is due to the patina subsequently accreted.[1]

[1] A patina is a crust that forms on a bronze (as on some other materials) during a long period of time because of the chemical action of the alloys that compose the bronze, and the atmosphere or material in which the article is buried. It may be thin or thick, rough or smooth, and variously colored.

ARCHITECTURE

Chinese architecture in its uniformity through the ages well illustrates the conservatism of the race. When once the Chinese had evolved a type of building elastic enough to fulfill various functions, he saw no reason for changing what had become a satisfactory tradition. This uniformity is a matter both of material and of design. For some inexplicable reason the Chinese has used timber as his chief building material, despite a plentiful supply of stone and of clay for brick. The harder materials were used only for substructures, for bridges and military defenses, and for the tiles which served universally as roofing. Such a heavy roof resting upon wooden supports made none too stable a building, one that was subject to col-

[A]   *Temple of Heaven. Peiping. 18th cent.*

lapse from earthquake or fire. So it is that no buildings from any period before the T'ang have survived; our knowledge of ancient Chinese architecture is garnered from descriptions in Chinese literature and from recent buildings which appear to continue the old traditions comparatively faithfully.

The type seems to have been set as early as the Chou period, and we read of Han palaces huge enough to accommodate thousands of people and resplendent with bronze columns, mural paintings, silk hangings, fine rugs, and lacquer work. The most striking feature of the design as it is used in recent buildings is the broadly projecting curved roof,[1] whose expanse, conspicuous because the entrance is on the long side, repeats the broad earth to which the building clings. Sometimes this roof is single; frequently it is double — that is, on two levels, the

upper level supported by interior columns not visible from the outside. The construction consists of columns, tie beams, and brackets, and an open timber roof covered with tiles laid in beds of mortar. The walls are not functional as supports, but merely fill in the space between the columns. Horizontality is the dominant note in the design, and any extensions consist of horizontal projections.

Ornament and color are especially stressed and are of great splendor. The approaches and the balustrades of the terrace are elaborately carved. The roof tiles of royal buildings are yellow, the imperial color in China. On other buildings the tiles are sometimes blue or green; and the choice, determined by strict laws, is indicative of the rank of the owner and symbolic in meaning. The ridgepoles are decorated with dragons, phoenixes, and grotesques, as if to break the long lines as well as to ward off evil spirits. The columns, the beams, and the undersides of the projecting roofs and the interior are elaborately

---

[1] The origin of the curved roof, often with upturned corners, is a moot question. Of many explanations suggested, none is satisfactory.

[A]   *Pagodas. Near Peiping.*

ornamented with gold and vermilion, carvings, lacquer, and inlay.

The *Temple of Heaven* (Fig. 213A) well illustrates symbolism in Chinese architecture. Its Chinese name means "Temple of Prayer for the Year," for here each spring the emperor went to offer sacrifices and prayer for a propitious year, not only to heaven but to the imperial forefathers, to sun, moon, and stars, and to the spirits of nature in winds, clouds, and rain. Here again color and form are determined by symbolism. As blue is the color of heaven, so the tiles of the temple are a deep cobalt. And during the ceremonies of the spring sacrifice blue dominates the interior, for the ceremonial vessels are of blue porcelain, the worshipers are

clad in blue; a blue tone is cast over everything by the Venetian blinds made of blue glass which cover all the doors and windows. Likewise, the unusual circular shape of the temple is symbolic of the spherical appearance of the heavens. The temple is an imposing structure, its triple roof with gilded ball pointing with assurance toward the heavens. This impressiveness is increased particularly by the location of the building; for it stands upon an elevation, surrounded by encircling marble terraces, and approached by broad stairways set at the cardinal points of the compass, which have ornamental balustrades.

A characteristic feature of Chinese landscape is the Buddhist pagoda, which originated in the umbrella, that symbol of royalty in India which usually terminated the stupa, often in a multiple form (Fig. 198A). Some of these pagodas are of a vigorous, massive type, with as many as thirteen stories. Others are more slender (Fig. 214A), with elegance of proportion, interesting variety in the shape of the stories, and elaborate ornamentation. One of the famous "porcelain"[1] pagodas is faced with glazed tiles in five colors — deep purplish-blue, rich green, yellow, red, and turquoise-blue — so that the effect as it stands in an open place surrounded with greenery is most charming.

The function of the pagoda is not clear, though it often formed a part of a temple group. But it is always so placed that it stands out prominently against the surrounding landscape. It has been compared to the Gothic spire. "Perhaps after all," says Mr. Silcock, "there is something in the notion that in periods of religious fervor the soul of

---

[1] "Porcelain" is a misnomer. These pagodas are faced with glazed tile, a method of ornamentation carried out effectively in Babylonia-Assyria; and it is quite probable that the Chinese of the Han dynasty, as they pushed their boundaries westward, learned of its use from these Western peoples.

man expresses aspiration by building towers pointing to the skies, whether he is a follower of Christ or Buddha"[1] — or indeed a worshiper of Quetzalcoatl, for whose worship the Maya placed his temples upon lofty pyramidal bases.

Another characteristic architectural form in China is the gateway, the *pailou* made of wood with tile roofs, or of stone imitating the wooden structure. These gateways appear to be derived from the gates of the stupas in India, but the silhouette of the upper part has been determined by the typical curved line of Chinese roof. Unlike the Indian stupa gate, these arches are not necessarily entrances but are often independent structures, erected as memorials to distinguished Chinese, both dead and living, and may be compared with the triumphal arches of Rome, which were erected for the same purpose.

SCULPTURE

Sculpture in ancient China before the advent of Buddhism seems to have functioned to serve the dead. There were tomb figurines of clay gaily painted — spontaneous and freely characteristic representations of people and animals. Stone sculpture decorated the tomb, the pillars that formed a gateway to the path leading to it, and the stone slabs set up along the walls of the anteroom of the burial chamber. At royal and princely tombs, massive stone lions or chimeral figures stood guard. In addition to the spirited figurines, the highly decorative Han reliefs are notable. Because of their strongly lineal character, they seem less like reliefs and more like drawings or engravings, with the background slightly cut back. The procession of mounted riders and carriages, which may represent the journey of the

[1] *Introduction to Chinese Art and History*, London, 1936, p. 124.

[A] *Buddhist Votive Stele. Erected in* A.D. *554, "as a means of securing the happiness and welfare of the donors, their ancestors, their posterity, their relations, and friends, the Emperor in particular and the Chinese people in general." H. c. 7 ft. Museum of Fine Arts, Boston. (Boston Museum) Note the two types of relief: flat with incised lines in the two lower zones and high relief modeling in the upper zones.*

[A]   *Maitreya. Limestone. H. 6½ ft. Northern Wei Dynasty. Early 5th cent.* A.D. *Museum of Fine Arts, Boston.* (*Boston Museum*)

[B]   *Kuan-yin. T'ang Dynasty. Memorial Art Gallery, Rochester, New York.* (*Memorial Art Gallery*)

dead to the spirit world, is filled with a vivacious pattern and swift linear rhythms (Fig. 212A). The curves of the wheels and the bodies of the horses are brought into sharp interplay with the angles and diagonals of the horses' legs; the vertical-horizontal arrangement of the umbrellas adds a quieting note. Among the guardian winged lions and chimeras, Figure 217A, with its full rounding forms, striding pose, strong curve of the head, open mouth, and long tongue, is equally imposing as related, rounded masses of

ponderous stone and as an expression of power and energy.

The influence exerted by Buddhism upon sculpture was a fusing of the new ideas with the traditional native art, creating a product that was inherently Chinese. The preliminary stages are seen in colossal figures of Buddha and the Bodhisattvas carved in the caves along the routes over which Buddhists worked their way eastward. Associated with these purely Buddhist themes are non-Hindu details, ornaments, and

[A]   *Winged Lion. From the Tomb of Hsiao Hsiu, near Nanking.* A.D. *518.* (*Segalen, Mission Archéologique*)

themes. The fusion of these styles appears in a richly decorative votive stele of the Wei dynasty (Fig. 215A). Above the inscriptions that make a broad, firm base are four seals forming a square that is surmounted by a reliquary; four donors with their horses; worshipers; and lions. In the middle zone Buddha, with the uplifted hand symbolic of his teaching, is seated in a canopied niche with two disciples, Bodhisattvas, and guardians. The upper zone contains Buddhas and Bodhisattvas under a canopy, and scenes connected with the life of Buddha. The figures of the donors and the reliquary in the two lower zones are incised and the ground is cut back for contrast, the traditional Han style of decoration. The Buddhist subjects in the middle and upper zones are carved in high relief, modeled; they show strong Indian influence.

A single figure of the Wei dynasty which expresses the Hindu theme in a style strongly Chinese is a *Maitreya* (Fig. 216A), the Bodhisattva who is destined to become the next Buddha. He is seated in an austerely frontal pose with legs crossed and hand uplifted in the traditional Indian pose of the teacher. The features are conventionally treated with planes sharply cut. Except for the head and the arms, the figure is so flat that it gives one more the impression of relief than of the round. The drapery, plaited and girdled high, and the streamers of the cloak that cross in front in an almost geometrical pattern, fall over the pedestal in a conventional way, with feeling for sweeping, rhythmic pattern. Here is an archaic art which by the use of symbols and conventions, with no attempt to create an illusion of natural appearance, makes all the more emphatic the spiritual fervor of the conception.

The evolution of these archaic forms into a classic climax took place in early T'ang. But even though the forms became full and rounding and the decorative details richly elegant, and though the poses relaxed from austere frontality into elegant and dignified grace (Fig. 216B), the sculptors never surrendered their traditional ideal of conventions and abstract form to an attempt to copy nature. The cutting of the stone is expert, though it may lack the energy of

[A]   *Ku K'ai-chih. Lady Feng and the Bear. Detail of the Admonitions of the Instructress.*
Probably a T'ang copy. Late 4th or early 5th cent. A.D. *British Museum, London. (British*
Museum) The seal impressions were added by later connoisseurs (see note 2, p. 219).

the crisp carving of Wei art; the folds tend toward naturalism, and although they still form a rhythmic pattern, it is a pattern that is not so tingling with life and meaning as in Wei.

CALLIGRAPHY AND PAINTING

The Chinese early began to develop one of his greatest expressions: calligraphy, poetry, and painting. We say "one" of his expressions, because the three are inextricably connected. Chinese writing evolved from pictographs; that is, it presented an image of the idea directly to the eye, in contrast with most systems of writing, which are based on sounds that are symbols of the idea. In time, the pictographs became more conventionalized and highly complex, yet they never lost their pictographic character. The abstract form of the character and the quality of the strokes that make it are of great beauty in themselves; and when they are joined with a poetic idea the result is a combina-

tion of form and content which makes one realize why the Chinese consider calligraphy one of their finest arts.

The painter used the same materials as the calligrapher: Chinese ink and especially prepared silk or paper. The process of making the finest ink was a secret, often a carefully guarded heritage. The characters were made with a brush, not a pen, and required a skill attained only through long years of practice. The brush was not held as we hold a pen, but vertically in the hand; its movement was sometimes controlled by the wrist, as in executing a delicate detail, and sometimes by the whole arm from the shoulder, as in making a broad sweeping stroke. Whatever their character, one quality permeates the line of all fine writing and painting in China — a living force. Whether functioning as an edge, a contour, or calligraphically, line has a life of its own which makes the writing or the painting dynamic.

As the same materials, technique, and habits of mind control the work of the painter and the writer, we may expect to find in painting the same simplification, suggestion, and abstraction as in poetry. Of the poet-painter Wang Wei a Chinese writer said: "I can taste in the poem something of the picture's flavor; and in the picture I see something of the poem."[1]

The chief forms of Chinese painting are frescoes, hanging scrolls (*kakemonos*), long scrolls (*makimonos*), and album leaves. The frescoes, which formed great series of wall decoration, majestic and hieratic like the *Ajanta Frescoes* and the early Christian mosaics, have disappeared from China proper, and we can judge of them only through the wall paintings of Turkestan and Japan, which reflect something of their nature.

One important difference between Eastern and Western painting lies in the method of exhibiting it. The framed picture, with which we are so familiar, is practically unknown in the Orient. The Chinese panel or scroll was not kept on view continuously, but formed a part of the family treasure, to be exhibited for a short time in a place of honor, or to be brought out for a brief period of enjoyment or for some connoisseur to examine and to affix his seal.[2] It was then rolled up and returned to a place of safety.

Of early Chinese painting only a few fragments remain. Something of its nature we learn from a makimono in the British Museum attributed to Ku K'ai-chih (c. A.D. 400),[3] whom the Chinese writers consider one of their great painters. The subject of the scroll was

[1] Arthur Waley, *An Introduction to the Study of Chinese Painting*, London, 1923, p. 144.
[2] There are seals of about fifty former owners or famous connoisseurs, for example, on the scroll in the British Museum attributed to Ku K'ai-chih.
[3] For interesting stories of this painter see H. A. Giles, *An Introduction to the History of Chinese Pictorial Art*, 2d ed. rev., London, 1918, p. 18; and Arthur Waley, *op. cit.*, p. 45.

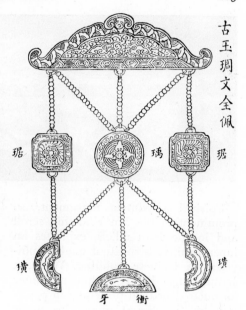

[A]   *Complete Jade Girdle Pendant. (Laufer)*

taken from a Chinese writer, who explains the principles that an instructress in the royal palace would teach to the princesses under her care. The detail reproduced in Figure 218A represents the lady Feng interposing herself between the Emperor and a bear that had broken loose from the circus ring. At the right sits the emperor, perfectly calm, surrounded by his courtiers; at the left two men are attacking the bear, in front of which the lady Feng stands fearlessly, her lithe figure, with its draperies billowing about her feet, an epitome of courageous self-sacrifice. The secular subject is interesting, but perhaps the most striking characteristic is the great amount of expression created almost alone by line. The line is delicate but firm and is used to model the figures and at the same time calligraphically, as in the draperies, to create pattern and movement. Light washes of color laid on flat within the contours create a pattern of light and dark to differentiate the areas.

[A] *Burial Girdle Ornament. Brown jade. L. 6 in. Han Dynasty. Chicago Natural History Museum. (Chicago Natural History Museum)*

Spirited rhythmic movement, so prominent in the Ku K'ai-chih scroll and in the Han reliefs, expresses an inner vitality, a spiritual quality, universal in Chinese painting. When, a century after Ku K'ai-chih, a painter formulated critical principles in painting in the Six Canons, he made "Rhythmic Vitality" the first canon.[1]

An accomplished school of painting, then, had developed in China before the coming of Buddhism. The earliest evidences of the infiltration of the new faith we see in the paintings of *Paradise* from the monastery caves of Turkestan. These paintings represent the paradise where Amida Buddha lived in gorgeous surroundings, attended by Bodhisattvas and believers.[2] Paradise and its pleasures were pictured in terms of an earthly court of great splendor and joy. Yet a lofty mood permeates all the figures, a mood of spiritual attainment and peace.

It was in the T'ang dynasty that there

came about an amalgamation of the powerful native Chinese tradition and the energizing spirit of Buddhism, for Buddhism had brought to China a new conception of deity. Buddha in his contemplative aspect, with his conquest over self and his universal love and pity for suffering mankind as expressed in the Bodhisattva Kuan-yin, was particularly appealing, and inspired an art concerned not with the visual facts of natural appearance but with those highly simplified, essential aspects of form that could express an inner life of calm intensity.

Greatest of the T'ang painters, the Chinese tell us, was Wu Tao-tzu (born about A.D. 700), and his greatest paintings were the series of frescoes in the Buddhist temples, destroyed in the revolution that ended the T'ang dynasty. Many are the stories told of him.[3] What stands out clearly in these tales is the great vitality of Wu's art. His brush strokes were so intense that they gave a sense not of realism, but of a reality so powerful that it far surpassed any visual copy.

Another aspect of Buddhism that influenced Chinese painting profoundly was its attitude toward nature. We saw in India how Buddhism recognized all life as a unit. Some of the poets and philosophers of South China had al-

[1] See Laurence Binyon, *The Flight of the Dragon*, Dutton, 1922, for the Six Canons.

[2] Amida, or Amitabha, Buddha means "Buddha of Boundless Light." This worship may have originated among the sun worshipers of Parthia, for Buddhism, as it penetrated northwestern India, there received some Greek and Iranian influences (see pages 198, 201), which it carried along into Turkestan. In Turkestan we see a mixed culture: Manichaeans, Buddhists, and Christians lived together peaceably. Yet Buddhism was the dominating element.

[3] See Giles, *op. cit.*, pp. 47 ff.; and Waley, *op. cit.*, pp. 112 ff.

[A] *Chimera. Brownish-green jade. L. 6¾ in. Han Dynasty. This monster, called p'i-sieh ("warding off evil influences"), was buried in the grave to dispel demons and protect its master from evil. Chicago Natural History Museum. (Chicago Natural History Museum)*

ready realized something of this kinship with nature, and their spirit, intensely augmented by the powerful Buddhist belief in the universal brotherhood of all forms of life, laid the foundation of those schools of landscape-painting which culminated in the Sung period in one of the great accomplishments of Chinese art.

JADES

Jade-carving is a very old art in China and may possibly be traced to the work of the lapidary in Babylonia. Jade is a relatively rare, tough, hard stone, usually greenish in color. It was obtained by the Chinese from the mountains of West China and from the rivers that had their rise near the quarries and washed the jade pebbles and boulders for some distance down their courses. In early days, particularly fine boulders were kept in the temples as precious relics, and some of these were carved in the eighteenth century into bells, vases, and bowls. Because of the numerous unusual qualities of jade, its appeals are many. Its reserved color, like diluted emerald, and its soft, waxy luster,

at times slightly translucent, appeal to the eye; and its resonancy when it is struck, to the ear, thus making it valued for musical instruments. But the quality which the Chinese prize most highly is its texture, a highly pleasurable waxy texture which they liken to mutton fat. Because of its toughness, jade-carving requires great technical skill. This was especially true for the Chinese, who was equipped with only a few simple tools — saws for cutting and shaping; iron disks and drills, worked by treadles, for carving; and for polishing, several kinds of abrasives, such as quartz, garnet, emery, and, hardest of all, ruby dust. These abrasives were applied with wood, leather, or gourd skin, because the entire surface, even in the deepest crevices, must be free from all irregularities and from all tool marks.

The uses of jade were varied. Sometimes unadorned boulders were prized for themselves, almost reverentially; more often they were fashioned into articles of personal adornment or into vases, cups, bowls, or various charms and symbolic figures. For the early jades, like the bronzes, were influenced by religious and emotional symbolism. This is seen in the personal ornaments, perhaps the most interesting of which are the girdle pendants (Fig. 219A). Seven pieces of jade formed this pendant, which tinkled as the bearer walked. Each was a token of love and friendship, as an old song says: "Who will give me a quince, I shall return to him a central side-ornament of fine jade for the girdle-pendant. It is not meant as an act of thanks, but I want to render our friendship everlasting. Who will give me a peach, I shall return to him the red jade *yao* . . ." (with the same refrain).[1] Such ornaments were sometimes buried with the dead, as emblems of the parting caused by death and also of an eternal love. Such a burial-girdle ornament is seen in Figure 220A. On the right is a phoenix on a cloud form, looking down toward the long slender hydra, with a bird's head, on the lower left side; above, along the upper edge, are cloud bands carved in long firm curves. To the eye the pendant presents a design of curves, repeated and opposed, built into the elliptical shape, with a pleasing angularity in the hatchings on the wings of the phoenix. Part of the design is in relief, part incised, and it is so strong and so lucid that one can follow it as easily with one's fingers as with one's eyes. This is true also of the monster of Figure 221A. What a pleasing alternation here between the smooth and broken surfaces and in the repetition of the large spirals of the haunches in the smaller spirals of the hair!

The symbolic and ritualistic jades from the Shang and Chou periods — rings, disks, axes, knives, etc. — approach pure geometry in the abstract simplicity of their shapes. They are often subtly modeled and always highly polished.

[1] Berthold Laufer, *Jade*, Chicago Natural History Museum, 1912, p. 198, by permission of the publishers.

SUMMARY

The arts cf China were the arts of a sober, patient, conservative people whose law was the custom of their ancestors. Art and education therefore looked to the past. Training consisted in copying the masters. The attitude of the Chinese on the matter of copying Dr. Laufer explains thus: "Where and what is the original, after all? Of these Chinese copies and copies of copies, the word of Holmes (*The Autocrat of the Breakfast Table*) holds good: 'A thought is often original though you have uttered it a hundred times.' . . . As everything Chinese is pervaded by an atmosphere different from our own, so also a Chinese copyist is framed of a different mould; his work is creative invention, not purely receptive, but partaking of the spirit permeating the soul of the master."[2]

The Chinese people early developed native arts of power and skill, notably their hieratic bronzes, and also their sculpture and painting. When Buddhism, coming from India, became a stimulating factor, it brought sculpture and painting to a lofty attainment. Sculpture in the Wei period was conventional and austere, but compelling in its spiritual significance; in the T'ang period, though it became more naturalistic, it still retained a conventional treatment. Painting and calligraphy, inseparable arts, early showed sureness of hand and spirited movement in the use of Chinese ink, and during the T'ang dynasty reached a mastery that was used to express surcharged reality — reality based not upon visual perception but upon a vital inner meaning objectified in a distinctively linear style by traditionally accepted conventions.

See the Bibliography on page 385.

[2] Laufer, *op. cit.*, p. 326, by permission of the Chicago Natural History Museum.

[A] *Horyuji. Near Nara.* A.D. *586–607. In the center is the kondo containing the shrine and behind it the pagoda. At the right is the entrance, and at the left the preaching hall.*

10

JAPANESE ART

(A.D. 552–900)

THE origin of the race of Yamato (the native name of Japan) is problematical. As far back as we can trace the Japanese, they are an energetic, warlike people, yet "gentle in the arts of peace"; possessed of a primitive religion, known as Shinto, which included the worship of the powers of nature, especially the sun goddess, and of ancestors.

Their country is one of great natural beauty. "The waters of the waving rice-fields, the variegated contour of the archipelago, so conducive to individuality, the constant play of its soft-tinted seasons, the shimmer of its silver air, the verdure of its cascaded hills, and the voice of the ocean echoing about its pine-girt shores — of all these was born that tender simplicity, that romantic purity, which so tempers the soul of Japanese art, differentiating it at once from the leaning to monotonous breadth of the Chinese and from the tendency to overburdened richness of Indian art. That innate love of cleanness which, though sometimes detrimental to grandeur, gives its exquisite finish to our industrial and decorative art, is probably nowhere to be found in Continental work."[1]

But profound as were the influences of the varied topography of the land, the chief energizing power in Japanese culture came from Buddhism. The impulse of Buddhism had already flooded and transformed Chinese thought, and then in the sixth century, under a Chinese rather than an Indian mode of expression, passed on with undiminished power of stimulation to Japan. With the religion came echoes of the art of India, and not only a strong influence but at first a close imitation of Chinese art by way of Korea. Korean artists came to Japan to execute works.

The story of Japanese art is a story of successive waves of influence from China, followed by periods of retirement. At no time, however, has Japan been a mere imitator. Just as China assimilated and molded to its own mode of thought and expression the ideas of India, so the native culture of Yamato, though a heavy debtor to both India and China, still is an individual product.

Buddhism first came in the Suiko period[2] from China of the Six Dynasties, especially the Wei, and manifested itself as something spiritual and mysterious, conceived in terms of abstract form. The second wave came from T'ang China, bringing with it a spirit of grandeur and exaltation that we discern in majestic, contemplative Buddhas and gracious and all-merciful Bodhisattvas.

ARCHITECTURE
AND SCULPTURE

Love of nature, and love and understanding of wood, nature's chief material in this land, are fundamental in the building art in Japan. Very little stone is to be found, but an abundance of timber. To make a building harmonious with nature and to construct it of the materials at hand constituted the builder's problem, whether the structure was a temple or a home.

Though Shinto temples are to be found in Japan,[3] the Buddhist temple and monastery are the highest expression of Japanese religious architecture. Many monasteries were built under the patronage of the court, and one of these, *Horyuji* (near Nara, the capital and center of Buddhist faith and learning) in its buildings, paintings, carvings, and equipment is an epitome of early Buddhist art (Fig. 223A). Here vermilion buildings rising from a white sanded ground are set in a spacious walled area in the midst of a mountainous, heavily wooded landscape. They are grouped along an axis leading from the gate to the preaching hall; the kondo or golden hall, containing the chief shrine, and the pagoda stand in balanced position on each side of the axis; and the entire group is surrounded by a walled corridor. Outside this wall are grouped subsidiary structures, such as administrative buildings, treasure houses, and cloisters, for the monastery served several purposes. Like the medieval monastery of Europe, it was a temple, a charitable institution, a hospital, and a center of learning where philosophy and music were taught as well as religious subjects.

The general style shows its Chinese

---

[1] Kakuzo Okakura, *The Ideals of the East*, 1920, p. 16, by permission of E. P. Dutton & Company.
[2] The chief periods of early Japanese art are: Suiko, A.D. 552–645; Hakuho, 645–709; Tempyo, 709–793; Jogan, 793–900.

[3] Notably the *Temple of Isé*, the sun goddess, in central Japan, which has been replaced every twenty years by an exact copy and hence, though built entirely of wood, preserves in excellent condition the original form.

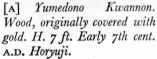

[A] *Yumedono Kwannon.*
Wood, originally covered with
gold. H. 7 ft. Early 7th cent.
A.D. *Horyuji.*

[B] *Maitreya. Wood. Suiko. Chuguji Nunnery, Nara.*
(Figs. 225A and B reprinted by permission of the Cleveland
Museum of Art from Japanese Sculpture of the Suiko
Period *by Langdon Warner, Yale University Press)*

origin. There is the same massiveness, especially in the dominating roofs, the same somber dignity despite the brilliant color. Yet one feels here, especially in the pagoda, a more subtle feeling for proportion and a delicacy in the sweeping curves of the eaves that indicate the Japanese influence. The details and the restrained decoration are refined, with careful spacing and proportioning of the members and an entasis in the columns. The construction is essentially of wood. Wooden columns from two to three feet in diameter support heavy beams, the angle of joining being filled with a simple bracket. On these rests the open timber roof covered with tiles. The wall space is filled partly by plaster and partly by sliding screens. Such a structure is not only suitable to the climate of Japan but is loosely yet firmly enough constructed to withstand the frequent earthquakes to which the country is subject.

The interior is splendid. On a platform is a gilded statue of the Buddha with attendant Bodhisattvas, above which hangs an elaborate canopy with angels carrying musical instruments. The timbers are decorated with vermilion, blue, and green, and with gilding and lacquer; the walls are covered with frescoes representing the paradise of Amida Buddha. The rich color harmony adds to the mystic calm of the Buddha, so that the whole effect sug-

[A] *Kwannon. Bronze. H. 8½ ft. Hakuho period. Yakushiji.*

gests a plastic representation of the paradise seen in the T'ang paintings.

The cult statues and the decorative figures of the shrine are chiefly of wood or bronze, as the scarcity of stone in Japan militated against its use as a medium for sculpture. The abundant timber of the country furnished several native woods suitable for carving, notably cypress and camphor wood. Many of the statues were originally covered with gold foil or painted, and thus harmonized with the colorful interior.

Sculpture, like architecture, had its rise in the coming of Buddhism from China by way of Korea, and its highest expressions were created under the stimulus of that faith. Thus its subject matter, objectives, and forms were similar to those of Chinese sculpture. A popular subject was the Bodhisattva Kwannon, the Japanese equivalent of the Kuanyin of China and the Avalokiteshvara of India. The *Yumedono Kwannon* (Fig. 225A)[1] is a tall, slender figure, which seen from the side is thin and flat, producing an effect of noncorporeality. The figure is clad in a long garment with conventional folds and ribbons hanging in loops from the arms. A lofty delicate crown of copper rests on the head, behind which rises a lotus-leaf halo decorated with flamelike motifs that swirl up to the apex, their movement and rough texture acting as a foil to the quiet surfaces and long unbroken lines in the figure. The features are carved crisply on the oval face, conventionally, as in all archaic art. The folds of the drapery, sweeping outward in long unbroken curves, form a broad base, and by terminating in a wavelike motif create a pattern of contrasting unbroken and broken lines, of slow and rapid movement. The aim of the sculptor has been an impersonal objectification of dignity and beneficence by means of a symmetrical organization of conventional motifs, many of which are symbolic — for example, the lotus pedestal, the position of the hands and the attributes, and particularly the large prominent halo so characteristic of Japanese Buddhist sculpture because of the special emphasis in Japan upon the light that radiated from the Buddha (an emphasis seen in the popularity of the *Amida Buddha*). Thus the placid rhythms in the figure move upward — in an

[1] The *Yumedono*, or *Hall of Dreams*, is a sanctuary at *Horyuji* where Prince Shotoku, founder of the monastery, practiced Buddhistic meditation. The statue has been held in great veneration in Japan even up to the present time.

[A] *Amida Trinity of Tachibana Fujin. Bronze. Early 8th cent. A.D. Horyuji. Named for the original owner, Tachibana Fujin (died A.D. 733), mother of Komyo Kogo, Empress of Shomu Tenno.*

accelerated tempo, a rapid crescendo that is symbolic as well as esthetic — to the tiny stupa at the apex, symbol of the Buddha.

The trend of Japanese sculpture was in the direction of naturalism, toward an approximation of visual perception. But in the Bodhisattvas of the Suiko age one does not think of the human form first. Most appealing is a mysterious, ethereal quality, suggesting perfect poise and gracious beneficence. Though the figure acquired solidity and its propor-

tions became more naturalistic, with details partly conventional and partly naturalistic, these changes were not made at the expense of the dominant theme. As in the art of India and China, the pre-eminence of the theme is inescapable. The theme may be abstract and expressed in an abstract form. But form for its own sake lies outside the Oriental's conceptions of art.

A seated *Maitreya*, for example (Fig. 225B), is an expression of inner peace, the consciousness of self-conquest, com-

bined with great tenderness. The Bodhisattva is seated upon a high lotus
pedestal; the left foot rests on a lotus,
the right is crossed over the knee and
lightly held by the hand; the chin rests
meditatively upon the uplifted right
hand. The figure has solidity and natural
proportions, modified by such conventional requirements as broad shoulders,
narrow waist, smooth round limbs
— all reminiscent of the Gupta statues
of India. The drapery is undercut rather
than engraved, as it is in the *Yumedono
Kwannon*. The whole figure is based
upon the interplay of cylinders: the
large cylinder of the base and the seat,
smaller cylinders in the torso and the
limbs. Note the vertical unity of the
left arm and leg at right angles with
the horizontal leg. This quiet balance
is opposed by the angularity and the
diagonal line of the left arm and of the
upper part of the drapery: the rest of
the folds fall in quiet vertical lines.
These relationships of volume and line
contribute to the calm, the tenderness,
and the vitality of the representation.
The statue is carved from one piece of
wood and shows traces of gold.

This Suiko sculpture derived from
that of the Wei dynasty and the Six
Dynasties of China. In the Hakuho and
Tempyo periods (also together known
as the Nara period), another wave of
influence appeared from T'ang China,
a Buddhistic art centering about Amida
Buddha. In the cult statues Buddha was
usually represented as seated upon the
lotus in the posture of meditation or
with one hand uplifted signifying his
preaching, and accompanied by standing Bodhisattvas. Behind the figures rise
the elaborate lofty halos shaped like
leaves of the bodhi tree[1] and decorated
with flame motifs and small seated Buddhas. Aims and conventions are dis-

[1] The tree under which Gautama sat when
he attained enlightenment; hence it was called
the tree of enlightenment (bodhi).

cernible here similar to those in early
T'ang — the same elaborations of costume, jewelry, and ribbons. The design
(Fig. 226A) is eminently suited to bronze,
and the sharp contours and linear
rhythms enabled the sculptor to tie the
figure, the great halo, and the finely
designed pedestal into an extraordinary
unity. There is a slight sway to the
figure, and there is vigor in the crisp
curves of ribbon, folds, and features,
with a contrasting delicacy of texture
in the necklace.

Most of the great *Trinity* groups are
of bronze and reveal the masterly skill
of the Japanese founders. An outstanding example is a small shrine (Fig. 227A)
in which the base represents the surface
of a lotus pool from which rise on curving stems three lotus flowers as pedestals
for the Buddha and two attendants, all
with the hands lifted in the "fear-not"
mudra. Behind the figures is a screen
with figures in relief and the halo for
the Buddha. Rotund forms and suavely
flowing lines dominate. The figure of
the Buddha, although in frontal position, is an outstanding example of
rounding masses and flowing surfaces
accented by crisp curving lines. On the
screen behind the figures are angels on
inverted lotuses, with ribbons floating
above them as if they had just alighted;
the intervening space is filled with lotus
flowers and stems in very low relief,
which produces a gentle movement over
the surface. In contrast to this easy flow
is the virile pattern of the halo, which
consists of a central lotus motif framing
the head of the Buddha, surrounded by
an open border of radiating lines and
an outer border with a floral design;
along the rim are flames which rise to
a point directly above the head of the
Buddha and symbolize man's aspiration from the lower life to the higher.
The rapid movement in the screen enhances the more placid rhythms of the
central figure.

PAINTING

Like architecture and sculpture, much of the painting of Japan shows a direct influence from China. Buddhism furnished the stimulation for the earliest paintings now known, the frescoes in the *Kondo of Horyuji*, which are as typically early T'ang as the building itself and thus, like the latter, strongly Hindu. In theme, execution, scale, and composition they appear to be closely related to the *Ajanta Frescoes*. A popular subject was one of those celestial scenes in which Amida Buddha is seated upon a lotus, wrapped in meditation and surrounded by saints, deities, and disciples representative of the "vast community" of the Buddhist faith. There is the same stateliness and tenderness, the same vitality born of religious conviction, the same dynamic line, as in the *Ajanta Frescoes*.

SUMMARY

Japanese art, though derivative from Indian Buddhist forms through recurring waves of Chinese influence, infused into the derived forms a flavor of its own. Japanese Buddhist architecture was close to that of China in material, construction, and form. But it showed subtler feelings for proportion, for quality of roof curves, and for decoration.

Early Buddhist sculpture, based on Chinese Wei and T'ang styles, expressed, by means of symbolism and archaic conventions, an intense fervor, tranquillity, and otherworldliness, a clarity of formal relationships, and a command of materials — wood and bronze.

Contributing rich color to the splendor of temple interiors, painting consisted largely of Buddhist frescoes much in the style of the *Atjana Frescoes*.

See the Bibliography on page 397.

American Art

11

MIDDLE AMERICAN ART

WHILE the early cultures of India and China were slowly evolving from the Neolithic stage, the same process was going on in the Americas. The outlines of development are equally dim. What is clear is that about the close of the last glacial age (from 25,000 to 10,000 B.C.) there began a long-continued series of migrations from Asia by way of the Aleutians (then probably a land passage) and Alaska. The migrants were Mongoloid nomads of the Stone Age, with no knowledge of agriculture but possibly some of basketry. Over the centuries they spread out, partly because of pressure from oncoming immigrants and partly because of the more favorable climate and living-conditions farther south, until they occupied the two continents. So widely and sparsely were they scattered over these great areas that, because of the differences of geography and climate and of lack of contact, there evolved from the same stem a great diversity of cultures. At some time (possibly about 3,000 B.C.) and at some place (some say on the Mexican highlands; others, on the Andean) some of these nomads learned to cultivate wild grasses and thus began the maize culture which is basic in aboriginal America. As agriculturalists

they became a settled people, learned to make pottery and figurines of clay with a lively realism, and probably textiles. On this base, which is known as the Archaic Cultures, there arose through long periods of time a large number of cultures, several of which reached a high level of attainment by the early centuries of the Christian era.[1] These are the Mayan and Toltec cultures in Middle America, the Chimu, Nazca, and Tiahuanaco cultures in South America.

Mayan Art of the First Empire

IN Middle America the (term frequently used by archaeologists to designate what is now Mexico and Central America) we find a great variety of geographical and climatic conditions. The country lies in the belt of dry and rainy seasons. Great reaches of arid plateau land, fertile for raising maize and wheat wherever water can be secured, rise to heavily forested mountain

[1] American chronology is in its infancy, and authorities differ widely. Hence all dates are tentative.

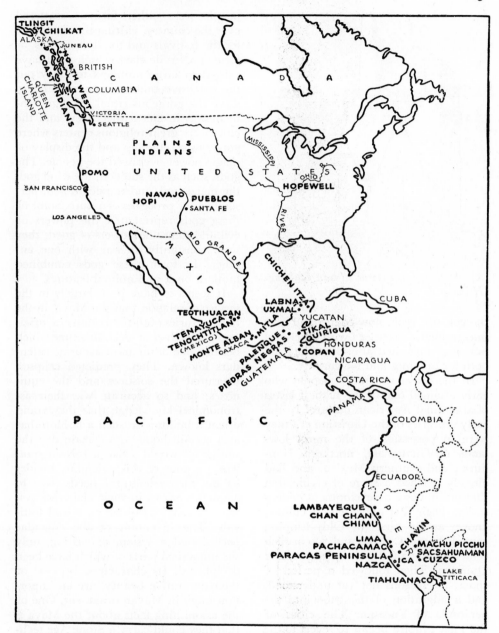

[A] *The Americas, Showing Important Centers of Aboriginal Art Activity.*

slopes and thence, at some places, to
perpetual snow; or they descend to the
moist tropical jungles of the coastal
plains, which are marvelously rich ag-

riculturally if man can only clear the
land and steadily pursue his battle
against the rank luxuriousness of nature. The country is a volcanic region;

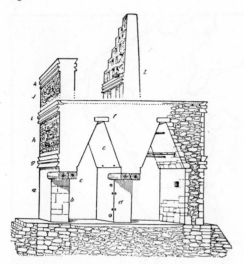

[A] *Section of a Typical Mayan Building.*
(*Holmes*)

the volcanic rock, now coarse and now fine-grained, together with plentiful limestone furnished abundant material both for building and for carving.

In the Maya we find a people who early attained one of the highest levels of aboriginal American culture. In the early centuries of the Christian era they were in possession of the moist lowlands of Guatemala, northern Honduras, and southern Mexico, and had already reached a stage of civilization that presupposes a development of centuries. Their first and greatest climax, known as the First (or Old) Empire, came between A.D. 450 and 700 at such centers as Copan, Tikal, Palenque, and Quirigua. Then followed a period of chaos, for reasons not yet understood, and a migration of the tribe into the peninsula of Yucatan. The cities of the First Empire began to revert to the jungle.

Though the Maya were an agricultural people, their activities were motivated by religious practices. Priests, astronomer-priests, and nobles comprised an upper class; the mass of the people were either farmers scattered over the country, visiting the cities only for the festivals and for the markets, or formed a servile class, which must have existed in large numbers to carry out the extensive building projects and to serve the gorgeous ritual. The government was in fact a theocracy, and the cities were great religious centers where gorgeous ceremonies and the display of magic power overawed the people. The gods, such as the sun god, the wind god, the maize god, and the death god, personified the processes of nature. Some of these gods represented the powers of evil and some the powers of good; they were constantly at war with one another. In form these gods combined human, bird, and animal features.

It seems to have been largely in the service of religion that the Maya, in the first centuries of the Christian era, originated a method of reckoning time which became one of the most accurate calendars known. They predicted eclipses, measured the solstices and the equinoxes; and so accurate was their astronomical knowledge that they could orient a building in such a fashion that at a certain hour on a certain day the sun's rays would strike a certain spot. The purpose of this calendar, besides its use for agricultural needs, was to assist the priests in their elaborate systems of religious observance and festivals. The invention of the calendar necessitated a system of writing, only the numerical parts of which have been deciphered. Its characters, because of their decorative beauty, are an important motif in Mayan ornament. One of the astonishing facts about the Maya is that they could carry a Stone Age technique to such levels. Copper was so rare that metal tools, if they existed at all, were negligible. Only stone tools, the hardest made of obsidian or flint, were used for the expert and intricate stone-carving.

[A] *Temple of the Cross. Palenque. Dedicated* A.D. *692. From a model in the Brooklyn Museum, Brooklyn, N.Y.* (*Brooklyn Museum*)

ARCHITECTURE
AND SCULPTURE

In a theocratic culture, temple-building is destined to be paramount. So it was with the Maya, though there remain so-called palaces, which seem to have been used for habitation, perhaps by the priests or the nobles. As for the people, their houses were thatched huts. An abundance of excellent building material favored the Maya. They had quarries of evenly grained limestone; plenty of weathered stone suitable for making cement and concrete; and huge forests to furnish timber and firewood for the preparation of lime.

The most characteristic building was the pyramid temple (Figs. 233A, 411A), a temple standing upon a high pyram-

idal base and approached by a broad flight of steps. The base was a solid mass of concrete faced with stone; the thick walls were concrete faced with stone blocks smoothed on the outer face but left roughly pointed on the inner, to hold more tenaciously in the concrete. On the interior the courses projected inward, forming two corbeled arches that sprang from wooden lintels (Fig. 232A). Rooms so constructed could not be more than about twelve feet wide, but might be of unlimited length. Hence the temples consisted of one or two long, narrow compartments. Where there was one only, it served as the sanctuary; where there were two, the inner served this function and was sometimes divided into smaller units. In some buildings, above the flat roof rose a false

[A] *Young Maize God. From Copan.*
Rhyolite. H. 18 in. c. A.D. 515. Peabody
Museum, Harvard University, Cambridge.
(Peabody Museum)

front or a pierced roof crest for decoration. The construction of such a building — the quarrying of the stone, the
transporting and lifting of it to its
high position — represents a prodigious
amount of labor. The stone tools were
primitive, and there were no transportation facilities, not even beasts of burden.

A small temple at Palenque illustrates
the type (Fig. 233A). As the First Empire
cities were located in a moist, devastating
climate where the jungle encroaches
overnight, the buildings are in such ruin
that models serve best for an understanding of the temple. The base consisted of
a series of receding terraces, with a stairway leading to the temple itself. The
building was rectangular, with a roof
that sloped inward, and was surmounted

by an ornate roof comb. Elaborately
costumed figures in relief flanked the
doorway; carvings ornamented the sloping roof and the roof comb. Instead of
being carved in stone, these figures were
built up in stucco, the stone at Palenque
being too difficult to carve with stone
tools. The rough wall was covered with
plaster, in which small stones were set
to form a framework for the figure.
Holes were cut in the wall at intervals,
to give a firm hold for this stone skeleton. On this the plaster was molded;
and the final coat of fine stucco was
polished and painted so that the surface was brilliant and shining. Color,
undoubtedly determined by symbolic
as well as artistic criteria, was used
lavishly, so that the temple must have
produced a jewel-like effect against the
jungle green.

The temple did not stand alone, but
was one of a group of other temples and
palaces built about a court. For the
Maya appear always to have placed
and related their buildings in an orderly
system.

Wealth of ornament is already evident in the architecture of the First
Empire. Where suitable stone was available, as at Copan and Piedras Negras,
it was carved with exuberance and
vitality, but with a tendency to fill the
space to overflowing. This is seen in the
peculiarly Mayan stelae, commemorative or calendrical stone shafts, from
five to twenty-five feet high, erected in
the plazas. Most of them are crowded
with carvings — usually a figure in ceremonial dress, probably some important
personage, in high relief, surrounded by
hieroglyphs and other motifs in lower
relief. The reliefs cover the four sides
of the shaft. Sometimes each side is a
unit in itself; sometimes the carving is
continued from side to side — a device
facilitated by the fact that the corners
are rounded off. Curvature rather than
angularity is inherent in Mayan art.

The *Corn Stele* (Fig. 235A) is unusual in its restraint and feeling for space. Against an unbroken ground the imposing figure of the corn god stands out in clearly defined planes. With a bag in one hand, he kneels to sow the kernels with the other hand. Notice how a sweeping curve connects the two figures, and how the hieroglyphs are square with rounded corners — again evidence of the fluidity, devoid of sharp angles, in Mayan ornament.

In the *Dragon of Quirigua* (Fig. 237A) ornament reaches flamboyancy. The purpose of the huge boulder is unknown. It is entirely covered with intricate carvings in both high and low relief. The most conspicuous part of the design on the north face is the human figure, dressed in rich garments with an enormous elaborate headdress, and seated in the mouth of a great dragon. The placing of a human figure in the jaws of a reptile is quite common in Mayan art and undoubtedly had a symbolic meaning — possibly the endowment of the serpent with human intelligence, thus combining in the god the highest type of mind with any type of material body. The top of the altar (Fig. 236A) presents an intricate decorative design based upon a highly conventionalized form of the serpent, in which the virile lines that indicate the features stand out from the intricate decoration about them with dominating power.

Sculpture in the round is rare. It appears to have been used, together with high relief, to give emphasis to important points in the decorative scheme, as at *Uxmal*. Such may have been the use of the head, practically in the round, of the *Maize God* (Fig. 234A), carved from rhyolite, a hard, roughly cleaving volcanic stone. The quiet spiritual intensity is all the more profound because of the monumental simplicity of the form. The head is a sensitively proportioned oval volume whose contour is clearly defined

[A] *Corn Stele. From Piedras Negras. Limestone. H. 13 ft. 8th cent.* A.D. *University Museum, Philadelphia.* (*University Museum*)

[A] *Great Dragon or Turtle of Quirigua. Top view. W. 11½ ft. A.D. 795. (Courtesy of the Archaeological Institute of America)*

[B] *Mayan Vase. From Copan. Peabody Museum, Harvard University, Cambridge. (Peabody Museum)*

by the framing hair that sweeps back in repeated curves and falls down by the ear plugs. The delicate play of light and shadow afforded by the broad plane of the forehead and the softly blended features is accentuated by the deeply cut curves of the hair and the counter-curves of the lofty headdress. The eyes are downcast, owing to the fact that the head was meant to be seen from below.

This intensity of inner life combined with an imperturbable aspect is even more dynamically seen in a half-length figure of the *Maize God* (formerly known as *The Singing Girl*). The features are more sharply cut into a masklike pattern, especially the eyes and the mouth, and the hair is more brusquely treated in comparison with the suavely curving locks of the *Maize God* of Figure 234A. This treatment of the face, the pose of the body, and the vital intensity of the figure are strongly reminiscent of Far Eastern sculpture, such as the Chinese Kuan-yins and Japanese Kwannons.

[A] *Great Dragon or Turtle of Quirigua. Carved stone monolith. Front view. H. 7¼ ft.* A.D. 795. (*Courtesy of the Archaeological Institute of America*)

POTTERY

The Mayan potter, like all aboriginal American potters, had no knowledge of the wheel but constructed his pottery by hand-shaping, by coiling, or by the use of a mold. Nor did he know of glazing, but obtained a polish and a certain degree of imperviousness by rubbing. The cylindrical vases of the Maya are boldly vigorous and richly warm in color: black against a yellow or orange ground, with details of red, brown, and white. Borders of hieroglyphs are frequent, as in Figure 236B, in which the chief decorative motif is derived from the quetzal. Again the decoration may be representational and narrative as in Figure 237B, which illustrates the visit of an inferior to his chief.

[B] *Drawing from a Mayan Vase.* (*Joyce,* Mexican Archaeology, *G. P. Putnam's Sons*)

[A] *Temple of Quetzalcoatl. Teotihuacan.*
Detail of sculptured mosaics.

Toltec Art

(ABOUT A.D. 500–1000)

ROUGHLY contemporary with the First Empire of the Maya was the Toltec civilization on the plateau of the Valley of Mexico, which developed a refined esthetic sensibility and skilled craftsmanship in all the arts. The Toltecs were an agricultural people who seem to have attained a cultural climax after a long series of archaic levels that are not as yet understood. They worshiped many nature gods, important among whom were the maize god and Quetzalcoatl,[1] a benevolent deity, in form a combination of the quetzal and the coatl, a serpent. In his bird mani-

[1] Quetzalcoatl seems to have been a historical and legendary personage, a great Toltec king who introduced many useful arts, sciences, and industries, and finally went away, promising to return.

festation he appeared to typify the winds and thus had to do with the sky and the four directions; in his serpent manifestation he was connected with water and rain. Sometimes he had the teeth of the jaguar and in his mouth a man's head.

In the worship of their gods the Toltecs practiced human sacrifice. This was practiced by all the tribes of Mexico, for their religion called for it as an obligation to the gods, who had sacrificed themselves to create man. The sacrificial ceremonies were carried out with elaborate pageantry, to which the great pyramidal temples with their vast courts lent themselves magnificently.

ARCHITECTURE
AND SCULPTURE

The great center of the Toltecs was Teotihuacan ("Place of the Gods"), founded about the fifth or sixth century A.D. and reaching a climax from about the seventh to the tenth century. This great sacred city was carefully laid out in such a way that its pyramid temples, each oriented for ritual by the accurate astronomical knowledge of the Toltecs, were all related and united by broad avenues. The largest and most imposing of the group is the *Temple of the Sun*. Though the temple itself is entirely gone, its pyramidal base, made in five tiers with one broad stairway, alternately single and double, leading from the base to the temple, must have provided, in its simple monumentality, a contrasting setting for the elaborate pageantry of the rites. A smaller temple, the *Temple of Quetzalcoatl* (Fig. 238A), furnishes the one remaining example of Toltec architectural sculpture. Its excellent preservation is due to burial by subsequent building. The pyramid consists of six terraces, each decorated with boldly projecting heads of the feathered serpent surrounded by leaves; these heads alternate with a masklike motif; and the

two are connected by highly conventionalized plumes, rattles, and shells carved
in much lower relief (Fig. 238A). Traces
of color indicate that the parts of the
design must have been clearly differentiated by this means and that in the
brilliant sunshine of this valley the total
effect must have been gorgeous indeed.

SUMMARY

Of the ancient American cultures, the
Mayan was the first to reach a high
level, probably the highest reached in
the Americas before the coming of the
Europeans. The Maya were a theocratic people and, in the service of ritual
and agriculture, scientific in that they
succeeded in evolving one of the most
accurate of calendars and a system of
writing. Their cities were chiefly ecclesiastical centers, and though they built
some secular buildings, their principal

concern was the erection of temples
raised on lofty pyramidal bases and decorated luxuriantly in reliefs and color
— fit settings for their elaborate ritual.
Wealth of ornament one discerns also
in the commemorative stele and boulders, highly conventional in style, dominated by curving lines and intricate
movement. Sculpture in the round is
rare, but when found is infused with an
intensity of inner life.

Another Middle American cultural
climax was the Toltec. Here also was
an agricultural people whose life was
dominated by a theocratic government
and whose ecclesiastical centers were
carefully laid out, and dominated by
pyramid temples; but these were less
luxuriantly adorned than the Mayan.
According to legend, from their plumed-
serpent god Quetzalcoatl, they learned
to become skilled and refined craftsmen.

See the Bibliography on page 417.

12

SOUTH AMERICAN ART

IN South America, high cultures developed in the Andean region,
chiefly in the area from Ecuador to
northern Chile. This area, like that of
Middle America, presents great contrasts of geography and climate. Three
well-defined belts run north and south,
roughly parallel to one another: (1) a
narrow coastal plain, where, as in
Egypt, a hot desert is intersected by
rivers from the highlands that create
habitable and prolifically fertile oases;
(2) the great Cordillera of the Andes,
whose high peaks hem in plateau valleys with a temperate climate; and (3)

the eastern slopes of the Andes, a hot,
humid jungle. Both on the coast and in
the highlands, cultures evolved, probably from an archaic base as in Middle
America, and perhaps with migrations
from the latter.[1] From before the Christian era to about A.D. 600 there flourished on the northern coast of Peru the
Early Chimu (Muchik or Mochica); on
the southern coast, the Early Nazca;

[1] The origin of the South American cultures
is a question on which authorities differ widely.
For opinions, see George C. Vaillant and Samuel
K. Lothrop, *The Maya and Their Neighbors*, Appleton-Century, 1940.

[A] *Duck Jar. Early Chimu. Larco Herrera Museum, Trujillo, Peru.* (*Larco Herrera Museum*)

on the highlands around Lake Titicaca, the Tiahuanaco. About A.D. 600 the Tiahuanaco culture fused with the coastal to form the Tiahuanacan Empire, which spread over the Andean and coastal regions and flourished until about A.D. 900.

Early Chimu and Nazca Art

(FIRST CENTURY B.C. TO A.D. 600)

IN South America, on the Peruvian coast lived the Early Chimu (Mochica) and the Nazca, the former makers of a lively realistic pottery with strong sculptural feeling, the latter producing ceramic products of a more colorful conventional style and textiles of an extraordinary quality both esthetically and technically. On the highlands lived the austere Tiahuanaco peoples, great workers in stone and architectural stone sculpture. A mingling of the coastal and highland peoples, brought about by the Tiahuanacans, produced an art combining elements of both.

[B] *Portrait Jar. Early Chimu. H. 11½ in. Henna and brick-reds on tan. American Museum of Natural History, New York City.* (*American Museum of Natural History*)

POTTERY

The Early Chimu, living in one of the fertile valleys, were agriculturalists, but their proximity to the sea made them fishermen also, as the sea motifs on their pottery reveal. Hunters and warriors they were too. Their proud chieftains lived in fine houses in large fortified towns. But as stone was not available, they built of adobe so that only mounds of ruin remain, many of which have not yet been excavated. They seem to have been a vigorous people, dramatic, with a lively interest in the daily activities of life and in the world of nature, which they translated, with high imagination and strong sculptural feeling, into clay forms which constitute the chief source of our knowledge of the Chimu and their art. As the wheel was unknown to them, this pottery was either coiled or hand-shaped. In fact much of it gives a strong impression of the hand shaping the clay. Figure work predominates. Parrots, owls, ducks, frogs, fish and crabs, a fruiting branch of a plant, the head of a llama, people singly or in groups pursuing various activities — all this wealth of material is adjusted to the needs of a jar. One constant element, almost a mark of Chimu style, is the stirrup handle. The adaptation of animate life — that is, its conventionalization to a globular shape — is particularly successful with the bird and animal figures, as in the *Duck Jar* of Figure 240A.

Probably the highest attainment of these sculptor-potters was the portrait jars (Fig. 240B), highly individualized portraits of haughty chieftains or nobles, modeled not only from the angle of representation but also from that of a fine feeling for clay, and then painted to vivify the impression. The Chimu did not appear to be interested in color as such, for their pottery is rather dull in that respect. All their lively imagination found expression in sculptural form.

The Nazca, on the contrary, though related to the Chimu and perhaps derived from them, reveal a very different habit of mind and therefore a different style. The drab pottery of the Chimu, imaginative and highly realistic in its content, gives way to Nazcan simple geometric shapes, decorated in colorful, highly conventional motifs. The globular shape is popular, as is the double spout connected by a bridge. Flat, linear designs derived from plant, animal, and sea life and from gods and demons follow the curving surfaces in a freely exuberant manner and with a wide range of color: white, yellow, black, violet,

[A]   *Nazca Jar. Black, white, red, orange, yellow, pink, and brown. Gaffron Collection, Berlin. (Lehmann)*

blue-gray, and intermediate tones on a ground of white, red, or black. (Fig. 241A)

TEXTILES

In the field of textiles, too, the Nazca reached one of the highest achievements of the aboriginal American. Many examples have been found in graves, preserved by the dry climate. The women were the weavers, and their materials consisted of cotton for the warp and the wool of the llama and the vicuña for the weft and for embroidery. The articles woven were not objets d'art, but articles of everyday use — pouches, girdles, mantles, tunics. Since their looms were of the most primitive type, they depended largely upon skilled fingers to produce an astonishing variety of weaves — tapestry, pile, gauze, minute embroidery — all worked with an incredible fineness which has never been surpassed. The range of hues was rather narrow — red, brown, blue, and green;

[A] *Peruvian Textile. Slit tapestry weave. Museum of Fine Arts, Boston. (Boston Museum)*

but these were used with the greatest subtlety of relationship and variation. Figure 242A is a border of slit tapestry of extraordinarily fine weave, in which the chief motif is a zoomorphic figure repeated at equal intervals but infinitely varied in its details, as in the arrangement of the light and dark strips forming the body of the zoomorph. The fine slits not only help to define the color areas clearly but also give the fabric a vibrating texture. Embroidery in wool on a cotton base reached an astonishing quality, both in its rare color harmonies and in its technical accomplishments. This is particularly true of the textiles found at Paracas, north of the Nazca area. As embroidery technique admits the use of the curved line, the motifs are more curvilinear and the variations of tone extraordinary. In a *Mantle* (American Museum of Natural History) the light border strongly contrasts with the dark ground; the repeat pattern of the ground, equally spaced in even rows,

carries the lighter colors into the dark area. This repeat motif, based on a human figure, is never exactly repeated, but filled with such variation in color and tone that the effect is one of exceeding richness. In chromatic richness, the Paracas textiles are among the world's most notable.

Tiahuanaco Art

(A.D. 600–900)

THE starkness of the bleak highland country around Lake Titicaca presents a different picture from the warm, luxuriant valleys of the coast. Isolated in these mountains, a people were paralleling the development of the coastal cultures until about A.D. 600, when they forced their rule upon the coastal as well as the highland areas from Ecuador to northern Chile. The

[A] *Monolithic Gateway. Tiahuanaco. L.*
c. 13 ft. H. c. 11 ft. c. A.D. 600–900. (Chi-
cago Natural History Museum and Archive
of Hispanic Culture, Library of Congress)

center of this culture was Tiahuanaco,
on Lake Titicaca. Though the Tiahuanacans dominated politically, they fused
culturally, and produced an art that
partakes of both the starkness of the
mountain culture and the warmth and
imagination of the coastal culture.

ARCHITECTURE
AND SCULPTURE

As the highlands furnished an abundance of stone, fine and hard, there developed a race of masons highly skilled
in cutting and joining these hard stones.
The *Gateway* at Tiahuanaco (Fig. 243A)

is monolithic, with a doorway cut
through it and a sculptured frieze across
the top. In the center of the frieze,
above the doorway, is the image of
Viracocha, the sky god, a short, squat
figure standing on a pyramid, facing
directly forward and holding spears and
weapons in both hands. From his angu-

[A] *Gold Cylinder. From Lambayeque,*
Peru. H. 9¼ in. Museum of the American
Indian, Heye Foundation, New York City.
(Museum of the American Indian, Heye
Foundation)

lar face project rays terminating in
circles and puma heads. This figure of
the god is in high relief and thus stands
out prominently against the low-relief
border, which consists of rows of figures
of condors and winged men, with
weapons, running toward the center.
A border of frets interspersed with
masklike heads ties the design together.
Each of the running figures with his
weapons forms a square motif that is
repeated with precision. Yet the movement within the square contributes action to what would otherwise prove
static. Thus a combination of high relief and low, of static and dynamic elements, produces a decorative element
that is in keeping with an austere gateway in an austere setting.

A similar style of carving in two shallow planes is found at Chavin in the highlands of central Peru. The *Greater Chavin
Stone* (Fig. 245A) (several others have
been found) gives one the impression of
an elaborate conventional pattern. This
consists of a central vertical motif, from
which radiate diagonal lines terminating alternately in spirals and serpent
heads, the whole forming a bilateral design. Closer study reveals that at the
base is a figure in frontal view, short,
and built on rectangular forms except
for the arms and the legs, which are
slightly modeled; the features are so
highly conventionalized that it is difficult to identify them; each hand holds
a bunch of staves. The panel above this
figure is occupied by three masks with
decorated protruding tongue and fangs.
To see them it is necessary to reverse
the illustration. This carving impresses
one with its severe symmetry, its angularity, and its highly abstract decorative quality — decorative, though so
much in contrast to the asymmetrical,
curving, luxuriant carving of the Maya.

POTTERY AND METALWORK

Tiahuanaco pottery presents a combination of highland and coastal elements. Large flaring cups show how
the luxuriant curvilinear designs of
Nazcan ceramics and the realism of
the Mochican were affected by the
sterner style of the highlands. This is
evident in a dish in which is seated a
figure whose simplified modeling and
conventional decorative motifs produce
an effect of startling vividness.

Gold, the lure of later conquerors,
was known by these early Peruvians
(being found plentifully in the streams
or in surface veins) and was used for
cups as well as for articles of adornment.
On a cylindrical object (Fig. 244A) we
see again the motif of the *Chavin Stone*,
worked in repoussé.

SUMMARY

During the first six centuries of the Christian era three civilizations arose in the Andean region.

The Early Chimu of the northern coastal valleys modeled stirrup-handled pottery jars of great vitality in the form of highly realistic representations of the life around them: animals, birds, human figures and groups, perhaps the finest being the expressive, individualized portrait heads of warriors. Though drably painted the jars often show ingenious adaptations of the subject to the shape and an understanding of clay as a medium.

The Nazca in the coastal valleys to the south produced less realistic, more geometric and decorative pottery, often globular with twin spouts joined by a handle. The colorful painted designs are stylized, fanciful representations of plant, animal, and human forms. Textiles, though produced by primitive means, were their supreme accomplishment, and have never been excelled either in the fineness of the weaving or in the rich, imaginative coloring of the embroidered designs.

The highland people of Tiahuanaco are notable for the austere, monumental grandeur of their stone sculpture and architecture. After 600 the Tiahuanacans extended their power till they dominated the whole Andean region with the result that their culture fused with the arts of the coast to produce an expression combining elements of both. About 900, when the Tiahuanacan power declined, the coastal peoples re-established their own political and artistic forms.

See the Bibliography on page 420.

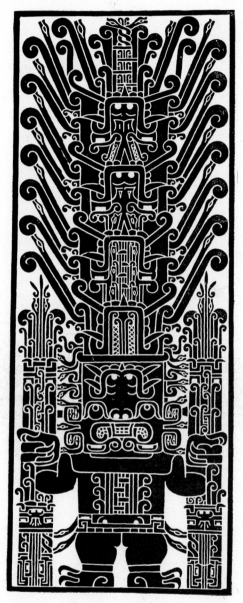

[A]   *Greater Chavin Stone. Carved greenish diorite monolith. H. 6 ft. National Museum of Archaeology, Lima.*

Part Two

[A]   *Ch'ên Jung. Wave and Dragon. Detail of the 36 ft. bamboo-paper Nine Dragon Scroll.*
Sung Dynasty. Museum of Fine Arts, Boston. (Boston Museum)

MEDIEVAL ART

WORLD PANORAMA

IN Europe and the Near East some of the ancient civilizations had run their course — the Egyptian and those of the Tigris-Euphrates Valley. Others — such as the Greco-Roman and the Iranian — though they had likewise completed their cycles, lay submerged, but later were to contribute ingredients to new cultures evolving under the energizing forces of the new religions: Christianity and Muhammadanism. After the recognition of Christianity as the state religion of the Roman Empire, Christian art spread its forms over most of the Roman Empire and into Russia, more widely in the Eastern areas than the Western because of the breakdown of the Empire in the West at the hands of the marauding Eurasian invaders. With the rise of Muhammadanism, and the advance of this military missionary faith from Arabia and Egypt as far as India in the East and Spain in the West, a new style of art arose alongside the Christian; and though predominantly assimilative, it spread over this vast area its own characteristic forms. Contacts between Christian and Muhammadan areas were frequent, and motifs, techniques, constructional methods, and stylistic qualities passed between them.

In the Far East, Gupta and Classic India and Sung China were probably the most highly civilized areas in the world. China, under the stimulus of Zen Buddhism, reached a Golden Age in all the arts as it expanded geographically south and west. India also attained one of its highest levels with the renascence of Brahmanism, and expanded into Indo-China and the East Indies. In the thirteenth century the rise and spread of the Mongol Empire from the Pacific to central Europe brought close intercourse between the khans and the Western peoples. This not only broadened the horizon of the Europeans as they learned of the magnificence and the luxuries of the East, but also led to a demand for those luxuries and hence to an increase in trade by land and sea, and of travel to those fabulous countries by such intrepid travelers as Marco Polo. Iran continued, as in ancient times, to be a crossroads by which Eastern forms came to Europe to find a place in European art. This movement was intensified by the activities of the Crusades.

Still completely isolated, and unknown to Eurasia, were the Americas. In Middle America the second empire of the Maya spread its influence to neighboring areas until it fell under the domination of the Toltecs, who in turn succumbed to the warlike strength of the Aztecs. In South America the Incas absorbed both highlands and coastal areas into an empire that marked a high level of civilization. Between these two areas the Isthmus of Panama seems to have been a link for interchange of influence. North of the Rio Grande, the Pueblos evolved the highest level of culture, though the Hopewell people of the Eastern United States created noteworthy works of art, in some of which appear motifs clearly derived from Middle America.

Two other isolated areas, Africa (except for the northern coast and Egypt) and Oceania, were to influence the modern world profoundly when contacts between them and the Eurasian and American peoples were established.

European and Near Eastern Art

13

EARLY CHRISTIAN
AND BYZANTINE ART

ABOUT the year A.D. 300 we see Rome still outwardly splendid — a highly organized despotism, internally decayed and externally hard-pressed by foreign barbarians or by cultivated indigenous peoples struggling for self-expression. Meanwhile the Christian Church, growing at first in secret, and strengthened by persecution, emerged victorious as the real successor of Rome. Constantine, by changing the capital in A.D. 330 to Byzantium, which he renamed Constantinople, cut the Empire into two rather sharply divided parts, the East and the West. Let us note a few of the important movements in each.

The lands about the eastern Mediterranean had always been Hellenic rather than Roman at heart. In many places the traditions of the older civilizations — those of Egypt and of Babylonia-Assyria, for example — were still dominant. Long before Christianity became officially the Roman state religion, vigorous Christian communities began to

flourish in Persia, Egypt, Asia Minor, and in Syria, that great highway of war, commerce, and ideas. Under the stimulus of the new faith, brilliant creative work began in church-building and was unhampered by the weakening Roman power. But Constantinople, because of its wealth and prestige, became the point at which the various Eastern influences coalesced with the Hellenic and the Roman to form what is known as Byzantine art, or, as it has well been called, the Christian art of the East. In the reign of Justinian (A.D. 527–565) this art reached its first climax under the patronage of the Church and the court. But some of the forces that were shaping it — the prejudice of the early Christian against everything pagan and of the Semitic peoples against the representation of sacred personages; the influence of Islam[1]; and the impersonal, mystic attitude of the East — these forces inevitably led to the iconoclastic (image-destroying) controversy (A.D.

[1] See Chapter 15.

726–824), which in denouncing the use of images guided creative impulses into the channels of rich ornamentation based upon floral and geometric motifs, and into a dependence upon richness of color and texture. But a compromise led, under Basil I and his successors, to a second climax of Byzantine art, whose purpose was "to render visible the mysteries of the supra-natural world. . . . If God might be painted after all, not only in innocence and majesty but in the commonplace and degradation of earthly life, then painting should be worthy and attempt the highest."[1] Hence arose "a mystical renunciation of the transient phenomena of earth for the universal in-being Reality — enshrined in a fixed iconography whose rigid apportionment of subject and space alone could put intelligible bounds to so immeasureable an aim."[2]

The Western half of the Roman Empire presented a different picture. For centuries the barbarians had been threatening the Rhine and Danube frontiers, and the decaying government could no longer hold out against the strong vitality of the North. On all sides the uncouth barbarians poured in, finally reaching Rome; and though they may have had some reverence for the magnificence they saw, with no capacity for appreciation they cared little about maintaining it. The *Colosseum* was merely a mine from the stones of which could be drilled out the iron clamp to tip the spear of a Goth. The one power to hold firm was the Church, the earnestness and zeal of whose leaders, such as Saint Augustine and Saint Gregory, laid the foundations for its supremacy in the Middle Ages.

Although the history of the two halves of the Roman Empire continued so differently, there were close relations between them. The establishment of the exarchate at Ravenna brought a flow of Byzantine work westward. Byzantine builders came to Italy at the summons of patrons whose own country was no longer producing trained artists. The iconoclastic outbreak drove artists to Italy to seek employment; and pilgrims and traders brought with them such portable objects as enamels, ivories, manuscripts, and textiles.

ARCHITECTURE

Rome, notwithstanding its pitiable condition,[3] offered ample incentive for building. Here were the sacred places, the sites of martyrdom and burial of saints. Hither came pilgrims from all Christendom, despite hazardous travel — throngs so great that men and women were trodden under foot. Ample building material was at hand, to be had for the taking — the finely cut stones, columns, and marble veneers of the huge Roman structures. With the emergence of Christianity from secrecy we observe a type of church established — the basilica — which, though known in the East,[4] became predominant in Italy.

Figure 251A illustrates the plan of the basilica, a rectangular building entered through an open colonnaded court, the atrium (f), one side of which forms the narthex or vestibule (e); the body of the church consists of a nave (a), aisles (b), an apse (d), and a transverse aisle or transept (c) inserted between the nave and the apse and slightly projecting beyond the walls, making the plan T-shaped. Figure 338A1 is simpler, with single aisles and no transept, but shows the place of

---

[1] Bréhier, *L'art chrétien*, quoted by Robert Byron and David Talbot Rice, *The Birth of Western Painting*, Knopf, 1931, p. 15.

[2] *Ibid.*

[3] See Grant Showerman, *Eternal Rome*, new ed., Yale University Press, 1925, for a good description.

[4] Particularly in Syria. See H. C. Butler and E. B. Smith, *Early Churches in Syria*, Princeton University Press, 1929.

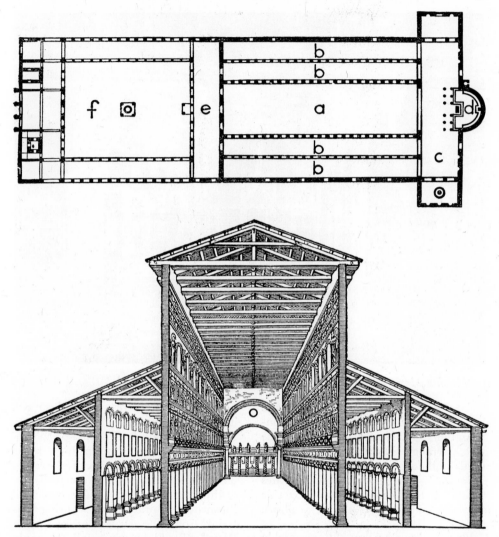

[A]   *Plan and Section of Section of Old St. Peter's, Rome. Restored. W. c. 215 ft. A.D. 326.*
Destroyed to make way for the present cathedral. a. nave; b. aisles; c. transverse aisle;
d. apse; e. narthex; f. atrium.

the altar immediately in front of the apse, and the choir with two pulpits occupying about half of the nave. The nave walls rest on columns (Fig. 251A) and rise higher than the side walls, forming a clerestory for lighting (Figs. 252A, 255A) and leaving wall space between the colonnade and the win-

dows. Both the nave and the aisles of such a basilica carried wooden roofs, but the apse was usually vaulted. The origin of the basilica is difficult to determine. In many respects it is close to the classical basilica, the name of which it bears; yet certain elements, such as the atrium and the transverse aisle, seem

[A]   *Santa Maria in Cosmedin. Rome. Late 8th cent. (Anderson)*

to be derived from the Roman private house, where the early Christian congregations met in secret and whose whole arrangement suited the liturgical needs of the service.

Santa Maria in Cosmedin well illustrates a modest basilica.[1] Its plain exterior shows an unadorned narthex, above

[1] Built in the sixth century A.D.; enlarged in the eighth century; restored in the twelfth. The bell tower (campanile) is Romanesque. The church has frequently been remodeled, notably in the late Renaissance, when a Renaissance façade was added; it was restored in 1894–99 to its eighth- and twelfth-century form. This continuous remodeling of churches, especially in Rome, each in the style of the period of the remodeling, makes many churches a confusing composite of early Christian, Romanesque, Renaissance, and Baroque, and leaves but few in the style in which they were originally built. For a sensitive understanding of the formal relationships in *Santa Maria in Cosmedin* see Le Corbusier, *Towards a New Architecture*, pp. 160 ff.

which rises the clerestory of the nave. The interior (Fig. 252A) is a rectangular space, so designed that interest focuses on the altar standing in high relief against the rich mosaics of the apse. The columns supporting the walls are of different sizes and designs, and well illustrate the practice of securing material from the structures of pagan Rome. Should one ruin fail to supply enough columns for a basilica, another would be stripped of its material, apparently with little concern for the matching of the columns. It was even the practice to prop up short columns to the required height with additional bases. Thence also were procured the fine marbles of the choir rail, pulpits, and floor for this church. The choir (for the clergy who participated in the service), with its two flanking pulpits, one for the reading of the Gospels and one

[A] *St. Paul's Outside the Walls. Rome. Founded* A.D. *386; rebuilt after the fire of 1823, which destroyed almost all except the transept. (Anderson)*

for the Epistles, occupied a considerable part of the nave (see also Fig. 338A1). The walls were originally covered with frescoes and the simple wooden roof was brightly painted. A large and elaborate basilica is that of *St. Paul's Outside the Walls* (Fig. 253A), built over the tomb of Saint Paul, very resplendent in colored marbles, gilded coffered ceiling, and mosaics.

The interior of a basilica was colorful. Of the many mediums used to obtain color, mosaic transcended all others. By means of mosaic the Byzantine builders clothed the surfaces of the apse and often of the walls too, if funds permitted, with mural decoration of unsurpassed splendor, equally satisfactory for decorating a dim interior and for conveying the ideas of the Christian faith. Its forms are conventional because of the nature of the medium, and symbolic because of the nature of the ideas ex-

pressed. By *mosaic* is meant a design worked out by means of small pieces of colored glass or stone, called *tesserae*, set in cement. It is clear that to carry out a design in this medium, the artist must make the drawing so simple that the form becomes almost a flat pattern, with sharp contours and little light and shade. It affords ample opportunity, however, for broad massing of color and for deep glowing tones, especially when gold is used liberally either as a background for the figures or as a backing for the tesserae (Figs. 255A and B, 256A, 257A, 258A).

As the basilicas in Rome have been so repaired and remodeled that few give an adequate picture of their original appearance, those at Ravenna will serve to illustrate how relatively barren, yet impressively frank and rugged, was the exterior of the early basilica (Fig. 254A); relatively, in contrast to the interior

[A]　*Sant' Apollinare in Classe. Ravenna.* A.D. *534–538.* (*Alinari*)

(Fig. 255A and B), where the half-light from translucent marble panels and perforated marble windows discloses rich colors, gold, carvings, and stately hieratic figures. Here is the atmosphere of another world, of enfolding peacefulness and mystic calm. With symbolism prominent in the mental outlook of the age, one wonders whether the early Christian thus symbolized the contrast between the hard externals of his life and the beauty of the inner spirit.

Early Christian art, both in the East and in the West, was an art of symbols. Prominent among Christian symbols are: the fish, not only an acrostic but a symbol of water, baptism, and in general of the faith; the ship (Latin *navis,* whence "nave"), symbol of the Church in which the faithful were carried over the sea of life; the vine, symbol of Christ; sheep, especially with the shepherd; the stag, the soul thirsting for baptism; and the peacock, emblem of immortality — an illustration of how the early Christians infused

pagan symbols (the peacock was the bird of Juno) with new meaning. Thus symbols constitute a language; and as they tend to isolate and emphasize some dominant element of the person or thing symbolized, they tend in their form toward the highly generalized and the abstract, and thus are more than likely to be peculiarly decorative as well as expressive of intense inner significance.

The iconography of early Christian art — that is, what is represented and how and where — was strictly regulated by the Church. Old Testament personages and scenes were plentiful: the patriarchs and the kings, the Genesis stories, the prophets. New Testament scenes focused on the childhood and the atoning life and death of Christ: the Annunciation, the Nativity, the Flight into Egypt, the Adoration of the Magi, the Crucifixion, the Resurrection, the Ascension, episodes which were celebrated in the festivals of the Church: Christmas, Epiphany, Lent, Easter

[A] *Sant' Apollinare in Classe. Ravenna. (Anderson)*

[B] *The Transfiguration. Mosaic of the apse of Sant' Apollinare in Classe, Ravenna.*

[A]   *San Vitale. The apse. Ravenna.* A.D. *526. (Anderson)*

Scenes from the public life of Christ were also used — among others, the Baptism, the Temptation, the Last Supper — as well as stories from the lives of the saints. For example, in the apse of *Sant' Apollinare in Classe* is a representation of the *Transfiguration* (Fig. 255B). The purpose is to tell the story symbolically in the language of conventions established by the Church and at the same time to decorate the surface of the apse. Against a gold ground is a large blue medallion with a jeweled cross, symbol of Christ. Just above, the hand of God and the dove issue from the clouds on an axis with the cross (the three together symbolizing the Trinity). On each side in the clouds appear the figures of Moses and Elias; below are three sheep, the three

Disciples who accompanied Christ to the foot of the mountain. Beneath, in the midst of green fields with trees, flowers, and birds, stands Saint Apollinaris with uplifted arms, accompanied by twelve sheep symbolizing the twelve Apostles and forming, as they march in regular file across the apse, a wonderfully decorative base. Thus in a language that was understood by all Christians the story is told, and the saint to whom the church is dedicated is brought before the observer. And at the same time the resplendence of the wall as abstract design intensifies the emotional reaction to the scene and hence its significance.

In *Sant' Apollinare Nuovo* (Fig. 257A) the side walls above the columns glow with mosaic. Here a procession of

[A] *Sant' Apollinare Nuovo. Nave wall with mosaic decorations. Ravenna. 6th cent. (Alinari)*

saints, stately and hieratic, moves in quiet rhythm toward the altar. Each saint, richly dressed and carrying a crown, stands isolated, separated from the next by a palm tree. Thus two themes interweave to carry the movement. Note that though the figures and the trees at first glance seem identical, they contain an infinite number of variations on the main theme. Here is an art of line and subdued mellow color which is highly successful not only as mural decoration but as an evocation of a mystic mood.

At Ravenna we meet the other important type of church building, — the type commonly called *central* — which, though not unknown in Rome,[1] seemed

[1] *Santa Costanza* and *San Stefano Rotondo* are examples.

less at home there than it did in Ravenna, which had direct connections with the East, where this type of building reached its highest development. A simple form we find in the *Mausoleum of Galla Placidia* (Figs. 258A and B, which is built in the form of a Greek cross, with a dome over the intersection of the two arms that is enclosed and concealed from the exterior view by a low rectangular tower. The building is of the plainest brick construction and unadorned except for the blind arcades and dentils along the cornices. But stepping within, we find ourselves enveloped in mellow light and quietly rich color. Above the yellow-marble paneling blue-ground mosaics sheathe the entire surface, deep-toned blues with accents here and there of other hues and with a restrained use of gold. The same incredibly rich interior we find in a church of the central type, *San Vitale* (Figs. 256A, 258B). The brick construction, presenting an almost barnlike appearance on the outside, is entirely concealed on the inside by marbles and glowing mosaics.

This central type reaches a climax in the East, specifically in *Santa Sophia*, or *Hagia Sophia, Church of the Holy Wisdom*, in Constantinople (Fig. 259A). The ground plan (Fig. 262A), however, reveals some features of the basilica. Though almost square, it contains a nave, with side aisles separated from it by columns, and is roofed with a combination of dome and half-domes. An apse, a double narthex, and an atrium complete the plan.[1] The ex-

[1] The minarets and heterogeneous buildings about the base were added by the Muslims when they converted the church into a mosque after the capture of Constantinople in 1453. The atrium no longer exists.

[A] *Mausoleum of Galla Placidia. Ravenna, c. A.D. 450. Floors and walls of marble; vaults, lunettes, drum, and cupola covered with blue ground mosaic. (Anderson)*

[B] *San Vitale (in the middle background) and the Mausoleum of Galla Placidia (in the foreground). Ravenna. (Alinari)*

[A] *Santa (Hagia) Sophia. Istanbul.* A.D. *532–537. (Publishers' Photo Service)*

terior view shows a compact mass of brick, of great solidity at the corners, covered with a low lead-covered dome and half-domes. But entering (Fig. 261A), one stands amazed at the wonderful spaciousness, obtained through the simple but daring design of the building, which consists of an arrangement of arches and half-domes moving rhythmically with increasing size and volume until they unite in the all-embracing dome, which seems to rest easily and lightly over the great space. Space is the first impression, then sumptuousness. The richest materials[1] of all kinds were used — rare marbles of all

[1] The mosaics, which were largely painted over by the Muslims, are now being uncovered. See Thomas Whittemore, *The Mosaics of St. Sophia at Istanbul*, Oxford University Press, 1933.

colors and literally acres of gold-ground mosaics — yet every detail is subordinate to the powerful space-organization. Listen to the poem of Paulus Silentiarius, court poet of Justinian, written to commemorate the dedication of the church, "About the center of the church, by the eastern and western half-circles, stand four mighty piers of stone, and from them spring great arches like the bow of Iris, four in all; and, as they rise slowly in the air, each separates from the other to which it was at first joined, and the spaces between them are filled with wondrous skill, for curved walls touch the arches on either side and spread over until they all unite above them. . . . The base of the dome is strongly fixed upon the great arches . . . while

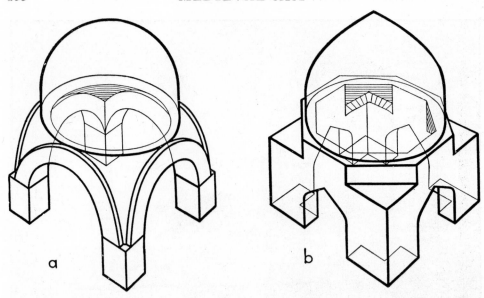

[A]   *Two methods of erecting a dome over a square area.   a. a dome on pendentives; b. a dome on squinches. In pendentive construction, the Byzantine solution of the problem, the dome rests upon what is in effect a second and larger dome from which segments have been sliced, to form the four arches bounding the square and to receive the base of the upper dome. By transferring the weight to piers rather than to the wall itself, pendentive construction enabled the builder to secure a lofty, unobstructed interior space (Fig. 261A). In squinch construction, the solution favored by the Muhammadan builders, the dome rests upon an octagon formed by building arches (or corbeling or lintels) across the four corners of the square. Squinches were frequently ornamented with stalactites and colored tiles (Fig. 303A).*

above, the dome covers the church like the radiant heavens. . . .

"Who shall describe the fields of marble gathered on the pavement and lofty walls of the church? Fresh green from Carystus, and many-colored Phrygian stone of rose and white, or deep red and silver; porphyry powdered with bright spots; emerald-green from Sparta, and Iassian marble with waving veins of blood-red and white; streaked red stone from Lydia, and crocus-colored marble from the hills of the Moors, and Celtic stone, like milk poured out on glittering black; the precious onyx like as if gold were shining through it, and the fresh green from the land of Atrax, in mingled contrast of shining surfaces.

"The mason also has fitted together thin pieces of marble figuring intertwining tendrils bearing fruit and flowers, with here and there a bird sitting on the twigs. Such ornament as this surrounds the church above the columns. The capitals are carved with the barbed points of graceful acanthus all gilt; but the vaulting is covered over with many a little square of gold, from which the rays stream down and strike the eyes so that men can scarcely bear to look."[1]

The decoration of *Santa Sophia*, however, is by no means merely abstract. It is filled with meaning. The characters or episodes move in hieratic suc-

[1] W. R. Lethaby, "Santa Sophia, Constantinople," *Architectural Review*, April, 1905, p. 122.

[A] *Santa (Hagia) So-*
phia. (Drawing by J. B.
Fulton in the Architec-
tural Review)

cession from the more human scenes on
earth, scenes relating to the life of the
Virgin and of Christ, through the figures of angels, saints, and prophets on
the walls, to the four cherubim in the
pendentives, and finally to the Pantocrator, the Ruler of the Universe, in
the crown of the dome: "Know and
behold that I am." Thus the movement
of lines and volumes is paralleled by a
literary movement of ever-increasing
sanctity and awe culminating in the
symbol of the heart and mystery of the
Christian faith.

The dome, as has been said, appears
to rest lightly and without effort, yet
we know that it exerts a tremendous
weight, which is met by the massive
masonry that we noticed at the exterior corners. For the dome of *Santa
Sophia* differs from that of the *Pantheon*
structurally in that its load is concentrated at four piers rather than distributed along a circular wall. The
triangular segments that carry the load
to the piers are known as *pendentives* and
a dome so constructed is called a *dome
on pendentives* (Figs. 260A, 9Ae). This
structural method solved the problem
of erecting a perfect dome over a square
area and of keeping the space free of
load-carrying walls; or, in other words,
of concentrating the load at the fewest
possible points, thus creating a largely
unbroken interior space. Though the
origin of this solution of the structural

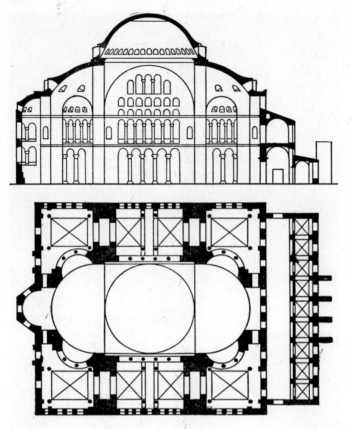

[A]   *Santa (Hagia) Sophia, Istanbul. Section and plan. The atrium, originally built in front of the church, no longer exists and is not shown in this drawing.*

problem is of uncertain date and place, it appears to have been the result of many experiments in vaulting by the builders of the Near East and to have been passed on by them to the West, where we meet it in *St. Mark's* in Venice, in the Romanesque churches of southern France, in the domed cathedrals of the Renaissance, such as *St. Peter's,* and in many domed buildings of modern times.

The stone carvings in *Santa Sophia* though often based upon the acanthus and other classical motifs (Fig. 263A), differ from the classical in their insistence upon the surface which they decorate (contrast Figure 157A). This type of carving is obviously of Eastern origin, as is apparent in the *Mshatta Frieze* (Fig. 263B). Richly carved mold-

ings finish the edges of a long border that is decorated with a zigzag and rosettes, which, together with the entire background, are luxuriantly carved with acanthus and vine scrolls in which are interwoven vases, animals, centaurs, and other fantastic beings. Here, as in *Santa Sophia,* the carving is done by drilling into the background, and leaving the original surface cut into a flat pattern, rather than by modeling with the chisel, leaving an uneven relief surface, as did the Greeks and the Romans. Zigzag and rosettes add vitality and rhythm to the delicate allover pattern.

Stone-carving played a large part in early Christian and Byzantine ornament, and was applied to capitals, screens, railings, and pulpits. Byzantine capitals (Figs. 264A, 256A) appear to be

[A] *Santa (Hagia) So-phia. Carvings of capitals and spandrels. Marble.*

derived from the classical Corinthian type, though they afford a great variety of detail. From the square abacus, the carver gradually merged his stone into the circular shape of the column and covered the surface with carvings — the basket type, so called because of its basketlike interlacings; the melon type, in which the stone is cut in ridges like those of a melon; or that with the inter-laced-circle motif which is so frequently found in medieval ornament. An en-tirely new feature, however, is the im-post block, of much the same shape as the capital itself, inserted between the abacus and the springing of the arch. The purpose of this is not quite clear. It may have been to obtain greater height, or to bring the weight of the arches directly upon the shaft rather than on the outer edge of the abacus. Sometimes the impost block was richly carved; sometimes it simply bore a monogram (Fig. 264A); and sometimes it was omitted, as in *Santa Sophia* (Fig. 263A). The stone railings afforded a large area for decoration. They were carved with patterns very much like those on the capitals; or with animals and birds in a balanced bilateral arrangement — a scheme of decoration that probably originated in the Near East and found

great favor in all the arts.

The central type of church on the Greek-cross plan continued, modified, in the second Golden Age of Byzantine art (Fig. 264B). The angles of the arms

[B] *Frieze from Mshatta, a Palace in the Syrian Desert. H. 15 ft. 4th–6th cent.* A.D. *Berlin. (Berlin Museum)*

[A]   *Byzantine Capitals. San Vitale, Ravenna. (Alinari)*

[B]   *Plan of a Byzantine Church of the Second Golden Age. North Church, S. Saviour Pantocrator, Istanbul. Early XII cent. Compare with Fig. 274Aa.*

were filled in and frequently covered with domes; the domes themselves became more conspicuous by being lifted up on high drums (Fig. 265A). External decoration found a place, in the form of patterned brickwork, sometimes polychrome, as well as in carvings. On the interior, colored marbles and mosaics or frescoes covered the walls (Fig. 266A). Even more strict now was the control over the iconographic scheme, the guides or manuals prescribing in detail the place of each subject, the composition, and the forms, even to the detail of the color of the Virgin's hair. Hence arose the similarity of type and composition seen in all Byzantine painting. Such a procedure precluded any study of nature and insisted upon continual copying and recopying until the figures were so fixed in the mind that they could easily be reproduced from memory. In other words, the painters were using a language understood by all and at the same time extraordinarily effective in its austere splendor.

[A]   *Church at Daphne, Greece. Late 11th cent. (Alinari)*

Besides the colored marbles, mosaics, and frescoes, many other features contributed to the richness of a Byzantine church interior: the iconostasis[1] with its elaborate decoration and colorful icons, the gold, ivory, and enameled vessels, and the rich stuffs of the vestments. When we see all these in the dim light of candles and through clouds of incense, we feel that the Byzantine artists did not fall short of their objective: "to render visible the mysteries of the supra-natural world."

St. Mark's in Venice, with its many domes, is an example of this type in Italy, for there was a close connection between Venice and the Near East. From Alexandria the body of Saint Mark, patron saint of Venice, was

brought secretly to the city, and the church was founded to house the relic. Marbles, mosaics, carvings, and the famous *Pala d'Oro* (Altar of Gold) — the retable of the high altar, a magnificent example of Byzantine goldwork rich with enamels and jewels — make the interior one of great splendor. Many of the materials for the church were brought from the East, including the four bronze horses above the main portal.

PAINTING

The function of the painter in the early Christian and the Byzantine world was to decorate the walls of the churches with mosaics and frescoes, to paint panels for the iconostases of private chapels and miniatures to illustrate books. The early paintings are strongly Hellenistic or Roman. Before the emergence of the Church from

---

[1] The panel or partition with doors and tiers of icons (whence the name) found in Eastern (Orthodox) Catholic Churches, which separates the sanctuary from the nave. Only the clergy may enter the sanctuary.

[A] *Church of the Monastery of Xeno-phontos, Mt. Athos, showing frescoes. 11th cent.* (*Millet,* Monuments de l'Athos)

secrecy, the early Christians decorated the walls of the catacombs with frescoes such as the vine, which is an echo of the carved floral pattern so common in Roman ornamentation and was a favorite Christian theme because of the frequent symbolic use of the vine in the New Testament. They also used figures, such as those representing brotherly love that are close to the Pompeian frescoes of Cupids and Psyches in the *House of the Vettii.* Thus there was no break with the classical tradition on the part of those who forsook the pagan faith; the early Christian painter merely gave the traditional forms new meaning. Among the mosaics, the apse of *Santa Pudenziana* (Rome) of the late fourth century well illustrates the Hellenistic phase. Among the paint-

ings, the *Joshua Roll* [1] (Fig. 267A) re-produces a detail in which Joshua, near the walls of Jericho, is prostrating himself before the angel; in the lower right-hand corner is a female figure crowned with a tower, the personifica-tion of the city. Though the subject is Christian, the method of expression is Hellenic — the personification of the city, the naturalism of the figures, the way in which they fit into the land-scape, and the perspective in the archi-tecture. But soon a change occurred, a trend away from Greco-Roman nat-uralism toward a conventional, highly abstract expression. In the *Good Shep-herd* mosaic in the *Tomb of Galla Placidia* the landscape is flattening out, though there is still some depth and some use of shadow in the rocks and the sheep to indicate volume. The complete reduction into one plane and to ab-stract form we find in the mosaics of the apse of *Sant' Apollinare in Classe* (Fig. 255B), and in the *Theodora* and *Justinian* portrait groups in *San Vitale.* In these mosaics the figures are thor-oughly noncorporeal, are gorgeous symbols of bodies, and are highly decorative because of their very flat-ness.

The effect of the iconoclastic con-troversy and the compromise that fol-lowed it has already been noted. A rigid iconography; materials rich in color, texture, and gold; impersonal forms far removed from an illusion of

[1] This manuscript was originally a continu-ous roll 32 feet long and 1 foot wide, with pen-and-ink and color illustrations of the Hebrew conquest of the Promised Land, which occupy most of the space, interspersed with the text in Greek. It has now been cut into sections and mounted for preservation. The manuscript be-longs to the period when the long roll used by Egyptians, Greeks, and Romans was being superseded by the *codex* — a book made of separate pages bound together, the usual modern method. The change was probably due to prac-tical considerations, since passages can be found much more readily in this form.

[A] *Joshua before the Walls of Jericho. Detail from the Joshua Roll. 5th–6th cent.* A.D. *Vatican, Rome. (Muñoz)*

the actual world; abstract representations of this world and symbols of another world — all these combined to produce mosaics and frescoes which were monumentally austere but quite definite in their objective. "The pictures have the same object as the liturgy; they possess the same sacramental character and form the requisite setting for the mystery of the Eucharist."[1]

Mosaic[2] met perfectly the Byzantine requirements of splendor of effect, but was costly. Fresco, it is often suggested, was used when economic conditions demanded a less expensive substitute.

Whatever the reason, there developed a great school of Byzantine painting that paralleled the mosaics, both of which were strongly affected by a revival of the study of Plato and of Greek humanism in general. Forms became less austere, more human; otherworldliness partook somewhat of this earth. For three centuries, from the thirteenth to the fifteenth, the Byzantine painters covered the walls of the churches and monasteries of Greece with frescoes in which the forms, though humanized, are still abstract, built up of light and color.[3] In the *Lamentation over the Body of Christ* (Fig. 268A) a dramatic subject is expressed with emotional intensity through "a tempestuous rhythm of light and dark." The faces, the gar-

[1] Bréhier, *L'art chrétien*, quoted by Byron and Talbot Rice, *op. cit.*

[2] *Daphne* in Greece (eleventh century), *Palermo* in Sicily (twelfth century), *Kahrie Djami* in Istanbul (fifteenth century) are examples of mosaics.

[3] For a detailed exposition see Byron and Talbot Rice, *op. cit.*

[A] *Pietà (Lamentation over the Body of Christ). Fresco. Xenophontos, Mt. Athos. 1544. (Millet)*

[B] *Christ Crowning Romanus and Eudocia, Rulers at Constantinople. 1068–71. Ivory. Bibliothèque Nationale, Paris.*

ments, the body of Christ, and the rocks are constructed into various patterns of light and dark, sharply darting areas of light against dark, a contrast emphasized by the juxtaposition of complementary hues; and these individual patterns are organized into long sweeping curves and sharp angles.

STONE–CARVING
AND IVORY–CARVING

Monumental sculpture was produced only to a very limited extent in early Christian art, because the statue in the round was even more closely akin than painting to the graven images of the pagan. In a rare example, the *Good Shepherd* of the Lateran Museum (Rome), we recognize an archaic Greek motif, imbued with a new sig-

nificance. This again is a striking example of the continuity of the old tradition.

One of the chief expressions of sculpture we find in the sarcophagi. In some the surface is entirely covered with reliefs representing scenes from the Old and New Testaments, crowded together one upon another for the purpose of narration, with little regard for design, a continuity again of Roman third-century style, and the use of classical figures, to express Christian ideas.

Another style is represented by the *Sarcophagus of Theodore* (Fig. 269A). Here there is no crowded relief, in fact no figures, but a piece of beautiful decoration composed of symbols, each of which by itself and in conjunction with the others carries a clear, definite message. In the center of the side is the

[A]   *Sarcophagus of Theodore. 7th cent.* A.D. *Sant' Apollinare in Classe, Ravenna. (Alinari)*

sacred monogram[1] in a circle, facing which are two peacocks, symbols of eternity. Behind them are scrolls of fruiting vines and birds; on the lid are the inscription and three wreaths enclosing sacred monograms; carved moldings frame the design.

The ivory-carver was important, not only for the intrinsic quality of his work but also because his craft carried on the tradition of sculpture until its emergence as a major art, hundreds of years later, about the portals of the churches. The carved figure followed at first the general idiom of the Hellenic style. But Hellenic naturalism soon yielded to Eastern influence. This is very pronounced in the so-called *Throne of Maximian* (Fig. 270A), an episcopal chair covered with panels of

[1] This monogram consists of the first two letters in the Greek name of Christ, chi and rho; in the side angles formed by the chi are the Greek letters alpha and omega, frequently used to symbolize the divinity of Christ.

richly carved ivory. On the front are five niches, containing figures of Saint John the Baptist and four Apostles which have markedly individual characteristics, vary in pose and drapery, and appear to have been studied from nature. The borders above and below, however — with the monogram, the spiraling vines which enclose figures of peacocks and various animals, and (in the lower panel) the rampant lions flanking a central vase from which issue vines interspersed with animals — recall in their flat patternlike forms against a dark ground the stone carvings of *Mshatta* (Fig. 263B) and of *Santa Sophia* (Fig. 263A).

The iconoclastic controversy affected ivory-carving much as it did the other branches of art. The trend was from naturalism to austere conventionalization, then to a modified naturalism. The last stage we see in *Christ Crowning Romanus and Eudocia* (Fig. 268B). In the center, Christ, with the halo of

[A]   *Bishop's Chair, Called the "Throne of Maximian." Wood, inlaid with ivory panels and borders. 6th cent.* A.D. *Archiepiscopal Palace, Ravenna. (Anderson)*

divinity, elevated on a dome-shaped pedestal fringed with windows like the dome of *Santa Sophia*, is placing crowns upon the heads of the emperor and the empress, who by their gestures acknowledge His sovereignty. The royal pair are dressed in garments of rich stuff, which form a flat pattern in contrast to the simple unadorned robe of Christ that falls in seminaturalistic folds with long unbroken lines. The group is fitted with acute sensitiveness into the shape with its oval top, a theme repeated insistently along the vertical axis in the halo and the circles of the pedestal, and in the pedestal and in the lower border

interweaving with the square theme seen in the garments. Insistent verticals balance equally insistent horizontals; roughly textured areas act as a foil to smooth. Everywhere is a balance of components, viewed with even greater clarity when seen in the original color. For ivories could not remain uncolored in a total cultural expression that was so colorful. In this ivory, then, one finds a particular flavor of style compounded of the austerity of the early Byzantine and the naturalism of the Hellenic.

ENAMELS AND TEXTILES

Great demands were made upon craftsmen in this period by the luxurious courts of the East and by the Church. Both needed fine fabrics for costumes and for hangings; jeweled ornaments; books, which, to suit current tastes, might be written in gold letters upon purple-tinted vellum or decorated with bright miniatures on gold grounds, and bound in gold, ivory, enamel, and jewels; vessels for the service,[1] which must be of the finest material and workmanship to be worthy of the Church.

A craft to contribute color and sumptuousness was that of the enameler. Most of the Byzantine enamels are of the cloisonné type. Because of the precious material used and the long, tedious process, the enamels were small and were used chiefly to adorn larger objects (Fig. 271B). To an even greater extent than the mosaic-worker, the enameler must reduce his design to its simplest terms, for the beauty of the finished product is dependent upon its line, pattern, color, and texture. To

[1] See W. R. Lethaby and Harold Swainson, *The Church of Sancta Sophia, at Constantinople,* Macmillan, 1894, for a description of the great quantities of sumptuous vessels used in this church.

[A] *Saint Peter. Enamel and gold plaque. D. 4 in. 10th cent. Metropolitan Museum of Art, New York City. (Metropolitan Museum)*

[B] *Chalice. 11th cent. Treasury of St. Mark's, Venice. (Alinari)*

attempt to represent the human figure in so difficult a medium is daring; for the technique requires not only the utmost economy of line but, even within that, the greatest precision in placing the cloisons — a slight deviation in the face, for example, would bring about a ludicrous expression. Yet the Byzantine craftsman did not hesitate, as is seen in the plaque representing *Saint Peter* (Fig. 271A), in which a surprising amount of character has been expressed in the face framed by the white hair and beard. Geometric or more abstract design, however, emphasizing as it does the massing of color and texture, was usually found more suitable to this medium. These enamels are so satisfactory because the Byzantine craftsman in enamel, as in mosaic, never overstepped the severe laws that govern the technique.

The application of enamel plaques to larger objects is illustrated by a chalice (Fig. 271B) made of sardonyx, mounted in silver and decorated with enamels, gilt, and pearls — an illus-

tration of the sumptuousness of the age.

Weaving also was an important art in early Christian times, both for the quality of its products and for its influence on the arts of western Europe. In the early centuries of the Christian era, the Coptic textiles of Egypt show patterns in wool upon linen, sometimes woven directly in the garment or hanging, and sometimes on borders or medallions to be appliquéd. In Figure 272A, the design is made up of a vine scroll with leaves and fruit — at which birds are pecking — on a black ground. In both plant and bird forms there is a fine underlying observation of nature; yet all the forms have been subordinated to the decorative scheme, so that the birds, the leaves, and the grapes have been flattened out, simplified, and so massed that they are splendidly adapted to fill without crowding the spaces made by the undulating wave line of the stem.

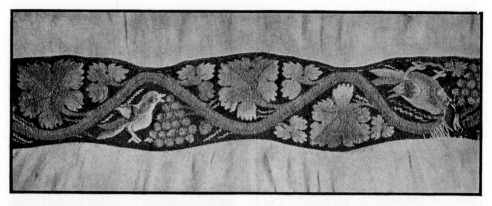

[A] *Coptic Textile. Linen, with tapestry weaving in colored wools on black. W. 3¾ in. 4th or 5th cent. A.D. Victoria and Albert Museum, London. (Victoria and Albert Museum)*

Silk fabrics, however, were the most important textile product of the East and were used for garments, hangings, vestments, and furnishings; and as wrappings for the dead and for the bones and other relics of numerous saints, which must be shrouded in the finest material procurable. For several centuries before the time of Justinian, Persia had held a monopoly of the silk industry, controlling not only the manufacture of these fabrics but their sale as well. Because of this monopoly in the trade of an article much desired by the wealthy Byzantines, Justinian introduced the industry into the Empire, with the help of two monks, so the story goes, who smuggled the eggs of the silkworm out of China in hollow staves. A hunting scene is frequently found on these stuffs and is evidently of Persian origin (Fig. 273A). The design is a medallion repeat pattern within which hunters and game offer materials for a symmetrical composition of flat decorative units. In all the surviving textiles of the Byzantine period the pattern reveals its salutary dependence upon the basic technique of any textile — the creation of a surface by interlacing fibers at right angles.

SUMMARY

Early Christian and Byzantine art was a natural consequence of the fusion of the East and the West: the impersonal, mystic East whose ideal was transcendental and whose forms were abstract; the individual, anthropocentric West, whose ideal was humanistic and whose forms were naturalistic. In this fusion originated an art based upon nature yet with no intention of producing an illusion of natural appearance. It consisted of a convincing formalism free from the accidents of actuality and in perfect accord with the ideals of the Church: "to render visible the mysteries of the supranatural world." It was a hieratic and aristocratic art, in the service of the Church and of the courts. To carry out its aims, two types of church evolved, the basilican and the central, the latter of which, with its domical construction, displayed an extraordinary feeling for interior space organization. Both types, austerely plain on the exterior, on the interior concentrated a lavish use of low-keyed mosaics, colored marbles, carvings, and gold and silver vessels set with jewels and enamels — all of which through symbols and conventions

[A] *Byzantine Textile. Silk. Detail showing one of a series of circular medallions, interspersed with floral motifs, which covered the fabric. D. $9\frac{1}{2}$ in. Syria. 7th cent. Metropolitan Museum of Art, New York City. (Metropolitan Museum)*

were intended not only to decorate sumptuously but also to teach clearly the lives of sacred personages and the tenets of the faith. At its best, under the spiritual power and driving force of a new faith all forms of this art expression were remarkably successful in evoking an ineffable mood of otherworldliness.

BIBLIOGRAPHY

Anthony, Edgar W., *A History of Mosaics*, Sargent, 1935

Bayley, Harold, *The Lost Language of Symbolism*, 2 vols., Lippincott, 1913

Brooklyn Museum, *Coptic Egypt*, Museum, Brooklyn Institute of Arts and Sciences, 1944

———— *Pagan and Christian Egypt: Egyptian Art from the First to the Tenth Century A.D.*, Museum, Brooklyn Institute of Arts and Sciences, 1941

Butler, Howard C., and Smith, E. B., *Early Churches in Syria*, Princeton University Press, 1929

Byron, Robert, *The Byzantine Achievement*, Knopf, 1929

———— *The Station, Athos: Treasures and Men*, Knopf, 1928

———— and Talbot Rice, David, *The Birth of Western Painting*, Knopf, 1931

Conant, Kenneth J., *A Brief Commentary on Early Mediaeval Church Architecture*, Johns Hopkins Press, 1942

Cunynghame, Henry H. S., *European Enamels*, London, 1906

Dalton, Ormonde M., *Byzantine Art and Archaeology*, Oxford University Press, 1911

———— *East Christian Art*, Oxford University Press, 1925

Diehl, Charles, *Byzantine Portraits*, tr. by Harold Bell, Knopf, 1927

———— *History of the Byzantine Empire*, Princeton University Press, 1925

———— *Manuel d'art byzantin*, 2d ed. rev., Vols. I–II, Paris, 1925–26

———— *La peinture byzantine*, Paris, 1933

Diez, Ernst, and Demus, Otto, *Byzantine Mosaics in Greece: Hosios Lucas & Daphni*, Harvard University Press, 1931

Early Christian and Byzantine Art, Walters Art Gallery, Baltimore, 1947

Frothingham, Arthur L., *The Monuments of Christian Rome from Constantine to the Renaissance*, Macmillan, 1908

Glück, Heinrich, *Die christliche kunst des ostens*, Berlin, 1923

Hamilton, John A., *Byzantine Architecture and Decoration*, Scribner, 1934

Jackson, Sir Thomas Graham, *Byzantine and Romanesque Architecture*, 2d ed., 2 vols., University of Chicago Press, 1920

Jacobus de Varagine, *The Golden Legend*, tr. and adapted from the Latin by Granger Ryan and Helmut Ripperger, 2 vols., Longmans, Green, 1941

Jameson, Anna B. Murphy, *Sacred and Legendary Art*, 2 vols., Houghton Mifflin, c. 1911

Lanciani, Rodolfo Amadeo, *Pagan and Christian Rome*, Houghton Mifflin, 1893

Lethaby, William R., *Mediæval Art*, new ed., Scribner, 1913

———— and Swainson, Harold, *The Church of Sancta Sophia, Constantinople*, Macmillan, 1894

Lowrie, Walter, *Monuments of the Early Church*, Macmillan, 1901

Maskell, Alfred O., *Ivories*, Putnam, 1905

Millet, Gabriel, *Le monastère de Daphni*, Paris, 1899

Morey, Charles R., *Christian Art*, Longmans, Green, 1935

———— *Early Christian Art*, Princeton University Press, 1942

———— *Mediaeval Art*, Norton, 1942

Muratov, Pavel Pavlovich, *La peinture byzantine*, Paris, 1935

Peirce, Hayford, and Tyler, Royall, *Byzantine Art*, Stokes, 1926

Porter, Arthur K., *Medieval Architecture*, 2 vols., Baker and Taylor, 1909

Rivoira, Giovanni Teresio, *Roman Architecture*, Oxford University Press, 1925

Schultz, Robert W., and Barnsley, S. H., *The Monastery of Saint Luke of Stiris, in Phocis*, London, 1901

Sherrill, Charles H., *Mosaics in Italy, Palestine, Syria, Turkey and Greece*, London, 1933

Showerman, Grant, *Eternal Rome*, rev. ed., Yale University Press, 1925

Strzygowski, Josef, *Origin of Christian Church Art*, tr. by O. M. Dalton and H. J. Braunholtz, Oxford University Press, 1923

Swift, Emerson H., *Hagia Sophia*, Columbia University Press, 1940

Talbot Rice, David, *Byzantine Art*, Oxford University Press, 1935

Van Millingen, Alexander, and Traquair, Ramsay, *Byzantine Churches in Constantinople*, Macmillan, 1912

———— *Byzantine Constantinople*, London, 1899

Victoria and Albert Museum, *Catalogue of Textiles from Burying-Grounds in Egypt*, 3 vols., Museum, London, 1920–22

Warner, George F., *Illuminated Manuscripts in the British Museum*, ser. 1–3, Museum, London, 1910

Whittemore, Thomas, *The Mosaics of St. Sophia at Istanbul*, Nos. 1–3, Oxford University Press, 1933–42 (Report of the Byzantine Institute)

See also the General Bibliography, pp. 791–92

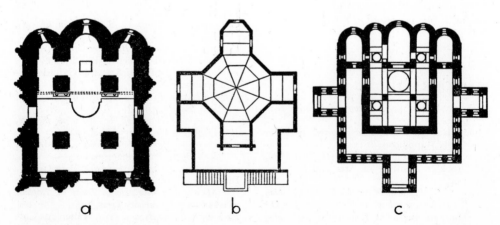

[A]   *Plans of Russian Churches.*   a. *Church of the type of St. Dmitri, Vladimir (Fig. 277A);* b. *Church of the Transfiguration, Kizhi (Fig. 278A);* c. *Church of St. John the Baptist, Yaroslav (Fig. 280A).*

[A]   *Iconostasis. Uspenski Cathedral, Moscow. 17th cent.*

14

RUSSIAN ART

(TENTH TO EIGHTEENTH CENTURY A.D.)

WHENCE came the original Slavic peoples of Russia? This is a moot question. The peoples who early colonized along the Black Sea and who roamed the great steppes were Hellenic or Iranian. Whatever their origin, these early pagan Russians were settled in Kiev and other cities along the western rivers when Vladimir I (about 956–1015), through close relations with Constantinople, accepted Eastern Orthodox (or Greek) Catholicism as the state religion and imposed this faith upon his subjects.

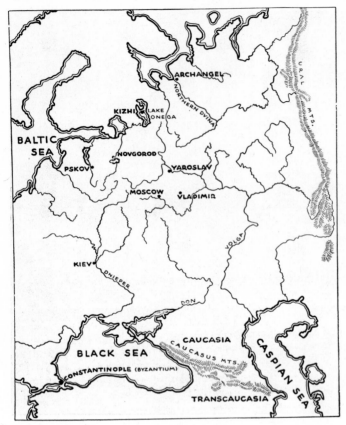

[A]   *Russia*

Russia at this time consisted of a group of loosely federated cities situated on the great water trade route between the Baltic and the Black seas. This route lay along the Dnieper and northern lakes and rivers, with Kiev the chief city of the south and Novgorod that of the north (Fig. 276A). In this land of sweeping areas — vast steppes in the south and unmeasured swamps and woodlands in the north — the natural trade routes of long navigable river systems connected by short portages determined the city sites. These great distances, as well as differences of climate and geography, on the one hand militated against unity, political and cultural, but on the other, enabled the northern cities to remain comparatively independent and out of reach of the Asiatic invaders who were surging west over the great steppes.

At first Byzantine influence was strong. But inevitable expansion eastward (eleventh and twelfth centuries) into the valley of the Volga, another great trade route, and the change of the capital from Kiev to Vladimir (1109) brought the Russians into relations with Caucasia and Transcaucasia. In the thirteenth century the great cultural development at Vladimir was halted by the invasion of the Mongols (1238),[1] who held sway over Russia until the rising principality of Muscovy at first defied and then defeated the in-

[1] The same westward movement of the Mongols under Jenghiz Khan which captured and destroyed Baghdad in 1258 and set up the Mongol dynasties in Persia. See Chapter 16.

vaders (1480) and finally, under Ivan the Terrible, expelled the last of them (1552).

In the meanwhile northwestern Russia, centering at Novgorod and free from the Tatar domination, developed its native arts, into conformity with which it brought the imported Byzantine traditions. Though Novgorod was a member of the Hanseatic League and was on the direct trade routes to the East, it was in a comparative isolation, so far as cultural influences were concerned, that the arts evolved. In the fifteenth century, with the eviction of the Tatars, Russia again established close relations with the Byzantine Empire. Byzantine painters came to Novgorod and Moscow, and Novgorod painters and Pskov builders helped build the new Moscow. So that as Moscow became a cultural as well as a political center, here was consolidated a truly Russian style, which translated borrowed forms into its own modes of expression.

ARCHITECTURE

The architecture of medieval Russia was chiefly ecclesiastical, at first strongly under the influence of Constantinople, if not actually produced by Greeks.[1] Examples are *Santa Sophia* at Kiev and a similar though less pretentious *Santa Sophia* at Novgorod. Both are built on the posticonoclastic plan of the Byzantine church (Fig. 264B) — that at Kiev with five apses and some

[1] The only book in English which adequately treats medieval Russian architecture is D. R. Buxton, *Russian Mediaeval Architecture*, Macmillan, 1934, to which the author is largely indebted for the material in this section. The basic authority on Russian art is the history by I. E. Grabar, which unfortunately has not been translated from the Russian but which is invaluable for its illustrations and to which the author is indebted for many of the illustrations in this chapter.

[A]   *Church of St. Dmitri. Vladimir. View showing the three apses. 1194–97. (Buxton)*

very fine Byzantine mosaics[2]; that at Novgorod with three apses, bulbous domes, and frescoes instead of mosaics — for Novgorod was not so affluent as Kiev, not being the seat of royalty. At Novgorod and at near-by Pskov the bulbous dome vividly colored had already appeared,[3] as had external galleries, covered stairways, and separate bell towers — all characteristic features of Russian churches.

Two churches at or near Vladimir, *St. Dmitri* (Fig. 277A) and the *Church of the Intercession*, are built on the typical plan of a square enclosing a Greek cross and crowned with a dome (Fig. 274Aa), in these churches a single dome on a high drum. They are built of stone,

[2] Only the central part of the present church at Kiev, with apses, belongs to the original church of 1037.

[3] Apparently a native Russian form. Its origin is uncertain, though a plausible explanation is that it sheds the snow.

[A] *Church of the Transfiguration. Kizhi, Lake Onega. Early 18th cent. For plan see Fig. 274Ab. (Grabar)*

which is rare in Russia, where brick, stucco, and wood are the usual materials. With very few openings, the wall spaces are decorated effectively with moldings, some of which, rising unbroken from the ground to the roof, divide the wall into panels; others, much shorter, form blind arcadings. At *St. Dmitri* the surface within the arcadings is elaborately carved in low reliefs peculiarly adapted to stone, and in subject matter and form close to Sassanian and other west-Asiatic carvings.

A truly native style[1] of church building originated in the north in the vast

[1] Though these timber churches all date after 1600, Mr. Buxton feels that they are the culmination of a long tradition, the earlier expressions of which have been lost through the perishable nature of the material, and particularly through fire.

rural districts dotted with villages, where timber was abundant. Free from Byzantine and Eastern influences and undisturbed by Mongol invaders, the Russian evolved out of his simple domestic buildings constructed of tree trunks laid horizontally the type of church seen in the octagon "tent-roofed" church of *St. Nicholas* (Fig. 279A), of which the *Church of the Transfiguration* at Kizhi (on an island in Lake Onega) is an elaboration (Fig. 278A). In the latter the octagon plan has been converted into a cross by extending four of its sides (Fig. 274Ab), and the mass of the church is as compact as its plan, notwithstanding the fantastic covering of roofs, which look like horizontally extended bulbous domes. Each roof carries a dome, and together they mount vivaciously to the crowning

members — an extraordinary grouping of twenty-two domes into a compact conical mass.

So deeply traditional was this native
wooden type that when requirements
of greater permanency demanded
brick or stone, the type was translated
quite literally into the new medium, as
we see in the *Church of the Ascension*
(Fig. 280B) at Kolomenskoe (near Moscow). This practice reaches a fantastic
expression in *St. Basil* at Moscow, in
which all the elements noted above are
used in excess, in exaggerated form
and with intense color. Yet "a rare
beauty of proportion emerges from
apparent confusion — an impression
of tranquility, not chaos," especially
when the building is "seen from the
distance in some happy play of sun or
moonshine." [1]

The fusion of Byzantine, Eastern, and
native timber styles [2] took place in
Muscovy, where at Moscow and Yaroslav one finds, from the fifteenth to
the seventeenth century, the climax of
the national style. In Moscow, the
Cathedral of the Annunciation (Fig. 281A)
is an example. It is built on a square
plan with eastern apses and is covered
with bulbous domes. Around three
sides run external galleries approached
by covered stairways; on the roof,
leading up to the domes, are "encor-
beled" arches. [3] In this cathedral there
is also evidence of the fact that as early
as the late fifteenth century Italian

[1] Buxton, *op. cit.*, p. 44.
[2] The relation of the timber style to that of
Moscow, like the origin of the bulbous dome, is
controversial, as are, in fact, many points of
origin and influence connected with this art,
which has received but little attention up to
the present time.
[3] This extraordinary external decorative
feature originated in a structural device, on the
part of builders in Pskov, of superposing corbeled arches above the four great arches of the
crossing in order to make the transition from the
square base to the dome — a problem solved by
the Byzantine builders with pendentives.

[A] *Church of St. Nicholas the Wonder-
Worker. Panilowo, Gov. Archangel, 1600.
(Grabar)*

architects were arriving in Moscow and
were introducing into the native style
Western elements — classical moldings,
for example.

In Yaroslav, however, a great trade
center still free from foreign influence,
these Italian elements are lacking, and
the church of *St. John the Baptist* (Fig.
280A) is consistently Russian, following
closely the standardized plan which,
according to an edict issued in 1650 by
the Patriarch of Russia, required all
churches to use the square plan with
five domes — a central one over the
crossing and one over each angle between the arms of the cross (Fig. 274AC).
Notable in this church are the external brickwork, the glazed tile decoration around the windows, the fine
porches, and the general magnificence
of the church as a whole.

[B] *Church of the Ascension. Kolomenskoe (near Moscow). 1532. (Grabar) This brick church derives from its wooden prototypes a conical tower, superposed arches, and a high base with covered stairways and galleries.*

[A] *Church of St. John the Baptist. Yaroslav. 1687. See plan, Fig. 274AC. (Buxton)*

Only the exteriors of these Russian churches have been described. As the window openings are few and small, the interiors are dim. However, the great wall spaces lend themselves to mural decoration, as did those of their prototypes, the later Byzantine churches (Fig. 266A). A few wealthy churches used mosaics, the others fresco, but in either case according to a strict iconography. An important feature was the iconostasis (Fig. 275A), the many-tiered screen that separates the sanctuary from the main body of the church, with three doors, the central one — the royal door — reserved for the priests only. The iconostasis contains the sacred images, arranged according to rigid regulation. It is deco-

rated elaborately with carvings, gilding, and metalwork, and before it hang magnificent candelabra. Very resplendent is such an interior, its very dimness adding to the effect. The congregation stands, the liturgy contains long chants and a cappella music, with frequent censing. In flickering candlelight and through clouds of incense the rich vestments of the clergy combine with the brilliant color and ornament of the iconostasis to create a focal point, which is surrounded by dim walls covered with figures that rise in hieratic succession to the Pantocrator of the dome. Thus every element contributes to produce the effect of otherworldliness, the aim of the Byzantine artists.

[A] *Cathedral of the Annunciation. Moscow. 1482–90.*

PAINTING

To decorate the walls of churches, to paint icons for private shrines and for iconostases and miniatures for the sacred books, were the functions of the painter. Again, it was an ecclesiastical art. Like the buildings, the early mosaics, frescoes, and icons are Byzantine in style. Some icons were probably imported from Constantinople or Greece. This was probably the case with the *Vladimir Madonna* (Fig. 283A), one of the icons held most sacred because it was believed to protect the Russians against the Mongols. For this reason it held a place of honor in the lowest tier of the iconostasis of the church at Vladimir. It is a typical Byzantine painting,[1] in

[1] There are at least six layers of repainting; only the faces show the original surface. As the icons were quickly blackened by the incense, it was a usual practice to repaint them, which was often done, unfortunately, by an inferior painter. For the cleaning of this and other icons by the Central National Restoration Workshops of the Soviet Government, see M. S. Farbman, ed., *Masterpieces of Russian Painting*, London, 1930.

which two figures are compactly united into a majestic group that fills the panel with its flat pattern, a silhouette with unbroken sweep of virile contour within which the figures are tied together both as to form and as to sensitive feeling.

The development of the iconostasis into the elaborate screen with more than five tiers had an important effect on icon-painting. For the purpose of these paintings was to enable the worshiper to read pictorially. Clear pictorial legibility in wavering candlelight and through clouds of incense required strong pattern, firm lines, and intense color. For this reason the relatively sober hues of the early Byzantine paintings gave way to the more characteristically Russian colors, intense and contrasting.

This style we find in the work of the Novgorod and Pskov painters, in the *Saint Basil* (Fig. 283B), for example, which is dynamic in feeling, and startling in its angularity and contrasts. The sharp angles and strong curves repeated in every detail, the precise out-

[A]　*Rublëv. Old Testa-
ment　Trinity.　Trinity
Cathedral in the Mon-
astery of Sergievo. c. 1410.
(A. H. Barr, Jr.)*

lining of the parts of the head and of the features, the sharp color-contrasts, the elongated proportions — each of these elements contributes to an abstract pattern of brusque forcefulness and vigorous movement that is little concerned with a representation of visual perception.

As in architecture, it was the assimilation of outside influences with this native dynamism that produced a Russian style. As in architecture, again, with the waning of the Mongol domination, during which Byzantine influence was cut off, Greek painters again appeared at Novgorod and Moscow, among them Theophanes of Mistra. Under this renewed Byzantine

influence and through the requirements of the iconostasis, which was just at that time reaching its highest development, a climax of Russian painting was reached in the work of Andrei Rublëv (about 1370–1430) whose monumental *Old Testament Trinity* (Fig. 282A) is a masterly design in line and color. About a table are seated the three angels who appeared to Abraham near the oaks of Mamre. The figures, each framed with a halo and sweeping wings, almost fill the panel, and are clearly and definitely related to each other and to the space by a design of horizontals and peculiarly suave curves, free from clashing oppositions, which produces a tranquillity like that of the *Vladimir*

[A] *Vladimir Madonna. 11th cent. Historical Museum, Moscow. Formerly in the Cathedral of the Assumption at Vladimir but removed to Moscow in 1395 to protect the city from a Tatar invasion.*

[B] *St. Basil the Great. Right half of a pair of royal doors. 14th cent. Museum of Tver. (Figs. 283A and B, A. H. Barr, Jr.)*

Madonna. Yet sufficient angularity in the table, the chairs, and the folds of the garments provides contrasting motifs. These forms are constructed of color, each detail an area of color, which is frequently intensified by the juxtaposition of a complementary hue. The intense blue and green folds of the cloak of the central figure stand out starkly against the deep-red robe and gilded orange wings. In the figure on the left the high lights of the orange cloak are a pattern of opalescent blue-

green: "one is amazed at a recurrent *gamme* of color different from any that Western art has produced or attempted to produce until recent years, in the extraordinary copy of Rublëv's Trinity, the unforgettable Saint Demetrius robed in vermilion with a vermilion shield, the black-winged archangels, Michael and Gabriel. The dominant scale of color is distinctly Oriental — parchment white, golden buff, turquoise, blue, vermilion, malachite green, an occasional note of plum heightened by the uncompromising accent of unrelieved black. It could be matched by grouping Chinese, Korean, and Persian ceramics. The enamel-like purity and brilliance of the pigment constitute an almost unparalleled triumph in the technique of painting."[1] We should not forget in considering this rich ecclesiastical art of medieval Russia the indispensable part played in the entire ensemble of a church interior by other arts: the carvings and rich metalwork of the iconostasis and the finely wrought jeweled halos and other ornaments on the icons; the candlesticks and candelabra; the miters and ecclesiastical robes stiff with gold, embroidery, and jewels; the illuminated books bound in gold or ivory inlaid with jewels and enamels; the crosses, croziers, sacred vessels, and processional banners. Each contributed with its amazing richness of texture and color to the total effect.

SUMMARY

The common objective of Russian art in the Middle Ages — to create visibly and emotionally an effect of transcendent otherworldliness — produced one of the loftiest expressions of Eastern Christianity. It was an art that took much from other cultures, yet by adapting these borrowings to its own vernacular produced something strangely individual. In the quiet, if not monotonous, landscape a vivid, picturesque mass of domes and steeple-

[1] Lee Simonson, *Metropolitan Museum of Art Bulletin*, January, 1931, p. 6.

like tent roofs "gleams like a jeweled clasp on a sober robe." The dim, resplendent interior, to whose effectiveness builder, painter, and craftsman contributed, is perhaps the most comprehensive expression of the common objective.

BIBLIOGRAPHY

Bunt, Cyril G. E., *A History of Russian Art*, Studio, 1946

Buxton, David R., *Russian Mediaeval Architecture*, Macmillan, 1934

Eliasberg, Alexander, *Russische Baukunst*, Munich, 1922

Farbman, Michael S., ed., *Masterpieces of Russian Painting*, London, 1930

Halle, Fannina W., *Alt-russische Kunst*, Berlin, 1920

Kondakov, Nikodim Pavlovich, *The Russian Icon*, tr. by E. H. Minns, Oxford University Press, 1927

Lukomskii, Georgi; Kreskentevich, *History of Modern Russian Painting*, Hutchinson, 1945

Maskell, Alfred O., *Russian Art and Art Objects in Russia*, London, 1884

Metropolitan Museum of Art, *A Catalogue of Russian Icons*, with introduction by I. E. Grabar, Museum, New York City, 1931

Miliukov, Paul N., *Outlines of Russian Culture*, 3 pts., University of Pennsylvania Press, 1942: Pt. III, *Architecture, Painting and Music*

Muratov, Pavel Pavlovich, *Les icones russes* Paris, 1927

——————— *La peinture byzantine*, Paris, 1935

Newmarch, Rosa J., *The Russian Arts*, Dutton, 1916

Olsufiev, Yoori A., "The Development of Russian Icon Painting from the Twelfth to the Nineteenth Century," *Art Bulletin*, December 1930

Talbot Rice, David, ed., *Russian Art: An Introduction*, London, 1935

Voyce, Arthur, *Russian Architecture*, Philosophical Library, 1948

See also General Bibliography, pp. 791–92.

[A]   *Mosque of Ibn Tulun. Cairo. 876–78. (Creswell)*

15

MUHAMMADAN ART[1]

(A.D. 622 TO DATE)

WHILE the early Christian and Byzantine culture was evolving from a fusion of Greco-Roman, Near Eastern, and Northern elements, another culture, energized by an extremely dynamic religious force, was also rising. This was destined to meet the Christian religion at certain points and to fuse some of its forms, especially in Spain and Hispanic America, with those of Christian medieval art; in the Far East it met and fused with the arts of Far Asia. This was the Muhammadan religion.

When we think of the Muhammadans, we think not of a nation in the modern sense of the word, with sharply defined geographical boundaries, but of groups of people of varying cultures, widespread geographically but bound together by a burning and at times fanatical religious faith. The Mu-

[1] Also called Mohammedan, Muslim (Moslem), or Islamic.

hammadans call this faith Islam, which means obedience to the will of Allah (God); and their creed is embodied in the prayer chanted by the muezzin from the minaret as he calls the faithful to worship: "God is great, God is great, God is great. I bear witness that there is no god but God. I bear witness that there is no god but God. I bear witness that Muhammad is the Apostle of God. I bear witness that Muhammad is the Apostle of God. Come to prayer. Come to prayer. Come to security. Come to security. God is great. God is great. There is no god but God." This religion, originating in Arabia, spread both east and west with amazing rapidity, chiefly by means of the sword; for the Muslim became an invincible soldier because of his fatalistic belief in the will of Allah, and because he was lured by the promise of immediate entrance into the Garden of Paradise if he died upon the field of battle fighting for the Islamic faith.

Because of geographical extent and lack of traditional unity, Muhammadan art has manifested itself in diverse ways, strongly affected by local traditions, sometimes merely grafting upon the native art a few of its requirements. At first the Muslim conquerors, Arab nomads with no arts of their own,[1] did just what the Persians under Cyrus did when they conquered the older civilizations — borrowed or adapted what they found at hand. For example, when they conquered Constantinople they converted the church of *Santa Sophia* into a mosque merely by inserting a niche, whitewashing the mosaics containing figure work, and erecting the minarets. Soon, however, they so transformed their adaptations by their own means of expression that Muhammadan art became a strikingly individual thing. Because of this di-

versity, our discussion will be confined chiefly to Egypt[2] and to noting some of the characteristic features of Islamic art.

Egypt was a province of the Byzantine Empire at the time of its conquest by the Muslims in 641, and already the early Christians of Egypt, the Copts, had evolved from the strongly entrenched Hellenistic art centered at Alexandria a very vital nonmaterialistic expression much more consistent with their own traditions. It was an expression augmented by influences from the East, as we saw in their textile designs (Fig. 272A). Ruled first by governors appointed by the caliphs of Damascus or Baghdad, Egypt finally set up an independent government under the Tulunids (868–904), which continued under the Fatimids (969–1171), who founded a new capital at Kahira (Cairo) in 969 and in their art expression reached a climax of refinement and dynamic vitality. Succeeding them as rulers were the Mamelukes (1252–1517) — Tatar slaves of the sultan who rose from servitude to become for nearly three hundred years independent Muslim sovereigns of Egypt. Politically it was an age of intrigue and murder. The Mamelukes were still barbarians and merciless cutthroats; rarely did a Mameluke reign more than a few years, and very few died a natural death. Yet the arts flourished with an amazing vigor and displayed a rare and refined taste — one of the startling contrasts of history, as Mr. Lane-Poole suggests.

Against sumptuousness and license of all kinds the Koran decreed puritanically. Yet the Muhammadans, particularly the Mamelukes, with their Oriental love of color, fine silks, jewels, and richly inlaid vessels, managed in var-

---

[1] No visual arts. Pre-Muhammadan Arabic poetry is of a high order.

[2] Although possibly the finest early mosques and fortified palaces important for their stone construction are to be found in Damascus and Aleppo. For Muslim art in Persia see Chapter 16, and for Indian Art, Chapter 19.

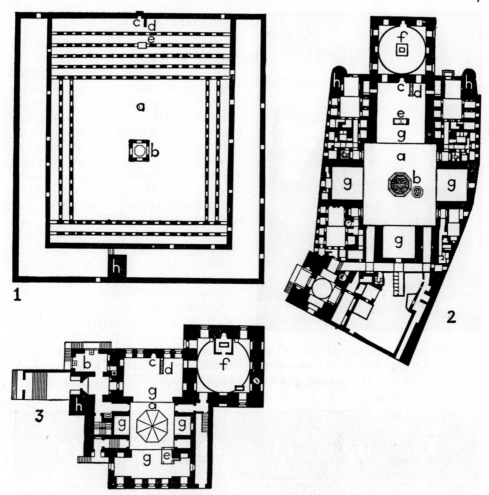

[A] *Plans of Mosques. 1. Mosque of Ibn Tulun (Fig. 285A); 2. Tomb-mosque of Sultan Hassan (Figs. 288A, 289A); 3. Tomb-mosque of Sultan Kait Bey (Figs. 290A, 291A). Although apparently diverse in plan they have several features in common: a. court; b. fountain; c. niche* (mihrab) *indicating the direction of Mecca; d. pulpit* (mimbar); *e. tribune* (dikkeh); *f. tomb; g. recess* (liwan); *h. minaret. In* (1) *covered arcades instead of recesses surround the court, which is 300 ft. square; in* (2) *the angles formed by the recesses of the court are filled with rooms for schools, offices, and apartments for the attendants.*

ious ways to circumvent these decrees. With great wealth at their command, they adorned their homes, and even their traveling tents of gold-shot silk, with rich hangings, fine rugs, and exquisite utensils; and they clothed themselves in the most splendid apparel. In spite of many fastings, prayers, and pilgrimages demanded by the Koran, life was gay with festivals, feasts, and sports.[1]

[1] For a picture of Muhammadan life, see Stanley Lane-Poole, *The Art of the Saracens in Egypt*, London, 1886, Chap. I.

[A] *Mosque of Sultan Hassan. Cairo.*
1356–59. The dome indicates a tomb-mosque.
Of stone taken from the Pyramids of Giza.

ARCHITECTURE

Since the Muhammadan was fanatical in religious belief and at the
same time zealous in the pursuit of
pleasure, it is natural to find his architecture devoted chiefly to the mosque
and the palace. As far as worship was
concerned, his needs were simple: a secluded place, away from the noise of
the streets, where a fountain provided
water for ablution (for he must bathe
before going to worship), and a place
protected from the hot sun where, with
face turned toward Mecca, he could
pray. This direction was indicated to
him by a niche in the wall of the
mosque, beside which was a pulpit
from which the Friday (the Muhammadan Sunday) sermon was preached;
a little in front of these stood the raised
platform from which the Koran was
recited and prayers were chanted.
These simple but universal features constitute the sanctuary of a mosque (Figs.
287A, 291A).

[B] *Decorative Border with Arabesques and Kufic Lettering. Mosque of Sultan Hassan*
(*Fig. 289A*)

[A]   *Mosque of Sultan Hassan. Court, looking toward the sanctuary.*

The early cloistered mosque of *Ibn Tulun* (Figs. 285A, 287A1) adequately supplies these needs. It consists of a great open court with a fountain in the center, surrounded by covered arcades two deep on three sides but five deep on the sanctuary side (the end facing toward Mecca), the special place of prayer; and a girdle wall standing fifty feet outside the mosque walls on three sides, which gives the building added seclusion. The exterior presents a plain, massive wall with a row of small windows and simple unadorned doorways, the only decoration being a crenelated parapet. At one side rises the minaret, the tower from which the muezzin calls to prayer; it is rectangular, partaking of the same simple boldness and massive-

ness as the rest of the mosque. An external ramp provides a means of ascent which carries the mind back to the ramp towers of Babylonia (Fig. 83A).

The mosque of *Sultan Hassan* (Fig. 288A) is more complex in plan (Fig. 287A2). On each side of the court is a barrel-vaulted recess (*liwan*) with pointed arch, the largest constituting the sanctuary, behind which is the dome-covered tomb. The angles of the recesses are filled with rooms for schools, offices, and apartments, for Muslim educational institutions are usually connected with the mosque. This mosque is an austere mass of stone (appropriated from the *Pyramids of Gizeh*, just as the early Christians appropriated stone and marbles from the classical Roman

[A]   *Tomb-mosque of Sultan Kait Bey. In the environs of Cairo. 1472–76. Of red and white freestone. (Photoglob)*

buildings to build their churches), with decoration concentrated at the lofty portals and in a frieze beneath the crenelation. The interior (Fig. 289A), except the great arches, is made of brick stuccoed with decorative carvings and a particularly fine border (Fig. 288B) at the spring of the vault.

Smaller mosques enabled the builders to decorate more lavishly; as we see in the mosque of *Kait Bey* (Fig. 290A), the small size, lightness, and elegance of which contrast with the grandeur and unadorned simplicity of *Ibn Tulun* and *Sultan Hassan*. The mosque with its minaret and the tomb with its dome are massed asymmetrically, as is indicated in the nonaxial plan (Fig. 287A3). The tall arched portal, a characteristic feature of the mosque, is elaborately ornamented with carvings and

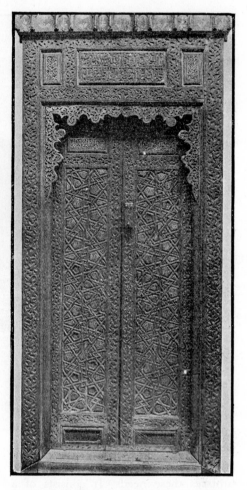

[B]   *Pulpit of Kait Bey. Door. Wood and ivory. H. 7 ft. Late 15th cent. Victoria and Albert Museum, London. (Victoria and Albert Museum)*

stalactites.[1] Shallow recesses enclosing the windows break up the wall surface. The slender, graceful minaret, with projecting galleries from which stalactites depend, is ornamented with niches and carvings; the contrasting dome with its virile sweep of line is covered

[1] Pendent architectural ornaments resembling the icicle-like deposits (stalactites) found in caverns.

[A]   *Tomb-mosque of Sultan Kait Bey (Figs. 290A, 287A3). Sanctuary showing the pulpit* (mimbar), *the niche* (mihrab), *and the richly colored glass windows; at the upper left is a segment of the horseshoe arch.*

with arabesque carvings. The usual crenelation finishes the walls, for the overshadowing cornice rarely finds a place in Muhammadan architecture. In this mosque the place of ablution is a small room at the left of the entrance. The court is roofed with a hexagonal lantern rich in color and gold, and on it opens the sanctuary, with a pointed horseshoe arch of alternating light and dark stone (Fig. 291A). The floor is paved with marble slabs, and the lower part of the walls is faced with variously colored marbles through which gleams mother-of-pearl. The niche is ornamented sumptuously with marble and mosaic, and the pulpit with carvings. Above, the wall is pierced with small windows of brilliantly colored glass. From the ceiling are suspended chains

that originally held inlaid metal or enameled-glass lamps. The impression of such a sanctuary with its subdued light is one of great richness of material and splendor of color.

Even a superficial glance at Islamic art — not building only but all the arts — discloses its love of an ornamentation which impresses one with its dynamic vitality and decorative beauty. Its motifs were very limited. Islam forbade the representation of human and animal figures, and though the decree was not followed except by the orthodox and except in the case of objects used in the mosque, still it turned the eye of the artist to geometry and the world of plant life for subject matter.

From plant life — no one has discovered just where or when — was

[A]   *Carved Wood Panel. From the mosque-hospital of Sultan Kalaun, Cairo. 1284. (After Prisse d'Avennes)*

derived the arabesque, that universal Muslim motif which is one of the most characteristic marks of the style. The arabesque is a flowing, spiraling, interlacing pattern with palmette- or half-palmette-like motifs, suggestive but not at all imitative of leaf forms (Fig. 293A). It was adaptable to almost every material, and with its capacity for spiraling with infinite variations well satisfied the Muslim's strong impulse to cover surfaces. For a horror vacui

possessed him. Another universal motif in Islamic ornament was Arabic calligraphy. Writing was a fine art and both styles, Kufic and Neskhi,[1] revealed decorative possibilities, the Kufic (Figs. 288B, 297B) providing contrasting angularity, the Neskhi flowing into the curves of the arabesques (Fig. 295A). A third Islamic motif found from Spain to India was the stalactite used with such effectiveness in the mosque portal.

Plaster, used wet, was a particularly adaptable medium for the freely flowing line that distinguishes Muhammadan ornament, for here the hand could move easily and spontaneously. It appears in the earlier buildings — for example, about the arches in the mosque of *Ibn Tulun* — but was largely replaced by stone or marble about the fourteenth century. The Kufic frieze (Fig. 288B) that decorates the sanctuary of the mosque of *Sultan Hassan* well illustrates stucco ornament. The bold, angular letters are particularly monumental, and contrast effectively with the delicate floral arabesques from which they emerge.

Though plaster and stone were used largely in architectural ornament and even occasionally for a pulpit, wood was the material most favored for decorating the furnishings of both mosques and palaces. It was not only carved but frequently inlaid with ivory and ebony. This is well illustrated by a mosque pulpit, which stands at the right of the niche as one faces the sanctuary (Fig. 291A). Approached by a high door, it consists of a stairway that leads to a small covered platform surmounted by a cupola. Elaborate decoration, geo-

[1] Kufic: the older, formal, angular style, so called from the city of Kufa in Mesopotamia, where the best calligraphers lived. Neskhi: a cursive script. Kufic was used for inscriptions and for copying the Koran, though later Neskhi was used for the latter purpose, with Kufic reserved for chapter headings.

metric, floral, and stalactite, covers the surface. A door from one of these pulpits (Fig. 290B) illustrates the abundance of the carving. Arabesques, with panels inserted for the inscriptions, cover all the surfaces except the panels of the doors, which are filled with geometric patterns whose incisive angularity affords a happy contrast to the gliding lines of the rest of the carving. The geometric patterns are made up of many small polygons, each framing a floral motif and finished with a molding. The polygons are ingeniously fitted together so as to allow for warping, which is expected in the Egyptian climate. In these geometric designs we see the same fertility of invention as in the arabesque.

In an example of Fatimid wood-carving which is notable for the virility of its design (Fig. 293A) the wood is undercut so as to create a light pattern on a dark ground, thus bringing into prominence the strong central motif terminating in the horses' heads, and its integration, carried out with such inevitability, into the lighter rapid arabesques. Another panel (Fig. 292A), from the *Hospital of Kalaun*, makes greater use of human and animal figures, some of which are suggestive of Eastern textiles. Broad sweeping bands form a heart-shaped motif repeated with variations and playing into the narrower spirals. Thus two systems of movement interplay throughout the panel. Broadly sweeping lines intertwine and knot, now terminating in floral forms that fill the ground and now forming geometric areas that contain human, bird, animal, and griffin forms. In the large central medallion is a kneeling man carrying a slain deer on his shoulders; above him are two eagles in balanced position, and at the sides two cockatoos whose long sweeping tails repeat the curves of the scrolls; the four circular medallions are filled

[A] *Wood Door Panel. Carved with arabesques and the heads of two horses. W. c. 9 in. 11th cent. Metropolitan Museum of Art, New York City. (Metropolitan Museum)*

with griffin or deer on whose backs are eagles with outspread wings. Details are omitted, and the forms are flattened out, simplified, and pleasingly adapted to the curving lines of the geometric areas.

Color and gilding played an important part in Muhammadan ornament. Both stucco and wood-carvings were vividly painted. Another method of obtaining color was by marble inlay and stained glass. Panels of variously colored marbles — red, yellow, black, green — perhaps combined with blue tile, or bordered with a geometric pattern of colored glass and mother-of-pearl, faced the sanctuary of the mosque or formed a dado around the palace room. A most brilliant effect of color came from the windows, which were

[A] *Window. Stucco and glass. H. 30 in. Victoria and Albert Museum, London. (Victoria and Albert Museum)*

made by filling a wooden frame with plaster about an inch thick, scooping out a pattern in the plaster while it was still soft, and then filling in the perforations with bits of colored glass. In Figure 294A the design consists of a palm tree with spreading branches that curve to fit into the arch in which it stands; below are plane trees and flowers. The process is very simple and crude in comparison with the leaded windows of the Gothic period (Fig. 354A); but the masses of color when penetrated by the Egyptian sunshine are rich and jewel-like in their effect.

The Cairene house was, and is today, a flat-topped structure of several stories built about an open court — the typical Mediterranean house plan — with one part reserved for the women, who live in seclusion. It stands flush with the narrow street and often has a

carved, metal-studded wooden door and overhanging windows with infinitely varied wooden lattice. Although provided with these windows, the house faces the court, which in the better homes is a garden with fountains. The furnishings are extremely simple, but the carpets and cushions, inlaid metal, and carvings produce the same richness of effect that we have observed in the mosque.

The palaces of the Muslims, from India to Spain, are magnificent houses for luxurious living. In Spain the Moors established themselves in the southern part of the country, though their influence penetrated the entire peninsula. Cordova in the tenth century was one of the most enlightened cities of Europe and, with its great libraries, a center for learning. Its astronomers, mathematicians, musicians, and surgeons were famous, and in the *Great Mosque* its architects had worked out a system of ribbed vaulting two centuries before the Gothic builders. Here in Iberia was firmly implanted a style that was to continue after the expulsion of the Moors and was to be influential in the Hispanic colonies in America. Marks of this style are: the horseshoe arch; geometric ornament with an insistent surface character; carved and polychromed wood ceilings and doors. The *Alhambra* illustrates the Moorish version of the Muhammadan palace. It is built about several courts, with tiled fountains and shaded porticoes along the sides. The lower part of the walls is covered by tiles decorated with geometric designs in subdued tones harmonizing with the shady part of the court. Slender columns support arches and walls, the surfaces of which are richly covered with stalactites, intricate geometric ornament, and inscriptions, molded in stucco and painted and gilded. This decoration, though profuse, is orderly, and each motif is sensitively related to the area — wall space, soffit of an arch, spandrel, or capital — and held to that area, and its delicacy is brought out clearly by color.

METALWORK, GLASS, TEXTILES

The furnishings of the palaces as well as of the mosques satisfied the Muslim's love of rich and sumptuous effects. With both painting and sculpture banned, he must needs depend upon the carvers in stone and wood, the mosaicists, the workers in various metals, the glassmaker, and the weaver to satisfy his needs. The same motifs — the arabesque, floral, and geometric designs and interlacings, calligraphy — appear in all the crafts, and are a revelation of the flexibility of this narrow range of ornament, for rarely does one find exact duplication.

Islamic metalwork maintains the high quality that has characterized this art in the Near Eastern lands throughout the ages. Basins, often huge in size, ewers, candlesticks, trays, perfume-burners, jewel cases, writing-boxes — many objects for use in the mosque and the home — were made of wrought copper or brass, engraved and inlaid with silver, with the base sometimes covered with a black substance to set forth the silver inlay more sharply and

thus create a resplendent effect. In Figure 295A, for example, effective use is made of the Arabic calligraphy; the chief band of decoration consists of an inscription in large letters, broken by rosettes which are made of a central whorl surrounded by a ring of flying ducks. A narrower band of scroll pattern, broken at intervals by whorls, separates the broad band from the diaper pattern of flowers and birds on the bottom.

Very brilliant was the enameled glass, particularly effective in the mosque lamps. The glass of these lamps is blown, with many bubbles and streakings, and is usually slightly yellow or green. In Figure 296A, the broad, tall neck tapers toward the rather squat body, which carries six loops or handles for the silver chains by which it was suspended to the beam or ceiling of the mosque. The surface is covered with bands of arabesques and arabesque-entwined inscriptions worked in enamel — blue, white, yellow, green, red — with a liberal use of gold. Inside the lamp a small glass vessel, with oil and wick, is hooked to the rim, so that the light brings out the decorations with a rich soft glow. The effect of a considerable number of these lamps in such a sanctuary as that of *Kait Bey* must have been magnificent.

Woven fabrics and leather were of great value for their contribution of

[A] *Brass Bowl. Inlaid with silver. The inscription reads: "His Excellency, generous, exalted, lordly, great Amir, wise, ruler, leonine, fighter for the Faith, warden of Islam (liegeman) of El-Melih En-Nasir"* (a Mameluke ruler of 14th cent.). *British Museum, London.*

[A] *Mosque Lamp. Enameled glass. H. 13 in. The inscription on the neck from the Koran reads, "In the house that God hath permitted to be raised for His name to be commemorated therein, men celebrate his praises morning (and evening)." 14th cent. Victoria and Albert Museum, London. (Victoria and Albert Museum)*

texture and color. When the Arabs came into Egypt, the weaving craft had already reached a high level of attainment among the Copts, as it also had in Sassanian Persia,[1] whose fine silks not only were highly prized but dominated textile design throughout the Near East.[2] At first the Arabs employed the Copts to work for them, and from these expert weavers they learned the craft. By the time of the Fatimids Arab fabrics were famous (Fig. 297A).

[1] See Chapter 16.
[2] It is interesting to note how many of our names for textiles originate in Near East weaving centers — *damask, muslin,* and *taffeta* are examples — indicating the fame of these centers for producing fabrics.

The fabrics were made usually with a fine linen warp and silk weft, and the patterns were based upon the usual Islamic motifs — the arabesque and calligraphy — and upon Coptic and Sassanian designs of interlaced circles containing birds and animals or two bilaterally balanced figures.

CALLIGRAPHY

Two peoples, at least, practiced the art of writing as a major art: the Chinese and the Muhammadans. With the latter, fine writing was used not only for books — for at this period all books were written by hand — but also, as we have seen, as one of the peculiarly Islamic decorative motifs. Perhaps the highest point of achievement was the Koran (Qur'an), the sacred book of Islam. The calligrapher's work consisted not only in the shaping of the letters but also in illumination as rich as the decoration of the mosque sanctuary (Fig. 297B). The first and last two or three pages generally contain a richly decorated panel with the usual inscription — "Let none touch it save the purified" — in Kufic letters, and a margined medallion. Frequently the text is written in gold letters. Vivid blue predominates in the decoration, with a little red and white, black or green, and a great deal of gold. The splendor of the effect is perhaps equaled by the delicacy of the infinite detail, even more intricate than the carvings and engravings, for the brush is more facile than the carver's tools.

SUMMARY

Among the Muhammadans we find an art with unusually narrow restrictions. The mosque and the palace with their sparse furnishings illustrate the range of art expression. There is a conspicuous absence of pictures and sculpture and few representations of the human or animal figure except for secular use, and then infrequently. In their stead are delicate carvings of stone, stucco, wood, and ivory or marble inlay, rich stuffs, brilliantly colored glass, and resplendent metal. Everywhere is line, pattern, color. All the arts are inextricably interwoven, not only in creating the ensemble but in interchange of ideas and motifs; for the geometric inlay on the helmet finds its way to the carvings of the dome; the stone or stucco carved band on the mosque, to the pages of a Koran; and the textile design, to the silver inlay of a bowl. The very restrictions of this art, however, seem to be responsible for its particular bent. For with concentration upon decoration, and with that, too, dependent upon a few fundamental geometric and floral motifs, the Muslim created an endless variety of carvings, now the angular geometric pattern, now the smoothly flowing, intricate arabesque. But each work, no matter what the medium, was apparently a fresh and vital creation, displaying, in spite of narrow bounds, great inventiveness and amazing exuberance.

[A]   *Fatimid Silk Textile. 13th cent. Metropolitan Museum of Art, New York City. (Metropolitan Museum)*

BIBLIOGRAPHY

Arnold, Sir Thomas Walker, *Painting in Islam,* Oxford University Press, 1928
———— and Guillaume, Alfred, eds., *The Legacy of Islam,* Oxford University Press, 1931
Briggs, Martin S., *Muhammadan Architecture in Egypt and Palestine,* Oxford University Press, 1924
Creswell, Keppel A. C., *Early Muslim Architecture,* 2 pts., Oxford University Press, 1932
Dimand, Maurice S., *A Handbook of Mohammedan Art,* Metropolitan Museum of Art, New York City, 1944
Fry, Roger Eliot, *Vision and Design,* Brentano's, 1924, "The Munich Exhibition of Mohammedan Art"

[B]   *Illuminated Page from a Koran. 1368–88. Khedivial Library, Cairo. (Moritz)*

Glück, Heinrich, and Diez, Ernst, *Die Kunst des Islam*, Berlin, 1925

Grousset, René, *The Civilizations of the East*, tr. by C. A. Phillips, 4 vols., Knopf, 1931–34, Vol. I

Hobson, Robert L., *A Guide to the Islamic Pottery of the Near East*, British Museum, London, 1932

Kendrick, Albert F., *Catalogue of Muhammadan Textiles of the Medieval Period*, Victoria and Albert Museum, London, 1924

Kœchlin, Raymond, *L'art de l'Islam: Les céramiques*, Paris, 1928

————— and Alfassa, Paul, *L'art de l'Islam*, Paris, 1928

Lane, Edward W., *An Account of the Manners and Customs of the Modern Egyptians*, 3d ed., Dutton, 1908

Lane-Poole, Stanley, *The Art of the Saracens in Egypt*, London, 1886

Migeon, Gaston, *Les arts musulmans*, Paris, 1926

Nicholson, Reynold A., *Translations of Eastern Poetry and Prose*, Macmillan, 1922

Rivoira, Giovanni Teresio, *Moslem Architecture*, tr. by G. McN. Rushforth, Oxford University Press, 1919

Ross, Sir Edward Denison, ed., *The Art of Egypt through the Ages*, Studio, 1931

See also General Bibliography, pp. 791–92.

16

PERSIAN ART

Sassanian Persian Art

(A.D. 226–641)

IN the third century A.D. a new power had arisen in Persia, the Sassanian, so called from a priestly Iranian family who lived in a secluded part of southern Persia and there maintained the old traditions and religion of their race. Having conquered the Parthians, the Sassanians, notwithstanding the welter of Hellenistic, Roman, Parthian, and early Christian influences in the Valley of the Two Rivers, brought about a revival of Iranian culture, especially of the ancestral faith of Zoroaster. This Sassanian empire, with capitals at Istakhr (near Persepolis) and at Ctesiphon (near Baghdad), reached a climax under Chosroes (Khosrau) I (A.D. 531–579) and Chosroes (Khosrau) II (590–628), when Ctesiphon became a fabulously rich city and one of the most influential centers of the Near East. These rulers were great patrons of the arts and encouraged all workers in the crafts, particularly the weavers of fine silk textiles, which were in demand by the luxurious Byzantine court and which, through their introduction into the West, became a strong influence in the evolution of European ornament. When Justinian, in his zeal to propagate the Christian faith, closed the pagan schools of Athens, the artists and scholars fled to the court of Chosroes I, carrying with them the classical traditions and learning, with the result that the Sassanian court was one of the broadest and most enlightened of the Near East. But, notwithstanding its power and vigor, this empire was short-lived, for it was one of the first to fall before the fanatical invincibility of the Muslim invaders (A.D. 641).

[A]   *Palace at Ctesiphon. Sassanian. (Sarre and Herzfeld)*

ARCHITECTURE

Sassanian art is an example of the great assimilative capacity of the Iranian. Whatever he took he translated into his own idiom and infused with his own dynamic vitality. As with the Achaemenids, the palace is the type building, of which the *Palace at Ctesiphon* (Fig. 299A) is the outstanding example. Though the columnar Hellenic style had penetrated the East through the conquests of Alexander the Great and had continued under Roman and Parthian rule, the Sassanian revived the native tradition of vaulted construction, though Western influence is seen in details. What little is left of the *Palace at Ctesiphon* is eloquent of monumental grandeur, and when one recalls the stucco decorations and — upon reading of the booty taken by the Muslim — the marvelous carpets and furnishings, one can easily believe in its fabulous magnificence. An imposing elliptical barrel vault of brick which roofs the throne room dwarfs human beings by the magnitude of its scale. It is buttressed by a solid façade, and decorated with engaged columns and blind arcadings, which do not follow the superimposed system of the Roman style, but show a striking variety of arrangement in the stories that reveals an unhampered versatility.[1]

SCULPTURE

Monumental vigor through largeness of design distinguishes Sassanian rock-cut sculpture: the colossal equestrian reliefs of Ardashir I and Shapur I at Naksh-i-Rustum near Persepolis, and of Chosroes II at Tak-i-Bostan, a villa near the modern Kermanshah that was a famous park in Sassanian times. Here, in an arched recess cut in a rock at the base of a cliff which borders a small lake, is the statue of *Chosroes II.* His char-

[1] Excavations at Ctesiphon have brought to light a large number of fragments of stone and stucco ornament and other objects. See the *Metropolitan Museum of Art Bulletin*, August, 1932. See also reports of excavations by the University Museum at Damghan and by the Oxford-Field Expedition at Kish.

[A]   *Stone Carving with Winged Griffin. Detail from a relief of Chosroes II. (Sarre)*

ger Shabdiz (a name meaning "Black as Night") is heavily caparisoned, and the rider is clothed in armor. Though the statue has been badly mutilated by the Muslim, it still impresses with its monumentality, with its feeling for stone, and with the virility of every line and detail, which are so carved that they imbue the entire figure with an intense vitality as well as surface decorative beauty — qualities that are evident also in the recently discovered stucco fragments of horses and decorative panels.

SILVERWORK AND TEXTILES

This same pulsating vitality, combined with a sensitive relationship of forms, controls the work of the silversmiths and weavers. Behind the Sassanian metalworker lay a long tradition of extraordinary quality, which his own cups and plates maintain. The winged griffin is a popular motif, in early examples expressed with all the vigor of the carvings (Fig. 300A). Later this acquires more elaboration, elegance, and ease of line, as in the shallow cup with a plumed griffin in

the Victoria and Albert Museum. An easy facility of line combined with a vigor of conventional form is seen in a *Silver Plate* (Fig. 301B), which is decorated with a lithe animal walking along the banks of a river, indicated by swirling lines, from which rise lotus flowers to fill the vacant spaces. Another popular motif is the hunter. In Figure 301A six figures are composed into a unit determined by a circular space. Dynamic curves and countercurves, now flowing together, now meeting at sharp angles, create a forceful pattern through which conventional motifs for drapery, muscles, manes, and fur carry rapid minor rhythms.

Weaving reached a high stage of accomplishment. The silk-weaving craft had made its way westward from China and became a flourishing industry in Persia, where the craftsmen wove fabrics not only for home use but for Byzantium and western Europe as well. An all-over pattern based upon large medallions connected by small ones is a distinctive feature of these stuffs. In Figure 301C the hunter motif appears. Two kings on winged horses, arranged with perfect bilateral balancing, are

[A] *Silver Plate. Partially gilt. Chosroes I hunting ibexes. D. 8⅝ in. 6th cent. Metropolitan Museum of Art, New York City. (Metropolitan Museum)*

[B] *Silver Plate. Partially gilt. Carved and engraved with a fantastic animal and lotuses. D. 10 in. 9th–10th cent. Bibliothèque Nationale, Paris. (Giraudon)*

holding aloft the cubs of the lioness they have been hunting. The forms of all the figures are so highly generalized that they have become decorative patterns splendidly adapted to the circular space. The astounding amount of vigor in the forms, and the highly simplified drawing necessary for a successful textile pattern, are harmonized with extraordinary skill in the Sassanian fabrics.

Muhammadan Persian Art

(A.D. 641–1736)

THE kingdom of the Sassanids was short-lived because of the invincible fighting power of the Muslims, who swept eastward in their conquests in the seventh century A.D. and in 762 established Baghdad as the seat of the caliphate, a final blow to the life of Ctesiphon. Baghdad became the center not only of a gorgeous and pleasure-

[C] *Silk Textile with the Hunter Motif. Sassanian. c. 600. Kunstgewerbe Museum, Berlin. (Lessing) Compare this with the more naturalistic rendering of the same motif on a Byzantine textile (Fig. 2734).*

[A]   *Royal Mosque. Isfahan. 1612. (Arthur Upham Pope)*

loving court, the famed city of the Thousand and One Nights, but also of a culture and art that was ostensibly Islamic but at heart Iranian. For it was the age of the Iranian Abbasids, of that famed ruler Harun-al-Rashid (786–809); the age of Firdausi (940–1020), the great epic poet who gathered together the heroic legends of the Iranian people into the *Shah-nama*, or *Book of Kings;* of Nizami (1141–1203), the famous romantic poet of Persia; of Omar Khayyám (died 1123), who took for the setting of his quatrains the luxurious, pleasure-seeking aspect of life; and of the Sufi mystics, who provided the poets a complete contrast to the sensuous element in Omar Khayyám in their concepts of a joyful, ecstatic apprehension of divinity permeating all animate life.

Meantime the Mongols, or Tatars, moving westward under Jenghiz Khan (1162–1227), captured Baghdad in 1258, and came to rulership, bringing with them the traditions of China.

Thus Persia has been the melting-pot of many influences: the Babylonian, the Assyrian, and the Achaemenian, with an admixture of Egyptian; through the conquests of Alexander and the Romans, the Hellenic influence, the Roman, and their successor the Byzantine; after the revival of the Iranian by the Sassanids, the Islamic influence; and with the Mongol invasion, the Chinese. But despite these converging influences, one feels the constancy and the tenacity of the Iranian tradition. The Mongol rulers of the thirteenth and fourteenth centuries, with their capital at Samarkand, accepted Islam. The dynasty of the Timurids (1396–1500), founded by Timur (Tamerlane), was a period of prosperity and wealth, and under their patronage were produced some of the finest books, carpets, and metal. The Safavids (1502–1736) at the time of Shah Abbas I (1587–1628) reached another climax. But already overelegance, easy grace, and a naturalistic trend were foretelling the decline.

[A] *Recess Decorated with Stalactites of Colored Tile. Royal Mosque, Isfahan (Fig. 302A). (Arthur Upham Pope)*

ARCHITECTURE

In Islamic Persia it is the mosque as well as the palace that engages the builder. And the garden assumes extraordinary importance in this semi-desert land, an importance that finds expression in poetry as well as in painting and in the garden carpets. For Persian art "is inseparable from the very land of Persia, where, against an ever-present background of mauve and golden desert, set in a frame of rosy mountains, a few dead mountains standing out against the horizon like some landscape in the moon, a slender stream of water, a few poplars, and an old crumbling wayside inn suddenly assume a totally unexpected artistic value.

"And in addition to this incessant reminder of the desert there is the light air of the high plateaux with its incomparable purity, which adds an unvarying delicacy to every tone. Against this sky of a tender blue the favorite colors of the Persian architects acquire an extraordinary value — the mellow tone of the brick of the ancient mosques of Hamadan and Varamin or the fairylike blue of the great domes of Isfahan or the gold of the dome of Qum, brooding and solitary in the infinite space of the desert. A profound harmony exists between this country and its art, an intimate relation which transcends human factors and will survive them, for here ruin assumes the aspect of the very soil of the country, while the desert itself possesses the tones and appearance of its ruins."[1]

The *Royal Mosque* (*Masjid-i-shah*) of Isfahan (Fig. 302A) reflects this description. It faces a great open square about which are located the imperial palace, mosques, and markets. Rising from a group of subsidiary cloisterlike buildings and courtyards with gardens and fountains, it presents a composition of pointed, bulbous dome, pointed arches framed by rectangles, and cylindrical minarets — all sheathed in brilliantly colored glazed tile. There are evident here several traditions of the Valley of the Two Rivers: brick, with a limited use of stone, for material; the arch sys-

[1] René Grousset, *The Civilizations of the East*, 2 vols., Knopf, 1931, Vol. I, p. 393.

[A]　*Mirak. Laila and Majnun. 16th cent.
Metropolitan Museum of Art, New York
City. (Metropolitan Museum)*

tem of construction; and intensely colorful ceramic decoration. Structurally,
the erection of a dome on a rectangular
or polygonal plan brings the problem
of the transition from angular to spherical volumes, a problem met by the
Byzantine builders with the pendentive
(Fig. 261A), by the Persian with the
squinch (Figs. 260A, 290A).

The ceramic decoration at Isfahan
(Fig. 303A) is a continuation of the tradition we have followed in the Valley
of the Two Rivers from the blue tile of
the sanctuary of the *Ziggurat* at *Ur*
(Fig. 83A) by way of *Khorsabad* (Fig.
91A) and the *Ishtar Gate* (Figs. 96A, 97A)
to *Susa* and *Persepolis*. The motifs are
geometric patterns, arabesques, or inscriptions, sometimes slightly in relief,
and the colors are rich blues of many

tones, green and yellow, black and
white — now used with strong contrast, such as a white arabesque on the
deepest blue or black ground, now more
nearly in the same key. Yet whatever
the color combination and however intricate the design, the surfaces are
never broken. The clear, definite organization of a few simple masses, with
the help of the shadows in the arched
recesses, keeps the rich surface decoration entirely subordinate, just as in
Santa Sophia (Fig. 261A), where the
rhythmic movement of arches and
domes holds under control the sumptuous detail.

PAINTING

Although frescoes are by no means
unknown,[1] our chief criterion of Persian painting and probably its greatest
expression is found in the miniatures.
The shahs were great lovers of fine
books. They spared neither time nor
money to obtain them and maintained
trained calligraphers at court; often
these included the most famous artists
of the day. Among the early books,
in addition to splendid copies of the
Koran, are copies of the *Manafi al-
Hayawan* (or Bestiary). In the *Bullock*
(Fig. 305A) the bulky figure, with its
firm lines and its strong dark stripes
and horn balanced by dark areas in the
hoofs and the tail, stands massively
against the lighter wavering movement
of the foliage, which is painted in the
style of Chinese ink painting (which
came to Persia with the Mongols).

The truly Persian style and some of
the greatest triumphs of Persian painting are found in the secular books of
the Timurids and the Safavids, such
as the poems of Firdausi and Nizámi

[1] For the recently discovered frescoes at
Isfahan, see *Persian Fresco Paintings*, American
Institute for Persian Art and Archaeology, New
York, 1932.

[A] *Bullock. From a Manafi al-Hayawan (Bestiary). Late 13th cent. Pierpont Morgan Library, New York City. (Metropolitan Museum)*

illustrated by a whole galaxy of painters, famous among whom were Bihzad (about 1440–1553) and Mirak and Sultan Muhammad, court painters of Shah Tahmasp (1524–1576), a great art patron. Although the shahs were Muslims, orthodox Islamic restrictions regarding the figure did not affect their secular arts, so that the gay scenes of their life of pleasure — the hunt, the feast, flowers, music, and romance — and battle scenes fill the pages of their books. One looking at them feels the luxury, the splendor, and the fleeting happiness of Omar. The cool gardens with fruit trees always blossoming and tall slender palm trees waving gently against the blue sky; the palace or mosque that gleams with enamel-like walls of lustrous faïence; or the rocky hillsides where the hunters or warriors dash by on slender horses — these form the setting for the tales.

From one of Nizami's romantic poems is the *Laila and Majnun* (Fig. 304A). The scene represents a school, apparently in a mosque. Seated on a rug is the turbaned priest, the teacher, lash in hand, listening to a youth reading; round him are other youths studying, all seated on their knees and heels or with one knee raised, the customary sitting postures in the East. Here and there are the cross-legged bookrests. In the foreground one boy is pulling his companion's ear, and at the left, near the large water jar, two are playing ball. In the middle distance are the lovers Laila and Majnun, each obviously aware of the other's presence. There is a good deal of vivacity in the narrative element. The figures are drawn expressively with delicate, flowing lines; but they are flat, with no chiaroscuro and with but a hint of perspective; the tiles in the court and the rugs on the floor appear to be hanging vertically. The painting is conceived from the point of view not of natural appearance but of pattern and vivid color. To this end the tones are kept bright and clear. The decorative quality of the miniature is emphasized by the broad margins of the page, which is tinted pale-blue and flecked all over with gold. The opposite page of the

METALWORK, POTTERY, TEXTILES

The tradition of the metalworker, as has been said, is very old in the Valley of the Two Rivers and seems never to have ceased in spite of the rise and fall of dynasties and the influence of foreign invaders. In the twelfth and thirteenth centuries, after a period of suppression at the hands of orthodox Muslims, there appears to have been a revival of this work, probably due to the coming of the Tatars, who though converted to Islam still held but slight regard for its decrees. The center of the craft was near great copper mines at Mosul, from which it spread to other localities, appearing in Egypt in such a work as a brass bowl (Fig. 295A), in which inscriptions and arabesques furnished the motifs of decoration. In the Mosul products, however, figure work is an important element, as we see in a ewer (Fig. 306A) in which the figures of men, animals, and birds in hunting, fighting, and feasting scenes are inlaid in silver on an engraved brass ground. On the silver also were engraved details such as features, drapery, plumage of the birds, and manes of the horses, so that the effect of the contrasting metals and the delicate chasing is one of rich splendor.

Behind the products of the ceramist, as of the metalworker, lay a long tradition, including ceramic wall decoration on a large scale as well as the more usual smaller products. And as the former made the walls of mosques and palaces glow with color, so the latter provided accents of texture and color to the interior. For shape and color were the potter's objective, and to its realization he brought a spontaneity and an ease of expression based upon an innate sensitivity and a technical ability handed down from generations. In short, these Persian potters were

[A] *Ewer. Brass inlaid with silver and ornamented with inscriptions and festal scenes. H. 11 in. 1232. British Museum, London. (British Museum)*

book is designed to harmonize with the illustrated page, for the area containing the writing is equal to that of the miniature and the margins are of the same gold-flecked pale-blue. The writing, a beautiful example of the Arabic script, is the work of a famous calligrapher who says in the colophon that the book was "finished with God's help by the hand of the poor and obscure Sultan Muhammad Nur." The binding of brown leather, embossed and gilded, gives an impression of quiet richness and elegance and is an example of the rare skill of the craftsman in gold-tooled leather.[1]

[1] See H. A. Gardner, *Understanding the Arts*, Harcourt, Brace, 1932, pp. 253 ff., for a description and illustrations of this book.

[A] *Rhages (Ray or Rayy) Bowl Showing a Court Scene. 13th cent. Metropolitan Museum of Art, New York City. (Metropolitan Museum)*

[B] *Lustered Rhages (Ray or Rayy). c. 1200. Metropolitan Museum of Art, New York City). (Metropolitan Museum)*

master ceramic designers. Their shapes — bowls, cups, bottles, pitchers, plates, jars — are usually true clay shapes, not sharply precise like metal, and their decorations in every detail relate to the shape. The vital lines and contours are in perfect harmony with and in purposeful contrast to the rim of a plate (Fig. 307B) or to the curving surface of a pitcher; and all appear to be dashed on the surface spontaneously and with great ease, yet with a perfect conviction of their exact rightness.

The coarse base of most of this pottery required a slip or coat of opaque enamel to provide a surface for the painting. In the *Rhages* (Ray)[1] bowl (Fig. 307A) the ground is turquoise-blue, on which are painted in many colors, with dull red and blue predominating, and a little gold, a sultan on his throne with courtiers on each side and seated figures in the surround-

[1] So called from the city of Rhages, near Teheran, a great center of pottery-making, and one of the most splendid cities of Persia before its destruction by Jenghiz Khan in the thirteenth century.

ing compartments. About the rim runs a Kufic inscription, and on the outside, in cursive hand: "Glory, triumph, power and happiness, generosity and safety, to the owner." Many of the jars and plates have a creamy glaze with decorations in a soft brown that has a peculiarly fleeting charm when covered, as it often is, by a transparent luster. For then, viewed at a certain angle, there appears an iridescence of violet, dull gold, and copper. Move slightly, and the sparkling color disappears. Thus is produced a subtle, evanescent form of decoration highly suggestive of the joy of the passing hour. There is none of the sobriety of Egypt or China, or of the intellectuality of Greece, but rather the restless joy of Minoan art. Delight in the happiness of the present hour expresses itself in the sparkling, fleeting beauty of the luster vases.

In the *Rhages* bowl (Fig. 307A) one notes that the faces are Chinese in type; and in other examples we find motifs (phoenixes, peonies, and scrolls) and color schemes of Chinese origin. Persian shahs and nobles imported

[A]   *Ardebil Carpet. Detail. Wool. 34½ x 17½ ft. Made by Shah Tahmasp for the tomb-mosque of his family at Ardebil. Victoria and Albert Museum, London. (Victoria and Albert Museum) The inscription at the bottom of the field reads:*
"I have no refuge in the world other than thy threshold;
There is no place of protection for my head other than this door.
The work of the slave of the threshold, Maqsud of Kashan in the year 926 (A.D. 1540)."

Chinese porcelain, which their ceramists succeeded in imitating. Yet the Persian potter, like other Persian artists, was able to assimilate these influences from the Far East and to produce a unique fabric that ranks among the world's finest.

This pottery was an aristocratic art, and like the books and many of the fine carpets was produced under royal patronage. Carpets, however, were peculiarly expressive of the people as a whole. The land itself produced all the necessary materials, and the need of

[A]   *Wool Animal Rug. Detail. c. 1520–30. Metropolitan Museum of Art. New York City. (Metropolitan Museum)*

protection against the winter cold made them indispensable both in the nomad shepherd's tent and in the shah's palace. And in each case the intimate relation of the carpet to its makers and to its function determined its design, as we realize in comparing a small shepherd rug of bold primitive pattern with the huge royal carpets of subtle richness. In the houses and palaces of Persia, built of brick, stone, plaster, and glazed tile, the carpets contributed a contrasting texture as floor and divan coverings and wall hangings.

Carpet-weaving was an inherited craft among the Persians, attained through generations of effort. Many a pattern, or perhaps the secret of making a particularly fine dye, was handed down from father to son. The wool was obtained from the sheep which grazed on the mountainsides of this rugged country; and the dyes, few in number, from plants.

The success of a Persian carpet results from color massing and texture. The royal *Ardebil Carpet* (Fig. 308A), a large example of the medallion type, depends for its effectiveness upon a simple massing of large elements of design enhanced by a wealth of subordinated detail. These main elements are the single unifying tone of the field, the central and corner medallions, and the finishing borders. The field is a rich blue and is covered with leaves and flowers (chiefly peonies, a Chinese influence) attached to a framework of delicate stems which weave a spiral design over the whole field. The central medallion is of yellow, surrounded by small oval panels of yellow, red, and green, from one of which is suspended a mosque lamp; quarter-sections of this medallion group fill the corners. The broad border has alternating medallions of red and yellow on a deep-purple ground; the narrow borders make a happy transition from field to border.

In the *Ardebil Carpet* there are no human or animal figures, since it was made for a mosque; but another carpet (Fig. 309A) from Ardebil illustrates how the Persian weavers used the animal form. Lions and other animals are attacking spotted gazelles while boars are running rapidly away; other animals and various flowers fill the field; and Chinese cloud banks carry a rapid movement in the border. All these forms, whether flora or fauna, show an extraordinary combination of simplification with naturalism, for each can be clearly identified. The decorative pattern enabled the weaver to mass shapes and colors into an underlying abstract design whose movement is confined by the borders, each of which contains in its motifs rhythmic movements of varying tempo around the central field.

Technically, these great royal carpets represent the work of a group of weavers, probably a group belonging to the court. Pile weaving is a slow process at best, and since a carpet like the *Ardebil* often has more than three hundred knots to the square inch, it would have taken one skilled weaver (according to an estimate) about twenty-four years to weave such a carpet — an unthinkable length of time for a shah to wait.

SUMMARY

Scale and monumentality mark the buildings of the Sassanian Persians; dynamic vitality, their sculpture; and virile strength, their fine textile designs. Islamic Persian art in all its manifestations — the mosque, the carpet, the illuminated page, the *Rhages* bowl, inlaid metal — reveals its delight in the massing of color to obtain brilliant effects. It delights in the flat pattern suggested by human, animal, or plant form as an element of decorative power, as is evident in the hastily sketched figures on the pottery, in the silhouettes of the slender-legged horses that dash across the pages of the manuscripts, in the flat swaying palm trees, in the infinitely varied flowers of the rugs, and in the inscriptions of silver that shine forth from a dark metal ground. Nor are there, in this art, profound abstract expressions. It is rather a frank reflection of a life of luxury, splendor, and romance, delighting in the pleasures of the present — lively, joyous, worldly, and transitory. It is the spirit of Omar Khayyám expressed by the potter, the weaver, and the metalworker. Influences from all directions converged upon Persia, where great highways crossed. But the Iranians, always successful in assimilating foreign elements, preserved their identity and traditions. Though they accepted the mosque from the Muslims, they used their traditional materials and constructional methods, and made it colorful by sheathing all its surfaces with their traditional glazed tile. For their palaces they produced equally colorful pottery and carpets; and to lighten their leisure, some of the most beautifully written and illustrated books ever made. The meeting of the Far East and the Near East is evident in the Chinese motifs found in the carpets and in the Mongolian types and motifs seen in the pottery and miniatures. These influences, however, were absorbed into a truly Muhammadan Persian type of expression.

BIBLIOGRAPHY

Arnold, Sir Thomas Walker, *Painting in Islam,* Oxford University Press, 1928

Binyon, Laurence, Wilkinson, J. V. S., and Gray, Basil, *Persian Miniature Painting,* Oxford University Press, 1933

Blochet, Edgar, *Musulman Painting, XIIth–XVIIth Century,* tr. by C. M. Binyon, London, 1929

Bode, Wilhelm von, *Antique Rugs from the Near East,* tr. by R. M. Riefstahl, 3d ed. rev., Weyhe, 1922

Dimand, Maurice S., *A Guide to an Exhibition of Islamic Miniature Painting and Book Illumination,* Metropolitan Museum of Art, New York City, 1933

Firdausī, *The Shāh-nāmah,* described by J. V. S. Wilkinson, Oxford University Press, 1931

Gray, Basil, *Persian Painting,* London, 1930

Hannover, Emil, *Pottery & Porcelain,* 3 vols., Scribner, 1925

Hawley, Walter A., *Oriental Rugs, Antique and Modern,* new ed., Tudor, 1937

Jackson, Abraham V. W., *Persia Past and Present,* Macmillan, 1906

Kendrick, Albert F., *Catalogue of Muhammadan Textiles of the Medieval Period,* Victoria and Albert Museum, London, 1924

———— and Tattersall, C. E. C., *Fine Carpets in the Victoria and Albert Museum,* London, 1924

Kœchlin, Raymond, and Migeon, Gaston, *Oriental Art: Ceramics, Fabrics, Carpets,* tr. by Florence Heywood, Macmillan, 1928

Martin, Fredrik R., *The Miniature Painting and Painters of Persia, India, and Turkey,* 2 vols., London, 1912

Mayer, Leo A., *Saracenic Heraldry,* Oxford University Press, 1933

Mumford, John K., *Oriental Rugs,* rev. ed., Scribner, 1915

Nizami, Ganjavi, *The Poems of Nizami,* described by Laurence Binyon, Studio, 1928

Persian Fresco Paintings, American Institute for Persian Art and Archaeology, 1932

Pope, Arthur U., *An Introduction to Persian Art since the Seventh Century A.D.,* Scribner, 1931

———— *Masterpieces of Persian Art,* Dryden Press, 1945

———— and Ackerman, Phyllis, eds., *A Survey of Persian Art from Prehistoric Times to the Present,* 6 vols., Oxford University Press, 1938–39

Ross, Sir Edward Denison, ed., and others, *Persian Art,* London, 1930

Sarre, Friedrich P. T., and Trenkwald, Hermann, *Old Oriental Carpets,* tr. by A. F. Kendrick, 2 vols., Vienna, 1926–29

Tattersall, Creassey E. C., *Notes on Carpet-Knotting and Weaving,* rev. ed., Victoria and Albert Museum, London, 1933

Victoria and Albert Museum, *Brief Guide to the Persian Woven Fabrics,* Museum, London, 1922

———— *Guide to the Collection of Carpets,* with an introduction by A. F. Kendrick, 3d ed. rev., Museum, London, 1931

See also the General Bibliography, pp. 791–92.

[A]   *Church at Moissac. Tympanum of the south portal. c. 1100. Contrast, in style, with the tympanum of Fig. 321A. (Giraudon)*

17

ROMANESQUE ART

(ABOUT A.D. 500–1150)

WHILE the long-continued Byzan-tine tradition was following a more or less unbroken course in the Near East, chaos ruled in the West from about A.D. 500 to 1000. Through the close relations of Constantinople with Venice and Ravenna, and through trade and pilgrimages, especially the Crusades, interchange was constantly bringing Byzantine and Far Eastern ideas westward. During this period of

chaos the elements that were to form the foundation of western Europe were meeting and mingling — Roman, bar-barian, and Christian. Rome, through its provincial system, had built cities over a large part of western Europe, connecting them by magnificent roads, and there had established its customs and culture. In swept waves of bar-barians, illiterate but of the fresh, vig-orous blood of the North. In their new environment they continued to govern by tribal methods instead of accepting Roman law; and when this law ceased, and with it order — for their kings were usually powerless — a natural outcome was feudalism, because people of necessity bound themselves to anyone who could provide some measure of safety from the dangers and outrages of the times.

The one power to remain strong was the Christian Church. It was steadily perfecting its organization and increasing both its spiritual and its temporal power. At the head of each unit of its organization stood the bishop, who lived in the largest city of his diocese. In the church of this city was the bishop's chair, called the *cathedra*. Hence his church was known as the *cathedral*. As feudalism was the dominant system, the bishop became practically a feudal baron. With the increase of its power and wealth, the Church was weakened by elements of decay, and in protest against its degradation arose the monastery. This institution, with its triple vow of poverty, chastity, and obedience, had originated in the East; it was introduced into Italy by Saint Benedict in 526, and thence spread rapidly over western Europe. At the head stood the abbot, and his church was known as the abbey church.

In Figure 315A we see the plan of a typical monastery of the period. Near the center, dominating the group, is the abbey church, of basilican type with an apse at either end and a cloister at one side. About it are grouped the living-quarters, the bakehouse, store-rooms, shops for the goldsmith, the blacksmith, the fuller, and other craftsmen, gardens and cattle yards, hospitals and schools — a complete community in itself where daily needs were supplied without communication with the outside world. As a protection against robbers and feudal barons, some monasteries were surrounded by a fortified wall. Thus the monastery was much more than a church. In it centered most of the learning of these centuries, for it was the industrious monks who kept alive whatever ancient culture had survived. It was, in fact, church, school, library, and hospital all in one; furthermore, it was the steadying hand throughout this whole formative period.

With the exception of the large cities, which could withstand the attacks of the barbarians, there were few towns up to about the year 1000. The people lived in rural communities, and were attached, practically as serfs, to the estate of some feudal lord, abbot, or bishop. Because of the dangers of travel, there was little intercommunication or commerce. But the members of feudal society — the lord, the bishop, and the abbot — were far from secure in their positions. There was constant warfare. The strife between the bishops and the abbots, who were jealous of each other's power, added to the turmoil.

The one brilliant spot in the early part of this period was the reign of Charlemagne, when for a short time order was restored, education and learning were revived, and the arts were stimulated. But after his death Europe descended to its lowest level, and even the Church sank to deepest degradation, from which it was ultimately rescued through the influence of such monasteries as that of Cluny, which was established in 909 and for two hundred years served as the spiritual guide of Europe.

About the year 1000 a new spirit began to infuse Europe. We hear of uprisings against the feudal barons, the establishment of towns, the opening-up of communication, the organization of trade guilds, and the growth of commerce. Religious faith developed into a religious enthusiasm of great vitality. This culminated in the First Crusade, which, though participated in by many for the sake of adventure, was nevertheless an indication of the religious faith of the age. This new spirit caused a vigorous artistic activity which swept all Europe.[1]

Universities and schools of learning were founded. The various vernaculars were becoming mediums of literary expression. The troubadours were singing their songs at the gay feudal courts of southern France, while the *Song of Roland* and the legends of the Grail were stirring men with the ideal of chivalry.

Thus while five centuries were years of chaos, during which the different basic elements were fusing, the eleventh and twelfth centuries were the early flowering of this fusion, a powerful archaic age with institutions and art forms centered in the monastery and the feudal court, peculiarly expressive of the entire outlook of the age as well as a prelude to the full flowering of medieval culture in the Gothic age.

ARCHITECTURE
AND SCULPTURE

As the monastery was the predominating power during the Romanesque period, it is chiefly the abbey church that furnishes examples of building and sculpture. In fact, with its furnishings and equipment, it illustrates the entire range of the arts, as does the mosque in Islamic art. Before the year 1000 there was little building, as the barbarians were incapable of it and the Latins inactive in it because of the disorder. But the new spirit discernible about that year was an incentive to church-building.

[1] Note that this synchronizes with the second Byzantine Golden Age; and it now seems probable that not only the stimulation but also many of the forms in building, sculpture, and other arts are directly attributable to the East.

In studying the architecture of the Romanesque period, one important fact must always be kept in mind: Very little remains in its original condition; there are few structures with no additions or restorations of a later period. Another important fact is that the architecture is not homogeneous, but manifests itself differently in different parts of Europe. Hence we shall look at a few examples in several countries, beginning with Italy.

In the sixth century the Po Valley had been occupied by the Lombards, whose name to this day designates this part of Italy. Of the buildings that they erected in the eleventh century, the most important is *Sant' Ambrogio* (Fig. 316A). It is a plain building, with an unbroken sloping roof which shows that there is no clerestory. The façade, which is approached through an atrium, consists of a two-storied arcade flanked on either side by a sturdy square tower. The decoration consists of a corbel table along the cornices and on the tower. The whole design is one of dignity, with no suggestion of elaboration, and is saved from heaviness by its reserved decoration.

The plan (Fig. 338A2) shows a Christian basilica without a transverse aisle. Now the early Christian basilica had a wooden roof, which the builders realized was neither permanent nor fireproof. Hence a central problem of the Middle Ages was to roof over the basilica with a vault. This means two things — to construct the vault and to support it adequately. The Romans had constructed great barrel and groin vaults (Figs. 174A, 179A) that rested upon massive walls heavy enough to withstand the thrust of the vault. The Byzantine builders preferred a domical vault on pendentives (Figs. 260Aa, 261A) and the Persians, a domical vault on squinches (Fig. 260Ab). The Byzantine type, though found in western Eu-

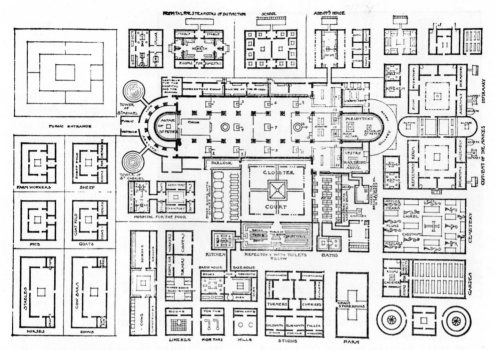

[A] *Monastery of St. Gall. Switzerland. Plan, drawn from a manuscript. The various activities indicated here constitute a complete social unit. (Porter,* Medieval Architecture, *Yale University Press)*

rope,[1] did not appeal to the medieval builders so much as did the basilica.

Let us see how this problem is met in *Sant' Ambrogio*. As we look at the nave (Fig. 317A) we see that instead of carrying a long barrel vault it is divided into sections, or bays, by transverse arches or ribs; and that each bay is covered by a groin vault with four diagonal ribs built along the lines of the groins. Why are these ribs here, and of what value are they in the construction of the building?

In building a barrel or a groin vault, a large amount of centering — wooden scaffolding to hold the vault during its erection — is necessary. Soon the builders discovered that by separating the long barrel vault into bays by trans-

verse arches, they could vault one section at a time, thus economizing on the centering. Next they noticed that these arches offered a convenient ledge on which to rest the vaulting; and then it occurred to them that it would be equally convenient to build ribs diagonally across each bay, following the lines of the groins and intersecting at the crown, on which to rest the four sections of the vault. Thus they discovered that they could erect a skeleton of ribs to support the vaulting which could be made of much lighter material than that used in a barrel or a groin vault without ribs, and hence afford much greater freedom in construction. In fact, the application of the rib vault to the roofing of a basilica was the greatest constructional discovery of the Middle Ages. The builders now had

[1] *St. Mark's*, Venice, and *Angoulême* and *Périgueux*, France are examples.

[A] *Sant' Ambrogio. Milan. Early 12th cent. A rare example of the survival of the atrium. (Alinari)*

the means of lightening and raising the skeleton framework; two hundred years later, it reached the majestic height of the nave of the Gothic cathedral (Fig. 345A). But they were not guided by the structural problem alone. With a sensitiveness to design, they appreciated the rhythm and the decorative effect of the ribs. Compare, for example, the heaviness and barrenness of the barrel vault with the lightness, rhythm, and emotional uplift of the Gothic nave.

We have now studied the principles on which the vault in *Sant' Ambrogio* was constructed. Let us see how it is supported. In Figure 317A, it will be noticed that the transverse arch springs from a pilaster rising from the floor; the diagonal rib, from an engaged column also rising from the floor; the longitudinal rib that encloses the double arcade separating the nave and aisle, from a thin pilaster; and the smaller arches of the arcade, from pilasters or engaged columns. That is, each rib of the skeleton frame of the vault is supported by a member rising either from the floor or from the second story, all of which

unite to form a compound or clustered pier.

These piers, however, are not adequate of themselves to support the weight of the roof. Cross walls are built over the transverse arches of the aisles at right angles to the clustered pier, where the thrust of the vault is concentrated (Fig. 340A2). These, together with the vaulted aisles, carry the thrust to the outer thick walls, which in turn are reinforced by pier buttresses at the points where the cross walls meet them. Thus while we have in *Sant' Ambrogio* a structural principle worked out for constructing the vaults, we still have the heavy walls for buttressing them. How this latter problem was met, we shall see later in France.

Sant' Ambrogio is important, therefore, because it is an early example of rib vaulting and clustered pier. These innovations, however, did not appear at once. The rib was known to the Roman and to builders in the Near East, and possibly its use was a rediscovery rather than a discovery. First these principles were tried out timidly in the

[A] *Sant' Ambrogio. Nave. (Alinari)*

aisles, then finally some courageous builder ventured to apply them in the nave. Even here at *Sant' Ambrogio* timidity is seen in the fact that there is no clerestory, as if the builder did not dare raise the ribs high enough to allow for that. Hence the interior is low and dark.

These important structural innovations, however, did not develop further in Italy. The Lombards themselves were perhaps too much embroiled in political strife to continue a development so splendidly begun, and builders in general seemed to be more interested in mitigating the rugged austerity of the basilica by means of decorative elements. These elements were: porches with sculptured decorations; open arcadings; brickwork and contrasting light and dark stone; and marble inlays. It was chiefly in northern Italy, in the *Cathedral of Modena,* for example, that

we see a successful attempt to enliven the plain façade by open arcades and by the addition of a porch, with sculpture about the doorways. All of this not only accents the entrance but, with its projections and recessions and broken surfaces, creates a pattern of light and dark and infuses movement into the design. Recumbent lions serve as bases for the columns (a common motif in medieval art), and reliefs representing scenes and characters as various as those in actual life — Biblical and legendary scenes, romantic and military, imaginative monsters, and everyday people intertwined with foliate spiralings — are carved on pilasters and arches and on the capitals of the interior. All this ornament is filled with a spirit of great energy and vitality and is carved in a consistently clear manner in rather low relief. In these portals, sculpture as a major art began to revive.

[A] *San Miniato. Florence. Façade of marble inlay and mosaic. Begun 1013. (Alinari)*

[B] *St. Paul's Outside the Walls. Rome. Detail of the cloister. (Anderson)*

Arcadings as a decorative element were used more elaborately in the *Cathedral of Pisa*, a basilica with vaulting over the aisles and a small dome over the crossing, but with a wooden roof over the nave. The group as a whole — cathedral, campanile, and baptistery (chiefly Gothic) — impresses one with its splendor when compared with the more rugged *Sant' Ambrogio*. Blind arcades with colored marbles fill the ground story, and open arcadings, subtly irregular in height and spacing, the stories above.[1] It is not surprising to find arcading on many of the Italian churches, for this was one of the most characteristic elements of Roman architecture, and the numerous examples of it in Italy could hardly fail to impress the Northerners and to suggest to them its use as a means of impressive decoration. The campanile (the famous

[1] See Ruskin's detailed analysis in his *Seven Lamps of Architecture*.

[A] *Marble Inlay on the Façade of San Michele. Lucca.*

"Leaning Tower") repeats the decorative scheme of the cathedral.

This external embellishment and attention to proportions transformed the campanile from the almost unbroken cylinder at *Sant' Apollinare in Classe* (Fig. 254A) into the generally rectangular (at Pisa, round) towers, still free-standing, lightened by openings, and enlivened by moldings and colored inlays which are one of the most stirring forms in Italy in their fine balance between solidity and grace.

In central Italy, notably in Tuscany, open arcadings and sculptured doorways tend to disappear in favor of a one-plane façade encrusted with marble inlays of a severely geometric symmetrical pattern, chiefly angular even when enclosed by arches, as we see in *San Miniato* (Fig. 318A) and the *Baptistery* of Florence. In the *Cathedral of San Michele* at Lucca (Fig. 319A), however, we find a combination of Romanesque decorative elements: contrasting courses of light and dark stone; and open arcadings, whose shadows effectively set forth the rhythmic movement of the arches, which holds together the almost

fantastic richness of minor elements in columns, capitals, and inlays. Each column and each capital is different in design, and the spandrels are filled in a lively fashion with geometric, animal, and imaginative figures.

Marble inlay was carried into the interior of these buildings also, and forms a contrasting note to the gaily colored wooden-beamed ceilings above. Floors as well as walls were covered with marble, but with a greater variety of design than that found on the exterior, including both animal and geometric forms. Some of these — especially the bird or animal figures enclosed in circles — closely resemble the textiles of the Near East. The spiral flutings found in the colonnettes of such a cloister as that of *St. John Lateran* or *St. Paul's Outside the Walls* (Fig. 318B), repeating the inlaid surfaces above, lend a note of shimmering richness to the court. These cloisters constitute one of the most charming elements of the Romanesque building.

Farther south, especially in Rome, interior marble inlays take the more elaborate and more colorful patterns

[A]   *Pulpit Decorated in Cosmati Work. Ravello. 13th cent. (Alinari)*

that are known as *Cosmati* work.[1] Altar fronts, pulpits (Fig. 320A), and candelabra are sumptuously decorated with a design composed of squares or circles of red porphyry or green serpentine surrounded by borders, frequently interlacing, made up of small pieces of marble and glass cut into various shapes.

The richly colorful quality of Cosmati work rises to greater resplendence in Sicily. This island, at the crossroads of conquerors, had been occupied by Greeks, Romans, Lombards, Muslims, and Normans. The last-named accomplished the remarkable feat of assimilating these various cultural elements, so that Sicily, like Spain, became a great center of learning, with Islamic scientists and Greek scholars, Christian and Muslim, equally patronized by the court. The *Cathedral of Monreale* incorporates these diversified elements.

[1] So called from the Cosmati family in Rome, who were particularly skillful in this technique.

In the nave, the floor and lower part of the walls are covered with marbles, above which the walls are entirely incrusted with Byzantine mosaics which culminate in the magnificent *Pantocrator* in the apse. Columns with Corinthian capitals support Islamic stilted and pointed arches. Yet all these diversified elements are blended into a resplendent unity. On the exterior of the apse the interlacing arcades sound a note of Normandy.

In France, the southern part of the country had been thoroughly Latinized by the Romans. Flourishing cities existed at Nîmes, Arles, and Orange, whose theaters, arches, temples, and baths could not but influence the medieval builders. We see their influence in the churches of *St. Gilles* (Gard) and *St. Trophime* (Arles). In plan *St. Trophime* is basilican with a cloister, as is usual in abbey churches. It is roofed with a barrel vault, as are the covered passages of the cloister. This plan and constructional system, with variations, is common in southern and central France as in the *Madeleine* (Vézelay), which has transverse arches with groin vaulting. Other plans and constructional systems are illustrated by *St. Front* (Périgueux), the central type with the Greek cross roofed with domes on pendentives; and by *St. Pierre* (Angoulême), basilican in plan, and roofed with a series of domes.

To return to *St. Trophime*, the façade (Fig. 321A) reveals the basilica type with nave, clerestory, and lower side aisles, and is quite barren except for the richly carved portal. Above the plain base runs a broad band of decoration, with columns resting on the backs of lions or grotesques, and with statues of saints in niches tied together by a continuous frieze. Above the door a sculptured tympanum surrounded by concentric, slightly pointed arches breaks the upper part and accents the

[A] *St. Trophime. Arles. Portal. 12th cent.*

entrance; a bracketed cornice parallel to the roof finishes the design. Thus the builder divided his space effectively, concentrating his ornament on the central band like a piece of embroidery on a plain garment, and setting it off by the contrasting plain surfaces about it and by the vigorous arches above the door. A closer inspection of the details shows that the brackets of the cornice, the Corinthian capitals, the fluted pilasters, the acanthus, and the fret are classical; the figures in the niches, the tympanum, and the friezes are related stylistically to Byzantine ivories and miniatures.

In the tympanum is the seated figure of Christ, surrounded by an aureole, one hand holding a book, the other raised in blessing. About him are grouped the four beasts of the Apocalypse, which symbolize the four Evangelists — the winged man, Saint Matthew; the winged lion, Saint Mark; the winged ox, Saint Luke; and the eagle, Saint John. On the lintel below are the twelve Apostles, seated; to the left are the blessed going to heaven; to the right, the damned, chained together and being led to hell. The representation of Christ surrounded by the symbolic beasts had already become a conventional representation in Christian art and is found very frequently, not only over the doorways of the churches but in the illuminated manuscripts, the ivories, and the enamels. For art in the Middle Ages was subject to the authority of the Church. As in Byzantine art, certain subjects must be represented in a certain way and placed in a certain position on the building, and the au-

[A] *St. Peter. On the jamb of the south portal of the church at Moissac (Fig. 312A). Contrast with the static figures of Fig. 321A.*

thorized use of symbols and attributes must be strictly followed. Yet while the medieval sculptor or painter was limited by convention, he could use his individual imagination to a surprising extent.

To illustrate this let us look at the south portal at *Moissac* (Fig. 312A), which consists of a vestibule covered by a barrel vault, with both doorway and sides richly carved. In the tympanum we find the same subject and the same general arrangement as at *St. Trophime*, except for the addition of angels and of the twenty-four elders arranged in zones below and on each side of the central group. But at *Moissac* the figures are filled with life and movement; they are even twisting and writhing; the draperies flutter, and the elders strain their necks toward the figure of Christ. Thus, while the subject matter, the

arrangement of the figures, and such details as the attributes are the same in both, yet the feeling is diametrically opposed. *St. Trophime* is tranquil and static, with all parts harmoniously related and balanced. *Moissac* is energetic and dynamic, with forceful oppositions in the movement surging through; the lower relief has a lineal quality (a mark of Northern art) peculiarly fitted in its dynamic rhythms to express the fervor of the Northerners, and for the sake of which the figures are twisted and distorted. A comparison of the *St. Peter* (Fig. 322A) on the door jamb with one of the saints of *St. Trophime* will illustrate the difference, though in both styles the forms are archaic, and the drapery, clouds, hair, and other details are expressed by conventions with a linear beauty which adds to their decorativeness.[1]

At *Angoulême* (Fig. 323A) the sculpture, instead of being concentrated at the portal, is more widely spread over the surfaces and, with the blind arcadings, enriches the broad unbroken surfaces and at the same time, because it is carved in the actual masonry, retains a unity with it. *Angoulême*, like most Romanesque churches, is solid, firmly rooted, and presents a picturesque massing of volumes — a rectangular basilica, domes, and a bell tower which is incorporated into the structure rather than free-standing, as in Italy.

Romanesque ornament (Figs. 319A, 325A, 326B) is always spirited, infinitely varied, and highly decorative. On the lintel of the doorway of *Moissac* (Fig. 312A) we see, at each end of the lintel, a chimeralike creature from the East, out of whose mouth issue cords that enclose finely carved rosettes, all slightly different and unequally spaced. Fantasy manifests itself particularly in

[1] See Jurgis Baltrušaitis, *La Stylistique Ornamentale dans la Sculpture Romane*, Paris, 1931, for analyses of Romanesque tympani.

the "storied capitals," where characters from the Bible, and creatures of the imagination, centaurs, and hunters — many of Eastern origin — find a place, often intertwined with scrolls and foliage. Strikingly effective are many of the Romanesque recessed portals, about which was concentrated much of the decorative carving. We note in particular that all this carving is an integral part of the stone capital or the stone masonry. In fact it *is* the stone, with its original surface retained but enlivened by the vigorous carving of conventional motifs of a calligraphic character organized into a highly decorative pattern.

Romanesque architecture and sculpture in Spain are similar to those of southern France, largely because of the famous pilgrimage route to the shrine of Saint James the Great at Santiago de Compostella, along which art conceptions and forms, if not actual copies, were conveyed by the pilgrims and by the traveling builders and craftsmen.[1] But the style was first modified by climatic conditions. Roofs were flatter and windows fewer, even to the suppression of the clerestory to dim the strong light of the Southlands. In the second place, the presence of the Moors and the rich exuberance of their ornament influenced the carvers toward a more abundant, complex expression. This is evident in *Santiago* (Compostella) and in *San Isidoro* (León).

Turning to northern France, we recall that this part of the country had been occupied by the Normans, who, like the other barbarians, had no notable arts of their own. Furthermore, the dwellers in northern France, unlike those in the southern part of the coun-

[A]   *St. Pierre. Angoulême. 1105–28. Note the domical vaulting. See p. 315, note 1.*

try, had no large Roman cities to teach them. Their own accomplishment, in which they were probably aided by builders from Lombardy who settled there, is illustrated by the *Abbaye-aux-Hommes* (Fig. 324A). The first impression of the church, as we think of *St. Trophime* and *Angoulême*, is its plainness and its rugged vigor. We notice that the façade with its two flanking square towers is divided into three vertical sections separated by pilaster buttresses and emphasized by a triple doorway, indicating a triple division of the interior — a nave and two side aisles; the doorways and two rows of windows indicate that the structure is three stories high. We notice also the almost entire lack of decoration except the arcading in the upper stories of the towers. There is no monumental portal, no figure sculpture.

As we look at the interior (Fig. 324B) we realize that here is something that

[1] See A. K. Porter, *Romanesque Sculpture of the Pilgrimage Roads*, 10 vols., Marshall Jones, 1923, pp. 171 ff., for a discussion of the pilgrimage as one of the most vivid and influential institutions of the Middle Ages.

[A] *Abbaye-aux-Hommes (St. Etienne).*
Caen. 1064–77. The spires were added in
the 12th and 13th cent.

[B] *Abbaye-aux-Hommes (St. Etienne). Nave.*
Vaulting constructed c. 1135.

we have not seen since we left *Sant'*
Ambrogio in Milan (Fig. 317A). There is
a similarity in the principles of structure, such as the ribbed vaulting, the
division of the nave into bays, and the
clustered pier. On the other hand, there
is a distinctive difference in the height
of the vaults. At *Sant' Ambrogio*, in his
timidity the builder omitted the clerestory; in the *Abbaye-aux-Hommes* the daring Norman had the courage to add it
and thus to obtain both height and
light.[1]

Let us see how the Norman buttressed
his vaults. A cross section of this abbey

[1] The present vaults of the *Abbaye-aux-*
Hommes are later than the original roof, but the
arrangement of the piers indicates that the
original plan must have been on the Lombard
principle.

(Fig. 340A3) shows us that the principle
adopted was similar to that of *Sant'*
Ambrogio (Fig. 340A2); that is, the heavy
vaults and cross walls of the aisles are
strong enough to hold the nave vaulting. But in the *Abbaye-aux-Hommes*, instead of a complete barrel vault over
the aisle, a half-barrel vault springs
from the outer wall to abut on the nave
wall. Here it is evident that the builders
realized that the thrust from the nave
vaults was not equally distributed along
the entire length of the nave wall, but
concentrated at the points where the ribs
converged; that is, at the clustered piers.
Hence it followed in their understanding that much of the half-barrel buttressing vault was unnecessary; so when
they built a neighboring church, the
Abbaye-aux-Dames, they cut away, as it

were, the unnecessary parts, leaving those sections only that abutted on the nave wall where the piers stood, and thus created a rudimentary flying buttress. But it was still concealed under the sloping roof of the aisle.

Thus in Normandy we find further development of the principles established at *Sant' Ambrogio*. The nave vaults have been lifted higher, admitting the clerestory as a means of lighting; the principle of the flying buttress has been applied, making the whole structure much lighter; the triple façade, with its two flanking towers and triple portal, has become an acknowledgment of the internal structure. These principles, we shall see, reach their culmination in the Gothic cathedral.

The Norman builders carried with them to England the principles evolved in northern France and there, usually in a picturesque setting, built massive, sturdy structures characterized by a heavy rectangular tower over the crossing, such as *Durham Cathedral*. Norman ornament, originating away from the highways of trade — which, as we have said, are always highways of ideas — was used at first very sparingly, and consisted of conventional motifs, among which the zigzag, with variants, was important. In England, the Norman builders produced some very delightful doorways, such as those at *Iffley* and *Kilpeck* (Fig. 325A). The thick Norman wall permitted a deeply recessed doorway, with a series of decorated shafts in the jambs and several orders of decorated arches surrounding the semicircular tympanum.

In Germany, the Rhine Valley became an active center of building as well as of other arts, for the German has always been pre-eminent as a thorough craftsman. An abundance of excellent building stone led him early toward vaulted structures, although the great forests of Germany tempted him to

[A]   *Doorway of the Church at Kilpeck. 12th cent. (The County Studio, Monmouth)*

wooden roofs. The cities of the valley were strongly organized politically and economically, and had rapidly become a firm stronghold of Christianity, with many abbey churches, such as the *Church of the Holy Apostles* at Cologne (twelfth to thirteenth century), and cathedrals, such as *Speyer* (eleventh to twelfth century), *Mainz* (chiefly thirteenth century), and *Bamberg* (Fig. 327A). As the Rhine Valley was one of the great trade routes between northern and southern Europe, close relations with Italy, especially Lombardy, are reflected in the fine vaultings based upon the Lombard system, and also in the exterior arcadings reminiscent of *Pisa*. These cathedrals show not only structural excellence, but a massive, picturesque appearance that results from the multiplicity of structural ele-

[A]   *Stave Church of Gol. 1000–1500. Now in the*
Bygdoe open air museum near Oslo.

[B]   *Carved Doorway. Wood.*
c. 1200. Oslo Museum.

ments boldly and interestingly grouped.
For the apse and the towers are frequently used at both ends of the nave[1];
a polygonal tower rises over the crossing and also at the west end of the nave.
But when the apse is repeated, it de-
prives the building of the spacious
portals that so distinguish the façade
designs of the French cathedrals.

Mention at least should be made of
an individual variant of the Romanesque basilica in another material, the
stave churches of Norway (Fig. 326A).
The wealth of timber in the forest-
covered mountains of this land led to
its almost exclusive, in fact prodigal,
use in both secular and ecclesiastical

[1] The reason for the double apsidal plan of
the German Romanesque churches has not
been satisfactorily explained.

building. With the coming of Christianity about 1000 the basilica plan
was adopted, a low enclosing passage,
like an extended narthex, being added.
The church was of solid timber construction, strong posts providing support, with upright planks (staves) between — a vertical timber construction
in contrast to the horizontal used in
secular buildings and in the wood
architecture of northern Russia (Fig.
279A). Externally, the building emphasizes verticality in its proportions and
in its steep-pitched roofs. The additional
passage affords not only ample gather-
ing-space and protection for the supports of the building against rain and
snow, but also repeats the roofs above,
and makes the building more compact
and the base broader and more solid.

About the portals the heavy timber is carved into low relief of great decorative beauty and of a peculiarly architectural quality, for it is carved in practically two planes and retains an extraordinary feeling of identity with the doorpost (Fig. 326B). The designs are frequently very intricate, and combine natural, geometric, and zoomorphic motifs into linear patterns. The roof lines were made fantastic by affixing conventionalized dragon heads and tails — the same motifs that the Viking builders and carvers attached to the prows and the sterns of their ships.

PAINTING

Although great series of frescoes decorated the stretches of wall space in the Romanesque churches, they have almost all disappeared,[1] so that very little can be determined concerning them, except that they show the same type of work that we see in the manuscripts of the period, which therefore serve as the best criterion of Romanesque painting.

The manuscripts, largely religious in subject — copies of the Bible, in whole or in part, prayer books, and liturgical books — were written in Latin.

A highly individual kind of illumination was that of the Celtic monks of Ireland and Britain, who had a preference for intricate initial letters that sometimes cover an entire page, as we see in the *Quoniam* page of the *Book of Lindisfarne*[2] (Fig. 328A). The circular

[1] A considerable number of Romanesque paintings have been recovered from overpainting and whitewash, especially in Italy and Spain. Easily accessible are the frescoes from the apse of *Santa Maria de Mur*, Catalonia, now installed in the Boston Museum of Fine Arts.

[2] This page contains the Latin word *Quoniam*, with which the Gospel of Saint Luke begins. The *Book of Lindisfarne* is also known as *Saint Cuthbert's Gospels*, because it was written in honor of Saint Cuthbert, Bishop of Lindisfarne.

[A] *Cathedral. Bamberg. 1185–1274. For the plan of a church with two apses see Fig. 315A. Compare with Figs. 323A, 324A.*

part of the Q is decorated with particularly fine spirals; the motif of the all-over pattern filling the irregular space below is made by interlacing four birds. The stems of the letters and the borders are filled with spirals, interlacing birds, and elongated dogs, with dottings and delicate diaper patterns as a background for the letters.

Perhaps the most famous of the Celtic books was the *Book of Kells*.[3] Some of its pages contain textual material with interlaced zoomorphs along the borders. Others are elaborately decorated with letters filled with various motifs —

[3] The *Book of Kells* is a book of Gospels and miscellaneous matter that came from the monastery of Kells in Ireland. Records tell of a gold cover now lost.

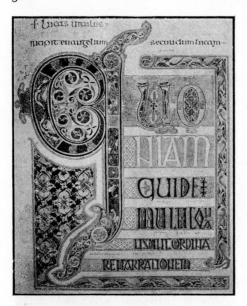

[A] *Quoniam Page from the Book of Lindisfarne (St. Cuthbert's Gospels). H. 13½ in. c. 700. British Museum, London. (British Museum)*

some geometric, such as interlaced bands and knots, spiral and quatrefoil; others naturalistic, such as foliage, birds, reptiles, grotesques, and occasionally a human form. All are interwoven with a facility, an intricacy, and a fine sweep of line that leave us astounded at the possibility of such execution, and also at the vigor, the fancy, and the infinite variety found in one initial. Comparable with Celtic illumination in intricacy of design and delicacy of brush work are some of the *Korans* (Fig. 297B). But in comparison with the latter, the Celtic work is more varied, more sweeping in its linealism, and more restrained in effect because it employs almost no gold. And one should mention the fact that, like the *Korans*, these Celtic manuscripts, in particular the *Book of Kells*, contain some of the most beautiful calligraphy of the Middle Ages. The mo-

tive for the incredible patience and utter disregard of time which must have characterized these artist-monks is well epitomized in the colophon of the *Book of Lindisfarne* — "For the love of God and Saint Cuthbert."

Important work was produced also at Canterbury, and particularly at Winchester, then the capital of England. Some of the illuminations are close to Byzantine models and some show an art of vigorous penwork with light washes of color, in which the figures have the same twisting movements, elongations, energy, and linear decorativeness as those in the carvings at *Moissac* (Fig. 312A).

METALWORK, IVORY–
CARVING, TEXTILES

As we looked at the ground plan of the monastery of *St. Gall* (Fig. 315A), we noticed that rooms or separate buildings were provided for the various craftsmen, so that while some of the workers were clearing the land, planting the gardens, and tending the cattle, others were carving ivory crosiers, shaping gold chalices and reliquaries, and decorating them with jewels and enamels; others were copying and illuminating manuscripts, painting miniatures to illustrate the text, and fashioning splendid covers for them of gold and silver, ivory, jewels, and enamel. The point of view of these monks, and the relation of their art to their religion, are seen in a treatise on painting, enameling, metalworking, and other crafts written by a monk named Theophilus in the eleventh or twelfth century. The prologue to the third book reads:

"David, that most excellent of prophets . . . collecting himself with all the attention of his mind to the love of his Creator, uttered this saying among others: 'Lord I have loved the beauty of Thine house.' And — albeit a man

[A] *Gospel Cover. Of oak covered with plates of gold set with enamels and stones. H. 10 in. 12th cent. Victoria and Albert Museum, London. (Victoria and Albert Museum)*

of so great authority and of so deep an understanding called this house the habitation of the court of heaven . . . yet it is certain that he desired the adornment of the material house of God, which is the house of prayer. . . . Wherefore, most beloved son, make thou no long delay, but believe in full faith that the Spirit of God hath filled thine heart when thou hast adorned His house with so great beauty. . . . Work therefore now, good man, happy in this life before God's face and man's, and happier still in the life to come. . . . Kindle thyself to a still ampler art, and set thyself with all the might of thy soul to complete that which is yet lacking in the gear of the Lord's house, without which the divine mysteries and the ministries of God's service may not stand; such as chalices, candelabra,

thuribles, chrism-vases, crewets, shrines for holy relics, crosses, missals and such like, which the necessary use of the ecclesiastical order requireth. Which if thou wouldst fashion, begin after the manner thus following." [1] This spirit of devotion and reverence not only permeated the monastery but was basic in the social solidarity of the community as a whole.

It was "the adornment of the material house of God" that motivated the metalworkers and ivory-carvers also. Liturgical books were as sacrosanct as the vessels on the altar, and their covers equally sumptuous. In Figure 329A, the rich effect is obtained through the com-

[1] Quoted by G. G. Coulton, *A Medieval Garner*, London, 1910, p. 166. See also A. P. Laurie, *The Materials of the Painter's Craft in Europe and Egypt*, Lippincott, 1911, p. 152.

[A]   *Ardagh Chalice. Of silver, brass, and gilt bronze, with decoration in gold and silver filigree with enamels, blue glass, and amber. D. $9\frac{1}{2}$ in. c. 700. Royal Irish Academy, Dublin. (Royal Irish Academy)*

bination of many materials. In the center panel is the figure of Christ, done in gold repoussé, surrounded by a narrow border containing an inscription in cloisonné enamel in opaque white on a luminous blue ground. The wider border is decorated with a conventionalized floral pattern, and both borders are set with stones irregular in size, shape, and color. The broad outer border is made up of gold plaques decorated alternately with various jewels and with filagree and enamel. The shimmering gold, enhanced by the massing of color, the luminous blue of the enamel that is all the deeper because of the opaque white and the rich color of the other stones, produce a richly decorative effect. Other covers were made entirely of carved ivory or of ivory surrounded by a gold and jeweled border.

Among the metalworkers — and they were many and important — the Celtic craftsman again produced individual work, in style akin to the illuminations, with regard for difference of medium. Brooches, staffs, and ecclesiastical vessels of all kinds were constructed of various materials and decorated with

enamels, jewels, repoussé, and filigree. The *Ardagh Chalice* (Fig. 330A), for example, is of a round bowl shape, with two handles, a short stem, and a broad base — a design of strength rather than of elegance. The rich ornamentation neither overloads nor interferes with the structural lines, being concentrated about the handles, on the two disks on the body of the chalice, and in the borders that decorate the top and the foot. In the details we discern the spirals and the interlaced animal forms of the *Book of Kells* executed in gold and silver, worked both in repoussé and in filigree of almost incredible finesse.

The bronzesmiths and ironworkers of Hildesheim in Germany were another group of great craftsmen. Their bronze church doors and candlesticks were famous for both their spirited designs and their masterly execution.[1]

Fine textiles were in great demand for reliquaries and vestments, and those of the East were highly prized. The Muslims, always skilled weavers, had made Palermo famous as a weaving center

[1] See the doors of *St. Michael* at Hildesheim, and the large Paschal candelabra at South Kensington, London, and in Milan.

and thus not only introduced into Western manufacture Eastern design, but built up a lively traffic in fabrics to meet the demands of a West awakening to the luxuries of the East. This traffic was much accelerated by the Crusaders, who returned with whatever was portable from their pilferings of *Santa Sophia* and other Eastern buildings.

SUMMARY

In every aspect of the Romanesque period we have observed enthusiasm, experimentation, accomplishment. Out of the chaos that marked the early part of the period order was emerging, largely through the steadying hand of the monastery. The barbarians, Christianized, were going to school to the old traditions of the Mediterranean civilizations, but were transforming them with the fresh vitality of the North. North, South, and East were mingling.

Romanesque was an ecclesiastical art and manifested itself differently in different countries. In architecture, in Italy it contributed to the revival and the advance of vaulting, and added decorative elements — arcadings, marble inlays, and sculptured portals — to soften the austerity of the basilica. In southern France and in Spain, the builders erected solid, massive structures, but laid still greater stress upon the sculpture at the portals, upon carvings about doors, windows, and on capitals. All of these were conventional in style, and of great decorative beauty as well as profound symbolic meaning. In northern France, Germany, and England interest again centered, as in Lombardy, on construction. The need to furnish the "House of God" with worthy equipment led to making books with the finest calligraphy, illustrations, and covers; and

vessels of gold, silver, ivory, and jewels. All this Northern expression is permeated with a characteristic dynamic, highly decorative linealism.

BIBLIOGRAPHY

Adams, Henry, *Mont-Saint-Michel and Chartres*, Houghton Mifflin, 1913

Allen, John R., *Celtic Art in Pagan and Christian Times*, Jacobs, 1908

Baltrušaitis, Jurgis, *La stylistique ornementale dans la sculpture romane*, Paris, 1931

Baum, Julius, ed., *Romanesque Architecture in France*, 2d ed., Westermann, 1928

Belloc, Hilaire, *The Book of the Bayeux Tapestry*, Putnam, 1914

Clapham, Alfred W., *English Romanesque Architecture after the Conquest*, Oxford University Press, 1934

——————— *English Romanesque Architecture before the Conquest*, Oxford University Press, 1930

——————— *Romanesque Architecture in Western Europe*, Oxford University Press, 1936

Coffey, George, *Guide to the Celtic Antiquities of the Christian Period*, Royal Irish Academy, Dublin, 1910

Coulton, George G., ed. and tr., *A Medieval Garner*, London, 1910

Cunynghame, Henry H. S., *European Enamels*, London, 1906

Dawson, Edith B. (Mrs. Nelson), *Enamels*, McClurg, 1911

Focillon, Henri, *L'art des sculpteurs romans*, Paris, 1931

Hammett, Ralph W., *The Romanesque Architecture of Western Europe*, Architectural Book Publishing Company, 1927

Jackson, Sir Thomas Graham, *Byzantine and Romanesque Architecture*, 2d ed., 2 vols., University of Chicago Press, 1913

Jameson, Anna B. Murphy, *Sacred and Legendary Art*, 2 vols., Houghton Mifflin, c. 1911

Lethaby, William R., *Mediæval Art*, rev. ed., Scribner, 1913

Maritain, Jacques, *Art and Scholasticism*, Scribner, 1930

Markham, Violet R. (Mrs. James Carruthers), *Romanesque France*, Dutton, 1929

Maskell, Alfred O., *Ivories*, Putnam, 1905

Millar, Eric G., *English Illuminated Manuscripts from the Xth to the XIIIth Century*, Paris, 1926

——————— *English Illuminated Manuscripts of the XIVth and XVth Centuries*, Paris, 1928

——————— ed., *The Lindisfarne Gospels*, Oxford University Press, 1924

Porter, Arthur K., *Medieval Architecture*, 2 vols., Yale University Press, 1915

———— *Romanesque Sculpture of the Pilgrimage Roads*, 10 vols., Marshall Jones, 1923

Ricci, Corrado, *Romanesque Architecture in Italy*, Brentano, 1925

Robinson, Stanford F. H., *Celtic Illuminative Art*, Dublin, 1908

Saunders, O. Elfrida, *A History of English Art in the Middle Ages*, Oxford University Press, 1932

Strzygowski, Josef, *Early Church Art in Northern Europe; with Special Reference to Timber Construction and Decoration*, Harper, 1929

Sullivan, Sir Edward, *The Book of Kells*, Studio, 1914

Swartwout, Robert E., *The Monastic Craftsman*, Cambridge, Eng., 1932

Warner, Sir George Frederic, *Illuminated Manuscripts in the British Museum*, ser. 1–3, Museum, London, 1910

Whitehill, Walter M., *Spanish Romanesque Architecture*, Oxford University Press, 1941

Zervos, Christian, *L'Art de la Catalogne*, Paris, 1937

See also the General Bibliography, pp. 791–92.

18

GOTHIC ART

(ABOUT A.D. 1150–1550)

THE word "Gothic," in the sense of "barbarian," was a term of reproach applied to medieval buildings by the architects of the Renaissance, who found their ideal in the architecture of Greece and Rome. The Gothic cathedral, however, is the highest expression of an age that was vigorous in its civic life, intensely religious, and profoundly intellectual. Rising in the midst of the houses that huddled closely about it (Fig. 333A), not only did it dominate the town, but it stood as a center for the activities of the people — all of whom it was large enough to hold when the whole town gathered for the Christmas or Easter celebration, or to see a mystery play. The market place, the shop, and the home were situated literally in the shadow of the great church; and so interwoven were religious and secular activities that life presented a unified whole rather than the segregations of modern times. Let us look at some of the factors in the civilization which thus manifested itself.

Politically stronger kings, such as Philip Augustus (1180–1223) and Louis IX (Saint Louis; 1226–70), were holding in check the feudal lords, though here and there such a baron as the Sieur de Coucy, protected by moat, thick walls, and a great donjon, could support his boast — "I am not king, nor prince, nor duke, nor even count; I am the lord of Coucy." In distinction from the Romanesque period, when life was chiefly rural and monastic, the Gothic age was one of towns, with their merchant guilds, growing in number and power. Revolting from the feudal domination of the baron or the bishop, one by one they became independent communes, robust and vigorous with a growing sense of freedom and expansion resulting from the opening-up of intercourse with neighboring countries and the Near East through the Crusades.

[A] *Chartres, the Town and the Cathedral.* (*N. D. Photo*)

Economically, this intercourse stimulated commercial activity and brought wealth.

Religiously, the thirteenth century saw the culmination of enthusiasm that had been developing since the year 1000. Under a strong line of Popes the Church reached a pinnacle of temporal as well as of spiritual power. The existing monasteries, having fulfilled their purpose of reforming the Church from within, declined in power, while attention was focused upon the churches of the towns where the bishops lived. Hence we see the rise of the great cathedrals. The higher clergy had developed the creeds and the ritual until they had become subtle and complex, far above the comprehension of the mass of the people, whose religion nevertheless was intense, manifesting itself in the mystery and miracle plays and in the veneration of relics. Many of the latter were believed to be miracle-working and, carefully protected in reliquaries (Fig. 359A) of gold and silver inlaid with precious stones and enamels, were carried through the land, curing the sick and stimulating the contribution of large sums of money for the erection of a church to house the relic. So intense was the enthusiasm that at Chartres, for example,[1] all the people, old and young, prince and peasant, hitched

---

[1] For a full account, see the letter of Haymo, an eyewitness, as translated in A. K. Porter, *Medieval Architecture*, 2 vols., Yale University Press, 1912, Vol. II, pp. 151 ff.

themselves to carts and dragged great loads of stone to build the cathedral.

But a new far-reaching element was altering religious ideas — the Franciscan movement. In 1210 Saint Francis of Assisi, in protest against the growing internal degradation of the Church, clad in a rough peasant's cloak, barefoot, with no money, began traveling about with his small band of followers, preaching the creed of poverty, chastity, and obedience and inspiring the people with his own gentleness and radiant love for all life. The birds, the animals, the insects, the trees, and the sun — everything in nature was a part of God's great universe, a brother, to be loved and respected. Gradually there came about a change in point of view — a change from the medieval ideal of focusing upon the life to come, for which this life was but a preparation, to a realization of the value of this life for itself, for the beauty to be seen all about and for a legitimate joy in nature. Such a realization turned men's eyes toward an observation of nature that revealed itself in the Gothic age, and found its culmination in the individualism and secularization of the Renaissance.

Another aspect of medieval life revealed itself in the cathedral — the intellectual. It was a period of great learning. Universities were springing up, and the passion of the age for encyclopedic knowledge we observe in the work of Vincent of Beauvais, who attempted to classify all knowledge under four headings, which he called *The Four Mirrors:* first, the mirror of nature, which included scenes of creation, vegetable and animal ornament, monsters, and grotesques; second, the mirror of science or instruction, which included human labor, the handicrafts, and the seven arts; third, the mirror of morals, which revealed the vices and virtues; and, fourth, the mirror of history, which related the stories of the Old and New Testaments, the tales of the apocryphal books, and the lives of the saints. And the age, not content with gathering this knowledge into a book, carved it all in stone on the portals of the cathedral, on the capitals, and high up on the buttresses and towers, and pictured it in vivid colors in the windows.[1]

Everyday life in the towns was vigorous and democratic, each person contributing to the life of the community. To be sure, the streets were narrow and dark; and there was little sanitation, so that plagues, once started, easily wiped out great masses of mankind. At the feudal courts life was festive and gay, and from hall to hall the troubadours and the trouvères traveled, singing their songs of love and adventure.[2]

This thirteenth century was the classic period of Gothic art, as the twelfth had been its archaic period. Though the style continued into the sixteenth century and even longer in some countries, after the thirteenth the trend was toward greater engineering achievement, elegance, and overelaboration.

ARCHITECTURE AND SCULPTURE

As has been said, the highest achievement of the age was the cathedral, which is an epitome in stone of medieval life. Unlike Romanesque architecture,

[1] For a fuller description and symbolic meaning, see Émile Mâle, *Religious Art in France, XIII Century,* Dutton, 1913.

[2] Vivid pictures of life in this period are found in the manuscripts, especially the calendars, in which the activity typical of the month is illustrated — the feast and the hawking party; sowing and reaping; and hunting the wild boar for the Christmas feast. Henry Adams, *Mont-Saint-Michel and Chartres,* Houghton Mifflin, 1930, is especially recommended for its sympathetic insight into the spirit of the age.

[A]   *Cathedral of Notre Dame. Chartres. Chiefly 12th–13th cent.*

which was diverse and widely scattered, Gothic architecture is distinctly French and in its purest form narrowly restricted to the Île de France, though it manifested itself in varying forms in other localities.

To understand the cathedral, let us travel about fifty-five miles southwest of Paris to Chartres and there study in detail, as a typical example, the cathedral of *Notre Dame de Chartres*.[1] As we approach (Fig. 333A), we notice how it

[1] The present cathedral dates from the fire of 1134, which destroyed the old basilica on the site. The west façade was built by 1150. To gain space in the nave (Fig. 337A), this façade, which had been built behind the towers, was moved forward until flush with the west end of the towers, its present position. The south tower was completed between 1180 and 1194, when a great fire destroyed all the church except parts of the western end. Rebuilding proceeded rapidly and the new cathedral, the present one, was dedicated in 1260. The northern and southern portals were added during the thirteenth century, and the northern spire between 1506 and 1512.

looms above the compact town, a bulky mass culminating in two spires. An air view (Fig. 335A) shows that this mass consists of two lofty, narrow rectangular volumes, the longer one terminating in a semicircular end, the shorter interpenetrating the longer at right angles, somewhat nearer the circular end. These volumes organize an interior space, just as the dome and the drum of the *Pantheon* (Fig. 176A) and the domes, half-domes, and walls of *Santa Sophia* (Fig. 261A) organize the interior space of these buildings. But the space is of a different character. As we enter Chartres, it is too dim for us to see at first. Then we become aware of a narrow lofty space, in which the eye is carried upward by swiftly rising verticals into mysterious shadows, and down the deep vista of the nave to a high light near its end. The surfaces of the walls glow with the rich colors of glass, which spreads its radiant luminosity over the gray stone. Proportions, emphasis of line di-

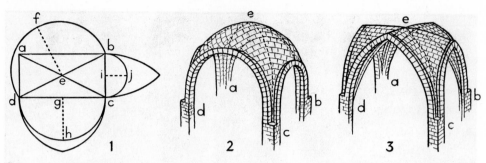

[A]   *The Value of the Pointed Arch.*   (1) abcd *is an oblong bay to be vaulted; bd is the diagonal rib; dc, the transverse; and bc, the longitudinal. If circular ribs are erected, their heights will be ef, gh, and ij. The result will be a domical vaulting* (2) *irregular in shape because of the unequal height of the ribs; and with the longitudinal arch too low to admit of a clerestory. A building so vaulted is low and dark, like Sant' Ambrogio (Fig. 317A). The problem, then, is to bring the crowns of all the ribs to the same height as the crown of the diagonal rib* e. *This can be done by pointing the lower ribs. The result is a lighter, more flexible system* (3), *affording ample space for a clerestory.*

rection, thematic repetitions, such as the pointed arch and compound pier — these are components of an interior space organization that overwhelms the onlooker with a feeling of mystery and exaltation.

The plan (Fig. 339A4) generated this spatial organization and it, in turn, was determined by utilitarian considerations. It is an elaborated basilica, in which liturgical considerations so lengthened the choir that the transept is near the center of the nave, thus transforming the T-shape of the early basilica into a cross shape. The apse has developed into a complicated form called the *chevet*,[1] which includes not only the apse itself but the surrounding aisles, known as *ambulatories*, or apsidal aisles, and the chapels opening from them (Fig. 335A). The constructional principles which enabled the builders to create such a structure are clearly evident on both the exterior and the interior. As we think back to *Sant' Ambrogio*

[1] Note that the apse is the full height of the nave, but the ambulatories and chapels, though vaulted, are but one story high, and over them spring the flying buttresses. See also Figure 350A.

(Fig. 317A), low, dark, and heavy, and even to *St. Etienne* (Fig. 324B), where advance over *Sant' Ambrogio* came about through the daring of the Normans, we ask ourselves what enabled the Gothic builders to erect their lofty naves. It was three things primarily — ribbed vaulting, the pointed arch, and the flying buttress — by means of which they produced buildings that were not only uplifting in their emotional appeal, but highly intellectual in their engineering.

Let us look at Chartres from the engineering angle. In the nave, we recognize the ribbed vaulting, but we see that the arches are pointed rather than round. By studying Figure 336A we understand why the pointed arch could give height and light where the round one could not; and that was what these builders were trying to secure — height for expression, and light because of the dull Northern climate.

Given, then, a method of securing these two essentials, how is the vaulting stably supported in its lofty position? In Figure 337A we see that the great piers at the crossing are of the

[A] *Chartres. Nave, looking east. L. 236 ft.; with choir, 367 ft. W. 54 ft.; with aisles, 107 ft. H. 112 ft. (Clarence Ward)*

clustered or compound type such as we saw in *Sant' Ambrogio* — each rib of the vaulting, diagonal, transverse, and longitudinal, has its individual supporting member in the clustered pier. The consistent application of this principle makes a massive pier necessary at the crossing, to support the tower over the crossing that the original plans called for but which was never built. Such a pier also affords an effective accent at this part of the cathedral. Along the nave and transept, however, the builders used a single shaft with four engaged columns (Fig. 337A) — quite adequate to carry the load. Three of these rise one story only to support the arches of the ground-story arcade and the trans-verse arches of the aisle; the fourth — that facing the nave or the transept — rises from the base to the vaulting, interrupted by stringcourses only, and at that point meets the downward thrust of the great transverse ribs of the nave. Smaller shafts, which carry the diagonal and longitudinal ribs, rise from the capitals of the ground-story arcade.[1] The same deviations from regularity that are found in the buildings of many peoples — in the *Ziggurat of Ur*, the *Parthenon*, the arcades of *Pisa*, to cite a

[1] A comparison of the piers of several of the great cathedrals, such as *St. Denis, Senlis, Sens, Paris, Amiens*, and *Reims*, will reveal an interesting variety of methods of treating the problem of the compound pier.

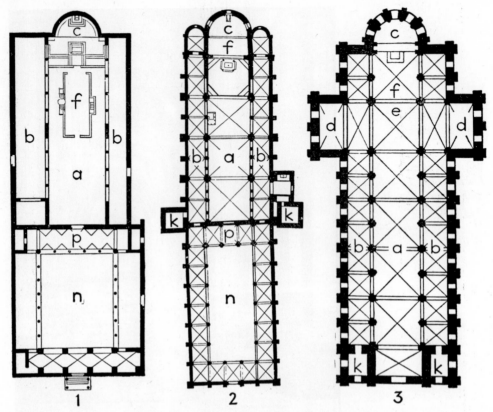

[A]   *Steps in the Development of the Gothic Plan.* (1) *San Clemente, Rome. An early Christian basilica. A timber roof, light in weight and with no side thrust, is carried on slender, uncomplicated supports. The development of liturgy has resulted in a low-walled choir occupying about half the nave.* (2) *Sant' Ambrogio, Milan (Fig. 316A). Italian Romanesque. While the plan closely follows that of the early Christian basilica (with atrium, detached towers, and no transepts), the stone roof vault necessitates heavier walls and columns for support, and the concentration of buttressing to support the rib vaulting divides the interior into bays.* (3) *Abbaye-aux-Dames, Caen. French Romanesque. While round-arched rib vaulting results in a plan of square bays similar to that of Sant' Ambrogio, the larger window openings, obtained by further concentration of buttressing, indicate the requirements of a northern climate. The atrium has disappeared; the towers have become part of the building and a*

few — appear in Gothic in the unequally spaced piers, and in the curved stringcourses.

A study of one bay in detail indicates a clearly marked division into three stories: (1) the ground-story arcade that separates the aisle from the nave; (2) the triforium, a low second story pierced with four arched openings separated by

colonnettes;[1] and (3) the clerestory, which consists of tracery filled with glass, reaching to the crown of the vaulting (Fig. 337A). An obvious characteristic of the system is the relatively small

[1] As this story frequently had three openings, it became known as the *triforium,* meaning *three-pierced.* Sometimes a gallery is built here over the aisles.

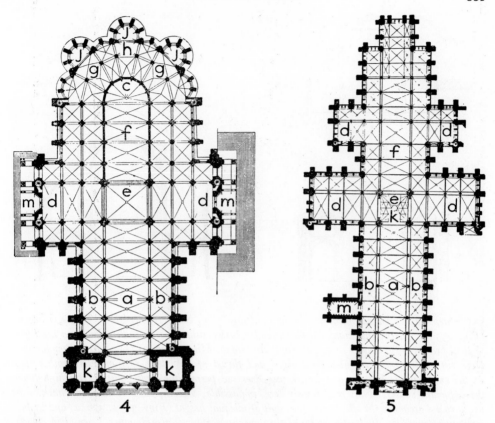

4   5

dominating feature of the façade; a transept with exterior projections separates the nave from the choir and gives the plan the shape of a cross. (4) Chartres Cathedral (Figs. 333A, 335A). French Gothic. Enlargement of the choir leaves the transept in the middle of the church. The once separate towers are integrated. Deep triple doorways front the transepts. Gothic buttressing makes possible the complexities of the chevet and double aisle and, by removing all weight from the walls, converts them into window areas. Pointed arches permit an oblong bay (Fig. 336A) and thus widen the nave. (5) Salisbury Cathedral (Fig. 352A). English Gothic. A long narrow plan, deep, double transepts, single aisles, a square instead of apsidal east end, shallow portals, and a dominating tower over the crossing are characteristic English features.

*   a. nave; b. aisles; c. apse; d. transept; e. crossing; f. choir; g. chevet; h. ambulatory; j. apsidal chapel; k. tower; m. porch; n. atrium; p. narthex.*

amount of wall space in comparison with the openings. The long reaches of uninterrupted surface in the basilica have given way to this light, open arrangement, with the clerestory entirely filled with apertures for admitting light. But this suppression of wall also eliminated any space for such mural decoration as the frescoes or mosaic that enriched the interiors of the early Christian churches. Compensation for this the Gothic builders found in stained glass, which was just reaching a climax in its development. Eagerly seizing upon its possibilities, they substituted great areas of glass for stone, producing a decoration of deep, glowing color, even richer than the Byzantine mosaics.

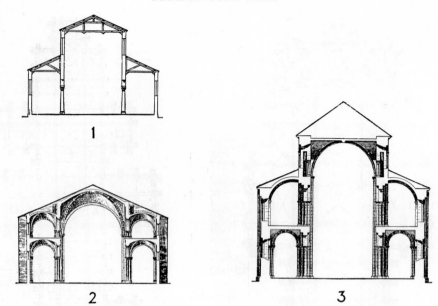

[A]   *Steps in the Development of Gothic Vaulting.*   (1) *Sant' Apollinare in Classe, Ravenna*
(Fig. 255A). Early Christian. Slender arcades easily support a high clerestory and the light,
vertical pressure of a timber roof. (2) Sant' Ambrogio, Milan (Fig. 317A). Italian Romanesque.
Here rib vaulting concentrates the weight and thrust of the stone roof on piers rather than
on the entire wall, but the pier buttressing does not permit the nave vault to rise high above
the triforium vaults. Thus a clerestory was impossible, and the nave is low and dark. The
use of round arches in the ribs makes the vault of unequal height (Figs. 317A, 336A2) and by pre-
scribing a square bay limits the width of the nave. (3) Abbaye-aux-Hommes, Caen (Fig. 324B).
French Romanesque. A concealed half barrel vault over the loftier triforium acts as a flying
buttress and props the nave vault high enough to permit a small clerestory. (4) Chartres

We now have the explanation of the pointed arch, the ribbed vaulting, and the clustered pier from which the latter springs. The third vital element involved, if the vault is to stand, is efficient buttressing; otherwise the thin walls will be pushed out by the great weight and the whole structure will collapse like a house of cards. We have already learned that buttressing is needed only at the points where the thrust of the vault is concentrated. This thrust, which exerts pressure both downward and outward, is concentrated partly on the piers and partly at a point about a third of the way up the curve of the rib, a point called the

haunch, so that here the thrust must be met by a counterthrust. This is the function of the flying buttress.

With this in mind, let us study the buttresses (Figs. 335A, 341A4). From the ground rise massive buttresses, each on the axis of a clustered pier, in line with the transverse arches of both the nave and the aisle (Fig. 339A4). They diminish in thickness as they rise, and from each spring two half-arches — the flying buttresses — which abut on the nave wall, one at and slightly above the capital of the pier and the other at the crown of the ribs. The lower arch is double, with an open arcade between — an unusual feature. Furthermore, the nave

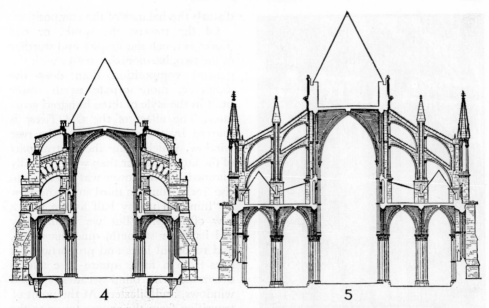

4   5

Cathedral (Fig. 337A). French Gothic. Pointed arches permit a vault of even height and a high clerestory. Flying buttresses, frankly revealed, permit the nave vault to rise high above the aisle vaults and, by providing support only at the points of greatest stress (where the ribs converge), eliminate the necessity for support from a vault over the triforium or from the walls below, thus making it possible to fill the walls with windows and to reduce the triforium to a low, mural gallery. (5) Reims Cathedral (Figs. 349A, 350A). French Gothic. Flying buttresses here transfer the weight and thrust of the high nave vaulting across two aisles to the pier buttresses. Note the use of pinnacles at the tops of the piers to provide stabilizing weight to balance the outward thrust of the flying buttresses. In this drawing all the naves are represented as the same width in order to show the effect of construction upon proportion.

wall between is stiffened by engaged columns. The buttresses of the *Abbaye-aux-Hommes* (Fig. 340A3), hidden beneath the roof with their place of abutment too low, have here come out into the open, frankly revealed and efficiently constructed. Thus the thrusts of the vaults are counterbalanced and the whole structure is dynamically stable.[1]

[1] As in the case of the clustered pier, no two cathedrals show the same treatment of the flying buttress, though the underlying structural principle is the same. *Sant' Ambrogio, Abbaye-aux-Hommes, Abbaye-aux-Dames, St. Germer de Fly, Soissons, Chartres, Amiens, Notre Dame de Paris, Reims,* and *Beauvais* illustrate the general evolution. The trend is toward lightness without sacrifice of structural stability.

Engineering alone, however, though fundamental, deals with but one aspect of Gothic architectural form. The treatment of the surfaces that bound the volumes, and the decorative elements, contribute equally to the unity. Two kinds of ornament were used: stone sculpture and stained glass, the former to enrich the portals and the latter to provide luminous color for the interior.

The local gray stone, which was used for both the masonry and the sculpture, integrates the surfaces of the constructional walls and the carvings into a compact unity. This is particularly evident in the western façade, whose dominant note is a quiet strength that

[A] *Chartres, Western Portal: Kings and Queens.* (*Monuments Piot*)

results from large areas of unbroken masonry (evidence of its Romanesque ancestry), from the thematic repetition of the rounding arch in the fenestration, and, with the exception of the northern tower, from its restrained decoration, which breaks the surface only enough for vivifying contrasts. The façade is divided vertically into three parts. A central division contains the portal, three lancet windows, a rose window, and an arcade; and on either side a flanking tower that reaches up into a tall spire. The design, however, is not symmetrical, the most striking irregularity being in the towers, one of which is sturdy and plain, the other higher, more slender, and ornate; and the division into stories is not uniform. These irregularities, however, which are due to different periods of building, do not

disturb the balance of the composition.

Of the towers, the south, or *Old Tower*, is much the simpler and sturdier of the two, harmonizing better with the general composition than does the slenderer, more ornate north tower built in the style of three hundred years later. The effect of the *Old Tower* is marred by the arcading and the rose window, which bring the central part of the façade higher than was originally planned; for the tower was intended to rise freely from the third story and now is "hunched up by half a rose and a row of kings."[1] But we instinctively feel its sober strength, quiet harmony, and reposeful lines and proportions. It rises from a firm, square base and is decorated with blind arcades, splayed windows, and pilasters. At the point of transition from the square tower to the octagonal spire (the builder's most difficult problem), the work becomes lighter, with more frequent openings and small pinnacles that lead directly to the towering spire; but so skillfully is this transition made that one is quite unaware how gradually and subtly it has taken place.

On the triple portal (Fig. 343A), which is confined to the central division of the façade, is concentrated the elaborate sculpture, carved of the same material, which enlivens the stone masonry and accents the entrance. The first impression is that of perfect architectural unity. In the central tympanum is the figure of *Christ* surrounded by the four beasts of the Apocalypse, in every respect very close to *St. Trophime* (Fig. 321A). The linealism of the conventional forms contributes to the decorative value, and the austerity of the central figure, combining benevolence and pity for humanity (expressed by the gesture of benediction) conveys to one entering the church the innermost meaning of that for which the Church stood. In

[1] Adams, *op. cit.*

[A] *Chartres. Western, or Royal, Portal. So called because on the central tympanum is represented Christ as King of Kings. c. 1145. (Houvet)*

the rows of kings and queens on either side of the doorway (Fig. 342A) we see elongated figures standing rigidly erect, compact, with arms close to the body, never projecting beyond the contour.[1] The long lines of the drapery are predominantly vertical, reminiscent of flutings, so that the whole effect is that of a column. And this is what the artist was striving for — to use the human figure to adorn a column and yet not lose the feeling of the column. This effect is still further enhanced by the background of rich carvings on the pedestals and the intermediate shafts. As representations of kings and queens,

they are richly clad in embroidered robes, befitting royalty; each carries a scepter, a book, or a scroll, and many wear crowns. In the heads are expressed great variety and marked individuality. At the same time these figures are primarily of stone, of the same material and texture as that of the building itself and carved in a manner that is suitable to a rather coarse stone. The sculptors have consistently carved this stone to serve a definite function and not to produce a realistic representation of kings and queens.

Throughout the portal, then, first, there is a feeling for function, as seen in the restraint and the conventionalization of each figure which adapted it to the place that it was to occupy; second, there runs through the figures

[1] The unequal height of the figures is probably due to the fact that after the fire they were assembled from different parts of the building. The plain shafts indicate repair.

[A]   *Chartres. Northern Porch, detail. c. 1205–70. (N. D. Photo)*

a living quality of marked individuality, with a serene emotionalism born of sincere religious conviction.

The details of the left and right doorways deserve notice. On the arches about the left tympanum is carved a calendar. Why should such a subject be represented on a cathedral? Recalling the *Four Mirrors* of Vincent of Beauvais, we read in the *Mirror of Instruction* that while man can be saved only through a Redeemer, still he can prepare himself for redemption by labor and knowledge. Hence the sculptor pictures man's typical occupation for each month, together with the appropriate sign of the zodiac. In all these little pictures there is a mingling of the fanciful and the simple homely scenes of everyday life, very spontaneous, and very close to the heart of the people.

Another glance at the ground plan of *Chartres* (Fig. 339A4) shows that the transepts terminate in deep porches approached by a broad flight of steps. In Figure 344A we see the north porch, a large open portico, each of its triple divisions vaulted over and capped with a pediment. As on the western portal, rows of figures flank the doorways; the tympani are filled with sculptured reliefs; all the arches are carved with figures and the intervening spaces are decorated with trefoil ornament. The south porch is similar in general design. Both form effective entrances, rich in detail and harmonious in design with the whole façade.

The subject matter of the sculpture of the north porch is taken from the Old Testament and the life of the Virgin, fitting subjects for the portal which

[A] *Amiens. Nave, looking east. 1220–36. L. 240 ft.; with choir, 370 ft. W. 49 ft.; with aisles, 108 ft. H. 138 ft. (Clarence Ward)*

looks to the cold and dark of the North, forming a prelude to the life of Christ that finds its place on the portal which faces the warmth and sunshine of the South. On both porches are found representations of scenes from the creation, the Vices and Virtues, and the lives of saints and martyrs, thus continuing the illustrations from the *Four Mirrors*.

As we look at some of the figures from these north and south portals (Fig. 344A), we realize that this is a different art from that of the western portal. The figures are well proportioned; they appear to stand upon their feet and turn their bodies and heads, so that we feel that a bodily structure exists beneath the drapery, which falls in naturalistic

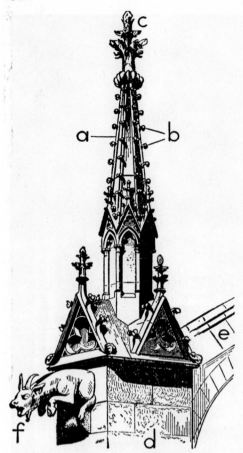

[A] *Pinnacle. St. Etienne, Châlons-sur-Marne. 13th cent.* a. *pinnacle;* b. *crockets;* c. *finial;* d. *pier buttress;* e. *flying buttress;* f. *gargoyle. Although utilized as an ornament, the pinnacle originated as a constructional necessity — to provide stabilizing weight at the top of the pier buttress where it receives the thrust of the flying buttress.*

folds. So, too, the carvings on the capitals and the bases reveal a tendency away from the conventional to the naturalistic. During the century that intervened between the building of the western and the side portals, the Gothic sculptor had been turning to nature, and in his eagerness to imitate it had sacrificed that complete subordi-

nation to architectural needs which characterized the western portal. He has not lost his sense of design, however. The beautiful long sweeping lines of the drapery give the figures something of an architectural feeling; but they are not so impressive or so essentially a part of the building as are the kings and queens at the western doorway. In the *Visitation* particularly we notice the sweep of line in the delicate, almost clinging drapery.

Beneath each statue, or underneath the bracket upon which it stands, are small figures which not only are decorative but also bear some symbolical or historical relation to the statue above. Beneath the feet of *Christ*, for example, are the lion and the dragon — "The young lion and the serpent shalt thou trample under foot." These little figures are added to symbolize Christ's conquest over evil. Thus we see on these portals not only stories from the Bible and the legends and the illustrations from the *Four Mirrors*, but also, interwoven with them all, a whole world of figures and attributes which are symbolic.[1]

Sculpture, we have seen, was used chiefly on the exterior, to adorn the portals. The second factor in decoration, the stained glass, ornamented the interior. As we stand in the nave of *Chartres* and look up at the three lancets and the rose window of the western façade, we are aware of a mass of the richest color imaginable, glowing like a cluster of brilliant gems. The *Tree of Jesse* window (one of the western lancets), for example, or *La Belle Verrière* ("The Beautiful Window") in the ambulatory gives us the impression of an area of radiant vibrating blue, stabilized by the adjacent opaque stone. Closer inspection shows that other colors — deep red and green relieved by

[1] For the symbolic interpretation of Gothic sculpture, see Mâle, *op. cit.*

lighter tones of the same hue or by a little white — contribute equally to the design. Why then the effect of blue tonality? The art of working in colored glass involves a knowledge of the action of light upon color. Red areas, for example, tend to present ragged edges, whereas blue spreads out over adjacent differently colored areas. Thus the window at a distance presents an over-all blue tonality.[1]

A detail of these twelfth- and thirteenth-century windows reveals a two-dimensional design, based upon line and color areas and upon the transparency of glass and the opacity of lead and iron, each a foil to the other. There is no landscape, no feeling of depth, and the figures are quite Byzantine in style. The purpose of the glassmaker was not to produce a naturalistic representation, but to keep his design flat with all parts subordinated to color organization.

Let us follow a glassworker as he makes such a window. With the dimensions of the window in hand, he draws his design in full size on the whitened bench upon which he is building up his window, indicating with heavy black lines the iron bars that are necessary to hold the window firmly; for a large area of glass and lead is too pliable to withstand the force of storms. These bars must play into the design and not obstruct it; hence they determine the main lines of the composition. Having drawn in the figures, he begins putting in the glass. At hand he has sheets of glass which have been colored, not by being painted, but by having coloring matter, chiefly metal, added while the glass was in a molten state. From these sheets he cuts tiny pieces, often not more than an inch long, to fit his designs, a separate piece for each color or shade of color. He pieces them together

[1] For an explanation of this action of light upon color see C. J. Connick, *Adventures in Light and Color*, Random House, 1937.

[A]   *Grotesques. Notre Dame, Paris.*

with strips of lead, because this metal is pliable, and solders the strips where they join. Thus he builds up his design, piece by piece, mindful first, as he works in his reds and blues with whites, yellows, and greens, of color relationships. Hence when his design calls for an illustration of the Prodigal Son feeding the swine, he does not hesitate to make one pig green, two blue, and one red, because it is more important for the final effect to have those colors at certain spots than to follow the color of nature. And again, with the final effect in mind, when he wants a rich purple, instead of making purple glass, he places side by side bits of red and blue, allowing the eye to mix them at a distance, and so obtains a much richer hue than he could get by color-

[A]   *Notre Dame. Paris. 1163–1235. (Clarence Ward)*

[B]   *Notre Dame. Amiens. 1220–88. (N. D. Photo)*

ing the glass purple. Thus the twelfth-century glassmakers used the same principle as the French Impressionists of the nineteenth century, who juxtaposed their red and blue pigment cn the canvas for the eye to mingle into purple from afar. Here and there in the designs he needs somewhat larger pieces of glass, on which must be painted a face, a hand, or a bit of drapery. With a brownish enamel, in fine, firm strokes he draws these details and fires the pieces (thus fusing the enamel with the glass) and then leads them into the design. Thus the glassworker is guided by the same principle as the sculptor; namely, decorative value determined by architectural needs. At the same time, a vital content coheres with visual effectiveness. The windows were contributed partly by the royal house and the Church, and partly by the guilds, each

of which had its patron saint, who, naturally, would figure in the design. In fact, the windows of Chartres furnish a gorgeously illustrated Golden Legend for all the people to read.

While sculpture and stained glass formed the chief decorative elements of the cathedral, polychromy and certain accessories also played an important part. Color and gilding were applied, apparently, to any available wall space, to capitals, to ornamental details, and to statues. Of this, because of time and the destructive Northern climate, nothing but faint traces now remains. The accessories of the service, too — the rich robes of the clergy, the gold and silver jeweled crosses, reliquaries, and chalices, the carved ivory crosiers, and the great tapestries — contribute to the magnificence expressive of the religious exaltation of the times.

[A] *Notre Dame. Reims. 1211–90. Restored after extensive damage during World War I.*

[B] *Notre Dame. Rouen. From c. 1200; façade, 1507–30. The tower on the right is the Tour de Beurre (Butter Tower), so called because it was built with funds secured in return for permission to eat butter during Lent, 1485–1507. Badly damaged during World War II. (N. D. Photo)*

Many other great Gothic cathedrals were built, particularly in the thirteenth century in France, noteworthy among which were *Notre Dame* in Paris (Fig. 348A), *Amiens* (Fig. 348B), and *Reims* (Fig. 349A).[1] Each was constructed on the same basic principles as *Chartres*. Only in detail and ornamentation do they differ. All are incomplete, and the impression of squatness noted by some observers would have been eliminated had the towers been carried up by spires to the intended height. In façade composition, the tendency is toward elaboration. *Notre Dame* has sobriety and repose, due to the almost classic balance of line and the quiet unadorned spaces of wall and buttress; at *Amiens* there is richness of detail, effective interplay of line, and richness of light and shade; at *Reims* decoration has become excessive and the vertical line is stressed. We notice in all of these façades the decorative effectiveness and the suggestion of welcome in the deeply recessed portals that extend the width of the façade. The flying buttress also developed from the simple, robust type of *Chartres* (Fig. 341A4) into the lighter and more elaborate type of *Reims* (Fig. 341A5), which, with its niches, pinnacles, crockets, and finials (Figs. 346A, 349A, 350A), contributes to the soaring quality of the cathedral.

[1] As each of these cathedrals bears the name *Notre Dame*, it has become the habit to designate them by the towns in which they are located, with the exception of the Paris cathedral, which has always retained its original name.

[A] *Reims. North side. Reims, as planned, would have carried seven spires, two at each of the portals and one, the highest, over the crossing.* (*N. D. Photo*)

[B] *An Ogee Arch with Flamboyant Detail.*

The sculpture of these great thirteenth-century cathedrals, while akin to that of the north and south portals of *Chartres*, still shows marked differences. The *Vierge Dorée* (*Amiens*), a gracious virgin, stands holding the child and playfully smiling; three angels, two in rapid movement, hold the shell-adorned nimbus. She stands so that the figure is built on a great sweeping curve; the drapery, girded high, falls in broad folds. The delicate naturalistic carvings and the fluttering angels enhance the graciousness of this gentle, smiling queen. In his tendency toward naturalism, the sculptor has altered his type, and for the symbolic austerity and dignity of the Queen of Heaven of the eleventh and twelfth centuries has substituted elegance and the serene joy of the more human type of mother and child.

[A]   *Church of Notre Dame. Louviers. South porch. 1494.*

[B]   *Smiling Angel. Reims. Detail of the Western Portal. 13th cent. Practically destroyed during World War I. Contrast with Fig. 342A. (Levasseur)*

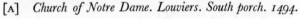

A highly characteristic example is the *Smiling Angel of Reims* (Fig. 351B). The tall, slender figure stands in an attitude of ease and grace; the swing of the body is accentuated by the long sweeping curves of the drapery. The tilt of the head, the movement of the uplifted hand, the sweep of the wings that frame the head — all these lend charm to this angel who is so tender and so joyful. While the statue is not as impressively architectural as the kings and queens of the western portal of *Chartres*, it still retains with its naturalism a sense of decorative fitness; with the exception of the wings, it stands within the space bounded by the two engaged columns, the straight verticality of which, repeated in the fold of the cloak, acts as

a foil to the dominant curves of the design.

Although, as has been noted in the preceding chapter in regard to monasteries, the subject matter, general treatment, and location of the major sculpture of the cathedrals were dictated by the Church,[1] the imagination of the carvers found free play in the carvings on the capitals, on pedestals, up on the towers — in all the nooks and corners. This decorative carving, as well as the statues of the portals, reveals a return to nature. The capitals of the clustered

[1] See Mâle, *op. cit.*, for a full exposition of this.

[A]   *Salisbury Cathedral. 1220–58. (Aerofilms Ltd., London)*

piers of *Reims* are covered with foliage in which animals and fantastic figures are intertwined; the leaves, deeply undercut or standing out in the round, appear to have been just fastened up on the stone. Naturalism has destroyed the surface of the stone and has supplanted the organization of stone as stone with an illusion of natural appearance. The grotesques (Fig. 347A) that live high up on the balustrades of the towers, peering out over the city — half man, half beast, crow, elephant, the three-headed Cerberus — were born probably of pure fancy, and show that the fantastic and chimerical forms of the world of imagination also belonged to the mirror of nature, and thus are found tucked away in corners all over the cathedral.

The Gothic cathedral reached its culmination in the thirteenth century, continuing in the fourteenth without great change. The fifteenth-century cathedrals, however, such as *Rouen* (Fig. 349B), reveal quite a different aspect. The feeling of structural significance has given way to lightness and elegance and an overemphasis upon decoration for its own sake. In the lacelike carving of the portal of *Louviers* (Fig. 351A), the restless line finds recurrent expression in the ogee arch (Fig. 350B), which is not structurally an arch but is formed by two moldings with reversed curves that unite and terminate in a finial. So too the foliage, departing from the naturalism of *Reims*, now twists and turns in wavy, flamelike lines, so that the work

[A] *Gloucester Cathedral. Transept, Choir, and Lady Chapel. 1331–37.*

of the late Gothic period became known as flamelike or Flamboyant.

Although Gothic architecture was primarily French, its influence spread to England, the Low Countries, Germany, Spain, and Italy, with variations according to local conditions. The English Church was long monastic, and thus, in contrast with the French, was originally situated apart from the town in the open country (Fig. 352A) and included a close and a cloister, forms so ingrained in the English tradition that they were used with the secular cathedrals as well. The plan (Fig. 339A5) shows a long nave, a square end — probably a Saxon inheritance — and deep, usually double transepts, which provide opportunity for a complex massing of volumes that culminate in the rectangular tower over the crossing (Fig. 353A), sometimes, as at *Salisbury* (Fig. 352A), crowned with a spire. One misses in the English church that characteristic French feature, the flying buttress. For the English is not so consistent a style as the French, because many of the English churches were rebuilt Norman (Romanesque) structures whose solid walls and pier buttresses were sufficient support for the vaultings. Where the flying buttress was used, it was insignificant and often concealed beneath the roof. Thus the English cathedral retains much of the Romanesque sturdy solidity and seldom shares the French

[A] *Winchester Cathedral. Nave, looking west from choir. Remodeled (1346–1486) by encasing the 11th cent. Norman walls and columns with a Perpendicular veneer and adding a vaulted roof. L. 250 ft. W. 40 ft.; with aisles, 88 ft. H. 78 ft. (Jerry Hennigar) Compare the large window, the* lierne *vaulting, and the unbroken piers here with the smaller windows, the simple rib vaulting, and the use of stringcourses in Fig. 345A.*

restless, emotional, aspiring quality.[1] But the need for light tended to increase the size of the openings and to stimulate the development of tracery to hold huge areas of glass (Figs. 353A, 354A).

In window tracery and vaulting the English builders went beyond structural requirements in the direction of decorative elegance. In the nave of *Winchester* (Fig. 354A), for example, the compound piers rise in one sheer sweep, without a break by stringcourses — compare *Amiens* (Fig. 345A) — to the vaulting where the ribs spread out in great sweeping lines, and with the help of intermediate ribs weave an elaborate design — a system known as *lierne* vaulting. A few of these ribs are structural, but most of them are decorative only. A climax of multiplying nonfunctional ribs, as in the *Oxford Divinity School*, is reached in the fan vaulting of the *Chapel of Henry VII* (Fig. 355A).

In the Low Countries, particularly Flanders, although typical Gothic churches were built, the most individual expression was the secular building, especially the town halls and the cloth halls of Flanders.[2]

In Germany, Gothic building was generally imitative of the French. In the Romanesque period the builders in the Rhenish cities had developed a particularly virile, original style of church architecture. The Gothic was arbitrarily accepted rather than naturally

[1] Most English cathedrals show various periods of building and rebuilding and thus are seldom homogenous in style. *Canterbury* and *Winchester* are excellent examples of all styles, which are: Late Norman or Romanesque (twelfth century), *Durham;* Early English (thirteenth century), *Lincoln* nave and chapter house, *Canterbury* choir, *Salisbury;* Decorated (fourteenth century), *Lincoln* Angel Choir; Perpendicular (fifteenth to sixteenth century), *Winchester* nave, *Gloucester* Lady Chapel, *Oxford* Divinity School, *Westminster Abbey* Chapel of Henry VII, *Cambridge* Chapel of King's College, *Windsor* Chapel of St. George.

[2] See Chapter 30 and Figures 532A, 533A.

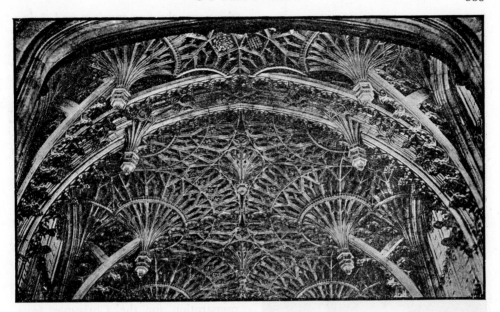

[A] *Chapel of Henry VII. Westminster Abbey, London. Detail of the ceiling. 1503–19.*

evolved. Hence *Cologne Cathedral* (1248–1880) imitates *Amiens* quite consistently. The most original accomplishment of Gothic Germany was the *Hallenkirchen* or *Hall Churches*, in which the vaults of the aisles equaled in height those of the nave, giving the building a simple outline and mass.

In Spain, the Gothic style — *Burgos* (founded 1226, spires begun 1442) and *Seville* (begun 1401) may be taken as typical — shows distinct contrasts with the French, due partly to different climatic conditions. The hot, dry climate did not require steeply pitched, protecting roofs; hence the vaults were either left exposed or covered with tiles, giving a flat or low-sloping shape to the roof. Because of the hot, brilliant sunshine, the large number of openings needed in the North was diminished, thus increasing the plain wall space. Frequently the clerestory was omitted or the windows blinded, making the interior gloomy. Decoration, especially in the late period, shows characteristic

Spanish exuberance and love of overloading, especially about the choir and the altar, and, because of the employment of Moorish craftsmen, frequently combines Moorish and Christian motifs.

In Italy the essentially Northern Gothic was still less at home than in Spain. In the hill towns of Assisi, Orvieto, and Siena are found characteristic examples which in some respects seem more Romanesque than Gothic. Possibly more successful adaptations of the style were the secular Gothic buildings, the town halls of Florence and Siena, and the polychrome Venetian palaces.[1]

PAINTING

Because of the great reduction of wall space, the Gothic style offered but little opportunity for mural painting. Hence book illustration was the chief function of the painter. The craft of bookmaking no longer centered in the

[1] See pages 433–442.

[A] *Chapter House. Westminster Abbey,*
London. Begun 1250. (From an engraving)

monastery. A flourishing school had
developed in thirteenth-century Paris,
where the university was attracting men
of learning. Although such secular
books as treatises on medicine, romances, and histories were appearing,
the most usual volumes were still liturgical and theological, such as the
psalter, and the book of hours — a
varied collection of calendars, lessons,
prayers, and psalms for private devo-
tional use.

A culmination of bookmaking was
reached in France in the fourteenth
and fifteenth centuries. In looking at
the manuscripts of the time (Fig. 357A),
one is impressed with the vivid color
(probably influenced by the stained-
glass workers), the shimmer of gold over

the page, the fine spacing, and the exquisite delicacy and refinement of every
part. The ivy was a popular form of
border decoration. The foliated sprays
were seminaturalistic, spreading out in
delicate curves to form a flat pattern.
Occasionally a single leaf was covered
with gold slightly raised, giving a delicate richness to the page. In among the
sprays one frequently finds tiny figures
of animals, birds, and grotesques that
are another evidence of the fancy of the
medieval artist that revealed itself in
the cathedral grotesque.

The tendency toward naturalism that
we saw in sculpture appeared in painting also. The miniature representing
December from the *Très Riches Heures*
(Fig. 358A) gives us a naturalistic and
intimate picture of the boar hunt in
preparation for the Christmas feast.
In the foreground the hunters in gay
costumes with their dogs are closing in
upon the boar. Behind them is a dense
forest with leaves in their autumn color
of golden bronze, above which rise, in
the distance, the towers of one of the
Duke's châteaux, over against a deep-
blue sky. The gold background of the
miniatures of earlier centuries has
given way to landscape. Naturalism has
entered, as in sculpture; but, as in
sculpture, it is subordinate to organization. Clearly defined areas of reds and
blues balance each other; vertical lines
are repeated in the château and in the
trees which swing around the tightly
integrated central group, where the
areas and the lines of the light dogs
converge upon the fallen prey — the
climax both of the composition and of
the content.

Out of the school of the miniaturists,
independent painting as a major art began to arise, and soon the miniature
school waned as the coming of the printing press impinged upon its very life,
— the life of one of the most vigorous
and beautiful arts of the Middle Ages.

[A] *Page from a Book of Hours. With a miniature of Saint Eutropius. French. First half 15th cent. C. L. Ricketts Collection, Chicago. (Harold Allen)*

IVORY– AND WOOD–CARVING, METALWORK, TEXTILES

Besides the bookmaker, many other craftsmen — ivory-carvers and wood-carvers, metalworkers, enamelers, and weavers — were needed to supply both ecclesiastical and rapidly increasing secular needs. Notwithstanding the revival of sculpture and the consequent relegation of the ivory-carver to secondary importance, his services were still in demand for small shrines and for statuettes of the Virgin. Secular objects also claimed the attention of the carvers, such as ivory covers for the little mirrors

that ladies carried attached to their girdles by gold and silver chains. These covers were decorated with love scenes, popular among which was the storming of the Castle of Love.

The work of the wood-carvers we see in furniture, both secular and ecclesiastical. Gothic furniture impresses one with its sturdy simplicity and strength. Great oak forests supplied an abundance of timber of superior quality and massiveness; one feels to what an extent this medium has determined the general character of the product. There were not many kinds of furniture made. Rooms were rather bare, one piece —

[A] *Pol de Limbourg and His Brothers. December, from the* Très Riches Heures (*the Very Rich Book of Hours*) *made for the Duc de Berri, c. 1416. Musée Condé, Chantilly. (Giraudon)*

a great oak chest, for example — serving not only as a receptacle but also as a seat and a bed. Almost any example of Gothic furniture possesses a simple massiveness which seems the direct result of the use of heavy timber. For decorative elements, carved panels, derived from Gothic tracery and ornament, sufficed.

In ecclesiastical furniture, the choir stalls gave the wood-carver ample opportunity to exercise his craft. In the misericords and the arm rests particularly, the carver gave free rein to his fancy and fashioned the knoblike rests to represent the washerwoman, the baker, or Reynard the Fox.

The ceremonial vessels needed for church rites demanded especially the skill of the metalworker. Chalices we have noted in each period since the founding of the Christian Church (Figs. 271B, 330A). The *Chalice of St. Remi* (Reims) in comparison with these reveals a departure from the ruggedness of the earlier examples toward a greater elegance in shape and proportion, a certain regularity and precision of detail. In this chalice a larger amount of the surface is decorated than in the earlier ones; the filigree, stones, and cloisonné enamels cover much of the broad base, the stem, and the cup. The shimmer of the gold, the light and shade in the filigree bands, deepened by the rich color of the stones and the deep luminous tones of the enamels, make this chalice a superb example of the skill of these goldsmiths.

Cloisonné enameling was still used, but another type, the *champlevé,* was practiced very successfully. The reli-

[A] *Reliquary. Limoges champlevé enamel on copper. 13th cent. Metropolitan Museum of Art, New York City. (Metropolitan Museum)*

quary seen in Figure 359A is made by this process. It is architectural in form, suggesting the steep roofs of the North. In the long panel are the figures of Christ in an aureole and four saints in niches; in the sloping panel above are angels on either side of a circle containing a lamb and the cross. The figures are in dark-blue, light-blue, green, and red enamel on a delicately chased metal base.

A metal used with highly artistic results was iron, which when hammered partakes of the pliability of softer metals and is free from the feeling of rigidity which results from casting in a mold. A fine example is found in the iron hinges of *Notre Dame.* Here the elaborate, elegant design, like that of the *Chalice of St. Remi,* has retained just enough reserve to save it from the weakness of overdecoration. The fine, strong scrolls, uniting firmly with the main stem, suggest the strength that should characterize a hinge. Within and about these scrolls, but subordinate to them, are minor details of naturalistic decoration, such as birds and serpents, which reveal the fancy of their designers.

Of great importance were large tapestries, which added color to the interior of the cathedral when, on festal occasions, they were hung from the triforium, and which decorated the great stone halls of the châteaux and with their firm texture helped retain whatever warmth was afforded by the fireplace. They were often made in sets, as in *The Lady and the Unicorn* series. Figures and animals stand out as clearly defined areas against a ground of trees and flowering plants of infinite variety; and though all are drawn with the greatest freedom and naturalism, each functions as one element in a harmonious massing of color — a frankly decorative design which could well be relied on, with its contrasting color and texture, to enrich a stone wall.

SUMMARY

The cathedral is the summation of the Gothic age. All the enthusiasm of a vigorous town life, in which civic pride and religious fervor were fused, poured itself into the erection of the cathedral. It became the symbol of the social solidarity of the age, in which individuals, great personalities though they often were, were submerged. As a construction, the cathedral consisted of a stone framework of rib vaulting supported by piers and flying buttresses, with walls largely of tracery and glass, which created an interior space of lofty proportions eminently expressive of the exalted feelings of the age. Contributing to produce this effect, in addition to the proportions, were: the predominantly vertical lines and repeated pointed arches, restless and upreaching; the ever increasing height of the nave lost in mysterious purple shadows; the radiant beauty of the glass with its own note of exaltation; the sculpture, architecturally satisfying and profoundly significant; all the multitude of accessories, "the adornment of the material house of God"; and the liturgy, with its plainsong and already developing polyphonic music. Though the involved theology of the Church lay beyond the intellectual grasp of the people, they were offered a visible evidence of its meaning that enabled them to share the feelings of the Abbé Suger when he said as he entered *St. Denis*, his own cathedral, upon whose construction and decoration he had labored earnestly: "When the house of God, many-colored as the radiance of precious stones, called me from the cares of the world . . . I seemed to find myself, as it were, in some strange part of the universe, which was neither wholly of the baseness of the earth, nor wholly of the serenity of heaven; but by the grace of God, I seem lifted in a mystic manner from this lower, toward that upper sphere."

The Gothic style evolved from its early ruggedness to lightness in construction, and from archaic, architecturally fitting sculpture to flamboyant elaboration and naturalism — a trend equally discernible in glass, ivories, metalwork, tapestries, and manuscripts.

BIBLIOGRAPHY

Ackerman, Phyllis, *Tapestry, the Mirror of Civilization*, Oxford University Press, 1933

Adams, Henry, *Mont-Saint-Michel and Chartres*, Houghton Mifflin, 1913

Arnold, Hugh, *Stained Glass of the Middle Ages in England and France*, Macmillan, 1940

Bond, Francis, *The Cathedrals of England and Wales*, Scribner, 1912

———— *An Introduction to English Church Architecture*, 2 vols., Oxford University Press, 1913

Bushnell, Arthur J. de H., *Storied Windows*, Macmillan, 1914

Connick, Charles, *Adventures in Light and Color*, Random House, 1937

Coulton, George G., *Art and the Reformation*, Knopf, 1928

———— ed. and tr., 2d ed., 4 vols. in 1, *Life in the Middle Ages*, Macmillan, 1930

Cram, Ralph Adams, *The Substance of Gothic*, 2d ed., Marshall Jones, 1925

Cunynghame, Henry H. S., *European Enamels*, London, 1906

Davis, William S., *Life on a Mediaeval Barony*, Harper, 1933

Day, Lewis F., *Stained Glass*, London, 1913

Delaporte, Yves, *Les vitraux de la cathédrale de Chartres*, 3 vols., Chartres, 1926

Ffoulkes, Charles J., *Decorative Ironwork from the XIth to the XVIIIth Century*, London, 1913

Francis of Assisi, *The Little Flowers of St. Francis*, Dutton (Everyman's Library), 1908

Gardner, Arthur, *French Sculpture of the Thirteenth Century*, Medici Society, 1915

———— *Mediaeval Sculpture in France*, Macmillan, 1931

Hahnloser, Hans R., *Villard de Honnecourt*, Vienna, 1935

Herbert, John A., *Illuminated Manuscripts*, Putnam, 1911

Houvet, Etienne, *Cathédrale de Chartres*, 7 vols., Chelles, 1921

Jackson, Sir Thomas Graham, *Gothic Architecture in France, England, and Italy*, 2 vols., University of Chicago Press, 1915

Jameson, Anna B. Murphy, *Sacred and Legendary Art*, 2 vols., Houghton Mifflin, c. 1911

Karlinger, Hans, *Die Kunst der Gotik*, Berlin, 1927

Lethaby, William R., *Mediæval Art*, rev. ed., Scribner, 1913

Macquoid, Percy, *A History of English Furniture*, 4 vols., Putnam, 1904–08

Mâle, Émile, *Art et artistes du moyen âge*, Paris, 1927

———— *L'art religieux du XIIᵉ siècle en France*, Paris, 1922

———— *Religious Art in France, XIII Century*, Dutton, 1913

Marriage, Margaret S. and Ernest, *The Sculptures of Chartres Cathedral*, Putnam, 1909

Martin, Henry M. R., *Les peintres de manuscrits et la miniature en France*, Paris, c. 1909

Maskell, Alfred O., *Ivories*, Putnam, 1905

———— *Wood Sculpture*, Putnam, 1912

Moore, Charles H., *Development and Character of Gothic Architecture*, 2d ed., Macmillan, 1899

Muratoff, Paul, *La sculpture gothique*, Paris, 1931

Parkhurst, Helen Huss, *Cathedral: A Gothic Pilgrimage*, Houghton Mifflin, 1936

Pollen, John H., *Ancient and Modern Furniture and Woodwork*, rev. by T. A. Lehfeldt, Vol. I, London, 1908

Prentice, Sartell, *The Heritage of the Cathedral*, Morrow, 1936

Read, Herbert E., *English Stained Glass*, Putnam, 1926

Salzman, Louis F., *English Life in the Middle Ages*, Oxford University Press, 1926

Saunders, O. Elfrida, *A History of English Art in the Middle Ages*, Oxford University Press, 1932

Sherrill, Charles H., *Stained Glass Tours in England*, Lane, 1909

Sherrill, Charles H., *Stained Glass Tours in France*, Lane, 1908

Smith, H. C., *Catalogue of English Furniture & Woodwork*, Victoria and Albert Museum, London, 4 vols., 1923–31: Vol. I, *Gothic and Early Tudor*

Street, George E., *Some Account of Gothic Architecture in Spain*, 2 vols., Dutton, 1914

Taylor, Henry O., *The Mediaeval Mind*, 4th ed., 2 vols., Macmillan, 1925

Thomson, William G., *A History of Tapestry*, 2d ed., rev., London, 1930

Victoria and Albert Museum, *A Picture Book of English Mediaeval Wall-Paintings*, Museum, London, 1932

Vitraux des cathedrales de France, XIIᵉ et XIIIᵉ, siècles, pref. by Paul Claudel, introd. by Marcel Aubert, Paris, 1937

West, George H., *Gothic Architecture in England and France*, Macmillan, 1911

Worringer, Wilhelm, *Form in Gothic*, ed. by Herbert Read, London, 1927

See also the General Bibliography, pp. 791–92.

# Far Eastern Art

19

HINDU ART: BRAHMANICAL
AND MUHAMMADAN–HINDU

THROUGH the Gupta[1] age, India
gave more than it received.
Buddhism, already being decentralized
by the missionary zeal of its followers,
had begun to move eastward to motivate peoples in the East Indies, China,
and Japan. With this decentralization
came a renascence of the cults of Vishnu
and Shiva and a florescence of Brahmanical art. Meanwhile Tatar invaders
penetrated the northern plains and took
over the power there under the name
of Rajputs; and the Muhammadans,
pushing eastward about A.D. 1000, over-
ran large sections of the country and by
1526 had established the Mughal, or
Mogul, Empire, which was the ruling
power over large areas until the coming
of the English and the French in the
eighteenth century. India has never
been totally united. Thus in the Middle
Ages we find flourishing side by side
different styles resulting from different
faiths and different traditions, yet not
entirely unrelated. For Muhammadanism brought a dynamic force and, as
was its wont, assimilated local forms.
Thus with its coming arose what one
may call a Muhammadan-Hindu art.

[1] See note 1, page 198.

ARCHITECTURE
AND SCULPTURE

Builder and carver worked in close
unity in meeting the demand for temples of Vishnu and Shiva, for abundant
carvings, and for cult statues. The
Brahmanical temples were not intended
for congregational worship, as were the
Buddhist assembly halls. The essential part was the shrine, with a passage
around it for circumambulation — a
rite found in all Hindu worship. Only
the priest entered the sanctuary, the
dwelling-place of the god. As the people
lived chiefly out of doors, so they worshiped, singing, dancing, offering flowers, doing reverence outside, not inside,
the sanctuary. For this reason also the
decoration, which was intended for an
illiterate people and was didactic as
well as ornamental, was placed on the
exterior of the shrine and on the exterior and interior of the *mandapam*, or
assembly hall, which was attached to
the shrine. For the Hindu temple usually served a much wider purpose than
that of a shrine. Here the king gave
audience, the village assembly met,
and religious and philosophical dis-

[A]   *Temple at Halebid, near Mysore. Detail of the carving. Between 1117 and 1268.* (*W. E. Clark*)

cussions took place, as well as recitations of the great epics, songs, and dances. Hence many temples had one or more mandapams, roofed over but open on the sides.

Of these Brahmanical temples there are three important classes: those dedicated to Vishnu, found chiefly in the north, where this sect was strongest; those dedicated to Shiva, found chiefly in the south; and a group in the Deccan, sometimes called the Chalukyan,[1] that combines features of the other two, implying use by more than one sect.

A typical temple of Vishnu (Fig. 366A) shows that the essential parts are the shrine and the mandapam, which takes the place of the simple portico of the temple consisting of a shrine only. The walls and roofs are thick and massive, and sometimes contain a hollow chamber as insulation against the heat; the

[1] So called because they are found in the district once ruled by the Chalukya dynasty.

cornices are deep and hollow for the same reason, and awnings frequently are added to shield the interior from glare and dust. The shrine is square and is covered by a high tower, the *shikara*,[2] with curving ribs. It is crowned by a flat round member (derived in shape from the fruit of the blue lotus)[3] surmounted by a vase; the lower courses of the tower are richly carved with statues of gods and goddesses. In front

[2] The origin of the *shikara* seems to have been the bamboo framework of a primitive shrine translated into stone.

[3] The lotus was the favorite flower of India and was used symbolically. It was "the flower of Vishnu." Growing up out of the mud undefiled, it blossoms in the pure light of the sun. Just so the human spirit growing out of the material conditions of life finds liberation in Nirvana. The open lotus with down-turned petals, frequently found in domes, capitals, and the pedestals of the statues of Buddha, suggested the vault of heaven. The section of the fruit, which is the shape of a wheel, symbolized the universality of Buddha's law.

[A]   *Temple of Vishnu. Khajuraho. L. 109 ft.; H. 116 ft. c. 1000. (India Office)*

of the shrine stands the mandapam, the roof of which is built up into a truncated pyramid in order to cover the elaborate ceiling, which symbolizes the dome of the world. On the mandapams the Hindu builders lavished their decorative skill. Some were made of white marble, with every inch of the surface of the ceiling and the supporting columns carved in all kinds of ornament — figure work as well as floral and geometric design — so that the effect was one of lavish richness.

An elaborate temple of this type is found at *Khajuraho* (Fig. 364A). It stands on a platform, which, with the rather plain base, unifies all the parts of the building. The roofs, rich and complex,

culminate in the lofty tower over the shrine. The tower itself has become complex by the addition of smaller towerlike members which encircle the base, fill the angles, and with their varying height carry the eye upward rhythmically.

In the second class of Hindu temple, the southern, the shrine is enclosed in an immense walled quadrangle (Fig. 366c) and surrounded by minor temples, halls, and evidences of a hot climate — bathing-pools and shaded porticoes. The great towering gateways, *gopuras*, bear a load of ornament — gods, monsters, animals, floral and geometric motifs — from base to summit, yet control it with simplicity of mass and plane

[A]   *Gopuras. Madura. 17th cent.*

and with a fine sweep of contour (Fig. 365A).

The third class of Hindu temple is like the northern in plan except that it has become star-shaped (Fig. 366B), thereby presenting a varied and picturesque outline from whatever point it is viewed. Like the southern temple, however, it is built horizontally and roofed with low towers. The decoration is very profuse, as at *Halebid* (Fig. 363A), where the horizontal zones are deeply undercut and carved with elephants, grotesques, mounted horsemen, gods, human figures, and floral motifs. Here one realizes how Hindu temple sculpture, as prolific as nature itself in the jungle, pours forth with intense vitality and ceaseless rhythm, and includes in its conceptions all animate life. "It is

to symbolize this universal fellowship of man, the unity of all creation, that the Indian loves to crowd into his picture all forms of teeming life ... uses every constructive feature to symbolize the universal law of the One in many."[1]

The Hindu predilection for cave temples, due to the heat of summer and the torrential rain of the monsoons, we have seen in the Buddhist assembly halls and in the *Ajanta Caves*. A culmination of this type is found in the *Kailasa Temple* at Elura (Ellora), dedicated to Shiva,[2] which was carved out of a hillside as a complete unit,

[1] E. B. Havell, *The Ideals of Indian Art*, London, 1911, p. 112.

[2] Mt. Kailasa is the mountain throne of Shiva.

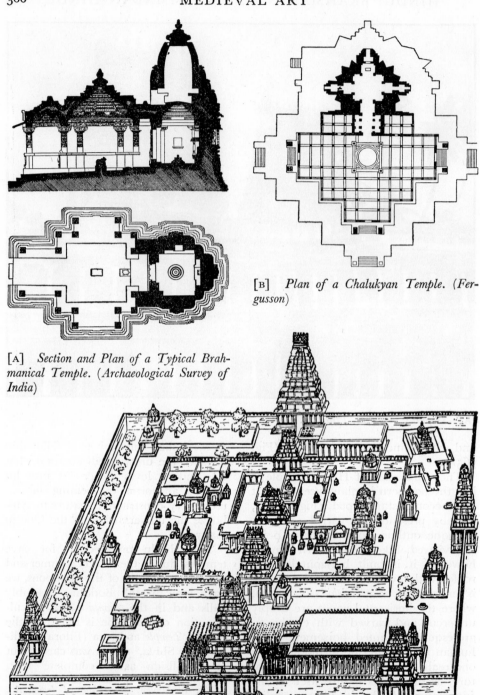

[A]   *Section and Plan of a Typical Brahmanical Temple. (Archaeological Survey of India)*

[B]   *Plan of a Chalukyan Temple. (Fergusson)*

[C]   *Bird's-Eye View of a Southern Temple. (Fergusson)*

with gopura, court, mandapam, and shrines; and, withal, lavishly decorated. The carvings are more dramatic than those of the Gupta age, more humanly emotional, suave and elegant. In the *Ravana under Mount Kailasa*, Shiva and his consort Parvati are seated upon their mountain throne surrounded by attendants. The thousand-armed giant Ravana, who sought, unsuccessfully, to dethrone Shiva, is represented below, in a niche cut back so deeply that the giant stands out forcefully against the dark while the lesser contrasts and suaver lines of the group above indicate the ease with which the god overcomes his foe.

This same dramatic use of light and dark appears in the caves at Elephanta where, however, the *Trimurti*[1] (Fig. 367A) retains more of the large monumentality of the earlier age. Its three heads rise from a single blocklike base and nearly fill the niche, where cavernous darkness brings the massive stone into bold relief. The two figures which flank the niche enhance its colossal scale and with their swaying rhythms accentuate its perfect symmetry and imperturbable monumentality. The faces are carved with the austere simplicity of a mask, and the elaborate headdresses and necklaces supply the needed movement and contrasting texture.

The *Trimurti* might be brought into comparison with the *Bodhisattva* of Ajanta, both superlative examples in different mediums of the Hindu theory of art as the expression of an inner dominating passion.

Cult statues of Shiva in bronze represent a popular aspect of the god as the *Lord of the Dance*, or *Shiva as Nataraja* (Fig. 368A). Shiva is poised with one foot upon a dwarf. He has four arms. In one hand is a drum, in another is fire.

[1] Formerly thought to represent Brahma, Vishnu, and Shiva, but also interpreted as a trinity of Shiva alone.

[A]   *The Trimurti (Brahma, Vishnu, and Shiva). Colossal size. 8th cent. Cave temple at Elephanta, near Bombay.*

A ring of fire rising from the lotus pedestal surrounds the figure, touching it at the hands with the drum and the fire. The meaning is that when Shiva dances with the drum and the fire, he awakens the powers of nature to the dance; that is, to life. But in turn he destroys these powers with fire and they return to rest. The movement of the dance symbolizes the rhythmic energy of the cosmos, whose purpose is perpetual creation and then destruction, but a destruction that is change, not annihilation, and results in the release or salvation of the soul. In the movement of this dance, we see that an orderly rhythm controls every part of the figure. The body, an S-curve, is poised firmly upon one foot. The other limbs move freely and form an asymmetrical design, composed of cylindrical and jagged shapes (the flames, the hands, the headdress), which is an objectification of the ceaseless move-

[A] *Shiva as Nataraja, Lord of the Dance. Bronze. H. 46 in. 14th–16th cent. Cleveland Museum of Art, Cleveland, Ohio. (Cleveland Museum of Art)*

ment of this vital rhythm.[1] Particularly noticeable is the use of bronze for a subject that is in no way adaptable to stone.

A utilization of stone in its native site is illustrated at Mamallapuram, in the monolithic temples and particularly in the gigantic relief carved on a great cliff and representing *The Descent of Ganga,* or *The Birth of the Ganges River* (Fig. 369A).[2] Birds, deer, elephants, men and gods, the hermit in his shrine — all are present and all are moving toward the cleft in the cliff where Ganga is descending to bring water to the dying earth. The slender figures above, arranged in irregular zones, create a light rapid rhythm in contrast to the

slow ponderosity of the elephants below, where the stone is cut back deeply, as at Elura and Ajanta, to create a deep shadow. The profound love and understanding of animal life is expressed here in a tempered naturalism which attains an unusual balance between the material and the content.

A great Hindu expression beyond the confines of India is the work of the Khmers, who, apparently of Indo-Chinese origin, had settled in Cambodia (Fig. 207A), whither came Hindu colonists who became the ruling class and developed a high type of civilization from the ninth century to the thirteenth, when they seem to have been annihilated by some other race. In the tropical jungles they built their capital city, Angkor, with magnificent temples and palaces of a fine native limestone, cut and laid precisely and carved lavishly (Fig. 370A).

[1] For a detailed description of the statue and of its symbolism, see Coomaraswamy, *The Dance of Śiva,* new ed., Sunwise Turn, 1925.

[2] For the story see Frederika Macdonald, *The Iliad of the East,* Lane, 1908, Chap. III.

[A]   *Birth of the Ganges River. Detail of the cliff carving at Mamallapuram. 8th cent.*

The great temple, the Angkor Wat (Fig. 371A), is laid out on a vast scale. It stands as the focal point of a rectangular area divided into smaller rectangular areas all related to the long axis. The various parts — low buildings, courts, avenues, and stairways — form a logical progression from the moat-protected outer walls and the outer court to a higher inner court surrounded by porticoes and accented by corner towers, and thence to the highest court. Here the shrine, resting on a lofty platform, lifts its five pagodalike pointed towers to dominate the surrounding jungle. The lavish carvings, which in their style seem to show an influence from Java, are subordinate to the architecture and at the same time highly enriching. Low reliefs cover the walls inside the porticoes, animating their surfaces but remaining an inseparable part of the stone masonry.

Figure 370A is a detail representing a battle scene from the *Mahabharata*. The army is marching through the jungle, whose lacelike foliage carved in a pattern of very low relief forms a contrasting background for the vigorous figures in higher relief. The unchanging rhythm of the marching troops is broken by the spirited movement of the horsemen and the elephant; and the delicate carving of the foliage is opposed by the strong accents of the umbrellas and the animals. The effect of such opposition and interweaving is analogous to that of a musical composition in which the cellos weave a deep-toned melody through the more delicate tones of the wind instruments. The highly decorative quality results partly from the conventional, linear character of the forms, partly from the shallowness and clear definition of the planes that indicate depth, and partly from the manner in which these planes reflect the light in a pattern of contrasting broken and unbroken areas.

When the Muhammadans had established their empire in India, their wealthy rulers, the great Mughals, or Moguls, erected magnificent tombs and mosques, palaces and audience

[A]   *Angkor Wat, Cambodia. Detail of the carving showing a scene from the Mahabharata.
12th cent. (Giraudon)*

halls, according to certain traditions from the West — a dome over a tomb, the pointed arch, the minaret, the absence of sculpture — fused, as was the wont of the Muslim, with local features.

The highest embodiment of Mughal architecture is the *Taj Mahall*[1] (Fig. 371B), a cubical structure surmounted by one large and four small domes, standing upon a high platform with four minarets, and set in the midst of a rich tropical garden. The impression of lightness, delicacy, and grace results from at least four elements: the material, the control of light and dark, the open design, and the setting in a

larger design of contrasting elements. The material is white marble inlaid with delicate floral designs worked out in precious stones, with inscriptions about the arches, and delicately carved panelings and low relief of floral motifs, all of which produces a subtle modulation of surface. Everything tends to a diffused light, with no strong contrasts such as are found when strongly salient cornices and moldings are used. The deep recessing of the portal and the windows provides just enough shadow to set forth clearly the dominant motif of the pointed arch that leads to the pointed lotus dome contracted at the base (contrast Figs. 177A, 259A), which springs from a row of conventionalized lotus petals and terminates in an inverted lotus. A lightness in design is secured through the large open spaces, subtly proportioned, between the solid

[1] Meaning "Crown of Palaces," the tomb built by Shah Jehan, one of the great Moguls, for his beautiful and gifted young wife, Mumtaz-i-Mahall, a name that means "Exalted of the Palace," from which the name of the building is derived.

[A]   *Angkor Wat. Cambodia. 12th cent.*

[B]   *Taj Mahall. Agra. 1632–53. (Kaufmann & Fabry)*

[A]   *Carved Marble Window. Ahmadabad. 15th cent.*

central mass and the minarets, which are tied together by the platform. Though the tomb is itself a complete unit of design, it attains its entire effect only when seen in its setting of tropical foliage and gardens with flanking mosques and gateways of red sandstone. By means of such contrasts a floating, almost evanescent quality is given the focal point of the entire design — the tomb itself — with the result that its total impression becomes a symbol of the grace and beauty of the queen for whom it was built. It was symbolical rather than representative, since Shah Jehan and the other Mughal rulers, while they were not strict Muhammadans and had adopted much of the Hindu thought and point of view, still had deeply ingrained in their tradition the Islamic aversion to representing the human figure, especially in

connection with a tomb or a mosque. Furthermore, to Muslim and Hindu alike the highest kind of expression employed the symbol, with its emphasis upon inner significance, rather than that representation which aims to copy outward appearance.

In the interior of the *Taj*, which is of the same materials and workmanship as the exterior, a mellow light filters through carved marble windows upon the cenotaphs of Mumtaz-i-Mahall and Shah Jehan,[1] which stand beneath the dome surrounded by a screen of marble carved into a lacelike design and bordered with floral inlays.

The marble window, which played an important part in Hindu build-

[1] Shah Jehan's plan for his own tomb to be built on the other side of the river and connected with the *Taj* by a bridge was never carried out because of disasters in the latter part of his reign.

[A]   *Krishna Quelling the Serpent Kaliya. Rajput. 18th cent. Coomaraswamy Collection, Boston. (A. K. Coomaraswamy)*

ing, was made by carving a slab of marble until it was perforated by tracery, sometimes with geometric and sometimes with naturalistic motifs (Fig. 372A) of infinite variety.

PAINTING

After the time of the *Ajanta Frescoes,* Buddhist in theme, a great gap occurs in the history of painting in India, except for traces of the tradition in Turkestan and Tibet, where the art was practiced as it spread along the great highways toward China in the early centuries of the Christian era. It is not until about 1550 that we again find examples of Indian painting. In the meantime important events had taken place. Buddhism had been absorbed by Brahmanism and the cults of Vishnu and Shiva had been developing. The

Muhammadans had conquered large parts of the country and established the Mughal Empire, bringing with them strong influences of the art of the West. The paintings fall into two classes: Rajput and Mughal.

The Rajput, so called because it was practiced chiefly in the Rajput domain, particularly in the Himalaya valleys beyond the reach of the Muhammadan power, was a purely indigenous art and seems to continue the traditions of the *Ajanta Frescoes,* though in it we find a wider expression: themes from secular life, often romantic, stories from the heroic days of the *Mahabharata* and *Ramayana,* and illustrations from the lives of the gods, particularly Vishnu. Another difference between these paintings and those at Ajanta is that they are small, though their largeness of design may well suggest lineal descent

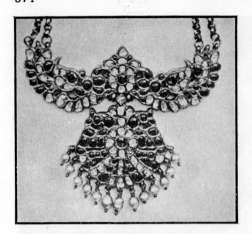

[A]   *Necklace Pendant. Polished stones set
in gold.* (*A. K. Coomaraswamy*)

from the great Buddhist frescoes. *Krishna
Quelling Kaliya*, a poisonous serpent
(Fig. 373A), is a typical example.
Krishna, one of the numerous incarnations of Vishnu, stands holding the
body of the serpent easily, through his
godlike power, pressing upon it with
his foot. On each side are grouped the
wives of the serpent, half human, half
reptile, tenderly grieving for him and
pleading with Krishna to spare him;
on the bank Krishna's family and the
cowherds are frantically rushing to the
edge of the pool; in the background
herds are peacefully grazing. The color
is clear and intense; the color areas
meet sharply, and thus accentuate the
linear character of the design, which
consists of two asymmetrically balanced
groups. In the Krishna group the god
himself, framed by the serpent, forms
the center of interest, with the wives
arranged symmetrically on either side,
each expressing by pose and gesture her
tender love or earnest pleading. At the
same time each figure, especially the
long sweeping curve of the reptilian
form, plays its part in a composition of
repeated lines and shapes set over
against the conventionalized waves of

the pool. By repetition of color areas
and shapes, unity is established between the two groups and the two areas,
sharply divided though they are by a
great curving edge.[1]

The second group, the Mughal or
Mogul, is less Indian than the other.
When the Mughals came to India, they
brought with them painters who had
been trained in the Persian school, and
their art, combining with the native
Hindu elements, formed the foundation
of Mughal painting. But while Rajput
painting was lyrical and religious, having its roots deep in the soil of native
traditions, Mughal painting was secular. It was a miniature art chiefly. Its
interest lay primarily in the picturesque
aspect of human life, chiefly that of the
palace; for it flourished under the
patronage of the Mughal rulers and
nobles, and aimed to give a vivid picture of court scenes and persons, hunts
and night scenes, animals and flowers.

METALWORK, CARVING,
    TEXTILES

The Hindu craftsman was an important member of Indian society and
was provided for economically by the
system of that society. The monastery
had its guilds of painters, sculptors, and
metalworkers to decorate its buildings,
and perhaps sent them on to another
monastery when its own work was done.
The noble had, as part of his household,

[1] Reproduced in color in the *Burlington Magazine*, Vol. XX (1911–12), p. 315. For the story
see Sister Nivedita (M. E. Noble) and A. K.
Coomaraswamy, *Myths of the Hindus and Buddhists*, p. 226. An interesting aspect of Rajput
painting is its relation to music. Many examples
display a deep feeling of tenderness, and are of
a lyrical mood that evokes the same emotion
as music. Thus they are known as *ragas*, or
raginis, that is, a melody or a musical theme.
On this see A. K. Coomaraswamy, *Rajput
Painting*, 2 vols., Oxford University Press, 1916,
or his *The Arts & Crafts of India & Ceylon*, London, 1913.

[A]   *Ceremonial Dipper. Silver and ivory. L. 18 in. Victoria and Albert Museum, London.*
(Victoria and Albert Museum)

his goldsmith to make the jewelry and plate for his family. The boy inherited his father's calling and belonged to the guild, which was under the protection of the king.[1]

Among the metalworkers the goldsmith was of great importance, for jewelry played a considerable part in Indian costume, both for men and for women.[2] It was used not only for personal adornment but for the trappings of state elephants and for palace hangings. Girdle chains originated in the old Hindu custom of decking the body with garlands of flowers and seeds. In order to keep the chain light in weight, the beads were made hollow and in filigree. Like the Greek, the Indian recognized the value of gold and silver as a medium for expression in itself without the addition of jewels. When he used gems, he did not facet them but only smoothed them off, thus obtaining a deep and glowing rather than a flashing effect. A special use of gems was made by inlay. Tiny pieces of ruby, sapphire, emerald, or topaz were embedded in a thin gold plate, producing

the effect of enamel. In this the Indian revealed his skill in massing color harmonies, and out of almost valueless bits created an unsurpassed piece of rich decoration. The pendant to the chain in Figure 374A is an example of this. The general shape is suggested by a bird with outspread wings. There is no thought of giving a realistic representation of the bird form; the aim is to use only the essential elements to obtain decorative beauty. "To wear a real bird . . . would be barbarous; to imitate a real bird very closely . . . would be idle; but all that is beautiful in the general idea of a bird, colour, form, and poise, can be suggested."[3]

Further evidence of the Indian love of ornament we see in the wood and ivory carvings. The sacrificial dipper (Fig. 375A), for example, is an elaborate design of curves. One great sweeping curve forms the structural line of the handle; but it is varied and emphasized by minor curves, swirling now this way and now that but entirely subordinated to the main line of direction. The bowl of the dipper shows the skill of the silversmith, for the rich design is superbly executed. The union of the two parts, however, is not successfully accomplished by the curious, elaborately be-

[1] On this situation see A. K. Coomaraswamy, *The Indian Craftsman*, London, 1909, and *Mediæval Sinhalese Art*, Broad Campden, 1908.

[2] See Coomaraswamy, *The Arts and Crafts of India and Ceylon* p. 151, for a description of the costume of the maids of honor of an Indian queen.

[3] Coomaraswamy, *Mediæval Sinhalese Art*, p. 211.

[A] *Embroidered Muslin. Collection of
Leslie de Saram, Colombo. (A. K. Coomaraswamy)*

jeweled little figure that distracts and
weakens the construction at that point.

One of the most important crafts of
India has always been weaving, and the
chief material, cotton. The muslins
from Dacca are so sheer that they have
received poetic names such as "running
water" or "evening dew," the latter
because the fabric is so delicate that if
laid on wet grass it is scarcely visible.
When these delicate muslins are embroidered they have the effect of exquisite lace (Fig. 376A). Cotton textiles
served not only for garments and tur-
bans but also for hangings, bedspreads,
and other furnishings. From their native names are derived many of our
own words for cotton fabrics, such as
chintz and *bandanna*. For decorating
these cottons, several processes were
employed, chiefly printing and painting. In one, cotton was first sized with
buffalo milk to keep the color from running. The design was drawn on paper
and punched on the prepared cloth.

Some of the colors were painted in by
hand; others, especially the blue, were
dyed so that the color would be more
permanent. To do this, all the parts
except those to be colored blue were
covered with wax, and the entire piece
put into the dye pot. After the material
was taken from the pot, the wax was removed with boiling water, and successive colors were added with paint or dye.
In a repeat pattern, wood-block stamps
were sometimes used. The colors of
the old Indian cottons are very lasting,
and their soft tones of rose, blue, and
blue-green have been acquired through
time and frequent washing.

Many of the woven fabrics were made
of silk interwoven or brocaded with
gold. The beauty of their designs arises
from the same attitude toward natural
appearance as that seen in the jewelry:
the ability to see in the bird or the animal form a pattern suitable for the
weaving technique.

One other kind of textile needs mention, the *Cashmere*. The weavers of
Cashmere, well up in the Himalayas in
northern India, used goat's wool for
their shawls, weaving them on small
looms in long strips, which they sewed
together so skillfully that the seaming
is scarcely perceptible. The characteristic motif is the pine pattern, probably originating in the cypress tree of
Persian art, while the ground or border is filled with small floral designs.
The beauty of color and design in
these shawls is equaled by the supreme
skill shown in the weaving.

SUMMARY

Hindu art from the earliest times to
the recent decadence of India has been
chiefly a religious art, strictly obedient
to accepted canons of technique and
representation. An exception was the
stronger secular element brought by
the Muslim. Thus it does not surprise

one to find the same ideology and attitudes toward form in Hindu art in both ancient and medieval times. Though Buddhism was submerged in a renascence of Brahmanism, temple-building continued on a great scale: towering stone temples, as well as cave temples of Vishnu and Shiva, lavishly decorated both inside and outside with sculptural ornament which was an integral part of the structure both as ornament and as subject matter: scenes from the lives of Vishnu and Shiva and from the *Mahabharata* and the *Ramayana*.

Painting also, in the tradition of the *Ajanta Frescoes*, but small in scale (illustrated by Rajput painting), represented both Brahmanical and secular themes, in a form constructed chiefly of line and brightly colored areas. The coming of the Muslim brought Islamic elements which, mingling with Hindu, culminated in the *Taj Mahall* in architecture and in the paintings of court life which are definitely influenced by Persian painting. Through all Hindu and Muhammadan-Hindu art runs the thread of skilled craftsmanship — in the metalwork seen in sumptuous jewelry; in fine weavings in silk, cotton, and brocaded fabrics for garments and furnishings; in wood-carvings and ivory-carvings for ritual as well as household use.

BIBLIOGRAPHY

Baker, George, *Calico Painting and Printing in the East Indies in the XVIIth and XVIIIth Centuries*, London, 1921

Bezemer, Tammo, J., *Indonesian Arts and Crafts*, The Hague, 1931

Bhagavad-gita, tr. by A. W. Ryder, University of Chicago Press, 1929

Bhagavad-gita, tr. by Swami Prabhavananda and Christopher Isherwood, Marcell Rodd Company, 1944

Binyon, Laurence, *The Court Painters of the Grand Moguls*, Oxford University Press, 1921

Birdwood, Sir George Christopher Molesworth, *The Industrial Arts of India*, 2 vols., London, 1880

Brown, Percy, *Indian Painting*, 2d ed., Oxford University Press, 1929
———————— *Indian Painting under the Mughals, A.D. 1550 to A.D. 1750*, Oxford University Press, 1924

Burlingame, Eugene W., tr., *Buddhist Parables*, Yale University Press, 1922

Cohn, William, *Indische Plastik*, Berlin, 1923

Coomaraswamy, Ananda Kentish, *The Arts & Crafts of India & Ceylon*, London, 1913
———————— *Buddha and the Gospel of Buddhism*, Putnam, 1916
———————— *The Dance of Śiva*, with preface by Romain Rolland, Sunwise Turn, 1925
———————— *History of Indian and Indonesian Art*, Weyhe, 1927
———————— *The Indian Craftsman*, London, 1909
———————— *Mediæval Sinhalese Art*, Broad Campden, England, 1908
———————— *Rajput Painting*, 2 vols., Oxford University Press, 1916
———————— *The Transformation of Nature in Art*, Harvard University Press, 1934

Cumming, Sir John Ghest, ed., *Revealing India's Past*, London, 1939

Fischer, Otto, *Die Kunst Indiens, Chinas und Japans*, Berlin, 1928

Frazer, Robert W., *Indian Thought Past and Present*, Stokes, 1916

Giles, Herbert A., tr., *The Travels of Fa-hsien (399–414 A.D.); or, Record of the Buddhistic Kingdoms*, Cambridge University Press, 1923

Grousset, René, *The Civilizations of the East*, tr. by C. A. Phillips, 4 vols., Knopf, 1931–34: Vols. I–II

Grünwedel, Albert, *Buddhist Art in India*, tr. by A. C. Gibson, London, 1901

Havell, Ernest B., *The Ancient and Medieval Architecture of India*, Scribner, 1915
———————— *A Handbook of Indian Art*, Dutton, 1921
———————— *The Ideals of Indian Art*, new ed., Dutton, 1921
———————— *Indian Sculpture and Painting*, 2d ed. rev., London, 1928

India Society, *Ajanta Frescoes*, Oxford University Press, 1915

Jataka Tales, ed. by H. T. Francis and E. J. Thomas, Putnam, 1916

Kālidāsa, *Translations of Shakuntala, and Other Works*, by A. W. Ryder, Dutton (Everyman's Library), 1913

Kramrisch, Stella, *Indian Sculpture*, Oxford University Press, 1933

Lin Yutang, *The Wisdom of China and India*, Random House, 1942

Macdonald, Frederika Richardson, *The Iliad of the East*, new ed., Lane, 1908

Mackay, Ernest J. H., *Further Excavations at Mohenjo-daro*, 2 vols., London, 1938
———— *The Indus Civilization*, London, 1935
Marshall, Sir John Hubert and others, *Bagh Caves*, London, 1927
———— *Mohenjo-daro and the Indus Civilization*, London, 1931
———— and Foucher, Alfred, *The Monuments of Sāñchī*, 3 vols., London, 1940
Monier-Williams, Sir Monier, *Indian Wisdom*, 4th ed. enl., London, 1893
Mukul Chandra Dey, *My Pilgrimages to Ajanta and Bagh*, Doran, 1925
Mulk Raj Anand, *The Hindu View of Art*, London, 1933
Nivedita, Sister (M. E. Noble), and Coomaraswamy, A. K., *Myths of the Hindus & Buddhists*, Holt, 1914

Oman, John C., *The Great Indian Epics: The Stories of the Ramayana and the Mahabharata*, London, 1899
Rowland, Benjamin, and Coomaraswamy, A. K., *The Wall-Paintings of India, Central Asia & Ceylon*, Merrymount Press, 1938
Smith, Vincent A., *A History of Fine Art in India and Ceylon*, 2d ed. rev. by K. de B. Codrington, Oxford University Press, 1930
———— *The Oxford History of India*, 2d. ed. rev. and enl. by S. M. Edwardes, Oxford University Press, 1928
With, Karl, *Java*, Hagen, Germany, 1920
Yazdani, Ghulām, *Ajanta*, 2 vols. in 4 pts., Pts. 1–2 Oxford University Press, 1930–93
Zimmer, Heinrich, *Myths and Symbols in Indian Art and Civilization*, (Bollingen Series VI) Pantheon Books, 1946
See also General Bibliography, pages 791–92.

20

CHINESE ART

(A.D. 960 TO DATE)

THE plateau of Iran formed a bridge between the West and the Far East, over which, in early times, the technique of metalwork and later of tiles and enamels passed eastward to China, while Chinese silks and various decorative motifs moved westward and on into Europe, especially with the spread of the Mongol conquests.

To medieval Europe, still chaotic and generally poor, there were coming, by sea as well as by land, the products of the East, together with tales of fabulous wealth and luxuries, enough to stimulate a few intrepid travelers to attempt to reach these fabulous lands. The most famous of these was Marco Polo, the Venetian, who eventually made his way to China, where he visited the palace of the Khan in Cathay

(Peking), and the city of Hangchow. Though Jenghiz Khan overthrew the Sung dynasty, his son Kublai Khan fostered the continuity of its culture. This civilization, called the second Golden Age of China, was an age of peace and introspective contemplation; of pursuing the arts of peace; of refusing to realize the growing menace of the Tatar hordes in the north. When these Mongols began their conquests, the Sung moved south, established their capital at Hangchow, and continued their peaceful course until the dynasty was overthrown by Jenghiz Kahn in 1280.

The three-hundred-year span of the Sung dynasty produced an age of great refinement, one of exquisite painting, poetry, and porcelain. Its capital at

Hangchow was one of the most civilized cities in the world in the twelfth century. This age, in one aspect, is analogous to the Renaissance in Europe in that both ages produced great statesmen, philosophers, poets, art critics, painters. Like the Renaissance, the Sung dynasty found its ideal in earlier periods, as we see in the deep study that the commentators made of the canonical books of Confucius, and in the Chou motifs that we find on the slender, typically Sung-shaped bronzes. In this period, philosophy, poetry, and painting together produced the finest of the Chinese landscape paintings.

An important source of inspiration of this art was Zen Buddhism. Zen, meaning "meditation in supreme repose," was brought to China by an Indian prince in the sixth century, and since many of its ideas were close in spirit to those of the Taoists, took deep root, especially in South China. "Their [Zen Buddhists'] training was centered on the methods of that self-control which is the essence of true freedom. Deluded human minds groped in darkness, because they mistook the attribute for the substance. Even religious teachings were misleading, in so far as they set up semblances for realities. This thought was often illustrated by the simile of monkeys attempting to seize the reflection of the moon in water; for each effort to snatch at the silvery image could but ruffle the mirroring surface, and end in destroying not only the phantom moon but also themselves. ... Freedom, once attained, left all men to revel and glory in the beauties of the whole universe. They were then one with nature, whose pulse they felt beating simultaneously within themselves, whose breath they felt themselves inhaling and exhaling in union with the great world-spirit."[1]

[1] Kakuzo Okakura, *Ideals of the East*, Dutton, 1921, p. 162, by permission of the publishers.

"The fundamental principle of ... Zen Buddhism may be summed up in the expression that *the Universe is the scripture of Zen*. ... Actual scripture is worthless in the letter, and only valuable for that to which it leads; and to that goal there are other guides than the written page or spoken word. It is related, for example, of the sage Hüen Sha that he was one day prepared to deliver a sermon to an assembled congregation, and was on the point of beginning, when a bird was heard to sing very sweetly close by; Hüen Sha descended from his pulpit with the remark that the sermon had been preached. ...

"It is the very heart of 'culture' and religion to recognize the eternal, not as obscured but as revealed by the transient, to see infinity in the grain of sand, the same unborn in every birth, and the same undying in every death. These thoughts find constant expression in the poetry and art inspired by Zen thought. The Morning Glory, for example, fading in an hour, is a favorite theme of the Japanese poet and painter. What are we to understand by the poem of Matsunaga Teitoku?

" 'The morning glory blooms but an
    hour, and yet it differs not at heart
From the giant pine that lives for a
    thousand years.'

"It is the same with the pine as with the morning glory, but as the life of the latter is shorter, it illustrates the principle in a more striking way. The giant pine does not ponder on its thousand years, nor the morning glory on its life of a single day. Each does simply what it must. Certainly the fate of the morning glory is other than that of the pine, yet their destiny is alike in this, that they fulfil the will of Providence, and are content."[2]

[2] Coomaraswamy, *Buddha and the Gospel of Buddhism*, Putnam, 1916, pp. 254 ff., by permission of G. P. Putnam's Sons.

[A]　　*Tung Yüan. Landscape. Sung Dynasty, late 10th*

PAINTING

In content and in spirit, Sung paint-ing is largely an expression of Zen Buddhism. The painters were motivated by their great love of nature, by their belief in the universal brotherhood of all forms of life, in which man is not the apogee but merely one of countless equally important animate beings. "Wherein lies the reason that good men so much love landscape?" asks Kuo Hsi, born about 1020 A.D. "It is be-cause amid orchards and hills a man has ever room to cultivate his natural bent; because streams and rocks never fail to charm the rambler who goes whistling on his way. It is because fish-ing and wood-gathering are the natural vocations of the hermit or recluse, hard by where the flying birds and chatter-ing apes have made their home. Noise and dust, bridles and chains — these are what man's nature is ever weary of. Haze and mist, saints and fairies — for these man's nature pines eternally, and pines in vain."[1] Thus the Chinese

[1] Quoted in Arthur Waley, *An Introduction to the Study of Chinese Painting*, 1923, p. 189, used by permission of Charles Scribner's Sons.

reached the concept of landscape as suitable subject matter for painting hundreds of years before the Euro-peans, with their strongly humanistic attitude, began to realize its value for its own sake. The Chinese word for "landscape" means "mountains and rivers." This is not surprising to anyone who has looked over a considerable number of Chinese paintings. Upon close inspection, however, he realizes that the forms of the mountains and the waters are highly conventional. For the Chinese had evolved certain formu-las based upon intimate knowledge and keenly realistic observation of nature, distilled until the result is an abstract convention.

For example, there were sixteen ways of drawing mountains, differing accord-ing to the geological formation, the flora, and the season — the sixteen "mountain wrinkles," the Chinese called them. The names of a few of them — "wrinkled like hemp fibers," "wrinkled like tangled hemp fibers," "wrinkled like confused brushwood," "wrinkled like a thunderhead," "wrin-kled like eddying water," "wrinkled like horses' teeth" — reveal a keen observa-

cent. Museum of Fine Arts, Boston. (Boston Museum)

tion of nature and also a direct, suggestive method of expressing the idea. Likewise there were laws governing the painting of water. "In regard to painting moving waters, whether deep or shallow, in rivers or brooks, bays or oceans, Chinanpin [a Chinese teacher] declared it was impossible for the eye to seize their exact forms because they are ever changing and have no fixed definite shape, therefore they can not be sketched satisfactorily; yet, as moving water must be represented in painting, it should be long and minutely contemplated by the artist, and its general character — whether leaping in the brook, flowing in the river, roaring in the cataract, surging in the ocean or lapping the shore — observed and reflected upon, and after the eye and memory are both sufficiently trained and the very soul of the artist is saturated, as it were, with this one subject and he feels his whole being calm and composed, he should retire to the privacy of his studio and with the early morning sun to gladden his spirit there attempt to reproduce the movement of the flow; not by copying what he has seen . . . but by symbolizing according

to certain laws what he feels and remembers."[1]

This discussion is valuable not only because it gives one an insight into the conventions that governed the painters, but also because it explains something of Chinese methods of working. Fundamentally, the method consisted of long contemplation — that is, mental and visual preparation — followed by rapid execution as a result of highly trained technical skill and the indelible nature of ink painting. The great Wu Tao-tzu, a well-known story says, was ordered by the emperor to paint for him one of his favorite scenes of river and mountain landscape. Thither the painter went. When he returned and was asked for his sketches, he replied, "I have it all in my heart," and then, in a single day, he threw off a hundred miles of landscape.

Technical training required complete control of brush strokes, which are the elemental and visual means of

[1] H. P. Bowie, *On the Laws of Japanese Painting*, Elder, 1911, p. 61, by permission of the publishers. For illustrations of these conventions see Benjamin March, *Some Technical Terms of Chinese Painting*, Waverly Press, 1935.

[A] *Ma Yüan. Bare Willows and Distant Mountains. Sung Dynasty, 13th cent. Museum of Fine Arts, Boston. (Boston Museum)*

expression. Each stroke has its character and vitality, and each is an embodiment of that which the creative mind and spirit are trying to objectify. "Brush strokes . . . indicate the movement of the mind, its direction, its speed, its duration, its strength. . . . Expression in a picture, as in writing, is the result of the action of the mind travelling through the brush. . . . Perfect control of the brush coupled with fine thought makes a picture worthy."[1]

A scroll (Fig. 380A) will illustrate these matters. Here is a typical landscape of mountains, rivers, and illimitable distance. As you slowly unroll the painting, there is spread out before you a panorama of great spaciousness, strongly characteristic of the bold mountainous country of China: a foreground of sparsely wooded country traversed by streams, with a pavilion and a few fisher-

[1] Kojiro Tomita, "Brush Strokes in Far Eastern Painting," *Eastern Art.* Vol. III (1931), pp. 29 ff.

men casting their lines where the land juts out into the sea. Behind, rise majestic mountains, rocky, partly wooded, with intermittent valleys filled with mist, and in the highest, a pagoda, in the distance, another range of mountains. What perhaps impresses us first is the bold rhythm in the upward thrust of the massive mountains, which slows down as the land tapers off into the quiet water and then is repeated by the distant range. Notice how these rhythms are interwoven like the contrasting themes in music, each evoking in the spectator a changing mood. This comparison between Chinese landscape painting and music Dr. Laufer expressed when he said: "We shall better appreciate Chinese painting, if we try to conceive it as having no analogy with our painting, but as being akin to our music. Indeed, the psychological difference of Chinese painting from our own mainly rests on the basis that the Chinese handle painting, not as we handle painting, but as we handle music, for the purpose of lending color to and evoking the whole range of sentiments and emotions of humanity. In depth of thought and feeling, the great T'ang masters, in their symphonic compositions, vie with Beethoven, and in line and color almost reach Mozart's eternal grace and beauty."[1] Looking at the scroll in detail, we see that the rocks and the various kinds of trees are all painted according to the Chinese pictorial language of brush strokes, and that distance is suggested by gradations in tone.

Highly expressive of the quintessence of mood, and also of skill in the use of space and asymmetrical balance, are the album leaves and the small paintings of birds and flowers, which are exquisite as expressions of nature and as compositional masterpieces. In Figure 382A, against open space and mountains soaring above the mist rise two willow trees, whose branches sweep over a foot bridge that leads across a quiet water to buildings in a wood at the foot of the mountain; at the extreme right, a traveler approaches the bridge. "The important thing about willows is that their branches hang down, for if they did not hang down, they would not be willows. It is important that the branches be long, for otherwise they cannot sway gracefully in the wind. What then would be the use of their hanging down? This tree is a place where the cicadas love to rest, as well as the birds. It is to the credit of this tree that we often hear music in the air and do not feel lonely in summer."[2]

Here again the rhythm of nature and the meaning of nature are distilled into a quintessence and objectified picto-

[1] Berthold Laufer, "A Landscape of Wang Wei," *Ostasiatische Zeitschrift*, 1912, p. 54.
[2] Lin Yutang, *My Country and My People*. John Day, 1939, p. 326, quoting a Chinese writer of the seventeenth century.

[A] *Ting Porcelain Bowl. D. 9½ in. Sung Dynasty. Art Institute of Chicago. (Art Institute)   The carved decoration shows two ducks swimming in a lotus pond.*

rially by brush strokes which, delicate in the willow, sweep downward in graceful curves toward the more forceful angular strokes in the lower branches and the gnarled trunk, and suggest the living quality in all parts of the tree. In the mountains, the strokes and broad washes suggest their massive solidity. Thus two dominant contrasting rhythms interweave, and as they interweave they incorporate minor rhythm, as in the trees and shrubs. Compositionally, the painting is a design of light and dark and line — predominantly curved lines, stabilized by verticals in the willows and horizontals in the bridge and the low-lying part of the landscape. The mass of mountains is balanced by space, and both are skillfully tied together by the willow. Such a masterly use of space as an element of design is one of the contributions of the Chinese painters. Though we may see the painting as flat pattern, it actually suggests great depth. By means of line, but primarily by gradation of tone, the eye is carried from the foreground willow diagonally in to the buildings and the nearer woods; then to the farther woods and, after an upward leap to the crest of the nearer mountains, to the far-distant peaks.

Such paintings are as evocative of mood as Chinese poems:

"On Lady's Table Mountain-top spring
    snows melt;
By the roadside apricot-flowers bud
    on tender twigs.
My heart is ready; I long to go. Yet
    when shall the day be?
Sadly I watch the homeward coach
    roll over the field-bridge."
    — *Yang E-Shih* (about 800, written when detained in the city)

"From the thick bamboos the last rain-
    drops drip;
On the high hill-top lingers the eve-
    ning light."
    — *Hsia-Hou Shen* (8th century, 2nd half)[1]

This purpose on the part of the Chinese painters to emphasize the vital essence of things rather than their external appearance is particularly true of the paintings of flowers and birds. Probably no other people have felt so deeply and so sympathetically as the Buddhists the unity and harmony of all animate life. The Zen Buddhists in particular arrived at an expression of this significance that is amazing in its intimate knowledge of form, its simplicity and subtlety. It is interesting to note that these lovers of nature did not personify its forms. The mountain, the bird, or the flower is an entity with its own attributes as individual, as majestic, or as delicately graceful as human life, and as important a member of the universe as man. Hence it was not necessary to visualize it in terms of man. Technically, these paintings of the Zen Buddhists are astonishing. Color

was usually abandoned and ink only used, applied with a few quick but amazingly vital strokes. Rarely has the world seen an expression so ephemeral, and at the same time so quivering with life, accomplished with such a minimum of means.

POTTERY

Sung porcelain reflects the same spirit as Sung painting — an exquisiteness, a quiet elegance, reflecting a highly refined taste. True porcelain was made in the T'ang dynasty, when we hear of cups used as musical instruments because of their resonancy. Famous wares were made for the royal and princely families, with experiments in glazing at the requirement of the emperor to the end that the fabric be as "blue as the sky, as clear as a mirror, as thin as paper, and as resonant as a musical stone of jade." Judging from the extraordinary praise with which Chinese writers describe this ware, this imperial order must have been well met. No example of it is extant so far as we know. It evidently served as a challenge to the Sung potters, as we discern some of these qualities in the wares of that period.

In the Sung dynasty porcelain reached a climax. Though some of the fabrics were functional — bowls, flowerpots, teapots, and tea bowls — many were fashioned to be enjoyed simply for their intrinsic beauty of form. Every Chinese gentleman owned a few pieces which, together with his paintings and bronzes, constituted the family heirlooms. According to Sung taste, these fabrics were of a subtly simple shape with a monochrome glaze. Many were small in size. Attention focused on proportions and relationship of parts; on turning to a meticulous finish and often to an eggshell thinness; and on the selection of just the right color of glaze to

---

[1] Waley, *op. cit.*, pp. 193–94, by permission of Charles Scribner's Sons.

set off the shape. One of the most delicate wares was the *Ting* (Fig. 383A). Ting bowls are thin, often translucent, covered with white glaze of subtly various tints, such as cream or the palest blue; and sometimes decorated with an almost imperceptibly incised or relief pattern. Very different is the stout *Chün* ware (Fig. 385A), a porcellaneous stoneware with thick walls and covered with a thick glaze richly colored in purplish hues varying from deep-red to pale-blue. Much of the Chün ware consisted of flowerpots frequently used in the garden — hence the need of a stout fabric. One of the wares best known in the West was the celadon,[1] glazed in a soft green color that the Chinese likens to young onion sprouts. In the color, and in the smooth texture of the glaze, the celadons are not unlike jade and may have originated in an attempt to reproduce the more valuable stone in a less expensive medium. If a person wanted to compliment a potter highly upon his vase, he would tell him that it looked like jade. In a typical *Celadon* (Art Institute of Chicago) there is quiet elegance and refined taste. It has a sturdy strength because of the careful proportioning of the parts, especially of the finely curved lip and the slightly spreading base. From this rise conventionalized lanceolate leaf forms, the severity of which emphasizes the easy grace of the peony scroll on the body; on the neck a tapering peony pattern meets a broad band of concentrated ridges. This decoration is all in low relief and everywhere plays into the structural lines of the vase. It is covered by a soft green glaze, which, though uniform in hue, is lighter on

[1] *Celadon,* meaning "sea-green," was originally the name of a shepherd in a seventeenth-century French novel. In the plays of that period the shepherds usually wore sea-green costumes, and the name was applied to the color and then to the Chinese ceramics of this color, which were then coming to the notice of Europeans. The term is European, not Chinese.

[A] *Chün Flower Pot. H. 8 in. Grey green to purplish blue. Sung Dynasty. Art Institute of Chicago. (Art Institute)*

the parts in relief and darker where it has collected in the hollows, producing a quietly vibrating harmony.

After the Mongol conquest, a return to a native dynasty, the Ming, stimulated a revival of the arts, with particular emphasis on color. Hence in pottery, while the Sung monochromes continued to be made in a white ware, the trend was toward polychrome fabrics made at the imperial kilns, where the potters reached a zenith of technical skill in the difficult problem of keeping the areas of color cleanly separated. Large jars of sturdy proportions were popular, and the colors were kept from running into each other either by incising the design so that any superfluous glaze would be held in the furrows, or by running a tiny ridge of clay around the color areas to form a cell (as in cloisonné enamels) to hold the glaze.

SUMMARY

The Golden Age of the T'ang dynasty, with its dignity and dynamic energy, bequeathed to the Sung dynasty conventions and techniques which the Sung artists carried to great refinement. In this dynasty China again reached a Golden Age, and was one of the loftiest civilizations in the world in the twelfth century. Sung China was the Cathay visited by Marco Polo, whose accounts of his travels accelerated contacts between a still chaotic, rugged Europe and the refined, luxurious, cultured East. In the allied fields of calligraphy, poetry, and painting, and in that of ceramics, Sung art attained its climax. Mountain and water landscapes, sympathetic interpretations of nature, painted according to the old conventions with the utmost skill in Chinese ink on silk and paper; exquisite bird and flower paintings executed with a few highly skilled strokes of the brush — these perhaps represent the climax, though figure work and portraits are not lacking. Porcelain reached its pinnacle both technically and esthetically in the subtly simple Sung fabrics, which relied for their effects on shape, proportion, and one-color glaze alone. In the following Ming dynasty these monochrome porcelains gave way to polychrome wares, which, despite their display of technical skill, fell short of the exquisite refinement of the Sung porcelain.

BIBLIOGRAPHY

Andersson, Johan Gunnar, *Children of the Yellow Earth: Studies in Prehistoric China*, Macmillan, 1934
Binyon, Laurence, *The Flight of the Dragon*, Dutton, 1922
———————— *Painting in the Far East*, 4th ed. rev., Longmans, Green, 1934
Bushell, Stephen W., *Chinese Art*, 2 vols., Brentano's, 1924
Carter, Dagny Olsen, *China Magnificent: Five Thousand Years of Chinese Art*, Reynal and Hitchcock, 1935
Carter, Thomas F., *Periods of Chinese History* (chart), Ginn, 1925
Cohn, William, *Asiatische Plastik*, Berlin, 1932
———————— *Chinese Art*, Studio, 1930

Cranmer-Byng, Launcelot A., tr., *A Lute of Jade*, Dutton, 1926
Creel, Herrlee Glessner, *The Birth of China*, London, 1936
Driscoll, Lucy, and Toda, Kenji, *Chinese Calligraphy*, University of Chicago Press, 1935
Encyclopædia Britannica, *Chinese Art* (Britannica Booklet No. 1)
Ferguson, John C., *Chinese Painting*, University of Chicago Press, 1927
Fischer, Otto, *Die Kunst Indiens, Chinas und Japans*, Berlin, 1928
Fry, Roger Eliot, and others, *Chinese Art*, Weyhe, 1925 (Burlington Magazine Monograph)
Giles, Herbert A., *An Introduction to the History of Chinese Pictorial Art*, 2d ed. rev., London, 1918
Glaser, Curt, *Ostasiatische plastik*, Berlin, 1925
Hannover, Emil, *Pottery & Porcelain*, 3 vols., Scribner, 1925
Hirth, Friedrich, *Scraps from a Collector's Notebook*, Stechert, 1905
Hobson, Robert L., *Chinese Art*, Macmillan, 1927
———————— *Chinese Pottery and Porcelain*, 2 vols., Funk & Wagnalls, 1915
———————— and Hetherington, A. L., *The Art of the Chinese Potter*, London, 1923
Kelley, Charles Fabens, and Ch'en Meng-chia, *Chinese Bronzes from the Buckingham Collection*, Art Institute of Chicago, 1946
Koop, Albert J., *Early Chinese Bronzes*, Scribner, 1925
Kümmell, Otto, *Die Kunst Ostasiens*, 2d ed., Berlin, 1922
Kuo Hsi, *An Essay on Landscape Painting*, tr. by Shio Sakanishi, Dutton, 1936
Laufer, Berthold, *Jade*, Chicago Natural History Museum, 1912
Lin Yutang, ed., *The Wisdom of China and India*, Random House, 1942
March, Benjamin, *Some Technical Terms of Chinese Painting*, Waverly Press, 1935
Metropolitan Museum of Art, *The China Trade and Its Influences* (pamphlet), Museum, New York City, 1941
Museum of Fine Arts, Boston, *Portfolio of Chinese Paintings in the Museum*, text by Kojiro Tomita, Harvard University Press, 1933
Okakura, Kakuzo, *The Ideals of the East*, Dutton, 1921
Petrucci, Raphaël, *Chinese Painters*, tr. by Frances Seaver, Brentano, 1920
Silcock, Arnold, *Introduction to Chinese Art*, Oxford University Press, 1935
Sirén, Osvald, *The Chinese on the Art of Painting*, Peiping, 1936
———————— *Chinese Paintings in American Collections*, Paris and Brussels, 1928
———————— *Chinese Sculpture from the Fifth to the Fourteenth Century*, 4 vols., Scribner, 1925

Sirén, Osvald, *A History of Early Chinese Art*, 4 vols., London, 1929–30
———— *A History of Early Chinese Painting*, 2 vols., London, 1933
Taki, Sei-ichi, *Three Essays on Oriental Painting*, London, 1910
Waley, Arthur, *An Introduction to the Study of Chinese Painting*, Scribner, 1923

———— tr., *A Hundred and Seventy Chinese Poems*, Knopf, 1919
———— *Zen Buddhism*, London, 1922
Warner, Langdon, *Buddhist Wall Paintings*, Harvard University Press, 1938
Yetts, Walter P., *Symbolism in Chinese Art*, Leyden, 1912
See also General Bibliography, pages 791–92.

21

JAPANESE ART

(A.D. 900 TO DATE)

THE influences from Korea, China, and even from India and Iran, had been assimilated when the Fujiwara family rose to power as the head of an aristocratic oligarchy centralized at Kyoto.[1] In the *Tale of Genji* by Murasaki, a gifted writer of the period, one reads of an exquisitely refined society, of a sophisticated etiquette, of conversing in improvised poetry; of music and festivals and buildings, gardens, paintings, and costumes — all in a style consistent with the ideals of the period.

With the Kamakura and Ashikaga eras two new elements entered to reshape this art, one militaristic and one religious. The barons had been usurping the political power of the emperor, and were setting up a military feudalism, when early in the thirteenth century they vanquished the Mongol hordes of Kublai Khan by the help, legend says, of their sun goddess. The shoguns, their commanders in chief, became military regents and established a complex feudal system, which under the

Tokugawas became a tyrannical autocracy. The astute statesman Iyeyasu, founder of the line, and his followers strengthened their own power by creating a new nobility of daimios (landed barons) and samurai (military barons), who were loyal because they were under obligation to the shogun for their existence. The Tokugawas also consolidated and increased the power of the people, and granted religious toleration. Partly through an appeal to patriotism and partly because of the Mongol and the Muslim power in China, the Tokugawas cut off relationship with the rest of the world and established that policy of isolation which continued until the downfall of the shogunate in 1868. The religious element which caused a change in art expression consisted of another wave of influence from China, in the form of Zen Buddhism, with its revolt from ritual and its emphasis upon contemplation, through which one attained insight into the essence of the universe and recognized in transient effects and in every seemingly insignificant manifestation of nature the underlying ultimate reality.

[1] The periods of later Japanese art are: Fujiwara, 900–1190; Kamakura, 1190–1383; Ashikaga, 1383–1603; Tokugawa, 1603–1868.

ARCHITECTURE

Characteristic buildings were palaces for the nobility and Buddhist monasteries. The *Howodo,* or *Phoenix Hall* — which is the kondo of *Byodo-in,* one of the few Fujiwara monasteries extant — represents both, as it was originally a residence and was later converted into a monastery. As a residence, it faced south and overlooked a garden pond. Even a humble Japanese home without a garden is unthinkable. One is immediately struck by the beauty of the site of the *Howodo,* and by the feeling of unity between the building and its environment. The heaviness and the somber massiveness of the Chinese model have given way to lightness and delicacy; the roofs have become lower and less dominating; there is a quiet grace throughout and an exquisite curve of line. The structure consists of a central hall, the highest part, and two projecting pavilions connected with the hall by open corridors; another corridor runs back of the hall at right angles to it. This plan suggests a phoenix with outstretched wings, symbolic of the paradise of Amida Buddha. Hence the name.

Though the building is long and low, it conveys no suggestion of monotony. On the contrary, it is filled with a delicate rhythmic movement. The verticals of the slender columns, together with the predominant horizontals of platform, steps, and entablature, serve as a support both structurally and esthetically for the roofs, which form a rhythmic interplay of low-swung curves. The vermilion color of the structure, with accents of gilded metalwork, is reflected in the pool and enhanced by the interplaying green of the trees. The interior, like that of *Horyuji,* is gorgeous in its splendor. Carvings and black lacquer inlaid with ivory, mother-of-pearl, and silver cover the coffered ceiling, from which a canopy of wood, carved to a lacy delicacy, is suspended above the great gold-bronze Trinity group. On the walls are paintings of multitudes of Bodhisattvas worshiping Amida. The whole effect in the softened light is one of rich, somber glow, comparable to that of Byzantine mosaics.

With the ascendancy of the feudal lords, far more attention was concentrated on domestic architecture. Feudal palaces, built on lofty stone walls surrounded by moats for the purpose of defense, consisted of a group of stately residences connected by galleries and facing an inner court, with towers for lookouts. The Japanese house, palace or modest home, followed a general plan which is peculiarly Japanese. Love of nature impelled the Japanese to bring nature into his everyday life by means of gardens, with which he so combined the house as to attain an extraordinary unity within a variety of forms and textures, even when working on a small scale. In plan, the house had one room slightly higher than the others, with an alcove (the *tokonama*) for the display of some treasure. The other rooms were separated from it by sliding screens, frequently decorated with paintings. The ceiling, as in the temples, was resplendent with rich color, gold, and lacquer. The floor, on the other hand, was most unobtrusive, for it was covered with simple straw mats. Equally unpretentious were the furnishings. To the eye of the Westerner, a Japanese house looks unfurnished (Fig. 389A). But he is compelled to admit that it has a satisfying serenity. The Japanese seemed to need but little in order to live comfortably. Cushions and a low table (for chairs were nonexistent), a pad for a bed, put away in the daytime — such simple arrangements sufficed. Another fact bears witness to this ideal of simplicity: in the tokonama only one or two treasures at

[A]   *A Japanese Domestic Interior.*

a time were displayed — a kakemono, or a fine vase with one rare flower or one carefully selected branch of a blossoming fruit tree.

The tranquility of Japanese interiors[1] is due partly to this simplicity in furnishings and partly to the unerring Japanese recognition of the intrinsic qualities in materials. Great craftsmen in wood, far from hiding its quality with paint, they used every resource to bring out its color, texture, and graining. Likewise with every material. Tile, stucco, and paper were used with a sureness of command over the potentialities of the materials, and also with an astonishing ability to integrate them into a form rarely equaled in the field

of domestic architecture. The rooms of the house opened on a long veranda equipped with sliding screens of translucent paper, for the admission of light when closed and for a view of the garden when open. For the unity of the house and the garden was the heart of the structure. Japanese gardens were laid out according to traditional formulas. We must not compare them with the flower gardens of the West, but think of them as arrangements of trees, shrubs, stones, water, sand, bridges, lanterns, all skillfully related to one another and to the house, both as to material and as to line, texture, color, and shape, so that together they form an inseparable unity.

Another kind of building also now began to receive the attention of the architects — the mausoleum, of which the tombs at *Nikko* are perhaps the

[1] For Japanese domestic interiors see R. A. Cram, *Impressions of Japanese Architecture*, Baker and Taylor, 1905, and Kakuzo Okakura, *The Book of Tea*, Duffield, 1906.

[A] *Bishamon, the Guardian King of the North. Kuramadera Temple, Kyoto. Wood. Early Fugiwara period.* (Japanese Temples and Their Treasures)

outstanding example. Here magnificent old cryptomeria trees on a hillside serve as a setting into which the buildings with their gorgeous decorations are fitted. Gateways, shrines, and treasure houses are so loaded with polychrome carvings and black-and-gold lacquers, that despite our admiration for the magnificence in itself and for the technical skill shown, we yearn for the greater simplicity of Suiko and Fujiwara buildings. For here at Nikko we witness the floridity of a style that is entering a decadence.

SCULPTURE

Zen Buddhism by its very nature would not incline toward sculpture for expression, but toward the more ephemeral art of painting. Hence with the decline of the need for Buddhistic statues — though the Kamakura age produced the impressive *Daibutsu* (*Great Buddha*) of Kamakura — we see the emergence of two kinds of sculpture. One kind consisted of portraits — again an influence of the individualistic strain of Zen — which were realistic in detail, but which subordinated this detail to a vivid, forceful characterization. The other kind consisted of militaristic subjects. A martial, nationalistic spirit, exemplified in statues of the god of war, had already appeared even as early as the Nara period. These statues were as vital an epitome of forceful power as the Suiko Kwannons were of calm beneficence. In Figure 390A, what impresses us first is an intense energy. As in the portraits, details of modeling are amazingly realistic. Yet this realism is subject to the dominating swing of the firmly planted figure and the dynamic sweep of the drapery.

This sculpture (the portraits and the militaristic statues) constitutes a thoroughly nationalized expression, probably the most characteristically Japanese expression in the sculptural art. From this time on sculpture waned with the rise of the popular schools of painting.

PAINTING

With the ebbing of the tide of Buddhist impulse from T'ang China, Buddhist themes changed in character, especially in the Fujiwara age, when, as we would expect from the delicate and almost feminine quality in Fujiwara culture, the more lofty, austere Bodhisattvas of Suiko and Nara art became

[A] *Heiji Monogatari. The Burning of the Sanjo Palace. Detail. 13th cent. Museum of Fine Arts, Boston. (Boston Museum)*

humanized, even individualized. Their tranquillity and otherworldliness gave way to movement, a delicate movement with gentle rhythms. And now appeared the more characteristically Japanese painting known as Yamato-e (the painting of Yamato). Though at times it dealt with religious themes, it was largely a secular art: portraits and illustrations of contemporary life and literature. It thus took for its theme the social, ceremonial, and military life of the aristocracy, as in the scrolls which contain the text and illustrations of the *Tale of Genji.* Here are scenes from the life of the palace drawn with firm lines which define areas of bright color and gold; and vivacious battle scenes filled with movement (Fig. 391A).

Parallel to Yamato-e was another school, closely allied to Chinese Sung painting and, like the Chinese, inspired by Zen Buddhism. This school produced exquisite and refined landscape and genre paintings. The simplicity and directness of Zen thought led these painters to use ink rather than the sumptuous color and gilding char-acteristic of Yamato painting. Important among these painters was a Zen priest, Sesshu (about 1420–1506), who painted landscape scrolls that were clearly inspired by Chinese Sung landscape painting. Sesshu and other painters were particularly successful in their paintings of animals (Fig. 393A), flowers, and birds, in which the artist, by a few strokes of the brush applied with consummate mastery of the ink technique, implies and suggests rather than specifically states the content of what he is painting.

A great demand for paintings of both the Yamato and the Sung styles came from the feudal lords, who wanted to decorate the walls and the sliding and folding screens of their palaces. Landscapes, tree, flower, and bird subjects were popular — now rich in color and gold, even with entire gold grounds, now austerely simple in uncolored ink. The folding screen, by its very make-up of several sections hinged together and used in various positions, posed a compositional problem, one so successfully solved by the Japanese painters that

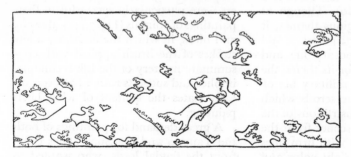

[A] *Korin. Waves at Matsushima. The analyses isolate various repeat motifs. Museum of Fine Arts, Boston. (Boston Museum)*

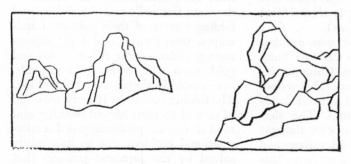

[A]   *Monkeys. Ashikaga period (1383–1603). Ryusen Collection, Kyoto. (Kokka)*

these screens constituted a peculiarly Japanese contribution. For the painting required unity not only in the entire composition but in each section as well, very much as in the makimono. In the *Waves at Matsushima* (Fig. 392A) of Korin (died 1716), for example, each of the six sections is a unit of design, largely asymmetrical yet as a whole united into a vigorous pattern that is quite consistent with the theme. The traditional conventions for rocks, water, clouds, and trees express the solidity of the rocks, the tumultuous movement of the surging waves, the gentler motion of the clouds, and the quiet security of the pines on their lofty sites. The effect of the rapid repetition of the restive wave and crest motifs in juxtaposition to the quiet unbroken areas of the rock motif illustrates Korin's implicit following of the Oriental tradition of painting moving water,[1] and also makes

¹ See page 381.

the screen both in parts and as a whole superbly decorative.

While Yamato-e depended for its content upon historical scenes and genre, it was the life of the aristocracy that it depicted, not that of the people. In the late Ashikaga age there rose demands for an art whose content was based upon the life of the middle and lower classes. In the early part of the Tokugawa period, when these classes were coming into position and wealth, this led to the Ukiyo-e, "pictures of this fleeting world," illustrations of the everyday life of the people in the streets, trade houses, theaters, and countryside, and in a form within the purchasing ability of the masses. Thus arose in the seventeenth century the Japanese print, made from wood blocks, which was sometimes an illustration in a book and sometimes an individual print. At first the impressions were made in black-and-white only, and if color was used

[A]   *Tōshūsai Sharaku. The Actor Segawa Kikunojō III as O-Shizu. 1794. Art Institute of Chicago. (Art Institute)*

it was added by hand. Then came the invention of printing in two colors and then, in the eighteenth century, the full polychrome process. The output was prolific, the subject matter and the style were varied. There are the strong single figures of actors and beauties by Moronobu (1625–1694), the first of Japanese painters to enter the field of designing for the wood block. and by Kiyonobu (1664–1729), large figures which fill the space, and which show in their firm accomplished drawing a sound training in the use of Chinese ink. There is an easy grace of line and a charm of pattern in the feminine subjects of Harunobu (1725–1770) (Fig. 395A), who is thought to have invented the process of polychrome printing. Notable is the successful design of his pillar prints and of those of Koryūsai

(active 1760–1780), very high narrow prints proportioned to fit the pillar of the chief room in the house. There are the powerful dramatic portraits of actors by Shunshō (1726–1793) and Sharaku (active 1794–1795) (Fig. 394A) and of popular beauties by Utamaro (1753–1806). With Kiyonaga (1752–1815), the designs became more complex, and though the figures are on a smaller scale and less monumental, their grouping and elaborate costumes offer material for complicated patterns, and landscape takes the place of the flat ground. With Hokusai (1760–1849) and Hiroshige (1797–1858), landscape became a dominant note. While these prints are not considered fine art by the Japanese, they nevertheless show the fundamental principles of the fine art of painting. In their sensitive feeling for space relations; in their skillful maintenance of asymmetrical balance of flat patterns, often very complicated and with marked linear quality; in their accomplished draftsmanship with a supreme command over line, usually calligraphic but at times so modulated as to express the mass of the figure; in their strangely beautiful color combinations and unusual point of view, especially in landscape — in all these excellences they reveal a democratic art of very high attainment.

METALWORK, LACQUER, TEXTILES, AND POTTERY

The bronze-workers of Japan have always been skillful to an unusual degree. The craft was inherited, and the most famous families of craftsmen traced their ancestry back to mythical times. The casting was done by the cire-perdue process, and the finishing by a considerable use of the chisel. Evidences of this skill we have already seen in the Buddhas and Bodhisattvas that compose the *Trinity* groups, and in the

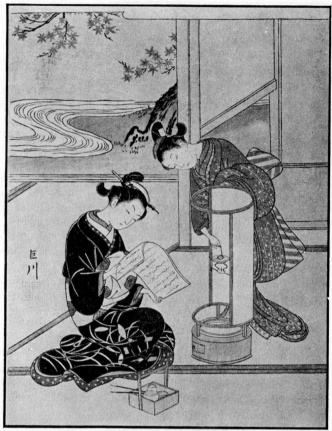

[A] *Suzuki Harunobu. The Evening Glow of the Andō (Night Lantern). 1765. Art Institute of Chicago. (Art Institute)*

screens, lanterns, and decorative figures of the shrines. Important among these metalworkers were the armorers, for the powerful samurai created a demand for the finest sword blades and sword furniture. A thorough knowledge of the properties of metals and alloys enabled the swordsmith to obtain various colors and textures; for decorations he employed a variety of metal processes in casting, chasing, stamping, and damascening. The blade was made of many layers, each forged and tempered with all the expert skill of generations.[1] This multiplicity of layers causes the watered effect seen in fine blades.

[1] For a detailed account of this forging of a sword see Stewart Dick, *Arts and Crafts of Old Japan*, McClurg, 1905, p. 85.

Lacquer of a distinctive type, black and gold chiefly, sometimes with inlays of mother-of-pearl, played an important role in Japanese interiors. The art of lacquering, like the other arts of Japan, was derived from China, but in the hands of the Japanese attained a quality, both technical and esthetic, exceeding that of any other people in the Far East. Various useful objects — trays and boxes of all kinds, for example — contributed to the elegance of the sparse furnishings of the homes of the nobles. On a larger scale lacquer was used, as we have already noted, as a decorative element in palaces and temples, whose coffered ceilings provided one of the richest decorations possible. Lacquer is a natural varnish

[A]   *"Three Day Moon" Tea Bowl. By Ninsei, a famous 17th cent. potter. Blue, green, and brown glaze on white slip. H. 3½ in.* (Tojiki Hyakusen)

of exceptional hardness derived from the lac tree. The Japanese usually made the object to be lacquered of thin white pine; covered it with paper or thin hempen cloth; and rubbed and polished it with a whetstone to provide a firm surface for the lacquer, a process reminiscent of the preparation of a panel for tempera painting. The lacquer was then applied, layer after layer, with much rubbing and polishing. The design was worked out in gold dust in a variety of ways to produce a variety of effects. It was then covered with a layer of translucent lacquer and again polished (as in the case of cloisonné enamels). The finished object, by its translucence and polish, appealed both to the eye and to the tactile sense.

Designs of Japanese lacquer range from the simplest patterns to complex pictorial compositions, which are sometimes worked out in relief (a technique unique with the Japanese). But, skillful though lacquer relief may be technically, its suitability as a decoration for a flat surface is questionable.

Japanese textiles are sumptuous, particularly when metal threads and embroidery are used to attain such rich effects of color and texture as one finds

in the costumes of the upper classes and especially in the kimonos used in the Nō plays, in which the patterns are designed to harmonize with the rhythms of the dancers. The Nō drama was a highly formal, dignified performance, appealing to the aristocracy chiefly, in which there was a complete lack of stage setting except perhaps for a gold screen decorated with a pine tree which brought into sharp focus the actors' elegant robes.

The ceramic art developed late in Japan. For many centuries importations from Korea and China satisfied the demands of the aristocracy. But with the introduction of Zen Buddhism and the development of the tea ceremony, the Japanese potters made great advances, especially under the influence of the Sung ceramists of China. Their tea bowls were of an almost ostentatious simplicity, to harmonize with the austerity of the ceremony, and often were made by amateurs in an attempt to avoid sophisticated forms. Their sensitive feeling for coarse pottery shapes, variety of textures, and simplicity of decoration is without parallel elsewhere. The tea bowl of Figure 396A has a simple, functionally efficient shape, which provides an effective foil for the decoration — the crescent moon over waves — painted with concise but freely flowing lines, a design of deceiving simplicity. This drastic use of stylized forms is typical of the Japanese potters' work. Polychrome porcelains achieved a distinctively Japanese style, although they were never so popular with the Japanese as were simple pottery forms.

SUMMARY

Though Buddhist architecture continued, emphasis shifted to secular building — the Japanese home, both palatial and modest. Here appears the

Japanese gift for a sensitive use of materials; for an appealing simplicity in furnishings; and for a highly satisfying joining of the building with a garden or natural environment — unity of exterior and interior space, prophetic perhaps of Western twentieth-century domestic building.[1]

With the coming of Zen Buddhism sculpture turned in the direction of portraiture, and with the rise of the samurai, to representations of warlike gods.

Painting held a high place in the art of medieval Japan, and was of two chief kinds. The first was secular in theme, representing the life of the aristocracy, and was rich in color and gold. The second, derived from Sung China under the influence of Zen Buddhism, followed its Chinese prototype in the ink technique as well as in its subject matter — landscapes, and animal, flower, and bird paintings. Both were arts of the aristocracy.

Other arts contributed to the ensemble: the metalworker provided, among other objects, the fine swords and sword furniture for the samurai; the lacquerer, exquisite objects and decorations in black and gold; the weaver, sumptuous costumes for the theater; the potter, under the influence of Sung China, utensils of subtle simplicity for both ceremonial and daily use. With the rise of the middle and lower classes, however, there arose an art of the people which dealt with their everyday life and in a form economically possible for them — the Japanese print, an art which made use of the same sensitive linear and textural pattern and subtle color relations that constantly recur in Japanese art.

[1] It may be illuminating to recall that Frank Lloyd Wright, one of the pioneers in the unification of exterior and interior space in modern domestic architecture, lived for several years in Japan.

BIBLIOGRAPHY

Anesaki, Masaharu, *Art, Life, and Nature in Japan*, Marshall Jones, 1933

———————— *Buddhist Art in Its Relation to Buddhist Ideals*, Houghton Mifflin, 1915

Binyon, Laurence, *Painting in the Far East*, 4th ed. rev., Longmans, Green, 1934

Cram, Ralph Adams, *Impressions of Japanese Architecture and the Allied Arts*, Baker and Taylor, 1905

Dawson, Edith (Mrs. Nelson Dawson), *Enamels*, McClurg, 1911

Dillon, Edward, *The Arts of Japan*, McClurg, 1909

Ficke, Arthur D., *Chats on Japanese Prints*, Stokes, 1915

Fischer, Otto, *Die Kunst Indiens, Chinas und Japans*, Berlin, 1928

Fujii, Koji, *The Japanese Dwelling-House*, Tokyo, 1930

Gunsaulus, Helen C., *Japanese Textiles*, Japan Society of New York, 1941

Harada, Jiro, *The Lesson of Japanese Architecture*, Studio, 1936

"Juraku," *Graphic Collection of Ancient Architecture and Gardens of the Orient*, 4 vols., Tokyo, 1928–33

Kishida, Hideto, *Japanese Architecture*, Tokyo, 1935

Kümmell, Otto, *Die Kunst Ostasiens*, 2d ed., Berlin, 1922

Minamoto, Hoshu, *An Illustrated History of Japanese Art*, tr. by G. Henderson, Kyoto, 1935

Murasaki Shikibu, *The Tale of Genji*, tr. by Arthur Waley, 2 vols., Houghton Mifflin, 1935

Okakura, Kakuzo, *The Book of Tea*, Duffield, 1906

———————— *The Ideals of the East*, Dutton, 1921

Priestley, Anna F., *How to Know Japanese Colour Prints*, Doubleday, Page, 1927

Sadler, Arthur L., *A Short History of Japanese Architecture*, Sydney, 1941

Seidlitz, Woldemar von, *A History of Japanese Colour-Prints*, Lippincott, 1910

Taki, Sei-ichi, *Japanese Fine Art*, Stechert, 1931

———————— *Three Essays on Oriental Painting*, London, 1910

Tamura, Tsuyoshi, *Art of Landscape Gardens in Japan*, Dodd, Mead, 1936

Tanaka, Yusaku, *Nō Costumes of Japan, 1573–1829*, Tokyo, c. 1920

Tatsui, Matsunosuke, *Japanese Gardens*, Bruce Humphries, 1936

Toda, Kenji, *Japanese Scroll Painting*, University of Chicago Press, 1935

Tsuda, Noritake, *Handbook of Japanese Art*, Dodd, Mead, 1936

Victoria and Albert Museum, *Japanese Colour Prints*, 6th ed., London, 1931

Waley, Arthur, *The Nō Plays of Japan*, Knopf, 1922

———— *The Craft of the Japanese Sculptor.* Japan Society of New York, 1936

———— *Japanese Sculpture of the Suiko Period*, Yale University Press, 1923

With, Karl, *Buddhistische Plastik in Japan*, Vienna, 1919

Yanagi, Sôetsu, *Folk-Crafts in Japan*, tr. by Shigeyoshi Sakabe, Tokyo, 1936

Yoshida, Hiroshi, *Japanese Wood-block Printing*, Stechert, 1939

See also General Bibliography, pages 791–92.

African and Oceanian Art

22

PRIMITIVE ART

IN our survey of the Middle Ages we have seen an art arise in the Near East under the stimulation of a new faith, Christianity. Coincident with the decline of the Greco-Roman civilization, the rise and spread of Christianity across Europe stimulated communication between the East and the West and at the same time provided the motive for vigorous new expressions. Almost parallel, though slightly later, another energizing religion, more militant, spread with amazing rapidity both east and west from its center in Arabia — Muhammadanism. As it expanded, we saw it meet and assimilate influences from China and in turn contribute to the art of India in the East, and to the Mediterranean cultures in the West. In this lively intercourse between the Far and Near East and Europe, we see the world shrinking and can already speak of an Eurasia.

Three large areas of the world, however, we saw lay isolated, evolving indigenous cultures which were to meet, some centuries later, the Eurasian civilizations, influence them profoundly, and in turn be influenced by them. These areas were Africa (except for Egypt and the coastal fringe of the Mediterranean), Oceania, and the Americas.

African Negro Art

IN west-central Africa (Fig. 400A) — on the coast, in the river basins of the Niger and the Congo, in the southern reaches of the Sudan — live a great number of primitive Negro tribes whose origin and history are largely unknown. Some are nomadic or seminomadic herdsmen on the grasslands fringing the forests; some are settled agriculturalists in clearings of the heavily forested regions of the river valleys; all are hunters and fighters. With an animistic religion they people all forms of nature with spirits for whose placation or supplication fetishes are in great demand. Dancing and chanting, to the accompaniment of a boldly rhythmic music, and elaborate and awe-inspiring costumes, in which masks feature prominently, are important in their ritual.

SCULPTURE

The exigencies of their life, in which a primitive hut serves for a dwelling, and the materials at hand have given rise to a remarkable art of woodcarving: the making and embellishing of objects of everyday and ceremonial

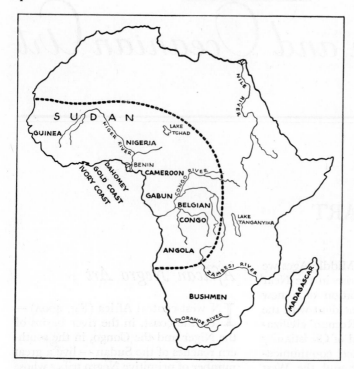

[A]   *Africa, Showing the Regions (inclosed by a dotted line) Where Negro Sculpture Is Produced.*

use out of the abundant native timber during the abundant leisure time that this way of life affords. Occasionally the carvers have used stone, and more frequently ivory or bronze, the technique of whose working the Benin people learned from the Europeans.

As these African tribes vary in language, customs, religion, and social organization, so the styles of their carving vary, a fact that precludes generalizations that are applicable to all, except that similar habits of visualization, and hence a similar basic style, are observable in their carvings. Practically none of the carving has a copy of nature as its objective. On the contrary, the African dissected and distorted the parts of the human or animal figure, and reassembled them not according to nature but according to an esthetic pattern related to the material he was using, the space to be filled, the function of the object, and its symbolic significance. The carving has nothing to do with a verisimilitude of natural appearances, though occasionally it may tend thither; but it presents a type of visualization long established by tradition and thoroughly intelligible to both the artist and his public.

"Every part in a typical, fully realized Negro statue functions as an element in plastic design: an embodiment, a repetition in rhythmic, varied sequence, of some theme in mass, line or surface. To be transformed into a design, the human figure must be regarded in a way quite different from that of ordinary life and of most sculpture. It must not be seen as an inviolable whole, treated as one unit and merely posed in this attitude or that. The figure must be dissociated into its parts, regarded as an aggregate of distinct units: the head, limbs, breasts, trunk and so on, each by itself. So distinguished and usually marked off by a surrounding groove or hollow, each part can be moulded into a variation of some chosen theme — a sharp, slender projection, or perhaps a smooth, bulbous swelling — never exactly the same as its neighbors, for that would be monotonous; never too far from nature, or completely abstract, for that would destroy its interest as representation, its relevancy to the world of human experience. In the same figure an artist may introduce two or more radically different shapes, perhaps repeating and slightly varying each one. Such contrast gives, as in music, an arresting and interesting shock to the observer. It carries with it a possible loss of unity; the whole piece may seem to fall apart, to be confusingly unrelated. Then the genius of the artist consists in finding means to weld the contrasting themes together by some note common to both.

"Constructed like a building of solid blocks, a typical Negro statue is itself a solid, a full, substantial block, set with convincing, massive reality in its own space."[1]

Take for example a table with a figure support (Fig. 401A). The cylindrical piece of wood, from which just enough has been cut away to allow the figure to emerge, is clearly felt as a determinant of the basic design; its section is retained in the top and the base and its diameter is maintained in the horizontal reach of the arms; its shape is repeated in torso, neck, and arms. The figure, compressed into a kneeling position, emerges from, yet remains rooted in, the semiovoid base through the flattening and distorting of the feet, thus bringing unity and stability to the table as a whole. It then rises through a series

[1] Paul Guillaume and Thomas Munro, *Primitive Negro Sculpture*, Harcourt, Brace, 1926, p. 35, by permission of the publishers. This book presents a lucid exposition of the artistic qualities of Negro sculpture, with detailed analyses of individual pieces. See also Roger Eliot Fry, *Vision and Design*, "Negro Sculpture."

[A] *Figure Supporting a Table. Wood. Congo. 17th cent. Barnes Collection, Merion, Pa. (Morgan Photo) Note the play on contrasts of circular and angular motifs united by the repetition of cone-shaped volumes.*

of outward- and inward-moving masses conoidal in shape and thus with a zigzag contour, to support the top firmly by the head and the uplifted arms, and by this action secures a vertical as well as a horizontal balance. This play upon masses — ovoids, conoids, cylinders — is repeated in the surface treatment, in which highly polished surfaces contrast with carved ones. Thus the table as a whole is basically a three-dimensional abstraction in which the parts are as closely related, structurally and esthetically, as in any building.

This three-dimensional organization so markedly characteristic of Negro

[A] *Ivory Coast Mask. Wood.*
14th cent. Barnes Collection,
Merion, Pa. (Morgan Photo)

[B] *Portrait of a Benin King. Bronze. Originally sur-*
mounted by a large carved tusk. University Museum,
Philadelphia. (University Museum)

sculpture is based upon a generally cylindrical mass — at times starkly geometric, as in the Gabun figures; at times with richly carved surfaces. In contemplating these compositions upon the theme of the cylinder, one ponders on the influence of a naturally cylindrical material upon the carver and on his daily life among the trees, which furnish him with a material that is soft and easily carved in comparison with stone, and whose continuous rounding surfaces suggest movement in depth to both his visual and his tactile perception. How different will be the work of a carver confronted with a four-sided block of hard, weighty stone that re-

sists every stroke of the chisel and hammer! Most of the African carvings are relatively small, and though extraordinarily firm and stable, have none of the mighty solidity of stone sculpture.

After the perplexity or even aversion felt by a non-African upon first seeing these carvings has given way to a desire for insight and at least a partial understanding, he becomes aware of their intense vitality. Likewise he recognizes a superb craftsmanship, and a design which may be entirely abstract to the foreigner but is so obviously filled with intense meaning to the African that it is bound to impress the unprejudiced observer, however little he may

[A] *Bushman Paint-ings.* (*Obermaier and Kuhn*, Bushman Art, *Oxford University Press*)

grasp its full import. The masks are an excellent illustration. Masks serve the same function, or rather contribute to the same objective, as the ceremonial chant and dance. They are one of the visual parts of a ritual whose purpose is to inspire awe or fear, and thus must present to the eye of the observer a form that will function to that end. Since the masks are actually worn, they are life-sized or larger, and are highly simpli-fied arrangements of the parts of the face, combined perhaps with a head-dress; and, though in relief only, they show the same attitude toward natural forms as the carvings in the round. In Figure 402A, for example, there is an interplay of the oval — in the face and its details repeated on a small scale in the headdress — and of the sharply angular zigzag on a large scale above and a small scale below. Likewise, the strong vertical accent balances a rhyth-mic repetition of horizontals.

Metal was used to a limited extent and in primitive ways by the Africans, but in Benin the metalworkers, having learned from the Portuguese the more

advanced process of cire-perdue, created as fetishes bronze heads (Fig. 402B), which probably were ancestor portraits. They were surmounted by elephant tusks elaborately carved with represen-tations of the king and his attendants. Since ancestor worship was an essential part of religious belief and rites, these heads with tusks stood on the altar and symbolized the spirits of the ancestors who were potent in bringing good or evil into the lives of their descendants, and to whom therefore sacrifices were made for the welfare of these descend-ants. In these heads we discern not only a great vitality, but a sensitivity to material in the rounding forms with flowing surfaces, the interplay of smooth and broken surfaces and rounding and angular motifs.

PAINTING

Among the Bushmen of the Kalahari Desert south of the Congo, who were very primitive nomad hunters living in a naturally poor land, paintings on rocks have been found of a character quite different in point of view from the African art of which we have been speaking, and strangely like that of the Paleolithic cave painters of France. A visual perception of their world reduced to essentials and expressed with directness and economy seems to have been their objective (Fig. 403A). These are not generalized men and animals and movements, but individualized men and animals in an infinite variety of naturalistic poses, even those involving foreshortening, such as front and three-quarters views, which indicates an extraordinarily keen vision and memory.[1]

Oceanian Art

THE peoples of Oceania are a mixed race compounded of the aboriginal inhabitants of the islands and Asiatics who migrated there. While Paleolithic and Neolithic remains in Java, Sumatra, and Celebes carry human habitation far back into prehistoric times, migrations from the continents appear to be relatively recent, some possibly as late as a few centuries B.C. So vast is the ocean area covered by these islands, and so varied the race and life patterns and art forms, that few generalizations can be made even in one of the main divisions into which they are grouped: Polynesia, Melanesia, and Micronesia.

The Polynesians are a finely built brown people organized socially into the family and the clan, with the chiefs, of attributed divine birth, as rulers. Their religion consists of spirit and ancestor worship, infused through and through, as is their social system (for the social and the religious are hardly

separable) with a highly developed system of taboo (*tapu*), which means "prohibited" for sacred or other reasons. "The true inwardness of the word *tapu* is that it infers the setting apart of certain persons or things on account of their having become possessed or infected by the presence of supermaterial beings."[2] Magic, too, plays a considerable part in the ceremonial, often highly elaborate, which attends many of their everyday activities, their fishing for example. Economically, fishing ranks first; agriculture is important where possible; and warfare employs a considerable part of their time.

The art forms of such a people are dependent upon the materials at hand and the tools they have evolved; and they are inextricably knit into the whole pattern of everyday life. The chief material is wood from the rich growth of timber, which supplies material for houses and canoes and for furnishings of all kinds, and pulp and fibers for bark cloth and mats; the feathers of colorful tropical birds for feather ceremonial robes; bone for carvings; and abalone and other shells for inlays. They have no metal and no pottery. Their tools are very primitive: an adz with a blade of jade or shell; knives of flaked obsidian or set with a row of shark's teeth; drills with points of stone, shell, or shark's teeth.

Their buildings of wood and thatch, adapted to the climate of the South Pacific and unusually craftsmanlike in details of construction, reach a climax in the *Maori Council Houses*, particularly because of their carvings. The chief Polynesian art expression, however, consists in the making and decorating of articles for everyday or ceremonial use — mats, baskets, bark cloth for

---

[1] See Fry, *op. cit.*, "The Art of the Bushmen," for a discussion of perceptual and conceptual images.

[2] *Ethnology of Polynesia and Micronesia*, Chicago Natural History Museum, p. 147. Continue this quotation for a detailed account of *tapu*.

[A] *Tapa. From Samoa. Rubbed and painted design in yellow, black, and reddish brown on white. Chauvet Collection, Paris.*

[B] *Ancestral Shield. Painted wood. Melanesian. Chauvet Collection, Paris.*

garments and hangings; paddles, clubs, spears, and other implements of warfare; all kinds of woodenware for house-furnishing — and in decorating their own bodies by tattoo and scarification. On the whole it is a richly decorative art, at times symbolic with a magic purpose. Most of the designs, as in aboriginal American art, have specific names which relate them closely to the milieu of their makers.

DECORATIVE PAINTING AND CARVING

Mats are an important article of furnishing because they serve for floor and wall coverings as well as for beds and sails. Mat-making is done by the women, who obtain their material from

sedge and from the leaves of the pandanus tree; and by a change in the plaiting or in the width of the fiber or by the introduction of colored fibers they create an infinite variety of patterns. Bark cloth, or *tapa*, which is used for clothing and hangings, is not a textile, for it is made by beating together strips of the inner bark of the paper mulberry tree until they form a sheet of fabric, sometimes thirty feet long by fifteen feet wide. The sheet is then painted in bold geometric designs in black, yellow, or red-brown. The simple geometric pattern of Figure 405A is filled with unexpected variations, as if the creative activity were too vital and prolific to repeat itself, though it adheres sternly to the basic pattern.

The boldly free and varied brush

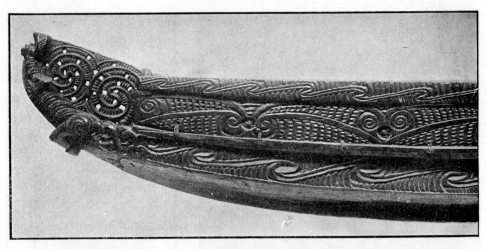

[A]   *Carved Prow of a Canoe. Polynesian. British Museum, London. (British Museum)*

work in the tapa-painting shows the same understanding of materials and techniques, as does the wood-carving, which is probably the highest expression of the Polynesian people. Boxes and food dishes, paddles and staves, both ceremonial and utilitarian, killing clubs and weapons of warfare — all these objects of daily and ceremonial life are carved lavishly. Frequently the entire surface is covered with an intricate pattern of curving motifs inlaid with abalone shell. It reveals a great virtuosity in carving, especially when one recalls the primitive tools with which the work is done. In Figure 406A, the carving covers the surface almost too exuberantly with a continuous movement in spiraling motifs like the unending rhythm of a tom-tom. In the orator's staff of Figure 407B (extempore oratory about gods and legends accompanied by the wielding of this ceremonial object is a privileged art expression among the Maori nobles), the carving is confined to the upper part, is adjusted in scale to the part that it decorates, and serves to enhance rather than to obliterate the form and its surfaces.

In contrast to the suavely elegant, accomplished carvings of the Polynesians are the starkly decorative carvings and paintings of the Melanesians, a Negroid race of lower civilization, a cannibalistic people, but one of an extraordinary esthetic sensibility. It is a boldly decorative art, at times purely ornamental, at times with totemic significance, that is lavished upon wooden shields and commemorative tablets, carved coconut-shell cups, bamboo boxes, bark belts, wooden spatulas, paddles, spears, dancing shields and dancing sticks, ceremonial masks — all objects of everyday and ceremonial use. In the great *ravi*, or men's house (for the women and children live in small family houses), hang many of the shields and tablets (Fig. 405B), elliptical in shape and painted or carved in designs which commemorate some event or have a totemic meaning. Ample timber provides suitable material, which is felled and roughly shaped by stone axes, adzes, and chisels and finally carved by stone, shell, teeth, or boar's tusk. The boldness of the ornament results partly from the designs themselves and partly from the use of contrasting

[A] *Carved Cocoanut Shell. Melanesian. Chicago Natural History Museum. (Chicago Natural History Museum) On the opposite side the shell is cut away to form a hemispherical cup with a handle left spanning the middle.*

[B] *Head of an Orator's Staff. Maori. University Museum, Philadelphia. (University Museum) Besides carving and inlays of abalone shell many staves were decorated with sleeves of bright-colored feathers and tassels of hair. They were carried by chiefs as insignia of rank.*

color. For after the wood is carved it is painted red or black and the incisions are filled with lime. The masks are made from the bright feathers of tropical birds; or from bark cloth (the tapa of the Polynesians) stretched over a light frame and painted in black, white, red, and yellow — colors which are obtained from the native soil and from shells and charcoal. These masks play a prominent part in initiation ceremonies and at religious festivals, where they represent ancestors or bear a totemic significance. Rising loftily above the mass of shredded palm leaves or grasses that covers the figure of the wearer, they produce a startling effect in the tropical surroundings. The decorative motifs used by the Melanesians show an almost constant use of spiraling motifs opposed to sharp dentils and chevrons; of the human or animal face highly conventionalized; and of an infinite variety of geometric shapes and variations thereof adapted most skillfully to the space to be filled, with a sensitive regard for scale. In a *Cocoanut Shell* (Fig. 407A) contrasts, both of light and dark and of circular and angular motifs, together with the free, exuberant quality of the carving, produce a highly dramatic effect.

SUMMARY

The forms of "primitive art" often appear to the outsider to be merely conventional or highly abstract. On the contrary, these works of art are objects used in daily living, in ritual, and for magical purposes, and their designs are symbols of the spirit world. Hence they must be understood against a background of purpose and symbolism, and with some knowledge of a culture in which social, economic, religious, and esthetic factors are too tightly interwoven to warrant separation. Form and decorative motifs were determined, within broad limits, by tradition and available material, which in both Africa and Oceania was chiefly wood. In Africa, wood-carving attained a remarkable three-dimensional quality; in Polynesia it was a surface art, richly decorative, suavely elegant, with infinitely varied carvings covering the surfaces. This creative ability appears also in the varied play upon geometric motifs found in Polynesian tapa. Melanesian art, by contrast, though primarily decorative and totemic, is bolder and more colorful.

BIBLIOGRAPHY

Bell, Clive, *Since Cézanne*, Harcourt, Brace, 1922

Burkitt, Miles C., *South Africa's Past in Stone and Paint*, Macmillan, 1928

Clouzot, Henri, and Level, André, *L'art nègre et l'art océanien*, Paris, 1919

Cossío, Manuel Bartholomé, and Pijoán, José, *Summa Artis*, Vols. I–X Madrid, 1931–46: Vol. I

Covarrubias, Miguel, *Pageant of the Pacific*, Pacific House, San Francisco, 1939

Einstein, Carl, *Afrikanische Plastik*, Berlin, 1921

Firth, Raymond W., *Art and Life in New Guinea*, Studio, 1936

Fry, Roger Eliot, *Vision and Design*, Brentano's, 1924, "The Art of the Bushmen" and "Negro Sculpture"

Golden Gate International Exposition, 1939, *The Pacific Cultures*, Exposition, San Francisco, 1939

Guillaume, Paul, and Munro, Thomas, *Primitive Negro Sculpture*, Harcourt, Brace, 1926

Haddon, Alfred C., *The Decorative Art of British New Guinea*, Dublin, 1894

Holmes, John H., *In Primitive New Guinea*, Putnam, 1924

Lewis, Albert B., *Carved and Painted Designs from New Guinea*, Chicago Natural History Museum, 1931

———— *Decorative Art of New Guinea: Incised Designs*, Chicago Natural History Museum, 1925

Linton, Ralph, Wingert, Paul S., and d'Harnoncourt, René, *Arts of the South Seas*, Museum of Modern Art, 1946

Obermaier, Hugo, and Kühn, Herbert, *Bushman Art*, Oxford University Press, 1930

Portier, André, and Poncetton, François, *Les arts sauvages*, 2 vols., Paris, c. 1930

Reichard, Gladys A., *Melanesian Design: A Study of Style in Wood and Tortoiseshell Carving*, 2 vols., Columbia University Press, 1933

Sadler, Sir Michael Ernest, *Arts of West Africa*, Oxford University Press, 1935

Sweeney, James J., ed., *African Negro Art*, Museum of Modern Art, New York City, 1935

Sydow, Eckart von, *Die Kunst der Naturvölker und der Vorzeit*, Berlin, 1923

———— *Handbuch der afrikanischen Plastik*, Vol. I, Berlin, 1930

Tongue, M. Helen, *Bushman Paintings*, Oxford University Press, 1909

See also General Bibliography, pages 791–92.

American Art

23

MIDDLE AMERICAN ART

IN the Americas, we have already seen the rise of ancient cultures on both continents. In Middle America, the Maya and the Toltecs reached the highest level. For some reason as yet not satisfactorily explained, the First (Old) Empire of the Maya declined and the tribe moved from the tropical lowlands of Guatemala and Honduras northeast into the high rocky peninsula of Yucatan, where they built new cities and spread their influence over neighboring tribes. From the north, however, the Toltecs, hard-pressed by northern tribes, in particular the Aztecs, began, about the eleventh century, to infiltrate and then to predominate.

Mayan Art: The Second Empire

ARCHITECTURE AND SCULPTURE

IN Yucatan great new cities arose — Chichen Itzá, Uxmal, Labna — which, like those of the First Empire, were great ecclesiastical centers carefully laid out on a grandiose scale. At Chichen Itzá, the pyramid temple of El

Castillo[1] (Fig. 411A) rose above the nearby jungle to dominate the group. Four stairways, carefully oriented to the four cardinal points, lead up the nine terraces to the temple of Kukulcan, the Toltec Quetzalcoatl, god of the wind and rain, who became the patron god of the Maya as the influence of the Toltecs increased. These stairways spread out over the ground several feet beyond the lowest terrace, giving the structure an effect of unity with the earth.

Near *El Castillo* stands the *Temple of the Warriors* (Fig. 411B), a temple of Kukulcan but so named because of the figures of warriors carved on its piers. The approach to the temple is across a plaza and through a great open hall, the roof of which was supported by rectangular piers decorated with life-sized figures of priests and warriors in ceremonial costume, carved in low relief and painted in vivid color. The temple itself rests on a base of four terraces, each with a carved frieze, and is approached by a broad stairway with carved stone balustrades. At the entrance are feathered-serpent columns, and immediately before the doorway is a chacmool

[1] The castle or fort, a name given the temple by the Spanish explorers, who did not understand the function of the structure.

[A] *Nunnery, East Building. Uxmal. (Middle American Research Institute, Tulane University, New Orleans)*

figure.[1] On the façade are masks, with feathers spreading out in relief from the serpent heads in the round. All this carving was brilliantly painted, and, with the frescoes on the interior depicting domestic, military, and religious scenes, constituted an elaborate and brilliant decorative entity. When we see such structures as *El Castillo* and the *Temple of the Warriors* as a whole, in the midst of a luxuriant tropical setting, as places for the performance of elaborate rites and ceremonies by priests in still more elaborate costumes, when we see the surfaces of these geometrically simple sculptural masses lightly broken by a decoration whose teeming richness is organized, unified, and given emphasis by its linear quality and particularly by the use of color — when we see all this, we realize the entire unity and consistency of the whole.

At Chichen Itzá, and especially at Uxmal, is a secular type of building, the so-called palace. The *Nunnery* at Uxmal, for example, consists of four separate buildings (Fig. 410A) set about

[1] A half-reclining figure with a flat disk which may have been used for sacrifices. Such figures are relatively common in Middle American art.

a court, all on a broad platform. Each building is a long rectangular volume, whose walls are broken by doorways only (windows are very rarely found). Each is divided into a lower band broken by several doorways and faced with stone finely cut and laid, and an upper band of uninterrupted stonework. The design consists of an inverted triangular shape made up of bars set over against a uniform diaper pattern, with a series of masks over the main doorway, and at the corners hieroglyphs and masks with projecting hooked noses which round off the corners and thus break their angularity. This same type of decoration is even more intricate in the *Governor's Palace*, in which particularly fine unbroken stonework below effectively sets off the rich band above, whose chief motif is a bold fret pattern. These borders, except for the door and the end ornaments, are made of stone mosaic; that is, of small pieces of stone, each individual piece cut and fitted to its own place in the design, and set in mortar — a process involving an enormous amount of labor, both in the cutting, since stone tools only were available, and in the laying.

[A] *El Castillo, Pyramid Temple of Kukulcan. Chichen Itzá. H. 105 ft.; the base covers one acre. 13th or 14th cent. (Carnegie Institution of Washington)*

PAINTING

The work of the Mayan painter, like that of the sculptor, was closely coordinated with building. His work could hardly be separate, for most of the reliefs were colored. On the inside of the temples, however, the walls were smoothed and given a coat of fine plaster for true painting. Here the painter first outlined his figures in red, then filled in the areas with flat colors, and

[B] *Temple of the Warriors. Chichen Itzá. (Carnegie Institution of Washington)*

[A] *A Seacoast Mayan Village. Reconstructed fresco in the Temple of the Warriors. L. 12½ ft. (Carnegie Institution of Washington)*

finally outlined the figure again in black — a process (reminiscent of the *Ajanta Frescoes*) which makes line emphatic and tends to make the design two-dimensional. Figure 412A reproduces one of the wall paintings that is as informative in subject matter as it is decorative as a mural. Here is a *Seacoast Mayan Village*, with village folk going about their everyday life in their boats on the sea and around their huts on the land. Figures and objects are strongly outlined areas of contrasting color, placed one above the other, covering the surface without crowding and keeping it unified in one plane. Thus results an extraordinarily decorative pattern, informal in composition, made up of the conventions for water, boats, fish, trees, roofs, people, clearly differentiated because of the contrasting color yet definitely united because closely keyed in tone. The convention for trees lends itself particularly

to repetition with variety, for it consists of a trunk dividing into two branches which support two circular areas of foliage, different in detail to indicate different kinds of leaves.[1]

Another function of the painter was the making of codices, which, like the stele, recorded both religious and historical events. A codex was a long sheet of deer hide or maguey paper, about six inches wide, which folded up accordion-wise and was protected by wooden covers. Unfortunately only three Maya codices are in existence, owing to the overzealous Spanish friars who, in an effort to destroy "paganism," burned them, as the T'sin of China had burned the Chinese classics.

[1] For a color reproduction see E. H. Morris, Jean Charlot, and A. A. Morris, *The Temple of the Warriors at Chichen Itzá, Yucatan,* 2 vols., Carnegie Institution, 1931. An abbreviated account, with two color plates, is given in the *News Service Bulletin* (School edition) of the Carnegie Institution, Vol. II, Nos. 17–21.

In one other field the work of the painter is evident. On a number of pieces of pottery scenes are pictured (we are reminded of Greek practice) in which can be seen not only the general style of painting but the draftsmanship of the Maya, the firm quality of his line as line, his skill in foreshortening, and his ability to express with line alone the mass of the figure.

Ceremony and ceremonial costume would naturally create a demand for objects of many materials and fine craftsmanship. A cursory glance at Mayan sculpture and painting would indicate a need for weavers, feather-workers, makers of jewelry and jade ornaments. Most of their work has disappeared, thanks again to the Spanish looting. Although the use of the wheel was unknown in all aboriginal America, Mayan ceramists constructed — by hand-shaping, coiling, and the use of molds — a great variety of pottery: figurines, effigy vases, and vessels of many shapes, the decoration on which might be painted, engraved, or in relief.

Zapotec and Mixtec Art

ARCHITECTURE
AND SCULPTURE

WEST of the Yucatan peninsula, in the province of Oaxaca in Mexico and close enough to Yucatan for mutual influences, lived the Zapotecs and the Mixtecs. Their culture, as old if not older than the Mayan, centered at Monte Alban (The White Mountain)[1] and at Mitla near by. For cen-

[1] Knowledge of this culture is recent and conclusions about it tentative, because the great discoveries at Monte Alban began only in 1931. Dr. Alfonso Caso, the discoverer and the director of excavation, is the chief authority in this field. Much of the area remains to be excavated.

turies these two tribes were at war with each other. The Zapotecs seem to have been the dominating element until toward the end of their life span, when the Mixtecs were in the ascendancy.

Though some influences of the Maya are evident, the Zapotecs were still highly original in their architecture. They built upon hills, for example, rather than on the plains — which presented the difficult problem of building on more than one level — and they grouped their buildings about a court from which broad stairways led to structures which seem to have functioned in religious ceremonies. At Mitla, in the so-called *Palace II*, a building whose function is uncertain, one can judge of the Zapotec style: a simple, long rectangular mass with walls unbroken by windows, like those of the Maya, but with an entirely different kind of ornament. Here are no mythological or naturalistic subjects. Sculpture is entirely eliminated. The long walls are broken into ribbonlike panels filled with a stone mosaic of purely geometric motifs which have the appearance of textile design. The tough yet easily worked stone of this vicinity lent itself well to this technique. The small pieces of stone, at most a few inches in size, were carefully cut and finished on the face, which projected only about one and one-half inches, with the back left rough and deeply triangular so as to adhere more firmly to the mortar bedding. There is great variety in the mosaic, and each panel is framed by finely cut stone bands, molded so as to produce an unbroken line of shadow, which holds the movement within the panel. This decorative scheme is carried out on the interior as well. As the building spreads at the base, like *El Castillo*, it gives the impression of being rooted firmly in the ground.

One aspect of life differentiates Za-

[A]   *Zapotec Effigy Urns. H. $7\frac{1}{4}$, $7\frac{1}{2}$, and $7\frac{3}{4}$ in. University Museum, Philadelphia. (University Museum)*

potecs and Mixtecs from the other tribes of Middle America — their attitude toward a future life, which manifests itself in innumerable tomb buildings and elaborate burial rites. The finest examples of Mixtec jewelry and carvings have been found in the tombs. At Monte Alban, the tomb was a small stone chamber, with painted walls and over the doorway a niche in which rested a funerary urn. The function of these urns is unknown, according to Dr. Caso, as nothing has been found in them. They may have contained offerings to the dead, such as liquids or substances that would have entirely disintegrated. A common design is made of a reddish clay in the form of an ornately garbed seated figure with crossed legs whose body is a cylindrical jar (Fig. 414A). Sometimes the face is naturalistic enough to suggest a portrait; again, it may be covered with a mask with long hooked nose and eyes of gleaming obsidian. The plumed headdress balances the broad base, and the whole figure is an inseparable part of the cylindrical jar. Here we see a virtuosity

in the use of clay as a plastic medium and in the interplay of cylindrical shapes.

GOLDWORK

The fabulous *Tomb 7*, discovered accidentally by Dr. Caso in 1932, plays the same role in the knowledge of Zapotec and Mixtec art that the tomb of Tutankhamun plays in Egyptian art. For here was found a great treasure which not only illustrates the elaborateness of the burial equipment but indicates an exquisite refinement in the culture that produced it. Here were gold and silver armlets and necklaces enriched with pearls and turquoise; gold pectorals; onyx and rock crystal vessels carved to unbelievable thinness; carvings in obsidian, jade, jet, and amber; and bone carved intricately with historical and mythological scenes. The origin of the goldworker's craft in the Americas is believed to have been in the northwestern corner of South America, for we note a diminishing number of examples as we move northward from

Central America, while from nearer areas in Central America, such as Panama, magnificent examples have come. The Mixtecs seem to have had great command over the use of gold, both technically and esthetically. A *Pectoral* (Fig. 415A) gives one the impression of filagree work, but is actually all made by the cire-perdue process. The total design is contained within a rectangular shape with rounding corners, and consists of an interplay of rectangular and circular motifs, straight and curving lines. The point of emphasis is the head, in high relief, which probably represents the death god; the rest of the pectoral is in low relief. The god wears a mask, a tiger or serpent helmet, a lofty headdress of quetzal feathers, and other ornaments.

Toltec and Aztec Art

THE Toltecs, at Teotihuacán, hard-pressed by wild hunters from the north, after a period of chaos were finally overwhelmed by a small but fiercely warlike tribe, the Aztecs, who arrived in the valley of Mexico about 1325, set up their capital at Tenochtitlan (now Mexico City), and became the dominant tribe of the region. They were as fierce in their religious as in their military practices, and carried to extremes human sacrifice, a practice generally followed by the Middle American peoples. As has already been noted, their religion demanded it. For, as the gods had sacrificed themselves to create man, man was under an obligation to requite the gods in like manner. And as the Aztecs were the chosen children of the sun god, they had laid upon them the peculiar obligation of supplying the god with nourishment — human blood. This ritual was carried out with gorgeous ceremonial, which required

[A]   *Gold Pectoral. From Tomb 7, Monte Alban. H. 4½ in. Museo Nacional, Mexico.* (*Museo Nacional*)

not only a fitting temple setting but equally magnificent costumes and accessories. In this, as in much of their culture, they appropriated from the Toltecs, as the Romans did from the Greeks.[1]

ARCHITECTURE AND SCULPTURE

Pyramid temples continued to be built, such as that at *Tenayuca*, many times rebuilt from Toltec to Aztec times, a double temple, dedicated to the sun god and some other god and hence with a double stairway leading up the pyramid to the temples. Fringing the base on a narrow platform is a row of massive stone serpents.

[1] For this reason it is difficult, at present, to separate the art of the Toltecs and the Aztecs. What we know of the Aztecs comes chiefly from the chronicles of the Spanish conquistadors. See W. H. Prescott, *History of the Conquest of Mexico*, Modern Library, 1936.

[A]   *Coatlicue (Lady of the Skirt of Serpents), Goddess of Earth and Death. Andesite. H. c. 8½ ft. Aztec. 15th cent. Museo Nacional, Mexico.*

It was in massive stonework that the Aztecs excelled, as well as in carving jade and other hard stones, and in mosaic inlay of turquoise, coral, and obsidian. Quite in contrast to the Mayan sculptors, who apparently were interested in surface richness, the Aztecs had a feeling for mass that was monumental and filled with savagely intense power. The Aztec's intensely religious nature, combined with his theocratic political organization, impelled him in this direction. An example is found in statues of *Coatlicue (Lady of the Skirt of Serpents)*, mother of the gods and earth goddess in the double role of creator and destroyer. Possibly the most forceful and savage is Figure 416A, a ponderous mass of stone shaped into the most elemental rectangular masses, upon which have been carved in both low and high relief the entwined serpents of the skirt, the necklace of hands and hearts with a skull pendant, the claw feet and hands, and the tusked mask — all of which are highly symbolic. This *Mother of the Gods* combines both savagery and tenderness, for out of destruction arises new life — an ideology analogous to that found in the Hindu dancing *Shiva* (Fig. 368A). Equally powerful masses of stone with conventional details and a strong tactile feeling are salient factors of Aztec animal sculpture.

That the Aztecs had a gift for surface enrichment as found in relief is seen in the *Calendar Stone*, a huge circular disk that stood before the *Temple of the Sun* in the central plaza of Tenochtitlan (now the civic center of Mexico City). It was placed in a horizontal position, probably for sacrificial use connected with the cult of the sun god. We feel a distinct orderliness in the rich carving. In the center is the face of the sun, from which radiate four squares which illustrate four former suns, or epochs, which were destroyed by tigers, wind, rain of fire, and flood. On either side of the sun god are claws clutching human hearts, symbolic of the fact that the sun god lives on human blood. Around this central group are concentric bands, which contain the days of the calendar, solar rays, ornaments, and the serpents who carry the sun across the sky and whose heads, at the base, hold human faces in their jaws. Every detail appears to have meaning, and it is all expressed with clarity and in a conventional form that enhances the stone's decorative quality.

BIBLIOGRAPHY

American Sources of Modern Art, Museum of Modern Art, New York City, 1933

Blom, Frans F., The Conquest of Yucatan, Houghton Mifflin, 1936

Brown, Frederick M., America's Yesterday, Lippincott, 1937

Caso, Alfonso, The Religion of the Aztecs, Mexico City, 1937

———————— Thirteen Masterpieces of Mexican Archaeology, tr. by Edith Mackie and Jorge R. Acosta, Mexico City, 1938

Davis, E. C., Ancient Americans, Holt, 1931

Gann, T. W. F., Ancient Cities and Modern Tribes, Scribner, 1926

———————— and Thompson, John E., The History of the Maya from the Earliest Times to the Present Day, Scribner, 1931

Holmes, W. H., Archaeological Studies among the Ancient Cities of Mexico, Field Columbian Museum, 1895–97; issued in parts

Joyce, Thomas A., Central American and West Indian Archæology, Putnam, 1916

Keleman, Pal, Medieval American Art, 2 vols., Macmillan, 1943

Lothrop, Samuel K., Pottery of Costa Rica and Nicaragua, 2 vols., Museum of the American Indian, Heye Foundation, New York City, 1926

MacCurdy, G. G., A Study of Chiriquian Antiquities, Yale University Press, 1911

Mason, Gregory, Columbus Came Late, Century, 1931

———————— Silver Cities of Yucatan, Putnam, 1927

Mason, John A., The Ancient Civilizations of Middle America, Bulletin of the University Museum, University of Pennsylvania, June 1943

The Maya and Their Neighbors, Appleton-Century, 1940

Médioni, Gilbert, and Pinto, Marie-Thérèse, Art in Ancient Mexico, Oxford University Press, 1941

Middle American Archaeology, Tozzer, Alfred M., "The Greater Cultures," Lothrop, Samuel K., "The Lesser Cultures," Bulletin of the Museum of Art, Rhode Island School of Design, Vol. XXIX, Nos. 1 and 2, 1941

Morris, Earl H., The Temple of the Warriors, Scribner, 1931

Saville, Marshall H., The Goldsmith's Art in Ancient Mexico, Museum of the American Indian, Heye Foundation, New York City, 1920

———————— Turquois Mosaic Art in Ancient Mexico, Museum of the American Indian, Heye Foundation, New York City, 1922

Spinden, Herbert J., Ancient Civilizations of Mexico and Central America, 3d ed. rev., American Museum of Natural History, New York City, 1943

———————— A Study of Maya Art, Peabody Museum, Cambridge, Mass., 1913

Thompson, John E., The Civilization of the Mayas, Chicago Natural History Museum, 1942

———————— Mexico before Cortez, Scribner, 1933

Toscano, Salvador, Arte precolombino de México y de la América Central, Mexico City, 1944

Totten, G. O., Maya Architecture, Maya Press, 1926

Tribes and Temples, 2 vols., Tulane University, 1926–27

Twenty Centuries of Mexican Art, Museum of Modern Art, New York City, 1940

Vaillant, George C., Artists and Craftsmen in Ancient Central America, guide leaflet 88, American Museum of Natural History, New York City, 1935

———————— The Aztecs of Mexico, Doubleday, Doran, 1941

Wiener, Leo, Mayan and Mexican Origins, Cambridge, privately printed, 1926

Willard, T. A., Bride of the Rain God, Burrows, 1930

———————— City of the Sacred Well, Century, 1926

[A] *Poncho. From an island in Lake Titicaca. Cotton and vicuña wool. H. 39 in. Red, green, black, buff, and violet with silver tinsel yarn in the border figures. Inca. American Museum of Natural History, New York City. (American Museum of Natural History)*

24

SOUTH AMERICAN INCA ART

WITH the decline of the Tiahuana-can Empire, the coastal Chimu and Nazca became independent, built great cities, such as Pachacamac and Chan Chan, and revived in particular their arts of weaving, pottery, and met-alwork.

In the highlands a remarkable growth took place through the efforts of the Incas, a small highland tribe who set up their rule in the valley of Cuzco, with the city of Cuzco as their

capital, and gradually extended their power until, in the early fifteenth century, it reached beyond the boundaries of the old Tiahuanacan Empire. It was a tolerant, benevolent rule, with religious practices free from the human sacrifices which characterize those of the Middle American peoples. Their religion centered about the worship of the powers of nature, primarily the sun, whose temple in Cuzco, the *Coricancha* (Place of Gold), was the most

[A] *Machu Picchu. Inca.* (*National Geographic Society — Yale University Peruvian Expedition. Copyright National Geographic Society*)

resplendent building in the Inca Empire. In their stark valley they wrung food from the barren soil by terracing the mountainsides, as the Peruvians do today.[1]

ARCHITECTURE

The Incas, even more than their Tiahuanacan predecessors, were supreme masters of cutting and fitting hard stone, a material that was plentiful in this high mountainous region. As a militant, conquering people, they selected sites fortified by nature, and strengthened them further by various structures for defense; as a religious people, they built temples, especially to the sun god, whose cult constituted the state religion; for their kings they

erected palaces befitting their status. Illustrative of their uncanny ability to select a naturally defended site and adapt it to function as a community, as well as of their amazing skill in masonry, is the city of *Machu Picchu*[2] (Fig. 419A), which is perched on a ridge between two jagged peaks high above the canyon of the Urubamba River in the heart of the Andes, some fifty miles north of Cuzco. Here in this isolated, wildly majestic environment the Incas built a city so ingeniously adapted to the site that it seems a part of the mountains themselves. At Sacsahuaman and Cuzco also are still to be seen the somber dark walls of the Inca temples and palaces, powerful walls made of precisely cut stone held firm — even in the curving walls of cylindrical structures — not by mortar but by cramps, a system of great advantage structurally in a land subject to earthquakes. From the esthetic viewpoint, they are highly

[1] As the Incas never invented a system of writing, our knowledge of them is derived from their works of art and artifacts and from the Spanish chroniclers. For the latter see P. A. Means, *Ancient Civilization of the Andes*, Scribner, 1931; *Pre-Columbian Art and Culture in the Andean Area, Bulletin of the Museum of Art*, Rhode Island School of Design, December, 1940; and W. H. Prescott, *History of the Conquest of Peru*, Modern Library, 1936.

[2] Discovered and excavated by Hiram Bingham in 1911. See Hiram Bingham, *Machu Picchu, a Citadel of the Incas*, Yale University Press, 1930; and the *National Geographic Magazine*, April, 1913, and February, 1915.

[A]   *Alpaca. Of sheet silver modeled in re-poussé. H. 9 in. Inca. American Museum of Natural History, New York City. (American Museum of Natural History)*

impressive for their feeling of solidity, for their texture, and for their finely cut angles and meticulously precise joinings.[1] Instead of embellishing their temples and palaces with paintings and colored carvings such as we found in Middle America, the Incas relied upon the decorative element of a material so abundant and so characteristically their own — gold. Dark granite and gold — it was a combination befitting these highland people. Gold was also symbolic of the sun god. His temple, according to the Spanish chronicles, was covered on the interior with sheets of gold beaten thin and encrusted with emeralds — a decoration lavish beyond imagination. And temples throughout the Inca Empire gleamed similarly, though not to the same degree.

[1] When the Spaniards captured Cuzco, razed the city, and on its ruins built their cwn, they did not level all the thick stout Inca walls completely, but utilized them in the construction of their houses and churches — fortunately for our knowledge of Inca building.

TEXTILES AND METALWORK

Like the palaces and the temples, the garments of the people and their ceremonial costumes were designed starkly, usually with geometric motifs, occasionally representational. Figure 418A reproduces a poncho worked off into squares, each filled with a geometric motif which, by variations in color value and a stress upon diagonal line, vivifies an otherwise monotonous checkerboard design. The same simplicity, bordering on geometry, permeates the goldwork and silverwork that was produced, according to the chroniclers, in unbelievable quantities — ornaments and utensils of all kinds and sizes, as well as representational objects such as the *Alpaca* of Figure 420A. The smooth surfaces of the head and feet throw into contrast the vertical ridges of the metal (made by the repoussé process), which so effectively suggest the heavy wool of the animal and at the same time accent the characteristically long neck.

BIBLIOGRAPHY

American Sources of Modern Art, Museum of Modern Art, New York City, 1933
Bennett, Wendell C., *Chavin Stone Carving*, Yale Anthropological Studies, Yale University Press, 1942, Vol. 3
Bingham, Hiram, *Machu Picchu, a Citadel of the Incas*, Yale University Press, 1930
Brown, Frederick M., *America's Yesterday*, Lippincott, 1937
Joyce, Thomas A., *South American Archæology*, Putnam, 1912
Lehmann, Walter, and Doering, Heinrich, *The Art of Old Peru*, London, 1924
Lothrop, Samuel K., *Inca Treasure as Depicted by Spanish Historians*, Southwest Museum, Los Angeles, 1938
Markham, Sir Clements R., *The Incas of Peru*, 3d ed., Dutton, 1912
Mead, Charles W., *Old Civilizations of Inca Land*, 2d ed., American Museum of Natural History, New York City, 1935
Means, Philip A., *Ancient Civilizations of the Andes*, Scribner, 1931

Means, Philip A., *Pre-Columbian Art and Culture in the Andean Area*, *Bulletin* of the Museum of Art, Rhode Island School of Design, Vol. XXVIII, No. 3, Dec. 1940
——————— *A Survey of Ancient Peruvian Art*, Yale University Press, 1917
——————— *A Study of Peruvian Textiles*, Museum of Fine Arts, Boston, 1932
——————— *Peruvian Textiles*, Metropolitan Museum of Art, New York City, 1930
Posnansky, Arthur, *Tihuanacu, the Cradle of American Man*, tr. by James F. Shearer, 3 vols., Augustin, 1945
——————— *Tihuanacu y la civilización prehistórica en el altiplano andino*, La Paz, 1911
Radin, Paul, *Indians of South America*, Doubleday, Doran, 1942
Rowe, John H., *An Introduction to the Archaeology of Cuzco*, Peabody Museum, 1944
Stafford, Cora E., *Paracas Embroideries*, Augustin, 1941
Thompson, John E., *Archaeology of South America*, Chicago Natural History Museum, 1936
Wassermann-San Blas, B. J., *Cerámicas del antiguo Perú de la Colección Wassermann-San Blas*, Buenos Aires, 1938

25

NORTH AMERICAN ART

Pueblo Art

OF the many tribes inhabiting the great area north of the Rio Grande, the Pueblo (village) people reached the highest cultural level. They lived in the region about the Four Corners — where Colorado, Utah, New Mexico, and Arizona meet. This semiarid plateau is cut by canyons and buttes, an austere land of brilliant color and tremendous spaces. As far back as we can trace the tribe, they were nomadic hunters and seed-gatherers, known as the Basket Makers because of their skill in this craft. The introduction of maize, probably from Middle America, and later of beans and squash (possibly about A.D. 500) led them to a more settled life devoted to agriculture, to the building of permanent houses, to the making of pottery and textiles. The Pueblo culture reached its apogee in the Great Pueblo age (about 950–1300). Each village lived a self-contained communal life — nonindividualistic, profoundly religious, but not theocratic like the Mayan, the Aztec, and the Incan. They worshiped the powers of nature, especially those concerned with rain and fertility — winds, clouds, and rainbow — which they supplicated with elaborate ceremonial. All the daily activities of life — religious, social, industrial, creative — combined into an extraordinary unity. The planting of corn, for example, was a ritual; and prayers for rain were expressed not only in the chants and dances, but also in the costumes of the dancers and in textiles and ceramics.

ARCHITECTURE AND PAINTING

In contrast to the Middle and South American peoples, the Pueblos built no great religious centers and no temples, despite their deeply religious character. Except for the parts of the ceremony which took place in an under-

[A] *Wall Painting from a Kiva. Awatovi, Arizona. Detail from a continuous decorative band. Replica. (Museum of Modern Art)*

ground room, the kiva, their ritual was performed in the open, with elaborate costuming, chanting, and dancing. So their architecture was confined to building houses, and to protecting these from the marauding nomads, even to the point of providing entrance by ladder only. Their materials were the local sandstone, adobe, and timber. The stonework was remarkable, considering that they possessed stone tools only and no draft animals. In the canyons, reaching up into the mesas, they found well-protected natural caverns large enough to house an entire community. Such are the hundreds of

cliff villages of the *Mesa Verde* (Green Tableland), so named because of its unusually thick covering of piñon). *Cliff Palace* (a name given by its discoverers), for example, occupies a cavern high above the valley floor. It consists of about two hundred round or rectangular rooms built of stone that was laid with great skill, or of adobe and timber, many of them several stories high. These constitute a communal domicile. Along the outer edge of the cavern floor are about twenty circular kivas. Not all Pueblo houses were built in caverns. On the contrary, villages rose in the river valleys, as in

[B] *Hopi Jar. Sikyatki ware. Red and black on yellow. D. 13 in. H. 7 in. 16th cent. National Museum, Washington. (Bureau of Ethnology, Smithsonian Institution)*

the *Chaco Canyon* with its eighteen or more major and innumerable minor villages. Along the river bottom the villagers farmed by irrigation, and in the kivas and the courts they carried out elaborate ceremonials to supplicate the gods for rain and abundant harvests. *Pueblo Bonito* (Beautiful Village), one of the largest and wealthiest, consisted of nearly a thousand rooms built on a semicircular plan about a court, and terraced back from one story in front to five at the back, which abutted the canyon wall. In the court were large kivas, which, together with those of *Chetro Ketl* (Rain Village), illustrate in their walls a climax of stonework. For the highest skill was expended on the construction of the kiva, a sacrosanct structure in which were performed the most sacred parts of the ritual on which not only the welfare but the very existence of the people were believed to depend.

Sometimes the walls were made of large smooth blocks of the local sandstone, smoothed on the face and laid in courses rather far apart, the interstices being filled with small thin chips — all laid in adobe mud; or of squarely cut blocks rather uniform in size and evenly laid. In some of the kivas, the curving wall demanded expert cutting, especially when we recall that only stone tools were known. In addition, when corners of large stones alternate with those of smaller ones, the decorative and textural effects, combined with precise laying, result in an unusually beautiful wall surface. Sometimes the walls of the kiva were painted, as recent excavations have shown, in a highly conventional though at times a naturalistic style. Figure 422A is a part of a continuous band running around the walls of a kiva, and seems to represent some ceremony. In fact, some of the details of the costumes are almost identical with those worn by these peo-

[A] *Mimbres Bowl. Black on white. D. c. 9 in. 13th cent. Peabody Museum, Harvard University. (Peabody Museum)*

ple in ceremonies today. It is an art of line, and light and dark color, on a flat surface, predominantly angular, as though influenced by textile designs, with no background and no accessories to detract from the directness of the presentation. It is thus extraordinarily decorative. But it was in costuming and personal adornment that the love of color and embellishment found expression in a contrasting setting furnished by the simple, almost barren architecture.

BASKETRY AND POTTERY

Early in their culture the Pueblos were expert in making finely coiled baskets for household and burial use and in inventing designs in red and black with zigzag, terrace, and other geometric motifs. The early black and white pottery, with an angular textile-like design not always suitable for curving surfaces, or with the constructional coils left unsmoothed, suggests an origin in basketry. Ceramics was a major art in all the Southwest, and an art whose practice, like that of basketry, was strictly confined to the women. It was a utilitarian art, whose function was to provide the water jars, and the storage and serving vessels necessary to everyday life. All pottery was made by the coiling method, for the wheel was unknown. Different pueblos developed individual styles, of which the *Sikyatki* ware is noteworthy (Fig. 422B). It consisted chiefly of large bowls with a broad flattened shoulder, and shallow bowls made of a yellow or orange clay decorated with geometric designs or highly conventional birds and animals in red or brown. Here again is seen a predilection for angularity in design, though the *Sikyatki* ware combines the curved and the angular with peculiar felicity in the designs within the shallow bowl. A unique ceramic expression one finds in *Mimbres* pottery. The black-and-white food bowls of this ware are decorated with figures of birds, insects, fish, and even human figures, drawn with a vivacious naturalism but with a conventionalization sufficient for filling the space (Fig. 423A).

Hopewell Art

OF the other cultures found north of the Rio Grande, we should at least mention one of the Eastern woodland groups, the Hopewell, which centered in Ohio, but was widespread in the eastern United States.[1] We know relatively little of these people in comparison with our knowledge of the Pueblos. Among the Pueblos, the most imposing art expression was the communal village, together with the objects essential for communal living;

among the Hopewells, great mounds and earthworks and the ceremonial objects placed in them.[2] Some of the mounds served for burial, and in these the finest works of art have been found; some were foundations for temples or domiciles; and some, perhaps the most spectacular, were effigies, such as the *Great Serpent Mound*. All the mounds probably had some social or religious function or, as in the case of the earthworks, a defensive role. Of the objects found in the mounds, the copper ornaments and stone sculpture are noteworthy. Copper, secured from the Lake Superior region, was hammered, cut, engraved, or embossed by the repoussé method into various ornaments with geometric and conventionalized human, bird, and animal motifs handled with rare ability in two-dimensional designing. At the same time the Hopewell people, unlike the pictorial-minded Pueblos, were sculptors. Stone pipes, carved with flint tools into the shape of birds and human and animal figures (Fig. 425A), show great vitality in forms generally naturalistic but tempered by material, size, and adaptation to function. Their carved shell gorgets and stone disks reveal in their designs a contact with Middle America.

SUMMARY

While the Eurasian civilizations of antiquity were evolving into the medieval cultures, and in the process were making more intimate contacts one with another, the American continents remained isolated and unknown to Europe, and their cultures evolved with merely regional contacts through trade, infiltration, and conquest. The

[1] This culture derives its name from the owner of a site in Ohio where the remains of it were first discovered and where some of its finest products have been found.

[2] The theory that the "Mound Builders" were one coherent people who preceded the Indian is no longer held. Mound-building was characteristic of many aboriginal groups in the Eastern half of the United States.

[A]   *Tobacco Pipe in the Form of a Wolf. Soapstone. L. 10½ in. Hopewell. Ohio State Museum, Columbus. (Ohio State Museum)*

Maya, after abandoning their cities in Guatemala and Honduras, moved into Yucatan, where they built great ecclesiastical centers with pyramid temples and secular buildings having lavish decorations, colorful and suavely curvilinear. They made pottery, richly warm in color, which was influential, probably through trade, among their neighbors. The Zapotecs and the Mixtecs were builders of stone "palaces" and tombs with a highly individual type of decoration, stone mosaic; they were masters of clay sculpture; and they produced jewelry and other objects of gold, turquoise, and jade intricately carved, all of great elegance and refinement and of high technical skill. In the Valley of Mexico, the Toltecs, the most gifted people in this area, were overwhelmed by the militant Aztecs, who appropriated much of the Toltec culture. Both built massive pyramid temples and were master stonecutters. The Aztecs in particular produced massive stone sculpture with an almost savage forcefulness. In South America, the highest level was reached by the Incas, who were masters in stonework, in erecting fortifications, and temples

and palaces with magnificently cut masonry and ablaze, on the interior, with gold and jewels. They were also expert in fashioning objects of gold and silver and in weaving. All of these cultures succumbed in the sixteenth century to the invading Spaniards.

North of the Rio Grande were two outstanding cultures: the Pueblo and the Hopewell. The Pueblos, instead of erecting temples, built great communal domestic structures, developed a high level of pottery and weaving, and found expression religiously in costume and in ceremonials performed largely out of doors. The Hopewell peoples built imposing mounds for social, religious, and defense purposes. They were skilled designers of copper ornaments, and carved stone pipes based on bird, human, and animal figures, which tended in the direction of naturalism but were conventionalized enough for their function.

BIBLIOGRAPHY

Brown, Frederick M., *America's Yesterday*, Lippincott, 1937
Chapman, Kenneth M., *Pueblo Indian Pottery*, 2 vols., Nice, France, 1933 and 1936

Clarke, Eleanor P., *Designs on the Prehistoric Pottery of Arizona, Social Science Bulletin No. 9*, May 15, 1935, University of Arizona

Douglas, Frederic H., ed., *The Indian Leaflet Series*, Denver Art Museum, Denver, Colo., 1930–44

———— and d'Harnoncourt, René, *Indian Art of the United States*, Museum of Modern Art, New York City, 1941

Hewett, Edgar L., *Ancient Life in the American Southwest*, Bobbs-Merrill, 1930

———— *The Chaco Canyon and its Monuments*, University of New Mexico Press, 1936

Jenness, Diamond, *The Indians of Canada*, Ottawa, 1932

Kidder, Alfred V., *An Introduction to the Study of Southwestern Archaeology*, Yale University Press, 1924

———— and others, *The Pottery of Pecos*, Vol. I, 1931, Vol. II, 1936, Yale University Press

Krieger, Herbert W., *Aspects of Aboriginal Decorative Art in America, Annual Report*, 1930, Smithsonian Institution, Washington, D.C., 1931

Mason, Otis T., *Aboriginal American Basketry, Annual Report*, 1902, Smithsonian Institution, Washington, D.C., 1904

The Maya and Their Neighbors, Appleton-Century, 1940

Morris, Ann A., *Digging in the Southwest*, Doubleday, Doran, 1933

Morris, Earl H., *Archaeological Studies in the La Plata District*, Carnegie Institution of Washington, 1939

Roberts, Frank H. H., Jr., *A Survey of Southwestern Archeology, Annual Report*, 1935, Smithsonian Institution, Washington, D.C., 1936

Shetrone, Henry C., *The Mound-Builders*, Appleton, 1930

Vaillant, George C., *Indian Arts in North America*, Harper, 1939

Wissler, Clark, *Indians of the United States*, Doubleday, Doran, 1940

———— *The American Indian*, 3d ed., Oxford University Press, 1938

Part Three

[A]   *Botticelli. Birth of Venus. c. 1485. Uffizi, Florence. (Alinari)*

RENAISSANCE ART

WORLD PANORAMA

THE five-hundred-year period from about 1400 to 1900 witnessed the rise of the Renaissance movement in Italy, its spread to all the countries of Europe, including Russia, and its decentralization to the Americas and other parts of the world. In these movements, the partitions of cultural areas began to break and the world to shrink strikingly in the direction of closer unity. Revival and expansion of scientific knowledge stimulated travel and exploration to search for new routes to secure the luxuries of the East. With the accidental discovery of America, expeditions set forth from many of the European nations with various motivations, but all with a desire to secure a share of the wealth — not now of the East, but of the New World, though a passage to the East was still a desirable objective. Europe and America now became united, in that the European nations expanded into colonial empires to which European civilizations were transplanted. The colonists went to varying environments. In the Americas they encountered indigenous cultures which were dissimilar in ideology and form from their own. Where the Indians were not exterminated or pushed back into the interior, the impact of the one group on the other produced the American-European art of the Colonial age.

Exploration and colonization were not confined, however, to the Americas. To Africa and the Far East the trading companies set forth. In China, after a renascence in the Ming dynasty, flamboyancy and decay were accelerated until, with the end of the Ch'ien Lung period, 1796, no art was produced that could be called noteworthy. India also experienced the decline of the Mogul Empire and generally decadent, unsettled conditions. Japan went into isolation in 1638, but within its own confines continued creative activity. Infiltration of Europeans into the Far East began with the trading companies, who established themselves at ports for economic advantage only, without any attempt either to transplant European culture, as did the colonists in the Americas, or to understand the cultures with which they made contact. To be sure, traders brought home various products which led to the vogue of chinoiserie in France and England; to the manufacture of true porcelain in Germany and France; to the appearance of Chinese motifs in Mexican pottery; to the use of lacquer in furniture and of Chinese wallpaper. With the arrival of the Jesuits in China in the seventeenth century, however, a sincere beginning was made to understand something of the nature of the Oriental civilization. But it was only a beginning, and whatever contacts resulted were superficial, a mere opening of the door to the great arts of the East, which were to be known only in the late nineteenth and the twentieth centuries.

Renaissance Art in Italy

RENAISSANCE (literally, "Rebirth") is the accepted though too restricted name given the complex movement that began stirring Italy in the thirteenth and fourteenth centuries, reached a climax there in the fifteenth and sixteenth,[1] and spread with different manifestations over Europe. Out of its complexity at least two general aspects emerge which affect its art expression: the discovery and enjoyment of the individual and his world, and the revival of classical culture. The trend in the Gothic age from the transcendent to the empirical, manifested in an increasing naturalism and given great impetus in Italy by Saint Francis and the Franciscan movement, eventually turned the tide of thought from the medieval point of view, which focused upon a future life, to a realization of the value of man in his actual present and to a vision of the delights and beauties of this life. This humanistic and individualistic point of view found a great source of stimulation in the Humanistic classical literature, philosophy, and art, whose study was one of the intense passions of the day.

The Renaissance, then, meant essentially a new attitude toward life, which led to a development of the individual, a greater freedom of thought, and a consequent curiosity about man and his

world. Hence we find ourselves in an age of scientific research and invention. The introduction of gunpowder, probably early in the fourteenth century, changed methods of warfare; the invention of the printing press, about the middle of the fifteenth century, meant the gradual substitution of printed books for manuscripts. Interest in man's surroundings naturally led to voyages of travel and discovery, such as those of Columbus (1492–1504), which had been prompted by the earlier journeys of Marco Polo in China (1260–1295) and by the tales that he brought back of the fabulous riches of the East. The result of such voyages was a wider knowledge of geography; colonization; and the development of commerce, with the wealth that followed. Leonardo da Vinci (1452–1519), with insatiable curiosity about man, animals, plants, and mechanical devices, attacked great engineering problems, even discovering some of the principles of flying machines and submarines. Copernicus, the Polish astronomer (1473–1543), rediscovered the revolution of the Earth and the planets about the Sun, a concept that had been lost since the Greeks; and Galileo (1564–1642), watching a swaying lamp in the cathedral of Pisa, deduced from its movement the law of the pendulum.

This freedom of thought was often opposed by the Church, which saw in it the undermining of its authority. The early Renaissance, largely medieval, still shared the fervor of the preceding

---

[1] The evolution of the Renaissance falls roughly into divisions marked by the centuries in their Italian names: Dugento (thirteenth), Trecento (fourteenth), Quattrocento (fifteenth), Cinquecento (sixteenth).

centuries, under the stimulation of the two great monastic orders founded in the thirteenth century — the Franciscan and the Dominican; and the religious and the secular were inseparably interwoven. But with the new freedom, secularization and revolt against authority, especially in the face of the pomp and circumstance and at times intrigue and profligacy of the papal court, brought about on the one hand reform within the Church and on the other skepticism; a break in the social solidarity of the Middle Ages; and a growing emphasis upon secular life.

Socially, democratic tendencies led toward an equalization of classes and with the advent of cheap printed books, toward more nearly equal opportunities for education. The social ideal was the many-sided gentleman, and toward its attainment were produced such remarkable individuals as Leon Battista Alberti[1] and Leonardo da Vinci.

Politically, it was an age of turmoil. For the communes found it necessary to ally themselves with one or the other ruling power, the Papacy or the Empire; they fought each other fiercely for commercial advantage, and within their own walls kept up local warfare over the lordship of the commune. These lords — tyrants, as they were known — were frequently enlightened paternal rulers; frequently they were not. In either case, many of them were remarkable personalities with equal capacity for war, business, and culture.

Notwithstanding the enthusiasm and the prolific accomplishments of the Renaissance, its contributions to science, its great outburst of expression in literature, music, all the arts, and in the amenities of outward life, there is the contrasting picture of its brutality and violence, profligacy, treason, poisonings, and assassinations.

The heart of the Renaissance was Florence (Fig. 431A): "Fair and gay Florentine city, the fount of valor and joy, flower of cities, Fiorenza . . . [yet in appearance] proud and dark and threatening . . . her hundred and fifty great towers and her battlemented walls surrounded by a moat, against a somber background of hills not yet brightened by houses and olive gardens but covered with cypresses, oak, ash, and fir trees." [2] This walled, compact city with narrow streets and tall threatening towers was a thriving commercial center, and its bankers and cloth-finishers were known all over Europe for their shrewdness as well as for their products. Florence prospered amazingly though it fought continuously, if not with Pisa and Siena for commercial supremacy, at home over local politics, for it had no gift for managing its civic affairs. Whatever stability it had was due largely to its highly organized guilds,[3] whose power extended far beyond the limits of industry. The noble families, each keen for power, kept the city in a turmoil with their feuds, not at all deterred by the sight of the bodies of the vanquished hanging in the public square or, hardly less gruesome, painted on the walls of the palace of the chief magistrate. This last became the custom, so that one artist commissioned to paint these effigies after one of the periodic uprisings won for himself the name "Andrea of the Hanged."

In spite of these frequent upheavals, the various activities of life continued uninterrupted and with amazing vitality. The people were industrious and

[1] For a brief statement, see J. C. Burckhardt, *The Civilization of the Renaissance in Italy*, Harper, 1929, pp. 149 ff. For a contemporary discussion of this ideal, see Baldassare Castiglione, *The Book of the Courtier*, Scribner, 1903.

[2] Guido Biagi, *Men and Manners of Old Florence*, McClurg, 1909, p. 16.

[3] See J. E. Staley, *Guilds of Florence*, McClurg, 1906, for a full description of the guilds as well as interesting illustrations.

ambitious; intellects were keen and quick; anything mediocre failed to satisfy.[1] For this reason the sculptor Donatello refused to remain in Padua after he had completed his commissions there with great success, because, he said, he was too much praised by Paduans and felt the need of the continual censure of the Florentines as an incentive to greater excellence.

Thus the city flourished materially and flowered culturally. Outwardly, life was festive.[2] The great palaces of the nobles (Fig. 438A), though massive and fortresslike for defense, contained many comforts and luxuries. Festivals and pageants of various kinds were frequent.[3] Now we hear of an Adoration of the Magi or an Annunciation; now of an Age of Gold or the Car of Death. Jousts and weddings not only furnished entertainment for the people, but together with the pageants kept the artists busy decorating banners, fashioning jewelry,[4] painting the marriage chests, designing scenery, costumes, and cars for the festivals — all of which in turn quickened the fancy.

The artist, with the Church, the nobles, and the wealthy merchants thus in constant need of his wares, had a place as well defined and as natural as that of the silk merchant, the butcher, or the baker. Supply and demand presented no problem. An artist was a versatile craftsman, and specialization was the exception, not the rule. His

[1] Read the introductory paragraphs to Vasari's life of Perugino.
[2] George Eliot's *Romola* furnishes a fairly accurate picture of Florentine life in the fifteenth century. For contemporary illustrations of everyday life, see Paul Kristeller, *Early Florentine Woodcuts*, London, 1897; Burckhardt, *op. cit.*; Julia Cartwright, *Isabella d'Este*, Dutton, 1903, 2 vols.; and J. A. D.-G. Ross, *Florentine Palaces and Their Stories*, Dutton, 1905.
[3] See G. B. Brown, *The Fine Arts*, Scribner, 1927, Pt. I, Chap. III, for a description.
[4] See Benvenuto Cellini's *Autobiography*, Modern Library, 1927.

[A]   *Italy. Centers of Renaissance Art.*

shop was a place where a patron could come to consult about building a palace or carving a statue or painting an altarpiece or decorating the walls of a chapel; where he could order a jewel set in a miter, a chest carved and

[A] *Nicola d'Apulia. Pulpit in the Baptistery of the Cathedral of Pisa. 1260.* (*Alinari*)

painted, a banner decorated with the family heraldic device, costumes and properties made for pageants and church festivals, books illuminated, and tapestries designed for a palace or a church.

Training for such versatility was acquired through the apprentice system.[1] Each well-known artist had a shop, a *bottega*, as it was called — there may have been from twenty to thirty in Florence — and to the artist a boy was apprenticed when he was ten or twelve years old. He spent his time grinding the colors, preparing the gold, transferring the cartoons (the master's pre-

liminary drawings) to the panel or wall, preparing the panel of seasoned wood for a painting. In this way years were spent in laying a solid foundation of craftsmanship. As the apprentice became proficient in the fundamentals of these crafts, he was permitted to work somewhat more independently and even trusted to paint minor parts of a great altarpiece or to make the jewel-set brooch, according to his master's design; and finally, after many years of such training he might leave his master's shop to set up one of his own.

For the public and officialdom, art was a matter of civic interest and enthusiasm. The archives of fifteenth-century Florence reveal to us what a great amount of time the city council spent upon art projects, such as the competition for the dome to be erected on the *Cathedral*, or the bronze doors for the *Baptistery*, or the location of Michelangelo's statue of *David*. And the people as a whole felt and appreciated art as a vital part of life, so that much of the art criticism came from the masses. When Ghiberti was making his plaque in the competition for the doors of the *Baptistery*, he invited people to come to his shop and criticize his work as it progressed. When Leonardo had made his cartoon of the *Madonna with Saint Anne*, "the chamber wherein it stood was crowded for two days by men and women, old and young — a concourse, in short, such as one sees flocking to the most solemn festivals, all hastening to behold the wonders produced by Leonardo and which awakened amazement in the whole people."[2] When Duccio's *Majèsta* was completed, there was a holiday in Siena, and a great procession of priests and citizens in holiday dress, with candles and the

<hr>

[1] See Cennino Cennini, *The Book of the Art of Cennino Cennini*, London, 1922; Brown, *op. cit.*, sections on a Florentine workshop, Pt. I, Chap. III; and E. H. and E. W. Blashfield, *Italian Cities*, new ed., Scribner, 1912, "The Florentine Artist."

[2] Giorgio Vasari, *Lives of Seventy of the Most Eminent Painters, Sculptors, and Architects*, tr. by E. H. and E. W. Blashfield and A. A. Hopkins, Scribner, 4 vols., 1913, Vol. II, p. 393.

sound of bells and musical instruments, carried the altarpiece to its place in the cathedral.

The general appearance of the city had a stimulating effect upon both the people and the artists. In their love for it and in their pride, the Florentines adorned their city with works by the greatest artists, many of which were placed in view of the public along the thoroughfares and in the open squares. At the entrance of the municipal palace facing the piazza stood Michelangelo's *David;* niches in *Giotto's Tower* and *Or San Michele* held statues made by Donatello, Ghiberti, and Verrocchio; Ghiberti's *Gates of Paradise* faced the cathedral piazza, in the heart of the city; along a narrow street was a lunette filled with a Luca della Robbia *Madonna and Child* in rich blue-and-white glazed terra cotta, or a painted terracotta *Nativity* by Donatello; just inside the churches and the monasteries were great cycles of mural paintings; above all soared the powerful lines of Brunelleschi's dome. With mind and eye trained by daily acquaintance with all these, it is little wonder that the average Florentine was a keen art critic.

[A]   *Arnolfo di Cambio. Detail from the Baldacchino of St. Paul's Outside the Walls (Fig. 2534), Rome. 1285. (Alinari)*

26

ARCHITECTURE AND SCULPTURE

(ABOUT 1300–1600)

DURING the Dugento and the Trecento, and well into the Quattrocento, the Gothic style of architecture prevailed, modified by climatic conditions and by the tenacity of the Romanesque because of its peculiar suitability to Italy. In these centuries commercial expansion and material prosperity stimulated a large amount of building, civic as well as ecclesiastical: *San Francesco,* Assisi; *Cathedral* and *Palazzo Pubblico,* Siena; *Cathedral,* Orvieto; *Cathedral, Santa Croce, Santa Maria Novella, Bargello,* and *Palazzo Vecchio,* Florence; *Ducal Palace,* Venice; *Cathedral,* Milan; *San Petronio,* Bologna.

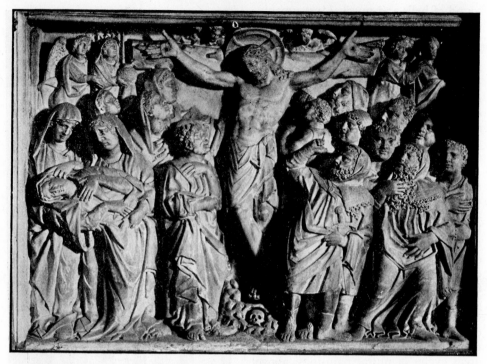

[A]   *Nicola d'Apulia. Crucifixion. From the pulpit in the Pisan Baptistery (Fig. 432A). 1260.*
(*Alinari*)

In the thirteenth and fourteenth centuries sculpture also was largely medieval, an integral part of the structure. Yet new forces were already affecting its character, earlier than that of building itself. For Nicola d'Apulia (Nicola Pisano; about 1206–1278), a sculptor who had been trained in southern Italy, where one of the earliest of classical revivals was in full swing, began working in Pisa, Siena, and Perugia. His *Pisan Pulpit* (Fig. 432A) combines Romanesque, Gothic, and classical elements. The panel reliefs (Fig. 434A) are crowded with quiet, imposing figures, flattened to maintain the frontal plane, and though Roman in type,[1] they achieve a decorative quality by the use of a conventional treatment of details. A fresh observation of nature, however, and a certain solidity in the figures are new notes.

In the work of Nicola's son, Giovanni (about 1250–1330), the discretion of Nicola, so truly sculptural in its effect, was submerged in tumultuous movement [2] (Fig. 435A). Through the restless groups rapid movement rushes hither and thither. In detail each figure, compared with Nicola's, is small in scale, and dynamically alive. Here Gothic naturalism and intricate linealism burst the bonds of architectural demands, but contributed to the evolving tradition a dynamic living quality. A comparison of Giovanni's *Madonna* in

[1] Nicola's immediate inspiration seems to have been late Roman sarcophagi, examples of which were to be seen in Pisa.

[2] Note the style of both these Pisani in the *Siena Pulpit* and in the *Perugia Fountain*, on which they collaborated.

[A] *Giovanni Pisano. Crucifixion. From the pulpit at Pistoia. 1298–1301. (Alinari)*

Padua with the *Vierge Dorée* at Amiens illustrates well Giovanni's use of the Gothic sweep of line.

Quite in contrast to Giovanni's confused agitation are the clarity, the calm rhythms, and the architectural fitness in every detail of the tombs and ciboria of Arnolfo di Cambio (died 1302; Fig. 433A). They show a perfect unity of various materials and forms — Gothic motifs, colorful Cosmati work and colored marbles, and highly decorative refined sculpture. Gothic linealism, again, marks the work of Lorenzo Maitani (about 1275–1330) in the low reliefs on the façade of the *Orvieto Cathedral* (Fig. 437A).

Sculpture seems to have been more actively pursued outside of Florence until another Pisano, Andrea (about 1270–1348), was commissioned by the Florentines to make a set of bronze doors for the *Baptistery* (Fig. 436A). Andrea

made his doors decorative by means of a repeated geometric motif, one found in Gothic sculpture and illuminations, within which he placed low reliefs of simple composition with smoothly flowing lines, admirably adapted to the spaces and in no way detracting from the main decorative pattern. In his reliefs on the *Campanile* of the *Cathedral* one feels the largeness of Nicola's style and the dynamic force of Giovanni's, plus an accomplishment in design not met before. The adequacy of design to material as illustrated in the bronze reliefs of the *Baptistery Doors* is paralleled by the stone carvings of the *Campanile* (Fig. 441A). The amplitude of the forms, which are based upon a direct observation of nature, their clear placement in shallow space, and their highly sensitive relation to the hexagonal shape seem to point to an influence upon Andrea of his contemporary

[A] *Andrea Pisano. South Doors of the Baptistery, Florence. Bronze. In the panels are scenes from the life of St. John, and allegorical figures. 1330. (Alinari)*

Giotto, who designed the *Campanile* and probably carved some of the reliefs.

In the fifteenth century the builders, whose eyes opened to the material remains of the ancient civilization that lay everywhere about them, began to study these ancient monuments as the Humanists were eagerly perusing the literature of the same culture. When the young Brunelleschi went to Rome with his friend Donatello[1] he was struck with amazement, and eagerly spent day and night among the ruins, drawing ground plans, vaults, cornices, and moldings. As a result of this new interest in classical remains, the architects began to introduce into their buildings classical decorative motifs, cornices, and stringcourses, and thus freely intermingled the old and the new with a freshness and at times a daring that are indicative of the free attitude of the early Renaissance.

This daring is characteristic of the young Filippo Brunelleschi (1379–1446) in his design for the dome of the *Cathedral of Florence* (Fig. 439A), which though not original in construction,[2] sounds a

[1] Read the account of this in Vasari's lives of Brunelleschi and Donato (Donatello).

[2] Read the account of the building in Vasari's life of Brunelleschi.

[A] *Lorenzo Maitani (?). Scenes from Genesis. Façade of Orvieto Cathedral. Early 14th cent. (Alinari) Maitani designed the façade and directed, if he did not actually share in, the carving of the reliefs.*

distinctive new note in its scale and external effectiveness. To roof a structure with a dome had been accomplished successfully many times before, notably in the *Pantheon* (Fig. 177A) and *Santa Sophia* (Fig. 259A); but a comparison of these two domes with that at Florence reveals at once a sharp difference — namely, that the former are partly concealed from the exterior view and aim at interior effect chiefly; the latter purposely emphasizes the exterior, to dominate not only the cathedral but the city. This dome is octagonal in shape, and rises from an octagonal base pierced with circular windows. The great stone ribs rise with a curve of great beauty and strength to converge on the circular apex holding the lantern. Because of its size and

simple design, the dome dominates by its grandeur. It does not possess the mystic, aspiring quality of the Gothic cathedral, nor yet the perfect equilibrium of the Greek temple, but rather the frankly pagan note of the mastery of power. But its effectiveness is external only, for the interior effect of well-designed space, such as one finds in the *Pantheon* and *Santa Sophia*, is lost when a long nave renders visible but a small segment of the dome (Fig. 438B. See Figure 459A; contrast Figures 176A and 261A). A realization of this failure led the architects of the Renaissance to abandon the basilica plan of church in favor of the central type, which found its fullest expression in *St. Peter's* (Fig. 460B). Thus the essentially medieval *Cathedral of Florence* stated, without

[A] *Medici-Riccardi Palace. Florence. Built for the Medici, 1444, and later taken over by the Riccardi family. (Alinari)*

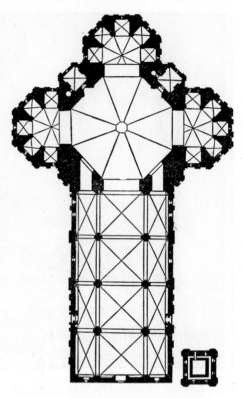

[B] *Cathedral of Florence.*

solving, one of the problems of church architecture of the Renaissance.

More characteristically Renaissance in design, and revealing direct inspiration from classical art, are the *Pazzi Chapel* of Brunelleschi (*Santa Croce*, Florence; Fig. 441B); *San Francesco* (Rimini); and *Sant' Andrea* (Mantua) by Alberti (1404–1472). In these one sees the classical balance of vertical and horizontal; round arches and arcadings; classical entablatures, pediments, and details; the combined use of the arch and lintel systems; and in *Sant' Andrea* the Roman triumphal-arch design with its triple division. Ornament is used sparingly and is quite subordinate to the quietly restrained design.

Another departure from medieval tradition was the greater attention given secular architecture, for, with the point of view shifted from aspiration for the

future to a consideration of the present, the palace and civic buildings claimed equal attention with the ecclesiastical structures. The early Renaissance is best illustrated by the Florentine palaces, those powerful piles of stone not only dignified but stern, for while feuds still menaced, a palace must serve as a fortress as well as a dwelling. In the compact city it stood flush with the street, and as a rule had but one doorway and only a few small windows in the massive ground story. For light and air it was built about an inner court. The *Medici-Riccardi Palace*, for example (Fig. 438A), built for Cosimo de' Medici by Michelozzo (1396–1472), is a simple massive structure whose strength is accentuated by the use of rusticated stone on the ground story.

[A] *Cathedral of Florence, or Santa Maria del Fiore (St. Mary of the Flower). So called because of the lily in the coat of arms of the city. 1296–1462. The present façade was added 1875–87. The design of the detached campanile is ascribed to Giotto.*

Its division into stories[1] by unbroken stringcourses, and its great cornice decorated with dentils, egg and dart, and acanthus, show classical influence; the mullioned windows flush with the wall, the great unbroken wall areas, medieval influence. In the *Rucellai Palace* (Florence) by Alberti, classical entablatures were added to each story, and pilasters between the windows. Thus in secular building as well as in ecclesiastical the fifteenth century was a century of transition, in which medieval forms were evolving, under the

impact of the revival of the classical culture and classical forms, into a new style.

A typical room in one of these Florentine palaces was spacious and dignified. The beamed ceiling was brightly painted, and the plastered walls, whose openings were without trim, furnished an unobtrusive background for the color accents of painted decorations or tapestries and majolica. An emphatic note was the fireplace with a high sloping hood. The furniture was simple and massive and consisted of only a few pieces, the most important of which was the great chest, or *cassone*, that served as a clothes closet, a storage place for the family plate or books, a seat, a bed, a table if high enough, and

[1] The great arches on the ground story, originally open entrances to a loggia, were later filled with windows in the style of the High Renaissance. The *Strozzi Palace* well illustrates an unbroken ground story.

[A] *Carving from the Ducal Palace, Urbino. 1468–82. Compare this Renaissance carving with the Roman decorative reliefs in Figs. 182A and B. (Alinari)*

[B] *Iron Grille. Palazzo Pubblico, Siena. 1445. (Anderson)*

a trunk if small enough. The early cassoni were very much like the Gothic chests in their almost severe rectangularity with simple carved decoration. Later this severity was modified by bracketlike carved ornaments covered with gesso and gilded, and by a brightly painted panel on the front. Rarely has an important piece of furniture attained the splendor and dignity of the Italian cassoni. The panels were frequently painted by the best artists of Florence.[1]

Wealth of ornament increased as the fifteenth century advanced. Frescoes covered the walls of palaces[2] as well as those of the churches. Carved pilasters, lintels, and cornices framed doors of inlaid wood (Fig. 445B). The motifs were chiefly classical — the acanthus, the rinceau, candelabra, garlands, Greek moldings — and, like the classical, naturalistic in form. They were carved crisply and spontaneously, as if by one who was finding his first delight

[1] Many of these panels have been stripped from the chests and now hang as isolated pictures in galleries and museums.

[2] The gay frescoes of Benozzo Gozzoli in the chapel of the *Medici Palace*, for example.

[A] *Andrea Pisano. Weaving. From the Campanile of the Cathedral, Florence. 1334-38. (Alinari)*

[B] *Pazzi Chapel. Santa Croce, Florence. Filippo Brunelleschi, architect. 1429. (Alinari)*

in rich and varied effects of light and shade (Fig. 440A).

Another feature of Renaissance architecture, equally functional and decorative, merits more than passing attention — the wrought-iron work. The strength of iron makes it valuable for grilles and gates where strong protection, and at the same time light and air, are needed. Technically, it can be worked by several processes, for it can be hammered, molded, welded, carved, chased, and stamped. The necessary tools are few and simple — forge and bellows, hammer and anvil, tongs and chisels. An important fact in designing in this medium is that the metal must be worked in the plastic state — that is, at red or white heat — and must be worked quickly. Hence virility and breadth must control a successful design, though the chased ornament may

be added at greater leisure. This harmony of material, process, and design is well seen in palace gates and chapel grilles (Fig. 440B); and in the standard-holders and the lanterns of the palaces. The lantern of the *Guadagni Palace*, for example, with its curving branches, is fittingly strong and architectural in feeling; and its decoration, done by fine chiseling, is entirely in keeping with the main design.

The Venetian palace forms a class by itself. Venice was as much Eastern as Western. The city had grown rich and luxurious because of its lucrative trade with the East. Its geographical position on a group of islands chosen as a place of refuge from the Huns isolated it from the other Italian cities, enabled it to develop more individually, to cling longer to medieval styles and delay the coming of the Renais-

[A]   *Ca d'Oro. Venice. 15th cent. (Alinari)*

sance. Being free from internal feuds because of its remarkably stable government and also from external foes because of its geographic location, Venice did not need to make its palaces fortresslike, as did Florence. The Gothic style, with its light, open tracery, as in the *Ducal Palace* and the *Ca d'Oro* (Fig. 442A), its warm color, and its rapid movement of light and dark reflected in the canals, was peculiarly adapted to the geographical situation. In the *Vendramini Palace* (Fig. 443A) we see the same influences at work that we saw in Florence: the ordering of the elements into a classically balanced symmetrical design and a substitution of classical detail for medieval. The ground story, with the door in the center, serves as a base for the lighter construction above, which consists to a large extent of two-light rounding windows with cir-

cular tracery. Each story carries a cornice which serves to finish and unify the entire design. The double shafts of the superimposed orders divide the façade into three parts, the central division containing three groups of windows separated by single columns, balanced on either side by a single group with double columns at the ends. Thus through symmetry, proportion, and rhythm of parts the façade presents an effective design. The windows with their mullions and tracery are Gothic; the superimposed orders, cornices, and decorative detail are classic.

The sculpture of the early fifteenth century still maintained its place as an integral part of architecture. A Sienese sculptor, Jacopo della Quercia (1375–1438), combined in his work something of the breadth of Nicola's style, Gothic linealism, and an individual ro-

[A]   *Vendramini Palace. Venice. Pietro Lombardo, architect. 1481. Contrast this open design with the solidity of the Florentine palace (Fig. 438A).*

bust energy. An early work, the sepulchral monument of *Ilaria del Carretto*[1] (Fig. 444B) shows him using French Gothic elements of style. As is fitting, a peaceful tranquillity permeates the monument. Ilaria lies easily, her head upon a double cushion and at her feet a dog, symbol of fidelity. The effectiveness of the monument is due to the insistent repetition of unbroken horizontals and to the long undulating rhythm in the reposeful drapery, interwoven with the quicker rhythms and stronger light and shade in the winged putti with garlands — a Renaissance motif.

An *Allegorical Figure* (Fig. 445A), one

[1] The attribution of this work to Jacopo is debatable.

of several which combined with reliefs to decorate the *Fonte Gaia* in Siena, introduces a new note. This is a powerful figure whose massive weight is enhanced by the boldly sweeping folds of the drapery, deeply undercut for strong shadows. Its dynamic quality is due to the fact that Jacopo here is attacking a central problem of the Renaissance, the conquest of space of truly three-dimensional design. Once before, in the work of Lysippus and the Hellenistic sculptors, we saw this sculptural problem attacked and solved. In the *Allegorical Figure* there is a controlling vertical axis about which the parts of the figure revolve, moving backward and forward in space. This conquest of space foreshadows more complicated

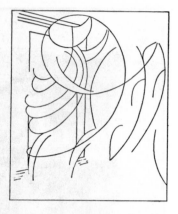

[A] *Jacopo della Quercia. Expulsion. Marble panel from the portal of San Petronio, Bologna. 1425–38. The idea of expulsion is expressed by a line organization which utilizes the sense of movement inherent in parallel diagonals and in radiating and spiraling curves.*

[B] *Jacopo della Quercia (?). Tomb of Ilaria del Carretto. 1406. Lucca Cathedral. (Alinari)*

[A] *Jacopo della Quercia. Allegorical Figure from the Fonte Gaia. 1409–19. The fountain, because of damage, has been replaced by a copy. Siena Museum.* (*Alinari*)

solutions by Michelangelo, who seems to have found stimulation in the work of Jacopo (compare Jacopo's *Allegorical Figure* and Michelangelo's *Delphic Sibyl*). The rugged, forceful energy in Jacopo's carving is seen in the *Expulsion* (Fig. 444A), a relief in which, combined with movement in shallow depth, is a linear and textural pattern which integrates the three figures tightly. This pattern, based upon long sweeping curves combined with diagonals and right angles, together with the intense robustness of the figures produces a dynamic organic structure which gives intensity to the dramatic character of the theme.

With Donatello (1386–1466) we are carried with an onward rush of adven-

[B] *Doorway from the Ducal Palace, Urbino. Showing door of inlaid wood. 1468–82.* (*Alinari*)

turous spirit into the wholehearted search for new forms to express new ideas which Donatello shared with Brunelleschi and Masaccio[1] and which definitely marks the Renaissance. In the early *Saint George* (Fig. 447A) this

[1] See p. 476.

[A]   *Donatello. Zuccone, meaning "Pumpkin-head," and Jeremiah. Marble. H. c. 6½ ft. 1427–36. Campanile, Florence. (Alinari)*

spirit already declares its daring. The youthful knight clad in armor[1] stands firmly on both feet and with furrowed brow looks keenly to the left. The naturalistically tied cloak, whose folds contrast with the rigid armor, and the shield simplify the contour and render the mass more compact. But though

[1] Saint George was the patron saint of the Guild of the Armorers, who commissioned the statue for a niche on the exterior of the guild church of *Or San Michele*. The original statue has been removed to the Bargello (the National Museum), and a reproduction placed in the niche.

the figure is firmly rooted to the ground, there is a turn in the torso as well as in the head; in fact there courses through the statue a great rhythm, visually stressed by the sweep of the cloak, which follows the turn in the pose. This movement is by no means the same as the sweeping surface rhythms of Gothic sculpture, but is the same in kind as that in Jacopo's *Allegorical Figure* (Fig. 445A), a movement which swings through space about the vertical axis and produces a dynamic living quality which is probably the reason for Vasari's famous statement — "Life seems to move within the stone."

Donatello, with Brunelleschi, had steeped himself at Rome in a study of classic remains. Of sculpture there were not as yet many examples; a large number of those well known today were then still buried in the ruins. Only small objects, such as gems and coins, were at all common. In fact Donatello and Brunelleschi while digging around the ruins in Rome, according to Vasari, found an ancient vase full of coins and thereafter were known as the "treasure-seekers"; but their real treasure was the stimulating ideas by which Brunelleschi was enabled to build the great dome of the *Cathedral* and Donatello to carve statues that were filled with energy and vitality. The lesson that the antique taught Donatello was a return to nature. Only by a careful observation of nature could he emulate what, to him, were the superlative accomplishments of the ancients. To his undying credit, he did not copy the Greeks. On the contrary, he learned from them how to make visual perception a starting-point. But he did not merely describe. Rather, he created a formal organization that not only expressed volume in space but also the individual character and significance of the figure. *Saint George* is a spiritually alive, chivalrous young knight. Of the figures on the *Campanile* of the *Cathedral* (Fig. 446A), the so-called *Jeremiah* is wholly restless in its pose, with tense articulations, abrupt meeting of verticals and horizontals in the arms, and unorganized drapery. The *Zuccone*, by contrast, shows a quiet, meditative character. His heavy mantle, falling in massive folds from the shoulder, conceals the figure except in the right arm and shoulder, and the throat, whose modeling reveals an intimate study of the human figure used not as an end in itself but as a means for the

[A] *Donatello. St. George. Marble. 1416. Originally on the exterior of Or San Michele. National Museum, Florence. (Alinari)*

expression of character. So the *Zuccone* is seen as a character whose intensity is cloaked by passivity. These massive, weighty figures, intended to be seen from below, not on the level of the eyes, in their compactness fit well into the slender pointed niches.

The *Gattamelata* (Fig. 449A), a bronze equestrian portrait of Erasmo da Narni,

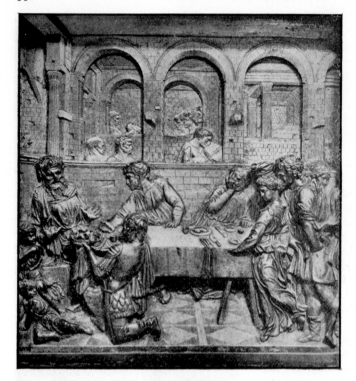

[A]   Donatello. Herod's
Feast. Bronze relief on
the baptismal font, Siena
Cathedral. 1425–27.

[B]   Donatello. The Mule before the Host. Bronze. Altar of Sant' Antonio, Padua. 1445–48.
(Alinari)

[A] *Donatello. Erasmo da Narni, called Gatta-melata, a nickname mean-ing "Honeyed Cat." Bronze. 1444–50. Padua. (Alinari)*

[B] *Donatello. Cantoria, or Singing Gallery. 1433–38. Museum of Florence Cathedral. (Alinari)*

[A] *Ghiberti. Temptation of Christ. Bronze. Panel from the North Doors of the Baptistery. 1403–24. Florence. (Alinari)*

a famous condottiere, stands in the open square of Sant' Antonio in Padua. As a group in space, it consists of a closely knit mass of man and horse set upon a lofty elliptical stone base; a slight turning movement in the figure of the man repeated in the head of the horse, noted particularly from the front view, indicates movement in space. But the dark color of the bronze stresses the contours and the linear pattern, which is built on curves with a dynamic diagonal in the sword and the baton; and the whole formal organization seems related to the domes and curved arches of the church of *Sant' Antonio* beside which it stands. As characterization, the statue shows a quietly powerful per-

sonality, not only in the features and in the relaxed bearing of the helmetless rider but also in the massive proportions, and in the harmonious relation of curvilinear volumes and curved lines.

Donatello adventured in the field of relief also, and here revealed a capacity for pictorial design had he chosen to work in the field of painting. In the early *Herod's Feast* (Fig. 448A), for example, he organizes a dramatic theme involving many figures into a dramatic composition confined to a shallow space, with movement largely lateral except at the left, where it cuts in at a diagonal in a Giottesque fashion; in the upper half of the panel parallel planes recede with clear precision. In the later *Mule before the Host* (Fig. 448B), crowds of people as they surge in from the sides toward the scene in the center create varied rapid movements accented by the reflective character of bronzes. This broken movement is chiefly lateral, is confined in shallow depth and to slightly less than half the height of the relief, and is set in a quiet architectural framework dominated by three great barrel vaults. In depicting these vaults, Donatello reveals his interest in one of the passions of the day — perspective — in that he seems to have been motivated by a desire to imitate visual perception. In his *Cantoria* (Fig. 449B), on the other hand, one is conscious only of surging rhythms playing through a static framework. Against a gold mosaic ground and behind mosaic colonnettes which define a shallow depth, putti swing from side to side with all the spontaneity and exuberance of children at play.

The influence of Donatello, which together with that of Brunelleschi and Masaccio constituted the modern movement of the fifteenth century, did not entirely overwhelm the conservative Gothic style, which lived on beside the new, as is inevitable in any age of

[A]   *Ghiberti. Episodes from the Life of Abraham. From the "Gates of Paradise" (Fig. 453A).*

transition, and found its highest expression in the work of Lorenzo Ghiberti (1378–1455). In the second *Doors of the Baptistery,*[1] Ghiberti followed the all-over pattern of Andrea Pisano (Fig. 436A). In the *Temptation* (Fig. 450A), we see that the sculptor was concerned chiefly with the swing of line and with the beautiful pattern that his figures could weave within the enclosed space, a pattern built on arcs of circles that approach but do not meet, symbolizing both a physical and a spiritual separation between Christ and the Devil. We notice the Gothic sway of line par-

ticularly in the drapery of the Devil, and the exquisite manner in which his wings are adapted to fill the space and to balance the group of ministering angels. Through the use of line and pattern, Ghiberti has succeeded not only in creating a beautiful design but also in exhibiting a great amount of dramatic power.

Ghiberti, however, was not untouched by the naturalistic movement of the day. Paradoxically, he was a great lover and collector of classical marbles, bronzes, and coins, evidence of which appears in his work. In the niche on the right of Figure 451A, for example, is a nude figure that appears to have been copied from some classical Heracles.

In the *Gates of Paradise* (Fig. 453A) Ghiberti abandoned the all-over pattern of the earlier doors and divided the space into rectangular panels, each containing a relief set in plain moldings.

[1] There are three sets of bronze doors to the *Baptistery* at Florence: the first (Fig. 436A), made by Andrea Pisano for the eastern doorway, which faced the cathedral, were moved to the south door to make way for those made by Ghiberti in 1403–24 (Fig. 450A); these in turn were moved to the north door in order that the second pair made by Ghiberti, the famous *Gates of Paradise* (Fig. 453A), might be placed in the eastern doorway, the most important entrance.

[A] *Luca della Robbia. Virgin Adoring the Infant Jesus. Glazed terra cotta. 15th cent. Philadelphia Museum of Art. (Philadelphia Museum)*

When gilded, these reliefs produced with their scintillating movement an effect of great elegance.[1]

Taking one panel in detail (Fig. 451A), we find several episodes welded into one design, not an uncommon practice in Renaissance art. In the upper right-hand corner Abraham is about to slay Isaac on the altar when the angel ap-

[1] It may have been this that called forth from the grim stonecutter Michelangelo the remark, "They are so beautiful that they might fittingly stand at the gates of Paradise."

pears to stay his hand; at the foot of the hill the servants and the ass are waiting for the master; on the left Abraham kneels before the three angels who appeared to him before his tent near the oaks of Mamre; in the background Sarah stands at the door of the tent. These groups Ghiberti united with astonishing ease. Emphatic lights and darks, as in the rocks and the trees, and the planes receding at angles to the foreground, as in the angels, the foreshortened ass, and the rocks at the

[A] *Ghiberti. "Gates of Paradise." Bronze. The scenes represented are taken from the Old Testament. 1425–52. Baptistery, Florrence. (Alinari)*

right, carry the eye upward and inward. So also do the higher relief in the foreground figures with sharper transitions of light and shade and the lower relief in the group of the sacrifice with gentler transitions. Thus is produced an effect of aerial perspective, a pictorial quality that shows an influence upon Ghiberti of the contemporary naturalistic movement, an influence seen again in the modeling of the figures in the lower right-hand corner, whereas the angels near by, with the subtly flowing lines in their drapery and wings, carry one back to the angels of *Amiens* and

Reims (Fig. 351B). By a comparison of this panel and Donatello's *Herod's Feast* (Fig. 448A), one realizes how sculptural is Donatello's conception in contrast to the pictorial quality in Ghiberti's work.

If sculpture in the first half of the fifteenth century was dominated by Donatello, with Ghiberti as a late flower of the Gothic style, the second half also was under the influence of the former, though the sculptors may be divided into two rather well defined groups. There was the gentle Luca della Robbia (1400–1482), whose simple unaffected naturalism has a certain appeal. He is

[A] *Desiderio da Settignano. Tomb of Carlo Marsuppini. c. 1455. Santa Croce, Florence. (Brogi)*

best known, however, for his introduction into Italian sculpture of the medium of glazed terra cotta, which was desirable both on grounds of economy, in comparison with stone and bronze, and because of color. The intense blues, yellows, greens, and purples with ivory-white made a very decorative note when used in a lunette over a doorway in a dull Florentine street. Luca's figures are the simply and broadly modeled clay forms necessary for glazing, and his types are appealing for their serene wholesomeness and tenderness, which is

neither profound nor sentimental (Fig. 452A).

In addition to Luca, there was a whole group of stonecutters who, though pupils or followers of the forthright Donatello, were interested primarily in securing exquisite surface effects, in catching a charming momentary pose of a youthful Tuscan aristocrat, in carving marble surfaces into beautifully cut patterns. Probably Desiderio da Settignano (1428–1464) best illustrates the group.[1] The alluring charm of his *Laughing Boy* or *Marietta Strozzi* results from subtle carving and exquisite surface modulation, from an impression of momentary alertness or of gracious personality. The uncompromising realism and formal structure of Donatello have given way to surface delicacy and technical virtuosity.

Nor is this smiling charm absent in the tombs designed and carved by Desiderio. Florence honored its dead — statesmen, humanists, artists, churchmen — with burial in its churches and with monumental tombs made by the greatest artists. In the *Tomb of Carlo Marsuppini* (Fig. 454A), the sarcophagus, with an effigy of the dead reclining on a bier, stands in a niche formed by two fluted pilasters that rise from a decorated base to the entablature, whence springs a round arch surmounted by a candelabrum, from which garlands are suspended. The back of the niche is filled with four panels of colored marble, which balance the horizontal line of the sarcophagus and the base and afford with their plain surfaces a restful contrast to the rich, delicate ornament, carved in low relief so that light and shade flit over the surface gently with no great contrasts, and produce an effect of elegance and refinement without a feeling of overloading.

[1] Others were Antonio Rossellino (1427–1478), Mino da Fiesole (1430–1484), and Benedetto da Maiano (1442–1497).

But the figures at the corners and the garlands, evidence of a superrealistic tendency, mar that perfect architectural unity found in Arnolfo's tombs.

A lone sculptor who stood apart from the generally naturalistic trend of the Renaissance was Francesco Laurana of Zara (about 1425–1502), who penetrated beneath the superficial surface beauty of the Desiderio group and at the same time substituted for the terse reality of the Donatello tradition the "proud unreality" of an austere architectural form. In the head of a *Princess* (Fig. 455A) the shoulders are one with the base from which they rise and their solid mass and unbroken impeccable contours support the slender neck and the spherical head. Every detail is a unit in a form; from the front view, one of repeated curves, horizontals, and a strong vertical axis, with diagonals, sharp angles, and definitely broken surfaces in the embroidered dress. Within this formal organization are the subtlest surface modulations, not used as ends in themselves or as naturalistic renderings of flesh or fabric but as contributory elements in a compelling abstract design.

Working side by side with the Desiderio group of sculptors was another group, the direct descendants of Donatello. Of especial importance was Antonio Pollaiuolo (1429–1498), who is an excellent illustration of the eager zeal of these Florentine artists in their search for the fundamentals of figure expression. In the case of Antonio, it was the figure in movement based upon an intensive study of anatomy. In his bronze statuette of *Heracles and Antaeus* (Fig. 456A) the two figures with tensely strained muscles are surcharged with vitality, and are so interlocked that their opposing movements and sharp angles, accentuated by the clear-cut contours and the reflections of the dark bronze, produce an almost abstract ex-

[A] *Laurana. A Princess of the House of Naples. Berlin (Clarence Kennedy)*

pression of Titanic conflict. Antonio worked in terra cotta as well, and to him is attributed a *Portrait of a Youth* (Fig. 456B), which combines a vivid aliveness, which he inherited from Donatello, with a simplicity of mass almost as abstract as that in Laurana's *Princess*, though the coarse clay from which the former is modeled does not lend itself to such nuances as are possible in the fine marble of the latter. Yet notice how in each case the material in itself is an effective element of expression.

Another important sculptor of this group was Andrea Verrocchio (1435–1488), who is best represented by the equestrian statue of *Colleoni* (Fig. 457A), one of the greatest soldiers of the age and at the same time a prince of great wealth, living part of the time in the midst of camp hardships and part of the time in the luxury of a magnificent court. We see Colleoni in full armor sitting rigidly in the saddle, from which he seems to be half-rising, the feet pressing firmly upon the stirrups which bear the weight of the body, in marked contrast to *Gattamelata*, who relaxes into the saddle. The violent twist of the

[A] *Antonio Pollaiuolo. Heracles and Antaeus. Bronze. National Museum (Bargello), Florence. (Clarence Kennedy)*

[B] *Antonio Pollaiuolo. Portrait of a Youth. Terra cotta. National Museum (Bargello), Florence. (Alinari)*

figure, the grim face, the piercing eyes, and the angularity of the group contribute to the impression of impetuosity; and every detail adds to a dramatic expression of forceful energy.

The fifteenth century, then, under the influence of individualism and a study of nature, took upon itself and solved problems which arose in connection with the structure of the figure, with its possibilities for spatial organization and for the expression of significant ideas. With these solutions came a relaxation into easy charm and surface subtleties on the part of one group of sculptors, but an uncompromising attitude with another group, who bequeathed the accomplishments of Donatello to his greatest follower,

Michelangelo. "Either the spirit of Donatello lives in Michelangelo," said Borghini, "or that of Michelangelo already lived in Donatello."

The sixteenth century, unlike the fifteenth, was dominated by one overpowering personality, that of Michelangelo Buonarroti (1475–1564), and that too in the fields of architecture and painting as well as in that of sculpture. With this century, the center of art activity shifts from Florence to Rome, where under the leadership of a large group of artists[1] working chiefly for

[1] Donato Bramante (1444–1512); Raphael (1483–1520); Baldassare Peruzzi (1481–1536); Antonio San Gallo the Younger (1482–1546); Michelangelo (1475–1564); Giacomo Barozzi da Vignola (1507–1573); and others.

[A] *Verrocchio. Colleoni, a condottière, or military leader. Bronze. 1481–88. Venice. (Anderson)*

the papal court and the Roman nobles, the Renaissance style reached a climax known as the High Renaissance. This was an accomplished age, one of splendor and magnificence in which wealthy Popes and princes created a great demand for churches and palaces, villas and gardens, all of which in their scale, in their princely dignity and splendor, reflected the worldly grandeur of the High Renaissance.

One palace, the *Farnese*, illustrates this sixteenth-century type; the *Cancelleria* is an interesting transition from the fifteenth-century Florentine to the sixteenth-century Roman. The princely dignity of the *Farnese Palace* (Fig. 458B) is the direct result of a design calculated to attain just that effect — a design of classical balance and symmetry. The long rectangle of the smooth façade is framed by quoins and a cornice, and across it march the long lines of windows, the regularity of which is broken by the strong central accent of the doorway built of rusticated stone and surmounted by a balcony and the Farnese coat of arms. The windows are no longer flush with the wall, as in the *Medici Palace* (Fig. 438A), but project beyond the surface, producing depth in the design; each window is a complete unit with engaged columns, entablature, and pediment. The different treatment of these units on each of the three stories, and the alternating curved and angular pediments, contribute the variations necessary to so symmetrical a design. The court is strongly classical in design, combining, like the *Colosseum*,

[A]   *Gardens of the Villa d'Este. Tivoli. 1549. (Provizi)*

[B]   *Farnese Palace. Rome. Architects: Antonio da San Gallo, 1530–34; Michelangelo, 1546, who designed the cornice; and Giacomo della Porta, who completed the palace c. 1580. (Anderson)*

[A]   *St. Peter's Cathedral. Rome. Nave.*

the arch and lintel systems, and using superimposed orders: Doric engaged columns on the ground floor, Ionic on the second, and Corinthian pilasters on the third, each order being finished with a complete entablature. But the windows with their pedimented niches are peculiarly Renaissance.

The interiors of these palaces are consistently regal, depending for their effect upon gilded coffered ceilings (sometimes containing painted panels), frescoes, and painted and gilded stucco.[1] The ceiling and the cornice received especial emphasis, as seen in the hall of the *Farnese Palace,* and the richest of stuffs in the furnishings — velvets, brocades, damask, taffeta — contributed sumptuousness, or overstepped into the pompous and grandiose.

[1] See the *Piccolomini Library* of the *Siena Cathedral* and the *Borgia Apartments* of the Vatican for paintings, and the *Villa Madama* at Rome, decorated by Raphael, for stucco.

As these wealthy princes sought the cooler air of the hills during the hot season, the villa assumed importance, and particularly its garden — a formal garden consisting of beds of flowers laid out geometrically, and usually, for the enjoyment of the color, situated near the house. Beyond these flower beds were regular compartments of greenery with closely clipped hedges of box; masses of trees, ilex or pines, or a stretch of wooded land in its natural state that served as a background for the formal parts and also afforded the desired shade; statues and stone benches; and, with especial emphasis, water: pools, fountains, cascades (Fig. 458A). All these elements were used as integral parts of a formal whole to which each, including the villa itself, contributed form, color, and texture.

Ecclesiastical building of the High Renaissance culminated in *St. Peter's,* the cathedral which replaced the early

[A] *St. Peter's Cathedral. Rome. Front view, showing the façade of Maderna and the great court by Bernini. (Anderson) The obelisk in the center was brought to Rome from Heliopolis, Egypt, by Caligula to adorn Nero's Circus, the scene of the martyrdom of St. Peter.*

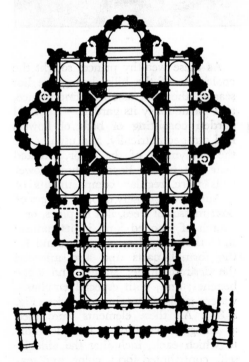

[B] *St. Peter's Cathedral. Rome. The dotted line shows approximately the front line of the building according to the plans of Bramante and Michelangelo.*

Christian basilica on the same site. The designers of *St. Peter's* abandoned the basilica plan, used in the *Cathedral of Florence* (Fig. 438B), in favor of the central type more suitable for a domical structure.[1] The dome, we have already seen, was one of the characteristic features of Renaissance architecture, and was used both for its exterior effect as a dominating symbol and for its capacity for creating interior space. These two objectives motivated Bramante and Michelangelo[2] in their plans for the cathedral, but the effectiveness of their design was later frustrated by the lengthening of the nave to gain space and by the addition of the wide, inharmoni-

[1] The conception of formal unity in a domed building, in which the body of the building serves as a base for the dome, is seen in Bramante's *Tempietto* of *San Pietro in Montorio*, Rome.

[2] Ten architects worked upon this cathedral. The plan is essentially that of Bramante, somewhat modified by Michelangelo, who designed the dome, which was completed from his drawings after his death. The façade was built by Maderna (1606–1626) and the great court with double colonnades by Bernini (1656–1663).

[A]   *St. Peter's Cathedral. Rome. View from the west. 1506–1626. (Alinari)*

ous façade which cuts off the view of the dome (Fig. 460A and B). Thus it is that only the back view of the cathedral gives some conception of the complete unity of masses which underlay Michelangelo's sculpturesque design[1] (Fig. 461A). The plan consists of a Greek cross with the corners made by the arms of the cross filled in (compare Figures 262A, 264B), and with apses on three sides and the entrance on the fourth side — a plan that is extraordinarily compact. As a volume, the cathedral consists of a closely knit unit of cube and half-cylinders, which in their volumes, surfaces, and contours form a harmonious base for the great dome that rises like a majestic symbol of universal au-

[1] See Le Corbusier, *Towards a New Architecture*, for a formal analysis from this point of view.

thority. On the base, gigantic pilasters carry an entablature which ties the parts into a unity. One wonders whether Michelangelo had in mind the *Colosseum* (Fig. 180A), in which cornices tie the arches together in a similar way. In *St. Peter's*, however, the cornices are not continuous, as in the *Colosseum*, but are broken. By advancing and receding they create movement in depth as well as laterally. This movement in depth, a three-dimensional quality, becomes stronger in the drum of the dome, where deeply projecting pairs of colonnettes crowned with a sharply broken cornice not only serve as bases for the great ribs of the dome but also carry the eye inward and outward as it sweeps around the drum.

Structurally, the cathedral offers no new problems, no new solutions, as is

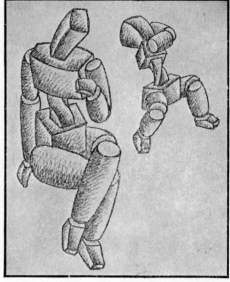

[A]   *Michelangelo. Medici Madonna. Marble. H. c. 7 ft. 1525–34. New Sacristy, San Lorenzo, Florence. (Alinari) Originally planned as part of a papal tomb in an ambitious project of Cardinal Giulio de' Medici, which was to include four Medici tombs, the Madonna was left an isolated figure when continuous changes in the plans resulted in the building of only two tombs. The analysis shows the organization of spiraling volumes.*

true of most Renaissance building. The arms of the cross are covered with barrel vaults and the dome rests upon pendentives. Spatial, not structural, problems concerned the builders: to bring movement in depth into the exterior as far as was consonant with solidity, but particularly to create an interior space as majestic as the exterior volumes, to harmonize exterior and interior effects. Had Bramante's and Michelangelo's designs not been tampered with, this effect would have been accomplished. Instead, the lengthened nave precludes such an interior space design as we find in the *Pantheon* and *Santa Sophia*.

Michelangelo's design for *St. Peter's* is primarily sculptural. He himself declared that he was a sculptor. Marks of his fully developed style are already apparent in his early *Moses*,[1] (Fig. 13B) with its restless movement backward and forward, and in the opposing movements of the drapery and beard. Yet the figure is extraordinarily compact, and the restless movement is sternly

[1] The *Moses* was carved to decorate the tomb of Pope Julius II, which was never completed as planned. The horns on the head, traditional in representations of Moses, are due to an incorrect interpretation of the passage in the Vulgate of Exodus xxxiv. 35 that describes the rays about the head of the prophet as he came down from Mt. Sinai.

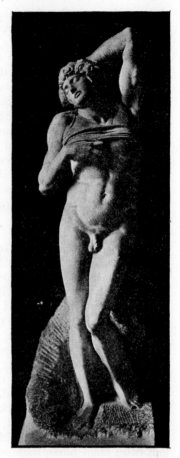

[A] *Michelangelo. Tomb of Giuliano de' Medici. 1524–33. New Sacristy, San Lorenzo, Florence. Never completed. (Alinari)*

[B] *Michelangelo. The Bound Slave. Marble. c. 1513. Louvre, Paris.*

confined within the space determined by the block of stone from which it was carved. The detailed modeling (here quite intent upon anatomical minutiae) later became broader, subordinated to a clearer enunciation of a three-dimensional organic structure, as in the *Bound Slave* (Fig. 463B). This figure is not as restless as the *Moses*, and every part is subservient to a great rhythmic movement which surges forward and backward from the foot to the uplifted arm and thence back into the figure, where it flows into another movement around the figure, made visible in the tight band about the breast. Both of these movements traverse, in their spiraling, the entire space determined by the sides of the block of stone.

All Michelangelo's sculpture was architectural, as his architecture was sculptural. Thus the two art forms came together in an extraordinary unity. This is best illustrated in the *Medici Tombs* (Fig. 463A), a work in which Michelangelo had charge of the entire design, both architectural and sculptural. The architectural setting is not only a framework of verticals, horizontals, and curves but is a design in depth, like that of *St. Peter's*, accented by strong shadow carefully controlled by overhead lighting. Into this setting the figures fit dynamically as a group, for they form a triangle which is repeated in the bent knees of the reclining figures. At the same time each figure, with its complex backward and forward movement, accentuates the spatial conception of the entire design.

Giuliano, seated with his head turned to his left, is clad in a suit of magnificent armor, and holds a marshal's baton somewhat listlessly. The whole figure, with its generalized features, is more a symbol of ineffectuality than a portrait of the Prince. Also symbolic are the two figures below. The Titanic *Day* has aroused himself and peers out upon the world with keen gaze. The head rises vertically erect above a mighty shoulder and a muscular arm that swings around the body and thus opposes a strong horizontal movement to the verticality of the head. Parts of the figure, such as the back and the shoulder, are highly finished, revealing the anatomical structure with scrupulous care; other parts, such as the head and the left hand, are still in the rough, giving one the feeling that this vigorous giant is trying to wrest himself from the block of stone. Yet such details are subordinate to the powerful rotation of masses about a central axis, which results in a design of maximum movement within the limited space marked off by the block from which it was carved. The same restlessness permeates the *Night*, whose drooping head brings her face effectively into the shadow. Despite the presence of the owl beneath the bent knee and a poppy wreath to symbolize slumber, the uneasy sleep of the restless figure is more truly symbolized by the mask, whose open eyes follow one with fascination.

In such figures as the *Bound Slave*, *Day*, and *Night* one realizes Michelangelo's purpose. His perfect understanding of and control over the figure as an organic structure, even in the most complicated movements, enabled him to use the figure not as an end in itself but for the creation of designs which by their formal value as well as their representational content translated into visual form the conceptions of a great imagination and intellect. The *Bound Slave*, for example, may suggest the futility of struggle and the *Night* the hopeless search for rest. Interpretation of sculpture, as of poetry, is not always satisfactory. But one notes that nowhere is there tranquillity. Something of Michelangelo's own tortured spirit permeates the tortuous movement of his designs.[1]

Perhaps the consummation of interlocking movements of a most complex organization in space is found in the unfinished *Madonna* of the *New Sacristy* (Fig. 462A), in which the two figures spiraling in opposite directions nevertheless compose into a unit of the utmost compactness. The complex, three-dimensional organization of Michelangelo's art, with its conquest of space, its ceaseless movement and great scale, foreshadowed, if it did not originate, the baroque style of the seventeenth century.

The new style did not develop without opposition, however. For another school, called the Academic, held fast, even rigidly, to the canons of building set forth by one whom they believed to be an infallible guide, the Roman Vitruvius, whose treatise on architecture had been discovered in the fifteenth century. This school is best represented by the work of Palladio (1518–1580), at

[1] One needs to recall the general background of the Counter-Reformation and Michelangelo's deep concern for the Church, to which he was devoutly loyal.

[A] *The Basilica, or Town Hall. Vicenza. Andrea Palladio, architect. 1549. A medieval building remodeled in Renaissance style. Partly ruined during World War II. (Alinari)*

Venice and Vicenza. His *Basilica* (Fig. 465A) was a Gothic town hall which he remodeled on the lines of a Roman basilica, hence its name. The building has a two-storied arcade around it with superimposed orders, Doric on the first story and Ionic on the second, thus combining in Roman fashion the arch and lintel systems. The intercolumniations, however, are not spanned by the arch alone, but contain smaller columns set two deep from which the arch springs.[1] The bays, whose width was determined by the old building, are unusually wide for their height; but in reducing the width to be arched by the insertion of the smaller columns Palladio not only attained superb pro-

portions for his arches but also brought about a rich play of light and shade where the smaller columns group around the larger pier. In both stories the entablature breaks about the columns, thus making more insistent the vertical lines, which form the main accents of the horizontal rhythm and also carry the eye upward to the statues adorning the balustrade. At the corners, Palladio narrowed the intercolumniation, but not the arch, by placing the smaller shafts nearer the large, and he doubled the columns at the corners, thus giving a feeling of solidity at these points. In the *Villa Rotonda* (Fig. 466A), Palladio established the classical two-storied portico, later so popular. His published drawings of Roman ruins spread the influence of the Academic school across Europe and eventually to the Americas.

[1] A form that has become known as the Palladian window. It is found frequently in American Colonial architecture, whither it came by way of England.

[A] *Villa Rotonda. Vicenza. Andrea Palladio, architect. (Alinari)*

SUMMARY

The Renaissance meant a change in point of view, the emergence of new ideas, and consequently the need of new forms for their expression. The social solidarity and the predominantly ecclesiastical outlook of the Middle Ages began to give way before an advancing individualism and secularization, with parallel changes in the art expression. Under the unlimited patronage of the wealthy and ruling classes, a great flowering developed in all the arts. Its beginnings appear in the fourteenth century, which was primarily medieval with a mingling of Romanesque and Gothic styles in its churches, palaces, and town halls, and with its sculpture closely allied to architecture. Sculpture, earlier than architecture, felt the influence of classical art — in fact deliberately copied those forms — but soon turned to the suave rhythms of French Gothic linealism.

The opening of the fifteenth century saw a great outburst in all art activity. Classical details appeared in buildings, and soon an increasing enthusiasm for the classical style as a whole became evident. The central plan, the dome, classical orders and ornament, and symmetry in the arrangement of all parts — all these traditional elements reappeared, used with vigor and originality. In architecture, interest centered not on constructional problems, as with the Romans, but upon basic abstract forms and particularly upon space organization. Sculpture also began to deal with problems of space. It was still architectural in function. Under the stimulation of classical art it moved toward the creation of forms based upon visual perception and a scientific knowledge of the figure, both of which would naturally lead toward a three-dimensional organization of the figure, and movement within the space determined by the material. These trends of the fifteenth century found complete fruition in the sixteenth, notably in the building and the sculpture of Michelangelo.

BIBLIOGRAPHY

Anderson, W. J., *The Architecture of the Renaissance in Italy*, Scribner, 1927

Baum, Julius, *Baukunst und dekorative Plastik der Frührenaissance in Italien*, Stuttgart, 1926

Biagi, Guido, *Men and Manners of Old Florence*, McClurg, 1909

Bode, Wilhelm von, *Die Kunst der Frührenaissance in Italien*, 2d ed., Berlin, 1926

———— *Florentine Sculptors of the Renaissance*, Scribner, 1909

Burckhardt, J. C., *The Civilization of the Renaissance in Italy*, tr. by S. G. C. Middlemoore, Harper, 1929

Cartwright, Julia (Mrs. Henry Ady), *Beatrice d'Este*, Dutton, 1903

———— *Isabella d'Este*, 2 vols. Dutton, 1903

Castiglione, Baldassare, *The Book of the Courtier*, tr. by L. E. Opdycke, Scribner, 1903

Cellini, Benvenuto, *Autobiography*, tr. by J. A. Symonds, Modern Library, 1927

Crichton, George H., and Elsie R., *Nicola Pisano and the Revival of Sculpture in Italy*, Macmillan, 1938

Cruttwell, Maud, *Verrocchio*, Scribner, 1904

Geck, F. J., *Bibliography of Italian Early Renaissance Art*, University of Colorado, 1932

———— *Bibliography of Italian High Renaissance Art*, University of Colorado, 1933

———— *Bibliography of Italian Late Renaissance Art*, University of Colorado, 1934

Goldscheider, Ludwig, *Donatello*, Phaidon ed., Oxford University Press, 1941

———— *The Sculptures of Michelangelo*, Phaidon ed., Oxford University Press, 1940

Gromort, Georges, *Italian Renaissance Architecture*, tr. by G. F. Waters, Helburn, 1922

Hill, G. F., *Portrait Medals of Italian Artists of the Renaissance*, Macmillan, 1912

Holroyd, Sir Charles, *Michael Angelo Buonarroti*, Scribner, 1904

Jackson, Sir T. G., *The Renaissance of Roman Architecture*, 2 vols., University of Chicago Press, 1922; Vol. I, *Italy*

MacLagen, Eric, *Italian Sculpture of the Renaissance*, Harvard University Press, 1935

Marquand, Allan, *Luca della Robbia*, Princeton University Press, 1914

Meyer, A. G., *Donatello*, Lemcke & Buechner, 1904

Moore, C. H., *The Character of Renaissance Architecture*, Macmillan, 1905

Odom, William M., *History of Italian Furniture*, 2 vols., Doubleday, Page, 1918–19

Ricci, Corrado, *Architecture and Decorative Sculpture of the High and Late Renaissance in Italy*, Brentano's, 1923

Ross, J. A. D.–G., *Florentine Palaces and Their Stories*, Dutton, 1905

Ruskin, John, *Stones of Venice*, 3 vols., Estes, 1913

Schevill, Ferdinand, *History of Florence*, Harcourt, Brace, 1936

Schubring, Paul, *Die Kunst der Hochrenaissance in Italien*, Berlin, 1926

Scott, Geoffrey, *The Architecture of Humanism*, 2d ed., Scribner, 1924

Staley, Edgcumbe, *The Guilds of Florence*, McClurg, 1906

Symonds, J. A., *A Short History of the Renaissance in Italy*, Holt, 1894

Taylor, H. O., *Thought and Expression in the Sixteenth Century*, 2 vols., Macmillan, 1920

Triggs, H. I., *The Art of Garden Design in Italy*, Longmans, Green, 1906

Vasari, Giorgio, *The Lives of the Painters, Sculptors and Architects*, tr. by A. B. Hinds, 4 vols., Dutton, 1927 (Everyman's Library)

Venturi, Adolfo, *A Short History of Italian Art*, tr. by Edward Hutton, Macmillan, 1926

Young, G. F., *The Medici*, Modern Library, 1930

[A]   *Duccio. Majestà. Detail of the center. Originally it had an elaborate Gothic frame.*
1308–11. Siena Cathedral Museum. (Alinari)

27

PAINTING

Sienese and Florentine Painting

IF sculpture in the early Renaissance was definitely architectural, painting was equally so. When not actual mural decoration, mosaic or fresco, for which Italian buildings with their large areas of unbroken walls were peculiarly adapted, it was an altarpiece or a panel commissioned for a definite site possessing a definite lighting. The painters were still working in the provincial "Italo-Byzantine," style which was a decadent form of early Byzantinism, though the contemporary Greek culture of the second climax with its great schools of painting seems also to have been felt in Italy, and in Rome a faint thread of Roman naturalism appeared now and then. Thus, as in architecture and sculpture, we find in early Renaissance painting medieval styles which through the impacts of new attitudes and new ideas evolved, after an age of transition, into a new style.

It is in Siena that the older style of the East blossomed into its finest flowering in Italy; in Florence that the new style was initiated and led to a brilliant climax. Reasons for this difference are not difficult to find. Siena, though situated only about thirty miles from Florence (Fig. 431A), always remained in temperament close to the mystic East,[1] and was too conservative to admit the new ideas and classical influences, as is illustrated by the story of the statue of Aphrodite that was discovered near the city and set up to decorate the public fountain. Because a long series of disasters subsequent to the coming of Aphrodite was laid to her malevolent presence, the city council decreed not only her removal but, in naïve faith, her burial far enough away from the city to be within the boundaries of its great foe, Florence.

Not only by temperament but by geographical situation Siena was destined to be out of the current of the Renaissance. In its lofty site on a triple hill it suffered a tragic disadvantage in comparison with the cities in the valleys on the great natural trade routes, such as Florence. Though important commercially in the twelfth and thirteenth centuries, and in close contact through Pisa with the East, it fell eventually but gloriously before mightier Florence, and the Renaissance swept by leaving it, in its emotional intensity and mysticism, isolated and still medieval.

Here, then, was congenial soil for Byzantinism, which reached a climax in Duccio di Buoninsegna (1255–1319), whose great altarpiece, the *Majestà* or *Madonna in Majesty* [2] (Fig. 468A), stood facing the nave on the high altar of the cathedral. In its original elaborate Gothic frame, with a liberal use of gold in the background and details, in the clear massing of large areas of color and definitely linear quality, it must have shared somewhat the sumptuous effect of a gold-ground mosaic. The Madonna and the Child, of majestic size, seated on an elaborate Cosmati throne and surrounded by four angels who bend over the throne and by row upon row of saints and angels, provide a clear central accent in a symmetrical, severely simple composition. Through clear areas of resplendent color gleams the gold of the ground, of the exquisitely tooled halos, and of small details — a beautiful example of tempera painting. The majesty of otherworldliness is combined with monumental splendor through the type of design that Duccio has used for a large altarpiece placed in a half-light.

Upon the reverse of the altarpiece was a series of small panels illustrating scenes from the life of Christ which show not only Duccio's power of narration — for these little pictures were meant to be read, as were the windows of *Chartres* — but also how, as in the front panel, he built his forms of light and color and organized them into a design whose very character achieved lucidity of statement and beauty of decoration. The composition of *The Three Marys* (Fig. 470A), for example, as a whole and in detail is traditional in Byzantine art,[3] using elements of a widely known pictorial language. The triangular pattern of the angel's figure framed by the triangular hill and resting upon a rectangularly paneled base is opposed to the blocklike group of the three Marys accented by a blocklike hill, and through both groups play curves and countercurves and sharp angles. Though the three figures pro-

---

[1] See the life and letters of Saint Catherine, the most venerated saint of Siena.

[2] For an account of the festive occasion when this altarpiece was carried from the shop to the cathedral, see Langton Douglas, *A History of Siena*, Dutton, 1902, p. 336.

[3] See Byron and Talbot Rice, *The Birth of Western Painting*, Pl. 59.

[A]   *Duccio. Three Marys at the Tomb. A panel from the back of the Majestà. Siena Cathedral Museum. (Alinari)*

duce an effect of solidity and the sculptured hills one of a considerable feeling for space, the sharply defined areas of color, often of contrasting hues, and the flat gold background and halos leave one with the impression of a sumptuously decorative panel.

In many of Duccio's figures we notice a limited use of light and shadow to suggest volume, naturalistic folds of drapery, some feeling for solidity and space — hints of the entrance, even into Siena, of the new naturalism which swept Europe in the thirteenth century, instances of which we noted in the sculpture at *Chartres*, and in the work of the Pisani and Arnolfo. On the whole, however, these evidences of the new approach do not alter the essentially Byzantine character of Sienese painting.

The followers of Duccio we find focusing now upon one aspect, now upon another, of his all-inclusive style. Simone Martini (about 1285–1344) created exquisite surfaces — gold grounds, with marvelously tooled borders, through which play gliding linear rhythms and charming color-patterns. His *Annunciation* (Fig. 471A), painted to be seen in the dim light of a chapel in the *Siena Cathedral*, has a mosaiclike,

[A] *Simone Martini (assisted by Lippo Memmi). Annunciation. 1333. Uffizi, Florence.* (*Alinari*)

sumptuous decorative quality, exqui-site and lyrical rather than epically monumental, as is Duccio's *Majestà* (Fig. 468A) near by. The angel has just alighted and eagerly presses forward with the olive branch to deliver his message to the Virgin, who, interrupted in her reading, shrinks away, thus af-fording the painter, by her pose, an opportunity to combine the suave curves and countercurves of her figure in its dark robe into a charming pat-tern of blue against the gold ground, and to carry the movement, with the help of the arches of the frame, back to the angel. Here the rapid movement in the fluttering draperies and in the bro-ken patterns of gold brocade, wings, and

cloak offers an effective contrast to the quiet dark silhouette of the Virgin; the vase of flowers, the olive branch, and the floor, as well as the gold ground, unite the disparate elements. With prac-tically no reference to visual perception Simone wove symbols of figures into this charming, almost abstract pattern whose very loveliness of form intensifies the idea to be conveyed.

This delight in the loveliness of sur-face and sinuous line given such im-petus by Simone was one of the constant elements in Sienese painting and is by no means lacking in an entirely differ-ent follower of Duccio, Ambrogic Lorenzetti (active 1323–1348), whose robust figures, humanized from the

[A]   *Sassetta. Marriage of St. Francis and Poverty. 1444. Originally one panel in an altarpiece. Musée Condé, Chantilly. (Alinari)*

hieratic Duccio type, vigorous color contrasts, and equally vigorous straight lines, as well as a lucid organization within a realized space,[1] are evidences of the fact that he worked in Florence and there came into contact with the Humanistic and naturalistic movement of Giotto.

When the fifteenth-century Sienese painters could scarcely avoid some influence from the powerful new movement permeating all Italy, it was still the traditions of their great Trecento forebears that dominated their work, onto which the new naturalism was

weakly grafted. To take the *Mystic Marriage of St. Francis* (Fig. 472A) by Sassetta (1392–1450) as an example; though the gold ground has disappeared before a landscape and terrestrial spaciousness, the slender Gothic figures provide an excuse for the use of rhythmically repeated calligraphic lines and a primary interest in pattern in which the use of space as an element of balance is matched only by the great masters of handling space, the painters of China and Japan. In fifteenth-century Sienese painting the monumental archaic form of Duccio was transformed into a frail loveliness that betokened a declining age.

In the invigorating air of cities in a ferment of changing ideas, the Byzantine style could hardly suffice as a means of expression. Cimabue (about 1240–1301) in the face of this inadequacy attempted to revitalize its forms by infusing them with a new energy. Cavallini of Rome (active 1250–1330) in both his mosaics and frescoes attempted to meet the problem in a revival of Roman naturalism; that is, by modeling his figures in light and graduated shadow and by making their garments deep folds of actual stuffs instead of flat linear constructions, and by imbuing the figures with a stately dignity. Cavallini was something of a Nicola d'Apulia in painting, as Cimabue, at least in his emotional content, was a Giovanni Pisano.

Here, then, were two general lines of approach which confronted the youthful Florentine Giotto (1276–1336) when he came to Assisi to assist in the decoration of *San Francesco,*[2] which had been

---

[1] See Ambrogio's frescoes in *San Francesco,* his narrative panoramic style in the *Palazzo Pubblico,* Siena; compare his *Majestà* of Massa Maritima with Duccio's *Majestà.*

[2] This church well illustrates Cimabue's work in the *Crucifixion* (Upper Church) and the *Madonna and Saint Francis* (Lower Church); see also his *Madonnas* (Uffizi and Louvre). The *Isaac* series (Upper Church) represents the Roman school; for Cavallini, see the mosaics in *Santa Maria in Trastevere* (Rome) and the frescoes of *Santa Cecilia in Trastevere* (Rome).

going on since its erection. And here was the very heart of one of the dynamic forces of the Renaissance — Saint Francis and the Franciscan movement. At Assisi Giotto seems to have created a mode of expression which he set forth fully developed in the *Arena Chapel*[1] (Fig. 473A) at Padua a few years later. Here one senses at once a great gulf between the old and the new despite Giotto's artistic ancestry in both Byzantine and Roman styles and his continued use of traditional Byzantine iconography and composition, his use of the contemporary fresco technique, and the usual practice of covering walls with narratives which served a combined didactic and decorative purpose.

The great difference between Giotto's work and that of his predecessors is the difference between two widely divergent attitudes in painting.[2] The proponents of the one (this is the Byzantine attitude) construct forms out of purely formal elements — line, light and dark, color, and texture — with little or no regard for the natural appearance of what is represented. The tendency is toward abstraction, and if carried to its logical conclusion would result in pure geometry. The proponents of the other, represented by Giotto, construct forms with direct reference to visual perception and spatial relations. The tendency is toward naturalism, and its logical conclusion is a photographic copy. Now what particularly impresses

[1] So named because it stands on the site of an ancient Roman arena or amphitheater. It is also called the *Scrovegni Chapel* because Enrico Scrovegni, the son of a wealthy Paduan, who was so avaricious that Dante placed him in the seventh circle of hell among the usurers, had built the chapel as if to atone for the reputation of the family.

[2] These two attitudes, which roughly divide all painting into two groups — with many border cases, of course — are highly important for an understanding of the evolution of European painting and particularly for its twentieth-century phase.

[A]   *The Arena Chapel. Padua. Decorated with frescoes by Giotto, 1305. (Anderson)*

one about Giotto's work, in comparison with the Byzantine, is its actuality, its wholehearted grasp of an actuality based upon visual perception. Other painters had groped in this direction. Perhaps Tuscany inherited more than its name from the Etruscans of long ago. Perhaps there still existed a slight thread of their vital human reality. One likes to feel this when looking at Cimabue's *Crucifixion*. But Giotto was the first to turn definitely to visual actuality, and so definitely that he set painting on the path of visual investigation that it was to travel for five hundred years.

Take the *Pietà* (Fig. 475A) as an example. The body of Christ is held and surrounded by mourners who are actual people, with real bodies in clearly defined space, united in their expression of intense human grief; in fact the entire fresco is permeated with this emotional quality. There is the mere suggestion of a barren landscape — a rocky hillside

[A] *Giotto. Obsequies of St. Francis. Fresco. c. 1320. Santa Croce, Florence. (Alinari)*

and a dead tree. The sky is filled with angels who are giving themselves up to unrestrained grief. The center of interest is the head of Christ, on which all the lines converge — the curves of the bending figures, and the forceful diagonal of the hill, which is broken by one of the figures and hence not too obvious, the vertical folds of the drapery just above the Virgin, and even the glance of the two upright figures on the right, whose function is to balance the group on the left and to form, in an almost architectural way, a framework for the central group. Every figure in the panel plays its part, as if it were an architectural member of an abstract construction to which every gesture and detail is a contributing element. Looking at the individual figures, we see how economically yet how convincingly the bodies are realized as masses existing in space, and with what discrimination their simplest aspects only are expressed. Line, chiefly, combined with a limited use of shadow, defines the

mass of the figures,[1] each of which is so placed that movement in shallow space radiates from the focal point elliptically; for the opportunity for movement is chiefly lateral, since the space is abruptly terminated by the flat blue ground. This blue, used consistently in all the panels, serves as the unifying element in the entire decorative scheme.

An arresting balance and coherence of static and dynamic elements appear in the *Obsequies of Saint Francis* (Fig. 474A), whose basic composition is expressive of deep calm. This is due to an emphasis upon symmetry and a bal-

[1] This kind of drawing might be called sculptural, and is found in the drawings of those artists who see and feel masses in three dimensions and thus is to be distinguished from the calligraphic line of such painters as Simone Martini and the Persian miniaturists. Roger Fry calls attention to the fact that when we realize the great significance of Giotto's line, the famous story of Giotto's O seems credible. For this story see Vasari's life of Giotto. See also Bernhard Berenson's essay stressing "tactile values" in *The Florentine Painters of the Renaissance*, Putnam, 1909.

[A]   *Giotto. Pietà. Fresco. 1305. Arena Chapel, Padua. (Alinari)*

anced use of verticals and horizontals, in contrast to the *Pietà*, in which the stress lies upon asymmetry and the diagonal. Indeed, almost every painting by Giotto shows his inventiveness, for each presents a different problem of integrating visually perceived figures and objects into just that type of abstract organization which will convey the significance of the event. In the *Obsequies*, the architectural framework and the static, columnar figures at the sides provide a setting for the central group, which is contrastingly dynamic because of the asymmetrical arrangement of the figures about the bier, the

backward and forward movement within the group, and the more emphatic use of curved and diagonal lines.[1]

Giotto's unique and powerful art produced imitators only, who were without his power of lucid synthesis. Sienese painting was at its climax, for Duccio and Giotto were contemporaries and Ambrogio Lorenzetti was

[1] Giotto's paintings are so clearly and precisely composed that few works offer better opportunity for careful analysis for the purpose of showing how every detail is an indispensable element in a closely articulated organic structure.

[A] *Masaccio. Tribute Money. Fresco. c. 1425–28. Brancacci Chapel of Santa Maria della Carmine, Florence. (Alinari)*

painting in Florence about the time of Giotto's death. Thus the painters of the second half of the Trecento vacillated between an attempt to copy Giotto's forms and a maintenance of the traditional medieval style, which was much more popular and more easily understood than Giotto's.

Hence it was not until the fifteenth century that the movement initiated by Giotto found further expression in Masaccio (1401–1428),[1] whose frescoes in the *Brancacci Chapel* of the *Carmine* (Florence) dominated the Florentine school of the fifteenth century as did the sculpture and building of his contemporaries, Brunelleschi and Donatello,

[1] Masaccio's real name was Tomaso; but because of his careless disregard for his personal affairs, his forgetfulness of his debtors and equally of his creditors, he won the nickname Masaccio, a shortened form of Tomasaccio, meaning "Clumsy Tom." The Florentines frequently gave expression to their fun-loving disposition by applying appropriate nicknames to their citizens, which became so current that they have taken precedence over the real name. Thus in the case of Donatello, this sculptor's name was Donato, to which the suffix *-ello*, denoting endearment, was added, signifying the loving esteem felt by the Florentines for him. See Vasari for the lives of Brunelleschi, Donatello, and Masaccio.

with whom he was closely associated.

To illustrate by the *Tribute Money* (Fig. 476A), we see a group in a rugged barren landscape of great depth and spaciousness, not abbreviated or symbolic, as in Giotto, into which the figures fit as in the world of actuality visually perceived. The Disciples are gathered about Christ, who is directing Peter to go and cast his line, saying that in the mouth of the first fish he will find a coin with which he is to pay the tax. In the foreground, with his back to the spectator, stands the publican. The two concluding incidents are also shown in the panel, for at the left Peter is seen dragging the fish from the water, at the right he is giving the publican the coin. The visual reality of the scene is what Vasari felt when he said that Masaccio was the first artist to attain to the imitation of things. But the scene is not merely an imitation of nature. Like Donatello, Masaccio is enhancing the significance of the theme by translating it into monumental form. Christ is the central figure among the Disciples encircling Him. But notice the construction of the group. It is compact, with all heads on a level, and is set definitely into a space created by the architecture and the landscape. The group accentuates this space because it is controlled by a spiraling movement which begins with the publican on the frontal plane and swings backward and around elliptically to terminate in the figure of Christ. To the enframing landscape, architecture, and lateral figures, the group is tied by repeating verticals and diagonals, by a consistent lighting, and, if one can judge despite overpaintings, by an all-pervasive atmosphere. The landscape carries one into deep space, in contrast to Giotto's flat blue grounds, which maintain the solidity of the wall and provide but shallow space for the figures. The individual figures are large and massive, as were Giotto's, but they also give evidence of bodily structure — as in the figure of the publican, in which one feels a bony framework, muscles, joints, and articulations which enable the organism to support itself and to move. As Vasari says, "Masaccio made his figures stand upon their feet." This detailed knowledge is incorporated into broad inclusive line and simplified planes of light almost sculptural in their effect. Note this in the *Expulsion* and the *Baptism*, both in the *Brancacci Chapel.*

In his *Trinity* (Fig. 477A), Masaccio again showed his keen interest in perspective as a means for creating both space and monumental design. Here he has broken down the wall and extended the actual space of the nave into an illusionary space, and thus has created a chapel covered with a coffered barrel vault. The figures he has composed into a triangular group, the donors in the frontal plane outside the chapel, the others within, in parallel receding planes. As the level of the eye is low, the vault encloses the group with great power; and the clear linear design of contrasting curvilinear and angular motifs contributes to the monumentality of the design.

[A] *Masaccio. Trinity with the Virgin, St. John, and Donors. Fresco. c. 1426. Santa Maria Novella, Florence. (Alinari)*

With Masaccio we enter the early Renaissance, with its eager enthusiasm for inquiry. The world of actuality, curiosity about man and his world, led to fresh observations and to a compelling need for new forms in which to express them. The supranatural grandeur of Byzantinism arose from an entirely different world from that in which the men of the Quattrocento found themselves. Hence there began a scientific search for a more adequate type of expression. This involved the study of anatomy for the structure of the figure; of light and shadow to show its volume; of linear and aerial perspective to determine its place in space; and of new technical methods of mixing and applying pigment.

Paolo Uccello (1397–1475) displayed a compelling enthusiasm for perspective in his battle pieces (Fig. 478A), but not as an end in itself. The foreshort-

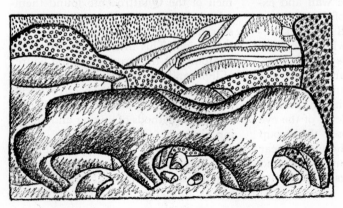

[A] *Paolo Uccello. Battle Piece. c. 1456. National Gallery, London. The analyses show* (a) *the organization of the foreground and background in depth by means of linear perspective, but they are not united by the middle distance, which is more or less a void as far as space is concerned; and* (b) *the composition of the main elements of the painting into planes generally parallel to the picture plane with the movement lateral.*

[A] *Andrea del Castagno. Youthful David. Painted leather shield. Widener Collection, National Gallery of Art, Washington. (National Gallery)*

ened figure, spears, and miscellany in the foreground carry one directly and insistently across space into the middle distance, whence the roads and the diminished figures continue the movement into the far distance. Thus is carved out a space for the action. A mass of soldiers, accented by their spears, moves in from the left, a movement balanced by the road moving forward diagonally from the depth at the right. The "impressionistic" crowd becomes more and more clearly defined until in the foreground simple

trenchant forms of horsemen stand fixed, their movement transmuted into immobility. Each form is clearly defined, of itself and in space, by juxtaposing highly contrasting values and by the sharp delineation of the forms by line. Thus an incident of complex movement becomes a clearly co-ordinate organization of formal and decorative beauty, in the search for which science was used only as the means to an end. In fact all the artists of this "scientific" group to which Paolo belonged sought scientific knowledge of the visual world

[A] *Antonio Pollaiuolo. Battling Nudes. Between 1465 and 1480. Paul J. Sachs Collection, Cambridge, Mass. (Paul J. Sachs)*

for this purpose, and because they were primarily great artists "their facts had to be digested into form."[1]

Important members of this group were Andrea del Castagno (1397–1457), whose David (Fig. 479A) reveals Andrea's tense incisiveness; Domenico Veneziano (1400–1461), an important innovator in the field of oil glazes; Antonio Pollaiuolo (1429–1498); Andrea del Verrocchio (1435–1488); Alesso Baldovinetti (1425–1499); and the Umbro-Florentines, Piero della Francesca (1416–1492) and Luca Signorelli (1441–1522).

Baldovinetti's workshop was an important center for the group about the middle of the century. Secular subject matter, especially the classical, and portraiture, emerging at a time of forceful individualism, was claiming attention. Experiments were going on in the use

[1] Fry, *Vision and Design*, "The Art of Florence."

of oil as a freer, more slowly drying medium than tempera; and in aerial as well as linear perspective. Part of this we see in Baldovinetti's *Madonna* (Fig. 481A). The figure of the Madonna is realized as mass and is constructed as tersely as Uccello's horses. Though it rises majestically into a great spaciousness, it bears no natural relationship to the landscape behind it. Yet the two tie into an organic design of complementary sharp angles and suave curves, of slow movements in unbroken contours balanced by the rapid rhythms of veil, hair, and meandering streams. These motifs are repeated all through the canvas with unmistakable clarity because of the sharp juxtaposition of lights and darks, which contributes to the generally decorative effect of the panel.

Antonio Pollaiuolo, trained first, like many Florentine artists, as a goldsmith, became equally successful as a sculptor,

[A] *Baldovinetti. Madonna. c. 1460. Louvre, Paris. (Giraudon)*

[B] *Antonio Pollaiuolo. Heracles Slaying the Hydra. 1460. Uffizi, Florence.*

as a painter, as an engraver, and as a designer of tapestries. In a small panel representing *Heracles Slaying the Hydra* (Fig. 481B), Heracles is rushing upon the monster, grasping one of the heads in the left hand and about to bring down his club with the right hand. The two figures nearly fill the panel and stand out against a low-lying landscape with winding rivers in much the same way as in Baldovinetti's *Madonna*. In the figure of Heracles we feel the tenseness of the muscles and the articulation of the joints as every part of the anatomy responds to the demand of the moment. One leg is bent to a right angle and firmly placed, with toes clutching the ground, the other is stretched to its utmost as he concentrates his energy upon the attack. As Berenson says, Antonio Pollaiuolo was "one of the greatest masters of movement that there ever has been and one

of the ablest interpreters of the human body as a vehicle of life-communicating energy and exulting power." We know that he made searching studies in perspective and in anatomy, especially through dissection. What interested him particularly was how the human figure would act in violent movement. For this reason he usually selected subjects that gave an opportunity for action. In his engraving of the *Battling Nudes* (Fig. 480A), each figure is an epitome of intense energy, a grimly realistic expression of human ferocity. Yet what a superb pattern these figures weave against the curtainlike background of plants and trees! This balance between visual perception and formal organization is well illustrated in a charming portrait (Fig. 485B), possibly by Antonio, a beautiful example of tempera technique with exquisite modulations and a decorative effect that

[A]   *Piero della Francesca. Visit of the Queen of Sheba to King Solomon. Fresco. Detail.
1452–66. San Francesco, Arezzo. (Alinari)*

results from the fine, precise brush strokes and the sharply defined edges.

Connected with this scientific group was an Umbrian, Piero della Francesca (about 1416–1492), who after a sojourn in Florence returned to his native province to execute some of the most monumental frescoes in Italy. At Arezzo he decorated a chapel with scenes from the legend of the cross on which Christ was crucified. Figure 482A shows a detail from the *Visit of the Queen of Sheba to Solomon*, in which the queen is kneeling before a bridge made from the tree that was destined to furnish the wood for the cross. The queen and her attendants form a compact group, accented by a tree. From figure to figure the

eye is carried by the alternating light and dark areas (compare Paolo Uccello's horses, Figure 478A), and by the long sweeping lines of the garments to the group on the left, that of the grooms and horses, also accentuated by a tree. Here the white horse turns the movement inward, where it is caught by the light hat and the black horse, and is taken up by the undulating hills, whose quiet rhythm is accented by the staccato of the trees. Every figure fits inevitably into the ample spaciousness, which is cut off in the middle distance, keeping the wall rather flat. Even the illimitable sky is held by the decisive trees. A profound calm devoid of human emotion pervades the austere figures, in which

[A]   *Piero della Francesca. Resurrection of Christ. Fresco. Gallery of Borgo San Sepolcro.*

Piero shows a lofty disregard of an illusion of natural appearance yet communicates a deeply convincing feeling of actuality. Every figure and every object is reduced to geometric simplicity and is placed with mathematical precision in space and in relation to every other figure — a relationship indicated precisely by the shapes and the movements of contrasted light and dark color-masses with sharply defined edges and tied together by an all-pervading cool tonality. "The lofty expanse of sky is an intense, unforgetta-

[A] *Fra Angelico. Coronation of the Virgin. c. 1430. San Marco, Florence. An example of beautiful tempera painting: gaily colorful, luminous, effectively organized in shallow space. The intense colors of the robes, interspersed with the gold of the halos and details, set against the gold ground produce the effect of a magnified cloisonné enamel.*

ble blue, not medievally flat, not filled with realistic clouds and haze, but varied a little in tone, so that it seems to recede into infinite distance. Its hue condenses to a deeper turquoise in some of the robes, and its pale dry light descends to reveal every figure with unflickering crystal clarity. It fills both highlights and background with a fresh, cool atmosphere, against which garments of deep red, green and gold

stand out here and there in warmer contrast."[1]

In contrast to this permeating light, Piero makes use of a highly concentrated light in the *Dream of Constantine* (Arezzo), which foreshadows Tintoretto and Rembrandt. Here is a framework as architectural as a building: the

[1] Thomas Munro, *Great Pictures of Europe*, Coward-McCann, 1930, p. 133. This book is excellent for clear concise statements on color.

[A] *Luca Signorelli. Last Judgment. Detail. 1500–04. Orvieto Cathedral. (Anderson)*

[B] *Unknown Artist. Portrait of a Lady. c. 1460. Poldi Pezzoli, Milan. (Alinari)*

cylindrical tent capped with a cone, a motif repeated in the tent opening and in the distant tents; the two columnar guards, the vertical spear and tent pole; the opposing horizontal bed and reclining figure. This stern regularity is given vitality by the angel, by the seated attendant, and by the strong light which radiates from the angel to the emperor and his servant. In his *Resurrection* (Fig. 483A), which Piero painted for his native town of Borgo San Sepolcro, an austere Byzantinesque figure stands above the tomb with imperturbable calm. The rigidly erect frontal pose, accented by the repeating verticals of the banner and the trees and the strong horizontals of the tomb, stands opposed to the inward and outward movement and the diagonal lines in the group of sleeping guards. The sternness of the standing figure is mitigated by the curves in the drapery, repeated in the hills, and its static quality is merged into the dynamic of the group by the movement in the bent knee, the hand, and the drapery. Note in this detail the fine integration of parts, definitely sculptural in feeling.

If in Piero scientific knowledge of mathematics, perspective, and anatomy was distilled to its essence and objectified in cool, impersonal, abstract forms infinitely precise in their relationships and architectural in quality as mural decoration, in his pupil Signorelli (1441–1523) this knowledge manifested itself in another direction, as we see in the frescoes of the *San Brizio Chapel* in the *Cathedral of Orvieto*. Here seething groups are carefully organized in space (Fig. 485A) and adapted to the lunette-shaped areas. But in contrast to the immobility and high simplification of Piero's figures, Signorelli's are filled with movement, muscular strain, and tense energy, like those of Antonio Pollaiuolo.

[A] *Fra Filippo Lippi. Madonna and Child with Two Angels. c. 1457. Uffizi, Florence. Compare with Figs. 484A, 500A.*

In this group of experimenters lay the fire of the Quattrocento. Yet it did not comprise all the painters in Florence. As in Ghiberti among the sculptors, the medieval style persisted in a more reactionary group, illustrated by Fra Angelico (1387–1455). As his name implies, he was a *frate*, a monk, brought up in the medieval tradition fostered in the monasteries. In his *Coronation of the Virgin* (Fig. 484A), Christ and the Virgin are represented seated upon a throne of clouds from which radiate golden rays, and about which circle angels and saints. The panel is a beautiful pattern of bright colors and gold organized by sweeping lines. We mark how effectively the drapery of the angels nearest the central group encircles it; how the rhythm is repeated in the outer circle of angels and saints, and relieved by the

kneeling saint in the left foreground and the angel with the harp on the right; and how the long trumpets very effectively fill the space above. Clarity of form always marks the work of Fra Angelico. His elements of organization are line, strongly calligraphic, and intensely bright color areas of dominant blues combined with rose and green and a liberal interspersing of gold. It is the art of the miniature translated into the tempera technique, and exemplifies admirably the glowing quality of that technique.

Fra Angelico could hardly escape, however, some influence from the innovations sweeping Florence. So we find his gold grounds giving way to landscape and to architectural details that are Renaissance, not Gothic, in style. In his late frescoes in Rome he reveals both volume in his individual figures and organization in depth.

While in a general way the painters of fifteenth-century Florence fell into the two groups typified by Masaccio and Fra Angelico, many did not, for the output of the shops, in this experimental age when life was all eagerness and spirits ran high, was too prolific, varied, and uneven to be so definitely pigeonholed. There was Fra Filippo Lippi (1406–1469), who profited from contact with Masaccio even if the calligraphic line of Fra Angelico found its way into his work. His own liking for the gracious, charming types and aspects of life which he saw in Florence led him to imbue the traditional religious themes with a gracious humanity (Fig. 486A). Benozzo Gozzoli (1420–1498) in the refreshingly gay decorations of the private chapel in the palace of the Medici represents ostensibly the *Journey of the Magi* but in reality a vivid pageant of the Medici court. Domenico Ghirlandaio (1449–1494) in *Santa Maria Novella* makes scenes from the New Testament excuses for the family portraits of rich merchants — a vivid picture of the "men and manners" of the Florence of that time. The popular, narrative style of this group with its gaiety and easy charm, infused though it is at times with the sterner aspects of the scientific group, is quite analogous to that of the Desiderio group of sculptors, which emphasized surface loveliness and decorative charm.

Thus this vividly alive century moves into its last quarter. Certain youths, then apprentices, were partly to continue its spirit of investigation and partly to take the results of its researches and by the strength of their individualities mold them into the more unified style of the sixteenth century — Botticelli, Leonardo, Raphael, Michelangelo, Fra Bartolommeo, Andrea del Sarto.

Sandro Botticelli (1444–1510), whose individual bent for calligraphic line was not crushed but rather was developed by his grounding in the realistic school, was a unique product of the Florentine school because he was out of its main current. Instead of accepting his visual perceptions as something to reproduce, he "conceived the visual world as an architecture of rhythmic line"[1] — not Giotto's sculptural line, which defines masses, but something akin to that of the Persian miniaturists. In *The Birth of Venus* (Fig. 427A), on the sea a classical goddess stands lightly on a shell that is being blown to the shore amid a shower of roses by two vigorous zephyrs; at the right a nymph is hurrying with a mantle to meet her. The composition is built on a great arc that rises along the figures of the winds, reaches its crown in the head of Venus, follows the fluttering hair, and is carried down by the arm of the nymph

[1] Yukio Yashiro, *Sandro Botticelli and the Florentine Renaissance*, Hale, Cushman & Flint, 1929 — a sympathetic interpretation from the point of view of an Oriental.

[A] *Leonardo. Mona Lisa. Portrait of the wife of Zanobi del Giocondo. 1503–06. Louvre, Paris. (Alinari)*

and the line of the mantle. This arc is repeated in the upper curve of the shell, and about it play quick nervous movements in drapery, hair, wings, and water. The tall, slender figure of Venus with its long, quiet lines, standing somewhat isolated against a low horizon, is rather flat, and the contour lines, while they model the form, as long graceful curves have a beauty of their own, and are emphasized by the movement in the great mass of hair twisting and fluttering and framing the drooping head, whose expression of wistful melancholy is characteristic of Botticelli. The flying locks lead to the nymph, where the impatient, whimsical curves of the drapery are all the more restless in contrast to the straight lines of the tree trunks, the little promontories, and the horizon. After all, the significance lies in line and pattern. The lines model,

[A] *Botticelli. Dante and Virgil in Purgatory. Drawing to illustrate Dante's* Divine Comedy, Purgatory XXV–VI. 1492–97.

insofar as they express the essentials of form, yet they have a quality of their own. Now they are long and quiet, now short and capricious, now whimsical, and always rhythmic. "My fancy is never checked: as the zephyr it flows smoothly along the gull-like pattern of waves on the green sea, along the facile lines of Venus' golden hair. You will soon forget the actual picture and you do not notice it: it is so evanescent and shy, as rare as a dream."[1]

The waning of medieval religious fervor and the increasing popularity of secular, and particularly classical, themes, especially under the stimulation and patronage of the court of the Medici, is well illustrated in Botticelli. The *Calumny* (Fig. 489A), for example, is an attempted reconstruction, with the help of classical literature, of a famous

[1] *Ibid.*

painting of the Greek painter Apelles. Calumny and Envy, accompanied by Treachery and Deceit, drag the innocent victim before the judge into whose asses' ears Ignorance and Suspicion are whispering; at the left, naked Truth protests in isolation while Remorse looks to Truth as she moves toward the vindictive group. The painting illustrates a break from the more usual symmetrical to an asymmetrical balance. Its movement is lateral and is set in the shallow space of an architectural framework whose perspective combines with the linear and light-and-dark organization to focus upon the group before the judge. The movement and the warm glowing color in the figures are heightened by being set over against the static architectural framework in neutral color and gold, through which is seen a cool sky and sea.

[A] *Botticelli. Calumny. Uffizi, Florence. 1485–90. (Alinari)*

Botticelli's feeling for line finds its purest expression in his drawings for the *Divine Comedy*. As illustrations for Dante, they are far in spirit from the profound, majestic, and dramatic poem. In Figure 488A, between a precipice in the foreground and high cliffs in the background, both indicated by freely sketched lines with no use of light and shade, runs a band of flame before which Virgil and Dante are walking, discoursing with the souls being purged in the fire. The form is in terms of line only, though Botticelli may have intended to use color in the figures. The broken, rapid, leaping lines, held in check by the firm straight lines in the figures and held between the cliffs, evoke an emotional reaction to movement per se, as in music or the dance; and they also suggest seething flames without actually imitating their appearance. Thus Botticelli's attitude toward natural appearance was very close to that of the Far Eastern masters [1] of India, China, and Japan (Figs. 247A, 380A, 392A).

Contemporary with, though far different from, Botticelli was Leonardo da Vinci (1452–1519), an epitome of the "myriad-minded" man of the Renaissance. For centuries Europe had been breaking away from the dogma and the authority of the Middle Ages. Finally, with the help of the newly discovered Humanistic classical culture, an entirely new world lay before man. It was not in view of everyone, but it strongly aroused the keen observation and eager curiosity of such a truly scientific spirit as Leonardo, whose myriad-sided curiosity is revealed best in his notes (comprising more than five thousand pages), jottings and studies, liberally interspersed with sketches, on botany, geology, zoology, optics; on hydraulic and military engineering and all kinds

[1] See pages 380–84.

[A]　*Leonardo. Last Supper. c. 1495–98. Refectory of Santa Maria delle Grazie, Milan. (Alinari) The doorway in the foreground was cut through later. The ruined condition of the Last Supper is due partly to careless restoration and vandalism and partly to the fact that in this painting Leonardo appeared to be experimenting, as was his habit, in media, and painted upon a wrongly prepared surface.*

of physical and mechanical sciences; on Latin and Italian grammar; on animal lore; on perspective, light and shade, color, anatomy; and on man — structural, emotional, and intellectual. Nothing of man and his world seems omitted. Painting and sculpture were merely two of a multitude of Leonardo's interests.[1]

In his notebook jottings on painting,[2] Leonardo says of the purpose of painting: "A good painter has two chief objects to paint — man and the intention of his soul. The former is easy, the latter hard, for it must be expressed by gestures and movements of the limbs. . . . A painting will only be wonderful for the beholder by making that

which is not so appear raised and detached from the wall" — that is, modeling with light and shadow is the heart of painting, and particularly a somewhat diffused light. "Towards evening or in bad weather I have noticed the features of men and women in the streets and marked what grace and softness can be seen thereon." For Leonardo combined with his scientific attitude a very subtle esthetic sensibility, and a predilection for the gracious aspects of the world.

Very early, perhaps while still in Verrocchio's shop as an apprentice, he seems to have become a master in transferring his images to paper with the greatest freedom and spontaneity. In Figure 491A, line alone models the baby form with its folds of soft flesh, and also expresses a single moment of delightful intimacy between mother and child, "the intention of the soul" as well as Leonardo's predilection for "grace and dignity."

[1] See the remarkable letter of self-recommendation which Leonardo wrote to the Duke of Milan in Osvald Sirén, *Leonardo da Vinci,* Yale University Press, 1916, p. 59.

[2] Later collected from all his manuscripts and put together into what is now known as his *Treatise on Painting.*

[A] *Leonardo. Drawing of Madonna and Child. Pen and ink. Louvre, Paris. (Giraudon)*

[B] *Leonardo. Adoration of the Magi, central figure. Unfinished. 1481–1504. Uffizi, Florence. (Alinari)*

In the unfinished *Adoration* (Fig. 491B) [1] Leonardo has placed the Madonna in the center, somewhat back from the frontal plane — a position emphasized by the inward movement of the kneeling king on the right — and has encircled her with the group of figures. In this painting he has posed and partly solved a spatial and a psychological problem: the formal unity in space of a dramatic group all of whose movement focalize upon the quiet, somewhat isolated central figures; and an emotional unity that binds the

dramatic figures together in the adoration of the *Christ Child*. The background is filled with miscellaneous objects — horsemen, ruined architecture, trees and landscape — and bears little compositional relation to the compact foreground group except that the large trees help tie them both together. Complete organization in deep space has not yet been attained.

Formally and emotionally, a great similarity exists between the *Adoration* and the *Last Supper* (Fig. 490A),[2] except that in the latter the highly dramatic action is made still more emphatic by the placement of the group in a quiet setting. In a simple, spacious room, at a long table set in the foreground parallel to the picture plane, Christ and the

---

[1] The underpainting, in browns, has been laid in, a few of the heads and the Child's figure quite completely modeled in light and shadow, the Virgin's and the kings' sketched only. The painting would have been completed by continuing the modeling and then adding the local color, either in tempera or in the newer oil medium which Leonardo used in his later works. Several preliminary drawings show the evolution of the design.

[2] See the preliminary drawings for this painting in most of the books on Leonardo or in Bernhard Berenson, *The Drawings of the Florentine Painters*, University of Chicago Press, 1938.

[A] *Leonardo. Madonna of the Rocks. Louvre, Paris. (Alinari)*

twelve disciples are seated. Christ, with outstretched hands, has just said, "One of you will betray me." At this statement a wave of intense excitement passes through the group as each asks, "Is it I?" The force and the lucidity with which this dramatic moment is expressed are due to the abstract organization. In the center is the figure of Christ, in perfect repose, isolated from the disciples, framed by the central window at the back, emphasized by the curved line over the opening (the only curved line in the architectural framework), and the focal point of all the lines in the composition. Into this reposeful framework are fitted four groups of agitated disciples, united within themselves and also to one an-

other by a movement of the hand, a gesture of the arm, or a turn of the head. The two figures at the ends are more quiet, as if to frame in the movement, which grows more intense as it approaches the figure of Christ, whose quietude at the same time halts and intensifies it. All this movement is lateral and confined to a plane parallel to the picture plane and but slightly removed from it in depth.

The ruined condition of the *Last Supper* makes it advisable to turn to other paintings, such as the *Madonna of the Rocks* (Fig. 492A) to illustrate the increasing depth and mystery of shadows and their tendency to break up the unity of the design. In this picture we see an arresting change in the use of pictorial elements. For the means by which the figures are knit together into a pyramidal group — a characteristic Renaissance design — is not so much line as areas of high lights and deep shadows, with subtle gradations of tone — which illustrates well Leonardo's theory of "modeling in light and shadow." Contrast the perfect clarity and architectural function of every detail in Piero's frescoes (Fig. 482A). Leonardo's predilection for high lights and deep shadows must have been highly stimulated by the use of oil as a medium, with its capacity for subtle nuances such as are found in the *Madonna of the Rocks* and the *Mona Lisa*, which have a loveliness of their own and at the same time a capacity for recording in the face enigmatic "intentions of the soul."

Mona Lisa (Fig. 487A) is seated in an armchair on a loggia whose stone rail and columns frame a misty landscape. She is simply dressed, with no ornaments, and her hair, falling in loose ringlets, is covered by a thin veil. The composition recalls Baldovinetti's *Madonna* (Fig. 481A) — a pyramidal mass sensitively related to the space and to the background. The powerfully realized figure with strong, almost unbroken contours rises against a vague dreamlike landscape whose elusive movement repeats itself in the subtle nuances of the face. Sharp high lights in the crumpled satin folds act as a foil to the extraordinarily subtle modeling of the hands. This interaction of the definite and the indefinite, the pyschological and the formal, controls the composition. A definitely felt vertical axis falls from the forehead to the crossed hands, connecting the two masses of interest, the face and the hands, each of which is an example of Leonardo's technical ability to objectify his visual perception realistically by means of infinitely gradual transitions from light to shadow. By this means also he could depict in the face that elusive expression[1] which reflects fleeting emotions into the mysteries of which Leonardo's curiosity led him to delve.

With Michelangelo, on the other hand, we meet a man who was interested in big generic ideas and who, building upon the researches of the scientists of the fifteenth century, in painting and sculpture alike used the figure as a vehicle for the expression of these conceptions. As has been noted, he considered himself a sculptor; and when Pope Julius II ordered him to decorate the ceiling of the *Sistine Chapel*[2] (Fig. 494A), he rebelled. But the Pope was insistent. The result looks as if Michelangelo had said, "Well, if the Pope will have his ceiling, let him have it; but," as Wölfflin suggests, "he will have to stretch his neck to see it." As a scheme

[1] Read Walter Pater's famous passage in his essay on Leonardo in *The Renaissance*, which is poetic prose on the theme of the *Mona Lisa* rather than a criticism of it as a painting.

[2] Frescoes in three chapels form epochs in the history of Italian painting: those in the *Arena Chapel* by Giotto, about 1405; in the *Brancacci Chapel* by Masaccio, 1424–26; in the *Sistine Chapel* by Michelangelo, 1508–12.

[A] *Michelangelo. Decorative Nude. Sistine Ceiling. 1508–12. (Alinari)*

of decoration, this ceiling is an absurdity, a penance alike to the artist while he painted it and to the spectator who wishes to look at it. A vast complex of humanity thunders down upon him, drowning out everything else, and the frescoes on the walls pale before it. Though the first impression is bewildering, a brief study easily resolves the mass into a great pattern, the motifs of which are rhythmically repeated and inextricably co-ordinated (Fig. 494A). The eye is carried from human figure to human figure; prophets and sibyls sit in niches flanked by pilasters on which are putti who serve, Caryatid-like, to hold up the painted cornice which runs the length of the vault and forms a framework for the central panels and a connecting link between the prophets and the panels; for on this cornice rest the blocks on which the nudes are seated, a pair at each corner of the smaller panels, holding be-

[A] *Sistine Chapel. Vatican, Rome. (Anderson)*

tween them, by means of bands, round medallions. These figures serve a decorative and unifying purpose, each pair with the help of the medallions carrying the eye, by their repeated rhythmic pattern, from the larger to the smaller panels all the length of the ceiling.

The marvel of gathering so many figures into a harmonious unit would have been impossible except for the extremely simple, though strongly marked, architectural framework, in monochrome, which holds the mass together, so that the eye can wander about among the figures and yet feel the unity of the whole. It is always the human figure, sharply outlined against the neutral tone of this architectural setting or the plain background of the panels. Why did Michelangelo decorate the ceiling

in this way? It was because to him the most beautiful, the most expressive, thing in the whole world was the human figure. It was beautiful not only because of its form but because of its spiritual and ethical significance, the state of mind or soul that its form could so successfully express. He represented it in its most simple, elemental aspect; that is, the nude or simply draped, with no background, no ornamental embellishment, and with an idealized physiognomy. It was upon the sheer power of definitely related masses that he depended. "Simple people," he called the prophets. *Jeremiah* (Fig. 496A), to take an example, sits with head bowed upon his uplifted hand, sunk in deep thought. The related masses of the figure are powerfully expressed by broad brush

[A] *Michelangelo. Creation of Adam. Sistine Ceiling. 1508–12. (Anderson)*

strokes, reminiscent of the sculptural drawing of Giotto except that in the *Jeremiah* the figure, instead of consisting of one mass, is a unit of organically related masses of legs, torso, arms, and head. With what ease and inevitability, for example, the prophet's left arm, as a mass, crosses and unites with the left leg as a mass. These backward and forward movements are stabilized by the sweeping contour of the shoulders repeated in the drapery across the lap and by the insistent verticals in the beard and the drapery. The pose of the figure — with the drooping right shoulder, the weight of the head on the right hand, the limp left hand, the ponderous weight of the whole — is determined by a desire to convey an impression of deep thought. There are no details to individualize this prophet; everything is so gen-

eralized that we feel that this is not only Jeremiah brooding over Israel, is not only Michelangelo himself pondering in isolation and melancholy, but is every human being who, probing with his own soul beneath the surface of things, loses himself in the contemplation of the problems and mysteries of life.

It was probably in the twenty *Nudes* that Michelangelo was happiest, for here he had the opportunity of reveling in his ideal — the human nude conceived sculpturally. Although all serve the same decorative purpose (Fig. 495A), still they are very different, each, perhaps paradoxically, a more or less realistic rendering of the human figure and at the same time an expression of a definite inner state of mind. In Figure 493A, strain and stress are symbolized by the mighty back, the thrust-out arm and

[A] *Michelangelo. Jeremiah. Sistine Ceiling. 1508–12. (Anderson)*

shoulder, the violent contrasts in the direction of movement, the tousled hair, the sharp profile with open mouth; in other figures, there is ease and complacency, lyric joyousness, the weight of burden-bearing.

As an illustration of Michelangelo's composition, let us examine the *Creation of Adam* (Fig. 495A), one of the larger panels of the ceiling. It is divided into two masses, which stand out clearly against the flat background. Adam, on a hillside — the hill is merely suggested, again a Giottesque quality — is just awakening. The physical potentialities of the reposeful figure are suggested in the balancing of broken jagged contours with those that are unbroken and suavely curving; and in the balancing of parts in movement — the thrust-back shoulder, the turned head, the sharply bent leg — with the relaxed outstretched arm and leg. This comparatively quiet figure is opposed to the second group,

that of God and His attendant spirits, which is full of vigorous movement; and the two are united by the two hands, each expressive of the mood of its possessor — Adam's limp and lifeless, God's tense with creative power.

In most of these figures on the ceiling, we can hardly fail to feel their inherently sculptural quality. Michelangelo himself says in a letter written while he was discouraged and depressed about the ceiling: "This is not my profession. I waste time without any results. God help me." Yet in the medium of painting he was motivated by the same desire as in sculpture — to organize the figure into a complex arrangement in space. And these arrangements usually involve strongly contrasting movements which produce a feeling of restlessness or even violence. It is futile to look for quietude in this artist.

In Michelangelo we reach a climax in painting so powerful that it overwhelmed the artists of the time, who forsook their own paths to follow in his — with the result that we have empty copying of his forms, lacking in creative spirit. Hence came the decadence which followed his death.

In Raphael (1483–1520) we find a rare ability to organize crowds of people in space. An Umbrian, a pupil of Perugino, he early acquired a feeling for spaciousness, characteristic of that master, a feeling that perhaps was partially acquired from the influence of the actual open reaches of this gently rolling hill country.[1] In Perugino's *Crucifixion* (Fig. 497A), for example, there is a dominant note of quiet repose, though the subject matter is dramatic and tragic. The painter has divided the wall space into three sweeping arches, which of themselves create a quiet rhythm. Into these the figures, uninteresting and even sentimental, are fitted as architectural

[1] See Gabriel Faure, *Wanderings in Italy*, Houghton Mifflin, 1919, Pt. III, p. 141.

[A]   *Perugino. Crucifixion. Fresco. 1493–96. Santa Maria Maddalena dei Pazzi, Florence.*
Compare the background with Raphael's in Fig. 497B. (Anderson)

units to form a triangle with a long base;
behind, unifying the whole composition, stretches a landscape of hills, valleys, rivers, and trees, above which are
reaches of sky, whose spaciousness is
suggested by the tall slender trees at the
left. The lines of this landscape are far-
extending and quiet, and the distance
is immersed in a bluish haze.

Apart from this Umbrian inheritance,
Raphael was a product of the Florentine
school. With great powers of assimilation, he profited not only from his
contemporaries, Leonardo and Michelangelo, but from Masaccio, Donatello,
Pollaiuolo. The whole series of Raphael's
Madonnas, from the *Granduca* to the
Sistine, is indicative of the way in which
the Florentine masters were shaping
this docile Umbrian talent. In *La Belle
Jardinière* (Fig. 497B), for example, the
influence of Leonardo appears in the
grouping of the figures[1]; that of Michelangelo, in the restless twisting pose of

[1] See the *Madonna of the Rocks* (Fig. 492A), and
the *Madonna with Saint Anne* (Louvre).

[B]   *Raphael. Madonna: "La Belle Jardinière." 1507–08. Louvre, Paris. (Braun)*

[A]   *Raphael. School of Athens. 1509–11. Vatican, Rome. (Anderson)*

the Christ Child.[1] The group is set naturalistically into, not in front of, a charming landscape with the Umbrian feeling for tranquillity and spaciousness. There is a compelling realization of this spaciousness, though the Madonna dominates the picture.

The *Sistine Madonna*[2] derives its effect from a carefully studied design in depth with effective contrasts in movement and in light and dark color. The design is based on the usual pyramidal grouping. The Madonna and the Child form a tight group with a gentle inward and outward movement set against a luminous sky, the highest light in the painting. This group is given further emphasis

by the lower kneeling figures with their stronger movement. One is turning inward, the other outward; one is looking up, the other down. Such abstract design in space is the basis of the *Madonna of the Chair*, "which, with its even pure volute, resembles nothing so much as some exquisite sea-shell. . . ."

"It is, however, in those compositions by Raphael that are laden with whole garlands of human bodies that we can best comprehend the genius for harmonic variations that combines over and over again those shapes wherein the life of forms has absolutely no aim other than itself and its own renewal."[3] Raphael's frescoes in the Vatican illustrate this best.

In the *Disputà* (Fig. 499A), two arcs, moving inward from the frontal plane,

---

[1] See Michelangelo's *Madonna and Child* (Bruges).

[2] Painted for the Sistine monks of Piacenza and called *Sistine* because of their ownership and the prominent figure of Pope Sixtus II.

[3] Henri Focillon, *The Life of Forms in Art*, Yale University Press, 1942, pp. 7–8.

[A]   *Raphael. Disputà. 1509–11. Vatican, Rome. (Anderson)*

approach each other at the central axis, about which all parts are balanced symmetrically. The upper arc encloses the scene in heaven, with Christ between the Virgin and Saint John, surrounded by saints, angels, and cherubim; with God the Father above, and the dove below. The lower arc contains a more varied group, each figure contributing by its pose or gesture and its line and color to the movement toward the four Fathers of the Church gathered about the altar on which stands, silhouetted against the highest light and on the vertical axis, the monstrance, symbol of the mystery of the faith, and the focal point of the design. A serene Umbrian landscape serves to unite the two groups.

Perhaps more imposing is the *School of Athens* (Fig. 498A). An effective architectural setting, which in form, scale,

and dignity is quite at one with sixteenth-century ideals,[1] furnishes a deep framework in which the figures are so placed that an elliptical movement swings from the front to each side and thence back to the figures of Plato and Aristotle framed by the series of arches. A supplementary movement inward directly from the picture plane to the focal point is carried by the receding lines of the inlaid floor, the steps, and the two seated figures.

The imposing dignity and plastic unity that we found in the architecture and the sculpture of the High Renaissance thus find their counterpart in painting: in the great series of frescoes of Raphael and Michelangelo, and in such

[1] Bramante was at this time working on the plans for the new *St. Peter's* and Raphael himself was about to assist in this great undertaking.

[A] *Andrea del Sarto. Madonna of the Harpies (from the figures of Harpies on the pedestal). 1517. Uffizi, Florence. (Alinari)*

panel paintings as those of Fra Bartolommeo and Andrea del Sarto (1486–1531). In Andrea's *Madonna of the Harpies* (Fig. 500A), the stately figures almost fill the canvas. We find an echo of the traditional symmetrical pyramidal grouping, but not the diffused lighting, the sharply defined contours, and the generally lateral movement of the Quattrocento. Instead we see dark shadows in which details are lost, blurred edges, and spiraling movements in a complete organization in depth which controls each figure as a single unit and as one unit of the group.

Northern Italian Painting

AMONG the cities of northern Italy (Fig. 431A) —Venice, Milan, Verona, Mantua, Ferrara, Bologna, Padua — Venice was chief. The islands on which it was built in the midst of salt marshes near the head of the Adriatic Sea had offered a refuge for the peoples of northern Italy from the barbarian invaders of the fifth century. Thus isolated and segregated from the rest of Italy, it developed, as we have seen, quite independently. The Venetians early became a seafaring people, establishing close relations with the East and sending their artists to execute commissions at the court of Constantinople. Venetian markets were full of the rich brocades, silks, jewels, metal goods, and slaves of the Near East. Politically, Venice was sound; and, though autocratic, it was peaceful and free from the periodic feuds that were constantly rending other Italian cities. Religiously, too, Venice was more independent. Safely remote from the papal power at Rome, it centered its religious life independently about the veneration of its patron, Saint Mark.

Venetian life was the antithesis of Florentine life, for it was dominantly gay and luxurious. A fervid patriotism made strong demands upon the citizens for the glorification of the state. There were gorgeous pageants and ceremonies, both religious and civil, besides private banquets and pompous balls (see the paintings of Giovanni Bellini, Carpaccio, Tintoretto, Veronese); the richest costumes of stiff brocades, gold embroidery, and lavish lace and jewels. This extravagance and love of display was not conducive to intellectual pursuits. A Humanist was shabbily treated and even starved in Venice, and a profoundly religious man found no sympathy there.

Gay and isolated as it was, however, its art did not remain uninfluenced by the great stirrings that were revolutionizing Italian art, though it clung longer than Florence to the Gothic style in painting, as it did in architecture. Up to the fifteenth century Venetian painting was strongly Byzantine and Gothic.

[A] *Mantegna. Crucifixion. 1459. Louvre, Paris. (Alinari)*

with the love of color a predominant quality, as we might expect in a city so closely connected with the East as well as in one located in a naturally colorful setting. Nevertheless it received strong enough influences from other Italian centers, particularly from Florence, to affect its art powerfully, though without changing its essentially Venetian character.

A new spirit first appears in the work of the so-called father of Venetian painting, Jacopo Bellini (died 1470). In his notebooks of drawings[1] we are struck by his fancy, and by his lively joy in nature — trees, hills, flowers, animals particularly, both real and fantastic. Jacopo had been touched by the naturalistic movement, and also by the growing passion for classical subjects,

[1] See Corrado Ricci, *Jacopo Bellini e i suoi libri di disegni*, Florence, 1908.

for sheet after sheet in these notebooks shows drawings of architectural details, antique statues, centaurs, and satyrs.

A still greater influence upon Venetian painting came from near-by Padua, an old Roman colony which had always had strong intellectual and religious strains in its culture. Its pride in being the birthplace of the great Roman historian Livy stimulated an enthusiasm for things classical; and its religious fervor led it to respond easily to Saint Bernard. Furthermore, Giotto had decorated the *Arena Chapel* about 1305; Paolo Uccello in the first half of the fifteenth century was working in this general locality; and in 1443 Donatello came to decorate an altar and to make the equestrian statue of *Gattamelata*. Under such influences Padua became an important center. The northern Italians, to be sure, had come under the

wave of naturalism but, unlike the Flor-entines, they did not "digest their facts into form." Instead, they (Pisanello, for example) took great delight in every newly discovered object, adding it to their decorative patterns without refer-ence to those fundamental structures and interrelations of parts which consti-tute the basis of Florentine painting.

The painter who was most influential in infusing the more descriptive north-ern Italian style with something of the stern realities of Florence was Andrea Mantegna (1431–1516), who as an ap-prentice in Padua came under the influ-ence of Donatello's realism and the Paduan passion for the classical culture. In his *Crucifixion* (Fig. 501A) we see both influences working. In the foreground on a rocky hill stand three crosses and

two groups of spectators, the Romans and the friends of Christ. The scene[1] as a whole is organized by two diagonal planes that recede from the two corners (an obvious exercise in perspective) and intersect behind the central cross, which thus receives additional emphasis to that given by the repeated verticals of the rocky hills, the soldier's spear, and the spacious sky against which it is sil-

[1] This small picture is part of the predella of Mantegna's *San Zeno Altarpiece*. The predella was the long, narrow panel that rested directly upon the altar and served as a decorative base for the altarpiece. It consisted usually of several small paintings related in subject matter to the large painting above. Many of these predellas were scattered when the altarpieces in course of time were dismembered. An example of an altarpiece that still retains its predella is the *Annunciation* of Fra Angelico at Cortona.

[A] *Mantegna. Gonzaga Family. A tablet in the room bears the following inscription: "To the illustrious Marquis Lodovico II, most worthy prince, invincible in the faith, and to his illustrious Lady Barbara of incomparable renown; their Andreas Mantegna of Padua has completed this humble work to their honor in the year 1474." Castello, Mantua. (Alinari)*

houetted. Mantegna's passion for everything Roman here finds opportunity to use Roman types and costumes; and his almost harsh realism reveals itself in the figures on the crosses, though he has not entirely broken from the Gothic stress on line.

Mantegna's penetrating observation and uncompromising fearlessness in recording facts is evident in the portraits painted on the walls of the castle at Mantua for the Gonzagas, whom he served for many years as court painter. In the *Gonzaga Family* (Fig. 503A), the group is placed rather compactly in a shallow space between two pilasters and a very naturalistic curtain is drawn aside and twisted about a pillar as if to present a view to the spectator. At the left sits the Marchese Ludovico Gonzaga, holding in his hand a letter just brought to him by his secretary, to

whom he turns as if giving some direction. At the right the Marchesa sits rather stiffly, looking toward the Marchese as if with some concern as to the contents of the letter; a little girl holds up an apple toward her, without attracting her attention; at her left is a dwarf whose task was to furnish amusement; grouped about are members of the family and court. Here is a quiet family scene, dignified and serious. The incident of the letter is a minor matter. What impresses the spectator is the exceeding reality of all these people, a reality that brings out sternly and incisively the character of each one, with no idealizing. The Marchese is a lofty-minded man, a conscientious and successful ruler; his secretary, with his squinting eyes and huge nose, a clear-headed, shrewd, and capable assistant; the stately Marchesa, a thoroughgoing

housewife and helpmeet. But while each portrait in itself is an astonishingly forceful characterization, as a whole the group lacks unifying formal relationships. Throughout the *Camera degli Sposi*, on whose walls the group was painted, Mantegna carried his realism to the point of breaking down the walls and substituting an almost complete illusion of space, especially in the ceiling (Fig. 502A), where by boldly foreshortened figures standing on the ledge, by others peering over, and by a light sky with clouds he creates a perfect illusion of an opening to the sky, an illusionism that was to reach a climax in seventeenth-century baroque.

In his austere and searching study of form, Mantegna accomplished for northern Italy what Donatello and Masaccio did for Florence. Classical sculptures, examples of which he had in his own collection, served as his models, and though at times his passion for

archaeology dominated his art, he nevertheless brought a tonic influence to schools whose predominant interests lay in the splendor of color, the texture of fine stuffs, the pride of their city, or the mood of the sunset hour.

Another energetic realist sojourning in northern Italy was Antonello da Messina (1430–1479), whose origin is uncertain but whose contact with northern European art is evident. His intensely real portraits have convincing mass, and his *Saint Jerome in His Study* is an unusual example of interest in genre and interior-lighting effects. In addition he brought a great stimulation to the already growing use of the oil technique, the capacities of which for securing rich color and surface effects he had learned from the Northerners.

While Mantegna was still in Padua, Jacopo Bellini and his family had traveled thither, with the result that Mantegna married Jacopo's daughter and

[A]   *Giovanni Bellini. Pietà. c. 1460. Brera, Milan. (Alinari)*

through his friendship with the sons brought the stern realities of his art directly into Venice. As Gentile Bellini's interest lay, apart from his portraits, in following his father's narrative turn, his expositions of Venetian pageants constitute his chief work.

This narrative interest finds a climax in the far more imaginative Vittore Carpaccio (1460–1522). For the staid groups of Gentile's pageants became full of lively action, as in the *Saint Ursula Series* (Venice), a vivid picture of contemporary Venetians whose costumes of magnificent stuffs provided an excuse for the use of vivid color-spots organized into a vivacious design and flooded with sunshine. In the *Dream of Saint Ursula* (Fig. 504A), how real is the space of the room and the interplay of

the outside and interior lighting which fills the room and with its varying values produces a feeling of the reality of the space! A very quiet design — a simple organization of vertical, horizontal, curve, and a sparse use of diagonal — is in harmony with the mood of the scene.

To return to the Bellini family, it is Jacopo's son Giovanni (1428–1516) who strikes out along new paths. In an early *Pietà* (Fig. 505A), a profound emotional quality combined with a terse, almost harsh drawing and cold color are evident. A low-lying landscape and an expanse of sky marked by horizontal cloudlets form a quiet background for concentration upon the tragic grief expressed by the three figures represented half-length in the foreground, just be-

[A] *Giovanni Bellini. Allegory, possibly from a medieval poem, the Pilgrimage of the Soul, and representing in the foreground the earthly paradise. c. 1490. Uffizi, Florence. (Alinari)*

hind a parapet. The Virgin and Saint John are supporting the body of the dead Christ, whose head is turned toward the Virgin's. The figures are brought together into a compact unity both formal and spiritual. Despite the angularity and the hard schematic lines and shadows, there is an intense searching for form and a relating of mass that is almost sculptural. Giovanni's evolution, however, was to be more Venetian, neither so profound in feeling nor so monumental in form as this early work. This truly Venetian quality becomes evident in the frankly gorgeous *Frari Madonna* (Fig. 507A). The composition suggests a scene in a church. In the center is the apse, decorated in gold brocade, where the Madonna sits on a lofty throne. On each side two saints, turning toward her, are standing in the aisles that surround the apse, separated from it by columns. Thus the architectural unity suggested by the church building, and the psychological unity

of the two groups of saints with the Madonna, bring about a singleness of effect. The elaborate frame covered with typically Renaissance carvings, the rich chiaroscuro, the sumptuous stuffs, and the glowing color produce a picture of truly Venetian splendor.

An important tendency not only in Giovanni but in the Venetian school as a whole is seen in a small *Allegory* (Fig. 506A). In the foreground is a paved enclosure in the center of which are children playing around a tree; men and women stand about apparently without unity of action. The rest of the panel is filled with a landscape in which there is a mountain lake surrounded by rocky hills. Here is a grasp of out-of-door space, not met before, in which the foreground with the figures is tied naturalistically with the landscape, a unity attained not only by the all-incorporating horizontal plane on which every object takes its place inevitably, by the movement of other planes and lines,

[A]   *Giovanni Bellini. Madonna. 1488. Church of the Frari, Venice. (Alinari)*

but particularly by the consistent scintillating light and by the enveloping atmosphere, which blurs the contours and unites all objects with its mellow tone.

Into the shop of Giovanni came two youths who were to take Venetian painting in new directions — Giorgione and Titian. Giorgione (1478–1510) left but few paintings, for he died young. His early *Castelfranco Madonna* reveals a break with the triptych style of altarpiece and a greater emphasis upon landscape. It also reflects a tranquil mood, a personal characteristic of this painter. The Madonna and the Child,

on a lofty throne, together with the flanking saints form a pyramidal group set in a rectangular framework of floor, wall, and throne; behind stretches a luminous landscape. Depth is expressed by parallel planes which recede quietly from the foreground to the horizon. A symmetrical surface pattern of triangles and rectangles is given force by the dynamic diagonal of the banner, frequently repeated and serving to connect the foreground and the background. Color too contributes to the mood, for the warm rich reds are set off by large areas of cool greens and blues.

[A]   *Giorgione. Fête Champêtre. Late. Louvre, Paris.*

In the *Tempest* (other titles are given this enigmatical painting) in the Academy of Venice, the figures are quite subordinate; they are integrated into a stormy landscape which seems to be the theme of the painting. Here an impressive space is carved out into which the eye is led, largely by light and dark, from the figure on the left to the distant clouds rent with lightning. In the *Sleeping Venus* (Dresden), figure and landscape act as a foil to each other yet are tied together in an extraordinary unity. The broad tranquil planes and unbroken lines of the figure are accented by the richly colored crumpled cloth (a classic example of contrasting textures) and repeated in the gently sloping hills. By a winding road the eye is led into the landscape, is caught by the trees silhouetted against a luminous sky, and then led by the dark branch back to the head of the Venus.

In the *Fête Champêtre* (Fig. 508A), the basic organization is much less obvious, less symmetrical, more subtle. The surface pattern consists of a quiet framework of verticals in the standing figure, the trees, and the houses; of horizontals in fountain, lute strings, background, and sky; of two sets of opposing diagonals, repeated in arms, legs, contours of the hills, and many details; and of sweeping curves of foliage and figures. These organizing lines, in contrast to those in Botticelli's *Calumny* (Fig. 489A) or Raphael's *School of Athens* (Fig. 498A), are intuitively felt rather than clearly visible, for most of the edges are blurred by atmosphere or lost

[A]   *Titian. The Man with the Glove. Early. Louvre, Paris. Compare with Fig. 509B for contrasting design motifs: sharp angles and diagonals versus curves and verticals.*

[B]   *Titian. Portrait of an Unknown Man. ("Young Englishman," or "Duke of Norfolk"). c. 1540–45. Pitti, Florence. (Alinari)*

in shadows. Yet the organization is as compelling as in the *Calumny* and the *School of Athens*, even if less evident at first glance and accomplished by different means — chiefly by spots of color of varying hues and values. But this organization is by no means a surface pattern only. Here is a grasp of space and an organization in space, particularly emphasized by the great plane that wedges in diagonally from the front on which the main figures are placed, yet without any lack of unity with the middle and far distance. A warm red in the cloak of the lute-player marks the center of interest, about which radiate somewhat less warm and cool hues. An additional richness of effect results from the varying textures of stuffs, flesh, stone, and foliage, but all are tied in a rich tonal unity by that pervasive "golden glow" which is a characteristic mark of Venetian painting. Color is no longer used as a decorative element to enhance the unity

of the design, but functions as an inseparable element in the construction of form. This richness of color and surface texture, the soft blending of light and dark, and the enveloping blurring atmosphere result from the oil technique, whose potentialities were peculiarly favorable for the expression of Venetian ideals.

One more element in the *Fête Champêtre* is both Giorgionesque and Venetian — a profound sensitivity to an idyllic charm and a tranquil brooding mood. Among the Italians it was the Venetian school that first expressed a love for nature and a realization of its potentialities for the painter, though this school never reached the point of eliminating entirely some figure interest.

The youthful Titian (1477–1576) followed rather closely, at first, in the style of Giorgione, as is evident in the *Concert* (Pitti, Florence), which may have been a collaboration of the two. But Titian's naturally robust, exuberant

[A]   *Titian. Education of Cupid. Late. Borghese Gallery, Rome. (Anderson)*

nature soon found more congenial expression in a more vigorous subject matter and more striking design, as in the *Bacchus and Ariadne* (National Gallery, London), the magnificent *Assumption of the Virgin* and *Pesaro Madonna* (Frari, Venice), and the *Entombment* (Louvre), though the means he employed were much the same as in the *Fête Champêtre* — organization by rich color masses, light and dark, warm and cool, which harmonize, contrast, and merge into sumptuous effects perfectly in tune with the Venetian love of pomp, splendor, and worldliness. Such surfaces were secured by a long patient building-up, usually upon a tempera ground painting, of layer upon layer of thin coats of pigment mixed with oil, some opaque, some transparent, with dryings and bleachings in the sun at every stage. The ground, in Titian often a warm red-brown, served to bind all the local colors into a dominant and consistent tonal unity.

It was not long, however, before Titian began restricting his hues and weaving them into more subtle organizations, as in some of his portraits. In the *Young Englishman* (Fig. 509B), so called though the identity of the subject is unknown, we see a young man represented half-length, dressed in a black costume relieved only by the heavy gold chain and the delicate white ruffles at throat and wrists. His right hand holds his gloves; his left is held somewhat restlessly on his hip. With the greatest simplicity and reserve, Titian reveals the pride and aristocracy of this young man, and his fine sensitive nature. The half-length figure admirably fills the square frame; the eye travels back and forth with the help of the chain and the contours of the arms from the face to the hands, which are as expressive of this young man's character as the face itself. In this portrait, and particularly in *The Man with the Glove* (Fig. 509A), a very restrained color

[A]   *Titian. Entombment. 1559. Prado, Madrid. (Anderson)*

scheme with close values conveys a re-strained impression. Yet the figure exists in an ample spaciousness made real by the background, which vibrates with infinitely subtle variations. The characterization in these portraits is accomplished not only by expression of the face and by characteristic details of costume, pose, or accessory that contribute to the creation of an environment which is as expressive of the individual as is the face itself; it is accomplished also by a basic design that says abstractly what features and details say concretely. For example, contrast the effect of the curves and the vertical of the *Young Englishman* with that of the sharp triangles in the *Man with the Glove*. For a group, one may take the *Pope Paul III and His Grandsons* (Naples), in which Titian's penetrating

vision and intellectual grasp of individual character and of the psychology of a situation find inescapably clear expression because of the perfect cohesion of every means available to the painter. Facial expression, pose, gesture, costume, line, color — each is one element definitely related to every other in order to attain the objective.

In his later works, such as the *Education of Cupid* (Fig. 510A), the late *Pietà* (Venice Academy), the late *Entombment* (Fig. 511A), and the *Crowning of Thorns* (Munich), the forms, which melt into a golden glow, are constructed of light and color with a use of pigment that foreshadows the great painters of Spain and northern Europe even into the days of Impressionism.[1]

[1] See Munro, *Great Pictures of Europe*, pp. 170-71.

[A]   *Tintoretto. Last Supper. 1594. San Giorgio Maggiore, Venice. (Anderson)*

As distinction and poise, even in movement, and elegance and grace, even in tragedy, were a manifestation of Titian's individuality, so dramatic force, impetuous movement, and vivid contrasts of color reflect the vehement Tintoretto[1] (1518–1594) — both, however, true Venetians. In the *Last Supper* (Fig. 512A), dramatic contrasts of light and dark control a design that is organized with a fully three-dimensional expression of deep space. The eye is guided by these startling high lights along an imaginary line of direction from the two figures in the left-hand lower corner across the foreground and back to the group of angels in the background; the same distance into space is reached more directly by the long table. In the *Miracle of Saint Mark* (Fig. 513A) the same energetic movement is subordinate to a great S-curve swinging backward and forward in space through the downward sweeping figures of Saint Mark, the executioner, and the slave; and another movement in depth swings from the judge on the right back through the group of spectators and forward to the lofty figures on the left. Along the entire course of these single controlling rhythms the eye is guided by light and dark spots of rich warm color, accented by the cooler hues of the quiet background, but all united tonally. Tintoretto's flashes of light, brushed in with apparent spontaneity and disregard for detail, were not haphazard, but often the result of many

[1] Tintoretto's impetuosity and his habit of working, at times, directly upon the canvas without preliminary sketches is well illustrated by Vasari's tale of the decoration of the ceiling of the *Scuola di San Rocco*. This confraternity had commissioned three painters, Tintoretto among them, to present competitive designs for the ceiling. When the council assembled to judge of the design and award the commission, they found that Tintoretto had painted his directly on a full-sized canvas and already had it put into place, saying that that was his way of doing it and if they did not wish to recompense him he would make them a gift of the painting.

[A]   *Tintoretto. Miracle of St. Mark. 1548. Academy, Venice.*

trials of a design and of single figures, as is seen in his drawings in the British Museum. And in his more direct method of painting he is closer to the modern school than any of the other Italians.

Truly Venetian in his expression of worldly pageantry, whether the subject was sacred or secular, and in his facility in handling pigment to create a magnificent surface, was Veronese (1528–1588). The narrative and descriptive painting of Carpaccio, naïvely joyous and clearly organized, became in Veronese a colossally grandiose expression of Venice's sophisticated pageantry. Into an imposing architectural framework, as in the *Feast in the House of Levi* (Fig. 515A), he placed animated groups of many figures all in movement, thus creating an impression of constant vibration of spots of color with little in-

ternal organization and little accent upon the focal point. As a unit, however, this movement is quite under the control of the dominant rhythm of the architectural framework. The surface texture in Veronese's canvases is subtly varied, and his color is less warm than Titian's and Tintoretto's, with more blue, less red, and less suffusion of warm golden tonality. A cool, more diffused luminosity and less contrast between light and dark stress the decorative aspect.

While Titian and Tintoretto were still youths, a painter who lived in comparative isolation in and around Parma, Correggio (1494–1534), was painting altarpieces of a certain lyric charm — when not too sweet and sentimental — and was experimenting in artificial and concentrated lighting, as in the *Holy*

[A] *Correggio. Assumption. 1520–24. Dome of S. Giovanni Evangelista, Parma. (Alinari)*

Night, or in the mythological panels, such as the *Danaë* (Rome) — creating a delicate kind of painting, not of rich surface textures like those of most of the Venetians, but of almost imperceptible modulations of light, filled with half-tints and of a cool silvery tonality. In the *Assumption* (Fig. 514A) in the dome of the *Parma Cathedral*, one is carried from the moderate movement in the pendentives, where saints and Church Fathers with angels are seated upon clouds, by way of a balustrade to which vigorous upward-gazing Apostles cling, into a whirling ecstatic flight of innumerable figures, an illusion of swift movement into infinite heights quite regardless of the material limitations of the stone dome. This illusion Correggio created partly by foreshortened figures but largely by the emotional force of a swirl of radiant light and color.

In these Parma frescoes, one is carried back to the boldly foreshortened figures and the illusionistic effect of Man-

tegna's *Camera degli Sposi* (Fig. 502A). In fact in all Correggio's work there are evidences of Michelangelo's drawing, of Raphael's types sentimentalized, of Leonardo's chiaroscuro, and of Titian's design and color, though the color is cooler.

Such eclecticism normally follows a period of such masters as those produced in Florence, Rome, and Venice in the sixteenth century. The Eclectics, or Mannerists, were centered at the art school which they established at Bologna. They attempted to combine into a perfect art the best qualities of the great masters — the drawing of Michelangelo, the noble types and composition of Raphael, the color of Titian, and the chiaroscuro of Correggio. Such a method, which copies external appearance and fails to grasp fundamental principles, is destined to become pedantic, or rhetorical, or melodramatic — as were many of the paintings of the Bolognese, particularly those of the Carracci.

[A]   *Veronese. Feast in the House of Levi. 1573. Academy, Venice. (Anderson)*

The other tendency was that of the realists, chief of whom was Caravaggio (1569–1608), who, in protest against the weakness of the Mannerists, selected his types from the lowest classes, and painted figures and scenes with a realism that at times approaches the photographic. His chiaroscuro, based upon that of Correggio in such a painting as the *Holy Night*, consists of picking out a detail here and there with a strong and concentrated lighting and sinking all else into shadow.[1]

Chiaroscuro we have seen developing in Italian painting from Giotto, who, though he used the shadow for modeling, still expressed both mass and space chiefly by line. The early fifteenth-century painters of Florence — Masaccio, Fra Angelico, Baldovinetti, and Pollaiuolo — used it moderately to express the structure and the volume of the figure in space, so that their work, whether in fresco or in tempera, had an even tonality without strong contrasts of light and shade. This was due partly to the medium and partly to interest in the structural line, for the Florentines were principally draftsmen. Leonardo, with the help of the oil technique, carried contrasting light and dark with soft transitions much farther in his attempt to secure a high-relief-like quality. Giorgione, Titian, and Tintoretto subordinated line and organized by light and dark color-masses in which figures and objects were constructed of light and color. Visible line hardly exists, though organizing lines of direction are clearly felt; edges are blurred and all figures are united by an enveloping atmosphere of dominant tonality. Michelangelo's remark that Titian could not draw, which might well have elicited the retort that Michelangelo could not paint, simply reflects a different way of seeing, feeling, and expressing form. To Michelangelo, the figure was an organic structure whose volumes arouse tactile sensations and can best be expressed by lines which indicate the movement of planes defining these volumes. To Titian, the figure was a mass perceived by light, which is color, and enveloped by atmosphere.[2]

[1] Painters who used this violent chiaroscuro are sometimes referred to as the Tenebrists, the shadow-painters.

[2] For an exposition of these contrasting attitudes towards form see Heinrich Wölfflin, *Principles of Art History*, Holt, 1932.

SUMMARY

Though architecture and sculpture, working in unison, constituted the dominant art of the Middle Ages, painting began, even toward the end of the medieval era, to usurp the primacy and held it for centuries. Like sculpture, painting was intimately allied with architecture. Its function was largely to decorate walls and produce altarpieces. For the former it employed the fresco technique; for the latter, the tempera until the emergence, in the second half of the fifteenth century, of an oil medium. Its content at first was chiefly religious, for such a content was commissioned by the Church, the nobles, and the guilds, all of whom were art patrons of the time. It then became increasingly secular, as did the whole cultural fabric.

Of the Italian painters of the thirteenth and fourteenth centuries, all of whom were working primarily in the Byzantine tradition, the Sienese remained rooted in that style, which they brought, with some modification because of the general naturalistic movement, to a climax in Italy — an art of exquisite surface patterns with suavely flowing calligraphic lines and areas of vivid color and gold; an art whose forms were imaginatively and conventionally constructed with but little regard for a visual perception of actuality. The Florentines, on the contrary, set themselves to the task of investigating the world of visual perception — the figure itself, its place in space, and spatial relations — not for the purpose of providing a perfect copy of man and his world but for the expression of the essential, monumental aspects of form and of the outward manifestation, through form, of generic or abstract conceptions. This last was the motivation of the fifteenth century. It was an art of the draftsman, with color largely a decorative adjunct, for drawing was the most suitable means of expressing the scientific facts of anatomy and perspective that were the passion of the century. Yet this enthusiasm did not overwhelm esthetic requirements, for the Florentine always "digested his facts into form." By the sixteenth century he had attained an accomplished and individually diversified style of great dignity and of great mastery over the figure itself, over spatial relations, and over the expression, through them, of the spiritually significant. The Venetians, differing from the Florentines because of different surroundings and attitudes, were worldly in their wealth and were frankly given to sumptuous magnificence and gorgeous pageantry. Such an impression the painters were able to create by complex designs in deep space in which the chief organizing means were the richest colors tied together by an all-embracing glowing light, a use of pigment made possible through the development of oil as a medium. Of all the Italians, the Venetians were most truly painters, not only in their construction of figures from color and light but particularly in their realization of the potentialities of pigment for creating surfaces that in color and texture have a distinctly emotional appeal in themselves, wholly without regard to the subject matter. Another contribution of the Venetians, seen early in their idyllic landscape backgrounds, was a revelation of nature; and though they never eliminated the figure interest, they opened up the great possibilities of nature as material for the painter.

As a result of the impact of the powerful personalities of the sixteenth century, an eclectic style arose in Bologna, in protest to which a school of realists, centered in Naples, took their subject matter frequently from the everyday life of the people and painted it in somber colors with violent chiaroscuro.

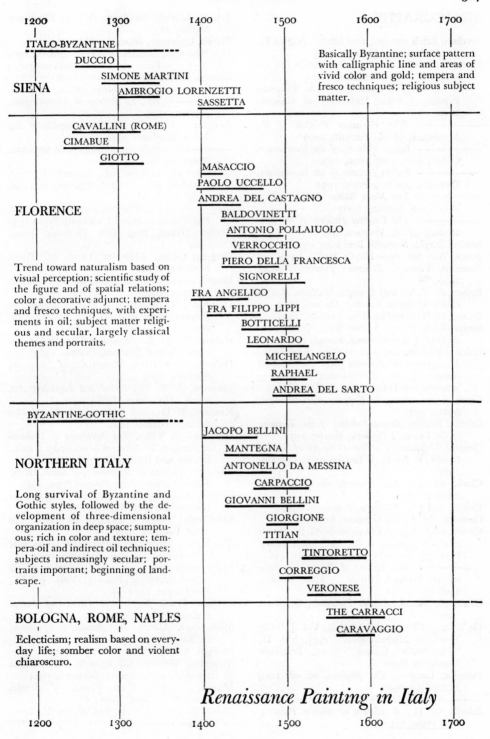

Renaissance Painting in Italy

The chart reads:

1200 1300 1400 1500 1600 1700

ITALO-BYZANTINE
DUCCIO
SIMONE MARTINI
SIENA
AMBROGIO LORENZETTI
SASSETTA

Basically Byzantine; surface pattern with calligraphic line and areas of vivid color and gold; tempera and fresco techniques; religious subject matter.

CAVALLINI (ROME)
CIMABUE
GIOTTO
MASACCIO
PAOLO UCCELLO
ANDREA DEL CASTAGNO
FLORENCE
BALDOVINETTI
ANTONIO POLLAIUOLO
VERROCCHIO
PIERO DELLA FRANCESCA
SIGNORELLI
Trend toward naturalism based on visual perception; scientific study of the figure and of spatial relations; color a decorative adjunct; tempera and fresco techniques, with experiments in oil; subject matter religious and secular, largely classical themes and portraits.
FRA ANGELICO
FRA FILIPPO LIPPI
BOTTICELLI
LEONARDO
MICHELANGELO
RAPHAEL
ANDREA DEL SARTO

BYZANTINE-GOTHIC
JACOPO BELLINI
MANTEGNA
ANTONELLO DA MESSINA
NORTHERN ITALY
CARPACCIO
GIOVANNI BELLINI
Long survival of Byzantine and Gothic styles, followed by the development of three-dimensional organization in deep space; sumptuous; rich in color and texture; tempera-oil and indirect oil techniques; subjects increasingly secular; portraits important; beginning of landscape.
GIORGIONE
TITIAN
TINTORETTO
CORREGGIO
VERONESE

BOLOGNA, ROME, NAPLES
THE CARRACCI
CARAVAGGIO
Eclecticism; realism based on everyday life; somber color and violent chiaroscuro.

1200 1300 1400 1500 1600 1700

BIBLIOGRAPHY

Bercken, Erich von der, and Mayer, August L.,
   Jacopo Tintoretto, Munich, 1923
Berenson, Bernhard, *The Central Italian Painters
   of the Renaissance*, Putnam, 1897
——————— *The Drawings of the Florentine
   Painters*, 3 vols., University of Chicago
   Press, 1938
——————— *The Florentine Painters of the
   Renaissance*, 3d ed., Putnam, 1909
——————— *Italian Painters of the Renaissance*,
   Oxford University Press, 1932
——————— *Italian Pictures of the Renaissance*,
   Oxford University Press, 1932
——————— *The North Italian Painters of the
   Renaissance*, Putnam, 1907
——————— *The Venetian Painters of the Ren-
   aissance*, 3d ed., Putnam, 1897
Bettini, Sergio, *Botticelli*, Bergamo, 1942
Boeck, Wilhelm, *Paolo Uccello*, Berlin, 1939
Borenius, Tancred, *Florentine Frescoes*, Nelson,
   1930
Brown, A. V. V., and Rankin, William, *A Short
   History of Italian Painting*, Dutton, 1914
Brown, G. B., *The Fine Arts*, Scribner, 1927
Byron, Robert, and Talbot Rice, David, *The
   Birth of Western Painting*, Knopf, 1931
Cairns, Huntington, and Walker, John, eds.,
   *Masterpieces of Painting from the National
   Gallery of Art*, Smithsonian Institution,
   Washington, D.C., Random House, 1944
Carrà, Carlo, *Giotto, La Cappella degli Scrovegni*,
   Milan, 1945
Cecchi, Emilio, *Sienese Painters of the Trecento*,
   tr. by Leonard Penlock, Warne, 1931
Cennini, Cennino, *The Book of the Art of Cennino
   Cennini*, tr. by C. J. Herringham, London,
   1922
Clark, Kenneth M., *Leonardo da Vinci*, Mac-
   millan, 1939
Coletti, Luigi, *Il Tintoretto*, Bergamo, 1944
Conway, Sir Martin, *Giorgione*, London, 1929
Crowe, Sir J. A., and Cavalcaselle, G. B., *History
   of Painting in North Italy*, ed. by Tancred
   Borenius, new ed., 3 vols., Scribner, 1912
——————— *New History of Painting in Italy*,
   ed. by Edward Hutton, 3 vols., Dutton,
   1908–09
Cruttwell, Maud, *Antonio Pollaiuolo*, Scribner,
   1907
De Tolnay, Charles, *Michelangelo*, Vol. I, "The
   Youth of Michelangelo," 1943, Vol. II,
   "The Sistine Ceiling," 1945, Princeton
   University Press
Douglas, Langton, *Fra Angelico*, 2d ed. rev.,
   Macmillan, 1902
——————— *A History of Siena*, Dutton, 1903
Edgell, G. H., *A History of Sienese Painting*,
   Dial Press, 1932

Faure, Gabriel, *Wanderings in Italy*, Houghton
   Mifflin, 1919
Fiocco, Giuseppe, *Mantegna*, Milan, 1937
Fry, Roger E., *Giovanni Bellini*, Longmans, 1901
——————— *Vision and Design*, Bretano's, 1924
Gamba, Carlo, *Botticelli*, Milan, 1936
——————— *Giovanni Bellini*, Milan, 1937
——————— ed., *La Pittura di Michelangiolo*,
   Novara, 1943
Gengaro, Maria L., *Il Beato Angelico a San
   Marco*, Bergamo, 1944
——————— *Raffaello, la Stanza della Segnatura*,
   Bergamo, 1944
Goldscheider, Ludwig, ed., *Leonardo da Vinci*,
   Phaidon ed., Oxford University Press,
   1943
——————— ed., *The Paintings of Michelangelo*,
   Phaidon ed., Oxford University Press, 1940
Graber, Hans, *Piero della Francesca*, Basel,
   1922
Gronau, Georg, *Titian*, tr. by A. M. Todd,
   Scribner, 1904
Hagen, Oskar F. L., *Art Epochs and Their Leaders*,
   Scribner, 1927
Hollanda, Francisco de, *Four Dialogues on
   Painting*, tr. by A. F. G. Bell, Oxford Uni-
   versity Press, 1928
Holmes, Sir C. J., *Raphael and the Modern Use
   of the Classical Tradition*, Dutton, 1933
Holroyd, Sir Charles, *Michael Angelo Buonarroti*,
   Scribner, 1904
Jameson, A. B. M., *Sacred and Legendary Art*,
   2 vols., Houghton Mifflin, 1911
Konody, P. G., and Wilenski, R. H., *Italian
   Painting*, Nelson, 1929
Leonardo da Vinci, *The Notebooks of Leonardo
   da Vinci*, tr. by Edward MacCurdy, 2 vols.,
   Reynal and Hitchcock, 1938
The Little Flowers of St. Francis of Assisi, tr. by
   Thomas Okey, Peter Pauper Press, 1943
Longhi, Roberto, *Piero della Francesca*, tr. by
   Leonard Penlock, Warne, 1930
MacCurdy, Edward, *Leonardo da Vinci: The
   Artist*, London, 1936
Marangoni, Matteo, *Gli Affreschi di Giotto nella
   Cappella degli Scrovegni*, Bergamo, 1943
Marle, Raimond van, *The Development of the
   Italian Schools of Painting*, Vols. I–XIX,
   The Hague, 1923–39
Mather, Frank J., Jr., *A History of Italian
   Painting*, Holt, 1923
Middeldorf, Ulrich A., *Raphael's Drawings*,
   H. Bittner, 1945
Morassi, Antonio, *Tiepolo*, Bergamo, 1943
Moschini, Vittorio, *Gli Affreschi del Mantegna
   agli Eremitani di Padova*, Bergamo, 1944
Munro, Thomas, *Great Pictures of Europe*,
   Coward-McCann, 1930
Muratoff, Paul, *Fra Angelico*, tr. by E. Law-
   Gisiko, Warne, 1930

Nebbia, Ugo, *Tintoretto, la scuola di San Rocco*, Bergamo, 1944

Neilson, Katharine B., *Filippino Lippi*, Harvard University Press, 1938

Offner, Richard, *Italian Primitives at Yale University*, Yale University Press, 1927

Ortolani, Sergio, *Raffaello*, 2d. ed., Bergamo, 1945

Paintings and Sculpture from the Kress Collection, National Gallery of Art, Smithsonian Institution, Washington, D.C., 1945

Pallucchini, Rodolfo, *Gli Affreschi di Giambattista e Giandomenico Tiepolo alla Villa Valmarana di Vicenza*, Bergamo, 1945

———————— *Veronese*, Bergamo, 1943

Pater, Walter, *The Renaissance:* Modern Library, Boni & Liveright, 1919

Phillips, Duncan, *The Leadership of Giorgione*, American Federation of Arts, 1937

Phillips, E. M., *Tintoretto*, London, 1911

Pope-Hennessy, John, *Sassetta*, London, 1939

Popham, Arthur E., *The Drawings of Leonardo da Vinci*, Reynal & Hitchcock, 1945

Ricci, Corrado, *Correggio*, Warne, 1930

———————— *Art in Northern Italy*, Scribner, 1911

———————— *North Italian Painting of the Cinquecento*, Harcourt, Brace, 1929

Richter, George M., *Andrea dal Castagno*, University of Chicago Press, 1943

Rinaldis, Aldo de, *Neapolitan Painting of the Seicento*, Harcourt, Brace, 1929

Rolland, Romain, *Michelangelo*, tr. by Frederick Street, 4th ed., Duffield, 1927

Ruskin, John, *Stones of Venice*, 3 vols., Estes, 1913

Sabatier, Paul, *Life of Saint Francis of Assisi*, tr. by L. S. Houghton, Scribner, 1927

Salmi, Mario, *Paolo Uccello, Andrea del Castagno, Domenico Veneziano*, Milan, 1938

———————— *Piero della Francesca, gli Affreschi di San Francesco in Arezzo*, Bergamo, 1944

Scharf, Alfred, *Filippino Lippi*, Vienna, 1935

Schmeckebier, Laurence, *A Handbook of Italian Renaissance Painting*, Putnam, 1938

Sirén, Osvald, *Giotto and Some of His Followers*, tr. by Frederick Schenck, 2 vols., Harvard University Press, 1917

———————— *Leonardo da Vinci, the Artist and the Man*, Yale University Press, 1916

Strutt, E. C., *Fra Filippo Lippi*, Macmillan, 1906

Taylor, H. O., *The Mediaeval Mind*, 4th ed., 2 vols., Macmillan, 1925

Taylor, R. A., *Leonardo the Florentine*, new ed., Harper, 1930

Tietze, Hans, *Titian, Paintings and Drawings*, Phaidon ed., Oxford University Press, 1937

———————— and Tietze-Conrat, Erika, *The Drawings of the Venetian Painters in the 15th and 16th Centuries*, Augustin, 1944

Toesca, Pietro, *Florentine Painting of the Trecento*, Harcourt, Brace, 1929

Venturi, Adolfo, *North Italian Painting of the Quattrocento*, 2 vols., Harcourt, Brace, 1931

———————— *A Short History of Italian Art*, tr. by Edward Hutton, Macmillan, 1926

Venturi, Lionello, *Botticelli*, Phaidon ed., Oxford University Press, 1937

Voss, H. G. A., *Die Malerei der Spätrenaissance in Rom und Florenz*, 2 vols., Berlin, 1920

Weigelt, Curt H., *Sienese Painting of the Trecento*, Harcourt, Brace, 1930

Wölfflin, Heinrich, *The Art of the Italian Renaissance*, new rev. ed., Putnam, 1913

———————— *Principles of Art History*, tr. by M. D. Hottinger, Holt, 1932

Yashiro, Yukio, *Sandro Botticelli*, 3 vols., Medici Society, Boston, 1925

———————— *Sandro Botticelli and the Florentine Renaissance*, rev. ed., Hale, Cushman & Flint, 1929

See also the background books of the bibliography on p. 467 and the General Bibliography, pp. 791–92.

[A] *Orazio Fontana. Majolica Plate. D. 10½ in. 16th cent. Metropolitan Museum of Art, New York City. (Metropolitan Museum)*

28

METALWORK, CERAMICS, TEXTILES, AND BOOKS

A STRIKING characteristic of the Renaissance artist was his versatility, the result of an apprenticeship system of education in a shop where many kinds of work were always going on. For the demands upon an artist's shop were various. All through the Middle Ages fine vessels and books were made of the most precious material for the Church: altar furniture, jeweled regalia for the clergy, and tapestries to decorate the cathedral. This need still continued; and to it were added the needs of wealthy nobles and merchants as secular life became more important and the mode of living more luxurious and ostentatious. Carvings, tapestries, and painted decorations were in demand for the palaces, as well as more elaborate furniture and gold and silver plate, and fine cloths, velvets, and brocades for costumes, and jewelry, and fine armor. Books in particular, with the widening of knowledge, scientific research, and passion for the literature of Greece and Rome, assumed an importance unknown before. As most of these things came from some *bottega*, it is easily seen that the artist must be versatile; and as public taste was of a

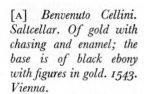

[A] *Benvenuto Cellini. Saltcellar. Of gold with chasing and enamel; the base is of black ebony with figures in gold. 1543. Vienna.*

high order, he must produce works of quality both in design and in technique.

METALWORK

Metal — bronze, iron, gold, silver — was an important medium, and skill in casting,[1] molding, chasing, and engraving was essential. The use of iron in lanterns and grilles, and of bronze in sculpture, we have already seen. Among smaller objects in bronze the commemorative medal became important as the individualistic strain manifested itself in portraiture. It reached a climax in the work of Antonio Pisano, known as Pisanello (about 1395–1455), in the medals of Leonello d'Este, Marquis of Ferrara.

The goldsmith was important. In fact it was as a goldsmith that many a painter and sculptor began his career. The processes used were substantially

the same as those employed in the Middle Ages — repoussé, chasing, jewel-setting, and enameling; and the character of the work in the early Renaissance had the same quality of sound design, with decoration subordinate and contributory, as in the best medieval work. But increasing luxury and desire for display in all aspects of life are reflected in the changed taste seen in the late Renaissance. Of this period, the famous bronze-worker and goldsmith Benvenuto Cellini (1500–1571) is typical, and the saltcellar (Fig. 521A) with figures representing the *Sea* and the *Land* that he made for Francis I well illustrates his work.[2] There is no question about the superb technical skill here shown, the great ease and facility in handling the medium and in finishing it. But who would conceive of this exquisite bit of work as a container for salt and pepper? To delight with accomplished handling of materials and to surprise with ingenious motifs seem to have been the aim of the artist. Thus Benvenuto as well as Michelangelo foreshadows the baroque.

[1] For an account of bronze-casting as practiced by the Renaissance sculptors, see Benvenuto Cellini's dramatic account of how he cast his *Perseus* (Loggia de' Lanzi, Florence) in his *Autobiography*, tr. by J. A. Symonds, Modern Library, 1927, pp. 413 ff.

[2] See the artist's own description, *Ibid.*, p. 347.

CERAMICS

The potter and the weaver contributed to the rich colorfulness of the age, the potter with his majolica,[1] which is earthenware covered with a whitish opaque glaze on which the decoration is painted. The colors used were intense, and their effect was heightened by a rich transparent overglaze and by a luster of amazing brilliancy. A particularly fine majolica was made in the sixteenth century at Urbino, exemplified by a plate by Orazio Fontana (Fig. 520A), in which borders with winged lions, birds, and half-human figures combined with garlands and scrolls surround a central medallion containing a mythological scene closely related in style to the paintings of Raphael. If one questions the use of three-dimensional painting as ceramic decoration, in the border designs at least he will find the fanciful motifs used as decorative color-units against the creamy glaze.

TEXTILES

From the weaver's shop came the fine fabrics — silks, velvets, brocades, tapestries — which were in such demand, as the paintings show,[2] for costumes, both ecclesiastical and secular, and for hangings. We have seen how Persia had been a center for weaving, especially of fine silks; how Justinian introduced the craft into Europe; and how the Muhammadans became expert weavers. In their conquests westward the Muslim brought the craft with them to Spain,

[1] The name is probably derived from Majorca, one of the Balearic Islands, a calling-place of the ships that brought to Italy the glazed and lustered wares of Spain.

[2] See particularly the paintings of Domenico Ghirlandaio, Benozzo Gozzoli, the Bellini, Crivelli, Titian, and in fact most of the Venetian painters, whose works reveal so clearly the love of the Venetians for fine stuffs.

to Sicily, and thence to Italy, where luxuriant stuffs were woven which in pattern, color, and motifs were entirely of the tradition of the Near East. In the fifteenth century, however, the Italian weavers, in accordance with the spirit of their times, broke with this old tradition, and introduced into their fabrics a pomegranate motif (Fig. 523A) used with many variations. The richness of color and vigor of pattern, in their velvets and brocades in particular, are in harmony with Renaissance art as a whole.

BOOKS

In the field of bookmaking, the Italians made valuable contributions. We have been following the evolution of the book from the long rolls of Egyptians, Greeks, and Romans to the codex, which became in the early Christian era very sumptuous in its writing, decoration, and binding, and throughout the Middle Ages remained a work in whose making a whole group of artists collaborated. Probably the highest expression of the Italian scribes and illuminators is seen in the great choir books that reached their culmination in the late fifteenth century. The most characteristic part of their decoration is the initial letter, painted in bright colors with white tracery, foliate ornament, and gold. Frequently because of its large size it was historiated — that is, adorned with a miniature within the form of the letter. Many of these were painted by well-known artists, as was the *Aeolus* (Fig. 523B). Within the letter and wonderfully adapted to the shape is a representation of Aeolus sweeping forward with all the energy of the north wind. The use of a classical subject is interesting here, as is the spontaneous, naïve conception so characteristic of the fifteenth-century attitude toward Greek and Roman subjects. The rich foliate

[A] *Brocaded Velvet. Italian. 15th cent. Metropolitan Museum of Art, New York. (Metropolitan Museum)*

[B] *Liberale da Verona. Aeolus. Historiated initial from a choir book. Piccolomini Library, Siena. (Alinari)*

decoration surrounding the initial is typical of Italian work, which often became too heavy and florid to have the perfectly decorative quality of the French manuscripts.

Meanwhile, one of the most far-reaching inventions was about to bring to an end the handmade book: printing, an invention not of one man or at one place, but the growth of centuries. Some of the underlying practices, such as using a stamp for initial letters, had long been known. Paper was becoming common in the fourteenth century, making inexpensive books possible, though vellum and parchment were long used for fine books. What we know is that in the decade from about 1450 to 1460 printing with movable type became established at Mainz, and by the end of the fifteenth century was being practiced in all the countries of western Europe. The early books (incunabula) closely resembled the manuscripts of the period in composition, form of letters, and decoration. Indeed printing was used for the small letters only; the initials and the decorations were added in color by hand after the printing was done, so that the general effect of the page was the same as that of the manuscript.

POLIPHILO QVIVI NARRA, CHE GLI PAR VE AN-
CORA DI DORMIRE, ET ALTRONDE IN SOMNO
RITROVARSE IN VNA CONVALLE, LA QVALE NEL
FINE ERA SERATA DE VNA MIRABILE CLAVSVRA
CVM VNA PORTENTOSA PYRAMIDE, DE ADMI-
RATIONE DIGNA, ET VNO EXCELSO OBELISCO DE
SOPRA. LA QVALE CVM DILIGENTIA ET PIACERE
SVBTILMENTE LA CONSIDEROE.

A SPAVENTEVOLE SILVA, ET CONSTI-
pato Nemore euaso, & gli primi altri lochi per el dolce
somno che se haura per le selse & prosternate mibre dif-
fuso relicti, me ritrouai di nouo in uno piu delecti bile
sito assai piu che el precedente. El quale non era de mon
ti horridi, & crepidinose rupe intorniato, ne saleato di
strumosi iugi. Ma compositamente de grate montagniole di nontro-
po alteria. Siluose di giouani querciuoli, di roburi, fraxini & Carpi-
ni, & di frondosi Esculi, & Ilice, & di teneri Coryli, & di Alni, & di Ti-
lie, & di Opio, & de infructuosi Oleastri, dispositi secondo laspecto de
gli arborisei Colli. Et giu al piano erano grate siluule di altri siluatici

[A] *Page from the* Hypnerotomachia
Poliphili, *or* Strife of Love in a Dream.
*Printed by Aldus at the Aldine Press in
Venice. 1499.*

For nearly a century the printed book
very closely followed the tradition of the
manuscript. It had no title page, no
chapter heading, no running title, no
pagination. The early printed books of
Italy show clearly the Italian sensitiveness for unity of design, which appears
especially in the small pamphlets issued
at Florence, known as *rappresentazióni*
because they reproduced the plays given
on saints' days. In place of a title page,
they had a woodcut with the representation of an angel as a herald to announce
the play, and perhaps a characteristic
scene from the life of the saint who was
being celebrated. These Florentine
books are among the most successfully
illustrated books ever made, because
the illustration illustrates and at the
same time harmonizes with the letterpress. Its purpose was to elucidate the
text or to emphasize some point by
visualization, and not to call attention
away from the text to itself as an end.
The Florentine realized that to keep
this unity his illustration must harmonize with the printing, and that nothing
could accomplish this end so adequately
as purely linear work. The *Hypnerotomachia Poliphili* (Fig. 524A) illustrates
these practices. Its high quality does
not lie in the content of the text, which
is dull and long-drawn-out, nor in the
woodcuts alone, but in the complete
and satisfying unity of letterpress, margins, type, and illustrations, a unity as
important in bookmaking as it is in
picture-making, unless one looks upon
a book merely for its content and not
as a work of art. As in the Florentine
pamphlet, so in the *Hypnerotomachia* the
linear quality of the woodcut adds variety to the printed page yet maintains
the unity of the page composition.

SUMMARY

Versatility in many arts rather than
specialization in one characterized the
artists of the Renaissance. All were
trained in several crafts and all joined
in making the furnishings for churches
and palaces; costumes; and the equipment for the pageants which were characteristic of Renaissance life. Ironwork
and goldwork; majolica, related to the
lusterware of Spain; tapestries designed
by painters but sent to northern Europe
for weaving; fine velvets and brocades
which show the influence of Muslim
weavers in Sicily — all these reveal the
richness of Renaissance art. Finally, a
landmark in the course of modern civilization was the coming of the printed
book, which in the hands of the Florentine and Venetian printers was a model
of unity of all the elements that enter
into the art of bookmaking.

BIBLIOGRAPHY

Ballardini, Gaetano, *Corpus della maiolica Italiana*, 2 vols., Rome, 1933, 1938

Cellini, Benvenuto, *Autobiography*, tr. by J. A. Symonds, Modern Library, 1927

Ferrari, Giulio, *Il Ferro nell' arte Italiana*, 2d ed., Weyhe

Gardner, J. Starkie, *Ironwork*, rev. and enl. by W. W. Watts, 2 pts., London, 1930: Pt. II

Herbert, John A., *Illuminated Manuscripts*, Putnam, 1911

Kristeller, Paul, *Early Florentine Woodcuts*, London, 1897

Orcutt, William D., *The Book in Italy during the Fifteenth and Sixteenth Centuries*, Harper, 1928

Podreider, Fanny, *Storia dei tessuti d'arte in Italia (secoli XII–XVIII)*, Bergamo, 1928

Pollard, Alfred W., *Early Illustrated Books*, Empire State Book Company, 1927

Rackham, Bernard, *Catalogue of Italian maiolica*, 2 vols., Victoria and Albert Museum, London, 1940

See also the General Bibliography, pp. 791–92.

29

BAROQUE ART

(SEVENTEENTH CENTURY)

BAROQUE is an excellent example of the necessity for looking at the culture that is responsible for a style of art and the reasons for the character of that culture. The coming of the seventeenth century marked the decline of the Renaissance in Italy, as the sixteenth marked its maturity and the fifteenth its youth. Hence one expects to find complexity and contradiction, technical virtuosity, and theatrical realism. A secular life centered in display found its needed stimulation in a grandiloquence that surprised and overwhelmed the senses. A complacent, decadent Church, threatened with disintegration by the progress of the Reformation in northern Europe, aroused itself into reform through the Counter-Reformation, and saw in the pomp and circumstance of the rising baroque style a type of expression that could overawe with splendor. This trend was confirmed by the Jesuits, recently established in Spain, whose influence was powerful not only in missionary endeavor but also in holding adherents loyal in the face of powerful heresies. Hence the motivation of both secular and religious interests was to feed strained emotionalism with grandiloquent brilliance. One is not surprised to find Italian opera developing rapidly, and the aria, with much florid embroidery, the vogue of the day; or the rise of the viol family among instruments, culminating at Cremona in the creations of the Stradivarius family.

Yet the seventeenth century was not completely unified in this objective. Its complexity admitted many contradictory elements, such as the emergence of the truly scientific spirit. For, stimulated by the Renaissance ideal of complete objectivity, men's minds turned from magic and the authority of the Church to independent observation. On the one hand the Church warmly reasserted the mystery of the Christian faith; on the other, Descartes with his *Cogito, ergo sum* displaced medieval faith with reason. It was the century of Galileo and Francis Bacon; of the invention of the telescope, the microscope,

[A] *Santa Maria della Salute. Venice. 1631–82. (Alinari)*

and the thermometer; of the discovery of the circulation of the blood. In other words, as the cycle of the Renaissance declines, the modern scientific age is being born.

ARCHITECTURE

Rome was the fountainhead of the baroque style, partly because of the religious situation in the city of the Mother Church and partly because the seeds of the style, sown in the sixteenth century, particularly in the work of Michelangelo, naturally grew quickly in native soil. But it spread rapidly to Naples and to northern cities, especially Venice, Genoa, Turin, barely touching, however, that stronghold of the early Renaissance, Florence. Great scale, restless movement, organization in depth, Michelangelo had held within bounds. With him relationships in all the parts were clear and definite. With the ba-

roque artists, movement became an end in itself. In a typically baroque church it is not the clear precise relationship of every part that the artist strives to set forth, but the total effect of many parts half-seen, moving, incoherent, provided the total effect is a "spectacle of never-ending movement" — not stability but flux.

Because of the powerful religious motivation it was a great age of church building and remodeling.[1] The elongation of the nave of *St. Peter's* and the addition of the present façade and of the colonnades which sweep around the piazza are thoroughly baroque in their scale and dramatic quality. The colonnades introduce a curving motif which finds repetition in the dome and diversification in the rectilinear character of the façade. Note how the two motifs are united by the straightening of the colonnades as they approach the façade. The scale of the piazza and the colonnades is colossal, and prepares one for the superhuman scale of the interior, to which all detail is tuned. Gigantic pilasters support broken cornices, as on the exterior; a colossal baldachino with huge twisted columns rises above the high altar; colored marbles, painted and gilded stucco reliefs, and richly gilded coffers adorn all the available space. When to these are added the colorful pageantry and the music of the religious festivals, the effect is overwhelmingly magnificent.

The façades of many of the baroque churches in Rome, such as *San Carlo alle Quattro Fontane* by Francesco Borromini (1599–1667) and *Santa Maria della Pace* by Pietro da Cortona (1596–1669), in general reveal an organization in

---

[1] This practice accounts for the baroque façade of *St. John Lateran* and of other early basilicas and for the refurbishing of many interiors, some of which are, fortunately, being restored. *Santa Maria in Cosmedin* (Fig. 252A) is one such case.

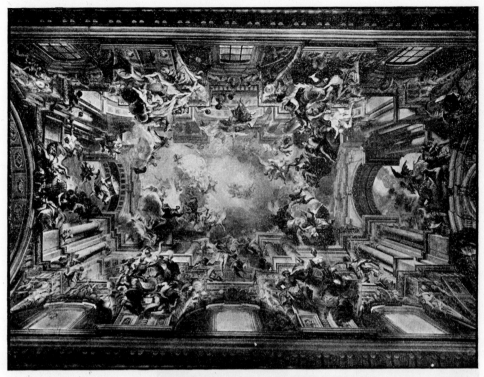

[A]   *Andrea del Pozzo. St. Ignatius Carried into Paradise. c. 1685. Sant' Ignazio, Rome.*
(Anderson)

several planes so that there runs through it an advancing and retreating movement.[1] Various architectural forms — columns, pilasters, pediments, moldings — are used to carry movement laterally, vertically, and in depth — a continuous flowing movement with occasional staccato accents, as in a broken or repeated pediment.

The central type of church with a dome still prevailed. Its external possibilities for expressing solidity and compactness of mass are well seen in *Santa Maria della Salute* in Venice (Fig. 526A), because of its open site at the head of the Grand Canal. It is octagonal in plan, with a great central dome and a

smaller one over the chancel; these are the climax of a restless design with complicated patterns and movements, and with indefinite broken upper contours because of the free-standing sculpture and great scrolls, which, however, unite the polygonal base with the circular dome. From this restless base rises the clear-cut mass of the dome, above which is repeated, in the lantern, the half-defined pattern below.

But the central type of church afforded opportunity for even more dazzling effects on the interior than on the exterior. For not only were all kinds of materials used to secure an effect of richness and all available spaces loaded extravagantly with marbles, reliefs, bronzes, gilding, and paintings, but the dome became the point at which crowds

[1] Contrast the single plane and quiet movement of the façades of the fourteenth- and fifteenth-century churches and palaces of Florence.

[A]   Bernini. The Episcopal Chair of St. Peter with the Four Doctors of the Church. St. Peter's, Rome. 1656. (Alinari)

of figures soar in a breath-taking sweep upward through the violently foreshortened architectural framework, which creates an illusion of reaching up to infinite heights (Fig. 527A). Here is the climax of the illusionism of Mantegna (Fig. 502A) and Correggio (Fig. 514A).

Secular architecture displayed the same general grandiose character. Imposing stairways, both external and in the interior, were a fertile motive toward this end, as is illustrated by the *Aldobrandini Villa* at Frascati, or by a sketch of the *Scuola di San Marco* in Venice by *Francesco Guardi* (1712–1765), which catches the whole spirit of the baroque as well as its forms. The Great Hall of the *Colonna Palace* in Rome or of the *Farnese Palace* is typical of the extravagance of ornament to convey a feeling of pomp and circumstance: paintings

and gilded stucco ornament with statuary below; above, rising from a heavy cornice, a cosmos of figures, statues, and paintings.

Besides the churches and palaces, supplementary piazzas, monumental fountains combining architecture, sculpture, and water, and imposing stairways, such as that of *Santa Trinità* — all are structures that in scale as well as form contribute to a general aspect of sumptuousness.

SCULPTURE

In sculpture, the dominating personality was Giovanni Lorenzo Bernini (1598–1680), architect as well as sculptor. To be a consistent part of an imposing, even theatrical building, sculpture must partake of similar qualities. The

[A] *Bernini. The Ecstasy of Santa Teresa. 1646. Santa Maria della Vittoria, Rome. (Anderson)*

Shrine for the bishop's chair in *St. Peter's* (Fig. 528A) well illustrates the dependence upon materials for their richness of color and texture, for the baroque sculptors freely combined colored and white marble and gilding. The indistinct half-realized forms — figures, clouds, rays — show a technical virtuosity in handling materials but an almost impudent disregard for their limitations — clouds and rays of light made of bronze. Yet the dazzling energy of this host of people, half sculptural, half pictorial, is held by an all-incorporating sustained rhythm and by the vast spaciousness in which it is placed and within which it therefore becomes a focal point. Bernini's papal tombs in *St. Peter's,* that of *Alexander VII,* for ex-

ample, and his *Santa Teresa* in *Santa Maria della Vittoria* (Fig. 529A) are prime examples of theatricality, manifesting the same kind of technical virtuosity and loss of feeling for stone that characterizes late Greek work. Intense facial expression, melodramatic poses, pictorial background, agitated voluminous draperies of white marble in juxtaposition with huge folds of variegated red marble — all these contribute to the desired effect. Michelangelo had expressed the utmost movement in his figures (Figs. 13B, 462A, 463A and B), but always sternly within the ideal space created by the original block of stone. Bernini abandoned this ideal space and allowed the figure to burst forth with great energy in all directions

Contrast with the clearly defined forms of the fifteenth century (Fig. 455A) a portrait by Bernini, with its movement, its realistic treatment of details, and its subtle modeling which causes the parts to flow one into another and the shadows to produce an almost pictorial effect.

Baroque painting involves carrying to a climax, at times to an extravagant climax under the stimulation of melodramatic ideals, many of the tendencies of the sixteenth century. Correggio's frescoes in *Parma Cathedral* are as truly, though less extravagantly, baroque as those in the domes of *Il Gesù* and *Sant' Ignazio* and in the *Barbarini Palace* in Rome. Caravaggio's realism and violently contrasted light and dark and the Mannerists' types become more sweetly sentimental. Tintoretto's conquest of space design set the three-dimensional organization as the normal type, with one or two great rhythms holding complex detail within their dominating sweep; and his rapid, more direct method in brush work was peculiarly suited to the expression of half-defined, dramatic effects. Veronese's use of a cooler, more silvery light and largeness of decorative quality reappears in Giovanni Battista Tiepolo (1696–1770). With him, though we are still in the baroque, we are also largely in the eighteenth century, when dramatic intensity eases into flowing grace.

SUMMARY

The consistency of the baroque style in all the arts, the perfect harmony of its forms and ideals, mark it as a style that consciously used a certain type of expression because no other could suitably serve its objective. Technical virtuosity, the result of centuries of endeavor, now became an end in itself.

The striving for effects, the theatricality — if these qualities are the object of unfavorable criticism, it should be criticism aimed at the age itself, at those forces which demanded in the declining years of the Renaissance cycle a type of expression that the artists must inevitably supply. When the exuberance of baroque was under control, its capacity for subordinating a multiplicity of complex movements into the sweep of an all-incorporating rhythm and its magnificent conquest of space in three-dimensional design were contributions of great value to the European tradition.

BIBLIOGRAPHY

Ayscough, Anthony, *Country House Baroque*, London, 1940
Briggs, M. S., *Baroque Architecture*, McBride, Nast, 1914
Fokker, T. H., *Roman Baroque Art*, 2 vols., Oxford University Press, 1938
Fry, Roger E., *Transformations*, Brentano's, 1927
Hagen, Oskar F. L., *Art Epochs and Their Leaders*, Scribner, 1927
Kimball, Sidney F., *The Creation of the Rococo*, Philadelphia Museum of Art, 1943
McComb, A. K., *The Baroque Painters of Italy*, Harvard University Press, 1934
Ricci, Corrado, *Baroque Architecture and Sculpture in Italy*, Dutton, 1912
Scott, Geoffrey, *The Architecture of Humanism*, 2d ed., Scribner, 1924
Sitwell, Sacheverell, *German Baroque Sculpture*, London, 1938
——————— *Southern Baroque Art*, Knopf, 1924
Voss, H. G. A., *Die Malerei des Barock in Rom*, Berlin, 1924
Waterhouse, Ellis K., *Baroque Painting in Rome*, Macmillan, 1937
Weisbach, Werner, *Die Kunst des Barock in Italien, Frankreich, Deutschland, und Spanien*, Berlin, 1924
——————— *Spanish Baroque Art*, Macmillan, 1941
Wölfflin, Heinrich, *Principles of Art History*, tr. by M. D. Hottinger, Holt, 1932
——————— *Renaissance und Barock*, Munich, 1926

Renaissance Art in Northern, Western, and Eastern Europe

30

FLEMISH ART

(FOURTEENTH TO SEVENTEENTH CENTURY)

WHILE the Renaissance was evolving its normal cycle from the archaic to decline in Italy, northern and western Europe — each country with local variations — was pursuing the Gothic tradition to its flamboyant decadence, which was reached when the Renaissance was just maturing — in the fifteenth century. Even that century, in its latter years, saw evidences of a centrifugal movement on the part of the Renaissance to all parts of Europe; but the sixteenth, seventeenth, and eighteenth centuries brought its direct impact. Sometimes its influence was assimilated; often it entirely transformed the native art or robbed it of its individuality. Frequently it was imposed by arbitrary monarchs, for the eighteenth century in particular was the heyday of the absolute monarch and the aristocracy, under whose influence art, and especially Italian art, became an artificial fashion rather than a genuine expression with vital significance.

But the Renaissance had a far wider influence than this. Its spirit of inquiry instigated travel, exploration, and colonization. Its love of independent thought permeated religious life, bringing about a revolt from the Roman Catholic Church and the establishment of Protestantism. It stimulated scientific activities, laying the foundation of observation and critical thinking that has resulted in unparalleled scientific development; in industrial and economic revolution; and politically, in the overthrow of absolutism and the coming into power of the middle classes and the masses. In the nineteenth century, as they began to emerge into the era of the present day, Europe and America were still struggling with the effects of the Renaissance. To watch the large aspects of this movement — for its complexity is too great to treat it in detail in one volume — let us begin with the flourishing Gothic art of the fifteenth-century Netherlands.

[A]   *Town Hall. Brussels. 1401–55.* (*N. D. Photo*)

The lowlands facing the North Sea near the mouth of the Rhine were the home of an industrious people, hardy because of their continual struggle with nature for self-preservation. Their knowledge of the sea and their courage in braving it early made them traders and manufacturers. Their ships brought raw wool and carried away the fine woolen cloth famous throughout Europe. Of the several provinces included in the Lowlands, or Netherlands, Flanders up to the seventeenth century was the most important, with many great manufacturing centers, such as Ghent, Louvain, and Ypres, and with Bruges not only the chief market of the Lowlands but one of the great trade centers of Europe. For an arm of the North Sea, now silted up, reached inland to

Bruges as late as the fifteenth century. Some of its trade went overland by the Rhine and the Brenner Pass; some went by sea around western Europe through Gibraltar.

Bruges (meaning "City of Bridges") was a typical Flemish city of medieval times, large, industrious, and wealthy. "In the fifteenth century buyers and sellers from every land resorted to Bruges for their trade. The merchant of Venice and the Jew of Lombard Street encountered one another on her quays and in her exchanges. Sailors and traders from all parts of the world made her streets lively with the varied colouring of their bright costumes. They came and went, and each left something behind him. The wealth of England met the wealth of the East in the market-halls of Bruges. The representatives of twenty foreign princes dwelt within the walls of this capital of the Dukes of Burgundy, at the crossroads of the highways of the North. 'In those days,' says Mr. Weale, 'the squares [of Bruges] were adorned with fountains; its bridges with statues of bronze; the public buildings and many of the private houses with statuary and carved work, the beauty of which was heightened and brought out by gilding and polychrome; the windows were rich with stained glass, and the walls of the interiors adorned with paintings in distemper or hung with gorgeous tapestry.' "[1]

Though technically Flanders was a fief, now of a duke and now of a king, these great Flemish industrial cities were only loosely united, for each was a strong civic unit, thoroughly organized through its merchant guilds, which were not only industrial but social, religious, and political as well. The cult of the individual, so prominent in Italy in the

[1] Sir W. M. Conway, *The Van Eycks and Their Followers*, Dutton, 1921, p. 85. For an excellent picture of Flemish life in the Middle Ages see Chaps. VII and VIII.

[A]   *Cloth Hall. Ypres. 13th cent. Destroyed, 1914, in World War I. (N. D. Photo)*

fifteenth century, had not yet reached Flanders. To pursue a craft, a man must belong to the guild controlling that craft — the painter, for example, to the Guild of St. Luke, which included the saddlers and glassworkers and mirror-workers as well. To secure membership in the guild, the aspiring painter was apprenticed in boyhood to a master, with whom he lived as a son, and who taught him the fundamentals of his craft: how to make implements, how to prepare the panels with gesso, and how to mix colors, oils, and varnishes — for there was no supply house where a painter could purchase ready-made pigments and implements. When the youth had mastered these problems and had learned to work in the traditional manner of his master, he usually spent several years as a journeyman, traveling about from city to city, observing and gaining ideas from other masters. He was then eligible to become a master

of his craft and was admitted to the guild. Through the guild he obtained commissions; the guild inspected his painting for honest, craftsmanlike materials and workmanship; and the guild secured him adequate payment.[1] The result of such a system was the sound craftsmanship that characterizes the best work of Flanders.

By the end of the fifteenth century Bruges was losing its prestige because of the silting-up of its harbors and because of political disturbances. Antwerp now became its successor as the center of the political, industrial, and artistic life of Flanders. Antwerp was more cosmopolitan than Bruges, and more eager to respond to the stimulation to trade that was being felt because of the discoveries in the New World. Life became more exuberant, and more sympathetic toward the new ideas that were penetrating northern Europe from Italy.

[1] For the guild system see *Ibid.*

Just at this time, however, Flanders, as a fief of the Spanish crown, was drawn into the religious wars. The Renaissance in northern Europe had emphasized the right of the individual in religious matters as opposed to the authority of the Catholic Church. Many of the provinces of the Lowlands had turned Protestant. Spain, strongly Catholic and Jesuitical, directed against these heretics the Spanish Inquisition. Antwerp, the center of the struggle, lost much of its wealth and vigor in these wars. In the seventeenth century, however, after the Peace of Westphalia, a renewed vitality under a stimulation from Italy produced the last great school of Flemish art.

ARCHITECTURE

Flanders in the fourteenth and fifteenth centuries was thoroughly Gothic; and though the Flemish built fine cathedrals, their most characteristic buildings were the town halls and the belfries, the guild and cloth, or market, halls, such as those at Bruges, Ghent, and Ypres. The *Ypres Cloth Hall* (Fig. 533A), of great vigor and dignity, was a large rectangular building with a steeply pitched roof, four small turrets with spires at the corners, and a massive tower with turrets which crowned the building. The small amount of decoration was inconspicuous. The impressiveness of the hall was due to the symmetrical massing of simple units (the rectangular body with pointed roof and the rectangular tower), to the quiet rhythm of repeated pointed arches and pointed turrets, and to the unbroken expanse of the roof, which balanced the large number of openings below.

This sturdy, restrained design became more slender, more elegant, and more ornate in the *Brussels Town Hall* (Fig. 532A) — an example of the same evolution of style that we saw in the cathedral. We note this in the tower and turrets, in the roof broken by frequent dormers, and in the light and shade of the façade made rich by the carvings and niches, the original statues of which were painted and gilded.

PAINTING

In northern Europe no great wall surfaces offered the painter an opportunity to develop a monumental kind of wall decoration such as the Italians produced in their mosaics and frescoes. For the evolution of the Gothic aimed ever to eliminate the wall by reducing the structure to a framework of piers and vaulting and by filling the open spaces with glass, the great mural decoration of the North. Hence the Northern painter's activity in the Gothic age was confined chiefly to painting miniatures and illuminations, unless one includes also the making of windows, which is handling of color, though not with the brush. In their colors, composition, backgrounds, and drawing the windows bear close relation to the miniatures, despite the difference of medium.

Suddenly, in the early fifteenth century, painting on a major scale appeared in the work of the Van Eyck brothers, Hubert (about 1370–1426) and Jan (about 1385–1440). Not that miniature-painting ceased. In fact the Flemings Pol de Limbourg and his brother were producing at the court of the Duke of Burgundy such books as the *Très Riches Heures* (Fig. 358A) at just about the time that the Van Eyck brothers were painting the *Ghent Altarpiece* (Fig. 536A).[1] This altarpiece is a good example of the folding altarpiece typical of the North. When closed it

[1] This was commissioned of Hubert in 1415, left unfinished at his death in 1426, and completed by Jan in 1432. It seems impossible to disentangle the work of the two brothers. It was carried off by the Germans during World War II, but has now been returned to Ghent, unharmed.

[A] *Jan van Eyck; also attributed to Hubert. Madonna of Chancellor Rolin. H. 27 in. c. 1432. Louvre, Paris. (Alinari)*

presents in monochrome the Annunciation and also, equal in scale and importance, realistic portraits of the donors. When it is opened, there is presented an intensely colorful rendering of the medieval conception of the redemption of man. In the center of the large lower panel — the *Adoration of the Lamb* — in a meadow gay with flowers, stands the altar with the Lamb, from whose heart flows a stream of blood into a chalice; around it are kneeling angels; in front is the fountain of life surrounded by kneeling Apostles. Toward the center, from the four corners great throngs of people approach, clad in rich robes, through a country where rosebushes and vines are laden with flowers; in the background stretches a varied landscape with richly wooded hills, rivers, and towns, and above this an early-morning sky. Over the altar appears a dove, from which rays descend to all the groups below. Above are the majestic figures

of God the Father, John the Baptist, and the Virgin, who sits tranquilly reading a book. Her hair falls loose over her shoulders; her elaborate crown is decorated with rubies, topaz, and pearls, with roses, lilies, and harebells, symbols of her virtues; seven shining stars scattered over the inscriptions of the arch form a supercrown. Her robe of blue is trimmed with an elaborately jeweled panel of gold-and-black brocade. The soft texture of the hair, the luster of the pearls, the gleam of the other jewels, in fact all the details, are indicated with extraordinary realism. But despite these realistic renderings of the detail, the *Adoration* scene is subordinate to a simple symmetrical organization with the Lamb as a focal point. The altar is placed on the vertical axis, and about it swing two concentric planes, the inner marked by the kneeling angels, the outer by the kneeling Apostles, the edge of the hosts, and the

[A] *Hubert and Jan van Eyck. Ghent Altarpiece, or Adoration of the Lamb. Central panel. W. 8 ft. 1415–32. Church of St. Bavon, Ghent. The analyses show (a) the organization of depth and the play upon texture; (b) the use of a sharp triangle as a basic unit shape.*

dove; from this outer circle the hosts radiate toward the four corners; the wavelike high horizon unites all the elements.

This minutely literal rendering of objective appearance strikes anyone forcibly in Flemish art if he approaches it with Italian painting in mind. Soon,

[A]   *Rogier van der Weyden. Descent from the Cross. 1435–50. Escorial, Spain.*

however, he realizes that all these de-tails and all the varying textures create a unity in which line and color are im-portant organizing means. Here is a smooth enamel-like surface of deep resonant color that has a strong linear quality, for the pigment is used with a precision that seems to be born of an innate sensitivity to line. It is, in fact, Gothic linealism.

In the small jewel-like *Madonna of Chancellor Rolin* (Fig. 535A), the wealth of detail is equally well controlled and organized. In a loggia with tiled floor, rich carvings, and stained glass the Ma-donna is seated, heavily draped in a richly bordered mantle which spreads in great folds over the pavement about her; an angel is holding a gold crown above her head. On the left, Chancellor Rolin, the donor of the picture, dressed

in the richest stuffs, kneels before a prayer desk. Through the columns one looks out on a garden with flowers and birds to a parapet where two passers-by are looking over toward the town on both sides of a winding river, where people walk about the square and across the bridge; beyond this scene the land-scape fades into distant blue hills. The eye delights in the rich color-harmony as it wanders from detail to detail, from texture to texture — stone, tile, glass, gold, hair, stuffs, flowers — but this wandering of the eye feels the co-ordi-nating influence of the arches and the columns of the loggia and of the con-sistently hard luminous surface.

The quality of color, the surface tex-ture, and the enduring quality of these paintings — for they are in an extraor-dinarily fine state of preservation — are

[A]   *Jan van Eyck. Gio-
vanni Arnolfini and His
Wife. 1434. National
Gallery, London.*

due to the technical methods of the Van
Eycks, who, though they did not invent
the oil medium, seem to have brought
earlier experiments to a climax. The
preliminary stages in painting such a
picture were the same as in tempera —
coating the wooden panel with gesso
upon which the figures were drawn and
modeled in light and shadow. Upon
this groundwork were added successive
coats of glazes, though the exact vehicle
used is not known, until a lustrous, hard,
enduring surface was produced.[1]

[1] See the unfinished *Saint Barbara* (Antwerp) by
Jan Van Eyck to illustrate the preliminary stages;
for Flemish technique consult Laurie, *The Materials of the Painter's Craft in Europe and Egypt.*

In the work of the Van Eycks we are
witnessing the same exploitation of the
visible world, the same break from the
imagery and symbolism of the medieval
world, that we saw in Italy, except that
in the North it took the form of a passionate interest in all the minutiae of
objective nature and an equally passionate desire to translate these details
into form. In details, we see an exact
copy of nature; in their unity, an organization not found in nature. The idea
of using everyday life as subject matter
for the painter was novel. The *Ghent
Altarpiece* is thoroughly medieval; in the
Madonna of the Chancellor Rolin the religious subject matter is hardly more

[A] *Memlinc. Marriage of St. Catherine. 1479. Hospital of St. John, Bruges.*

than an excuse; in the *Giovanni Arnolfini and His Wife* (Fig. 538A) a thoroughly genre scene shows the ability of Jan not only to satisfy the popular demand for realism but also to organize realistic detail into a coherent design in an interior space, partly by the subtle values of the space-defining and unifying light and partly by the pattern of line and unit shapes that repeat, contrast, and center upon the hands.

Rogier van der Weyden (about 1400–1464), whose home in the Walloon country in southern Flanders brought him into contact with the French, at times reveals a subordination of details and a predominant sense of design based upon sweeping line and balance of mass. In his *Descent from the Cross* (Fig. 537A), the eye is not lured from detail to detail, but is focused upon the central figure of Christ, to which the sweep of line and the area of light inevitably lead it. There is no landscape background. Against a flat surface the figures stand out in strong relief, and through the group runs a common intense emotion that unites them psychologically. Capacity for selecting essentials and setting them forth with emphasis enabled Rogier to paint portraits of forceful directness.

In the second half of the fifteenth century definite influences from Italy[1] brought certain changes in Flemish painting. In Hans Memlinc (about 1430–1494), for example, the linealism of the Van Eycks and Rogier van der Weyden was softened and the types became more ingratiating, yet without loss of the rich Flemish color and enamel-like texture. In the *Marriage of Saint Catherine* (Fig. 539A) the Madonna and the Child are enthroned in the center, a panel of rich damask behind them and a fine Oriental rug on the floor; saints and angels are grouped symmetrically on each side. At the top of the panel two small angels are floating down with a crown to place on the Virgin's head; on both sides are kneeling angels, one with a musical instrument, the other holding an open book, the leaves of which the Madonna is turning over. At the right Saint Barbara with her tower sits reading intently; at the left Saint Catherine reaches out her hand to receive the ring from the Christ Child; behind stand Saint John the Baptist with the lamb and Saint John the Evangelist with his poison cup; through the columns and piers we catch glimpses, in typical Flemish surroundings, of scenes from the lives of these saints. We feel the Northern realism here, in the detailed painting of the

[1] Hugo van der Goes (about 1440–1482) painted for Tommaso Portinari, agent of the Medici banking house at Bruges, an altarpiece (Uffizi, Florence) the advent of which in Florence is responsible for the realistic shepherds in Ghirlandaio's *Adoration of the Shepherds* (Uffizi). Florentine painters were making cartoons for tapestries to be woven in Flanders. These are but two of many mutual relationships between the two countries.

pattern and the texture of the fine rug, the rich brocade of the panel, the angel's robe and Saint Catherine's dress of black-and-gold brocade, the red velvet of the sleeves, and the delicate veil, so exquisite that it is scarcely discernible in a photograph. Still the total impression is not so much an insistence upon minute details as one upon the suave rhythms that control them, and the whole conception is lyrical, far removed from the austerity of the *Ghent Altarpiece*.

From even a cursory study of a group of fifteenth-century Flemish paintings it is apparent that there are certain well-defined types that govern the appearance of the figures, except in the case of an actual portrait. The Madonnas, for example, are much alike. The face with its high forehead, long nose, and small mouth is conventional. The Child is like a diminutive man with a large head, a face as mature as the Madonna's, and a wizened body quite without structure. These expressions are largely conventional, a part of the tradition of the school. The figure as an organic structure is something in which the early Flemings were not interested, as the Italians were.

The great century of true Flemish painting was the fifteenth, as we have seen it in the work of the Van Eyck brothers, Rogier van der Weyden, and Memlinc, centering chiefly in Bruges. During this century communication between Flanders and Italy was becoming much more frequent. Not only did these countries have a common trade interest, but the Flemish artists began to journey more frequently to Venice and Florence. Evidences of this contact we see creeping into Flemish art — an interest in the figure as expressed in the nude; Renaissance architecture and architectural details replacing Gothic in backgrounds; Italian types and landscape. With the coming of the sixteenth cen-

[A]   *Bosch. Temptation of St. Anthony. Middle panel of a triptych. c. 1490–1500. National Museum, Lisbon.*

tury, when Bruges lost its industrial prestige, the center of industry as well as of art shifted to Antwerp, an alert, more cosmopolitan city in which the new ideas of the Renaissance found more fertile soil than in conservative medieval Bruges. Thus the sixteenth century saw two main currents of art: first, the native tradition with its in- sistence upon realism which, when sev- ered from the religious subject, became genre, sometimes charming, sometimes satirical or fantastic; second, the Italian imitation, which resulted in paintings that were neither Mediterranean nor Gothic but a curious combination in which both racial styles were used, un- assimilated.

[A]   *Bruegel the Elder. Hunters in the Snow. 1565. Vienna.*

A unique painter in the Flemish tradition was Hieronymus Bosch (about 1450–1516). In his ideology medieval fantasy and grotesquerie reached a zenith. But his inexhaustible, audacious fantasy, which invented all kinds of diabolical creatures, found expression in clear, skillfully organized pictorial forms. Usually a landscape or an architectural framework, receding into space, provided the setting for figures that show Northern realism in detail and Gothic linealism in the crisp edges of the color areas, strongly opposed in value. All this is evident in any of his versions of *The Temptation of Saint Anthony* (Fig. 541A), a subject he painted frequently.

The native tradition appeared also in Pieter Bruegel (or Breughel) the Elder (1525?–1569), who showed that he could accept increments from other traditions without impairing his own integrity. As a journeyman, Bruegel traveled widely, particularly in Italy; and while in *Hunters in the Snow* (Fig. 542A), for example, one feels something of the Italian selective and organizing power, the Italian universalizing of the theme and familiarity with the science of linear and aerial perspective, yet every influence has been thoroughly assimilated. The eye takes in the scene and the mood at a glance, so directly and so convincingly are they conveyed. A few moments' careful observation, however, reveals that this impression is the result of a very precise organization that controls every detail. A cold blue-green dominant color with warm accents here and there, as in the fire and in the hunters and the dogs, sets forth the mood, as well as the visual appearance, of a village in winter. A clearly enunciated diagonal movement inward, marked by dogs, hunters, and

[A] *Bruegel the Elder. The Wedding Dance. 1566. Detroit Institute of Arts. (Detroit Institute) The analysis shows an asymmetrical organization of sinuous movement in depth. Compare with the static effect of the symmetrical organization of depth in Fig. 536A.*

trees, starts from the lower left-hand corner and continues, less definitely but none the less surely, by the road, the row of small trees, and the church far across the valley to the jutting crags of the hills. This movement is countered by an opposing diagonal from the lower right, marked by the edge of the snow-covered hill and repeated again and again in details. Verticals, prominent in the trees and houses, and horizontals in the skating-ponds stabilize the diagonals, as do the rectangular motif of the ponds and the

[A]   *Rubens. Rape of the Daughters of Leucippus. 1619 or 1620. Munich.*

sharp triangles in the hunter group, in the branches of the trees, in the roofs and the hills.[1]

The roistering peasant life of his own environment absorbed Bruegel, and whatever the theme, its vivid reality, at first glance so casually natural, is not the recording of visual perceptions, as with many Flemings, but the mar-

shaling of them into an abstract design which by distilling the merely perceived renders it far more effective to the eye. Particularly is this true in handling a large crowd, as in *The Wedding Dance* (Fig. 543A). The individuals in the foreground, while retaining all the actualities of type, costume, and environment, at the same time are drawn with such economy and emphasis at vital points that each becomes an abstract

[1] Compare with Giorgione's *Fête Champêtre* (Fig. 508A); a similar basic design.

expression of the rhythm of the dance. The group as a whole is firmly knit into interlocking curves in depth — movements that are carried partly by line and partly by shapes and color areas — which are held and accented by static trees and standing figures.

There was however but one Pieter Bruegel the Elder. Italianization seemed inevitable, and by it the truly Flemish art perished, while the Italianate form reached a pinnacle because of the sheer genius of Peter Paul Rubens (1577–1640), who lived in Italy for eight years as the court painter of the Duke of Mantua before he returned to Antwerp. After the religious wars, Antwerp regained its wealth and prestige and, still loyal to the Church, was ready to accept the expression of the Counter-Reformation, the baroque. Jesuit churches, patterned after their Italian prototypes, rose in Antwerp, Louvain, and Brussels. Baroque pulpits appeared, as at *St. Gudule* in Brussels, though they were hardly at ease in a severe Gothic interior; *Guild Halls* were remodeled to accord with the fashions of the day.

The exuberant painter Rubens was in perfect tune with this environment. Gifted in the handling of pigment, he brought painting to a climax in the history of painting in Europe and was a powerful influence for succeeding centuries. With an energy like that of Tintoretto, he usually chose dramatic themes, whether the subject was religious or mythological, landscape, portrait, or genre.[1] In the *Rape of the Daughters of Leucippus* (Fig. 544A), to take an example from the mythological pictures, the surface pattern consists of areas of extraordinarily rich contrasting textures — soft luminous flesh, silky hair, lustrous satin with scintillating reflections, swarthy masculine flesh, armor and heavy cloaks, the hide of the horses, the sky and the landscape — and is organized by intersecting diagonals and strong verticals; by light masses surrounded by dark. Yet it is not primarily surface pattern but a tightly knit group of solid masses existing definitely in space, with movement backward and forward in a truly baroque type of three-dimensional design. Each unit of this design is built up of color and light, as in Titian's late works; it is not drawn, in the Florentine sense of draftsmanship.[2]

Whirling movement carried on a diagonal off into space, quieted, and then brought back into a whirl is illustrated in the *Kermess* (Fig. 546A). Swirling units made up of two or three figures or of the still life are carried, by every kind of compositional device — line, light and dark, color, aerial perspective — from the lower left-hand corner to the distant right and thence inward by the lines of the hills and sky and by the strongly patterned trees and house back to the starting-place. The exuberant movement of the dancers is offset by the quiet spaciousness of the distance and by the solidity and repeated verticals of the trees and the house.

In Anthony van Dyck (1599–1641) we pass from the dazzling richness, impetuosity, and frequent coarseness of Rubens, his master, to a sobriety and refinement which, by comparison, is at times rather soft and empty. In his portraits, his chief work, at times he created a quietly rich surface of the textures of the rich fabrics, fine lace, jewelry, and feathered fan. Even the well-known portraits of the children of the court of Charles I in their overelegant satins and lace furnished Van Dyck an

[1] The huge number and the uneven quality of pictures attributed to Rubens are due to his well-known practice of composing or perhaps partly painting a picture and leaving the completion to some of his great number of assistants.

[2] See Munro, *Great Pictures of Europe*, pp. 217 ff., for excellent notes on Rubens's use of color in this and other pictures.

[A]   *Rubens. Kermess (Village Dance). c. 1623. Louvre, Paris. (Giraudon)*

opportunity for beautiful passages in the painting of stuffs. He displays in his figures no vigor either of character or of form, but, rather, an aristocratic detachment and somberness. For his sitters — much of his work was done for England's nobility, who invited him thither to paint portraits, to decorate their mansions, and to perpetuate their family pride — his sitters were a stately, elegant, self-centered people whose life was superficial. Van Dyck was not a satirist, like Goya.

METALWORK, WOOD CARVING, WEAVING

The carefully worked out details in Flemish painting serve to illustrate the versatility in many fields on the part of the Flemish artists, whose skill made them famous and influential throughout Europe. As in painting, everything was produced under the control of the guilds, with a like result of sound craftsmanship. Crowns and miters, jewels, and ceremonial vessels reveal the same skill of the goldsmith that we saw in the Gothic period. The pages of the illuminated manuscripts, glowing with color and gold, richly decorated initial letters, and miniatures, rival the panels of the altarpieces. The skill of the Flemings in the carving and paneling of wood made a wide market for their furniture and carried their workers to many parts of Europe to execute orders on the spot. But it is perhaps in the craft of tapestry-weaving that the Flemings showed their greatest skill.[1] In the Gothic tapestries

[1] There were two important centers for tapestry-weaving: Arras and Brussels. Arras was the chief center from early in the fourteenth century until 1447, when Louis XI seized the town. The Arras hangings were famous all over Europe, and some of them were designed by the Van Eycks and Memlinc. After the fall of Arras, Brussels became the center of the craft, which there operated under royal patronage. Painters such as Rogier van der Weyden and Rubens made cartoons for the weavers. Charles V required that the tapestries be signed by the master weavers. Of these Willem de Pannemaker was the most famous, and his signature appears on the great series made for Charles, such as the *Conquest of Tunis* in the Royal Palace at Madrid.

we saw that the same fundamental principles controlled the weaver that controlled the sculptor and the glass-worker; namely, decorative fitness through the insistence upon line, pattern, and color. Although the tendency toward naturalism was making itself felt and a love of minute detail was inherent in the Flemish artists, still they composed their figures skillfully into large units for the decorative effect, and kept detail subordinate. The tapestries became very large, and more complicated in composition. Classical, historical, and pastoral subjects entered. Dyes of intermediate tones, which were now becoming available, enabled the weavers to obtain more brilliant color and more pictorial effects. The borders became wider and more complicated and often gave delightful representations of foliage, fruit, and flowers as well as heraldic devices and inscriptions.

SUMMARY

In contrast to southern, or Mediterranean, man, with his search for the underlying principles of an expression of form that is clear, definite, with all parts precisely related, symmetrical, and reposeful, "Northern man knows nothing of repose; his entire power of configuration concentrates itself on the representation of uncontrolled, boundless agitation. The storm spirits are his nearest kin."[1] Thus the Gothic style, with its incessant movement, its feeling for infinite space, is the most fitting expression of the North, and the baroque, with similar indefiniteness and movement, found there a congenial home. Therefore in Flanders a splendid secular architecture, symbolic of the vigorous industrial and civic life, clung to the Gothic style; and out of the flourishing school of Gothic miniature-painters rose

[1] Wilhelm Worringer, *Form in Gothic*, Putnam, 1927, p. 83.

a school of painting whose strong linealism controlled its matter-of-fact actuality and literal presentation of the details of visual perception. The soundest of craftsmen, these Flemish painters, by creating magnificent surfaces of glowing color, hard and enamel-like, made an important contribution to the evolution of the oil medium; their fellow craftsmen, through the rigid control of the guilds, maintained an equally high quality in the fields of metalwork and weaving. With the inevitable movement of the Renaissance to northern Europe, a period of unsuccessful assimilation was followed by a complete control, in the hands of Rubens, of both Northern and Southern elements and a complete fusion into a great climax in European painting.

BIBLIOGRAPHY

Ackerman, Phyllis, *Tapestry, the Mirror of Civilization*, Oxford University Press, 1933

Barker, Virgil, *Pieter Bruegel the Elder*, Arts Publishing Corporation, 1926

Conway, Sir W. M., *The Van Eycks and Their Followers*, London, 1921

Elst, Joseph J. M. I. van der, Baron, *The Last Flowering of the Middle Ages*, Doubleday, 1945

Friedländer, M. J., *Die altniederländische Malerei*, 14 vols., Berlin, 1924–37

————— *Die niederländischen Maler des 17. Jahrhunderts*, Berlin, 1923

Fromentin, Eugène, *The Masters of Past Time*, Dutton, 1913

Fry, Roger E., *Flemish Art*, Brentano's, 1927

Glück, Gustav, ed., *Brueghel, Details from His Pictures*, tr. by Eveline B. Shaw, London, 1936

————— *Die Kunst der Renaissance in Deutschland, den Niederlanden, Frankreich, etc.*, Berlin, 1928

————— *Pieter Brueghel the Elder*, tr. by Eveline B. Shaw, Hyperion Press, c. 1936

Hourticq, Louis, *Rubens*, tr. by Frederick Street, Duffield, 1918

Hunter, G. L., *Tapestries, Their Origin, History and Renaissance*, Lane, 1912

Lambotte, Paul, *Flemish Painting before the Eighteenth Century*, Studio, 1927

Munro, Thomas, *Great Pictures of Europe*, Coward-McCann, 1930

Sterling, Charles, *La Peinture flamande, Rubens et son temps*, Paris, c. 1937

Stevenson, R. A. M., ed., *Rubens Paintings and Drawings*, Phaidon ed., Oxford University Press, 1939

Taylor, H. O., *Thought and Expression in the Sixteenth Century*, 2d ed. rev., 2 vols., Macmillan, 1930

Valentiner, W. R., *Art of the Low Countries*, tr. by Mrs. Schuyler Van Rensselaer, Doubleday, Page, 1914

Weale, W. H. J., and Brockwell, M. W., *The Van Eycks and Their Art*, Lane, 1913

See also the General Bibliography, pp. 791–92.

31

GERMAN ART

(FOURTEENTH TO SIXTEENTH CENTURY)

IN THE Middle Ages we noted the vigor of the Rhenish craftsmen in many of the arts. They built finely constructed and vaulted churches of bold picturesque mass and contour. Among the crafts their textiles and metalwork and wood-carving were equal to any produced in Europe. The impulse toward independent thought that was basic in the Renaissance movement in Germany touched chiefly religious and intellectual life, and resulted in a revolt from the authority of the Church of Rome and the establishment of the Protestant Church. The result of this Reformation was hostility to Rome and, perhaps unconsciously, to all things Italian. Probably it was for this reason that the traditions of the Middle Ages persisted so long in Germany.

It was not until the sixteenth century that German Renaissance expression reached a climax in Dürer, Holbein, and Cranach. Almost immediately after this Germany was plunged into a series of disastrous religious wars which so drained its energy and its resources that it was unable to make any notable contribution to the arts of Europe. In the eighteenth and nineteenth centuries, however, there arose another great expression of its people, perhaps its loftiest — the music of Bach, Händel, Mozart, Beethoven, Wagner.

ARCHITECTURE

German buildings seem always to have had a predilection for the picturesque — irregular outlines, abnormally high, steeply pitched roofs with dormers, and abundant decoration in the form of bright color, gilding, and carvings. When the influence of the Renaissance came — late, as we have said — it came in the form of the baroque, which with its excessive ornament and unceasing movement made a strong appeal to German taste. It was in secular architecture particularly, the town halls and the houses of the wealthy merchants, that this influence made itself felt. The Reformed Church had little zeal for building. In the houses — the *Peller House* in Nuremberg (Fig. 549A) was a typical example — the high gable had retained the essentials of the old traditions but had accepted some of the outward forms of Italy. The arrangement of doors and windows had become symmetrical; the doorway was placed in the center and was emphasized by a bay above it; the stories with superimposed orders to frame the openings continued up into the gable and were decorated fantastically with scrolls, pinnacles, and statues.

PAINTING
AND GRAPHIC ARTS

German painting, like that of Flanders, evolved from miniatures and stained-glass windows. It appeared early in the multiple altarpiece, which was usually the gift of some wealthy burgher, painted to please his taste and that of his friends. The *Isenheimer Altarpiece* (Colmar) by Matthias Grünewald (1485–1530) summarizes several important traits. There is something savagely grim, brutally realistic, in much of this early German painting, and intense color, at times as harsh as the portrayal of the incident. Crucifixions and scenes of agony were popular, and the *Danse Macabre* was peculiarly Germanic. Yet fairy gardens with the Madonna seated in the midst of roses in a mellow radiant light may be the scene upon which the wings open. But in all this painting there is never absent the controlling, intricate linealism of the North.

In the sixteenth century, however, Dürer, Holbein, and Cranach were able to soften the crassness of the native style without sacrificing its vigor, to infuse a feeling of structure into the forms, to eliminate much of the detail in favor of emphasis at essential points, without, however, loss of the restless, intricate Gothic line.

It was Albrecht Dürer (1472–1528) who first showed this reconciliation. While Dürer was still a young man, the printing press was beginning to make books available. Paper was becoming

[A] *Peller House. Nuremberg. 1605. An application of the Renaissance style to the high gabled house of the North. Jacob Wolff the Elder, architect. Destroyed in World War II.*

better in quality and cheaper in price. Illustrations began to be used commonly in printed books as early as about 1475. The extraordinary technical ability of the German in woodcarving and his feeling for line as the chief means of creating form, as well as for its intrinsic calligraphic possibilities, were pre-eminent potentialities for successful illustration. Thus Dürer's inherited tradition, together with his individual ability, fitted him to supply the illustrated religious books that were in demand because of the religious ferment of the Reformation. His conceptions, like those of Hubert Van Eyck, were of the Middle Ages, and his con-

[B] *Dürer. S. Christopher. Woodcut. 1511. Contrast with Fig. 550A for difference between woodcut and engraving.*

[A] *Dürer. St. Jerome in His Study. Engraving. 1514. Light is the real theme as well as the chief element of organization.*

victions were as sincere and intense as his imaginative powers, to take the *Apocalypse* series as illustration. Technically, Dürer used both the woodcut[1] and the copper engraving. In the *Saint Christopher* (Fig. 550B), the crisp lines create a surface pattern of large units of black, white, and intermediate gray in which the sweeping curves of the hills and the cloak hold in subordination the short, broken, jagged lines, which maintain a constant rapid movement and create varied textures.

The *Saint Jerome in His Study* (Fig. 550A) creates an atmosphere of peace, quiet, and orderliness — an atmosphere conducive to meditation. The sun streams warmly through the little round panes and envelops everything in the room with varying tones of light, thus

tying them into unity. The saint sits at his desk absorbed in work, quite disregardful of the movement of the sands in the hourglass behind him. The lion and the dog are dozing in perfect repose. The books, the cushions, and even the slippers underneath the bench suggest relaxation and comfort. Indeed, a mood as well as a light suffuses and submerges all the infinite detail, which, however, with its varying materials — knotty wood, glass, metal, fur, stuffs — creates a surface of interplaying textures. All the details feel the control of certain emphatic unifying elements, such as the beams of the ceiling, the arch of the window, the shadow on the floor repeating the curves in the animals.

Like Leonardo, Dürer was an inquirer. In his eager curiosity about everything he belonged to the Renaissance. He traveled in Italy, and was much impressed with the painters and with the beauty of the country. "How I shall freeze after this sun!" he wrote to one of his friends at Nuremberg. But Dürer's fiber was too strong for him to

[1] Some illustrators cut their own blocks; others do not. In Dürer's case it seems probable that this part of the work was done by a professional cutter.

be lured far away from his native traditions, though the influence of Italian forms appears in his *Adoration of the Trinity*, for example, in the absence of Gothic partitions and the pointed arches; and in a design strongly reminiscent of Fra Angelico's *Coronation of the Virgin* but with greater depth, more massive solidity in the figures, and less use of calligraphic line.

Hans Holbein the Younger (1497–1543), like Dürer, belonged to Renaissance Germany. But in his greatest work, his portraits, Holbein alone of his nation had the selective ability, the capacity to extract from the total visual impression a definite linear motif to which he subordinated whatever detail he used. In *Catherine Howard* (Fig. 551A), for example, notice how he states the dominant curve motif in the large brooch, repeats it again and again in the face and the headdress, expands it in the embroidery of the sleeves, and opposes it by the sharp angles of the collar. His lines are clear-cut and sustained, not broken, indefinite, and restless, as in many Northern painters. Technically, Holbein belongs to the fifteenth-century Flemish tradition, for the surfaces of his paintings are as lustrous as enamel; flat, for he uses shadow sparingly; and highly decorative.

Holbein's keen vision, his control over line, and his ability to select a pose, a costume, and a motif of composition that will emphasize characteristic aspects of personality are evident in his drawings, which are largely preliminary studies for the long series of portraits painted for the English court, whither he was called by Henry VIII. Drawn in red or black chalk, or with a silverpoint, with a light wash of color here and there or a few minutely worked details of pattern or color, sometimes the line is light, as in the designs for metalwork and jewelry; sometimes it is a strong continuous sweep; often it is

[A] *Holbein the Younger. Catherine Howard, Fifth Queen of Henry VIII. 1540–41. Toledo Museum of Art, Toledo, Ohio. (Toledo Museum)*

broken or wavering; usually it is definite, and always it attains its objective unerringly. In the *Man in a Broadbrimmed Hat* (Fig. 552B), the strong silhouette of the hat not only is interesting as pattern but serves to emphasize the sensitive face and keen eyes, and the suave curves in hat and hair are consistent with the almost effeminate character of the subject. The forty-one woodcuts known as the *Dance of Death* (Fig. 552A) not only illustrate Holbein's lucid thought and expression but disclose a remarkable dramatic power and an exuberant inventiveness. Death, in the form of a skeleton imbued with life and alert movement, always plays his part with grim irony as he mockingly enters into the activity of each individual.

[A] *Holbein the Younger. Dance of Death: "The Old Man." Woodcut. c. 1526. Metropolitan Museum of Art, New York City. (Metropolitan Museum)*

[B] *Holbein the Younger. Man in a Broad-brimmed Hat. Drawing with washes of color in the hair and face. Basel Museum.*

Lucas Cranach the Elder (1472–1553), an accomplished engraver as well as a painter, remained more German in his harsh realism, detailed individual heads, strong unmodulated color, and emphatically linear design. In the *Crucifixion* (Fig. 553A), the massing of the lights and darks — the three figures against the dark sky, the heads and spears against the light, the light masses of the horses and of the group of the Virgin — suggests an engraver's design. But the crass realism is permeated by a spiritual quality that results from the isolation of the crosses, as in Mantegna's *Crucifixion* (Fig. 501A), and from the symmetrical spatial organization that radiates from the central cross. The horses cut like wedges through the informally massed crowd with its indefinite, intricate, unending linear movement, which is echoed in the nervous drapery above.

SUMMARY

Although in architecture he enthusiastically accepted and adapted the baroque, the German found in the graphic arts and in painting, which remained essentially Gothic, an expression most in harmony with his nature. For in these arts line — with a reality of its own quite apart from its use in demarking areas and defining planes — abstract, intricate, interweaving line produced an indefinite, never-ending movement and texture that found a counterpart in the polyphonic music of Bach. Thus the typically Northern minute realism, intense, often harsh in feeling, was saved by its rhythmic lineal pattern and its stimulating color, so consistent in mood with both the content and the pattern. Their superb technical ability combined with love of decoration often led the artists to load with ornament not only

[A] *Cranach. Crucifixion. 1538. Charles H. and Mary F. S. Worcester Collection, Art Institute of Chicago. (Art Institute)*

their buildings, but the altars, the grilles, and even the pages of their early printed books. Technical virtuosity rather than esthetic effectiveness seems to have been their objective, though such masters as Dürer, Holbein, and Cranach, from contacts with the Mediterranean cultures, infused organization into Northern lineal realism. After the sixteenth century, production became negligible, because of the devastating religious wars, until creative activity again manifested itself in another form, the music of the eighteenth and nineteenth centuries.

BIBLIOGRAPHY

Bodmer, Enrico, *Dürer*, Novara, 1944

Carrington, FitzRoy, ed., *Prints and Their Makers*, Houghton Mifflin, 1916

Dickinson, H. A. S., *German Masters of Art*, Stokes, 1914

Dürer, Albrecht, *Records of Journeys to Venice and the Low Countries*, ed. by Roger E. Fry, Merrymount Press, 1913

Glaser, Curt, *Lukas Cranach*, Leipzig, 1923

———————— *Les Peintres primitifs Allemands*, Paris, 1931

Glück, Gustav, *Die Kunst der Renaissance in Deutschland, den Niederlanden, Frankreich, etc.*, Berlin, 1928

Hagen, Oskar F. L., *Art Epochs and Their Leaders*, Scribner, 1927

Hind, A. M., ed., *Albrecht Dürer, His Engravings and Woodcuts*, Stokes, 1911

Horst, Carl, *Die Architektur der deutschen Renaissance*, Berlin, 1928

Mather, Frank J., Jr., *Western European Painting of the Renaissance*, Holt, 1939

Panofsky, Erwin, *Albrecht Dürer*, 2 vols., Princeton University Press, 1943

Parker, Karl T., *The Drawings of Hans Holbein in the Collection of His Majesty the King at Windsor Castle*, Phaidon ed., Oxford University Press, 1945

Pollard, Alfred W., *Fine Books*, Putnam, 1912

Reinhardt, Hans, *Holbein*, tr. by Prudence Montagu-Pollock, Hyperion Press, 1938

Taylor, H. O., *Thought and Expression in the Sixteenth Century*, 2d ed. rev., 2 vols., Macmillan, 1930

Tietze, H. and Tietze-Conrat, E., *Kritisches Verzeichnis der Werke Albrecht Dürers*, 2 vols., Basel and Leipzig, 1937

Wölfflin, Heinrich, *Principles of Art History*, tr. by M. D. Hottinger, Holt, 1932

See also the General Bibliography, pp. 791–92.

32

SPANISH ART

(FIFTEENTH TO NINETEENTH CENTURY)

SPAIN, because of its geographical position and the mountainous character of its territory, is more isolated than most of the other countries of Europe. Yet it has been particularly the prey of the foreign conqueror — Roman, Goth, and Moor — and of foreign influences, from Flanders, Italy, France, and the Near East. The coming of the Moor and his long residence in the peninsula were a provocation to the Christians, whose long struggle against the infidels, combined with native conservatism, made them grim fighters for the faith and severe dealers with all forms of heresy. The Church, of a conservative type and with an overzealous priesthood, has always been a dominating power in Spain. Hence the Inquisition could flourish in Spain as in no other country of Europe. This constant struggle and religious fervor made the Spaniard brutal and fanatical on the one hand and emotional and mystical on the other.

It was not until after the fall of Granada in 1492 that any semblance of unity in the peninsula was possible. By the sixteenth century, largely through marriage and inheritance, Spain had become a first-rate power, holding large sections of Europe in fief and acquiring great wealth through its newly discovered possessions in America. Through Seville, the trade center of southern Spain, flowed gold and silver from the New World. Here, too, nature was less austere than in the barren, mountainous plateaus of the central part of the peninsula. The warm sunshine, the fertile soil, and the romantic temperament were more conducive to geniality. Southern and eastern Spain were also closer to Italy because of possessions in Naples and Sicily, and the great commercial seaports carried on a brisk trade with the East. But constant wars, mismanagement, and shortsighted policies controlled by an intolerant Church rapidly exhausted Spain's wealth. Its religious fanaticism led to the expulsion, in 1609, of the Mudéjares and the Moriscos, and deprived the country of its chief industrial class and its most skillful

[A]   *University of Salamanca. Portal and detail of the lowest zone, showing plateresque ornament with a portrait medallion of Ferdinand and Isabella. c. 1530.*

craftsmen, thus crippling the nation both economically and artistically. By the beginning of the seventeenth century the greatest days of Spain were past.

ARCHITECTURE
AND SCULPTURE

Spain, like other European countries, accepted the influence of the Renaissance upon its architecture, adapting it to local conditions and bringing about an ingenious fusing of it with the native style, especially in the matter of ornament. In the early Renaissance, when the continuity of the Gothic tradition in structure was still unbroken, a new spirit revealed itself in the plateresque style,[1] which is well illustrated by the *Town Hall of Seville* and by the entrance of the *University of Salamanca* (Fig. 555A). Plateresque ornament was usually concentrated about the doors and windows and its decorative value increased by the plain surfaces that surrounded it. At the *Salamanca* entrance a richly decorated panel rises above the double portal. The ornament is arranged in three zones separated by double string-courses and crowned by an elaborate cresting. Engaged clustered shafts frame the panel and furnish the needed vertical lines. The carvings increase in depth and boldness as they rise and are

[1] A name derived from *platero*, a silversmith, and applied to the style because of the delicate execution of its ornament.

[A] *Escorial. Near Madrid. Juan Bautista de Toledo and Juan de Herrera, architects. 1563–84. The building is a combination of monastery, church, palace, and tomb.*

broken by portrait medallions, heraldic emblems, and a sculptured group. The motifs include putti, masks, and grotesques, and predominantly the rinceau, showing an influence from Italy. More typically Spanish is the ornament of the *Archiepiscopal Palace* at Alcalá. The walls of the patio (the open court) give one the impression of richness and quiet taste. At first sight they appear to be rusticated, but on close inspection are found to be carved in low relief with animals, birds, masks, griffins, and putti expressed in vigorous movement that is characteristically Spanish.

The plateresque was the most original accomplishment of the period, and its short life of only about half a century was due to external causes. It was still vigorous and spontaneous when Philip II came to the throne in 1556. But it was too imaginative, too exuberant, too emphatic in its ornament, to please that austere, morose monarch. So, by royal order, a cold, unadorned classic ideal was imposed upon Spain, and the warm, typical Spanish style

gave way to a grim and solemn majesty exemplified by the *Escorial* (Fig. 556A), a huge, somber structure comprising church, monastery, and buildings of state. It was the work of Juan de Herrera (1530–1597) who set in this church a type that was to dominate not only in Spain but in the Hispanic colonies in the Americas as well: central in plan, often with an elongated nave, with a dome over the crossing and twin towers flanking the façade.

The severity of this Herreran style, however, did not appeal to the Spanish people, who turned to the rising baroque as a style more expressive of their native temperament, their love of luxurious ornament, and their religious zeal. The baroque infused the static Herreran style with movement and luxurious detail, particularly about the portals on the exterior and the altars in the interior, and under the influence of José Churriguera (1650–1723) reached a climax of elaboration known as the ultrabaroque or the Churrigueresque.

Of prime importance in this style was

[A] *Retable of Seville Cathedral. Detail of the central portion. Wood. 1482–1564.*

the retable, or altar screen, developed in Spain to a size and a magnificence met nowhere else in Europe. Its origin was in the simple altarpiece. But the native love of splendor and decoration and the extreme native religiosity seemed to pour itself forth in expanding the altarpiece until it spanned the bay or the nave and lifted its crest up into the vaulting. Sometimes it was carved of stone, more frequently of wood; invariably it was gorgeously painted and gilded, thus furnishing the richest possible background for the altar. In the *Retable* of the *Seville Cathedral* (Fig. 557A) vertical shafts and horizontal bands divide the space into panels with elaborately carved niches and figure sculpture. The motifs are chiefly Gothic, with an intermingling of Moorish. With the coming of the ultrabaroque, however, the retable abandoned the division into panels and became an area filled with never-ending movement, a surface excessively rich in gilded carvings, paintings, and highly realistic polychrome sculpture. The impression of overrichness with no contrasting reposeful areas perhaps finds partial compensation in the position of the retable in a spacious church with unadorned surfaces and dim light.

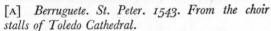

[A]   *Berruguete. St. Peter. 1543. From the choir*
stalls of Toledo Cathedral.

[B]   *Pedro de Mena. St. Francis.*
Wood. Toledo Cathedral.

Spanish sculpture is definitely allied
to architecture, either as architectural
sculpture or as religious equipment.
Wood was always a popular material
with Spanish sculptors, being plentiful
and cheap and offering a good surface
for the painting, which was considered
to be of equal importance with the carving. Well-known painters were employed for this part of the work and specialists developed, such as flesh painters,
drapery-painters, and gold-painters.

The advent of Italian influence is
illustrated by Alonso Berruguete (about
1486–1561), who studied in Rome not
only sculpture but architecture and
painting, was a pupil of Michelangelo,
and on his return to Spain produced a
melodramatic Michelangelesque style
in which the controlled movements
of the Italian were transformed into
uncontrolled contortions that suited
the Spanish love of realism and intense
emotionalism. Somewhat less emotional

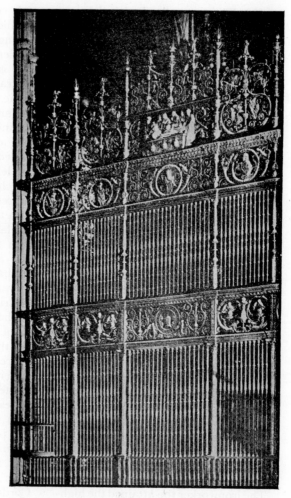

[A] *Custodia. Restored. Gold and silver. 1513. Cordova.*

[B] *Reja. Of hammered iron, gilded. H. 21 ft. 1518-33. Seville Cathedral.*

than some is the *Saint Peter* (Fig. 558A), though even in this figure there is a brittle tenseness in the lean, almost skeleton-like hands and feet and the expressive face. The drapery sweeps about the figure in massive folds, their broad simplicity accentuating the emaciation of the body. This high relief is a detail from one of the elaborate choir stalls which, like the retable, were a part of the church equipment that the sculptors carved lavishly.

The fervid piety of the Spaniard and his love of realism often led him to extremes, as in a wholly naturalistic polychromy, the use of actual hair and garments on figures, and glass tears. Restrained, by comparison, yet fervid in its emotional appeal, is the *Saint Francis* (Fig. 558B) of Pedro de Mena (1628–1688). The long monastic robe and hood completely clothe the quiet figure, and frame a face which in its expression of asceticism is typically

Spanish. The compact cylindrical shape, the deeply cut hood, and the manner of the carving are peculiarly indicative of the material, wood.

METALWORK, LEATHERWORK, WOODWORK, CERAMICS

Another artist who contributed to the richness of the church was the metalworker. Spain was rich in mines of gold, silver, iron, and jewels that supplied it with material even before the vast resources of America were opened to it. An important contribution of the silversmith, the *platero*, was the *custodia*, the large templelike receptacle that contained the monstrance and was carried in processions. The custodias made before the Renaissance illustrate well the Spanish love of ornament (Fig. 559A). From a polygonal base this gold and silver structure — for the design is primarily architectural — rises lightly and delicately, gradually diminishing in circumference. It is all decoration — reliefs with representations of both sacred and secular subjects, figure work, and Gothic ornament, all executed with great technical skill. Whether or not overloading with ornament is ever justifiable, here it is done with a fairylike grace that almost disarms criticism.

The ironworker too attained the highest skill, especially in the *reja*, or grille, which enclosed a chapel or altar in such a way that it could protect the treasures within and still leave them visible. To make such a grille it was necessary for the craftsman not only to work his material dexterously but also to have a sense of architectural fitness in his design. The *Reja* of the *Capilla Mayor* (Fig. 559B) of the *Seville Cathedral*, reaching from pier to pier, encloses the altar and its retable (Fig. 557A), and appears "glittering in the dim light like vast bits of gold lace heavy enough to stand of themselves on edge." Together with the rich colorful retable, it makes an ensemble of great splendor. The design is arranged in two stages, with decorative borders and a cresting. Vertically the reja is separated into five panels, the central one wider than the others. The vertical shafts on the lower stage are colonnettes covered with delicate reliefs reminiscent of silverwork, and carrying capitals; in the second tier they are carved balusters, and in the cresting, candelabra. In the decorative borders the chief motif is the scroll containing figures; the intervening space is filled with the typically Renaissance rinceau; similar motifs appear in the cresting with flying angels and cherub heads. The artistry of such a reja consists of the happy balance of vertical and horizontal lines; great richness of detail held in strict subordination to the main lines of the design; the architectural fitness of the design; the fitness of the material for the purpose; and the visible evidences of the hammer and tongs on the material when in a tractable state, and of the chisel when it is hard.

Besides the metalworkers, the craftsmen in leather, the woodworkers, and the potters added notes of color and texture to the stone and stucco buildings, more particularly in domestic and civic buildings. The leatherworkers of Cordova provided sumptuous painted and gilded leathers for hangings, cushions, furniture, and coverings for chests. The leather was moistened, and the designs were worked up in relief like repoussé by means of molds, the details added by engraving, and color applied — red, green, blue, black, and white. If silver or gold was used, the sheet metal was applied with oil sizing to the leather before the relief was stamped, so that the silver or gold relief stood out against the natural color of the leather or the brighter pigments. The Spanish love of color, stimulated by trade contacts with the East and by the

[A] *Mudéjar Wood Ceiling. Archbishop's Palace, Alcalá. 14th cent. (Moreno)*

long presence of the Arabs in the peninsula, found a means of satisfaction in polychrome woodwork and tiles. The Mudéjares were expert workers in wood and perhaps their supreme accomplishment, besides their fine furniture, is found in their ceilings, which were sometimes simply crossbeamed, sometimes coffered, or open-raftered, or three-planed, or of segments that simulated a dome. They were painted, gilded, carved largely with Moorish geometric ornament, and frequently served as the focal point of a room (Fig. 561A).

Balancing this colorful richness above, in a stone or stucco room with few openings, were tapestries and colored tiles below, or simple massive furniture with upholstery and cushions of sumptuously gilded and painted leather. The tilings, reflecting the influence of the ceramic

tradition of the Arabs, were often of interlacing geometric pattern or arabesque, or of animal and figure motifs — all painted in vivid colors on tin enamel with a spontaneous dashing quality. Climatic conditions favored a wide use of this cool material for interiors (Fig. 562A). The Hispano-Moresque pottery, which included plates, bowls, and jars with foliate and heraldic decorations painted in an exuberant colorful style and often heightened with luster, constituted a great industry in the Mediterranean coastal provinces, especially in Malaga and Valencia, and furnished the commercial cities with one of their important articles of trade. Cobalt and manganese on white enamel combined with a golden or iridescent luster, in designs that maintain surface continuity, produce a decoration that is highly colorful and peculiarly Spanish.

[A]   *House at Sitjes (Barcelona). A typical Catalan interior.*

In Spain as in Italy, all the arts were closely interwoven, for the artists were versatile craftsmen, members of the trade guilds. "The formula of admission to a Spanish brotherhood was very quaint in its punctilious and precise severity. . . . It was required that the candidate for admission should be a silversmith, married in conformity with the canons of the church, a man well spoken of among his neighbors, and not a recent convert to the Christian faith. The day prescribed for choosing or rejecting him was that which was consecrated to Saint John the Baptist, coinciding with the festival of Saint Eligius or San Loy, 'the patron and representative' of silversmiths, who in life had been a silversmith himself."[1] We hear of Berruguete assisting in the

[1] Leonard Williams, *Arts and Crafts of Older Spain*, McClurg, 1908, 3 vols., Vol. III, p. 222.

decoration of the palace at Alcalá, carving wooden panels for the choir stalls at Toledo, as well as making marble tombs for counts and cardinals and statues for altarpieces. Juan de Arfe is equally famous for the delicate workmanship of his silver custodias and for his bronze sepulchral statue of *Don Cristobal*. The famous makers of iron grilles were sculptors and architects as well.

PAINTING

A very close interrelationship and unity of style existed among the builders, the sculptors, and the various craftsmen, as we have seen. Spanish painting, on the other hand, seems more like sporadic outbursts in the hands of strong individuals, often working in alien traditions, rather than a normally evolving national expression. Before the sixteenth century locally differentiated groups of painters produced miniatures, frescoes (for Spanish churches, like Italian, provided large wall areas), and panels, largely religious, in a medieval style that was strongly Byzantine. They were painted in tempera with a lavish use of gold and frequently with details molded in relief in the gesso, and in their dramatic quality and grim realism are perhaps the most truly Spanish paintings. Foreign influence, however, infiltrated, now from Siena by way of Avignon, now from Flanders, now from France; and in the late fourteenth century and the fifteenth there evolved in Spain a late-Gothic style which is difficult to differentiate from that of Flanders, France, or Italy. Because of its lack of local characteristics this style of painting, which spread over large parts of Europe because of close communications and the journeying of artists, is sometimes called the international style.

In the sixteenth century, when Spain reached its zenith under Charles V and Philip II, Italian influence became stronger, partly because of the close political connection between the two countries and partly because of Charles's patronage of Titian and the large importation of Italian paintings to Madrid. Valencia, closely connected with Naples, produced painters who worked in that city with Caravaggio and other Tenebrists and through whom the strong chiaroscuro, limited color, and realism of those painters were transmitted to Spain. The forceful Jusepe de Ribera (1588–1652) exemplifies this group. His restless organization in depth, his violent contrasts of light and dark, often meeting with sharp edges, and his tense realistic drawing fittingly express his often violent subject matter — such as martyrdoms — and appealed to the piously fervid, if not morbid, element in Spanish life.

[A] *Murillo. Immaculate Conception. 1655–65. Prado, Madrid.*

More attuned to the warmly luxuriant and colorful plain of Andalusia, centering in Seville, were the paintings of Bartolomé Esteban Murillo (1618–1682). Despite a too-frequent soft, sentimental prettiness, Murillo revealed a technical ability in creating a surface of vibrating color; in bathing the canvas in a delicate glowing light; and in one or two of his *Immaculate Conceptions* — the most popular subject matter of Andalusia — an organizing power of some strength (Fig. 563A).

On the stark plateau of northern Spain, in the meantime, had arisen two

 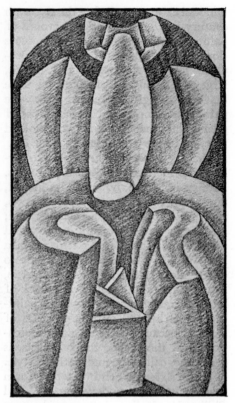

[A]   *El Greco. Assumption of the Virgin. 1577. Art Institute of Chicago. (Art Institute)*
The analysis shows the organization in space of cylindrical and cubical volumes.

of Spain's greatest painters — El Greco
and Velásquez. In Toledo Domenico
Theotocopuli, known as El Greco, "The
Greek" (1541–1614), found a congenial
home. His origin, highly important for
an understanding of his art, appears to
have been in a Greek — that is, a Byzantine — family long established in
Crete; and his training, in Byzantine
art of the second Golden Age, at Cretan
monasteries. When a young man he
sailed for Italy; after a few years in
Venice and Rome he left, for some unknown reason, for Spain, where he spent
the rest of his life at Toledo.

A double, and almost irreconcilable
basis — late Italian and Byzantine —
is evident in his early *Assumption of the*
Virgin (Fig. 564A). Some of the figures,
in particular that of the kneeling Disciple, in pose and drawing suggest
Michelangelo, and the composition obviously is based upon Titian's painting
of the same subject, though the three-
dimensional baroque organization is
close to Tintoretto. The panel is divided
into two parts. Below, the Disciples are
grouped about the empty tomb in a
circle from which, above, the Virgin is
rising in a floating, slightly spiraling
movement, which nothing impedes but
which, on the contrary, every detail accentuates: the sharp point of the sarcophagus lid, the break in the circle of
Disciples, the uplifted hands, the horns
of the crescent moon, the long slashes

[A] *El Greco. Burial of the Count of Orgaz. c. 1584. Santo Tomé, Toledo. (Anderson)*

of light on the Virgin's robe. As she rises she is surrounded by a group of angels whose lightness and agitation contrast with the solidity of the firmly rooted figures below. As surface pattern, sharp triangles furnish the dominant motif, marked chiefly by the sharp edges where color areas meet. For everywhere the eye is guided by abrupt transitions from color to color, from light to dark. This sharp cutting of areas and planes, often by the juxtaposition of complementary colors, boldly at variance with the Venetian practice of soft transitions, enveloping atmosphere, and dominant tonality, is evidence of El Greco's Byzantine training in building forms out of color and light and integrating them into a design that by its own abstract power makes forceful the inner signif-

icance of the incident pictured.[1]

In the *Burial of the Count of Orgaz* (Fig. 565A), we find a like division of a large curved panel into two parts, the one devoted to the scene upon earth, the other to that in heaven. As the priest is reading the service, Saint Stephen and Saint Augustine miraculously appear clad in gorgeous vestments, to take charge of the burial. The three figures form a compact circular group about which are massed, at the right, the priest who is reading the service, clad in a robe stiff with rich embroidery and

[1] To see the logical conclusion of this point of view applied to this subject matter, see the late *Assumption* (*San Vincente*, Toledo), in which the forms are completely etherealized in an attempt to objectify the ultimate essence in an ecstatic swirl of unearthly light and color.

[A]　*El Greco. Pentecost. 1604–14. Prado, Madrid. (Anderson)*

holding a jeweled gold cross, and beside him another of the clergy, in a filmy robe, standing with outstretched hands, transfixed by the vision above; at the left in balanced position, two monks, wondering at the miracle; and behind them a row of mourners dressed in black robes, with lacy ruffs about the neck and wrists. There is much solid painting in this lower group, and fine characterizations in the highly indi-

vidual portraits, which appear realistic in comparison with the painting above. A restrained mood suffuses the group, though the design is somewhat agitated in its sharp angles and dynamic contrasts of light and dark, in the rapid jagged movement of the ruffs and in the long sensitive fingers, and in the streaks of the filmy robe and of the torches, which help, with the drab color, to unite the two dissimilar parts. Above, swift lines leap up to the crown of the arch, creating an impression of tremendous movement and intense emotion. Here is the scene of the reception of the soul of the Count into heaven. Everywhere is restless movement, expressed by the same means that we saw in the *Assumption* — sharp cutting of planes, and high lights sharply picked out against the dark background with the startling effect of lightning.

As El Greco's emotional intensity became more concentrated, his design became more clearly abstract. His palette was often restricted, as in the *View of Toledo* (Fig. 567A), in which the same method of constructing forms out of light and color is applied to landscape.[1] In the *Pentecost* (Fig. 566A), on the contrary, the color is rich and varied. This panel is high and very narrow, curved at the top. At the head of a stairway is the Virgin seated, and grouped about her are the Disciples and the other two Marys, upon whom the Holy Spirit, symbolized by the dove, is descending in tongues of fire. The spectator is carried at once into that realm of fiery emotion which the group as a whole is experiencing. The figures form a rectangle enclosing a triangle made of the two foreground figures and the Virgin, and its upper edge is broken by the uplifted arm, which also connects the group with the effective space above that emphasizes the descent of the Spirit

[1] Compare Giorgione's treatment of a similar theme.

[A] *El Greco. View of Toledo. 1600–10. Metropolitan Museum of Art, New York City. (Metropolitan Museum)*

and is singularly suggestive of the meeting-place of the uplifted spirit of man with the descending spirit of the divine. At the same time the group exists in space, with agitated rhythms that move inward and outward in true baroque fashion. Visible line has practically ceased to exist. Light and color remain as organizing means and are used not naturalistically to represent form — its volume, structure, texture, and surrounding atmosphere; that is, an illusion of visual perception — but as something eerie, imaginative, entirely non-naturalistic, as a means of "rendering visible the mysteries of the supra-natural world." Thus the figures are significant partly for their representational values but largely as units in an abstract design, and hence are elongated or distorted, when necessary, to fulfill their function in the framework of light and color whose purpose is the expression

of an ecstatic emotional experience. And in this mystic quality El Greco is at home in the intensely religious Spain of the Inquisition.

In Diego Velásquez (1599–1660), on the other hand, we perceive a cool, objective, impersonal attitude toward visual appearance. In his *Surrender of Breda*[1] (Prado) Justin of Nassau, the Flemish governor, is handing to Spinola the keys of the town. The two commanders, elaborately dressed for the occasion and accompanied by their retinues, occupy the foreground against a hazy background of lowland country with marching troops, winding rivers, and smoke

[1] During the struggle between Spain and the Netherlands in the seventeenth century, the town of Breda, a key to Flanders, was still in possession of the Flemish. To the Marquis of Spinola the Spanish king Philip II had said, "Spinola, you must take Breda!" After a siege that was brilliant alike for defense and offense, the town surrendered.

[A] *Velásquez.   Inno-cent   X.   1650.   Doria Gallery,   Rome.   (Anderson)*

from conflagrations. Such an organization provided an opportunity to mass clear warm colors and varying textures against cool blue-greens with a decorative, tapestrylike effect. While each figure is objectively and naturalistically seen, the basic organization of repeated verticals, horizontals, and prominent diagonal in the central group and the flag, through which play wavelike movements in the men and horses, combined with the color organization — these raise it above the level of a mere historical document.

As court painter to Philip IV, Velásquez spent a large part of his life recording, in his cool, detached way, the objective appearance of this rigidly conventional royal household, with little interpretation but with the keenest eye for selecting what was important for

pictorial expression and with a control of paint to secure exactly the desired effect. Through acquaintance, while in Italy, with the work of Caravaggio and through contact with Ribera, he learned something of the potentialities of a very limited palette, black and neutrals, as is evident in many of his portraits, which are subtle harmonies of grays and blacks.

The *Maids of Honor* (Fig. 569A), which summarizes Velásquez' attack upon spatial problems, represents an apparently casual interior scene in which the little Infanta Margarita, accompanied by her maids of honor, by dwarfs and a dog for amusement, is posing for her portrait which Velásquez himself is painting on a large canvas at the left. In the background at an open door the grand marshal of the palace is pushing

Velásquez. Maids of Honor. 1656–57. Prado, Madrid. (Anderson)

aside a curtain; the king and queen stand in the same position as we, the spectators, and their likeness is reflected in the mirror in the background. Behind the casualness of this intimate scene is an organization built around the Infanta, upon whom the light falls from the window at the right and in relation to whom each figure takes its place in space, producing an impression of extraordinary reality of the space from the princess to the out-of-door light behind the marshal and from the floor to the lofty ceiling. This intense reality of the space is partly the result of a precise observation and the recording in pigment of the exact amount of light that each object receives and the effect of the light upon the distinctness of the form and its contours. Yet combined with and dominating this accuracy in the observance of values are the relationships among the different parts. The foreground group forms an S-curve in depth from the dog to the painter, and it is filled with bright light, color, and movement painted in dashing strokes, now of thin pigment, now of thick, which define exactly each texture and quality of light. This vivacious group is played off against a large quiet spaciousness of gray-green with quietly proportioned rectangles repeated on the walls, each detail of which is toned as precisely as the foreground group. And the two parts, which act as a foil to each other, are united by the enveloping light and also by the prominent edge of the canvas at the left.

Out of the extravagant costumes of the court Velásquez created exquisite harmonies of silvery gray, black, and rose and of varying textures put on in light, skillfully calculated strokes which

[A]   *Goya. Portrait of His Wife. 1811–14. Prado, Madrid. (Anderson)*

blend the tones and suggest rather than depict the forms. The portraits of the *Princesses Margarita* and *Marianna* (Prado) illustrate this.

In painting these royal portraits, whatever interpretation he made or whatever emotional reaction he experienced, Velásquez kept to himself. Royalty, courtliness of the most rigid character, it was his task to portray, not individual personality. But the portrait of *Innocent X* (Fig. 568A) leads us to suspect that there might have been more interpretation had the painter been free to express it. For in this Roman portrait there is not only objective reality in its tersest essentials, an arresting design of curves and angles, a masterly use of pigment in a play upon reds and whites in contrasting textures of satin, lace, velvet, and metals, but also a piercing penetration and forceful presentation of a personality.

After the seventeenth century there is little that is noteworthy in Spanish painting until it flames up once more in Francisco Goya (1746–1828), who for a considerable part of his life was the favorite painter of the Spanish court. In the *Family of Charles IV* (Fig. 571A) we see Goya as realistic as Velásquez; but in contrast to Velásquez' impersonal poise, Goya paints into these portraits his high scorn of this sham court degenerate in both body and mind. Prominent in the foreground is Charles, much bedecked with regalia, "the pompous futility of a king," and his queen Maria Luisa, masterful and dominating, surrounded by the other members of the royal family, whose elegance of costume only heightens their weakness. At the left in the background stands the painter at his canvas. How an artist who was so fearless of truth and so bold in his expression of it could be tolerated at such a court is a puzzle. Either Charles was too stupid to understand or he was too lazy to resent. Besides the caustic satire of the portrait, we here discern Goya's power to paint exquisitely silks, jewels, velvets, and lace, each with a brush stroke suitable to the texture represented and productive of a delicately colorful vibrating surface. The spatial problem here is not unlike that of Velásquez in the *Maids of Honor* (Fig. 569A). "There are no lines in nature," said Goya, "only lighted forms and forms which are in the shadow, planes which project and planes which recede." So each figure in the group takes its own place backward or forward in relation to its neighbor; and the group as a unit, filled with atmosphere, with varying lights and shadows which play over the richly colored textures, is set off against the quiet spaciousness of the room.

A contrasting characterization, as warm in its sympathy as the royal portrait was bitter in its satire, we find in the *Portrait of His Wife* (Fig. 570A), who

[A]   *Goya. Family of Charles IV. 1800. Prado, Madrid.*

is sitting stiffly with conventional propriety, her gloved hands folded over
her lap. The sharp triangles of the figure
and the ground are opposed to the
rounding motifs of the head, the shoulder, and the back of the chair. Over the
surfaces of the solidly realized figure a
light movement runs through the delicately painted hair, the transparent
shawl, and the stuffs of the dress and
upholstery.

Another example of sheer beauty of
painting as painting is the *Maja Nude*
(Prado), a masterly integration of light,
dark, color, and texture. The area of
light which cuts diagonally across the
panel is composed of the solidly built
and softly rounding figure, with its
warm blended flesh tones, set over

against the cool blue-white filmy pil-
lows and sheet, which contrast also in
texture and angular motifs. This light
area, standing out strongly against the
dark color of the blue couch and the
flat neutral ground, draws the eye to
concentrate upon it. Compare, for contrast, the effect of the landscape background in Giorgione's *Venus*.

Goya's life falls into the period not
only of the rapid decay of Spain but
also of the Napoleonic Wars, whose
grim horror he depicts and protests
against in his etchings *The Disasters of
War* and in such a painting as *The Shooting of the Rebels of May 3, 1808* (Fig. 572A),
in which the whole organic structure is
peculiarly fitting to the theme. The
scene cuts diagonally into space from

[A]   *Goya. Shooting of the Rebels of May 3, 1808. Prado, Madrid. (Anderson)*

the lower left-hand corner; on the right, the firing squad, in regular file, parallels the irregularly grouped terrified victims, upon whom the light from the lantern falls directly, producing an intensely lighted area around which sweeps the dark area of the soldiers, the town, and the sky. The striding movement of the soldiers, their shadows, and the light on their weapons carry the eye to the central figure of the victims, whose passionate gesture forms a sharp triangular motif that recurs endlessly throughout the canvas and is accentuated by the bold contrasts of light and dark. Color too contributes fittingly to the grimness. For Goya used neutral grays and browns with a splash of red in the pool of blood.

Goya's insight into the life about him and his fearlessness in expressing it with biting comment is clear in the *Caprices*. In this series he pictures with stinging satire the weakness of the State, the greed and corruption of the Church, the hypocrisies of the people, and the social rottenness. In the foreground of *Why Hide Them?* (Fig. 573A), a miser with snarling face tightly clutches his money bags, bending over them as if to protect them from the four men who stand laughing at him. He is probably one of the clergy, for the great wealth and greed of the Church at that time were commonly known. Goya's draftsmanship is as incisive as his satire is biting. With a few economical lines and a dynamic patterning of black and white he has trenchantly revealed the characters and has set forth the significance of the situation with amazing lucidity and startling power.

SUMMARY

The Spanish "national temperament, somber as it is, is a baroque temperament, full of fancies and extravagances, warlike, religious to the verge of superstition, yet inconsequential, and in Spain even the baroque style, carried to a degree of ornateness unparalleled elsewhere in Europe, compels admiration for its dignity and splendor."[1] The exuberant love of ornament was held in restraint in the short-lived plateresque and Herreran styles but burst forth in the baroque and Churrigueresque retables, choir stalls, metalwork, and vestments, in the creation of which the Spaniard was extravagantly lavish of both time and material. At the same time he was never free to develop a normal self-expression, limited as he was by an intolerant Church and a rigid court, and with his energy occupied in assimilating or combating aliens and alien influences. Particularly true is this in the field of painting. However, in El Greco's construction of form in light and color; in Velásquez' detached observation of life, his limited palette, and his abrupt brush work combined with subtle niceties of values to organize space; and in Goya's trenchant satire, enhanced by a consistently dynamic form, whether in pigment or in the graphic arts — in the work of these masters at least Spanish painting played a brilliant role in the evolution of painting in Europe.

[A] *Goya. Caprice: "Why Hide Them?"* (*Calvert*)

BIBLIOGRAPHY

Adams, Nicholson B., *The Heritage of Spain*, Holt, 1943

Barber, E. A., *Hispano-Moresque Pottery in the Collection of the Hispanic Society of America*, Hispanic Society of America, 1915

Beruete y Moret, Aureliano de, *Goya as a Portrait Painter*, tr. by Selwyn Brinton, Houghton Mifflin, 1922

————— *School of Madrid*, tr. by Mrs. Stuart Erskine, Scribner, 1909

————— *Spanish Painting*, ed. by Geoffrey Holme, Lane, 1921

Byne, Arthur, and Mildred, *Decorated Wooden Ceilings in Spain*, Putnam, 1920

————— *Spanish Architecture of the Sixteenth Century*, Putnam, 1917

————— *Spanish Interiors and Furniture*, 3 vols., Helburn, 1921–25

————— *Spanish Ironwork*, Hispanic Society of America, 1915

Byron, Robert, and Talbot Rice, David, *The Birth of Western Painting*, Knopf, 1931

Caffin, C. H., *The Story of Spanish Painting*, Century, 1910

Calvert, A. F., *Sculpture in Spain*, Lane, 1912

Dieulafoy, M. A., *Art in Spain and Portugal*, Scribner, 1913

Goldscheider, Ludwig, *El Greco*, Phaidon ed., Oxford University Press, 1938

Goya, Francisco, *The Complete Etchings of Goya*, foreword by Aldous Huxley, Crown, 1943

Gudiol, José, *Goya*, Hyperion Press, c. 1941

Hagen, Oskar F. L., *Patterns and Principles of Spanish Art*, University of Wisconsin Press, 1943

King, G. G., *Mudéjar*, Longmans, Green, 1927

[1] R. R. Tatlock, ed., *Spanish Art*, London, 1927, p. 97 (Burlington Magazine Monograph).

Lafuente, Enrique, ed., *The Paintings and Drawings of Velasquez*, Phaidon ed., Oxford University Press, 1944

Legendre, M., and Hartmann, A., *Domenikos Theotokopoulos Called El Greco*, Hyperion Press, 1937

Mather, Frank J., Jr., *Western European Painting of the Renaissance*, Holt, 1939

Meier-Graefe, Julius, *The Spanish Journey*, tr. by John Holroyd-Reece, Harcourt, Brace, 1927

Munro, Thomas, *Great Pictures of Europe*, Coward-McCann, 1930

Notes Hispanic, Hispanic Society of America, 1942–45

Peers, E. A., ed., *Spain: A Companion to Spanish Studies*, Dodd, Mead, 1929

Post, C. R., *History of Spanish Painting*, 3 vols., Harvard University Press, 1930

Rutter, F. V. P., *El Greco*, Weyhe, 1930

Stevenson, R. A. M., *Velasquez*, Macmillan, 1899

Stokes, Hugh, *Francisco Goya*, Putnam, 1914

Tatlock, R. R., ed., *Spanish Art*, Weyhe, 1927 (Burlington Magazine Monograph)

Trapier, Elizabeth du Gué, *Hispanic Notes and Monographs, Catalogue of Paintings in the Collection of the Hispanic Society of America*, 4 vols., Hispanic Society of America, 1929–32

Tyler, Royall, *Spain: Study of Her Life and Arts*, Kennerly, 1909

Van de Put, Albert, *Hispano-Moresque Ware of the XV. Century*, London, 1904

Weisbach, Werner, *Spanish Baroque Art*, Macmillan, 1941

Whittlesey, Austin, *The Renaissance Architecture of Central and Northern Spain*, Architectural Book Publishing Company, 1920

See also the General Bibliography, pp. 791–92.

33

DUTCH ART

(SIXTEENTH TO SEVENTEENTH CENTURY)

THE country now commonly called Holland constituted the northern and eastern part of the group of provinces known as the Lowlands or the Netherlands; Flanders occupied the southern and western part. There was a racial difference between the two, the Hollander being closer to the German, the Fleming to the French. Like Flanders, these northern provinces were the fief now of one lord and now of another. At the time of the religious and political struggle with Spain, however, the northern provinces, which had quite generally accepted Protestantism, revolted from the Spanish crown, forming the nucleus of the modern Netherlands, whose independence was recognized by Spain in the Peace of Westphalia (1648). Under the early part of the Spanish rule

the Dutch, like the Flemish, had flourished. The East India Company had been formed and the discovery of the New World had opened up to them further opportunities for trade and colonization. Their great commercial cities, such as Haarlem and Amsterdam, had thus been stimulated, and were rapidly acquiring great wealth. Life was not unlike that in the neighboring Flemish cities. Civic pride was strong, and supervision by guilds and similar organizations effective.[1]

Religiously, however, there was a great difference. Protestantism gained

[1] See G. B. Brown, ed., *Rembrandt*, Scribner, 1907, Chap. III, for a picture of Holland in the seventeenth century; also H. W. Van Loon, *Life and Times of Rembrandt: R. v. R.*, Garden City Publishing Company, 1932.

a strong hold among the Dutch and with its puritanical attitude toward art banned sculpture, religious pictures, pagan myths, and even historical subjects. As we think back over the art of the Middle Ages and of the Renaissance, we realize that to eliminate the religious subject means to eliminate most of the art and one of its chief motivations. What, then, was left for these wealthy Hollanders, under the stimulation of their recently won independence, their national pride, and their religious convictions? Fromentin has answered the question thus: "A writer of our time, very enlightened in such matters, has wittily replied that such a people had but one thing to propose — a very simple and bold thing, . . . and that was to require that they [the artists] should paint its portrait. This phrase says everything. Dutch painting, it is quickly perceived, was and could be only the portrait of Holland, its exterior image, faithful, exact, complete with no embellishment. Portraits of men and places, citizen habits, squares, streets, countryplaces, the sea and sky — such was to be, reduced to its primitive elements, the programme followed by the Dutch school, and such it was from its first day to the day of its decline."[1]

PAINTING

Thus it came about that the Dutch painters pried into the pictorial possibilities of this everyday life, yet with an eye to their patrons, the middle-class burghers, who were acquiring wealth and position and wanted paintings to hang on the walls of their houses as an evidence of their prosperity, and also to enjoy, with their inherited appetite for realism, a copy of actual appearance. What the artists supplied was a compromise, if it suited at all.

[1] Eugène Fromentin, *The Masters of Past Time*, Dutton, 1913, p. 130.

[A] *Hals. Laughing Cavalier. 1624. Wallace Collection, London.*

In the field of portraiture Frans Hals (1580–1666) met the demand, at least for part of his life, through the sheer drive of his style, which combined a slashing directness in the use of pigment and a robust naturalism with a knack of terse characterization and a contagious spirit of laughter and jollity. Thus in the *Laughing Cavalier* (Fig. 575A) a self-confident soldier with a suggestion of bravado looks out at us with a direct glance while over his face ripples a momentary expression difficult to analyze. The unbroken surfaces of the flaring black hat and of the cool blue-gray ground act as a foil to the ostentatious coat with its fine lace collar and cuffs, silk sash, and rich embroidery of warm red-browns and yellows, all dashed in with vigorous brush work. The simple pattern of sweeping curves and sharp angles, the color scheme, and the contrast of cool quiet and warm vivacious areas are in harmony with the nonchalance and bravado of the subject.

[A]   *Hals. The Archers of Saint Adrian. 1623–24. Frans Hals Museum, Haarlem. (Braun)*

Momentary surface expression, caught in passing and frequently of a jovial nature, is characteristic of much of Hals's work, and his technical methods are particularly suitable to his purpose. How much he could say by means of a few of his vigorous brush strokes the *Young Man with a Slouch Hat* (Cassel) illustrates.

Hals painted many group portraits of civic organizations, a type of portrait-painting popular in Holland. In those of *The Archers of Saint Adrian* at Haarlem (Fig. 576A) and *The Governors of the St. Elizabeth Hospital* (Haarlem), he has so grouped the figures that each is equally visible and each head is an individualized portrait — otherwise the picture probably would not have been accepted. But the artist has managed to tie them into a loose pattern and to rely largely upon creating a vivacious surface by his vigorous painting of the textures of lace, velvet, satin, metal.

In Rembrandt van Rijn (1606–1669) we find an entirely different type of mind from that of Hals, a totally different method of using paint, and a refusal to compromise with the ideals of the Dutch burghers, who failed to grasp his imaginative conceptions and could not understand his formal means. The immediacy of effect in Hals and the clear literalness of some of his minor contemporaries suited the current taste better.

Rembrandt's portraits of the 1630's, such as the *Old Lady* (National Gallery, London) or the *Elizabeth Bas* (Amsterdam), are precise, realistic descriptions with diffused lighting, though the group portrait *The Anatomy Lesson* (The Hague) already reveals a concentration upon light as the chief organizing element. By 1642, when Rembrandt painted *The Night Watch* (Amsterdam), he had found his formal means in a highly individual use of light and color which was not understood by his patrons, who refused

[A] *Rembrandt. Young Girl at an Open Half-Door. 1645. Art Institute of Chicago. (Art Institute)*

to accept the picture, hooted at it, and brought the prosperous Rembrandt to ruin financially.[1]

This personal use of light and dark reaches an early maturity in the *Young Girl at an Open Half-Door* (Fig. 577A). Subject matter was of importance to Rembrandt, both its visual appearance and its inner significance. In this painting the character of the form and the personality of the girl interest him equally. She is standing at a Dutch door with her hands resting on the lower part, and she faces the spectator directly, though her glance is averted to her right. She wears a tightly fitting bodice with a linen guimpe gathered

[1] For an analysis which lucidly explains the artistic problem involved, see Munro, *Great Pictures of Europe*, pp. 267–69; then compare with Hals's *The Archers of St. Adrian.*

closely about the throat, and a full skirt; about her neck is a double string of beads. Her youthful awkwardness rather than grace, and her shyness and reserve — which is not unfriendly, one judges from the suggestion of a smile about the mobile mouth — Rembrandt has pictured with an appropriate simple directness. A brilliant illumination concentrates upon the side of the face, one hand, and the wall behind the figure — against which the arm is sharply silhouetted — and submerges the other parts in shadow. Glowing light and shadow envelop the figure and blur its outlines. The most subtle gradations of tone within a very few hues — reds, red-browns, and yellows — create a deep space, define the volume of the figure, and place it exactly in that space. Light, then, is Rembrandt's basic means

[A]   Rembrandt. Supper at Emmaus. 1648. Louvre, Paris. Compare with Fig. 564A for a similar organization in the lower part. (Giraudon)

of expression, as line was Botticelli's — a light, usually warm, that throbs with infinite variations, entirely opposite to the cold, darting, untoned light of El Greco. This light penetrates the shadows as well, for they too throb with color in infinite variations and subtle gradations and are as vibrant as are the highest lights.

The *Supper at Emmaus* (Fig. 578A) is also organized in space by the same means — light. Four men are grouped about a table, Christ in the center. The Disciple at the left sits with hands folded in adoration as he recognizes the guest; the one at the right has made a quick movement as recognition dawns, but remains transfixed as if still doubting; the stolid serving-boy hesitates, puzzled at the scene. The room is dim except for the brilliant light that falls on the tablecloth and the face and hands of Christ, touches the hands of the Disciple at the left, and brings out the faces and hands of the two at the right. It plays

[B]   *Rembrandt. Man in a Gold Helmet. c. 1650. Kaiser Friedrich Museum, Berlin.*

[A] *Rembrandt. Christ Healing the Sick, Called the Hundred Guilder Print. c. 1649. Art Institute of Chicago. (Art Institute)*

upon surfaces — chairs, tablecloth, garments, stone — bringing out their textures. The highest light, about the figure of Christ, holds the eye to the center of interest and plays into the other figures, tying them into a psychological as well as a formal unity before it melts into the shadow. One sees here a typically baroque, asymmetrical balance (note the relation of the central figure and the arch to the vertical axis of the panel); a strongly felt linear pattern of verticals, horizontals, curves, and a dynamic diagonal, blurred, to be sure, by light; and a closely knit group of figures organized on a plane that swings around the rectangular table. All these visual elements are suffused with a warm vibrant yellow relieved with cooler grays.

We may question here why, after what has been said about the aversion of the Dutch Protestants to representing sacred themes, we have as the subject here an incident from the life of Christ. Rembrandt, as individual in religious thought as in artistic creed, evidently cared little for the dogmas of the times and the decrees of the Church. The fierce struggle of the Jesuits and the Calvinists did not trouble him. His representation of the Bible story was human, in terms of contemporary Dutch life. Many of the religious paintings of the Italian Renaissance, with their splendor and idealism, were made at the command of the Church as outward manifestations of its power. In the baroque painters, the Church, in its attempt to stem the tide of the Reformation, became pompous and grandiloquent. How very simple and sincere then, in contrast, is Rembrandt's everyday story told in the language of everyday man!

[A]   *Rembrandt. The Three Trees. Etching. 1643. Art Institute of Chicago. (Art Institute)*

Rembrandt's highly subjective and imaginative use of light reaches a culmination in the late portraits. The *Man in a Gold Helmet* (Fig. 578B) is a penetrating interpretation and a marvelous interplay of textures with the subtlest gradations of light. In the *Portrait of an Old Woman* (Leningrad), a high light is concentrated upon the face, the kerchief, and the hands, leaving the rest of the canvas an area of shifting dark. The bent figure combines with the chair into a curvilinear volume set in space, and makes a tranquil setting for the broadly modeled and highly lighted face and hands so eloquent of weariness. The significance of the picture lies not so much in its representation of some individual as in its abstract expression of an emotion, like Michelangelo's *Nudes* on the *Sistine Ceiling*. Carried still fur-

ther, almost to the point of disembodiment, is the last *Self-Portrait* (Munich), in which a few roughly brushed-in strokes of light impress upon us unforgettably the satiric laugh at his own loneliness, despair, and apparent failure.

That line also appealed to Rembrandt as a medium of expression is clear from his numerous etchings. His subject matter he took from the life around him — the landscape of Holland, the beggars of Amsterdam, peasants, and the common folk of all kinds — even when the title was religious, as in the *Hundred Guilder Print* (Fig. 579A).[1] The center of interest here is the figure

[1] The subject of the print is *Christ Healing the Sick. Hundred Guilder Print* is a title by which the print has been known since early in the eighteenth century. It is probably derived from the price that the print brought at an auction sale.

[A]   *Pieter de Hooch. Pantry Door. H. 27 in. 1658. Rijksmuseum, Amsterdam. (Braun)*

[B]   *Ter Borch. The Concert. Berlin.*

cf Christ, a concentrated mass of brilliant light set against a dark ground. The group on the right, the sick approaching to be healed, is strongly pictorial, due to the same kind of illumination that we have seen used in Rembrandt's paintings. On the left, in the group of Pharisees, line alone — a few economical lines — expresses not only the essentials of form but a penetrating characterization. Even more linear and more architecturally constructed is *The Three Trees* (Fig. 580A), in which the trees, in the middle distance, rising at right angles from the flat plane which stretches to the low horizon and from the dark area of the foreground, lift their rounding masses of foliage against a clear vast expanse of light sky which succeeds a passing storm, represented by firm diagonals — a prime example of the dynamic effect of the diagonal when it appears in conjunction with verticals and horizontals.

Contemporary with Hals and Rembrandt was a group of painters who were supplying the Dutch with another kind of small picture to hang on their walls, pictures of their homes, their courtyards, their streets, and their everyday activities. Genre, as subject matter for the painter, was infrequent[1] before these "Little Dutchmen" of the seventeenth century[2] not only popularized it but kept it on a high level of artistic treatment. In the *Pantry Door* by Pieter de Hooch (Fig. 581A), we are in one of these Dutch homes, and see a young woman just outside the pantry handing a small jug to a little girl. There is the usual beamed ceiling and tiled floor; in the room beyond, a chair, and above it a portrait near the half-open window where the light and air pour in, flooding the room and permeating even the darker corners of the

[1] Note Carpaccio's *Dream of Saint Ursula* (Fig. 504A); Van Eyck's *Jan Arnolfini and His Wife* (Fig. 538A); Dürer's *Saint Jerome in His Study* (Fig. 550A); and Velasquez' *Maids of Honor* (Fig. 569A).

[2] Important in the group are Pieter de Hooch (1629–1677); Jan Steen (1626–1679); Gerard Ter Borch (1617–1681); Jan Vermeer (1632–1675); Jacob Ochtervelt (1634?–1708?).

[A] *Vermeer. A Young
Woman at a Casement.
H. 18 in. c. 1664. Metro-
politan Museum of Art,
New York City. (Metro-
politan Museum)*

foreground. There is nothing monumental, nothing of profound significance, about the picture but much that
is quietly human. What interests us is
the masterful way in which the artist
makes us feel the interior. The bright
outside light coming through the windows emphasizes, by contrast, the dim-
mer light inside, and so true are the
artist's values here that we get a living
impression of the air-filled space and
distance. The two figures are placed
effectively against the wall and break
the almost monotonous angularity of
the design.

The textures of various objects afforded these painters opportunity to
create interesting surfaces. Ter Borch,
for instance, shows extraordinary craftsmanship in the painting of lustrous
satins and velvets, and heightens their
quality by surrounding them with contrasting hues and textures, and with

subtly modulated light organizes them
into deep space (Fig. 581B).

In Jan Vermeer of Delft we reach a
climax of Dutch genre painting. In his
Young Woman at a Casement (Fig. 582A)
there is pictured an everyday scene of
purely human significance; not merely
an illusion of visual perception, but the
organization of the elements of visual
perception into a formal unity: the human connotation, and the abstract form
— neither the one nor the other alone,
but a perfect union of the two. A young
woman is standing at a partly open
window by a table, one hand resting on
the window, the other holding a pitcher.
There is perfect poise and serenity in
the picture and a feeling of great coolness and restfulness. The informal, asymmetrical design is based upon rectangles,
in window, map, table, and still life,
countered by the curves of the figure,
the pitcher, and the basin; and upon

[A] *Ruisdael. Swamp. Hermitage, Leningrad.*

the interplay of various textures and qualities of the materials represented: smooth rigid glass and metal, stiffened linen, a thick rug that weighs down solidly. The light from the window falls upon the wall with the subtlest gradations of tone and fills the room, unifying all objects with its generally blue tonality. The dress is deep-blue; the cloak thrown over the back of the chair is lighter blue; blue plays through the linen headdress and the window glass. A cool white with infinite modulations covers the wall; the map and the rich red rug on the table furnish complementary notes of warmth and strength.

The importance given the objects on the table in this as well as in other paintings by the "Little Dutchmen" introduced a subject hitherto given but little attention in the field of painting, but soon to assume a prominent role

— still life. Painters were seeing that objects of everyday life offered great possibilities for the expression of pure form constructed out of related shapes, colors, and textures, which had of itself high esthetic significance apart from any subject matter.

In the field of landscape also the Hollanders made a great contribution, in that they saw in their native landscape, unidealized, as great possibilities for pictorial expression as in their homes. In the *Swamp* (Fig. 583A) of Jacob van Ruisdael (1628?–1682), we are looking across a marshy place in the woods, surrounded by great gnarled trees whose trunks are reflected in the open stretch. Water plants fringe the edge of the swamp and float on its surface; a duck flies off to the left where two others are swimming; the light illumines a great log half in the water, a slender birch sapling, and a gaunt oak; behind the trees the clouds roll up with an impression of movement in space. The calm and the stillness, tinged with melancholy, reveal the artist's sympathy and intimacy with nature, which have enabled him to interpret rather than merely transcribe its appearance. Despite an overattention to realistic detail, Ruisdael has massed his darks strongly at the corners, allowing the light and air to penetrate freely in the center; the high lights strike important accents and unify the scene. The color is somber, browns and greens predominating both in the light and in the shadow.

SUMMARY

It is in the field of painting primarily, and that for a brief century only, that Holland's creative activity produced magnificently and prolifically. The sturdy independent Dutch Protestants, who banned everything classical and Italian, made demands upon the painters that produced, besides portraiture, a new subject matter — genre and intimate landscape — in which unpretentious scenes found artistic expression. The jovial dash of Hals suited them well, as did the small pictures of Dutch life made to adorn the walls of small houses. The Dutch failed, however, to understand their greatest painter, Rembrandt, who developed a highly personal style based on baroque organization in deep space and on his own individual use of light with subtle gradations within a narrow range of color. All the Dutch painters were superlative craftsmen, and had a capacity to see everyday things as forms organized in space, as related and contrasted colors and textures, and not merely as visual perceptions to be faithfully described.

BIBLIOGRAPHY

Baker, C. H. C., *Dutch Painting of the Seventeenth Century*, London, 1926

Bode, Wilhelm von, *Great Masters of Dutch and Flemish Painting*, tr. by M. L. Clarke, Scribner, 1909

Bodkin, Thomas, *The Paintings of Jan Vermeer*, Phaidon ed., Oxford University Press, 1940

Borenius, Tancred, *Rembrandt, Selected Paintings*, Phaidon ed., Oxford University Press, 1942

Bredius, Abraham, *Rembrandt Gemälde*, Phaidon ed., Vienna, 1935

Caffin, C. H., *The Story of Dutch Painting*, Century, 1909

Coulton, G. G., *Art and the Reformation*, Knopf, 1928

Fromentin, Eugène, *The Masters of Past Time*, Dutton, 1913

Hagen, Oskar F. L., *Art Epochs and Their Leaders*, Scribner, 1927

Hind, A. M., *A History of Engraving and Etching*, 3d ed. rev., Houghton Mifflin, 1923

————— *Rembrandt*, Harvard University Press, 1932

Holmes, C. J., *Notes on the Art of Rembrandt*, London, 1911

Laurie, A. P., *Brush-work of Rembrandt and His School*, Oxford University Press, 1932

Lucas, E. V., *Vermeer of Delft*, 2d ed., George H. Doran, 1922

Mather, Frank J., Jr., *Western European Painting of the Renaissance*, Holt, 1939

Robins, W. P., *Etching Craft*, Dodd, Mead, 1923

Trivas, N. S., ed., *The Paintings of Frans Hals*, Phaidon ed., Oxford University Press, 1942

Valentiner, W. R., *Art of the Low Countries*, tr. by Mrs. Schuyler Van Rensselaer, Doubleday, Page, 1914

Van Loon, H. W., *Life and Times of Rembrandt: R. v. R.*, Garden City Publishing Co., 1932

Wilenski, Reginald H., *An Introduction to Dutch Art*, Stokes, 1929

See also the General Bibliography, pp. 791–92.

[A] *Compton Wynyates. Warwickshire, England. c. 1520. Service rooms, a great hall, a chapel, and private apartments are grouped irregularly about a central court.*

34

ENGLISH ART

(SIXTEENTH TO NINETEENTH CENTURY)

THOUGH the accomplishment of England in the arts since the Gothic age has been supreme in literature and admirable in some of its architecture, in painting it has seldom risen to the highest level, and its attempts in sculpture have been negligible, for the British have not evinced any marked feeling for sculptural form. Much of the fine vigorous art of the Middle Ages in England — cathedrals, carvings, illuminated manuscripts, embroideries — had been created under the stimulus and patronage of the Church. But when,

in the sixteenth century, Protestantism secured a strong hold and the monasteries were destroyed, this patronage ceased and England was deprived of a large class of skilled craftsmen. Protestantism in general was averse to religious representation, as in Holland; and its attitude became extreme among the Puritans, even iconoclastic under the Commonwealth. The Restoration, however, gave added zeal to the aristocracy, whose wealth and position, increased greatly through the acquisition of large colonial holdings, stimulated

[A] *Hammer-Beam Ceiling. Westminster Hall, London. 1397-98. (Viollet-le-Duc)*

effects upon the arts not only of England, but also of the world — the Industrial Revolution. For at that time the work of machinery driven by steam began to replace the handmade or literally the *manufactured* product. The movement spread rapidly to France, America, and other countries, and vitally affected all the arts, for it took away from the vast majority of the workers the creative faculty and the ideal of craftsmanship. Art was now confined chiefly to building, painting, and sculpture, and was fast becoming something apart, something that was looked upon as a luxury to be enjoyed at certain times and in certain places rather than as an integral factor of life.

ARCHITECTURE

Gothic art in England was strong, versatile, and long-lived. The first suggestions of the Renaissance were seen in decorative details, and in the greater symmetry of ground plan and of design, especially in the great houses of the Tudor age. For with the coming of Protestantism church-building almost ceased. At the same time the greater security throughout the country and the increasing wealth of both nobles and merchants from confiscated properties of the monasteries and from colonial possessions encouraged the building of country places. The typical Gothic manor, such as *Compton Wynyates* (Fig. 585A), is set in a great park with stretches of green lawn, masses of elms and oaks, and gardens, all carefully designed with an informality that is patterned after nature. There is an air of comfort, geniality, and freedom from conventionality about both the manor and the surrounding park that is peculiarly English. The variety of materials used in the construction — brick, wood, stone, and plaster — and the irregularity of the exterior and the plan

the building of fine mansions on great estates and the production of fine furnishings and portraits. Except in building there was so great a dearth of native talent that the kings and lords were forced to turn to foreign countries for artists. This need is especially noted in the field of portrait-painting. It was not until the eighteenth century, a hundred years after the Renaissance had begun to influence architecture, that a British school of painting evolved. This, like that of the Dutch, was devoted to portraiture and landscape; but, unlike the Dutch, it was under the influence of Italy and existed for the aristocracy.

The eighteenth century also initiated a revolution that was far-reaching in its

[A]   *State Room from Bromley-le-Bow. 1606. Victoria and Albert Museum, London.*
(*Victoria and Albert Museum*)

give the manor a picturesque appearance. In these Tudor mansions, a terrace was sometimes substituted for the
outer side of the court and the rooms
were grouped symmetrically on either
side so that the plan assumed an H-
shape.[1]

The Renaissance influence reveals itself more clearly in such a house as
Longleat, with its balance and symmetry,
fundamental to the Renaissance. The
exterior, with its flat roof, superimposed
orders, regularity, and proportions, reflects the Italian influence; the large
number of openings, the bays, and the
mullioned windows are due to the medieval English tradition.

[1] *Montacute House* and *Hatfield House* are good
examples of this plan.

The interiors of these English houses
indicate the wealth of the country in
timber — oak and other hardwoods —
and also the taste and skill with which
it was used. The open-timber ceiling,
the wainscoting, and the stairways were
perhaps the three most characteristic
uses. The hammer-beam ceiling,[2] which

[2] An open-timber ceiling in which pairs of
hammer beams (short beams that project from
the top of the walls and are supported by
brackets) support large brackets that rise to the
collar beam (a short tie beam connecting the
rafters near the top of the roof). The hammer
beam acts as a lever and dispenses with the tie
beam between the lower rafters, thus affording
height and spaciousness to the interior. It frequently terminates in some decorative carving,
and the space above is usually filled with
tracery.

[A] *St. Paul's Cathedral. London. Sir Christopher Wren, architect. 1668–1710.*

is ceiling and roof combined, is seen fully developed in *Westminster Hall* (Fig. 586A) and in its most elaborate form in the *Great Hall* of *Hampton Court.*

A fine example of wainscoting is found in the *Bromley* room [1] (Fig. 587A). The walls are entirely sheathed in panels of a fine quality of oak in a simple design. The center of interest in the room is the great fireplace with its carved stone lintel, above which rises the overmantel elaborately ornamented with the royal coat of arms. The ceiling of molded plaster harmonizes with the mantelpiece and adds another element of richness. Although the flat plaster ceiling had taken the place of the vault, it still retained the most obvious feature of the lierne vaulting (Fig. 354A) — the intricate design made by the ribs.

[1] The palace is now destroyed, but this room has been re-erected in the Victoria and Albert Museum, London.

When the Renaissance came as an effective force, it came quickly and was Palladian in form. This was due very largely to the dominating personality of Inigo Jones (1573–1652). The new style is evident in the *Banqueting Hall* of *Whitehall* (Fig. 589A). The façade is designed in two orders superimposed, with columns in the center and pilasters near the ends, doubling at the corners; the entablature of both orders breaks about the supporting members and is finished with a balustrade. All these characteristics are suggestive of Palladio's *Basilica* (Fig. 465A). The window treatment is peculiarly Renaissance, with alternating curved and angular pediments on the ground story and horizontal cornices supported by scroll consoles on the second. The rusticated masonry gives a feeling of strength and solidity, and the ample window openings furnish the light needed in a Northern climate. Inigo Jones, then, availing himself of the elements and principles of the Renaissance architects, combined and adapted them to the needs of London. Like all accomplished designers of buildings, he kept his decoration subordinate. Everywhere there is fine proportion, dignity, and restraint.

The second great architect of the English Renaissance was Sir Christopher Wren (1632–1723). Wren, like Inigo Jones, fell under the spell of Italy, as we see in *St. Paul's Cathedral* (Fig. 588A). Here the emphasis has been placed upon an effect of picturesqueness and majesty rather than upon a frank expression of structure. The artist realized that a church located in the heart of London with no open space as a setting but viewed from the irregular streets leading to it, and in a city whose climate is uncertain, dull, and foggy, must be vigorous and bold in its composition if it were to dominate. Wren used the basilica plan with a great dome spanning both the nave and the

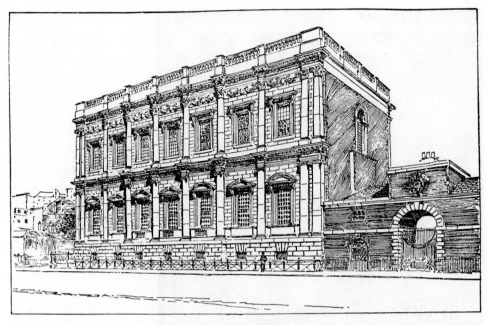

[A] *Whitehall Palace. Banqueting Hall. Inigo Jones, architect. 1619–22. London. (Blom-field) Compare the treatment of entablatures and corners with Fig. 4654.*

aisles. The classical portico shows some baroque tendencies in its superimposed colonnades, in their saliency, and in the inward and outward movement of the turret colonnades, which repeat the motif of the encircling colonnade of the drum of the dome and of the portico below. The two stories, which are carried consistently about the building, hiding the vaults, are rusticated, and are decorated with coupled pilasters and with strongly profiled and ornamented cornices to give the needed shadow. *St. Paul's* is an interesting example of a discreet use of the classical style with a frank acceptance of conditions of location and climate different from those of its original home.

The demand for small city churches[1] which resulted from the London fire of 1666 provided a new problem for the

[1] Many of these churches were destroyed or badly damaged by German bombs in World War II.

builders, for the congested conditions predetermined a plan that would be conformable to the restricted plot of land and also led the builder to place emphasis upon that part of the structure which would set the building apart from its crowding neighbors — the tower. Wren's *St. Mary-le-Bow* (Fig. 591A) would seem nonexistent were it not for the tower, which begins at the street level as a strong square structure no more pretentious than its secular neighbors. As it overtops these it takes on a more elegant character, evolves into increasingly slender polygonal and circular forms with encircling colonnades, and finally terminates in a slender spire. Thus it proclaims its symbolism above the roof level of the city. James Gibbs's *St. Martin's-in-the-Fields*, on the contrary, because of its open site on Trafalgar Square makes an effective use of a lofty classical portico, consistent with the contemporary classical revival but in-

[A] *Stone Hall. Hough-ton Hall, Norfolk. Built entirely of white stone. 1722–35. (A. Stratton, The English Interior, Batsford, London)*

consistent with the functionalism of the tower, which looks as if it were perched on the sloping roof (Fig. 591B).

Characteristic of this period that followed the Restoration were the mansions and country houses of the aristocracy, which vary from the great palaces — such as Wren's addition to *Hampton Court* (1689–1703), *Chatsworth* (1681), *Blenheim* (1705–24), and *Somerset House* in London (rebuilt 1776–79) — to the modest manors whose setting in spacious parks constitutes much of their charm. Renaissance styles were popular, particularly the Palladian design of the *Villa Rotonda* (Fig. 466A), in which a two-storied portico surmounted with a pediment formed a dominating feature of the design (*Prior Park*, near Bath, and *Chiswick House*). This late-Renaissance style was succeeded in the late eighteenth century and the first half of the nineteenth by the classical revival, illustrated by *Kedleston* (1761–65) in domestic architecture, and by the *Bank of England* (1788–1835) and the *British Museum* (1825–47) in civic buildings.

The interiors of the palaces and manor houses were perhaps more characteristic of the elegant formality of the times than the exteriors. Lofty proportions and fine materials contributed to their stateliness; classical sculpture, one of the passions of the aristocratic classes, filled the niches; and family portraits, perhaps by Reynolds or Gainsborough, stimulated family pride and added a colorful decorative note at the same time. The hall at *Houghton Hall* (Fig. 590A) illustrates the consistently monumental scale and the Renaissance treat-

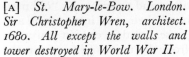

[A] *St. Mary-le-Bow. London. Sir Christopher Wren, architect. 1680. All except the walls and tower destroyed in World War II.*

[B] *St. Martin's-in-the-Fields. London. James Gibbs, architect. 1722. (Raymond R. Buckley) Compare with Fig. 644A, one of many American churches influenced by this design.*

ment of the strongly salient doors, mantel, and ornament. The hall at *Kedleston*, with its great height, alabaster colonnades, and rich ornament, has the grandiloquence of Italian baroque. Thus the desire for a dignified effect at times led to extravagant pomposity, a reaction to which found expression in the late Georgian age[1] in the work of Robert

---

[1] The period from about 1720 to 1780, covering roughly the reigns of the Georges.

Adam (1728–1792), an influential architect and designer. Adam retained the characteristic spaciousness but lightened the detail. Consonant with the classical revival, and with Roman stucco decoration (Fig. 593A) in mind, he based his stucco ornament on classical motifs — garlands, scrolls, vases, candelabra — kept it low, light, and delicate, and arranged it in panels, frequently oval, for curved lines predominated and the room was frequently designed on an oval plan. White was the prevailing hue, or the pale tones of green, tan, and gray. Invigorating color was supplied by rugs, hangings of velvet and chintz, and the mahogany of the furniture.

Robert Adam's influence is apparent also in the furniture used in these Georgian houses — *Chippendale, Hepplewhite,* and *Sheraton.*[1] A *Chippendale* chair was solidly constructed, though light in appearance, and finely carved; its legs were sometimes sturdily straight, sometimes curved or cabriole. The *Hepplewhite* was more delicate, with tapering legs and heart-shaped back. Of more extreme delicacy and severe balance was the *Sheraton,* which had inlays of various kinds of wood and daintily painted floral decoration.

PAINTING

In the field of British painting we feel an insularity that was due partly to its separation from the vitalizing influences current throughout the Continent, and partly to its frequent dependence upon foreign artists, whose influence lay, but little assimilated, on the surface while a contemporary native style was practiced weakly by its side. Not until the time of Reynolds did the art of painting become thoroughly professional. Then too, "the English temperament does not take kindly to the creation of monumental design in terms of three-dimensional form; but prefers a narrative and descriptive art based on close observation of nature, given a whimsical or dramatic turn, and put in terms of color and linear rhythm."[2] These characteristics

mark the source of one of England's highest accomplishments in the graphic arts, the English and Irish medieval illumination and miniature.

No school of British painting, however, evolved from this medieval basis, as in Flanders and France. To be sure, the miniature portraits painted by the Oliver family and others in the sixteenth and seventeenth centuries and the group of portraits, chiefly of royalty, by unknown painters of the fourteenth century to the sixteenth mark a beginning of great promise, over which swept the tidal waves of imported styles. First Holbein, in England from 1531 to 1534 at the invitation of Henry VIII, then Van Dyck, summoned in 1632 by Charles I, and Sir Peter Lely (1618–1680) set the styles in portrait-painting that were accepted by the chief patrons — the royal family and the aristocracy.

In the eighteenth century a sporadic expression of a more independent character was that of William Hogarth (1697–1764). A wide social gulf separated classes in seventeenth- and eighteenth-century England. The portrait-painters, whether native or imported, supplied the demands of the aristocracy, as did the builders and the furniture-makers. On the wave of classicism and consequent antiquarianism many classical statues and paintings by "old masters" found their way into manor and town houses; and a certain unity resulted from the unity of life within the limits of a given social class, such as existed in France under the later Louis. But it was not in this social stratum that Hogarth found his interest. His "moralities" were aimed at the London middle classes that he knew so well, and were strongly narrative and realistic. It was the age of Addison and Steele, the *Spectator,* and the early novelists. The middle classes had been growing in power at the expense of the court. Of the former class were the Puritans,

[1] Thomas Chippendale (died 1779) and George Hepplewhite (died 1786) were cabinetmakers with shops of their own; Thomas Sheraton (about 1751–1806) was primarily a designer, famous chiefly for his publications of designs for furniture.

[2] W. G. Constable in the catalogue of the College Art Association, *International, 1933,* p. 37.

[A] *Dining-Room. 20 St. James Square, London. Designed by Robert Adam.* (*Swarbrick*)

whose life was drab and intolerant; of the latter, the Cavaliers, who were trivial, artificial, and licentious. In the life and manners of these eighteenth-century people Hogarth, like Addison, found his subject matter. The dramatic situation, recalling stage productions, focuses attention upon narration, and the satire, though apparent, has a weakness of formal organization that prevents it from affecting the spectator with the unforgettable force of a Goya or a Daumier.

Evidence of Hogarth's feeling for pigment, however, is found when he was off guard, forgetful for a moment of his narrow moralizing. In a few portraits, notably in the *Shrimp Girl*, there is the sureness of a swift perception, and a sparkle and verve in its expression, attained through a spontaneous, swift,

and vigorous use of pigment — an artistic kinship with Hals — however rightly one may point to its lack of form, and to its lack of evidence that "the artist is preoccupied with purely visual values" (Roger Fry), both of which are permanent weaknesses of British painting.

It was the portrait-painting of Reynolds, Gainsborough, and their followers, however, that was the popular expression of the aristocracy. Sir Joshua Reynolds (1723–1792), despite a romantic sentimental vein and a futile attempt to adopt an Italian style, restored to painting — in his *Discourses* and his professional standards, acquired largely through study in Europe — the solid professional base which had been lost since the breakup of the medieval schools at the closing of the monasteries.

[A]　*Gainsborough. The Honorable Frances Duncombe. 1777-78. Frick Collection, New York City. (Frick Collection)*

More a theorist than an artist, overwhelmed by the color harmonies of the Venetians, he built up a "grand style" in which he painted the fashionable people of the day. An artificial society found in him its artificial painter, satisfied with superficial description containing little interpretation, structure, or organization, though he apparently saw these qualities in the prototypes he professed to follow.

Thomas Gainsborough (1727-1788), though he too painted the fashionable people of the time, tended to give their artificiality artistic expression (Fig. 594A). His portraits are usually composed after a Venetian formula, with masses of foliage, or a column, and a distant landscape in the background. But light and air play about the figures, which take their place in space in relation to the whole composition. Spontaneity and ease of line, and the textures of satin, lace, velvet, and plumes delicately brushed in with glowing iridescent color, together produce charming passages of surface. But it is largely surface painting, which in the followers of Reynolds and Gainsborough[1] weakened eventually into sweet prettiness.

If the British portrait-painters attained only a superficial excellence, the landscape school made definite contributions. The work of Richard Wilson (1714-1782), with its close dependence upon elemental nature, and of John Crome (1768-1821), with its quiet spaciousness filled with light and air, its direct and intimate relation to nature, often expressed with greater breadth and simpler realism than in Hobbema, by whom he was influenced — the work of these men was a prelude to the climax of British landscape-painting in Constable and Turner in the nineteenth century.

SUMMARY

In England we find a people who had developed strong traditions in the arts during the prolific Middle Ages and who through their insularity and tenacity of Gothic style were not easily influenced by Italian styles. Thus the Renaissance infiltrated gradually at first, without appreciably affecting the fine open-timber ceilings, for example, which were distinctively characteristic of the age. Eventually, however, the Renaissance — in particular the late Renaissance — overpowered this transitional type, and appeared in the churches and in the great manor and town houses of the aristocracy. This in

[1] George Romney (1734-1802); Sir Henry Raeburn (1756-1823); John Hoppner (1759-1810); Sir Thomas Lawrence (1769-1830).

turn gave way to the classical revival of the late eighteenth century and the early nineteenth. Painting was an imported art, confined largely to royal portraits until the rise in the eighteenth century of a truly English school, which, with the exception of illustrative satires on contemporary society and the beginnings of a landscape school, was confined to portrait-painting strongly under the influence of the Venetian portraitists.

BIBLIOGRAPHY

Armstrong, Sir Walter, *Art in Great Britain and Ireland*, Scribner, 1909
———— *Gainsborough and His Place in English Art*, Scribner, 1904
Baker, Charles H. C., *British Painting*, with a chapter on "Primitive Painting" by Montague R. James, Hale, Cushman & Flint, 1934
———— and Constable, W. G., *English Painting of the Sixteenth and Seventeenth Centuries*, Harcourt, Brace, 1930
Binyon, Laurence, *English Water-Colours*, Macmillan, 1933
Blomfield, Sir Reginald T., *A History of Renaissance Architecture in England, 1500–1800*, 2 vols., Macmillan, 1897
Borenius, Tancred, *English Painting in the XVIIIth Century*, Hyperion Press, 1938
Cescinsky, Herbert, *The Old-World House, Its Furniture and Decoration*, 2 vols., Macmillan, 1924
Dobson, Austin, *William Hogarth*, new ed., McClure, Phillips, 1902
Edwards, Ralph, and Jourdain, Margaret, *Georgian Cabinet-Makers*, Transatlantic, 1945
Fry, Roger E., *Reflections on British Painting*, Macmillan, 1934
———— and others, *Georgian Art (1760–1820)*, Scribner, 1929 (Burlington Magazine Monograph)
Gotch, J. A., *Early Renaissance Architecture in England*, Scribner, 1914
Grimsditch, Herbert B., ed., *Masters of Painting, William Hogarth*, London, 1926
Grundy, C. R., *English Art in the Eighteenth Century*, Studio, 1928
Hind, C. L., *Landscape Painting from Giotto to the Present Day*, 2 vols., Scribner, 1923
Jackson, Sir T. G., *The Renaissance of Roman Architecture: Vol. II, England*, University of Chicago Press, 1922
Johnson, Charles, *English Painting from the Seventh Century to the Present Day*, Dial Press, 1932
Macartney, M. E., *English Houses & Gardens in the 17th and 18th Centuries*, Scribner, 1908
Mather, Frank J., Jr., *Western European Painting of the Renaissance*, Holt, 1939
Mulliner, H. H., *The Decorative Arts in England, 1660–1780*, London, 1924
Richardson, A. E., *Georgian England*, Scribner, 1931
Russell, John, *British Portrait Painters*, Hastings House, 1945
Sitwell, Sacheverell, *Conversation Pieces*, Scribner, 1937
———— *Narrative Pictures*, Scribner, 1938
Swarbrick, John, *Robert Adam and His Brothers*, Scribner, 1916
Tallmadge, T. E., *The Story of England's Architecture*, Norton, 1934
Triggs, H. I., *Formal Gardens in England and Scotland*, 3 pts., Scribner, 1902
Vallance, Aymer, *Old Colleges of Oxford*, Scribner, 1912
Victoria and Albert Museum, *Panelled Rooms*, Vols. I–VI, London, 1914–24; Vol. I, *Bromley Room;* Vol. II, *Clifford's Inn Room;* Vol. V, *Hatton Garden Room*
———— *Catalogue of English Furniture and Woodwork*, Vols. I–IV, London, 1923–31
Wilenski, Reginald H., *Masters of English Painting*, Hale, Cushman & Flint, 1934

See also the General Bibliography, pp. 791–92.

[A]   *Château of Blois. Wing of Francis I. 1515–19. (N. D. Photo) Legend attributes the design of the spiral stairway to Leonardo da Vinci.*

35

FRENCH ART

(FIFTEENTH TO NINETEENTH CENTURY)

UNTIL the sixteenth century France was still Gothic, and each community was still a unit of civic and religious elements which found free expression in the work of the artists. But cosmopolitanism was taking the place of medieval local solidarity. The exchange of commodities and of ideas was establishing a broader attitude toward life. Political interrelations were taking the French kings to Italy and ended in bringing Italian ideas to dominate France. There is little wonder that the warmth and splendor of Italy captivated the Northerners, even those who came primarily on political missions, as did Charles VIII, who during his expedition to Italy in 1494 lived for some time in the Medici Palace in Florence. Even more influential was

Francis I (1515–1547), a great patron of all the arts, who not only brought ideas from Italy but induced Italian artists, such as Leonardo da Vinci and Benvenuto Cellini, to come to France and there execute commissions for him.

For it was the king and not the Church who now held power in France. The religious art of the Middle Ages was being superseded in an attempt to glorify the state and to flatter the monarchs, who were now arbitrary and now whimsical, and usually under the spell of Italy. Hence upon the native artists the kings usually imposed a foreign art.

Politically, socially, and economically, the rapid tendency toward the final suppression of the feudal lords and toward the concentration of power in the hands of the monarch reached its climax in the famous statement of Louis XIV, "I am the state." The burden of religious wars and persecutions, of unendurable taxation, and of the injustices of class privilege on the one hand, and on the other, a new mental outlook in which reason and the laws of nature challenged medievalism, combined in the great outburst of the French Revolution, one of the important signs pointing to a new era based upon a new social order.

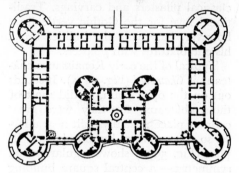

[A] *Château of Chambord. 1526–44. In the central building were the rooms of state; in the side wings, the servants' quarters, kitchens, and pantries. There was little in the way of convenience or sanitation. The stables were near the living-rooms and the kitchens far from the dining-room. (N. D. Photo and Du Cerceau)*

ARCHITECTURE

The tendency in France away from religious toward secular interests, even before the coming of a direct influence from Italy, brought about a greater demand for châteaux and civic buildings. Protection, an important function of the medieval château, was no longer necessary. Yet some of its features, such as the towers and battlements, had become so traditional that they still persisted. Climatic conditions also determined several features characteristic of Northern buildings — steep roofs, a large number of windows, chimneys and fireplaces.

The Italian influences we see emerging at *Blois* (Fig. 596A), in the wing built by Francis I. The steep roof with its dormers and chimneys, the large windows with mullions, the niches containing statues, the gargoyles — these are French. The Italian reveals itself in the greater regularity of design, the greater repose that comes from the balance of vertical and horizontal lines, and the classical pilasters and carvings. Traditional love for the Gothic verticalism, however, has made the builder break his entablatures with pilasters.

Typical of the early Renaissance châteaux is *Chambord* (Fig. 597A). It stands out on the open plain, as did most of these châteaux; for they were great country places, usually built near a forest so as to serve as hunting lodges. Its plan (Fig. 597A) shows regularity and symmetry — a central square building with four rounded towers at the corners, set in a court surrounded on three sides by an outer line of rooms, the whole surrounded by a moat. Horizontality dominates and ornament is sparse. As a mass, the building consists of interplaying rectangular and cylindrical volumes; in its fenestration it combines curving and angular motifs. To compensate for restraint in the lower part, the roof presents a fantastic group of steep surfaces, with dormers and chimneys, about a central lantern.

The rooms of the early Renaissance châteaux were large; the ceilings, when not vaulted, showed the structural wooden beams, which were richly painted; the walls, whether of stone or plaster, were covered with tapestries that served two purposes — decoration

and warmth. The only source of heat in this cold climate was the huge fireplace, which served not only functionally but also as a center of decorative interest; for the overmantel, which usually reached to the ceiling, was elaborately carved, giving a strong accent to the design and a note of elegance to the entire room.

Thus the architecture of the early Renaissance, as illustrated by *Blois* and *Chambord*, was still French at heart. In the reign of Henry II (1547–1559), came translations of treatises by Italian architects and even the architects themselves; and study and travel in Italy by the French. This brought about a more thoroughgoing revolution, though it never eliminated some French elements. In the *Louvre*, for example, the projecting central and corner pavilions are descendants of the tower pavilions and the central gate of the early fortress-like châteaux. At the same time the *Louvre* is one of the best illustrations of French Renaissance style, both early and late. The early period is found in that part of the *Louvre* (Fig. 599A) which was built by the architect Pierre Lescot (1510?–1578) and the sculptor Jean Goujon (died before 1568). The typically French details of this façade are somewhat lost in the large court that it now faces, four times the size of the original one; for the projections, the shadows, and the detail are too delicate to carry a great distance. Each story forms a complete order; the pilasters no longer break through the entablature as at *Blois;* the cornices project enough to furnish the balancing horizontal line. The arcading on the ground story reflects the Roman combination of the arch and lintel, and is recessed enough to produce more shadow than the upper stories, thus strengthening the base of the design. On the second story the pilasters rising from bases, and the alternating curved and angular pediments

[A] *Louvre. Court, showing the façade of Lescot and Goujon. 1546–76. Paris. (Giraudon)*

supported by consoles, have direct ante-
cedents in the Roman palace; but the
lower height of the stories, the larger
size of the windows, and the sloping
roof are Northern. Sculptured decoration verging on overornamentation
plays a large part in the composition.
This decoration is delicately carved in
low relief and is distinctly architectural
in its design. In this façade we have the
best of French Renaissance architecture, showing masterly design both in
the balance and in the proportions of
the large elements, as well as delicacy,
charm, and fine taste in the details and
the ornamentation.

A more literal dependence upon Renaissance design is evident in the façade
of the *Louvre* (Fig. 600A) built by Claude
Perrault (1613–1688) for Louis XIV.
This effective composition has strongly
influenced columnar façade design ever
since. The general impression is one of
imposing nobility combined with quiet
restraint. There are five divisions, bilaterally balanced — a projecting central pavilion, emphasized by a great
arched doorway and crowned with a
pediment; two projecting end pavilions;
and two connecting colonnades. A unifying line is the horizontal of the cornices, broken lightly by the projecting
pavilions and pediment. The severely
plain ground story with its light, unbroken surfaces not only serves as a
base but emphasizes by contrast the

[A]   *Louvre. Façade of Perrault. 1665. Paris.*

[B]   *Hôtel des Invalides. Chapel. Jules Hardouin Mansart, architect. 1692–1704. Paris. (Raymond R. Buckley)*

richness of the broken light and shade of the colonnade. This variation of light and shade is carefully regulated — deepest in the colonnades because of the open loggia behind the columns; lighter in the center, where the columns stand close to the walls; and lightest on the corners, where the columns are engaged or supplanted by pilasters, with a shadow accent in the central niche. Thus there comes about a varying degree of light and shade, like the different values in a painting, that adds richness and unity to the design.

In ecclesiastical architecture as well as in secular, the seventeenth century saw Paris definitely, not halfheartedly, transformed from Gothic to Renaissance; and this was true in sculpture and painting as well as in architecture. Everything Italian was the vogue of the day. In the chapel of the *Hôtel des Invalides* (Fig. 600B), which is typical of a large group of churches, we find a thoroughly Renaissance base surmounted by a dome that derives obviously from *St. Peter's.* Here the greater saliency in the parts of the façade, through their

[A]   *Versailles. Galerie des Glaces. Decorated, 1680, by Charles Le Brun for Louis XIV.*

organization in several planes, the more exaggerated play upon light and dark, the superimposed orders, and the broken cornices and ornament of the dome — all these elements show the influence of the baroque.

The French gardens that formed an integral part of the plan and the life of the château were as formal as the age itself. Those laid out at *Versailles* by André le Nôtre (1613–1700), the landscape artist employed by Louis XIV, illustrate how magnificent the gardens had become. Water played an important part, and its use demanded a knowledge of hydraulic engineering. Garden design called for great basins to catch the reflections of the buildings, and for fountains, large and small, cascades, and canals. Statues of river gods and of playing children and great ornamental vases of lead served as accents in the fountains or against the tall clipped hedges that bordered the gardens. Broad walks and long avenues afforded fine vistas and great masses of trees framed the design.

While the exteriors of these buildings were so purely imitative of the Italian Renaissance, the interiors were a freer expression of the personal taste of the monarch. This is particularly true of the buildings erected during the reigns of Louis XIV and Louis XV. Louis XIV (1661–1715) was a great builder who paid special attention to decoration and to furnishing, with the result that the ensemble was an unusually harmonious unit. Louis was able to do this because of the centralization of the arts in the Gobelins' establishment, purchased for him in 1662. At that time it did not limit its productions to tapestries but made furniture, metalwork, jewelry,

[A]   *Hôtel de Soubise.*
Louis XV. Paris.

and textiles. The Grand Monarch's ideal was somber dignity and magnificence; and as artists were at the service of the state for the purpose of pleasing and glorifying the monarch, the palace at *Versailles* in all its aspects, from the architectural design of the buildings to the metal decorations of the furniture, is sober, symmetrical, and stately. The *Galerie des Glaces* or *Hall of Mirrors* (Fig. 601A) is magnificent in its dignity and in its sober color enriched by brilliantly painted ceilings, by hangings of silk, velvet, and tapestry, and by an abundance of ornament, such as colored marbles, plaster relief painted and gilded, carvings, and metal fittings. The furniture is consistently heavy and rich (Fig. 603A), of massive construction but elaborately veneered with fine woods and usually decorated with metal ornaments of various alloys.

At the death of Louis XIV, the nobility threw off this heavy dignity, and turned to the gaiety and sparkling light-heartedness that characterized the reign of Louis XV. The age found a perfectly harmonious expression in the rococo.[1] Dainty rooms for conversation or card-playing or boudoirs are typical (Fig. 602A). Slender proportions and never-ending movement in easy curves with a definite avoidance of straight lines and angles; light color with much gilding; the use of many mirrors to add vivacity with their reflections — these, in general, constituted the rococo style, the light, sparkling, thoroughly French version of baroque. Such a room, however, is incomplete without the people for whom it was built, with their elegant costumes of lustrous satins and brocades, their equally elegant manners, and their sparkling wit. The furniture (Fig. 603B) shows a design based entirely upon curved lines. Its slender

[1] From *rocaille*, the rockwork or shellwork found frequently in rococo ornament.

[A] *Table. Louis XIV.
Of wood with metal
ornamentation. Metro-
politan Museum of Art,
New York City. (Metro-
politan Museum)*

proportions, its dainty decorations of flowers and garlands, and its gray-white color form a harmonious part of the rococo style. So also the paintings of a whole galaxy of painters of court life — Watteau, Boucher, Nattier, Fragonard, to mention a few — the brocaded satins, the Sèvres porcelain, music and literature, together constituted a unified expression, produced under the lavish patronage of the court and the nobility, that points to unity and consistency in French court life of the eighteenth century.

TAPESTRY AND PORCELAIN

The centralization of all the arts in the Gobelin factory forced the artists who were in the employ of the ruling aristocracy into the state-controlled system. This resulted in standardization and artificiality on the one hand and a high standard of craftsmanship and great unity on the other. The fine furniture made during the reigns of Louis XIV, Louis XV, and Louis XVI,[1] with its inlays of various fine woods and tortoiseshell, and gilt bronze mountings, was the work of craftsmen as well known as the painters and the sculptors:

[1] The Wallace collection in London is particularly rich in the arts of eighteenth-century France.

André Charles Boulle (1642–1732), for example, and Jacques Caffieri (1678–1755). Likewise the royal Sèvres porcelains were the products of potters who were masters of ceramic technique, and they harmonized with the artificial elegance of the interiors. Chinese porcelains had made their way to Europe perhaps as early as the eleventh or twelfth century and, because of their thinness and translucency, were greatly admired. But it was not until the eighteenth century that the potters in both

[B] *Console Table. Louis XV. Metropolitan Museum of Art, New York City. (Metropolitan Museum)*

[A] *Houdon. Louise Brogniart. Baked clay. Louvre, Paris.*

[B] *Houdon. Voltaire. 1781. Comédie-Française, Paris.*

Germany and France discovered the nature of true porcelain. One typical Sèvres vase is elegant in shape, is covered with a deep-blue enamel, flawless in its finish, and is heavily ornamented in gold. On the body of the vase in a reserved panel is a naturalistic painting of figures and landscape. In thus vying with the art of the painter it fails, despite its display of technical virtuosity and its perfect harmony with the table on which it stood, to maintain that integrity of medium which is the mark of the finest ceramic products.

This same transgression of the limitations of a medium is seen in the great tapestries made at the Gobelin establishment, which since its purchase for Louis XIV had been a center for the finest production. The tapestries of this period were of great size. Their subjects were taken chiefly from history and mythology, and the compositions were designed by the most important artists of the day. Technically, they show the great skill of the weavers in their complicated compositions, in the large number of colors and tones used, and in their elaborate borders. But artistically many of them fail to attain the highly decorative quality of the Gothic tapestries, because the designers came too much under the influence of painting, whose ever increasing importance tended to ally other arts with it in its concern with creating an illusion of space.

Some of the other textiles reveal a

[A]   *Pietà. Middle of 15th cent. Louvre, Paris. (Giraudon)*

more consistent textile design. The large repeat pattern that originated in the Near East began to break up into a lighter framework, and by the time of Louis XV had taken the form of a delicate pattern of vines, garlands, flowers, and ribbons that harmonized well with the interior decoration and the furnishings of the period. These brocades and silks were made largely at Lyon, an important textile center, and, like the tapestries, they show the great technical skill of the weavers.

SCULPTURE

Sculpture too follows the graph of style. Yet the native grace and swing of line in Gothic carving (Fig. 351B) still dominated in the somewhat Italianate and more naturalistic architectural sculpture of Jean Goujon (died before 1568). The nymphs which are carved in low relief on the *Fountain of the Innocents* are elongated to allow for the free sweep of the long sinuous lines, which are accented by the rigid verticals of the enframing vertical pilasters.

Much of the sculpture of the seventeenth and eighteenth centuries and into the nineteenth is feminine both in subject matter and in feeling — figures of goddesses all ease and grace and with exquisite surface finish expressive of the texture of flesh or fabric, too often mere superficial prettiness. This was the result of the autocracy of the French Academy, which narrowly restricted the subject matter and the technical methods of painters and sculptors. An outstanding figure is Jean Antoine Houdon (1741–1828), who used the current baroque and rococo forms with independent vigor, especially in his por-

[A] *Jean Clouet. Charlotte of France. c. 1540. Max Epstein Collection, Chicago. (Art Institute of Chicago)*

traits, which constitute his best work. A prolific portrayer of notables, he even traveled to America to model the *George Washington* (Virginia State Capitol). In the *Voltaire* (Fig. 604B) baroque qualities — restlessness, momentary pose, realism, the dependence upon heavy draperies for pictorial effect — are modified by the usual French poise and suave flow of line. In the terra-cotta portrait of *Louise Brogniart* (Fig. 604A), the vivacious turn of the head, the quick glance of the eye, and the mobile expression about the mouth are spontaneously caught and expressed in clay, the medium so suitable for momentary expressions, and made permanent by baking the clay. Such sparkling portraits parallel the rococo paintings and furnishings of the late eighteenth century and thus represent the sculptural phase of the rococo style.

PAINTING

French painting of the fourteenth and fifteenth centuries was largely in the Gothic style, which originated in miniature- and glass-painting, with the altarpiece the most conspicuous form until portraits began to appear as the individualizing tendency permeated the social structure. The French painter, though naturalistic, was not so insistent upon detail as the Flemish and the German artist. He was possessed of a larger, more selective way of seeing his world and a greater facility for organization; and his predilection for poise and gravity, for an easy flow of line, and for suave rhythms lent an air of graciousness to his paintings. Activity was localized in a number of sites, particularly around Paris; in Burgundy, for the Dukes of Burgundy were great art patrons; in Touraine; and at Avignon, where Italian influence was strong because of Italian painters at the papal court. So long as the demand for handmade books continued, well-known painters, such as Jean Fouquet (about 1415–1481), painted miniatures as well as altarpieces and portraits. From some unknown painter of southern France comes a *Pietà* (Fig. 605A) whose scale and monumentality show an influence of the Sienese frescoes in Avignon. Above a low-lying landscape, with the towers of Jerusalem at the left, three figures rise against a gold background: the Virgin, with Mary Magdalen and Saint John on either side, bending over the dead body of Christ, which lies, gaunt and angular, across the lap of the Virgin; in the left corner is the kneeling figure of the donor. The picture is filled with an intense emotion, expressed not by a realistic rendering of agonized grief in pose and facial expression, as in many Northern paintings, but by purely formal qualities: a large, striking pattern of light and

[A]   *Louis le Nain. Peasant Family. 1642. Louvre, Paris.*

dark masses of sober color and gold; great sweeping curves opposed by dynamic diagonals and sharply defined right angles; and quieting horizontals.

This vital late-Gothic art continued, in the sixteenth century, in the portraits of the Clouets and of Corneille de Lyon, in face of the Italianizing school which was fostered, if not arbitrarily imposed, by the French court. Ironically enough, when it came to portraits of himself and his family, the monarch seems to have preferred the native traditional style, while the school at Fontainebleau was producing pictures in an eclectic Italian style under the direction of masters imported from Italy. *Charlotte of France* (Fig. 606A), for example, by Jean Clouet (working about 1516–1546) is a relatively flat pattern of light and dark color areas of varying textures and shapes — curved shapes effectively opposed to angular — and sharply defin-

ing edges. The result is a strongly linear quality not unlike that of Holbein.

In the seventeenth century, as the Italianizing style continued into a baroque phase under Simon Vouet (1590–1649) and Eustache Le Sueur (1616–1655), the Le Nain brothers (Antoine, 1588–1648; Louis, 1593–1648; Mathieu, 1607–1677) were producing for the bourgeoisie a popular genre art similar to that of the Flemish and the Dutch.[1] Yet in this painting, to take the *Peasant Family* of Louis Le Nain (Fig. 607A) as an illustration, is a smaller unit of visual perception than in the Dutch and consequently a larger scale of figures. With the sober color of a limited palette, chiefly grays and red-browns, and with the skillful handling of light, both nat-

[1] See R. H. Wilenski, *French Painting*, Hale, Cushman & Flint, 1931, pp. 47–48, for the influence of a colony of Dutch and Flemish painters at Saint-Germain-des-Prés.

[A]   *Poussin. Funeral of Phocion. 1648. Louvre, Paris.*

ural illumination and firelight, the painter has constructed solid, almost sculptural forms placed firmly in space. Thus Le Nain shows a greater concern for massive forms related in space than he does for a description of the multitude of details present in unselective visual perception. At the same time he has recognized all the human values of the subject, and has portrayed both their immediate expression and their wider implications with a sincere directness.

In the field of landscape the French made a contribution through two painters, Poussin and Claude, who however lived most of their lives in Italy and whose paintings are markedly Italian Renaissance in their quiet architectonic structure, which is counter to the contemporary baroque of Rubens (Fig. 546A) and to the intimate realism of Ruisdael (Fig. 583A). In both, the interest of the figure and the title (usually mythological or religious) is submerged, almost lost, in a true landscape feeling — imaginative, to be sure, and based on the Italian and the classical. Nicolas Poussin (1594–1665) in his figure-painting was an eclectic derived from Italian masters, chiefly Raphael and Titian. In his landscape he carved out space, a deep spaciousness that is constructed by a few definite planes insistently stated and repeated with variations. In the *Funeral of Phocion* (Fig. 608A), for example, each figure, tree, and building is set firmly upon the basic horizontal plane or its variations, a plane which stretches from the foreground to the distant mountains; and each is constructed clearly of light and color with its component planes meeting rather sharply. Very definitely the eye is guided through the landscape by these lights and darks and by the shapes which they form — the angular patterns of the buildings and the rounding masses

[A] *Claude Gellée (Lorrain). Egeria. 1669. Naples. (Anderson)*

of the trees. In comparison with the melting atmospheric quality in Claude, Poussin's landscapes have a precise clarity often emphasized by an abrupt, almost clashing passage of color.

Claude Gellée (1600–1682), also called Claude Lorrain, though he too built up nature imaginatively, with classical subject matter, constructed architecturally. In the *Egeria* (Fig. 609A), Claude massed his trees and buildings to serve as a framework for the opening through which we are carried into a vast spaciousness by the light, whose highest value is here concentrated and thence radiates throughout the picture and ties together all parts by its enveloping tonality. At the right is a group of classical ruins, usual in Claude, and in the distance on a hill a ruined castle,

the dark mass of which carries the eye inevitably into luminous space. The trees on the right perform this same function by silhouetting interesting patterns against the high light. In fact, the composition is largely the skillful, balanced arrangement of light and dark masses, one which, despite its formality, gives an impressive sense of heroic grandeur and infinite spaciousness.

While Poussin and Claude were painting their ideal landscapes in Italy, art in France was becoming more and more the monopoly of the privileged class. The establishment in 1648 of the French Academy of Sculpture and Painting gave official sanction to the dictates of the autocracy which ruled France during the seventeenth and eighteenth centuries to further its own

[A]   *Watteau. Embarkation for the Island of Cythera. 1717. Berlin. (Braun)*

selfish interests. The pompous dignity of the court of Louis XIV and the elegance and light gaiety of those of Louis XV and XVI it was the business of the painters to portray. For the former there were Pierre Mignard (1610–1695) and Hyacinthe Rigaud (1659–1743); for the latter, Antoine Watteau (1684–1721); Jean-Baptiste Pater (1696–1736) and Nicolas Lancret (1690–1743); François Boucher (1703–1770); and Jean-Honoré Fragonard (1732–1806). Fragonard's typically rococo *Swing* (Wallace collection, London) or Watteau's *Embarkation for Cythera* (Fig. 610A) is representative of the spirit of the later period. In the latter, in the delightful cool shade of a park couples are idly loitering; winged loves hover about, cling to a statue of Venus, and dance around a dainty, gilded ship toward which the couples are making their way to journey to the island of love far away in the golden, misty distance. All is lightheartedness and gaiety, grace and elegance. But Watteau was too much of an artist to express merely this idea. Here are revealed his excellent feeling for balance; for the interesting pattern of trees against the luminous distance; for the easy rhythm of the undulating curve that begins in the figure of Venus, follows the groups across the canvas, and then turns inward again in the rollicking cherubs in the sky at the left; and, perhaps most of all, for the harmony of exquisite color, which the textures of the elegant stuffs gave him opportunity to exploit, and which is put on in light touches that melt in the enveloping glow.

Apart from this whole galaxy of court painters, whose pictures in theme and in style were in perfect harmony with court life and the rococo spirit, was a somewhat isolated artist who drew his subject matter from a different social stratum and sphere of life, Jean-Baptiste

Siméon Chardin (1699–1779). Not only in theme but in attitude toward form Chardin seemed to continue the tradition of the Le Nain brothers and the "Little Dutchmen" of the seventeenth century. Sometimes it is the interior of the French middle-class home, which Chardin, like the Dutch painters, saw as raw material with pictorial possibilities (Fig. 611A). The sober dusk of the small room provided an opportunity so to modulate the light that it would create a space in which to place the figures that catch the high light from an open door, and form a cylindrical mass cut across by repeated diagonals. The warm, vibrating brown ground modulates the rose, green, and yellow of the striped upholstery and garments; a contrasting note is the cool gray-blue, of large mass in the apron balanced by smaller areas in the details. The colors are not used with the light sparkling dash of Watteau but with a sober deliberation. Chardin's primary interest in genre as pictorial material for its own sake, exclusive of associational values, appears in his frequent use of still life. In Figure 612A, a large rectangular box, cutting into space on diagonals that are repeated in the pipestems and shadows, counters a number of cylindrical objects. Or as pattern, straight lines and angles oppose curves and ellipses; warm color, cool color; light texture, dark texture. With all the means at the painter's disposal these objects are built into an organization the unity and harmony of which have a power of their own quite separate from the representational content.

SUMMARY

The late-Gothic age saw France still vigorous in all the arts, though the heightened fervor of the Middle Ages had somewhat cooled and Italian influence had become increasingly strong.

[A] *Chardin. Saying Grace. 1740. One of several versions. Louvre, Paris.* (Braun)

Building, largely secular, combined, with the ever-present French good taste, native and Italian elements, notably in the châteaux and the palaces. Their more personalized interiors show all the arts at the service of the monarch and a consistent reflection of the mood of the court, as one sees in the heavy dignity of the Louis XIV style and the light sparkling rococo of that of Louis XV. Furniture, tapestries, porcelain, costumes, and paintings all contributed to the harmonious ensemble. Sculpture, though it functioned to some extent architecturally, tended to become an independent art and for the most part, in conformity to the dictates of the Academy, produced Italianate naturalistic female figures. Italian influence operated in the field of painting also as painters emerged from the medieval school of the miniaturists into secular painting — popular genre, landscapes, portraits, and court scenes, all showing baroque three-dimensional compo-

[A]   *Chardin. Still Life. Louvre, Paris.*

sition. Singleness of purpose, under the control of the court, infiltrated all the aristocratic arts, notably in the eighteenth century, and produced a total art expression of unusual unity both in its motivating spirit and in its consequent forms.

BIBLIOGRAPHY

Barnes, Albert C., and De Mazia, Violette, *French Primitives*, Barnes Foundation, 1931

Blomfield, Sir Reginald T., *A History of French Architecture from the Reign of Charles VIII till the Death of Mazarin, 1494–1661*, 2 vols., London, 1911

———————— *A History of French Architecture from the Death of Mazarin till the Death of Louis XV, 1661–1774*, 2 vols., London, 1921

———————— *Three Hundred Years of French Architecture, 1494–1794*, Macmillan, 1936

Brownell, W. C., *French Art*, Scribner, 1901

Cox, Trenchard, *Jehan Foucquet, Native of Tours*, London, 1931

Dilke, Lady E. F. S., *French Architects and Sculptors of the XVIIIth Century*, Macmillan, 1900

———————— *French Furniture and Decoration in the XVIIIth Century*, Macmillan, 1901

Les Fouquet, Verve, Vol. III, Nos. 9–12, Paris, 1943–45

Fourreau, Armand, *Les Clouet*, Paris, 1929

Fry, Roger E., *Characteristics of French Art*, Coward-McCann, 1933

———————— *Vision and Design*, Brentano's, 1924

Furst, H. E. A., *Chardin*, Scribner, 1911

Glück, Gustav, *Die Kunst der Renaissance, in Deutschland, der Niederlanden, Frankreich, etc.*, Berlin, 1928

Gromort, Georges, *Histoire abrégée de l'architecture de la Renaissance en France (XVIe, XVIIe, & XVIIIe siècles)*, Paris, 1930

Hind, C. L., *Landscape Painting from Giotto to the Present Day*, 2 vols., Scribner, 1923

Hourticq, Louis, *Art in France*, Scribner, 1911

Huizinga, J., *The Waning of the Middle Ages*, Longmans, Green, 1924

Jackson, Sir T. G., *The Renaissance of Roman Architecture*, 3 vols., University of Chicago Press, 1921–23; Vol. III, *France*

Konody, P. G., and Lathom, M. X., *An Introduction to French Painting*, London, 1932

Mather, Frank J., Jr., *Western European Painting of the Renaissance*, Holt, 1939

Moore, C. H., *The Character of Renaissance Architecture*, Macmillan, 1905

Munro, Thomas, *Great Pictures of Europe*, Coward-McCann, 1930

Osborn, Max, *Die Kunst des Rokoko*, Berlin, 1926

Réau, Louis, *French Painting in the XIVth, XVth and XVIth Centuries*, tr. by Mary Chamot, Art Book Publications, 1940

Ridder, André de, *J. B. S. Chardin*, Paris, 1932

Rocheblave, S., *French Painting in the XVIIIth Century*, tr. by George F. Lees, Hyperion Press, 1937

Royal Academy of Arts, *Commemorative Catalogue of the Exhibition of French Art, 1200–1900*, Oxford University Press, 1935

Terrasse, Charles, *Les Peintres français de la renaissance*, Paris, 1932

———— *Les Primitifs français*, Paris, 1931

Tilley, A. A., *The Dawn of the French Renaissance*, Putnam, 1918

Victoria and Albert Museum, *Panelled Rooms*, Vols. I–VI, London, 1914–24; Vol. III, *Boudoir of Mme de Sérilly*

Ward, W. H., *Architecture of the Renaissance in France*, 2d ed., 2 vols., Scribner, 1926

Wilenski, Reginald H., *French Painting*, Hale, Cushman & Flint, 1936

See also the General Bibliography, pp. 791–92.

36

RUSSIAN ART

(SIXTEENTH TO NINETEENTH CENTURY)

LATE in the fifteenth century, with the overthrow of the Tatars, Moscow became the capital of Russia. But it was not until the time of Peter the Great (1682–1725) that the Russian Government, if not the nation, turned wholeheartedly westward and came within the periphery of the European nations. Symbolic of this reorientation was Peter's abandonment of Moscow, center of traditional Russian culture, as his capital in favor of a new city to be built on the Neva, St. Petersburg (now Leningrad). He and his successors, Elizabeth (1741–1762), Catherine II (the Great; 1762–1796), and Alexander I (1801–1825), opened the doors wide to the West and not only accepted but solicited Western influence by inviting artists from various countries to work in Russia and by sending their own students to Western capitals

for training. The inexhaustible wealth of the extravagant, autocratic court made vast projects economically possible for the ruling class, with no regard for the vast number of Russians who were serfs. Even the French Revolution could not break through the hard crust of Russian reaction and absolutism until 1861, when the serfs were emancipated and the social stirrings began which were to end in the revolution of 1917.

ARCHITECTURE

When Russia accepted Christianity, in the tenth century, it accepted with it its outward expression, the Byzantine style, to which it eventually contributed its own indigenous type of wooden construction. The assimilation of the two styles, translated into stone construction, is typified by the *Cathedral of St. Basil* (1555) on the Red Square in Moscow. Before the building of *St. Basil*, however, Italian architects had been invited to Moscow to work on the walls of the Kremlin and on its churches and palaces. Although during the sixteenth and seventeenth centuries there was some attempt to integrate into the national style elements from the West — classical details and baroque ornament from Poland and other northern European countries — the accession of Peter the Great flung the doors wide-open to a whirlwind of lavish building based on Renaissance styles, though often in original Russian versions. In 1703, Peter began the erection of a capital that was to vie with, if not eclipse, every other capital of Europe. For more than a century work went on with the greatest intensity, as if to catch up on lost centuries, in laying out the city with wide avenues, open squares, and quays along the Neva, with monumental buildings — churches, palaces with vast gardens, and civic buildings — placed so as to create fine ensembles, and all on a grandiose scale. Great manor houses arose in the country, not only around St. Petersburg but in the Ukraine, in the Crimea, and in and about Moscow. In the early *Cathedral of Sts. Peter and Paul*, built by Peter, from a simple baroque base with a classical portico rises a lofty steeple (the tent roof of the medieval style); other churches are crowned with the Russian "onion" dome, *St. Andrew* at Kiev, for example. With Elizabeth, the rococo in an ostentatious version dominated. In her reign one of Russia's great architects, Count B. F. Rastrelli (1700–1771), built the Versailles-like *Imperial Palace* under her direction, and rebuilt and decorated *Peterhof* and *Tsarskoe Selo*.

The climax of the eighteenth century was reached in the reign of Catherine II, whose personal taste for the simple classical style was largely responsible for the spread of the classical revival over much of Russia. Catherine maintained close relations in all cultural matters with France and staffed the Academy of Arts, founded in 1758, with French instructors. She lured as many artists as she could from France and Italy with visions of vast building schemes supported by vast sums of money for carrying them out, and she sent Russian students abroad for training to fit them to share in the plans. Thus in her reign and in that of her successor, Alexander I, were erected: the *Academy of Arts*, which, with its rusticated ground story, central and end pavilions, and engaged columns, is so strongly reminiscent of the Perrault façade of the *Louvre* (Fig. 600A) that it does not surprise one to learn that a French architect collaborated in its design; the *Taurida Palace*, with its classical portico and colonnade; the *Cathedral of the Holy Trinity*, whose proportions contrast so markedly with the early lofty *Cathedral of Sts. Peter and Paul;* the *Kazan Cathedral*, a highly dignified domed edifice approached by curving colonnades, obviously inspired by Bernini's colonnades of *St. Peter's* in Rome; and *St. Isaac*, with its lavish use of rich materials, the *St. Paul's* of Russia. Further foreign influence came from England through Charles Cameron (1740–1812), who, influenced by both Palladio and Robert Adam, produced a style consistent, in its sobriety and simplicity, with the classical revival of the time and, in its prodigality, with the autocracy which demanded it. Thus Russia followed, though tardily, the same sequence of styles from the baroque to the classical revival as the other countries of Europe, but on a scale and with a pompous magnificence possible only to an absolute monarch and to which only the palaces of the French absolute monarchs at Versailles are comparable.

PAINTING

Medieval fresco and icon painting, with its exalted mood, symbolism, and mysticism, was zealously guarded by the authoritarian Eastern Orthodox Church, which condemned innovations that were creeping into painting from the West as they were into the buildings in the Kremlin. Rublëv (Fig. 282A) marked a high point in icon-painting, but any normal growth from this stage through vitalizing influences was stifled by the state. Copying of the traditional icon-painters was forced upon artists, with no opportunity for individual freedom. Despite this reactionary absolutism, some innovations had crept in, in the direction of naturalism, such as changes in traditional poses and in the introduction of architectural settings. Thus in the seventeenth century Russian painting seemed to be at the same stage as Italian in the fourteenth, when Cimabue and Giotto made the break from the Byzantine style. Natural development, however, came to a halt in the eighteenth century when the court introduced painters of the current academic schools of western Europe, exponents of the "grand style" of painting religious and historical subjects, nudes, and portraits. Though some Gainsborough-like portraits at the time of Catherine the Great were meritorious, this eclectic painting, as a whole — created entirely at the bidding and in the style demanded by the wealthy court and the nobles — was an empty thing. An exception was a thread of genre painting, spontaneously naturalistic both in subject matter and in mode of treatment, known as "common art" and unrecognized by the academic proponents of the "grand style." This trend was important, as it was sowing the seed of the realistic school of the nineteenth century.

SUMMARY

Although Russia had accepted a few ideas from the West before the time of Peter the Great, this monarch made a direct break with Russian traditions and repudiated the national styles in favor of a direct imitation of Western modes, with slight modifications and with the retention, at least in the beginning, of a few traditional motifs. The entire eighteenth century and the first half of the nineteenth made up a period of the imitation, on a grandiose scale for the benefit of the absolute state and the ostentatious court, of Renaissance styles from its early phases through the baroque and the classical revival. This imitative period was not, however, devoid of beneficial consequences, for it made a break, at least, in the hard shell of reactionary conservatism in all cultural life and by revitalizing that life played a part in the rise of a great independent age that reached a climax in the fields of literature, music, and the dance.

BIBLIOGRAPHY

Bunt, Cyril G. E., *A History of Russian Art*, Studio, 1946

Eliasberg, Alexander, *Russische baukunst*, Munich, 1922

Farbman, Michael S., ed., *Masterpieces of Russian Painting*, London, 1930

Grabar, Igor E., *Istoria Russkago Iskusstva*, 6 vols., Moscow, 1909–1916

Holme, Geoffrey, ed., *Art in the U.S.S.R.*, Studio, 1935

Loukomski, Georges, *Charles Cameron (1740–1812)*, London, 1943

Miliukov, Paul, *Outlines of Russian Culture*, ed. by Michael Karpovich, tr. by Valentine Ughet and Eleanor Davis, 3 pts.; Part III, "Architecture, Painting, and Music," University of Pennsylvania Press, 1942

Rubissow, Helen, *The Art of Russia*, Philosophical Library, 1946

Talbot Rice, David, ed., *Russian Art*, London, 1935

Renaissance Art in the Americas

THE Renaissance brought into the current of its thought and style not only all Europe, including Russia, but both the Americas as well. From its source in Italy, it was decentralized — quite normally in Europe because of intercommunication between Italy and the other nations and because with them, excepting Russia, it shared a common base: Romanesque and Gothic. This was not true in the Americas. While Europe was ready for growth in a new direction, the Americas presented an entirely different situation: a pioneering type of life; different climatic conditions and different materials, as a rule; and above all an unknown civilization that in its habit of thinking and in the character of its art expression was almost the antithesis of the European. This was the indigenous American, the Indian, culture. The resulting interaction sometimes led to the extinction or the isolation of the Indian and to implanting an adapted version of contemporary home styles, as with the French, the Dutch, the English, and, to some extent, the Hispanic. In some cases where it neither extinguished nor assimilated, it made vital contributions to the Indians, which enabled embryonic expressions to come to efflorescence, notably in the case of the Navaho, the Plains Indians, and those of the Northwest coast.

The aims of exploration and colonization, though varying in different countries, stemmed from the spirit of inquiry, individualism, and adventure so characteristic of the Renaissance; from a desire to secure a greater share of the world's goods, especially the luxuries of the Far East; and, in some cases, from a desire to find opportunity in a New World for realizing the individual freedom that was beginning to stir in Europe. Greater knowledge of geography combined with the revival of the ancient concept of a spherical world and the invention of the compass to mitigate the hazards of sailing enough to warrant voyages westward to find passage to the fabulous Indies, since the Mongolian invasions had cut off the usual routes eastward. When the true nature and great wealth of the new lands became known, other nationals than the Spanish and the Portuguese — the French, the English, and the Dutch — also sought their share of riches, trade, and lands. With the rise of great colonial empires — not confined to the Americas — European culture was decentralized. The resulting art expression was so modified through adaptation to new conditions that we are justified in speaking of American Portuguese, American Spanish, American French, and American English art.

[A]   *San Lorenzo. Potosí. Detail of the façade showing the carving above the doorway. 1728–44. The Indian figures carved in the columns, the guitar-playing sirens on either side, and the sun, moon, and stars are all Indian motifs. (Archive of Hispanic Culture, Library of Congress)*

37

LATIN AMERICAN ART

GOLD and the cross — these motivated the Spaniard and led him to attempt to impose upon the Indian the Spanish pattern of civilization, to transform the New World into a New Spain. This Spanish Empire included all South America except Portuguese Brazil, all Central America, and much of the southern and western parts of the United States. This huge area eventually was divided into five viceroyalties with their seats of government usually in the old capital cities, which the conquistadors wrecked and rebuilt in the Spanish style. It is illuminating to note that the highest attainments of Latin American art are found in the areas of the highest indigenous American attainment — in Mexico and Guatemala, the home of Maya, Mixtecs, Toltecs, and Aztecs; and in the Andean regions of Ecuador, Peru, and Bolivia, the site of the pre-Incas and the Incas. It should be stated at the outset that there is no such thing as a "Hispanic American

[A]   *Cathedral of Puebla. c. 1556–1649.*

art," in the sense of a homogeneous expression running through the Spanish colonies. Baroque art is one thing in Mexico City, quite another in Cuzco; one thing in a capital, quite another in a distant mission. Within broad limitations, however, the basic elements of Spanish baroque are there, but local conditions produced effective diversity.

ARCHITECTURE
AND SCULPTURE

Mexican

NEW Spain, the earliest of the viceroyalties, followed upon the conquest by Cortés, in 1521, of the Aztec capital of Tenochtitlan, on whose ruins

he built his own capital, Mexico City. A generation was needed to extend and consolidate the conquest, to lay out towns and cities, and to bring the Indians into conformity with the new pattern of life. Much of this was the work of the missionaries, who always accompanied the conquistadors,[1] and who strove not only to convert the Indians but frequently to protect them against the exploitation of the Spanish overlords. In building the churches and convents that rose in great numbers, the missionaries found their source of labor in the Indians, already skilled in many arts, and in this work taught them the Spanish styles. But the Indian, with no written language, possessed a keen memory and a tenacious hold on his ancient culture, with the result that when copying Spanish models he not only often introduced native motifs but also infused the European naturalism with something of his own conventional and abstract style, and in the villages the indigenous arts survived and continued.

The characteristic sixteenth-century building was the fortress-church, such as the convents[2] of *Huejotzingo, Acolman, or Actopan,* massive stone structures with thick walls, few windows, low towers flanking the portal, and a modicum of carving to accent the doorway. Gothic vaulting or finely carved Mudéjar ceilings, together with a lofty retable rich in gold and polychromed wood carvings, provided a colorful interior. The churches were set in large courts

[1] For the conquest of Mexico and for an account of the work of both the conquistadors and the missionaries, see W. H. Prescott, *History of the Conquest of Mexico*, Modern Library, 1936, and Bernal Díaz del Castillo, *True History of the Conquest of Mexico*, tr. by Maurice Keating, McBride, 1939. It is through the chronicles of the missionaries that we learn much of preconquest Indian life.

[2] In Mexico "convent" is used for both convent and monastery.

surrounded by a strong stone wall, with chapels at the corners and an open chapel near the entrance of the church. This is a new note, one not found in Spain. For mass, not individual, conversion followed the efforts of the padres, so that the court, with the open chapel for conducting services, was necessary for crowds too great for the church itself to accommodate. In the ornament of these early churches we find not only native motifs interspersed with Spanish but also a tendency to flatten the carvings, to give them a feeling of surface continuity, such as is inherent in indigenous reliefs. A good illustration is the convent of *Tlalmanalco*. Thus is the late medieval style of Spain modified by local conditions.

In the seventeenth century, the acquisition of wealth led to the building of fine mansions and, with the arrival of bishops from Spain, of cathedrals. The artists who were invited from the mother country for their construction brought the current Renaissance style, the plateresque. As a result, many a mansion or convent bears delicate carvings to accentuate its portal or to add a note of grace to its patio. This style was followed in the early seventeenth century by a brief period of the severe Herreran style (Fig. 556A), which the *Cathedral of Puebla* well illustrates (Fig. 618A). In general, it follows a basic type almost universal in Hispanic America: cruciform in plan, vaulted, with a dome over the crossing and twin towers to flank the main portal. In the *Puebla Cathedral*, one is impressed with the fine integration of the body of the church, the dome, and the towers, enhanced by clear profiles, unbroken surfaces, and reticent ornament, and by the surface contrast of the glazed tile covering the dome and the lanterns of the towers and the gray stone of the rest of the building. The

[A] *High Altar. Puebla Cathedral.*

sobriety of the exterior hardly prepares one for the sumptuousness of the interior, with its rich marbles on floors and walls, stone and wood carvings, rejas, polychrome and gilded sculpture, and paintings. The high altar in particular (Fig. 619A), spectacular in its combined use of many materials, in its broken cornices and obstructed profiles, in its constant movement, shows how the Mexican temperament, too restricted by the austerity of the Herreran style, found more suitable expression in the rising baroque.

The tile-covered domes which rise in such numbers above the roof levels of Puebla are witnesses of the great ceramic industry of the city. The Indians of the locality were already skilled in the craft when the Spaniard contributed

[A] *San Francisco Xavier. Tepozotlán. Façade redecorated by Lorenzo Rodríguez 1760-62. (Archive of Hispanic Culture, Library of Congress)*

new methods by introducing from Spain the Talavera ware, a tin-enameled fabric chiefly in blue, white, and yellow. This tile was used for wall facings, for fountains in patios and plazas, and for domes of churches all over Mexico. The tile-covered dome is a mark of Mexican colonial architecture. The designs are usually geometric or floral, but even include figure work. The use of tile spread until it sheathed entire exteriors, as in the *House of Tiles* (Mexico City), an example of a secular building, and the church of *San Francisco Acatepec*, near Puebla.

The *Cathedral of Mexico* (Mexico City)

was begun in the Herreran style, but because of the length of time taken in its erection took on elements of the baroque — witness the great volutes and the sumptuous façade — and in its *Sacristy* gave expression to a variant of the baroque, the ultrabaroque, or Churrigueresque. A climactic outburst of religious zeal, wealth, a never-ending supply of gold, skilled and inventive carvers, and, one likes to think, the Indian tradition of the gorgeous pageantry that accompanied native ancient religious rites — these at least were some of the ingredients of the Hispanic American ultrabaroque. It invaded all the arts, the furnishings as well as the buildings themselves. In the façades of the churches it manifested itself in lofty panels of stone carving; and strikingly on the interior, where the lavishly carved altarpieces glowing in gold and color, sometimes four or five in a nave, rose with rapid, intricate movement from altar to vaulting, now held by the framing edge of the reredos and the plain stone masonry, now bursting forth ecstatically to cover the entire interior. The *Convent of Tepozotlán* (Figs. 620A, 621A) illustrates these characteristics; or the church of *San Sebastian and Santa Prisca* at Taxco, built of the warm reddish volcanic stone so often used in Mexican architecture. The slender towers of the latter, largely unadorned on the lower stories to flank the elaborately carved baroque portal with a lofty wooden door of Moorish design, become richly carved as they rise loftily to balance the tile-encrusted dome. Churrigueresque altar-pieces and murals adorn the interior.

This spirited, lavish ultrabaroque style, so expressive of eighteenth-century Hispanic society, gave way in the latter part of the century to a strikingly different influence, the neoclassic, which was pervading not only Europe but all the American colonies as well. This transition is seen clearly in the work of two well-known architects, Manuel Tolsa, a Spaniard who settled in Mexico City, and Francisco Eduardo Tresguerras of Celaya (State of Guanajuato). Though baroque in his early work, Tolsa, head of the San Carlos Academy where the academic classical style was entrenched, shows a complete transition to the invading style in his *Palacio de Minería* in Mexico City. Tresguerras, though caught in the neoclassic wave, used it with more originality in his *El Carmen* (Celaya) — with perhaps more compromise, as seen in the tile-covered dome and the single tower rising above the Doric portal, and certainly with more graciousness and more sensitive proportions.

South American

FARTHER south in the Andean highlands were the two cities which, with Mexico City, constituted the great triad of art centers in Hispanic America: Quito and Cuzco. From Mexico the conquistadors, lured by gold, pushed southward to Peru, where in 1533–34 Pizarro overthrew the Inca Empire, laid out the new city of Lima, and upon the ruins of the Inca capitals Cuzco and Quito built Spanish cities.

The evolution of art in Mexico was duplicated in the viceroyalty of Peru in its broad outlines, with differences due to local conditions. Here appeared the same transplantation of Spanish ideology, religion, artists, and works of art, and the same silent but effective effort of the indigenous peoples to hold to their own traditional culture and art forms. In the high valleys of the Andes this Indian influence was particularly resistant, partly because this region was the heart of the Inca Empire and partly

[A] *Altar of San José. San Francisco Xavier, Tepozotlán. c. 1750–60. Thought to be the work of the wood-carver Jeronimo de Balvás.*

[A] *Cathedral of Cuzco. Completed 1564; reconstructed after the earthquake of 1650. Of granite taken from Inca structures. (Archive of Hispanic Culture, Library of Congress)*

because it was somewhat removed from the center of Spanish influence, Lima.

Lima was the symbol of Spanish power and culture in South America. Ships which left the harbor of Lima laden with gold and silver returned equally laden with statues, paintings, furniture, tiles, even whole retables in pieces ready to be assembled — the art of Spain literally transported to the New World. Hither, too, came architects and painters who could themselves paint Madonnas and portraits or could faithfully copy famous European works. This transplanted Spanish art felt no influence from the indigenous peoples, for the site of Lima was not a strong center of Indian culture. The churches and monastic institutions and the mansions of the aristocracy followed Andalusian types. *El Palacio de Torre Tagle* (Fig. 623A), now the *Ministry of Foreign Affairs*, is an example of the fine man-

sions of the ruling class. It is built flush with the street, its massive door flanked by projecting balconies of Moorish design; its gardenlike patio, carved Mudéjar ceilings, Sevillian wall tiles, and magnificent carved furniture might well be at home in Seville.

In Cuzco, on the other hand, a different situation affected this transplanted Spanish style. Though the conquistadors demolished this Inca capital, they did not rase it quite to the ground. The magnificently built Inca walls may have proved too solid for even the iconoclastic Spaniard; or perhaps, with an eye for practicality, he deemed the use of such fine masonry not too un-Christian. Whatever his motivation, he built the new city on the foundations and the walls of the old. The high valley of Cuzco, fringed by austere mountains and subject to frequent earthquakes; a long tradition of

[A]   *El Palacio de Torre Tagle. Lima. 1730–35. Originally a private mansion, now the Ministry of Foreign Affairs. (Archive of Hispanic Culture, Library of Congress)*

stone masonry as solid and somber as the mountains from which the stone was cut; highly skilled craftsmen of a lofty indigenous culture — this milieu gave direction to the Spanish style, brought it into harmony with itself, and produced what is perhaps the most original Hispanic American art.

Though most of the buildings in Cuzco date from the destructive earthquake of 1650, the *Cathedral* (Fig. 622A) survived the shock; it has however been subjected to much rebuilding. It is a low, heavy building with squat towers and solid masonry, much of it unbroken by windows. The projecting portal, soberly baroque, introduces a three-dimensional movement into an otherwise two-dimensional façade definitely Herreran in feeling. The low

interior, roofed with Gothic vaulting, unrelieved by any appreciable amount of color and texture except for paintings and wood carvings, is in keeping with the austerity of the exterior. Here in Peru we find not only the baroque but the ultrabaroque more reserved, more tranquil. And in such churches as *San Sebastian* (Cuzco) and *La Compañía* (Arequipa; Fig. 625A) we see evidence of indigenous influence in two directions: first, in the introduction of Indian motifs — local flora and fauna — even in religious buildings; and second, in the style of the carving. The naturalistic Renaissance style has flattened out, has taken on a strong feeling for the continuity of the surface, for oneness with the masonry. The crisp carving has a linear quality, and sharply defines the

Cuzco was a great center for producing paintings, metalwork, and especially wood carvings, both for its own churches, monastic institutions, and mansions and for those of the entire viceroyalty: richly carved, massive benches, cupboards, chests, and wardrobes for mansions; retables, pulpits, choir stalls, doorways, and screens for ecclesiastical buildings; and figures of saints and crucifixes for retables and chapels. Many of these figures approximated the Spanish realistic style; others were more abstract, like the stone figures on the façade of *San Sebastian*. The canopied pulpits in particular were lavishly carved (Fig. 624A) and, with the paintings and retables, lent a note of richness to somewhat sober interiors.

On the still higher, bleaker plateau of Alto Peru in the vicinity of Lake Titicaca (now chiefly Bolivia), in such cities as La Paz and Potosí, we feel even more than in Cuzco the intimate relation between man and the mountains. The thin, clear air sharpens the outlines against a metallic sky; the mountains are sheer masses of stone with but sparse vegetation; the cities of stone give the impression of being bound to their mountain environment. This is the locale, we recall, in which the austere Tiahuanaco culture developed. And we are not surprised to find that the deeper we penetrate this area, the stronger becomes the influence of the indigenous peoples. This we see in *San Francisco* (La Paz), low, massive, its baroque portal made tranquil by insistent horizontals and clean-cut angularity; and again in *San Lorenzo* (Potosí; Fig. 617A), once the great silver city of Charles V. Here the richly carved portal, set in a deep niche, contains all the elements of Spanish baroque, but the style has been transformed in two ways. First, it is permeated with Indian motifs to a greater extent than elsewhere — not only local

[A]   *Canopied Pulpit. San Blas, Cuzco.*

light and the dark. We recall the pre-Inca carvings from Chavin or Tiahuanaco, and remember that Moorish ornament, which so insistently emphasizes the surface, permeated all Spanish work. The figures also, as in the niches of *San Sebastian*, are strangely flat and abstract for baroque and are strictly frontal in pose, in strong contrast to the restless three-dimensional quality of baroque sculpture.

[A] *La Compañía. Arequipa. 1698.*

fauna and flora but the sun and the moon, symbols of Inca deities, angel-like figures playing native musical instruments, and, on the columns, figures of Indian dancers in feather costumes. Second, the manner of carving and of combining elements produces an even more tranquil effect than at La Paz. The basic organization of balanced vertical and horizontal lines combined with curves is set forth with the clarity of geometry, and within this framework the individual elements are simplified into abstract forms and carved flatly as integral parts of the surface they adorn. This same metamorphosis of the Spanish style is apparent in many of the rich carvings of retables and pul-

pits and in the figure sculpture in which in the expression of suffering Spanish theatrical realism takes on a restrained majesty.

As we move southeast along the passes into northwestern Argentina — to Jujuy, Yavi, and Salta, for example — the carvings and also the paintings become simple, direct expressions with passionate feeling through the use of highly conventional forms. Northwestern Argentina was on the periphery, culturally and artistically, not of the viceroyalty of La Plata, which was consistently European, but of that of Peru; and with the Spanish influence weaker in proportion to its distance from Cuzco, here we find the indige-

[A] *San Francisco. Quito. Late 16th cent. Towers rebuilt after the earthquake of 1868.* (*Archive of Hispanic Culture, Library of Congress*)

nous peoples retaining much of their own pattern of life, as did the Pueblos on the northern periphery of Hispanic America. Northward from Cuzco to Quito we find an inverse ratio of indigenous influence. Quito, though high in the Andes, is much farther north than Cuzco and hence enjoys a milder climate. Although a late capital of the Inca Empire, it was on its northern fringe, and upon its non-Incaic tribes the Inca culture had been imposed, whereas in Cuzco, the heart of the Inca Empire, it was autochthonous.

From its earliest days the Spanish city was an art center. In its numerous monastic establishments schools were established under the tutelage of the friars or of artists who came from Spain, so that the city became a center for making statues, carvings, and paintings for its own churches, monastic institutions, and mansions and for export to other Hispanic colonies, sometimes even to Spain itself. Churches and convents, which had followed the usual sixteenth- and seventeenth-century evolution of styles, suffered badly from earthquakes and in the process of repair and rebuilding developed in the eight-

eenth century an opulence unsurpassed in America.

From these churches without number, two will suffice for illustration — the Franciscan church and monastery, *San Francisco*, and the Jesuit church, *La Compañía*. *San Francisco* (Fig. 626A) is typical of the great monastic institutions; with its cloisters and subsidiary buildings it occupies an entire block. In external appearance it shares with all high Andean structures a low massiveness. Its heavy, severe portal prepares one but little for the richness of the interior, the work of the carver, the gilder, and the painter combined. In the apse (Fig. 627A) a framework of richly carved and gilded columns with a broken cornice, on which rests much free-standing sculpture, contains considerable flat area filled with paintings. All elements combine in leading to a lavish baroque altarpiece.

La Compañía (Fig. 628A) presents a strong contrast to *San Francisco*. Though low and without towers, it is lighter. The façade is a unit of design, with movement in depth — greater in the central section, less in the lateral; and with a delicate play of light and shade

[A] *Nave. San Francisco, Quito (Fig. 6264).*

over the surfaces from low reliefs accented by shadow-producing niches and openings and particularly by the typically baroque twisted columns at the entrance. One immediately turns to Rome, to *Il Gesù* and *San Ignacio* — the mother churches, stylistically, of the Jesuit order — and it is not surprising to learn that the plans of the church seem to have been made in Rome. If the façade of *La Compañía* is reservedly rich, the interior reaches a climax of opulence (Fig. 629A). For it is "sheer gold," not with a metallic glitter but with a warm glow, due partly to time and partly to the use of red and white pigment in the carvings, and accents of color in the paintings and in the polychrome sculp-

ture. Gold as a material was abundant; there was wealth to secure it; the zeal of the Jesuits was fervent, and their aim to overawe by sheer magnificence could here find ample outlet. At the same time we might be justified in asking whether the knowledge of Inca palaces and temples built of forbidding stone but lined with gold, and the description of these buildings given by the Spanish chroniclers, might be operating in the minds and the memories of the builders and the craftsmen. Though the surfaces are entirely sheathed in this rich decoration, there are effective contrasts. Large areas remain quite flat, are covered with angular Moorish ornament, and thus set off the more delicate

[A]   *La Compañía. Quito. 1722–65.*

curvilinear Renaissance carvings.

In creating these rich interiors, architects, sculptors, carvers, gilders, and painters worked in close collaboration. In fact sculpture hardly existed except in collaboration. Sixteenth-century carvers produced statues of a late-Gothic character. In the seventeenth century a style based on the Spanish baroque emerged: polychrome wood carvings. Some were realistically dramatic with brilliant color and gold in the voluminous drapery or in the actual fabrics with which the figures were clothed. Some, however, presented a more reserved character, best illustrated by the work of the well-known Indian Manuel Chili, also called Caspicara (eighteenth century). In his group representing *Saint Francis Receiving the Stigmata* one sees the baroque

almost transformed by a placid feeling which has been likened to that of late fifteenth-century Florence, but which may well find its roots in the character of the Indian bending the restless baroque in the direction of his own imperturbability.

Though ecclesiastical architecture perhaps represents the apogee of Hispanic American art, we must not forget that secular building as well engaged the attention of architects: to some extent municipal buildings, but more notably the mansions of the upper classes. These mansions were built on the Mediterranean plan, about patios, with only a portal, accented by carving, to hint at the magnificence within. The large, stately rooms tended to a barrenness which consciously set off the finely carved, massive furniture, the hangings and silver, the Sevillian tiles or the Mudéjar ceiling. In these furnishings — particularly in the carvings, the weaving, and the silver — we sometimes find pure Spanish designs, but frequently the same combination of Spanish and Indian as in the stone carvings.

Between or fringing the two great art centers in Mexico and the Andean highlands are other areas where varying conditions differentiate the basic pattern: Guatemala, where frequent earthquakes, a predominant, colorful Indian population, and the tradition of luxurious Mayan ornament condition a low, massive type of building, gay with colored plaster walls and ornament; the Caribbean, where, as in Santo Domingo, for example, plateresque and Herreran styles never gave way to the baroque, as there was no stimulation from either wealthy patronage or indigenous influence; the highlands of Colombia, where the transplanted Spanish retained a purely Spanish form of quiet dignity, with emphasis upon the Moorish element in its particularly fine *artesonados.*

[A] *Nave. La Compañía, Quito (Fig. 628A). 1605–89. (Archive of Hispanic Culture, Library of Congress)*

Eastward from the Andean Cordillera the terrain slopes down into vast tropical jungles in the north, with a salubrious plateau near the big eastern bulge, and into temperate plains in the south. This vast area was occupied by Indians who had never developed a culture comparable to that of the Andean tribes. The Portuguese traders, who explored the coastline of Brazil, hearing no tales and seeing no evidence of wealth, and obstructed by the dense tropical growth, clung to the fringe of the country and made little effort to penetrate the interior. Indeed Portugal did not push exploration and colonization as vigorously as Spain, because it became too deeply involved in similar enterprises in Africa and the Far East; nor did it exercise control so rigorously, or have such care for the souls or the welfare of the Indians. And although the Jesuits, the chief order of missionaries accompanying the Portuguese colonists, had zeal for their task, they had neither such wealth nor such skilled labor as the Spaniard found among the Aztecs and the Incas. Hence art expression developed slowly. In the northeast both the French and the Dutch secured footholds and for a time transplanted thither northern-European culture. Negroes were brought from Africa in large numbers to fur-

[A] *São Francisco. Ouro Preto. 1765–94. The planning and decorative sculpture are both attributed to Antônio Francisco Lisbôa. (Archive of Hispanic Culture, Library of Congress)*

nish labor. The Indians were pushed back into the interior, and their influence was insignificant.

Except in the French and Dutch settlements, whose art is known only through prints and paintings, and in one or two Portuguese cities whose buildings have been destroyed, there was little art activity in the sixteenth and seventeenth centuries. Thus Brazil experienced no succession of medieval and Renaissance styles such as occurred in the Spanish colonies. The earliest extant buildings, which date from the late seventeenth century, as well as those of the eighteenth, follow Portuguese styles closely, with adaptations due to climatic differences — such as the introduction of lattices to pro-

tect against the equatorial sun. In the coastal cities we find a brief period of Herreran building, as in the *Cathedral of Salvador* (Baía), which is heavy and austere, with a façade design strictly rectilinear except for the broken volutes over the windows and in the pediment. The interior, by contrast, is richly baroque, with its colored marbles, carved and painted wooden ceilings, and a sheathing of gilded carvings broken by brilliant blue Portuguese tiles and balcony rails of carved mahogany.

Later in the century appeared buildings of a very different character, not the Churrigueresque of Mexico and Quito but a style which closely followed Lisbon modes, with a French rococo

[A] *Rosario dos Pretos. Ouro Preto. José Pereira Arouca, architect. 1785. The plan is in the shape of two connected ovals. (Museum of Modern Art)*

flavor. The churches, the *Parish Church of Pilar* (El Salvador), for example, tend to be small, tall and slender, rectangular in plan, with no transepts, no vaulting, no dome. The lightness of the color, for they are usually plastered, the many openings, the delicacy of the rococolike ornament, produce an effect of lightness and elegance strongly in contrast to the heavy, dark, massive structures of eighteenth-century Andean buildings.

In the late seventeenth century and the eighteenth the discovery of gold and diamonds a few hundred miles inland led to a unique development in a group of isolated mining towns, the chief of which was Ouro Preto. In this heavily wooded, mountainous plateau, quite out of contact with European sources, a distinctive regional style evolved from Baían and Portuguese prototypes, rooted in the local environment and brought to fruition by a group of gifted artists.[1] As the great religious orders were banned in the district, the responsibility for building lay with the Third Order (a lay order) and the local churches. A native soapstone furnished excellent material for masonry, which was usually stuccoed, and for carving, and was augmented by an orange sandstone used in bases, pilasters, and cornices, which added a

[1] Ouro Preto has been made a Brazilian national monument to preserve the colonial character of the town, as Taxco does for Mexico and Williamsburg for the United States.

note of contrasting warmth to the gray soapstone.

Most of the churches were built on hilltops and stand out conspicuously as mass. Many are rectangular in plan, yet not a few are oval, even a double oval. This is seen in the *Church of the Rosary* (Fig. 631A) built for the large community of Negroes in Ouro Preto. The severely rectilinear design of the *Cathedral of Salvador*, based on rectangular volumes, seems to have been bent into a design based on cylinders and is highly sculptural in feeling. The plan consisting of two ovals and a convex façade; the cylindrical volumes tied together with an unbroken cornice; the skillful integration of the towers with the other cylinders; the triple doorway with unadorned rounding arches which accentuate the curving surface; the curving pediment and circular windows — all these elements denote a highly original designer.

Most of the churches, however, follow a somewhat different and fairly consistent style — rectangular in plan, with round towers and a single doorway with carved ornament flanked by two windows having a round window directly above, around which swings the cornice. The pediment is finished with broken scrolls. Such is *São Francisco* at Ouro Preto (Fig. 630A). Here the elegant carving about the portal and in the disk which displaces the window above is the work of the mestizo Antônio Francisco Lisbôa, known as O Aleijadinho ("The Little Cripple"). O Aleijadinho, whose hands and feet were badly crippled by some disease, was an architect as well as a sculptor, and while his actual work is a matter of dispute, there seems to be no doubt that both as an artist and as the trainer of a group of assistants his influence dominated. Portals, pulpits, fonts, altars, and stations of the cross, both in stone and in wood, in the churches in many towns of the province of Minas Gerais show an independent use of the rococo phase of baroque practiced in the coastal cities. Garlands, scrolls, ribbons, and figures are carved with a masculine strength and boldness; and the more-than-life-sized stone figures of the *Prophets* (Congonhas do Campo) possess a power and a vitality seldom met in Hispanic American art.

The interiors of these churches, which usually have wooden ceilings instead of vaults, are gay with accents of brightly polychromed and gilded altarpieces, carved pulpits, and paintings that swirl up in rapid movement, truly baroque in style.

North American

AS we turn to Hispanic America north of the Rio Grande, we find the southern and southwestern part of the United States constituting the northern fringe, corresponding culturally to Bolivia and northwestern Argentina on the southern fringe. From both the West Indies and Mexico Spanish expeditions set forth northward, motivated by the same desires as Cortés and Pizarro: gold and the souls of the Indians. Thus Florida and the Gulf Coast and all the Southwest as far north, roughly, as San Francisco became a part of New Spain. The climate along the Gulf and in California approximated that of southern Spain; the intermediate area was a dry plateau, more like Mexico, and its proximity to the latter country led to a more direct Mexican influence. The legend of "The Seven Cities of Cibola" led Coronado farther north into the Pueblo country in search of reputed fabulous wealth, such as had so richly rewarded Cortés and Pizarro. Finding none, he retreated, leaving the padres to carry out the work of Christianizing and Spaniardizing the Pueblos, most of whom were scattered along the Rio Grande Valley.

In the Gulf area, Spanish buildings of various kinds appeared, most prominently at New Orleans, where on the Plaza (now Jackson Square) rose the simple *Cathedral* and the *Cabildo*, or municipal building, both basically Spanish but later altered by the French, who in remodeling the buildings superimposed their own style on that of the Spaniard. More elaborate, though still provincial in comparison with their prototypes in Mexico, are the churches and the convents in Texas and Arizona. *San Xavier del Bac* (near Tucson) is the most elaborate example of the ultrabaroque style with a local idiom. Lack of stone and of skilled labor resulted in the use of adobe brick, the usual building material of the Indians, for the construction of walls, vaults, and domes. The walls were plastered white, and the ornamentation of molded plaster was concentrated as usual in the central part of the façade. The interior, rich in carvings, gilding, and color, though deriving from Spanish sources, shows many evidences of Indian conception and execution.

In California, which the padres penetrated in the late eighteenth century, economic conditions and lack of strong Indian building traditions led to one of the simplest expressions of the Spanish baroque — a unique and charming simplicity that fitted local requirements and climatic conditions admirably. In these missions — in their plans, massing of parts, and decorative elements — we see the final dilution of Spanish baroque, even more final than the similar simplification of the style found in somewhat similar conditions in the interior of South America. At times the usual towers are omitted and, as a substitute functionally, the gable is pierced to hold the bells, as at *San*

Gabriel. This is not a unique solution of the problem of the bell tower, for it is found in Mexico as well.

When we turn, however, to the Pueblo area, we immediately find this Spanish style strongly altered. Here the level of indigenous culture was high and the Pueblos were unusually tenacious of their heritage, so that the resulting pattern of life was largely Indian, modified by the Spanish contribution — sheep and draft animals, plants for an expanded food supply, metal tools, and Christianity. This is seen in the retention of the great communal houses, as at *Taos*, though in smaller adobe houses the addition of *portales*, or porticoes, and of chimneys reveal a Spanish influence. Everywhere, however, the continued use of the ceremonial kiva is evidence of the continuity of the old religious practices. Hard by stands the inevitable mission church, sometimes of stone, more frequently of adobe, with thick, unbroken walls, massive buttressing, and roofs of wooden beams which project beyond the walls and are covered with twigs and a layer of adobe. Low, squat bell towers usually flank the façade, which has an open balcony above the entrance that may have served the same function as the open chapel in Mexico and Peru and which breaks the austere surface with its shadow-filled recesses. The interiors with their whitewashed walls are as austere as the exteriors, except for the beams, or vigas, with their carved brackets and for the sanctuary, toward which the eye is inevitably guided through the dim light of the nave by the repetition of the vigas, by the focusing of light on the altar from a transverse clerestory, and by the painting and sculpture concentrated about the sanctuary.

In these paintings and sculptures we find Christian content given native form — a folk art, it perhaps should be called.

For while a limited number of pictures and carvings were imported from Mexico and instruction was given the Indians in European arts from which some creative work resulted, in the rebellion of 1680 most of this, together with the churches themselves, was destroyed, and for a period the Indians were free to express themselves without Spanish domination. Thus cut off from outside contacts, even after the return of the Spanish, Indian artists, notably in the more isolated villages, were thrown upon their own resources and, within the limitations of local materials and of poverty but with great intensity of feeling, produced *santos* that are almost hypnotic in their emotional power. The *santos* took the form of *retablos* (paintings) and *bultos* (carvings in the round), which were used on the altar or carried in rites and festivals. These were figures of saints, mostly Franciscan, as the Franciscans were the chief missionaries in this region, of the Virgin as *Mater Dolorosa*, and of Christ, with emphasis upon the Man of Sorrows. Somber in color and passionate in mood is the *Cristo* of Figure 635A, which, though based upon Spanish realism, in the hands of an impassioned local carver partakes strongly of the abstraction that permeates Indian art. The firm, clean-cut lines, the sharply contrasting light and dark areas, the large eyes, and the rhythmically repeated drops of blood create an effect more filled with anguish than the more realistic Spanish expression.

PAINTING

Painting in Hispanic America, though prolific in quantity, did not show the same inventiveness nor reach the same high level of accomplishment as architecture and carving. It was an almost purely derivative art, in which many painters were technically able, and a few were distinguished followers of the current Spanish styles. Some reasons for this are clear. It was easy to import paintings and painters, the colonial ideal. Painting was not dependent, as was architecture, on climate, geography, and materials, and hence received no challenge or stimulation from changing conditions, nor was it so dependent upon Indian craftsmen, another source of growth in a new direction. To be sure, soon after the conquest the friars undertook to teach the Indians the Spanish mode by giving them paintings to copy. Thus the sixteenth-century frescoes in some of the early fortress-churches, as at *Huejotzingo* or *Actopán* in Mexico, are copies on a large scale of woodcuts from Spanish religious books, carried out in the original black-and-white but never exactly copied.

Another early fusion of Spanish and Indian is even more evident in the post-conquest codices, for which there could be no model, yet which show the result of lessons learned. For here appear experiments in the use of light and shade to indicate volume, in linear perspective, and in the introduction of landscape and interiors in the backgrounds — all in combination with the traditional Indian flat linear style, in which depth was indicated by placing one figure above another with no diminution in size. There is a lively quality about many of these little drawings, as if the artist, though maintaining the integrity of his native style, was delighted to play with the new ideas. Given the opportunity, he might have been able to bring about, through assimilation, an art rooted in native soil yet reaching out in new directions. Instead, undiluted European art was imposed from above. But this fresh growth, submerged by the official art of the Church and the ruling class, was kept alive by the people and formed in the twentieth century a basis for a vital art rooted in its own traditions.

The official painters saw Spanish fashions only and followed first the current Flemish-Italian styles, or the tenebrist painting of Caravaggio, Ribera, and Zurbarán. Examples are Sebastián Arteaga (1610–about 1656), Baltazar Echave (1582–1650), and Miguel de Santiago (about 1620–1680) — a mestizo of Quito who is thought to have traveled in Spain and was versatile in turning to his own purposes as a fully independent artist not only tenebrist effects but the El Greco use of light, the luminosity and the high key of Murillo, and the realism of Velásquez. His contemporary Gorivar González (died 1671), however, based his style on that of the Venetians, Tintoretto in particular.

The clear bright color of Italianate painting and the melting light and color of Murillo made a far greater appeal to the Hispanic American than the somber style, and were in greater harmony with the sumptuously carved and gilded altarpieces. Sevillian art shaped the work of Gregorio Vásquez (1638–1711) of Bogotá, who was distinguished for his strong draughtsmanship and rich color, and for portraits of great dignity. Juan Rodríguez Juárez (1675–1728) of Mexico also painted in the luminous style of Murillo, as did the prolific Miguel Cabrera (1695–1768), often called the chief of Mexican painters. Cabrera is equally well known for his murals and for his portraits. In the latter he at times rises above the level of the official quality found in so many of his contemporaries and creates a painting which is sensitive both in interpretation and in structure. Such is the portrait of *Sor Juana Inés de la Cruz* (Museo Nacional de Historia, Mexico), a famous poet. José Ibarra (1688–1756) of Mexico shows how the influence of Rubens, through the importation of prints of his work, was adding to the sumptuousness of the baroque.

[A] *Cristo: "Man of Sorrows." Wood, covered with gesso and painted; natural hair; cloth garment. H. 65 in. Taylor Museum, Colorado Springs Fine Art Center. (Taylor Museum)*

There are two fields of painting, however, apart from that practiced in the viceregal centers of Mexico, Bogotá, Lima, and Quito, in which we find a more authentic expression of Hispanic American life. One is the so-called school of Cuzco; the other, the popular or folk art. In Cuzco we meet the same situation that we found in architecture and carving. Distance from the vice-regal centers, the presence of a powerful indigenous culture, and a predominant Indian element in the population conscious of a great tradition, brought about enough assimilation to produce a more autochthonous type of expression. An incredible amount of painting issued from the monastic schools, a great deal of it anonymous, to provide for the needs of the capital as well as for those of the other communities of the viceroyalty. Some of the painters followed the sequence of styles of the mother country; some, especially the mestizo artists, produced austere, hieratic Madonnas, flat, strongly linear, and richly decorative, with many details, especially in the garments and embroideries, of Inca derivation. Such is the *Virgin* of Figure 637A. And as we travel into Bolivia and northwestern Argentina we find, just as in the sculpture, further simplification, further intensity of feeling.

The other field of a more authentic expression may be illustrated by the Mexican *retablo*, a commemorative or votive picture that relates a miraculous escape from death or a cure from illness through the intercession of some saint. These are small in size, painted on wood, tin, or canvas. Though some were made by well-known painters for the aristocracy, on the whole this was an art of the people. With simple, dramatic directness, the story was set forth together with a picture of the interceding saint and an explanatory text. Some of the retablos were flat and linear, dramatic arrangements of bright color areas, and highly conventional. Others were somewhat more naturalistic, indicating some acquaintance with European methods of expressing depth and mass. Enormous numbers were made, of uneven quality. But in general they were infused with a spirit of sincere, fervid feeling and a vitality that springs from a sentiment deeply rooted in life and expressed by a people with a natural, high esthetic sensitivity.

SUMMARY

Latin American art was basically Spanish and Portuguese art transplanted to the Americas, where it existed sometimes in purely derivative form — though modified by different climatic and geographical conditions and available materials — particularly in the viceregal capitals and coastal cities; and sometimes so altered by contact with a people whose habit of mind and whose art were radically different that the blending of the two produced styles which may be truly called Hispanic American. This occurred in the areas where the aboriginal culture had reached a high level, as in Mexico and the Andean regions, and where the indigenous traditions were strong. It was an art largely at the service of the ruling aristocracy and of the Church and directed by these, but actually executed to a large extent by Indian craftsmen, who were endowed with no little technical skill before the coming of the Spaniard. A vast number of buildings were erected, at first chiefly ecclesiastical, later secular also; and they passed through the contemporary European phases of late-Gothic, plateresque, and Herreran, and reached a climax in the eighteenth-century baroque and ultrabaroque, which permeated all the arts.

Sculpture was inextricably allied to architecture — carvings for façades, retables, and altars — and though based on the Spanish polychrome realistic carvings, it frequently showed Spanish realism modified by the Indian and turned toward a simpler, more abstract form. Painting was definitely more derivative than sculpture, though in

[A] *Virgin Surrounded by Angels and a Donor. From Cuzco. 17th or 18th cent. International Business Machines Corporation Collection, New York City. (International Business Machines Corporation.) The stylized pose and drapery, the magnificent costume with added gold details, and the flat, static quality show Indian workmanship.*

Cuzco, Bolivia, and the northern and southern fringes of the Hispanic domain the strong indigenous element produced, through blending, original and vital painting. Among the people, especially away from the centers of Spanish influences, the native arts continued either in purely indigenous form or with assimilated Hispanic elements. Thus a pure Indian or Indian Hispanic art existed parallel to the neo-European art, and it played a decisive role in the vital twentieth-century renascence of Latin American art.

BIBLIOGRAPHY

Bandeira, Manoel, *Ouro Preto, the Old Villa Rica, Travel in Brazil*, Vol. I, No. 4, 1941

Documentos de arte Argentino, 21 vols., Buenos Aires, 1939–46

Hernández de Alba, Guillermo, *Teatro del arte colonial*, Bogotá, 1938

Kronfuss, Juan, *Arquitectura colonial en la Argentina*, Cordoba

Noel, Martín S., *El Arte en la América Española*, Buenos Aires, 1942

—————, and Torre Revello, José, *Estudios y documentos para la historia del arte colonial*, 2 vols., Vol. I, Buenos Aires, 1934

Pagano, José L., *Historia del arte Argentino*, Buenos Aires, 1944

Reis, José Maria dos, *História da pintura no Brazil*, São Paulo, 1944

Weiss y Sanchez, Joaquin, *Arquitectura cubana colonial*, Havana, 1936

See also the Bibliography on p. 702.

38

FRENCH AMERICAN ART

WHEN news of great wealth pouring into the coffers of Spain and reports of huge areas of rich, hitherto unknown lands reached the ears of other European countries, they too, quite naturally, became eager for a share, as well as for an opportunity to continue the search for some passage to the fabulous Far East not blocked by Spain and Portugal. Motivation differed with various countries as their backgrounds differed. France was interested not only in the search for a Northwest Passage, but in commercial enterprise, particularly the fur trade. Thus from Quebec and Montreal its traders pushed their explorations west and southwest until French forts and trading-posts were strung out over a vast area from the mouth of the St. Lawrence to the mouth of the Mississippi. Other expeditions, exploratory or piratical, established French communities along the Gulf of Mexico, in Florida, in Haiti, and on the northern coast of Brazil. As with the Spaniard, missionaries accompanied the explorers or frequently were themselves the exploring pioneers, seeking friendly intercourse with the Indians, if not their souls and their welfare.

While a small part of the colonists were landed aristocracy and constituted the ruling class, subject to and patterned after the absolutism of France, the bulk were loyal peasant people of the Roman Catholic faith — farmers, fisherfolk, and craftsmen — who transplanted to the St. Lawrence Valley the pattern of life in Normandy or Brittany, with little attention to the indigenous peoples. For the Indians, a woodland people with no cities, living in wigwams and with skill only in weaving, embroidery, and birchbark work, seem to have been more strongly influenced by the white man than he was by them, as is seen in the introduction of beads into their embroidery and in the change from an angular to a curvilinear design, apparently brought about by contact with the easy grace of French ornament.

ARCHITECTURE

The vast extent of the French domain, with such strongly contrasting climatic conditions as the rigorous cold of Quebec and the semitropical heat of New Orleans, with all shades of variation between, required adaptation to

climate as well as to local conditions of economy and materials. In the St. Lawrence Valley, stern economic conditions precluded nonessentials. The thrifty, industrious Norman and Breton peasants evolved a simple, direct, and thoroughly adequate type of home, church, and convent out of local material, to meet local needs. Based on inherent French good taste, a distinctive individual style arose. Out of local stone the builders built low, compact, rectangular houses, with walls several feet thick; small windows; steeply pitched roofs, sometimes broken by dormers to shed the snow; and stone end gables and chimneys. The *Château de Ramezay* (Montreal) is a somewhat elaborate version of the type.

The Church, a dominating element in the fabric of culture, gave importance to the building of churches, monasteries, and convents, which were of the same

materials as the houses and as austerely simple. The early churches were devoid of ornament, but their roofs bore a distinctive mark in the "tin tiles" with which they were covered. These consisted of sheets of tin laid diagonally, producing a tilelike appearance, and which, by acquiring a silvery or bronze patina with time, made the roof not only practical but uniquely satisfying. The interiors of these churches were as unpretentious as the exteriors except for excellent wood-carving about the altars. Schools of wood-carving had been established in the colonies, and the craftsmanship was on a high level. The designs were simplified current French styles. Monastic institutions were important. The *Ursuline Convent* (Three Rivers, Fig. 639A) well illustrates the neat, trim character of all this northern French Colonial building and the peculiar harmony between the style and its cultural setting. The quiet dignity of its plain walls; the symmetrical, well-spaced windows; its scorn, one is tempted to say, of ornament — these are peculiarly expressive of a simple, industrious people living in a rigorous climate.

In the large churches, especially in the cities, classic porches, a reflection of the neoclassic wave in Europe, and two towers were added. After the cession of Canada to England in 1763, English influence, notably Georgian, appears, as in the mansions and the churches of Montreal.

The southward movement into a less rigorous climate brought changes which are clearly evident in the vicinity of St. Louis. Here the combination trading-post and home became a more expansive structure, with the addition of porches, or galleries, and its walls were no longer two feet thick. However, plastered stone was still used for building material, though not to the complete exclusion of wood, and the steep gable roof and the stone chimney remained. Still farther south, at New Orleans, the semitropical climate, in combination with the Spanish influence already entrenched and with different social conditions, produced a style that is partly an adaptation of the French and partly a mingling of French and Spanish.[1] The *Ursuline Convent* and certain houses in the bayou country are evidence of the continuity of the northern French tradition, but the usual type of domicile is the Mediterranean, centering about an open court, a type eminently suited to the climate. The house was built flush with the street and served both as

a residence and as a shop. It was constructed of brick, covered usually with colored stucco, and carried iron balconies from which the inmates could view the narrow street or make contact with neighbors. Yet the house really faced the paved court, with its fountains and shade trees, which was entered by a passageway, at times large enough for an equipage, protected by heavy doors. The iron balconies (Fig. 641A), with their lacelike quality and repeated shadows, added grace and delicacy to the plain, rather stern walls. They were of two kinds, wrought and cast. Wrought iron, the older and often imported, is simpler in design and of painstaking craftsmanship. Cast iron lends itself to more intricate designs, which here include monograms and motifs of local flora. Other uses of iron were for elaborately designed benches and street lamps and for gracefully ornamented grilles which served as gates to protect the court and at the same time admitted a current of air.

Within, such homes of the wealthy had large, high, stately rooms with spiral staircases and carved balusters, fine paneling and mantles, and crystal chandeliers. The furnishings were predominantly French. Much of the furniture — tables, chairs, chests, and great wardrobes — was imported, but much also was made by skilled local craftsmen from the abundant local materials, such as cypress.

This, then, was a type of house well adapted to a compact walled city. Outside, extending over great areas of rich farm land, plantations developed, which produced great wealth for the owners and led to the building of houses as fine as those in the city but of a type adapted in both plan and arrangement to a different site. The plantation house was two stories high, the lower serving as a basement because of the water-soaked soil, the upper as the living-quarters of

[1] New Orleans was founded by the French in 1718 as a center for trade with the Indians, and was ceded to Spain by the treaty of 1763. It suffered great fires in 1788 and 1794. In 1801 it was ceded by Spain to France. Thus, as a result of the fires, most of the extant colonial building falls into the late Spanish and second French eras.

[A] *Cast-Iron Double Balcony. 805 Esplanade Avenue, New Orleans. c. 1850. (Clarence John Laughlin)*

the family. It was built of brick below and wood above, was rather long and rectangular, and instead of facing an inner court, opened outward onto wide verandas shaded by the overhanging roof. These verandas were supported by sturdy brick piers; the roofs, by slender wooden columns. Wide doors and windows opened on the shady verandas, thus providing a free current of air. These plantation houses resembled those of Haiti and Santo Domingo, whence refugees fled to Louisiana at the time of the revolution on that island, and also the plantation houses of northern Brazil. The urban French of New Orleans seems repeated in the colored stucco houses with delicate iron balconies seen in northern Brazil — in Belém and São Luiz, for example. Thus cultural areas do not coincide with national areas, but the two overlap at

many points under the controlling influences of forces other than political.[1]

SUMMARY

As the French colonies spread out loosely over a vast area from rigorous Quebec to semitropical New Orleans and tropical Haiti and northern Brazil, French colonial art was as diversified as its geography. On the northern fringe, in Canada, the style of Brittany and Normandy, adapted to a far more rigorous climate, produced compact, thick-walled stone houses and churches as simple and unpretentious as the industrious, devout people who built

[1] On this point of overlapping cultures, in its modern as well as its colonial aspect, see R. S. Platt, *Latin America, Countrysides and United Regions*, Chap. XII, Whittlesey House, 1943.

them, and sparse of ornament except for excellent wood-carving. In the middle Mississippi regions, the type expanded under the influence of a milder climate until in the semitropical and tropical regions of the Caribbean area it gave way, almost exclusively, to the Mediterranean type of house of colored-stucco finish and handsome iron balconies, built about garden patios. This was an urban shop-house. In the rich agricultural sections, the plantation house was compact, open to the out-of-doors, and shaded by verandas — a style arising out of its own environment. The furnishings of French colonial houses were usually in good taste, in harmony with the house as a unit, and ranged from the simple, robust peasant styles in Canada to the more elegant and aristocratic styles in New Orleans. Though secular art was predominant, ecclesiastical art was not neglected; but it was not as overpowering as in the Hispanic colonies — a reflection of the relative power of the Church in France and in Spain.

BIBLIOGRAPHY

Barbeau, Charles M., *Quebec, Where Ancient France Lingers*, Macmillan, 1936
——————— *Deux cents ans d'orfèvrerie chez nous*, in *Mémoires de la Société Royale du Canada*, 3rd Series, Vol. 33, Sect. I 1939
Carless, William, *The Arts and Crafts of Canada*, Montreal, 1925
——————— *The Architecture of French Canada*, McGill University, Montreal, 1925
New Orleans City Guide, Houghton Mifflin, 1938
Old Manors, Old Houses (Quebec), Historical Monuments Commission of the Province of Quebec, 1st Series, 1927
Ricciuti, Italo W., *New Orleans and Its Environs*, William Helburn, 1938
Spratling, William P., and Scott, Natalie, *Old Plantation Houses in Louisiana*, William Helburn, 1927
Traquair, Ramsay, *The Old Silver of Quebec*, Toronto, 1940
——————— *The Old Architecture of Quebec*, Toronto, 1947
——————— *Old Churches and Church Carvings in the Province of Quebec*, McGill University, Montreal, 1928
——————— *No. 92 St. Peter Street, Quebec, a Quebec Merchant's House of the XVIII Century*, McGill University, Montreal, 1930
———————, and Barbeau, Charles M., *The Church of Sainte Famille, Island of Orleans, Quebec*, McGill University, Montreal, 1926

39

ENGLISH AMERICAN ART

THE English were motivated not by the desire for gold and for exploitation of natural resources for the benefit of a European crown, but by a desire to trade in furs and fish and to settle and build communities in which they could pursue a way of life that would assure them a measure of independence politically, economically, and religiously. For these colonists came from those parts of Europe which had been affected by the Reformation and by a break in the feudal system. Thus they prepared a fertile soil for the development of complete self-government and religious freedom. There was no powerful Church-State to dominate their activities. Except in the moderate baronial life of the South, there was no entrenched feudal system with a landed aristocracy to dominate their economics, as in the Hispanic colonies. Greater social and political equality existed here, on the whole, than any-

[A] *Peirce-Nichols House. Salem. c. 1790. (Essex Institute)*

where else in the New World, and greater homogeneity despite local diversity. For diversity did exist between the Northern and Southern colonies, due to differences of climate and background. To the North came sturdy, thrifty middle-class colonists, including many craftsmen, with few from the educated classes and still fewer from the wealthy group. In this cold, nonagricultural, heavily timbered country, they built ships with which they developed a rich trade; and flourishing seaports arose, where most of the population centered and where democratic ideas flourished. In the warm, agriculturally rich South, on the other hand, the colonists came from the Cavalier class, and

on the basis of slave labor they developed plantations for the production of tobacco and cotton, from which they acquired great wealth. Thus in the country, to a greater extent than in the cities, rose the fine mansions of a more aristocratic people, who kept in fairly close touch with the home country and preferred to import thence rather than to encourage local talent.

Both North and South, however, took the same attitude toward the Indians, who were woodland tribes, with no cities, and with an art expression only in objects of daily life. There was no assimilation of cultures, no intermingling such as produced the mestizo class in the Spanish and Portuguese

[A] *St. Michael's. Charleston. 1752–61.*
Compare the portico and spire with those
in Fig. 591B. (Carolina Art Association)

colonies, but a consistent segregation,
a pushing of the aborigines ever farther
westward. Thus there was no indigenous
cultural influence upon the arts of the
colonists, which were English arts transplanted to primitive conditions and
adapted to a new climatic and a new
cultural environment.

ARCHITECTURE

Evidence of this background is seen
in the emphasis upon the types of
buildings erected by the colonists — the
home, the church, and the town hall —
and in the equality of treatment, as to
pretentiousness or unpretentiousness, of
the three types. The earliest buildings
were naturally in the style with which
the colonists were familiar, the late medieval of the Elizabethan and Jacobean
eras translated into a timber construction and adapted in the North to a more
rigorous climate. They were usually
clapboarded, had steep roofs, brick
chimneys, and small windows, few in
number and with leaded panes, as in
the *Whipple House* (Ipswich, Massachusetts; about 1650). All buildings and
their furnishings were simple, direct,
and functional, with sparse ornament.

With the coming of the eighteenth
century, the accumulation of wealth
and more frequent communication with
England were reflected in the introduction of the Renaissance, or Georgian,
style, then dominant in England.
Thence followed the full flowering of
the Colonial style, which appears in the
homes of the rich merchants of the seaport cities and in the mansions of the
Southern estates. The *Peirce-Nichols
House* (Salem, Massachusetts; Fig. 643A)
is an example of the former. Symmetry
of plan and elevation, flat roof, regularity of spacing in the façade, the
accent on the entrance, the individual
treatment of each window, the corner
pilasters, the cornice and roof balustrade — all these elements reflect the
Renaissance and can be traced, by way
of England, to such a distant ancestor
as the *Farnese Palace* (Fig. 458B), and as
in Rome, so in Salem, they produce an
impression of dignity and well-being.

A more genial dignity pervades the
houses in the Middle and Southern colonies. Life here was less drab, more gay

[A] *Woodlands. Philadelphia. Rebuilt 1788–89. (Detroit Publishing Co.)*

and luxurious. The two-storied pedimented portico of *Woodlands* (Philadelphia; Fig. 645A) strikes a note of stately hospitality. The strict regularity is broken by circular bays on the sides and by the arched windows of the ground story, Palladian in design. Most of these houses were placed with careful regard for natural surroundings. Trees, hedges, spacious lawns, and gardens contributed to the qualities of the building itself.[1]

As eighteenth-century exteriors accented the entrance, so the interiors emphasized the central hall, with its straight or winding stairway and rooms symmetrically arranged on each side. Here wood again predominated. Pine, locally abundant, and adaptable for carving because of its softness and fine

[1] Mention should be made of the restoration of Williamsburg, Virginia. Not only the buildings and their furnishings but also the grounds and gardens have been carefully restored to give as complete a picture as possible of an important eighteenth-century colonial city.

grain combined with its durability, was used extensively for stairways, overmantels, doorways, and paneling. The stairway was given especial attention by carved balusters and walnut or mahogany rails. The paneling was adapted to the area to be covered, with a high degree of sensitivity. Sometimes it sheathed the entire room, or again it was used only on the wall containing the fireplace — the chief feature of the room, about which were assembled the family portraits, silver, brasses, and porcelain. Carvings, classic or Renaissance in motif, accented the overmantel, the finishing cornice, and the doorways, thus enriching the simple geometric pattern of the walls. The skill and delicacy of the work of Samuel McIntire of Salem, one of the well-known carvers, reveal the influence of Robert Adam (Fig. 593A). The same carpenters and carvers who built New England houses also built the ships that produced the wealth which enabled merchants to build and

[A] *Paul Revere. Silver Creamer. H. 7 in. 1799. Museum of Fine Arts, Boston. (Boston Museum)*

furnish fine houses. These same crafts-men carved for the prows boldly strong figureheads — one of the few kinds of sculpture produced among the image-hating Puritans.

The churches were reproductions in wood or brick, with modifications, of English Protestant churches: a simple meeting-hall with a belfry or spire. At first, particularly in the Puritan North, they were as bleakly austere in appear-ance as the worshipers were uncom-promising in their religious faith and practice — for example, the *Old North Church* and *Old South Church* (Boston). Later, under the influence of Wren and Gibbs in England, the spire took on Renaissance details and a portico was added, as in *St. Paul's* (New York), *Center Church* (New Haven), and *St. Michael's* (Charleston; Fig. 644A).

The fine woodwork in the colonial homes was set off by, and itself set off, the dark walnut or mahogany furniture. Current European fashions dictated the furniture too — Chippendale, Hepple-white, Sheraton, French rococo — though much of it was the work of American craftsmen, and the products of some of the cabinetmakers' shops in Boston, New York, and Philadelphia were equal in design and craftsmanship to those imported from London. Such a shop was that of Duncan Phyfe of New York.

Within this framework of the room and its furniture the products of various craftsmen contributed notes of color and texture — iron, brass, pewter, silver, glass, textiles, costumes. Despite its Eu-ropean derivation, a new spirit in-fused this interior architecture, welding it into an extraordinary unity of vigor, restraint, and fine taste.

Especial mention perhaps should be made of the silver. For, in the absence of banks, family wealth often consisted of silver objects, and the family silver, the pride of the family for generations, proclaimed both its social and its eco-nomic position. Thus the silversmith held a more distinctive place in the community than the other craftsmen, and an exceptional quality was de-manded in his products. A pitcher by Paul Revere, for example (Fig. 646A), has an architectural quality in the fine relationships of its mass and contour, the subordination of the restrained or-nament to a direct clarity of form, and a fine balance between the smooth un-broken and the rough broken surfaces.

PAINTING

The family portraits which play a conspicuous part in the ensemble of the colonial interior reveal the chief func-tion of the painter in the English col-onies. At first a painter could find little

[A] *Unknown Artist. Mrs. Freake and Baby Mary. c. 1674. Private Collection. (Worcester Art Museum)*

demand for his services. What few pictures there were had been brought over from Europe. In Puritan New England strong religious prejudice against art, born of the Reformation in Europe, confined the painter to such activities as coach- and sign-painting.

To surmount this prejudice, however, became none too difficult when the colonists grew wealthy and wanted portraits not only to decorate their walls but also to hand on to posterity "lest their efforts to found families and states be forgotten."[1] Hence there arose a demand for the portrait that was met by untrained enthusiasts, or low-rate limners or face-painters, who had come to the New World perhaps for adventure.

[1] F. J. Mather, C. R. Morey, and J. H. Henderson, *The American Spirit in Art*, Yale University Press, 1927, p. 4.

The Cavaliers of the South, however, in closer contact with England, had their portraits painted in London, with personal sittings if possible, otherwise from verbal description. European painters, learning of this need, began to arrive to meet it. They not only painted portraits themselves but stimulated the development of the art by bringing engravings of European paintings and by giving instruction to the untrained local face-painters. Those who came from Holland to New Netherlands showed evidence of descent from Hals; those from England, the influence of the English portrait school.

An early arrival was John Smibert of Edinburgh (1688–1751), as "professor of drawing, painting, and architecture in the college of science and art which Berkeley proposed to found in

[A] *Copley. Lady Wentworth. 1765. New York Public Library. (New York Public Library)*

Bermuda for the benefit of the American Indian"[1] — a utopian dream soon blasted. Smibert's group portrait, *Bishop Berkeley and His Entourage*, in comparison with the work of the limners shows a certain amount of professional resourcefulness in drawing, handling pigment, and composition, notwithstanding his rather mediocre ability. The works of the local limners, however, often reveal a certain vigor, frank objectivity, and intuitive capacity, as one sees in such a portrait as *Mrs. Freake and Baby Mary* (Fig. 647A) by an anonymous painter.

Besides John Smibert, other painters arrived to contribute to the accumulating local endeavor, which reached a climax in John Singleton Copley (1737–1815). Beyond help in rudiments from his stepfather and opportunity to see some paintings and engravings, Copley was self-educated in his pre-European

[1] F. W. Bayley, *Five Colonial Artists of New England*, privately printed, 1929, p. 336.

work. In his *Lady Wentworth* (Fig. 648A) he shows some grasp of the figure, whose stiffness is an evidence partly of propriety and partly of a lack of ease on the part of a painter untrained professionally. There is a generally hard effect and an overemphasis upon contrasting lights and darks, and an inability to fuse them or to utilize them as pattern; a fondness for the texture of satin, laces, and other fine stuffs; and an intentional realism in details, for straightforward objectivity was the painter's purpose. Copley established his permanent residence in England after 1774; and in proportion as he gained professionally he lost in forthright candor of characterization. For despite their technical weaknesses, the portraits of his Colonial period possess an unpretentious directness and sheer force of characterization. Such an accomplishment, had it been grounded in the needed professional training, might conceivably have produced a truly indigenous art of high quality. But the potentialities of provincial life as a motivation of art expression passed unnoticed. Copley's choice to remain in England meant an increased facility in handling pigment, but a general weakening of his genuine ability. This was the first of a long series of similar choices that have throttled a normal evolution of art expression in this country.

Instead, "To London" filled the air. To be sure, it was necessary for technical training. But at that few stopped. Benjamin West (1738–1820), for example, after an adventurous and now legendary youth, set out for Italy in 1760 through the financial assistance of a rich patron and came to London at the time when Sir Joshua Reynolds was the revered president of the Royal Academy. Falling into the current styles, West became popular and wealthy, made a grandiloquent gesture by refusing knighthood, and upon the death of Sir Joshua in 1792 became president of the Academy. His studio was a mecca for American students during and for a generation after the War of Independence and thus brought American painting into close affiliation with English traditions. In addition, West introduced historical, mythological, and religious subjects in the "grand manner" — an influence of French Romanticism — but with none of the fire of a Delacroix and with little or no conviction.

Portrait-painting continued in the colonies, more and more under the influence of the English school, and also under that of the French.[1] Gilbert Stuart seems to be the most individual painter of the generation, and despite long residence in London, freer from imitating the styles with which he came in contact. With a real feeling for his medium, he built up a vibrant surface of loose virile strokes that has its own esthetic value. *Mrs. Yates* (Fig. 649A) for example, illustrates his sureness of technique and his use of it to set forth his subject with objective reality and interpretive probity.

SUMMARY

English colonial art was at first late-medieval English art (Elizabethan, Jacobean), and later Georgian, transplanted to a land where climatic and economic conditions required adaptation, such as the substitution of timber for brick or stone. As the Indians were either exterminated or pushed westward, there was no influence of the indigenous arts. The home, the church, and the town hall were the chief types of buildings erected, with the home perhaps claiming chief attention. Thus fine houses arose in the Northern seaports and on the Southern plantations — in

[1] Ralph Earle (1751–1801); Matthew Pratt (1734–1805); Charles W. Peale (1741–1827); and Gilbert Stuart (1755–1828).

[A] *Stuart. Mrs. Richard Yates. 1793. Mellon Collection, National Gallery of Art, Washington. (National Gallery)*

both cases Georgian in style, but more austere in the North, more expansive and genial in the South. Their interiors displayed fine woodwork, English styles of furniture (though much of it was made in the colonies), silver, and glass. Painting was confined chiefly to portraiture, at first the work of the limner, later that of painters in London or of American painters trained there. Sculpture, banned by the Puritans, was almost nonexistent except for the virile carvings found in hitching posts and ship figureheads.

BIBLIOGRAPHY

American Folk Art, Colonial Williamsburg, Inc., 1940

American Folk Art, Museum of Modern Art, New York City, 1932

Art in America from 1600 to 1865, University of Chicago Press, 1934

Avery, C. L., *Early American Silver*, Century, 1930

Barker, Virgil, *A Critical Introduction to American Painting*, Whitney Museum of American Art, New York City, 1931

Beard, C. A., and Mary, *The Rise of American Civilization*, 2 vols., Macmillan, 1927

Briggs, M. S., *The Homes of the Pilgrim Fathers in England and America, 1620–1685*, Oxford University Press, 1932

Burroughs, Alan, *Limners and Likenesses*, Harvard University Press, 1936

Caffin, C. H., *American Masters of Sculpture*, Doubleday, Page, 1913

——————— *The Story of American Painting*, Stokes, 1915

Cahill, Holger, and Barr, Alfred H., Jr., *Art in America*, Halcyon House, 1939

Chamberlain, Samuel, *New England Doorways*, Hastings House, 1939

Clarke, T. B., *Portraits by Early American Artists of the Seventeenth, Eighteenth and Nineteenth Centuries*, Museum of Art, Philadelphia, 1928

Cornelius, C. O., *Early American Furniture*, Century, 1926

——————— *Furniture Masterpieces of Duncan Phyfe*, Doubleday, Page, 1922

Cousins, Frank, and Riley, P. M., *The Colonial Architecture of Philadelphia*, Little, Brown, 1920

——————— *The Colonial Architecture of Salem*, Little, Brown, 1919

——————— *The Wood-Carver of Salem: Samuel McIntire, His Life and Work*, Little, Brown, 1916

Drepperd, Carl W., *American Pioneer Arts & Artists*, Pond-Ekberg, 1942

Eberlein, H. D., *The Architecture of Colonial America*, Little, Brown, 1915

——————— , and McClure, Abbot, *The Practical Book of Early American Arts and Crafts*, Lippincott, 1916

Embury, Aymar, Jr., *Early American Churches*, Doubleday, Page, 1914

Flexner, James T., *America's Old Masters*, Viking, 1939

Foote, H. W., *Robert Feke, Colonial Portrait Painter*, Harvard University Press, 1930

Forbes, Esther, *Paul Revere and the World He Lived In*, Houghton Mifflin, 1942

Great Georgian Houses of America, 2 vols., Architects' Emergency Committee, 1933, 1937

Hagen, Oskar F. L., *The Birth of the American Tradition in Art*, Scribner, 1940

Halsey, R. T. H., and Cornelius, C. O., *A Handbook of the American Wing*, Metropolitan Museum of Art, New York City, 1932

Hamlin, T. F., *The American Spirit in Architecture*, Yale University Press, 1926 (*Pageant of America*, Vol. 13)

Hipkiss, Edwin J., *Eighteenth-Century American Arts*, Harvard University Press, 1941

Index of American Design, *Folk Art of Rural Pennsylvania*, Pennsylvania Art Project, Works Progress Administration

——————— *Pennsylvania German Designs*, Metropolitan Museum of Art, New York City, 1943

Isham, Samuel, *The History of American Painting*, rev. by Royal Cortissoz, Macmillan, 1927

Jackman, R. E., *American Arts*, Rand, McNally, 1928

Kimball, Sidney F., *American Architecture*, Bobbs-Merrill, 1930

——————— *Domestic Architecture of the American Colonies and of the Early Republic*, Scribner, 1922

——————— *Mr. Samuel McIntire, Carver, the Architect of Salem*, Southworth-Anthoensen Press, 1940

La Follette, Suzanne, *Art in America*, Harper, 1930

Laughton, L. G. C., *Old Ship Figure-heads and Sterns*, Minton, Balch, 1925

Lee, Cuthbert, *Early American Portrait Painters*, Yale University Press, 1929

Lipman, Jean, *American Primitive Painting*, Oxford University Press, 1942

Mather, Frank J., Jr., *Estimates in Art, Series II*, Holt, 1931

——————— , Morey, Charles R., and Henderson, William J., *The American Spirit in Art*, Yale University Press, 1927 (*Pageant of America*, Vol. 12)

Mumford, Lewis, *Sticks and Stones, a Study of American Architecture and Civilization*, Boni & Liveright, 1924

Murrell, William, *A History of American Graphic Humor*, Vol. I, Whitney Museum of American Art, New York City, 1934

Neuhaus, Eugen, *History and Ideals of American Art*, Stanford University Press, 1931

Park, Lawrence, comp., *Gilbert Stuart*, with an appreciation by Royal Cortissoz, 4 vols., Rudge, 1926

Pinckney, Pauline A., *American Figureheads and Their Carvers*, Norton, 1940

Rosé, Grace N., *Williamsburg Today and Yesterday*, Putnam, 1940

Rourke, Constance, *Roots of American Culture*, Harcourt, Brace, 1942

Sherman, F. F., *Early American Painting*, Century, 1932

——————— *Early American Portraiture*, privately printed, 1930

Swan, Mabel M., *Samuel McIntire, Carver, and the Sandersons, Early Salem Cabinet Makers*, Essex Institute, Salem, Mass., 1934

Taft, Lorado, *The History of American Sculpture*, rev. ed., Macmillan, 1924

Tallmadge, T. E., *The Story of Architecture in America*, Norton, 1927

Walker, John, and James, Macgill, *Great Ameri-*

can Paintings from Smibert to Bellows, 1729–1924, Oxford University Press, 1943

Weitenkampf, Frank, *American Graphic Art*, new ed., Macmillan, 1924

See also the General Bibliography, pp. 791–92.

40

INDIAN ART

SEVERAL groups of Indians profited profoundly by the coming of the Europeans, because the white man brought them the material means whereby they brought their native culture into flowering without accepting European forms. Chief of these were the Northwest Coast, the Plains, and the Navaho tribes.

Northwest Coast Indian Art

THE Indians of the coasts of British Columbia and southeastern Alaska were a fishing and hunting people who lived on an irregular rocky coast from which heavily timbered mountains rose abruptly. This timber, largely cedar, which grows to an enormous size, and the products of their hunting provided them with the raw materials not only for food, clothing, houses, and canoes, but also for all those objects of everyday and ceremonial life which constituted their art expression. Shell, bone, horn, and skins were abundant, but above all wood, and as a result these Northwest Coast tribes were the best woodworkers in America. Wealth from the fur trade with the Hudson's Bay Company and metal obtained from the white man in the eighteenth century brought the art

of wood-carving to an apogee in the nineteenth. Since then the culture has so far deteriorated that its art is negligible.

How this material should be used was definitely determined by their religious and especially by their social patterns; and their decorative designs, though infused with religio-social symbolism, derived from their own immediate realm of nature — beaver and seal, hawk and eagle, killer whale and shark, bear, wolf, frog, snail, raven, and dragonfly. It was a highly conventional, in fact highly stylized, art. "This art style can be fully understood only as an integral part of the structure of Northwest Coast culture. The fundamental idea underlying the thoughts, feelings, and activities of these tribes is the value of rank which gives title to the use of privileges, most of which find expression in artistic activities or in the use of art forms. Rank and social position bestow the privilege to use certain animal figures as paintings or carvings on the house front, on totem poles, on masks and on the utensils of everyday life. Rank and social position give the right to tell certain tales referring to ancestral exploits; they determine the songs which may be sung. . . . A similar relation, although not quite so intimate,

[A] *Carved Goat Horn Spoon Handles. Northwest Coast Indian. American Museum of Natural History, New York City. (American Museum of Natural History)*

prevails in the relation of religious activities and manifestations of art. It is as though the heraldic idea had taken hold of the whole life and had permeated it with the feeling that social standing must be expressed at every step by heraldry which, however, is not confined to space forms alone but extends over literary, musical and dramatic expression." [1]

Notwithstanding its conventionality and heraldic significance, it was a purely utilitarian art. The largest of the trees were scooped out into canoes (at times forty or more feet in length), which served as the chief means of transportation for both hunting and pleasure. The Haida Indians of Queen Charlotte Islands were particularly famous for their canoes, which were not only seaworthy but also shaped with a feeling for proportion and for the qual-

ity of line in their curving prows and sterns, which were carved or painted with the heraldic devices of the owner, who considered his canoe one of his most-prized possessions. From the abundant timber they built also their sturdy wooden houses, for which they cut planks sometimes sixty feet long. They also cut single poles nearly a hundred feet high, to be carved with totems — that is, with heraldic designs (derived usually from animals or birds) — which were the mark and the prerogative of the family or clan, or which illustrated a story or a myth (Fig. 653A). In carving these poles the cylindrical mass and the rounding surface of the pole were never lost. Only enough was cut away to leave clearly defined, with the help of conventional color, the totems, which were large in scale and imposing in their simplified conventional form. Frequently additional totems, adapted to flat design, were painted on the front wall of the house (Fig. 655A).

[1] Franz Boas, *Primitive Art*, Harvard University Press, 1927, p. 280, by permission of the publishers.

Another closely allied field for the wood-carver was the making of the masks which served purposes of magic and played an important part in the ceremonial dances that often were dramatic presentations of legends. These masks were sometimes human, more often birds or animals or legendary monsters. They were frequently very large in size, were made of several parts, and so contrived mechanically that they could be manipulated with strings, thus enabling the actor to achieve strange effects, such as opening the mouth of one monster only to disclose another within. As for their esthetic significance, some possessed a superior quality as wood-carving, in which conventional color had been used as an additional element to clarify and accent.

In the furnishings of their houses, the Indians' first regard was for the purpose of the object, its material, and the rank of the owner. With pottery unknown, wood again was the chief material, and out of single pieces were carved killing clubs, grease and food trays, bowls, spoons, and ladles, large for ceremonial use, small for everyday use. Since fat was always an important item in the diet of these Northerners, the grease dish for the fish and seal oil was more elaborate than the other dishes and was often heavily carved, painted, and inlaid with abalone and other shells. Spoons and ladles sometimes had horn handles or were made entirely of the horn of the mountain goat by boiling the horn until it was pliable, then shaping it in a mold, and finally carving the handle with totemic designs (Fig. 652A). Among their sparse furnishings boxes and chests played an important part, and even in large chests the four sides were made of one plank, which had been steamed by very primitive methods until pliant, and then bent to form the corners. These boxes and chests were carved and painted in red, black and

[A] *Indian Village Street Showing Totem Poles. British Columbia. (American Museum of Natural History)*

blue (Fig. 655c). The blue was used least, since the material from which it was made was rare and difficult to obtain.

In these carvings, whether on wooden dishes, spoon handles, boxes, or totem poles, a unity of style is apparent, a common attitude toward the forms of nature that serve as the raw material of the artist. For it is not the animal's appearance from which the artist draws his material, but his knowledge of its essential parts, each of which he has reduced to a conventional unit and combined according to the space to be filled. Each unit is based upon its most characteristic aspect, quite regardless of a consistent point of view; some from

[A]   *Chilkat Blanket with Bear Design. Of wild goat's wool and cedar bark. Light yellow, turquoise blue, white, and black. Such blankets were used as ceremonial cloaks. Chicago Natural History Museum. (American Museum of Natural History)*

front view, some profile, some from above. For example, in the killer-whale design the essential features — the long head with large mouth and prominent teeth, the dorsal fin, the body, the tail — have been reduced to almost geometric patterns and combined to fill a rectangular space: the full-face head in the center at the top flanked on each side by the dorsal fin; below, the head in profile repeated bilaterally; at the bottom, the tail, the body, and the dorsal fin repeated and combined. So conventionalized are these parts that cedar stencils are made for each unit, allowing a great variety of grouping, depending on the shape and size of the space to be filled. In a similar way the head of an animal may be shown front view and the body cleft into two parts and spread out laterally (Fig. 655A), again forming a highly decorative pat-

tern. This is the same attitude toward treating the figure that one sees in Chinese bronzes (Fig. 211A).

So conventional a style is translatable into various mediums. Hence we are not surprised to find that the woven blankets are similar in style to the carvings and the paintings on skins. In the field of weaving the *Chilkat Blankets* of wild goat's wool and cedar bark were woven in designs similar to those found in the carvings, and usually with totemic significance. Figure 654A has the bear design, woven in yellow, white, blue, and black. The central panel contains the front view of the face and various parts of the body; the side panels contain the profile view, stylized to the point of unintelligibility — at times even to the Indian, as it was in the Pueblo pottery designs. These blankets were used only on ceremonial occasions and were worn

[A]   *Bear Design. Painting on a house front. Compare this painted design of curving shapes with the angular woven design in Fig. 655B, each excellently adapted to its medium.*

[B]   *Tlingit Basket. Alaska. Woven of spruce roots with design of colored grasses. Museum of the American Indian, Heye Foundation, New York City. (Museum of the American Indian, Heye Foundation)*

[C]   *Carved and Painted Wooden Chest. L. 19 in. Haida Indian. National Museum, Washington. (National Museum)*

about the shoulders over a tunic woven with a similar pattern. The accompanying leggings of skins were painted and decorated with bits of bone or ivory which clinked with the movements of the dance; and there was an elaborate headdress of abalone shell and ermine — a costume of elegance and taste and worthy to uphold the dignity of the family or the clan. These blankets were woven by the women on the most primitive looms according to designs drawn on boards by the men.

The *Tlingit Baskets*, exclusively the work of the women, were woven from grasses and fern stems and were used for various household purposes, for berrying in particular; they were woven finely and tightly enough to serve as drinking-cups. They were all decorated, by varying the weave or by the introduction of colored weft, or by wrapping colored grasses around the weft strand on the outside. The decorative motifs thus worked out look geometric but have names, showing that originally they had a meaning, although it has frequently been lost. Many of these baskets, especially those used for berrying, are cylindrical in shape, with the decoration concentrated in zones (Fig. 655B).

The Plains Indian Art

THE Plains Indians, numbering more than thirty tribes, occupied the Great Plains and Rocky Mountain regions. Before the arrival of the Europeans they were seminomadic peoples, small farmers and narrow-range hunters, dependent chiefly upon the buffalo for food, clothing, and coverings, and using only the dog for a draft animal. It seems to have been a pinched life, with a negligible art expression. The coming of the horse, however, which was brought into the country by Coronado in the sixteenth century, changed their whole pattern of life; it transformed them into wide-ranging, dashing hunters and, with the rise of competition among the tribes, into fierce warriors. Now they could range far and swiftly and thus secure plentiful supplies of food and materials from the great buffalo herds. With a flair for the dramatic, they proclaimed their wealth and economic status by the number of their horses and by the splendor of their costumes and trappings. In their new, fully nomadic life, they could use only nonbreakable and portable articles. Even their houses, tipis made of skins, were easily portable. So, with the exception of fashioning weapons and peace pipes, or calumets, which they decorated with hair, beads, and feathers, their art expression was restricted to the embellishment of everyday objects. On their clothing they lavished their decorative skill until they evolved a costume that was not only adapted to the climate but highly expressive of their dashing spirit. Made of the skins of buffalo, deer, elk, and various smaller animals, such as the beaver, it was ornamented with fringes, porcupine quills, beads, and painting, and crowned by an elaborate headdress of feathers which fell from the head to the feet.

Quillwork was a peculiarly American craft, found among other tribes as well as among the Plains Indians. It is a kind of embroidery, and because of the nature of the medium it is angular and geometric. In the rare cases in which representative motifs were used, they took on a highly abstract form.

Beadwork blossomed out into a major kind of ornament with the introduction of glass and porcelain beads from Europe. Before the coming of the white man, shells, stones, and seeds had been used. The new material provided both color and flexibility of design, and while the patterns continued to be chiefly

[A] *Painted Shield Cover. Kiowa, Oklahoma. D. 20 in. National Museum, Washington. (National Museum)*

angular and geometric, some floral motifs appear with curved flowing lines, probably due to the influence of the French with whom the Plains Indians traded in the Mississippi Valley.

Painting was used to decorate not only clothing but also tipis and shield covers, and to commemorate some fight or hunt by a pictorial representation on a buffalo skin. A design on a *Shield Cover* (Fig. 657A), perhaps of magical significance, contrasts light and dark areas and geometric and naturalistic shapes to produce a striking, virile effect. It was an art of line and flat areas of color, truly two-dimensional, full of life and vitality in the fighting and hunting scenes, quietly abstract in the nonrepresentational designs. It is interesting to note that these two widely varying kinds of painting were a sex variation in the craft, the men producing the representational scenes on shields and hides, the women the nonrepresentational or geometric designs on clothing, bags, and containers.

Navaho Art

ANOTHER Indian tribe which owed its flowering to the gift of the white man was the Navaho. The Navaho entered the Pueblo area from the northwest about seven hundred years ago, and as raiding nomads they had no little effect upon the harassed Pueblos' concentration in and final abandonment of their villages. The art of the Navaho was negligible until the Spaniards brought them animals, tools, plants, and, somewhat later, silver. The sheep and the horse became vital in their economy — the sheep both for food and wool, the horse for mobility, enabling them to roam more widely for pasturage in their semiarid plateau land. The addition by the Spaniards of a number of plants to those the Navaho had learned of from the Pueblos (for the Navahos were masters in the art of borrowing and assimilating) led some to become farmers, but the majority remained seminomadic, roaming widely with their sheep in summer but staying close to their hogans, or winter log houses, in the cold months. They had no villages. In this environment they developed three arts: weaving, silverwork, and ceremonial rites.

Something of the weaving craft they had learned from the Pueblos, with whom they came into more intimate contact in the rebellion of 1680. It was a craft pursued by the women only; it met a daily need in a cold country; and it could be carried on under the conditions of their seminomadic life. The loom, made of logs, could be set up in the open, often attached to a supporting pole of the summer tent. The blankets and rugs were of tapestry weave, usually interlocked, thick and strong, and the patterns were boldly geometric, straight and angular (Fig. 659A). The older blankets were designed in stripes, and the colors were few besides the natural black, white, and gray of the wool. Later the introduction of bayeta, an English cloth which they unraveled to secure red threads, enriched their color schemes and in combination with varied and effectively spaced geometric motifs brought the art to a climax in the nineteenth century.

Silver, introduced from Mexico about 1850, was used for making bracelets, buttons, necklaces, and bridles, and was enriched with contrasting turquoise and coral. The finest pieces were hand-hammered or cast; the turquoises were hand-cut and polished to a soft dull finish; and the designs were as boldly simple as those of the blankets.

In Navaho ceremonial rites, notably in their sand painting, we find a unique aboriginal art, whose rudiments may have been learned from the Pueblos but which reached, in the hands of the Navaho, a lofty climax in which ancient religious significance and high esthetic value are inextricably intermingled.

Sand painting was but one phase of a curative ceremonial which included chanting, dancing, and costuming. The more elaborate rites, such as the Mountain Chant or the Night Chant, lasted as long as nine days. Lacking a written language, by means of these ceremonials the Navaho kept alive the legends and beliefs, the rich mythology and poetry of their tribe, cured illnesses, and provided a focus for social life among a seminomadic people. The sand paintings (also called dry paintings) were made by the medicine man and his assistants on the floor of a hogan especially constructed for the purpose. Colored sands — white, red, yellow, black, and blue — were secured by grinding stones from the near-by cliffs. With incredible poise and dexterity the "painter" made the designs from memory and freehand, squatting on the ground and dropping the sand with his thumb and forefinger onto a smoothed surface of ordinary sand. The designs were highly abstract and in content had to do with the gods and spirits, the rainbow, mountains, plants, and animals — all having some religious or mythical significance. When the painting had served its function in the ceremonial, it was destroyed with the same traditional precision with which it was made. The design followed strict rules as to composition as well as in the single figures, with individual variations permissible only in small details.

SUMMARY

The coming of the white man contributed to several Indian cultures plants, animals, and tools which enabled these cultures to evolve to a flowering. The Northwest Coast Indians, fishermen on a coast with a great abundance of fine timber, had already shown ability at carving with stone tools. With the acquisition of metal they

[A] *Navaho Blanket. Detail. Museum of the American Indian, Heye Foundation, New York City. (Museum of the American Indian, Heye Foundation)*

produced an extraordinary art of wood-carving — canoes, totem poles, and objects of everyday and ceremonial life. It was a conventional art, highly abstract and superbly decorative. The Plains Indians, with the gift of the horse, became wide-ranging hunters and warriors and developed an art of a highly expressive costume, elaborate with feathers, procupine quills, and bead embroidery (the beads another gift of the European). On shields, tipis, and buffalo skins they gave expression to their vigorous life in paintings of hunts and fights filled with dashing spirit. The nomadic Navaho, with the gift of sheep, horses, and plants, became semi-nomadic sheep-raisers and with the wool they produced brought weaving to a high level. With the introduction of silver from Mexico they achieved a forthright expression in that medium, now using the silver alone, now combining it with turquoise or coral. Though the Navaho assimilated the new acquisitions, at the same time they retained in pure form many of their traditional ways of thinking and of living. Thus they brought to a climax one of the great purely indigenous American arts, that of sand painting and the ceremonial of which it is a part.

BIBLIOGRAPHY

Adair, John, *The Navajo and Pueblo Silversmiths*, University of Oklahoma Press, 1944

Amsden, C. A., *Navaho Weaving*, Fine Arts Press, 1934

Armer, Laura A., *Sand-painting of the Navaho Indians*, Exposition of Indian Tribal Arts, New York City, 1931

Boas, Franz, *Primitive Art*, Harvard University Press, 1928

Bunzel, R. L., *The Pueblo Potter*, Columbia University Press, 1929

Chapman, K. M., *Decorative Art of the Indians of the Southwest*, Bulletin No. 1, Laboratory of Anthropology, Santa Fé, N.M., July 1932

Cossío, M. B., and Pijoán, José, *Summa Artis*, Vols. I–X, Madrid, 1931–46; Vol. I

Cushing, F. H., comp. and tr., *Zuñi Folk Tales*, Knopf, 1931

Douglas, Frederic H., *Plains Beads and Beadwork Designs*, Denver Art Museum leaflets #73–74, December 1936

——— *Totem Poles*, Denver Art Museum leaflets #79–80, December 1936

Douglas, Frederic H., and d' Harnoncourt, René, *Indian Art of the United States*, Museum of Modern Art, New York City, 1941

Earle, Edwin, *Hopi Kachinas*, with text by Edward A. Kennard, Augustin, 1938

Emmons, George T., *Chilkat Blanket*, American Museum of Natural History, New York City, 1907

Ewers, John C., *Plains Indian Painting*, Stanford University Press, 1939

Gillmor, Frances, and Wetherill, Louisa, *Traders to the Navajos*, Houghton Mifflin, 1934

Gilpin, Laura, *The Pueblos*, Hastings House, 1941

Goddard, Pliny E., *Indians of the Northwest Coast*, American Museum of Natural History, 1924

Guthe, C. E., *Pueblo Pottery Making*, Yale University Press, 1925

Hewett, E. L., *Ancient Life in the American Southwest*, Bobbs-Merrill, 1930

Introduction to American Indian Art, Exposition of Indian Tribal Arts, New York City, 1931

James, G. W., *Indian Blankets and Their Makers*, McClurg, 1914

Keithahn, Edward L., *Monuments in Cedar*, Roy Anderson, 1945

Kidder, A. V., *An Introduction to the Study of Southwestern Archaeology*, Yale University Press, 1924

Klah, Hasteen, *Navajo Creation Myth*, recorded by Mary C. Wheelwright, Museum of Navajo Ceremonial Art, Santa Fé, N.M., 1942

Krieger, H. W., *Aspects of Aboriginal Decorative Art in America*, Annual Report, 1930, Smithsonian Institution, Washington, D.C., 1931

Mason, O. T., *Aboriginal American Basketry*, Annual Report, 1902, Smithsonian Institution, Washington, D.C., Part 2, *Report of the U. S. National Museum*, 1904

Matthews, Washington, comp. and tr., *Navaho Legends*, Houghton Mifflin, 1897

Mera, Harry P., *Navajo Blankets*, Laboratory of Anthropology, Santa Fé, N.M., General Series, Bulletin Nos. 2–16, 1938–45

———— *Style Trends of Pueblo Pottery in the Rio Grande and Little Colorado Cultural Areas from the Sixteenth to the Nineteenth Century*, Memoirs of the Laboratory of Anthropology, Vol. III, Santa Fé, N.M., 1939

Navajo Blankets, New Mexico Art Program, Works Progress Administration, Santa Fé, N.M., 1942

Newcomb, Mrs. Franc J., *Sandpaintings of the Navajo Shooting Chant*, with text by Gladys A. Reichard, Augustin, 1937

Oakes, Maud, *Where the Two Came to Their Father, a Navaho War Ceremonial*, Pantheon Books, 1943

Reichard, Gladys A., *Navajo Shepherd and Weaver*, Augustin, 1936

Underhill, Ruth M., *First Penthouse Dwellers of America*, Augustin, 1938

———— *Pueblo Crafts*, United States Indian Service, Education Division, 1944

Vaillant, George C., *Indian Arts in North America*, Harper, 1939

Wissler, Clark, *North American Indians of the Plains*, American Museum of Natural History, New York City, 1912

Woodward, Arthur, *A Brief History of Navajo Silversmithing*, Northern Arizona Society of Science and Art, Flagstaff, Ariz., 1938

Part Four

[A] *Léger. The City. 1919. Gallatin Collection, Philadelphia Museum of Art. (Philadelphia Museum)*

MODERN ART

WORLD PANORAMA

T HE expansion of the European nations in the Renaissance era into various parts of the world, and the consequent drawing of hitherto isolated areas more closely together, was a prelude to a world oneness brought about by the dominating force of today — science. Science, after groping its way for centuries, expanded in the nineteenth century to become the overpowering factor of the twentieth century. Because of its discoveries, transportation and communication have become so accelerated that no place on the earth is more than sixty hours distant by plane and but few places cannot be reached immediately by radio. Thus in a large sense all areas have been brought together into one total world. This, however, does not imply unification. For while every nation is now a close neighbor to every other, by no means does each understand its neighbors. Ideologies and their outward expressions differ so widely that, as a result of the world's greatest struggle, World War II, a vast field of pioneering has opened for man — to understand and to live peaceably with all kinds of next-door neighbors; and, by giving and taking, to preserve his own national elements within a larger international framework.

Artists, as always, are caught up in the spirit and tempo of the age — and are confused by its impacts. Just as scientists are engaged in epoch-making investigation and discovery, so artists are imbued with the spirit of investigation in form. Possibilities are being explored in every field of the arts: in music, literature, architecture, painting, sculpture, drama, and the dance. New arts have appeared: photography, the cinema, and the arts of the machine. Much of this search for new types of expression has been stimulated by the oneness into which the world has been drawn. For the first time, European and American artists have now been brought into direct contact with exotic peoples all over the world and have been brought to a recognition of the significance and the lofty quality of the arts of the past in the Far East, in Africa, and among the Pacific Islanders and the American Indians — all of them presenting different kinds of visualization and forms from their own. To eager investigators, these forms have proved to be highly stimulating. On the other hand, the influence of the Europeans and the Americans upon other cultures has often been deleterious; most of the cultures mentioned are now in decadence or in transition. In the field of the handcrafts especially, rapid decadence has resulted, except among the more stalwart and understanding who strive to adapt deeply rooted traditional forms to changing conditions. Thus the bringing of all parts of the world within one periphery is bound to be profoundly influential, sometimes for better, sometimes for worse. Yet it not only broadens horizons but stimulates the investigation of form in the spirit of scientific research, and in an age of transition is sowing the seeds of a new era in all the arts.

Nineteenth-Century Art

THE nineteenth century was a century of upheaval, of ferment of new forces and new ideas in conflict with the old. The two great storm centers were France, torn by its Revolution, with its political, social, and economic realignments; and England, disorganized by its Industrial Revolution, with its equally vast social and economic as well as cultural consequences. The freedom of inquiry and liberal thought born of the Renaissance bore fruit luxuriantly in France in the eighteenth century, notably in the work of the Encyclopedists and Rousseau, and voices were already raised in denunciation of social and economic injustice. By the end of the century this expression flared into action in the French Revolution. The Thirteen Colonies in North America had already separated from England, but it was the upheaval in France that caused repercussions throughout both Europe and the Latin American colonies, where French thought and influence had been strong, so that before the middle of the nineteenth century all the Middle, Central, and South American colonies of Spain and Portugal had severed political connections with their mother countries and set up republics. Europe saw the abolition or the limitation of kings and aristocracy in favor of constitutional monarchies or republics, and the consequent rise of the bourgeoisie and the lower classes into positions previously limited to the aristocracy — with a consequent shaking of traditional culture.

The Industrial Revolution, starting in England, where scientific research and applied science ushered in the Machine Age, spread rapidly. The half-century from 1800 to 1850 saw the first of many inventions: steamboat, locomotive, transatlantic liner, and passenger train as well as the telegraph and the camera — all which, with other factors, eventuated in a great expansion of industry; in the rise of the wealthy manufacturer to challenge the wealthy landowner; in the drift of population to the cities where the manufacturing plants were located, with consequent overcrowding; in the emergence of those social and economic conditions which gave rise to socialism and other attempts to alleviate their injustice. The application of the scientific viewpoint, with its critical observation of phenomena, produced Darwin's *The Origin of Species* (1859) and a consequent long line of research; and a weakening of religious faith.

The arts, meanwhile, were passing through two phases. The first, from about 1820 to 1850, was the romantic movement, whose fervor was symptomatic of a new age that was replacing the dying Renaissance. In the glorification by the romantic movement of human emotions and of subjective, individual reactions lay a basis for the expressionism of today; and its intense search for undiscovered beauties led it first out of doors and then into the paths of legends, primitive and medieval life, and exotic cultures. The second phase — a result of the scientific attitude — was a realistic movement. This meant not only a realistic imitation of nature on the part of some painters — an influence of the newly discovered camera — but a change in subject matter from the historical, legendary, and exotic themes of the romanticists to the scenes and incidents of everyday life, particularly the life of the people.

Not only were the artists subjected to these influences of a changing age, but their whole social and economic basis was thrown violently out of balance. In earlier times the artist had filled a normal niche in the economic structure, usually as a member of a guild, for the independent artist as an independent economic unit rarely existed. Kings, popes, nobles, the Church, and the guild provided steady patronage. Supply and demand balanced, and there was no economic problem. A work of art — a building, a statue, a picture, a textile, or a book — was ordered at the shop, made, paid for according to contract, and fulfilled the function which the purchaser had in mind when he ordered it. In the seventeenth and eighteenth centuries,

the establishment of the French Academy with its autocratically imposed official sanctions, the growth of museum collections, and the birth of the idea of salon or exhibition painting created an artificial market. At the same time the abolition of the classes and institutions that were the great art patrons, and the coming of the machine, which practically abolished the handcrafts, destroyed the artist's normal position and function and created an entirely new situation, to which, even today, the artist is not adjusted.

It is over against this complex, confusing, rapidly changing flux of the whole fabric of civilization that we must see the art of the nineteenth and twentieth centuries. It is a situation by no means novel. The late Roman Empire in the early centuries of the rising Christian civilization is a comparable situation; or the fourteenth and fifteenth centuries in Italy when medievalism was waning before the incipient Renaissance. These movements, however, were simple and almost local in comparison with the complexity and the cosmopolitan breadth of the situation of the nineteenth century.

41

NINETEENTH–CENTURY ARCHITECTURE

FROM the late fifteenth century to the middle of the eighteenth, all the countries of Europe, not excepting Russia, felt the impact of Italian Renaissance architecture in its various styles — early, high, baroque — and reacted, each according to local conditions. In the second half of the eighteenth century, classicism, no longer interpreted by

the Italian architects but actually seen through archaeological investigation and firsthand knowledge of Rome and Greece, swept Europe and the Americas. It affected all types of buildings — churches somewhat less than civic, commercial, and domestic buildings. Sometimes it appeared in details only, as in an egg-and-dart molding, or a Doric

[A]   *Marshall Field Wholesale House. Chicago. H. H. Richardson, architect. 1885–87. Demolished 1930. (Museum of Modern Art)*

portico. More frequently it determined the entire design of the building. Now it followed Roman styles, now Greek. So one sees *Sainte-Geneviève* (also called the *Panthéon*) in Paris and the library of the *University of Virginia*, modeled after the *Pantheon* in Rome; the *Brandenburg Gate* in Berlin after the *Propylaea* in Athens, and the *Arc de Triomphe* in Paris and the *Washington Arch* in New York after the Roman triumphal arches; railway terminals, such as the *Pennsylvania Station* in New York, after Roman baths. Almost every city can boast a bank or a museum patterned after a Greek or a Greco-Roman temple — the *Bank of England* and the *British Museum* in Lon-

don; the *Custom House (Sub-Treasury)* in New York; the *Casa de la Moneda* in Santiago, Chile; the *Palacio de Minería* in Mexico City.

These are but a few illustrations of a neoclassical tidal wave which swept over all parts of the world that came under the influence of Europe. Thus in the midst of a century of revolutions we see the curiously paradoxical situation of artists looking to the past while being carried along the current toward a new age. This was due partly to the romantic movement, which whetted the appetite for a deeper understanding of the past and set it up as a summum bonum. In addition, as there had not yet emerged a new age coherent enough to manifest itself, the disintegrating Renaissance revealed its decadence, as is normal, in an archaistic expression. That classicism took so strong a hold on the youthful United States is due partly to the wave of nationalism which permeated the country and demanded a break artistically as well as politically with England; and partly to the influence of Thomas Jefferson, who saw in pure classicism a style which seemed to answer that demand.

Thus was implanted the ideal of eclecticism — the arbitrary acceptance of a historical style without regard to dissimilarity of climate, material, and function, in lieu of a style that naturally evolved from the local environment. Before the nineteenth century had passed, architecture in Europe and the United States had run the gamut (sometimes called "the battle") of the styles: Italian Renaissance, baroque, Gothic, Romanesque, Byzantine, or, again, classical; even Chinese variations and details indicated an acquaintance with the Orient. The choice was not the same in all countries, but varied according to national preferences. Yet the result was that even today the main avenues of almost any European or American metropolis reveal, fraternizing in friendly proximity if not in stylistic unity, a French Renaissance mansion, a Gothic cathedral, a Venetian club, and a Greek bank. "Style" frequently meant a façade frontispiece. Architecture and engineering were completely divorced, and function bore little relation to the "style."

However, in the minds of a few architects who realized the artificiality and sterility of the eclectic ideal there began to revive the concept of architecture as an organic structure whose form is related to the materials of which it is constructed, to its use, and to its whole cultural environment. They realized that expanding industry was demanding new types of buildings. Under the stimulation of swiftly developing science and manufacturing methods, the use of older materials was revived or expanded, as with concrete, terra cotta, glass, and tile, whereas iron and steel, by themselves or in combination with concrete, were the great challenge of the century. Iron had been used constructionally in combination with glass as early as the middle of the century — as in the *Crystal Palace* in London, a great adventure in iron and glass which provided an interior space flooded with light, admirably fitted for exhibition purposes and for a Northern climate. In bridges iron was used openly and frankly as a constructional material. In fact it was the engineers who were the first to discover the potentialities of the new materials and new methods of construction. But engineering and architecture were still divorced, and in most buildings where these materials served in engineering construction their use was hidden by exterior coverings until in the *Eiffel Tower* (1889) it stood forth in complete freedom and pointed the way to new forms.

The pioneers of a new style came chiefly from the United States, Germany, Austria, Belgium, Holland, and France. England, Italy, Spain, Russia, the republics of Central and South America were as yet untouched.

In the United States, an eclectic, strangely enough, was a prophet: Henry Hobson Richardson (1838–1886). His work must be seen against the trends of the United States following the Civil War. That war marked the triumph of industrial and business enterprise and resulted in a great expansion of industry and transportation, the rounding-out of the continent, and the exploitation of the West. The growth of industry demanded centralization and consequently an urban rather than an agrarian type of civilization. Thus arose the American

[A]   *Transportation Building. Entrance. World's Columbian Exposition, Chicago, 1893.*
Louis Sullivan, architect.

metropolis with its enormous wealth and ostentatious display — the "Gilded Age" — an acquisitive society based upon "rugged individualism" and the building up of huge fortunes, such as those of Morgan, Carnegie, and Rockefeller. Many of the plutocrats were bourgeois in type, and in their hands wealth alone captured the social citadels of the remnant of the eighteenth-century aristocracy. Their tastes brought in the "heyday of the scroll saw, Rogers groups, and the dime novel."[1] Permeating this local situation was the world ferment of the late nineteenth century, the age of applied science and advancing technology, of research in pure sci-

[1] Lewis Mumford, *The Brown Decades*, Harcourt, Brace, 1931, a brilliant analysis of the period.

ence, of theories of evolution, social ethics, and social democracy.

But building did not keep pace with this changing world. Frequent travel to Europe, combined with pressure from architects with European training, brought all building into the current fashion of the historical styles. Richardson, too, was one of these eclectics — enthusiastic, after sojourning in Europe, over one style, the rugged Romanesque. Yet he was one of the thinkers who realized that function, site, and materials are determinants in the building art. This he showed in the *Marshall Field Wholesale House* (Chicago; Fig. 665A), a building of great strength and dignity. Here is a clearly defined single volume bounded by clearly felt planes. Its massiveness is accented by the use of rusticated stone and by the strengthening of the masonry at the corners. But in consideration of its function, the walls are largely broken by openings that do not disturb the plane of the wall but which in the larger rounded openings below create a sweeping rhythmic movement that is repeated in double tempo in the smaller rounded openings above and is contrasted by the rectangular windows of the top story.

Another pioneer was Louis Sullivan (1856–1924). In the midst of the classical revival of the World's Columbian Exposition in Chicago in 1893, Sullivan's *Transportation Building* was a conspicuous exception. The portal (Fig. 667A) was a simple rectangular block with a wide projecting cornice and long unbroken lines. Within the rectangular frame, we see concentric arches swing about the doorway, which is flanked by projecting terraces repeating the motif of the cornice. Low reliefs, designed by Sullivan on foliate motifs, ornament the arches and the cornices, and form a border to the rectangle. They are so low that they do not mar the feeling of the surface but add a note of varying texture and of wavering light and shade.

Sullivan's famous dictum that form results from function determined in his own work the preliminary stages of skyscraper evolution. The pre-eminent place of industry and the crowded urban site; the scientific developments in elevator service, in illumination, heating, and protection from fire; and the use of steel, reinforced concrete, and fireproof brick as structural materials, combined with advanced engineering technique — all these considerations contributed to produce the skyscraper. The problem of designing such a structure according to Sullivan's theory was not easy. To reveal the structural steel framework; to use stone or brick or tile so that its appearance indicates its function as a sheath and not a support; and

at the same time to give the tall façade balance, unity, and variety — these were problems in skyscraper design. One of the first successful solutions was Sullivan's *Prudential (Guaranty) Building* (Buffalo), in which one feels the framework of vertical shafts and horizontal beams in the lines of the sheathing and the massing of larger nonstructural units to form an effective base and to provide the necessary large window openings.

A little later, in the *Schlesinger-Mayer Building* (Chicago; now *Carson, Pirie, Scott and Company Building*), Sullivan eliminated all the sheathing except the narrow strips covering the framework, and filled the space between the uprights with glass. In this way the windows became horizontal instead of the usual vertical and expressed more logically the proportion of both the enclosed space and the inner framework. Unbroken cornices at the top of the building and above the second story, together with a band of ornament similar to that on the *Transportation Building*, emphasize horizontality. The rounding corner, whose windows stress verticalism, is a jarring note and is said not to have been part of Sullivan's design.

These forward-looking experiments of Richardson and Sullivan, however, were submerged by waves of revivals — chiefly the classical, stressed strongly at the World's Columbian Exposition, and the Gothic, employed in churches and collegiate buildings. Eclecticism ruled while the attention and the energy of the people went into the development of the country, into scientific industrialism and the creation of huge fortunes. Under these conditions, the creative impulse found comparatively little encouragement. And yet: "The American, while adhering closely to his utilitarian and economical principles, has unwittingly, in some objects to which his heart equally with his hand has been devoted, developed a degree of beauty in them that no other nation equals. His clipper-ships, fire-engines, locomotives, and some of his machinery and tools combine that equilibrium of lines, proportions, and masses, which are among the fundamental causes of abstract beauty. Their success in producing broad general effects out of a few simple elements, and of admirable adaptations of means to ends, as nature evolves beauty out of the common and practical, covers these things with a certain atmosphere of poetry, and is an indication of what may happen to the rest of his work when he puts into it an equal amount of heart and knowledge." [1]

In Europe as well as in America, innovators were seeking new solutions, each individually, not as a member of an integrated group, though all were foes of the historical styles. Peter Behrens of Germany, Hendrik P. Berlage of Holland, and especially Henri van der Velde of Belgium — an active center for innovation — were working toward simplification both in the basic volume and in its surface treatment. Others, experimenting in new decorative motifs, produced the short-lived art nouveau, whose freely invented curvilinear

ornament, derived from plant forms, tended to mask the basic structure. Others experimented in new materials, such as iron alone or iron and glass. Still others sought for new uses of old materials — for example, Auguste Perret, in his concrete houses and the concrete church at *Le Raincy*.

Thus were planted in the work of largely isolated, forward-looking individuals the seeds of what came to be known in the twentieth century as modern architecture.

[1] A strangely true prophecy of art in America today, written by James J. Jarves in 1864 and quoted by Mumford in *The Brown Decades*, p. 186, by permission of Harcourt, Brace and Company. Continue the quotation for an extraordinarily clear evaluation of eclecticism.

BIBLIOGRAPHY

Addison, Agnes E., *Romanticism and the Gothic Revival*, Richard R. Smith, 1938

Boas, George, ed., *Romanticism in America*, Johns Hopkins Press, 1940

Cahill, Holger, and Barr, Alfred H., *Art in America in Modern Times*, Reynal and Hitchcock, 1934

Hamlin, Talbot F., *Greek Revival Architecture in America*, Oxford University Press, 1944

Hitchcock, Henry R., *The Architecture of H. H. Richardson and His Times*, Museum of Modern Art, New York City, 1936

Morrison, Hugh, *Louis Sullivan*, Museum of Modern Art, New York City and Norton, 1935

Mumford, Lewis, *The South in Architecture*, Harcourt, Brace, 1941

———————— *The Brown Decades*, Harcourt, Brace, 1931

———————— *Sticks and Stones, A Study of American Architecture and Civilization*, Boni & Liveright, 1924

Sullivan, Louis H., *The Autobiography of an Idea*, American Institute of Architects, 1924

[A]   *Constable. Hay Wain. 1821. National Gallery, London. (Art Institute of Chicago)*

42

NINETEENTH–CENTURY PAINTING

English Painting

THOUGH France maintained a supreme position as a dynamic art center, in the early nineteenth century England made a valuable contribution to the evolving tradition of painting in Europe. This contribution is found in the work of Constable and Turner, a culmination of the landscape-painting of Wilson and Crome in the eighteenth century. John Constable (1776–1837),

like the Dutch and like Wilson and Crome, found delight in a direct contact with his native landscape — in the light and warmth of the sunshine, the cool of shadow, and the movement of the wind and rain. The *Hay Wain* (Fig. 670A) reveals the quiet charm of the countryside in a composition that is informal and unconventional. In the foreground a hay wagon is fording a stream near a house behind which are luxuriant trees that cast cool shadows; at the right stretch the meadows glowing in the sunshine; masses of clouds move rapidly through the spacious sky. Something of the vibrant quality of light and air that was lacking heretofore appears in this picture, and a rich varied texture rather subdued in color tonality. These effects Constable secured by substituting for the traditional smooth surface of greens, grays, and browns, short thick strokes or dots of pigment of various hues laid over the ground color, a method known as *divisionism*, or broken color. Thus he gained not only a vibrating quality of light and air but a rich texture of surface, which he sometimes enhanced by manipulating the pigment with the palette knife as well as with the brush.[1]

Joseph Mallord William Turner (1775–1851) was also interested in light and air. But in contrast to Constable's intimacy with and rather close transcription of nature, to the solidity of his forms and the reticence of his expression, Turner, after a preliminary direct study of nature, was swept off into a world of imagination, into limitless space filled with light, in which forms lost structure and solidity and existed merely for the sake of the golden misty light and air which enveloped them. He usually chose subjects as dramatic as his color. Yet whatever literary titles he bestowed on his work, the majesty of sun, sky, sea, and mountains and the vastness, power, and grandeur of light-filled space were his actual themes. Since he was enormously prolific — there exist thousands of his oils, water colors, drawings, the *Liber Studiorum* — the selection of two or three is obviously inadequate. In the *Fighting Téméraire* (Fig. 673A), he is preoccupied with titanic nature. In the light of a brilliant

[A] *Blake. When the Morning Stars Sang Together. From the Book of Job. 1825. Metropolitan Museum of Art, New York City. (Metropolitan Museum)*

sunset and a rising moon, the old battleship is being towed down the harbor to the wrecking-yards by an efficient, puffing tug. Here a romantic subject has found a consistent expression, with structure and organization present, though freely unconventional. While in this painting the human interest associates itself with the landscape in a highly imaginative way, later paintings reveal almost abstract visualizations of space and light. In *Rain, Steam and Speed* (National Gallery), the structure and solidity of all objects are lost in the effect of the swift movement of the train through a driving rain — an effect secured by using a rather thick pigment in broken color. In the water color *Norham: Sunrise* (National Gallery at

[1] To illustrate Constable's technical innovations, contrast his early painting of *Salisbury Cathedral* (Victoria and Albert Museum), exact in its descriptive details, with the later Salting and Ashton examples of the same subject.

Millbank) phantom shapes float in the opalescent mist as a result of the thinnest washes of transparent color drawn over a masterly, lightly sketched outline.

A solitary in English painting was William Blake (1757–1827), the mystic who lived the largest part of his life in the world of his visions (Fig. 671A). "There assuredly never was a more singular, more inexplicable phenomenon than the intrusion, as though by direct intervention of Providence, of this Assyrian spirit into the vapidly polite circles of eighteenth-century London. The fact that, as far as the middle classes of England were concerned, Puritanism had for a century and a half blocked every inlet and outlet of poetical feeling and imaginative conviction save one, may give us a clue to the causes of such a phenomenon. It was the devotion of Puritan England to the Bible, to the Old Testament especially, that fed such a spirit as Blake's directly from the sources of the most primeval, the vastest and most abstract imagery which we possess. Brooding on the vague and tremendous images of Hebrew and Chaldean poetry, he arrived at such indifference to the actual material world, at such an intimate perception of the elemental forces which sway the spirit with immortal hopes and infinite terrors when it is most withdrawn from its bodily conditions, that what was given to his internal vision became incomparably more definite, more precisely and more clearly articulated, than anything presented to his senses. His forms are the visible counterparts to those words, like *the deep, many waters, firmament, the foundations of the earth, pit* and *host*, whose resonant overtones blur and enrich the sense of the Old Testament."[1] With an intuitive sensitivity for linear rhythms, he ob-

jectified these internal visions in linear designs — woodcuts, engravings with a wash of color added, wash drawings — composed of symbols by which he wished to objectify the elemental forces with which he lived. His drawings and paintings are not illustrations of an incident, but objectifications of an experience of a man who has seen through the incident to its fundamental implications and who struggles for a form suitable for their expression. In his claim that the Byzantine style was revealed to him one discerns a realization that his own objective and that of the Byzantines were similar — "to render visible the mysteries of the supra-natural world." Yet his style of drawing shows affinity with contemporary neoclassical art.

A movement in English painting that is perhaps of greater value historically than for the intrinsic worth of its expression was that of the Pre-Raphaelites and their sympathizers. The Industrial Revolution had plunged the country into a profoundly chaotic state, socially, economically, and artistically, and had brought about a transitional period between the handcraft period and the Machine Age — a transition from which we have not entirely emerged. Art became segregated and lost its contact with life. Taste declined. In 1848 seven young men[2] formed the Pre-Raphaelite Brotherhood, whose purpose was to break away from the bad taste and empty artificiality of the times and to substitute real ideas, a sincere study of nature, and sound craftsmanship. The brotherhood sought to regain the spirit of the ages that preceded Raphael. In 1857, when Morris and Burne-Jones in-

[1] Fry, *Vision and Design*, p. 214, by permission of the publisher, Coward-McCann.

[2] The best known of the group were Dante Gabriel Rossetti (1828–1882) and William Holman Hunt (1827–1910); in close sympathy were Ford Madox Brown (1821–1893), Sir Edward Burne-Jones (1833–1898), and William Morris (1834–1896). A champion of the cause was John Ruskin (1819–1900).

[A]   *Turner. Fighting Téméraire. 1839. National Gallery, London. (Anderson)*

stalled themselves in London as "artists" (a profession then looked upon as odd and hardly respectable) and attempted to furnish their rooms, all the furniture and hangings that could be purchased were so ugly that they were driven to make everything themselves — the designs, the dyes, the textiles, and the furniture. Thus began the Morris movement, which sought to bring back the old ideal of the craftsman who could make things not only useful but beautiful in shape, line, pattern, and color. The Pre-Raphaelites, besides painting and writing poetry, worked as craftsmen along various lines: they made stained-glass windows, designed cartoons for tapestry and wallpaper, and printed and illustrated books. The value of the movement lay chiefly in its protest against the bad results of the segrega-

tion of art from life, and in its efforts to make art a vital, spontaneous expression which manifested itself in a chair and a book as well as in a building or a painting.

BIBLIOGRAPHY

Baker, Charles H. C., *British Painting*, Hale, Cushman & Flint, 1934
Figgis, Darrell, *The Paintings of William Blake*, Scribner, 1925
Hind, Charles L., *Landscape Painting from Giotto to the Present Day*, 2 vols., Scribner, 1923
Leslie, C. R., *Memoirs of the Life of John Constable, R.A.*, London, 1937
Sitwell, Sacheverell, *Conversation Pieces*, Scribner, 1937
———— *Narrative Pictures*, Scribner, 1938
Turner, Joseph M. W., *Golden Visions*, comp. by Charles L. Hind, Nelson, 1925
Wilenski, Reginald H., *Masters of English Painting*, Hale, Cushman & Flint, 1934

[A] Ingres. *Madame Rivière. 1805. Louvre, Paris. (Giraudon)*

French Painting

THE aristocratic painting of eighteenth-century France is the point of departure for the revolutionary changes of the nineteenth century. The gaiety, extravagance, and frivolity of the French court continued to disregard entirely the ever increasing rumblings that were soon to swell into the terrific storm of the thinkers and the masses rising against absolutism and class privilege. A reflection of the more serious mood of the day is to be discerned in an earnestness and a severity that was finding its ideal in classical subjects. Attention had already been turned in that direction by the excavations at Pompeii (1755), by the publication of Winckelmann's *History of Art among the Ancients*, the first ever written on the subject, and by the popularity of Piranesi's engravings of Roman buildings. Hence it is not surprising that the pictures of the classicists, such as the *Oath of the Horatii* (Louvre) by Jacques Louis David (1748–1825), were received with great enthusiasm. In contrast to the lilting rhythms and melting color of rococo, the cold harsh art of David, linear, drab, almost monochrome, and sculptural in feeling, furnished a gratifying change and a mood that was apposite to the changing temper of the times.

Another classicist, Jean Auguste Dominique Ingres (1780–1867), found his inspiration primarily in the Florentines. The *Odalisque* (Louvre) and the *Madame Rivière* (Fig. 674A) are linear patterns to which color has been added for decorative and clarifying effects. In the *Madame Rivière* what impresses us most is the harmonious rhythm of the sweeping lines of the shawl as it winds over the shoulders and falls across the figure in a single great curve through which minor harmonies interplay; and the admirable adaptation of the whole design to the oval frame. Ingres' famous saying laconically summarizes his artistic creed: "Drawing is everything; color is nothing." As a result he was charged, especially by his opponents the romanticists, with affecting Gothic primitivism, with belonging to the school of Cimabue.

Meanwhile the storm had burst into the Revolution, the result of which was to liberate powerful energy and tumultuous feelings that could not find expression in the cold severity of David's and Ingres's classical ideals. Here lay the origin of the romantic movement (about 1820 to 1850). Now it was human feeling and Rousseau's faith in nature rather than rationalism that served as a guiding principle. Wagner poured forth his tumultuous music in a glorification of intense human emotions; in England the Lake poets, in more restrained though individual subjective expression, glorified the beauty of nature. The inescapable task of

[A] *Delacroix. Entrance of the Crusaders into Constantinople. 1841. Louvre, Paris. (Giraudon) Compare with Fig. 546A for a similar organization and expression of depth.*

painters who were aware of a movement so surcharged with emotionalism and vitality was to give expression to its mood. This task was not accepted by the classicists, who clung to their traditional formulas in a rapidly changing world. The romanticists, on the other hand, offered both new subject matter and a new style of painting; and *The Raft of the Medusa* of Théodore Géricault (1791–1824) precipitated the long struggle between the two schools to defend their respective principles.

In Eugène Delacroix (1798–1863), perhaps the most gifted romantic painter, baroque compositions with tumultuous rhythms stem from Rubens or the Venetians (Delacroix was self-taught, in the Louvre), though with not so complete a mastery in the perfect subordination of a complex composition to deep spatial rhythms as we see in Tintoretto, Veronese, or Rubens. In contrast to the tranquil, linear patterns of Ingres, cold in color and with largely lateral movement, *The Entrance of the Crusaders into Constantinople* (Fig. 675A) is a restless design organized by strong color and light in space. It is a dramatic subject characteristic of the romanticists, who found their ideals in history and literature. In the foreground a group of mounted Crusaders are advancing with flowing banners; on every side are scenes of killing and pillage, or pleading for mercy; low-lying in the

[A] *Courbet. La Mère Grégoire. 1855. Art Institute of Chicago. (Art Institute)*

background is the city of Constantinople, with the smoke of fires rising from the houses and the ships in the harbor. A strong movement sweeping inward from the foreground and repeated again and again defines a space in which the figures are organized by light and dark, warm and cool spots of color. "Gray is the enemy of all painting," said Delacroix. . . . "Let us banish from our palette all earth colors — keep the brush strokes distinct, not fused, and thus secure energy and freshness — the greater the opposition in color, the greater the brilliance." The short distinct brush stroke, and the juxtaposition of complementary colors, already being practiced by Constable in England, and used earlier by Watteau, Rubens, and Titian, are on the direct path toward a climax in the impressionistic movement later in the century.

A by-product of the romantic movement, or perhaps more correctly a direct result, was the new attitude toward nature and therefore toward landscape-painting, an attitude foreshadowed in Ruisdael. With Poussin and Claude landscape was an artificial, imaginative visualization of nature, contemplated, to be sure, out of doors, but constructed in the studio into an architectural unity. Not so with the "men of 1830,"[1] who carried painting out of doors — a novel idea — and actually painted in the forest of Fontainebleau near the village of Barbizon, or at least made detailed drawings to be worked up into paintings in the studio. In their passion for, and close intimacy with, nature they faithfully interpreted its moods. They also pictured its actual appearance, using a considerable amount of realistic detail. This was, however, attributable partly to the influence of the Dutch school of landscape, and especially to a recent discovery, the science of photography. To copy nature as the camera does became more and more the objective of many painters, for in the minds of the public the novel idea of an exact copy of natural appearance was rapidly becoming an ideal.

Thus we find two Corots: the early landscapes, painted both in Italy and in France, together with the late figures, composing one group; and the intermediate, more photographic landscapes painted around Fontainebleau, the other. In the early landscapes the space is carved out almost as clearly as in a Poussin, each building taking its place in accordance with the planes defining the space, and with the values of its hues. But the popular landscapes were painted at just the time when Corot

[1] Important members of the group were Camille Corot (1796–1875); Théodore Rousseau (1812–1867); Charles-François Daubigny (1817–1878); Jules Dupré (1812–1889); Charles Jacque (1813–1894); Constant Troyon (1810–1865); Jean-François Millet (1814–1874).

was caught in the wave of romanticism on the emotional side and by the influence of photography on the visual side. Thus an honest, sincere love of nature, by no means always sentimental, was befogged by affectation; and the artist's vision, which he possessed in large measure, was blinded by the novel idea of the exactitude of the camera in reproduction.

The same influences turned the capacities of Millet into sentimentalities and overrealistic reproduction of detail. On the other hand, like Corot, he revealed at times, especially in his drawings, not only a grasp of form and its organization in space but also a healthy interpretation of his subject quite removed from romantic sentiment, and together with Courbet continued the tradition of the Dutch genre painters, of the Le Nain brothers and Chardin.

The situation in Paris about 1850 was a triangle of three mutually antagonistic groups. One consisted of the academicians, chiefly followers[1] of the classical and romantic traditions, who controlled the salons and formulated strict rules as to subject matter, which must be religious or legendary, and as to handling — "high art" or the "grand manner," it was called. A second group was the Barbizon school; a third, individuals of forthright independence. Of this last group was Gustave Courbet (1819–1877), who "didn't paint angels because he never saw one," and who called himself "a realist." By this he meant not that he reproduced nature with the eye of the camera, but that he reproduced the actualities of nature in the raw in protest against the empty artificialities of the academicians, and in such a way that the representation was more compelling than the visual actuality. His subject matter shocked

[1] Couture (1815–1879); Cabanel (1823–1889); and Bouguereau (1825–1905) are examples.

[A]   Manet. The Servant of Bocks. c. 1879. Tate Gallery, London.

the Academy — The Stone-Breakers, La Mère Grégoire (wife of the keeper of a brewhouse), The Funeral at Ornans — living actualities, often crude and harsh. The simple boldness in his limited sober palette is in harmony with the elemental character of the subject matter; lights and darks meet abruptly along the edges of simplified planes; and a surface richness results from the various ways in which Courbet used his pigment, often loading it on heavily with the palette knife (Fig. 676A).

Another independent was Honoré Daumier (1808–1879), who for forty years satirized Paris by his lithographs in Charivari, and in the meantime painted a few pictures. His daily task of reaching essentials through simplification — essentials of form to enforce the essential meaning — undoubtedly influenced his painting in the same direction. Within a limited range of color — a color scheme reminiscent of Rembrandt in its tonality of warm browns and yellows — large bold areas of pig-

[A] *Daumier. Tenants and Landlords: "After Midnight." Lithograph. 1847. Art Institute of Chicago. (Art Institute)*

ment cut highly simplified planes, and every detail is eliminated which does not bear on the central idea. In *The Uprising* (Fig. 679A), diagonal planes, moving in from opposite corners by means of sharply contrasted lights and darks, carve out a space filled with a mob, though but a few people can actually be seen. One dynamic figure in the foreground tersely carved in light and dark, with a forceful diagonal movement, repeated in the half-seen figure on the left, symbolizes the threatening mood of the mob. Daumier, like Goya, penetrated deeply into the contemporary life of all classes and represented it in a form that was terse, compelling, and caustically satiric. His means were line of tremendous energy, and forceful oppositions of black and white (Fig. 678A).

Other independents were protesting, rebelling, and experimenting in this experimental century. The alternative

which every painter faced was to conform or suffer the penalty of heresy. The majority conformed; the minority, eventually victorious, rebelled. An important rebel was Edouard Manet (1832–1883). Gifted with unusual vision and a healthy interest in the everyday life about him, he began to place upon canvas pictures taken from the real world and painted in the brilliant colors that he saw in nature, and at once found himself the object of ridicule and scorn on the part of the upholders of the old traditions. His subject matter shocked the academicians, for it was taken, like Courbet's, from the living world — a bullfight, a girl tending bar, a horse race, a group on a balcony, a man in a boat, everyday people in everyday clothes. The subject as a vehicle for interpretation did not interest Manet as it did Daumier and Millet, and in this respect Manet is on the way to abstractionism. Equally revolutionary were his technical methods. Influenced early by Ribera and Velásquez, he first used a very limited palette, and laid the color on in broad strokes, light and dark meeting abruptly, with a generally flat decorative effect (Fig. 677A). Thus the *Déjeuner sur l'Herbe* and the *Olympia* impressed Paris as vulgar and indecent, in subject and in method equally. In the seventies, although he broadened and brightened his palette and used, at times, short strokes and ragged contours and filled the canvas with luminosity, Manet never wholly abandoned his strongly linear, patternlike effects.

One of the other influences that were making themselves felt in Paris in the second half of the nineteenth century was the Japanese print, whose linealism and asymmetrical composition had some influence upon Manet, as it did upon Edgar Degas (1834–1917). Another influence was the wave of realism which, in reaction to the earlier romanticism and under the spur of science,

[A]   *Daumier. The Uprising. Thought to represent a scene from the political revolution of 1848. Phillips Memorial Gallery, Washington. (Phillips Memorial Gallery)*

emphasized cool objective observation of the entire visual world. Degas's coldly impersonal attitude toward the visual world made him such an observer, and together with his predisposition for linear forms strengthened his affinity with Ingres. Anything in the life about him served as subject, though race horses and dancers were favorite themes. Whatever it happened to be, Degas saw it as clear line and pattern caught in some casual moment. The awkward pose of a ballet girl tying her slipper became a sensitively realized decorative motif in an asymmetrical composition whose first impression is as casual as the theme. This informality, the unusual bird's-eye view, the cutting of a figure by the frame, and the total

linear decorative quality all show a strong influence of the Japanese print. Though he also worked in oil, his most characteristic work was pastel, whose chalky texture was the negation of realism and a medium for effects of line and color pattern. In Figure 680A, the cracks in the floor moving inward on a diagonal define the space into which fit almost immaterial figures, patterns created by slender means, in violent contrast to the tremendous bulk of Daumier's figures — a curious combination of two- and three-dimensional form. But this art is not abstract, for Degas with his bitter wit or dry satire was a commentator on certain classes of society.

The tradition of contemporary satire

[A] *Degas. Dancers Dressing. Pastel. c. 1878–80. Private Collection.*

on a high plane again manifests itself in the dynamic Henri de Toulouse-Lautrec (1864–1901), an individual as surcharged with the satirical viewpoint as Goya, his progenitor by way of Daumier and Degas. His subject matter is the sine qua non of his art. Steeped in his passion for observing life, gifted to an extraordinary degree as a draftsman, he became the caustic recorder of one slice of life, the dance halls of Montmartre. Unlike Goya and Daumier, who saw beyond the personal to the impersonal, the generic, and the universal, Toulouse-Lautrec dealt with definite individuals, penetrating to the very depth of their lives and expressing his interpretation in a style as terse and caustic as his observation. With a few lines he caught a characteristic pose, exaggerated or distorted to force a point of interpretation or form, but nevertheless creating a striking design. *At the Moulin Rouge* (Fig. 681A) shows charac-

teristics that are probably due to the influence of the Japanese print — the unusual point of view, the asymmetrical composition, the working into space on diagonals, the cutting of the figure on the right, the strong silhouette, and the linear quality. And while it is pattern it is also definitely organized in space, for the group around the table forms the focal point in a space the frontal plane of which is marked by the strong mask of the dancer in the foreground, and the back plane by the lights in the background. At the same time it is a pattern as forceful and striking in its line, its light and dark, and its color as is the characterization of the well-known persons of the central group.[1]

A painter who quietly pursued his own problems apart from contemporary conflict was Pierre Cécile Puvis de Chavannes (1824–1898). His chief concern, mural decoration, is illustrated by the paintings in the *Panthéon* of the life of Saint Genevieve, patron saint of Paris. These murals are a harmonious unit in interior design, holding their place on the wall yet breaking up the wall area and lending color to the gray stone interior. For they are linear, the figures are simplified and decorative, and the depth is shallow or controlled by planes generally parallel to the plane of the wall, with the movement lateral. The color has a silvery tonality, with no deep shadow or violent contrast, for the range of hue, value, and texture is limited. Even with oils, Puvis de Chavannes succeeded in creating something of the effect of fresco.

The radicals of the seventies and eighties were the impressionists: Edouard Manet (in his later work); Camille

[1] For a detailed description and identification of individuals see the Art Institute of Chicago, *Loan Exhibition of Paintings, Drawings, Prints and Posters by Henri de Toulouse-Lautrec, 1930–31*, with critical comment by D. C. Rich, Art Institute, 1931.

[A]   *Toulouse-Lautrec. At the Moulin Rouge. 1892. Art Institute of Chicago. (Art Institute)*

Pissarro (1830–1903); Alfred Sisley (1840–1899); Berthe Morisot (1840–1895); Claude Monet (1840–1926); and Pierre Auguste Renoir (1841–1919) — to mention notable examples. Impressionism[1] was not entirely novel. The realistic trend of the day aided and abetted its complete objectivity; its technical method, the chief center of

[1] This term was not invented by the impressionists themselves. In 1874 Monet exhibited a sunrise scene to which he gave the title, *Impression: Soleil Levant*. As this title seemed quite expressive of the methods of the group, the term soon became current, but it was used at first in a sense of reproach and scorn for the painters who were the "ignorant and extravagant iconoclasts of established principles."

the storm, had long been foreshadowed — in color theory even by Leonardo; in actual practice by Titian in his late years, by Rubens, Constable, Turner, and Delacroix. The objective of the impressionist was to create an illusion of light and atmosphere, of light enveloping objects, which required an intensive study of light as a compound of color and its action upon surfaces. Local color, the impressionists discovered, was but relative, because of reflections from other objects and because of modifications due to juxtaposed colors. Complementaries, for example, if used side by side in large enough areas, intensify each other; if used in small quantities, they fuse into a neutral. Shadows are not gray, but are composed of colors that are complementary to the hue of the object casting the shadow, if not modified by reflections or other conditions. Furthermore, it is not only the actual hue but its value and intensity that must be represented with exactitude — all of which is highly complex.

To express the living vibrating quality of light, a technical method had to be discovered which in the physical use of pigment would reach the same effect; and this was found in divisionism, or broken color. Approach an impressionistic picture and it becomes unintelligible — a rectangle of canvas covered with streaks and dabs of thick pigment, the colors of the spectrum chiefly, unmixed. But move across the room and the objects appear, enveloped in glowing, shimmering light. This has happened because the little dabs of pigment were placed so accurately as regards tone and value that when the eye mixes them at the proper distance, they reproduce the shape of the objects, the texture of the water, the color in the shadows, and (because of their rough surface) the vibrating quality of the light. Furthermore, the juxtaposition of colors on the canvas for the eye to mix at a distance produces a more intense hue than the mixing of the same colors on the palette; the same principle, we have seen, was employed in the making of Gothic stained-glass windows.

Monet may be taken to illustrate the group. He knew very well that light, and therefore the appearance of nature, changed every moment as the light shifted. So, in his insatiable desire to understand thoroughly the appearance of an object under varying lights and atmospheric conditions, he used to paint the same subject from the same point of view a great many times, going out at sunrise with twenty canvases so as to

be able to catch quickly the elusive changes. And the results are astonishingly different. Each is a realistic rendering of a fleeting impression, a painting of the light and air which envelop objects.

Landscape was the chief subject matter of the impressionist painters, and in addition to the sparkling, vibrating, colorful surfaces of their canvases there is sometimes a lyrical interpretative mood. Renoir, however, was possessed by an absorbing interest in the human figure; he took sheer delight in unaffected feminine charm and frankly expressed his joy in it; but eventually he used it as a point of departure for creating abstract designs in deep space. His early work with its long brush strokes is close to Courbet and Manet, but even then he displayed a feeling for color in the abstract in contrast to the usual impressionist's exact reproduction of the hues and values in nature. This innate love of color — which probably received its first development from Renoir's working as a boy in the porcelain factory at Limoges — when combined with the impressionistic technique produced such a painting as *At the Moulin de la Galette*,[1] which, though impressionist in technique and simple in formal composition, still is far from being an exact copy of objective vision. The color is by no means a reproduction of nature, but something imaginative, something that ties the dancing rhythms into a unity; and there is a gaiety and a frank joy in people, a hint of Renoir's concentration later upon the figure. The scintillating light and the shimmering color that hold together the many diverse elements in *At the Moulin de la Galette* give way in *The Luncheon of the Boating Party* (Fig. 683A) to an interest in single figures solidly constructed and

[1] See Munro, *Great Pictures of Europe*, pp. 73–76, for a detailed analysis.

[A]   *Renoir. Luncheon of the Boating Party. 1881. Phillips Memorial Gallery, Washington.* (*Phillips Memorial Gallery*)

placed rhythmically in a deep space organization. The asymmetrical design working in on diagonals, reminiscent of Degas and Toulouse-Lautrec, is based upon easy movements guided by the figures and stabilized by repeated verticals. Every hue of the spectrum is there, hue melting into hue and producing a marvelously rich texture and at the same time constructing solid forms and organizing them into suave spatial rhythms. This interest in abstract rhythms in deep space, which links Renoir with Rubens, led him to paint many pictures of bathers,[1] a subject of great potentiality for the expres-

[1] See W. H. Wright, *Modern Painting*, Dodd, Mead, 1927, opposite p. 126, for two of these *Bathers* showing Renoir's transition to his fullest expression.

sion of deep space design. Renoir, because of the solidity of his figures and their spatial organization, forms a bridge between impressionism and post-impressionism.

Another painter who carried forward the theories of impressionism was Seurat. Georges Seurat (1859–1891)[2] attacked the problem from the angle of the psychological effect of line direction and line relationship and of the science of related colors. Steeping himself in the color theories of Delacroix and of the color scientists of his time, Helmholtz and Chevreul, he worked out a system of putting the pigment on in tiny roundish dots, of about equal size, with scientific precision as to the color rela-

[2] Together with Paul Signac sometimes called a neo-impressionist.

[A]   *Seurat. La Grande Jatte. 1884–86. Art Institute of Chicago. (Art Institute)*

tion of dot to dot (a method known as pointillism) — an enormously difficult procedure, as severely disciplined and painstaking as the impressionist method was spontaneous and exuberant. Thus he transformed the illusion of natural appearance into a precise organization composed of people and objects that are solid and arranged with mathematical precision in a deep space filled with sunlight and air; and yet which, paradoxically, form an extraordinarily effective pattern. Such is *La Grande Jatte*[1] (Fig. 684A), the pattern of which is based upon the verticals of the figures and the trees, the horizontals in the shadows and in the distant embankment, the diagonals in the shadows and the shore line, each of which contributes the psychological

[1] For a full analysis with numerous preliminary drawings and sketches, which indicate how coolly premeditated his art was, see D. C. Rich, *Seurat and the Evolution of "La Grande Jatte,"* University of Chicago Press, 1935.

effect inherent in the character of its movement. At the same time, by the use of meticulously calculated values the painter carves out a deep rectangular space, and in creating both pattern and space he plays upon repeated motifs: the profile of the lady, taken from the costume of the day; the umbrella; and the cylindrical forms of the figures, each so placed in space as to set up a rhythmic movement into space as well as from side to side. The picture is filled with sunshine but not broken into ever changing myriads of scintillating colors. Light, air, people, and landscape are frozen into an abstraction in which line, color, color values, and shapes cohere into an organization as precisely as the parts of a machine. A calculating, intellectual art is this — in no sense a mechanical procedure, but an art which, being of the lineage of Paolo Uccello's and Piero della Francesca's, like theirs moves by its serene monumentality.

BIBLIOGRAPHY

Barnes, Albert C., *The Art in Painting*, Harcourt, Brace, 1937
——— and De Mazia, Violette, *The Art of Renoir*, Minton, Balch, 1935
Bell, Clive, *Landmarks in Nineteenth-Century Painting*, Harcourt, Brace, 1927
Cheney, Sheldon W., *A Primer of Modern Art*, rev. ed., Tudor, 1939
Delacroix, Eugène, *The Journal of Eugène Delacroix*, tr. by Walter Pach, Covici Friede, 1937
Duret, Théodore, *Manet and the French Impressionists*, tr. by J. E. C. Flitch, Lippincott, 1910
Florisoone, Michel, *Renoir*, tr. by George F. Lees, Hyperion Press, 1938
Fry, Roger E., *Characteristics of French Art*, Coward-McCann, 1933
——— *Transformations*, Brentano's, 1927
Hind, C. L., *Landscape Painting from Giotto to the Present Day*, 2 vols., Scribner, 1923
Hourticq, Louis, *Art in France*, Scribner, 1911
Jewell, Edward A., *French Impressionists and Their Contemporaries*, Random House, 1944
Lassaigne, Jacques, *Toulouse-Lautrec*, tr. by Mary Chamot, Hyperion Press, 1939
Mack, Gerstle, *Toulouse-Lautrec*, Knopf, 1938
Marriott, Charles, *Modern Movements in Painting*, Scribner, 1921
Mather, Frank J., Jr., *Modern Painting*, Holt, 1927
Mauclair, Camille, *Degas*, Paris, 1937
Mourey, Gabriel, *French Art in the XIX Century*, Studio, 1928
Munro, Thomas, *Great Pictures of Europe*, Coward-McCann, 1930
Rewald, John, *George Seurat*, Wittenborn, 1943
Rey, Robert, *Manet*, tr. by Eveline B. Shaw, Hyperion Press, 1938
Rich, Daniel C., *Seurat and the Evolution of "La Grande Jatte,"* University of Chicago Press, 1935
Rutter, Frank V. P., *Evolution in Modern Art*, rev. ed., London, 1932
Speed, Harold, *The Science and Practice of Oil Painting*, Scribner, 1924
Uhde, Wilhelm, *The Impressionists*, Phaidon ed., Oxford University Press, 1937
Vollard, Ambroise, *Degas, An Intimate Portrait*, tr. by R. T. Weaver, Greenberg, 1927
——— *Renoir, An Intimate Record*, tr. by H. L. Van Doren and R. T. Weaver, Knopf, 1925
Waldmann, Emil, *Die Kunst des Realismus und des Impressionismus im 19. Jahrhundert*, Berlin, 1927
Wilenski, Reginald H., *Modern French Painters*, 2d ed., London, 1944
——— *French Painting*, Hale, Cushman & Flint, 1936
Wright, Willard H., *Modern Painting, Its Tendency and Meaning*, Dodd, Mead, 1915

Painting in the United States

PAINTING in the United States in the nineteenth century (about 1815 to 1913) was even more profoundly affected than architecture by its environment, particularly after the Civil War. The commercial aristocracy of the North and the landed aristocracy of the South, which upheld good taste, declined in the era of great material expansion toward the West and gave way to an industrial plutocracy devoid of a cultural tradition. This group furnished the patrons whose tastes the artist must satisfy if he was ever given an opportunity. For the passion of the wealthy patrons was to collect, to spend huge fortunes in acquiring "old masters."

The school of portrait-painting, the chief expression in painting in the Colonial age, lingered on in the East in the work of Thomas Sully (1783–1872), who painted technically accomplished portraits imbued with all the mannerisms of the late English portrait-painters, and in that of Samuel F. B. Morse (1791–1872), who was trained in France and attained a vigorous style and forceful characterization, as in his *Lafayette* (Fig. 686A). But Morse abandoned painting for the scientific field, partly because of the general aridity of the art field for the American painter and partly because of the rising vogue of the daguerreotype, which almost abolished the demand for the painted portrait.[1]

---

[1] Other important portrait painters were Chester Harding (1792–1866) and Eastman Johnson (1824–1906).

[A] *Morse. The Marquis de Lafayette. 1825. New York Public Library. (New York Public Library)*

Historical and mythological painting was stimulated partly by the new spirit of nationalism and partly by Benjamin West's romanticism with a tinge of David's classicism. It proved, however, to be histrionics rather than historical probity, despite the shock caused by West's audacity in clothing his figures in historically correct costume. The huge canvases of John Trumbull (1756–1843) seem mediocre patriotic illustrations rather than creative art, and the classical subjects of John Vanderlyn (1776–1852) and Washington Allston (1779–1843), painted in the "grand manner," were merely technically proficient artificial canvases for which there was no demand.

Interest in the local scene found a dual expression. A general feeling of nationalism inspired by a youthful nation, together with the influence of the illustrated weeklies and the stories of the "Wild West," was producing the tales of

Irving and Cooper and giving rise to a parallel expression in native landscape and genre. This landscape found its beginning in the so-called Hudson River school.[1] A true love of nature and a fine feeling permeate their work. Many of their paintings, though realistic in detail, are composed with masses of trees and hills at the side through which the eye is guided into space in the manner of Claude Lorrain (Fig. 609A). Their green and brown tonality recalls the Dutch and the early English landscape-painters. In Doughty and Durand we find more intimate scenes; in Cole, more grandiose and romantic ones, as a result of travel in Europe and the influence of Turner. The panoramists sought their subject matter in the newly discovered majestic scenery of the Rockies and the Sierras, in Mexico, and in South America, whose grandeur they attempted to express, at times with questionable results but sometimes with no small degree of success in creating an impression of majesty.

From the Hudson River school emerged Homer D. Martin (1836–1897), Alexander Wyant (1836–1892), and George Inness (1825–1894), men who contributed both native ability and more thorough technical proficiency gained chiefly under the influence of the Barbizon painters. The comparison of an early Inness such as *Peace and Plenty* (Metropolitan Museum) with the late *Home of the Heron* (Fig. 687A) shows an evolution from a panoramic vision and

[1] This name was applied to a large group of painters because many of them lived in the vicinity of the Hudson and the Catskills, though they painted in various parts of the country and even in Mexico, South America, and the Mediterranean countries. Important among them were Washington Allston (1779–1843), Thomas Doughty (1793–1856), Asher Brown Durand (1796–1886), Thomas Cole (1801–1848), John Frederick Kensett (1818–1872); and the panoramists Frederick Edwin Church (1826–1900), Albert Bierstadt (1830–1902), and Thomas Moran (1837–1926).

[A]   *Inness. Home of the Heron. 1893. Edward B. Butler Collection, Art Institute of Chicago.* (*Art Institute*)

a painstaking recording of objective detail to a broad synthesis of essentials selected for the purpose of interpretation.

Similar in attitude toward the local scene were the genre painters,[1] who found their inspiration in the everyday scene within the home, in the yard, the city street, the country, the "Wild West." Their honest, frank pleasure in such scenes manifested itself in truth to objective appearance. With the advent of the camera they entered into competition to attain an actual verisimilitude. Such paintings as Hovenden's, as Brown's newsboys and Boughton's pilgrims, became merely storytelling snapshots. Not so the work of Johnson,

Homer, and Eakins, in which the genre content was expressed in a form founded upon visualization rather than upon vision and upon organization of elements rather than upon a reproduction of actuality.

Patronage, however, was moving in a different direction. The confusion which followed the Civil War and the rise of the "Gilded Age" with its wealth, its insistence upon European products, and its scorn of American products, had made "European" synonymous with "artistic." To Europe, therefore, American artists flocked in an effort to supply the demand. But in vain, for the patrons purchased names (European) rather than paintings. Some of the painters went to Düsseldorf and Munich,[2] where

[1] John L. Krimmel (1787–1821); Henry Inman (1801–1846); William S. Mount (1807–1868); George Caleb Bingham (1811–1879); Thomas Hovenden (1840–1895); Frederic Remington (1861–1909); Eastman Johnson (1824–1906); Winslow Homer (1836–1910); Thomas Eakins (1844–1916).

[2] Notably William Merritt Chase (1849–1916); Frank Duveneck (1848–1919); John W. Alexander (1856–1915); Walter Shirlaw (1838–1909).

[A] *Eakins. The Pathetic Song. 1881. Corcoran Gallery of Art, Washington. (Corcoran Gallery)*

they acquired a technique of bold vigorous brushwork, the use of black or dark colors, and strong contrasts in value. Chase's *Woman with a Shawl* exemplifies this style admirably. More went to Paris[1] into the ateliers of the popular academic painters and learned the formulas governing "proper" subject matter and a suave technique expended chiefly upon figure-painting based upon a visual perception of the model.

In both Germany and France these young men gained a sound routine

[1] Of this large group important examples are Kenyon Cox (1856–1919); Elihu Vedder (1836–1923); Abbott H. Thayer (1849–1921); Thomas W. Dewing (1851–1938); Edwin H. Blashfield (1848–1936); Edwin A. Abbey (1852–1911); Edmund C. Tarbell (1862–1938); Frank Weston Benson (1862–   ); George de Forest Brush (1855–1941). Their work is largely figure work and murals, with some portraits.

training and became able technicians. But imbued with European salon ideals and confronted with the Europeanizing of the United States, they found themselves at one point of an unfortunate triangle: a lusty new republic deep in the nineteenth-century ferment: a patronage with untrained, artificial (if any) taste, quite unconscious of, if not snobbish toward, a vigorous stimulating birthright in art, and quite blind to any role that the artist might play in the American commonwealth; and the painters themselves, caught between these divergent elements. In view of the situation some of the painters remained in Europe; others came home to practice what was largely art for art's sake rather than an art that grew out of and functioned in the culture which produced them. Some assimilated their European training better than others — a repetition of Stuart vs. Copley; some displayed more virility and independence, Vedder for example, in his strongly linear style, which he made personal even though it was based upon Ingres and the latter's Italian prototypes. John La Farge (1835–1910) was another independent who through his wide travel in the Far East as well as in Europe contributed a breadth of outlook and a feeling for sound craftsmanship that is seen particularly in his work in glass. In this medium, in protest against the degraded practice of painting pictures on glass, he revived the medieval conception of a mosaic of small units of glass colored in the pot and leaded into a flat decorative design.

Of the painters who remained permanently abroad, Whistler and Sargent are prominent examples. James Abbott McNeill Whistler (1834–1903) was one of the first to come within the periphery of the French revolutionary painters, with the result that Courbet, Manet, and through them Velásquez, Degas, Japanese prints, and the early impres-

[A]   *Sargent. The Wyndham Sisters. 1900. Metro-politan Museum of Art, New York City. (Metro-politan Museum)*

[B]   *Whistler. Portrait of Miss Alexander. 1872. W. C. Alexander Collection, London.*

sionists, are easily discernible influences in his work. In protest against the current realistic anecdotal painting, whose objective was the story and the snapshot, he became a champion of art for art's sake. But his method of protesting was characteristically personal, a mixture of individual irritation and sound fundamentals. He preached[1] and practiced the subordination of content in favor of "Harmonies," "Arrangements," "Nocturnes." Some of the portraits, especially *Miss Alexander* (*Harmony in Grey and Green*), *Mother* (*Harmony in Grey and Black*), and *Carlyle*, reveal a sensitive organization with an emphasis on pattern and with subtle harmonies

[1] For his theories see his *Ten o'Clock*, North, 1908.

through modulated values within a narrow range of hue. In the *Alexander* portrait (Fig. 689B), the young girl is standing before a paneled background of gray and black, wearing a white dress with a green sash and carrying a hat with a green plume. The gray and green, with black and gold, dominate the composition. In some parts they are massed strongly; in others they consist of faint strokes. Compositionally, rectangles, triangles, and circles repeat and contrast. His use of the bird's-eye point of view, the informal asymmetrical composition, the flowers breaking into the frame, the color relation, and the strong linear quality — these are evidences of the same influence that we found in Degas, that of the Japanese print; the

[A]　*Homer. Northeaster. 1895. Metropolitan Museum of Art, New York City.* (*Metropolitan Museum*)

full-length figure, so characteristic of Whistler's portraits, the use of black and neutrals, the emphasis upon values, and the brushwork reveal a strong influence of Velásquez. Despite his art for art's sake, Whistler was important in nineteenth-century painting because he struggled for the reinstatement of formal values in an art that had lost all sense of them as it tried to vie with the new realism attained by the camera.

John Singer Sargent (1856–1925), born in Florence and trained in the academic Parisian atmosphere, became the popular portrait-painter of socially prominent wealthy patrons. A virtuoso in pigment, he created surface effects with his brilliant dashing brushwork. But his paintings were devoid of formal significance and penetrating interpretation. In the *Wyndham Sisters* (Fig. 689A), for example, there is neither compositional value nor characterization, but only a superficial virtuosity in creating an effect of glamorous elegance.

In contrast to the Europeanized painters were the "solitaries," who assimilated whatever, if any, European training and travel they had had and pursued their profession frequently in obscurity or isolation, without regard to the popular tastes and fashions of the day. Characteristic of this group were George Fuller (1822–1884); Thomas Eakins (1844–1916); Albert P. Ryder (1847–1917); and Winslow Homer (1836–1910). Eakins, though thoroughly trained in Europe, kept his feet firmly planted on local ground and his eyes fixed unwaveringly upon whatever he was painting — chiefly the people and scenes of his own immediate environment — and produced the finished work after making a large number of preliminary drawings. The term "realist" is usually applied to Eakins.

[A] *Ryder. Moonlit Cove. 1890–1900. Phillips Memorial Gallery, Washington.* (*Phillips Memorial Gallery*)

He was a realist not in the sense of photographic verisimilitude but in his presentation of the essentials of objectivity based upon a thorough understanding of structure. His sober color and uncompromising fidelity to objective reality make his art austere. At times it displays weak passages esthetically or a lack of complete consistency and unity of the esthetic elements. For the *what*, vividly perceived, tended to overbalance the *how*. Yet its thoroughness and probity have been a steadying influence in the evolution of an American tradition (Fig. 688A).

Another sound influence in the latter part of the nineteenth century, though like that of Eakins not felt in the midst

of the "Gilded Age," was that of Winslow Homer. His work as an illustrator for *Harper's Weekly* until 1875 perhaps determined the strongly illustrative character of much of his painting. After some European travel during which he purposely avoided art centers, and a sojourn in the tropics, the result of which was some of his best water colors, he settled on the Maine coast and in isolation devoted himself to the interpretation of that locality. Like Eakins, he was firmly rooted in his own environment and did not scorn to use it as his raw material. While visual perception was his starting-point and his objective, he expressed it with economy and with as much concern for the organization

[A] *Unknown Artist. Glass Bowl with Fruit. c. 1820. Museum of Modern Art, New York City. (Museum of Modern Art)*

as a youth on the shores of Long Island Sound. Such a painting as *Moonlit Cove* (Fig. 691A) is a consistent expression of Ryder's imaginative rendering of actuality.

Close to the "solitaries" in distinction from the European-minded painters, and as untrained as the mystic Ryder, were the so-called primitives, whose work constituted a folk art, in which the subject matter was set forth with spontaneous directness. The untrained worker had to reach his objective in his own way, usually by means of conventions rather than naturalistically. Some of these paintings, in which intuitive esthetic feeling was joined with sound craftsmanship, attained a high quality. In landscape the work of Joseph Pickett (1848–1918) illustrates the type (Fig. 693A). Still life, reflecting an art of the home, was popular, and frequently exhibits no little sensitivity to formal values (Fig. 692A). The work of these folk artists is found in many mediums besides painting. It is largely anonymous, local, and much of it utilitarian — weathervanes, hitching posts, ships, figureheads, decoys, textiles and embroideries, and furniture.

Though impressionism had won recognition in Paris before 1886 and an exhibition of impressionistic pictures was held in New York in 1885, it had almost no effect upon the United States until the last decade of the century, when a few pioneers [1] began using the technique and thus opened up novel uses of pigment and a more intense and varied color. Basically, however, the

through which he expressed this raw material as for the material itself. In the *Northeaster* (Fig. 690A), for example, the relationship of lines and light and dark areas, the contrasts of movement and immobility, are largely responsible for the expression and interpretation of this storm-resistant shore.

If Eakins and Homer are more or less realists both in content and in manner of expression, Ryder was the visionary, the mystic, and the abstractionist — the Blake, as he has been called, of American painting, though he lacked Blake's great ability in drawing and in design. Clumsy in the use of his medium, for he was untrained even in the fundamentals of his craft, he reduced the elements of his composition to the simplest pattern and color, and labored over the surface, building it up thickly into a smooth texture. The sea, especially in moonlight — a favorite subject — was rooted in his own experience

[1] John H. Twachtman (1853–1902); J. Alden Weir (1852–1919); Willard L. Metcalf (1858–1925); Childe Hassam (1859–1935); Maurice B. Prendergast (1859–1924); Willis Redfield (1869–); Ernest Lawson (1873–1939); Frederick Carl Frieseke (1874–1939); Gifford Reynolds Beal (1879–); Jonas Lie (1880–1940); and Mary Cassatt (1845–1926), who, however, clung more to the style of Degas and Manet than to the truly impressionistic.

[A] *Pickett. George Washington under Council Tree, Coryell's Ferry, New Hope, Pennsylvania. 1914–18. Newark Museum. (Newark Museum)*

result was the substitution of one French technique for another, though the Americans used impressionism with considerable individual variations.

Professionally, the American painter was now well equipped. But on the one hand, he had lost contact with his own root actualities; on the other, affluent patrons were still purchasing European pictures, Dutch or French salon or Barbizon styles being particularly popular; while the public was captivated by the anecdotal, photographic picture, usually sentimental, such as Israels'

Alone in the World, or Hovenden's *Breaking Home Ties* (the prize painting by popular vote of the 1893 World's Columbian Exposition). Thus, apart from a few commissions for murals and portraits, there was no function for the painter and little demand for his product.

In protest against this almost exclusive patronage of European painters, in 1898 The Ten[1] organized and held an ex-

[1] Merritt Chase, Thomas W. Dewing, Childe Hassam, Edmund C. Tarbell, John H. Twachtman, and Alden Weir are the best known.

[A]   *Sloan. Backyards, Greenwich Village. 1914. Whitney Museum of American Art, New York City. (C. W. Kraushaar)*

hibition of their work. Another line of offense was developing among the young painters of the last decade of the century, with Robert Henri a leader in the attack. Individualists, soundly trained at home and abroad, they had sought stimulation wherever they could find it, in the Louvre and among the French rebels rather than in the academic ateliers of Paris; and at home their profession as newspaper illustrators had thrust upon them, as it had upon Homer and Daumier, immediate contemporary life in all its phases as raw material for the artist.

In 1908 The Eight organized in rebellion against the tyranny of authority in art in general and of Europeanized studio art in particular. The diversity of aim and of style in this group,[1] united though they were in their general objective, infused health and individuality into the evolving American tradition. Three of the group, Prendergast, Glackens, and Lawson, were luminists; Henri and Luks worked in the Chase and Duveneck tradition of vigorous brushwork with strong contrasts in values, though their objective in painting — human significance — differed from that of the

[1] Robert Henri (1865–1929); Maurice B. Prendergast (1859–1924); Arthur B. Davies (1862–1928); George B. Luks (1867–1933); William J. Glackens (1870–1938); Ernest Lawson (1873–1939); John Sloan (1871–   ); George W. Bellows (1882–1925).

[A] *Bellows. A Stag at Sharkey's. 1909. Hinman B. Hurlbut Collection, Cleveland Museum of Art. (Cleveland Museum)*

latter two, who were inclined to place technique and fine painting first. In this respect Henri and Luks were close to Manet, as they were at times technically. Davies, though in his personal life and work he lived in the realm of fantasy, was a wholehearted supporter of the movement, and made an individual pioneer contribution by working in a large number of mediums, and thus broke the narrowly specialized craft of the American painter.

The influence of Henri was felt upon his contemporary Sloan and the somewhat younger George Bellows. With these two painters — both were also accomplished etchers and lithographers — the objective became the interpretation of the American scene, the human actualities of their own milieu. Sloan's

keen observation was probably stimulated by Eakins's paintings, for his early training was in Philadelphia, but the satiric strain with which he infused his observations was his own (Fig. 694A). Much of his work is a faithful interpretative record of life in the alleys, back yards, bars, and harbor of New York, and some of his best productions are etchings.

Because of their subject matter, which shocked the academic painters and the public as well, the whole group associated with Sloan and Bellows was contemptuously dubbed the ashcan school. Of all the group Bellows perhaps plunged most wholeheartedly into the contemporary scene, and because of his forceful personality frequently selected vigorous and dramatic subjects, such as *A Stag at Sharkey's* (Fig. 695A), in which one sees the vigor of his brushwork, a technical use of pigment consistent with the energy of his personality, strongly contrasting values, and accomplished composition. It was members of this group who were responsible for bringing to the United States the International Exhibition of Modern Art (known as the Armory Show) of 1913, a show which was a definite landmark in the modern movement on this side of the Atlantic.

BIBLIOGRAPHY

American Folk Art, Museum of Modern Art, New York City, 1932

American Painting & Sculpture, 1862–1932, Museum of Modern Art, New York City, and Norton, 1932

Bushnell, David J., Jr., *Sketches by Paul Kane in the Indian Country, 1845–1848*, Smithsonian Institution, Washington, D.C., 1940

Cahill, Holger, and Barr, Alfred H., Jr., *Art in America*, Halcyon House, 1939

A Century of American Landscape Painting, 1800–1900, Whitney Museum of American Art, New York City, 1938

Cortissoz, Royal, *American Artists*, Scribner, 1923

Cowdrey, Bartlett, and Williams, Hermann W., Jr., *William Sidney Mount*, Columbia University Press, 1944

Drepperd, Carl W., *American Pioneer Arts & Artists*, Pond-Ekberg, 1942

Duret, Théodore, *Whistler*, tr. by Frank Rutter, Lippincott, 1917

Goodrich, Lloyd, *Thomas Eakins, His Life and Work*, Whitney Museum of American Art, 1933

———— *Winslow Homer*, Macmillan, 1944

Inness, George, Jr., *Life, Art, and Letters of George Inness*, Century, 1917

Janis, Sidney, *They Taught Themselves*, Dial Press, 1942

Life in America, Metropolitan Museum of Art, New York City, 1939

Lipman, Jean, *American Primitive Painting*, Oxford University Press, 1942

Mather, Frank J., Jr., Morey, Charles R., and Henderson, William J., *The American Spirit in Art*, Yale University Press, 1927, *Pageant of America*, Vol. 12

Mumford, Lewis, *The Brown Decades*, Harcourt, Brace, 1931

Pennell, E. R., and Joseph, *The Life of James McNeill Whistler*, 6th ed. rev., Lippincott, 1920

Peters, Harry T., *Currier & Ives*, Doubleday, Doran, 1942

Richardson, Edgar P., *American Romantic Painting*, Weyhe, 1944

———— *The Way of Western Art, 1776–1914*, Harvard University Press, 1939

Sixth Loan Exhibition, New York, May, 1930; Winslow Homer, Albert P. Ryder, Thomas Eakins, Museum of Modern Art, New York City, 1930

Whitney Museum of American Art, monographs by various authors on Bellows, Davies, Glackens, Luks, Prendergast, Twachtman, and others

See also the General Bibliography, pp. 791–92.

Latin American Painting and Folk Arts

EARLY in the nineteenth century, Spain was already decadent and was permeated by French influence through the coming of the Bourbons to the throne. The Spanish colonies, engulfed in oppression and intolerance, were becoming restless. Their leaders, notably Miranda, Bolívar, and San Martín, imbued with French liberal thought and witnessing the actual practice of freedom in the one-time English colonies followed by the great outburst of the French Revolution, eventually brought their own lands to independence. But their revolutions were much more formidable than that in the English colonies, which were relatively small and compact, politically and socially homogeneous, and had had some experience in self-government. The Spanish colonies, on the contrary, were spread over vast areas in which geographical diversity and almost insurmountable difficulties of travel and transportation militated against unity. There were racial differences, also. Large unassimilated elements were held in peonage by a small ruling class who, despite freedom from Spain, wished to perpetuate the existing social and economic system. Closely linked with this class was the Church, still wealthy and powerful. Thus the revolutions in Hispanic and Portuguese America lasted longer than that in the English colonies, varied in different parts of the continent, and, because of lack of experience in self-government under the oppressive Spanish rule, were followed by periods of disorder, or even chaos. In fact, in some of these countries this condition still exists. On the whole, culturally, the South American countries have clung more tenaciously to Europe than have those of North America.

In these circumstances — far more even than in the case of the English colonies — freedom in art did not follow political freedom. The colonial ideal continued. What happened usually was merely a shift from Spain to France; a few of the former colonies remained loyal culturally to the mother country. Important changes, however, did take place. The ecclesiastical art of the colonial age was largely superseded by an art that was secular both in content and in control, the control passing to lay institutions, frequently to the government itself. Government-sponsored academies were established, manned by Europeans who were mostly French, and pupils were sent to Paris for further training. Thus while art was liberated from the domination of the Church, it fell under that of the French Academy, with its official exhibitions, salons, and building-up of collections. Painters, instructors, and students alike clung to the academic wing of French art — the classicists, the romanticists, with perhaps a slight contact with the Barbizon group, or the atelier of Bouguereau — and imbibed the ideology as well as the technique of the French salon. On the whole they were quite untouched by the great revolution going on in French painting.

Thus classicism in painting followed closely on the classical movement in architecture that had already swept the Continent, and pupils of David were coming to most of the important Latin American cities both as painters and as instructors in the academies. But, as in Europe, the liberalizing effect of romanticism was more in accord with the spirit of the independence movement.

One cannot generalize about the complex art movements in this large number of countries,[1] all of which were living through revolutions and periods of chaos. Perhaps one outstanding fact is that no great art expression resulted from these upheavals in the nineteenth century. However, we can discern three general currents or trends.

First, there was the academic salon art, frequently but not always dull, derived in style and largely in content from Europe to satisfy the tastes of European-minded cities, and controlled by European-guided academies. Apart from some church murals, the subjects were portraits and battle or historical scenes or genre. Even with such local subjects the style was European.

A second movement was that of the regionalist and *costumbrista* painters. This was a result of the revolutions and the romantic movement, which inspired both individuals and scientific expeditions to seek out exotic peoples and places and record observations. Though on the whole not on the level of great art, not a few of the landscapes, street and country scenes, and studies of costumes and customs show fresh observation and a quality far above mere recording.

A third current was that of the arts of the people, in which were combined both deeply rooted indigenous and derivative elements. These arts tended to

[1] Still further complicated by the fact that little is known of many of the painters. It is a field still unexplored by scholars.

flourish away from the Europeanized cities, were functional in the lives of the people, and, though somewhat affected by European influences, carried on the long-lived indigenous traditions and eventually became a powerful stimulation toward — in fact an ingredient of — the great renascence of the twentieth century.

Let us discuss these three a little more in detail, beginning with the academic school. Portrait-painting flourished in the colonies, as it did in Spain and France. The influence of Goya was strong in every country and, side by side with it, echoes of French classicism. Prilidiano Pueyrredón (1823–1870) of Buenos Aires, one of the more original of the nineteenth-century painters, after studying with the neoclassical painters of the San Fernando Academy in Madrid, returned to Argentina to paint well-known personages of the aristocracy with penetrating interpretation. Genre scenes interested him as well, especially gaucho life, which he depicted with no little skill in the clear delineation and the careful balancing of line and light and dark color areas, and which he infused with a feeling broader in scope than the anecdotal painting then in vogue in France, England, and the United States. A French painter, Raymond Monvoisin (1794–1870), a product of the French Academy and very influential in propagating French influence in Argentina, Chile, and Peru, painted both the contemporary leaders and the gauchos with the incisive linear quality of Ingres. Carlos Enrique Pellegrini of Paris (1800–1875) also painted, in the Ingres style, the aristocratic ladies of Argentina; Antonio Salás of Ecuador (died, 1867), the heroes of the wars of independence; as did José Gil de Castro (1730?–1825?), a Peruvian mestizo who, in his capacity of official painter of Chile, portrayed not only Bolívar and San Martín but also Bernardo O'Hig-

gins, the Chilean hero of independence. Gil's work, based on that of the Cuczo school, has a simple directness, in the manner of folk portraiture.

Painters of battle and historical scenes were stimulated by a nationalistic fervor growing out of the wars of independence in much the same way as those in the United States. This fervor, not satisfied with simple portraiture, led to the perpetuation of heroes and events in huge canvases of battle and historical scenes which were national records rather than works of art. In the field of genre, the spirit of romanticism is evident in the painting which took as its subjects gauchos, Indians, and local historical events. This usually was a superficial recording of appearance rather than a sympathetic interpretation, except in the hands of a few of the more gifted painters, such as Pueyrredón and Juan Manuel Blanes of Uruguay (1830–1901). Blanes, trained in Italy, was accomplished in painting historical and genre scenes with dramatic fervor — scenes of gaucho life, of incidents in the career of San Martín, such as the *Review of Rancagua* (*The Military Review of 1885*), painted with an honest realism that lies between histrionic romanticism and the photographic anecdote. His *Incident of the Yellow Fever*, a scene from the great epidemic in Buenos Aires, illustrates his ability to heighten a tragic incident by a dramatic use of concentrated light and dark.

The second current was that of the regionalist and *costumbrista* painters — that is, painters of the local scene, of customs and everyday life, as well as of landscapes. This thread of regional painting began in the seventeenth century with the work of Frans Post and others who came to the Dutch colonies in Pernambuco to paint scenes of towns, plantations, and people. The thread was lost in the ecclesiasticism of the colonial age, to reappear with the coming of

[A] *Velasco. Valley of Mexico from the Hill of Tepeyac. 1905. Instituto Nacional de Bellas Artes, Mexico. (Philadelphia Museum of Art)*

Jean-Baptiste Debret, a pupil of David, who published a series of lithographs of people and places in his *Voyage pittoresque et historique au Brésil* (published in Paris, 1834); and with the coming of Johann Moritz Rugendas, a Bavarian painter and wood engraver who accompanied a scientific expedition as draftsman and traveled widely from Argentina and Chile to California. Captivated, like a true romanticist, by the picturesqueness of the land and the people, Rugendas painted and drew everyday people and everyday life in country and in city. Many of these paintings and drawings were reproduced in lithograph and so became widely distributed. Debret and Rugendas are but two of a considerable number of traveling painters and lithographers, who at least popularized a fresh point of view in that they turned

attention to the common people and to their environment as subject matter for the artist. Like them, the *costumbrista* painters, in every country, produced water colors, pen drawings, and lithographs depicting customs and modes of living, a genre painting of the people, in distinction from the genre painting of the aristocracy usually produced by the well-known artists, such as Pueyrredón and Blanes. Some of the best of this work is water color. In this medium Ramón Salás of Ecuador, son of the portrait-painter Antonio, depicted the customs of Quito; Pancho Fierro the life of the streets of Lima; Francisco Lasso (1810–1868) and Ignacio Merino (1817–1876), the Incas of Peru; Ramón Torres-Méndez, the costumes and daily activities of the Colombians. Some of this regional and *costumbrista* painting has no little freshness and charm about it in comparison with the generally sterile work of the academic painters. On the whole, however, it tended to be objective recording. To some degree, it is analogous to the work of Mount, Inman, Bingham, Eastman Johnson, and the early Winslow Homer, except that this latter group is rooted in the soil and though realistic, is deeper in understanding.

In the field of landscape, the same movement appears in Middle, Central, and South America as in the United States. As the spirit of nationalism stimulated not only the Hudson River school to paint the local scene of New York and New England but also the panoramists to penetrate the vast West, so landscape-painters in Middle, Central, and South America found subject matter for painting in the magnificence of nature in their own lands. Perhaps the most accomplished of these was José María Velasco of Mexico (1840–1912), who in painting the Valley of Mexico (Fig. 699A), his favorite subject, is far more an organizer than his contemporaries in the United States. For after holding the eye of the observer on the picture plane by the decorative use of the rich flora of the valley, he cuts his planes to the distant peaks with an almost Poussin-like clarity.

The third current or thread in this complex fabric of nineteenth-century painting was the art of the people and by the people, in distinction from the derivative European art produced mostly for the ruling classes. The latter was the art of the capitals and larger cities. But there were great areas of these vast lands either untouched and left to the Indians or penetrated only by the more sympathetic among the missionaries. Many towns and villages were fairly free from the influence of the cities and continued to produce a folk art rooted in their life that was vital, and esthetically of high value. In the field of painting this is well illustrated by the Mexican *retablos*, which continued to be important, and by paintings on the shop façades, an authentic expression of simple, untrained, naturally gifted artists. Some show a knowledge of European principles of perspective and sculptural use of light and shade. They are more likely, however, to reflect the tradition of flat linear design derived from the ancient codices and murals, and at times display a startling juxtaposition of brilliant color areas. This was an authentic art, spontaneous because it sprang directly from the experiences of living. And it later proved vitally important in that it carried the thread of an indigenous art into the twentieth century and served as one of the bases for the emergence of the great Mexican painting of this century.

The folk arts as a whole were bewildering in number, because they were devoted to making objects necessary to everyday living and hence were as varied as the activities of life. All were rooted in ancient traditions of technique and design but capable of absorbing new methods and motifs brought by the Spaniard. In Mexico, ceramics, textiles, and lacquer were perhaps the most important of the folk arts, though leatherwork, silver, masks, straw inlay, and basketry also deserve mention.

In the field of ceramics we find a derivative art in the talavera ware of Puebla. Puebla was a thoroughly Spanish city, and to it potters were brought from Spain to establish the making of this well-known fabric. Besides utilitarian objects for home use, we find tiles in blue, white, and yellow, for patios and fountains, church façades and domes. Technique and design were Spanish, with some Moorish elements and also some Chinese, the latter learned from traders landing at coastal cities on their way from the Far East. This was an art largely at the service of the aristocracy and the Church.

But pottery-making for home use and for trade had always been one of the most important arts of the people. Much of this indigenous ware was very plain and simple. In the nineteenth-century revolution, a new demand for better fabrics for the middle classes, together with new techniques introduced by the Spaniards, proved a great stimulation. Though pottery was made everywhere, perhaps the more important centers were the state of Guerrero; Tonalá, near Guadalajara; Oaxaca; the state of Michoacán; the state of Guanajuato; and Metepec. The Guerrero state produced strong bold water jars and bowls, cream in color with decorations in black stylized figures or linear patterns drawn with great vitality; Tonalá, more graceful water jars painted in soft colors with conventionalized flower or animal patterns. Oaxaca had its gaily glazed dishes, its black ware made in simple sensitive shapes and undecorated except for tool markings to give texture to the surface, and its black whistles in simplified animal shapes. In the state of Michoacán, in the midst of a great variety, the bird-shaped water jars were reminiscent of preconquest wares. The state of Guanajuato produced plates with flowers and animals in green and red-brown glaze on a cream ground. Metepec was the home of gaily painted ceramic toys. The making of toys, largely ceramic but in other materials also, reveals a deep wellspring in the Mexican, a need to make things for sheer joy — gay, humorous objects filled with life and always satisfying esthetically.

Almost as widespread as the ceramic art was the art of the weaver. In the more isolated regions primitive looms continued to be used, as well as traditional weaves and patterns, though at times Spanish motifs crept in. The articles woven were things for everyday use, chief of which perhaps were the serape, a man's cloak and blanket, usually of wool; the rebozo, the woman's shawl and headdress, sometimes made of silk, a fiber brought in after the conquest; and smaller articles such as belts, sashes, and carrying bags. As with the pottery, every region had its own distinctive color, which ranged from the neutral colors of the wool to the most brilliant hues daringly juxtaposed and interwoven, and also its individual design — both of which designated the origin of the fabric. The designs tended to be geometric, as in many of the serapes; or to use highly conventional bird, animal, and flower motifs, as in the cotton and wool embroideries of the Huichol and Otomi tribes.

The art of lacquering also continued from ancient times in two centers, Olinalá in Guerrero and Uruápan in Michoacán, both of which were situated where the needed materials were available. Gourds and wooden objects afforded a base, which was covered with a black lacquer coating in which the design was cut and the different colors were inlaid and then polished; or a sgraffito process was used, producing a raised design in two colors.

These native arts were to be found throughout Middle, Central, and South America. Only a few of them can be mentioned here: the textiles of Guatemala; the clay figurines representing everyday people or fruit and flowers of Ecuador; the silver of Peru and Chile, still partaking of the bold style of the unconquerable Araucanian Indians. All this folk art, with its high esthetic values, stood in sharp contrast to the crafts of Europe and the United States, which felt the impact of the machine and mass production, the immediate result of which was to end making articles by hand and to substitute copies made by the machine.

BIBLIOGRAPHY

Anderson, Lawrence, *The Art of the Silversmith in Mexico, 1519–1936*, 2 vols., Oxford University Press, 1941

Benavides Rodríquez, Alfredo, *La Arquitectura en el Virreinato del Perú y en la Capitanía General de Chile*, Santiago, 1941

Burr, Grace H., *Hispanic Furniture*, Hispanic Society of America, 1941

Buschiazzo, Mario J., *Indigenous Influences on the Colonial Architecture of Latin America, Bulletin* of the Pan American Union, Washington, D.C., May 1941

Chilean Contemporary Art, Toledo Museum of Art, Toledo, Ohio, 1942

Cossío del Pomar, F., *Pintura colonial, escuela Cuzqueña*, Cuzco, 1928

Fernández, Justino, *El arte moderno en México*, Mexico City, 1937

Goodwin, Philip L., *Brazil Builds*, Museum of Modern Art, New York City, 1943

Grant, Frances R., *Some Artistic Tendencies in South America, Bulletin* of the Pan American Union, Washington, D.C., October 1929

Griffin, Charles C., ed., *Concerning Latin American Culture*, Columbia University Press, 1940

Hanson, Earl P., ed., *The New World Guides to the Latin American Republics*, 2 vols., Duell, Sloan & Pearce, 1943

Hewett, Edgar L., and Fisher, Reginald G., *Mission Monuments of New Mexico*, University of New Mexico Press, 1943

Kelemen, Pál, *Colonial Architecture in Guatemala, Bulletin* of the Pan American Union, Washington, D.C., August 1941

Kilham, Walter H., *Mexican Architecture of the Vice-Regal Period*, Longmans, Green, 1927

Knee, Ernest, *Santa Fe, New Mexico*, Hastings House, 1942

Kubler, George, *The Religious Architecture of New Mexico*, Taylor Museum, Colorado Springs Fine Art Center, Colorado Springs, Colorado, 1940

Leão, Joaquim de Sousa, *Ouro Preto, Brazil, Bulletin* of the Pan American Union, Washington, D.C., November 1938

León, Francisco de P., *Los Esmaltes de Uruapán*, Mexico City, 1939

Means, Philip A., *Fall of the Inca Empire*, Scribner, 1932

Morris, B. T., "The Feather Art of Old Mexico," *House Beautiful*, April 1931, p. 368

Navarro, José G., *Art in Ecuador, Bulletin* of the Pan American Union, Washington, D.C., August 1925

——————— *Contribuciones a la historia del arte in Ecuador*, Quito, 1939

——————— *Quito, Bulletin* of the Pan American Union, Washington, D.C., September 1934

——————— *Religious Architecture in Quito*, Metropolitan Museum of Art, New York City, 1945

Newcomb, Rexford, *The Franciscan Mission Architecture of Alta California*, Architectural Book Publishing Company, 1916

——————— *The Old Mission Churches and Historic Houses of California*, Lippincott, 1925

Rippy, James F., *Historical Evolution of Hispanic America*, Crofts, 1940

Schiaffino, Eduardo, *La Pintura y la escultura en Argentina, 1783–1894*, Buenos Aires, 1933

Smith, Robert C., "XIX Century Painting in Argentina," *Gazette des Beaux Arts*, Series vi, Vol. 22, No. 909, p. 99, November 1942

——————— *The Colonial Architecture of Minas Gerais in Brazil, Art Bulletin*, June 1939

——————— *The Colonial Churches of Brazil, Bulletin* of the Pan American Union, Washington, D.C., January 1938

——————— "Latin American Painting Comes into Its Own," *Inter-American Quarterly*, July 1940

Solá, Miguel, *Historia del arte Hispano-Americano*, Barcelona, 1935

Toor, Frances, "Mexican Popular Arts" special number, *Mexican Folk-Ways*, Mexico City, August 1935

Toussaint, Manuel, *Tres siglos de arquitectura colonial*, Mexico City, 1933

Twenty Centuries of Mexican Art, Museum of Modern Art, New York City, 1940

Van Pelt, Garrett, Jr., *Old Architecture of Southern Mexico*, J. H. Jansen, 1926

Velásquez Chávez, Agustín, *Tres siglos de pintura colonial Mexicana*, Mexico City, 1939

Wilder, Mitchell A., and Breitenbach, Edgar, *Santos; The Religious Folk Art of New Mexico*, Taylor Museum, Colorado Springs Fine Art Center, Colorado Springs, Colorado, 1943

Wilgus, Alva C., *The Development of Hispanic America*, Farrar & Rinehart, 1941

Williams, Mary W., *The People and Politics of Latin America*, new ed., Ginn, 1938

SUMMARY

The nineteenth century was a century of complex and confusing dislocations. It was a century of revolution in society, economics, politics, technology, industry, and art. The Industrial Revolution, together with the segregation of art from the cultural fabric, deprived the artist of his earlier normal place in civilization.

In architecture two currents of thought were clearly discernible. One, the main broad stream found everywhere, was that of eclecticism, a following of the styles of the past. The other was a small but vital trickle, that of the engineers and a few forward-looking architects who rebelled against the "styles," and saw in the new methods of construction, the use of new materials, and the demand for new kinds of buildings suitable for an industrial age a challenge to original forms more in harmony with a rapidly changing era. Here were the beginnings of modern architecture. Painting broke more rapidly with the past; in Paris, the storm center and focal point of the century, it passed through a series of revolutionary movements: classicism, romanticism, naturalism, impressionism, each of which in turn took issue with conservative academism.

In all the Americas, painting followed the French school largely, and except for some imitation of the Barbizon school kept close to the academic wing until the last decade of the century, when impressionism became popular. In the United States a protest against derivative painting, the Colonial ideal, finally eventuated in the Armory Show of 1913, which, introducing postimpressionism, was a turning-point in the evolution of American painting. The other American countries, though now separated from Europe politically, remained firmly neo-European in their outlook in general and in their art, notably in their official art. But in both American continents there existed alongside neo-European painting a native folk art, together with the work of a few individuals who sought an expression rooted in their own environment. As with architecture, this current was to provide fertile ground for the growth of twentieth-century art. Its healthy growth involved the continuity of the tradition of many arts — pottery, weaving, metalwork, lacquer — in those lands not yet affected by the machine and where an aboriginal culture lay latent, yet vital. Thus the nineteenth century seems to have been a chaotic, transitional age, in which the lingering Renaissance came into conflict with the upsurging of a new and as yet unnamed era.

Twentieth-Century Art

CULTURALLY, no specific year and no specific event mark the passage of the nineteenth century into the twentieth, so part and parcel are they of one great transitional movement from the decadent Renaissance to the dimly discerned and as yet unnamed new age. At present the culture of the United States is witnessing unbelievable strides, probably not yet a climax, in science, technology, and industry. These make our civilization mechanistic, urban, and secular. At the same time great social changes are taking place. The roots of this culture are deep in the past and its growth was mightily accelerated by the French Revolution and the Industrial Revolution, with all their implications.

The same forces are now at work with accelerated speed. World War I, the Great Depression, and World War II have followed one another in swift succession, and the chaos of the nineteenth century has become the superchaos of the twentieth — a chaos, however, that is the outward expression of an evolutionary process. "The only normalcy is change." Culture is never static. Under the impact of inexorable forces it is constantly changing, at times imperceptibly, at times with the eruptive force of a volcano. The latter kind of change we are witnessing today. Ferment, confusion, and realignment have developed a faculty for -isms, -ologies, and -ocracies — necessarily, for only by experiment can the way out be found.

Because of the swiftness and ease of intercommunication, a new concept has emerged out of the present tumult — that of one total world, inextricably interrelated. On the one hand, nationalism is rampant; on the other, an earnest endeavor struggles to control nationalism within the larger framework of internationalism. An additional note heard is the world-wide voice of the people, "the common man," in protest against the old order of the favored few.

All these trends are reflected in the arts. A hopeful sign is that socially and economically the artist is again, though slowly, finding a place in this evolving order; he is coming closer to his audience, the people. Consider his position before the nineteenth century. The State, the Church, princes, and guilds kept up a steady demand for his products. Works of art seem to have been created but rarely unless commissioned for a specific function. Thus the artist performed a definite, necessary role in the social organization and had few, if any, economic worries, because supply and demand balanced. By the nineteenth century, however, such patronage had almost ceased, and the advent of the machine, which began to eliminate the handcrafts, completed the segregation of the artist from the cultural fabric. Now, however, there are signs that the artist and his twentieth-century patron, the people, are coming together. Artists are breaking down the walls of specialization. Painters are designing machine-made articles as well as ballet settings, and are reaching out into the fields of weaving, ceramics, and glass.

[A] *Falling Water. Bear Run, Pennsylvania. Frank Lloyd Wright, architect. 1936. (Hedrich-Blessing Studio)*

Painters and sculptors are collaborating with builders in providing murals and decorative accents. The people, on their part, when they thrill at the *RCA Building,* an airplane, or a streamlined railroad train, or when they take delight in a mechanized kitchen or in a simple, gaily colored gadget from the five-and-ten, or when they select an automobile on the basis of its lines and color, are beginning — barely beginning — to participate with the artist in a common understanding, and may be laying the foundation of a new style that will be expressive of the new emerging order. At the same time there exists the lag of the old order. For traditions are strong, and even in chaotic times they tend to evolve slowly. We need to keep in mind also that just as the arts seemed to be making strides in new directions, the United States was plunged into World War I, and then, after a decade of boom, into the Great Depression, and on into World War II — a course of events which, with social and economic implications, has vastly affected all the arts.

[A]   *Robie House. Chicago. Frank Lloyd Wright, architect. 1908–09. (Ryerson Library)*

43

TWENTIETH–CENTURY ARCHITECTURE

THE divergent trends which, as we have seen, characterize the twentieth century, became clearly differentiated in architecture as the century came into its third decade following World War I. Eclecticism continued — and still lingers — though somewhat invigorated by new ideas and new forms. We still are building, almost the world over, classical banks, Renaissance homes, Gothic or Byzantine churches, and Gothic universities. But among adventurous artists the break with eclecticism has been sharp and clean, a break with its philosophy as well as its forms. In place of something authoritative, a desirable pattern to be copied, the modern architect has substituted a look at his own world, a search for its needs in the light of its own changing milieu. He is aware of a primarily industrial, urban, technological Machine Age that requires new kinds of buildings — factories, stores and offices, apartment houses, large housing projects for "the common man" — in place of the temples and palaces that predominated in the architecture of the past. He is aware of huge cities in which these buildings are packed into small, overcrowded areas. He is aware of a bewildering number of materials, old and new; of new tools, new methods of construction, and mass production. He is

[A] *S. C. Johnson and Son Administration Building. Racine, Wisconsin. Frank Lloyd Wright, architect. 1936–39. (Johnson's Wax)*

aware of a close tie between the architect and the engineer, and realizes that they may be, in fact often are, synonymous. He is aware of overwhelming scientific discoveries, of swift, world-wide communication, and of forces that are reshaping society. In frankly facing such a world, the architect realizes that older methods, materials, and techniques will hardly suffice. He must explore. But he also realizes that esthetic values are still to be attained, as they always have been, by certain qualities of proportion, balance, contrast, coherence of parts; by fitness for function and adaptability to site.

The challenge to meet the needs of this changing world was felt by indi-

vidual pioneers in the late nineteenth century and the early twentieth in Germany, Austria, Belgium, France, and the United States. Influential in the United States and even more so in Europe in the transitional period between the pioneering stage and the fully developed modern age was Frank Lloyd Wright (1869–   ). In domestic architecture in particular his work has been significant. His early *Robie House* (Fig. 706A) shows an emphasis upon horizontality that results from his principle of tying the house closely to its site, of establishing continuity between the house and the out-of-doors. Continuity between the parts of the interior space is established by the suppression

[A]   *Row of Houses. Hook of Holland. J. J. P. Oud, architect. 1924–27. (Museum of Modern Art)*

of partitions wherever possible. Canti-levering the roofs eliminates outside vertical supports, which would appear to enclose the house, and thus enables it to open more expansively to its environment. We see and feel here the predominance of horizontal lines and horizontal planes — obvious, for example, in the overhanging roofs, which intersect and interplay with vertical lines and planes, and in the massive chimney. The structure is an organic unit in which the parts of the interior space flow one into another and thence by way of the exterior to the surrounding site. "I still believe that the ideal of an organic architecture forms the origin and source, the strength and, fundamentally, the significance of everything ever worthy the name of architecture. By organic architecture I mean an architecture that develops from within outward in harmony with the conditions of its being as distinguished from one that is applied from without."[1]

[1] Frank Lloyd Wright, *Wendigen*, p. 25.

In his California and Southwestern houses Wright has responded to different conditions of topography and climate. The *Millard House* (Los Angeles) is a geometric block with flat roof, solid walls, and few windows, and is tied closely to its hilly site, to its gardens and lofty trees. Its material is concrete blocks, some of which are molded into decorative patterns and thus enable the builder to secure contrast of broken and unbroken surfaces. Again in his design for a lodge among the firs at Lake Tahoe, and in one for a camp on the cactus-covered desert of Arizona, he exhibits his capacity to apply his principle of organic architecture to each individual problem and to use materials for their intrinsic qualities and for their suitability to the project in hand. *Falling Water* (Bear Run; Fig. 705A) shows a subtle relation to environment. The house is built on a rocky ledge over a stream in the midst of thick woods. Two contrasting materials are used in its construction: rough local stone, the

[A] *Savoye House. Poissy-sur-Seine, France. Le Corbusier, architect. 1929–30. (Museum of Modern Art)*

same as that of the ledge, laid in narrow strips to form the walls and chimney, and smooth reinforced concrete in the cantilevered balconies which project over the stream. The color and texture of these materials again offer contrast to the falling water and the trunks and foliage of the trees, yet all tie into an intimate unity. In this house even more than in the *Robie House* one sees intersecting planes, predominantly horizontal, and feels the continuity of space, the reaching of the interior out into its environment, with enough contrast to provide virility.

In the field of industrial buildings Wright has experimented in external problems of simplified geometric volumes and internal problems of lighting, as in the *Larkin Building* (Buffalo, New York) early in his career, and the *S. C. Johnson and Son Administration Building* (Fig. 707A) of recent years. In the latter, he introduced slender tapering columns of hollow reinforced concrete which spread out, treelike, into large disks

which form the roof except for the interstices, which are filled with glass. The circular motif of the disk is repeated in the furnishings. The walls of the building, which include strips of glass, are nonfunctional as supports.

The pioneering and the exploration which continued up to World War I in both Europe and America were the achievements of individuals working more or less in isolation rather than in a general movement. After the war a trend toward a coherence of these efforts into a general movement became evident, and in this trend Wright's work became influential — more so in Europe than in America and signally so in Holland. There Willem Marinus Dudok (1884–   ) was already experimenting, in his *School* and *Municipal Bathhouse* at Hilversum, in simple volumes of brick laid so as to secure plain surfaces with richly vibrating texture.

Housing projects were in great demand in the decade following the war; for reasons of economy they had to be

[A]   *Bauhaus. Dessau. Walter Gropius, architect. 1926. (Museum of Modern Art)*

as simple as possible and constructed of standardized units. This challenge was met in Holland most successfully by J. J. P. Oud (1890–   ). The early tendency of the modern builders was to go to the extreme of functionalism and geometry expressed by Le Corbusier — "The house shall be a machine in which to live"; and by Bruno Taut — "the perfect and therefore also beautiful efficiency." While such a philosophy led to the erection of buildings of a stark character, the esthetic impulse soon began to infuse pure efficiency, just as in Paleolithic times, when the quality of the curves of a flint was as much a matter of concern to the maker as the sharpness of its edges.

This quality appears in the *Row of Houses* which Oud built at the Hook of Holland. He had passed through the stage of stark geometry under the influences of the neoplasticist painters and sculptors, Mondrian and van Doesburg, that of the suprematist Kasimir Malevich, and that of the Russian constructivists, who in their constructions made out of various materials were experimenting in problems of interrelated and interpenetrating

spaces, applicable both to architecture and to sculpture and as completely nonobjective as Mondrian's. It is noteworthy that a similar purpose was motivating the painters at this time — the cubists. In fact the whole situation was analogous to that of early fifteenth-century Florence when Masaccio in painting, Brunelleschi in architecture, and Donatello in sculpture were all seeking solutions of spatial problems. Oud, in his *Row of Houses* with corner shops (Fig. 708A), by his use of concrete, brick, glass, and iron and by accents of color and contrasting textures and by a complete absence of ornament, created buildings whose refreshing clarity and conciseness, whose sensitively realized proportions and related parts, produce a satisfying result. The long two-story block with a ribbon arrangement of windows and a wide cornice over the first story, paralleling the unbroken horizontal of the flat roof, suggests in its emphasis upon horizontality the influence of Wright. This rectangular volume Oud saved from rigid regularity by bending it at the end into cylinders, like abstract sculpture, and by playing

[A]   *Tugendhat House. Garden façade. Brno, Czechoslovakia. Miës van der Rohe, architect. 1930. (Museum of Modern Art)*

subtly upon the theme of the cylinders in the details — as in the cylindrical supports — and upon the curved line, in contrast to the straight angularity of the rest of the building.

A similar evolution from "a machine in which to live" to a work of art is seen in the work of Le Corbusier himself. Le Corbusier, also a painter and in that field known as Charles Edouard Jeanneret, has been widely influential through his writings as well as through his buildings. About the same time that Oud was building his houses at the Hook of Holland, Le Corbusier was softening the severity of his earlier buildings, such as the *Vaucresson House* near Paris. In the later *Savoye House* (Fig. 709A), though the structure is contained within a space determined by a clean-cut rectangular volume lifted on slender piers, within this space there is a lively interplay of volumes, of curved and straight lines, of color and texture, and of exterior and interior space. A person whose eyes are habituated to strongly supporting stone walls may feel a sense of instability in the slender supports until

he begins to realize the tensile strength of steel (the framework is of ferroconcrete) and the possibilities of cantilevering. The house is conceived as a hollow rectangular volume within which open terraces and roof gardens — something like a patio — take up considerable space. But in the patio plan, the house, more or less sealed off from the outside world, opens inward upon its patio, whereas the *Savoye House*, because of its broad ribbon of openings, gives visual access to the environment in all directions, thus uniting the outside and the inside.

In Germany the early work of Eric Mendelsohn explored the possibilities of concrete, as seen in his *Einstein Tower* (Potsdam; 1920–1921). In his *Schocken Store* (Fig. 716B), the design of alternating broken and unbroken ribbons is a mode of fenestration widely used everywhere in modern architecture.

Walter Gropius of Germany (now a resident of the United States), like Oud, was drawn toward a study of abstract volumes and spatial relationships through contact with the neoplasticists

[A] *McGraw-Hill Building. New York. Raymond Hood, architect. 1931. (Museum of Modern Art)*

jections which jut out from the ferro-concrete framework. Here the concept of corner solidity, implicit in the masonry wall and even continued in some steel construction buildings, is entirely eliminated. The glass planes meet so lightly and cleanly that the outside and the inside space merge into each other.

The work of Ludwig Miës van der Rohe (1886–   ) of Berlin (now a resident of the United States) shows an architect intent upon a study of space — but not so much of space as defined by the planes of a volume as, again, of the continuity of space both within the volumes and also as flowing into external space. The *German Pavilion* at the Barcelona Exposition is an example of the flow of one part into another, the continuity of interior space rather than its division into tightly separated units. In addition, the artist has made effective use of different textures, including that of the water and the trees, and of a contrasting element to the smooth planes in the single statue standing in the pool of water. The *Tugendhat House* is a rectangular volume with clean unbroken lines and surfaces, austerely geometric. The garden side (Fig. 711A) consists of a wide ribbon of glass with unbroken borders and with an effective diagonal in the stairway. The interior space is a continuous unit with the various rooms marked off by partial or movable partitions. In this way it is possible to retain the continuity of one spatial unit and at the same time to divide it into smaller units as function or convenience may require. A wall of plate glass, which can be lowered electrically to open the house to the out-of-doors, or across which velvet curtains can be drawn; a half-partition of onyx supplemented by silk and velvet curtains on chromium rails; fine woods in the furnishings — the interplay of the colors and textures of these materials produces an impression of subdued ele-

of Holland. This is evident in the *Bauhaus* (Fig. 710A), a structure consisting of three parts, each with a distinct function: workshops, classrooms, and living quarters, each designed according to its use and all united into an asymmetrically balanced group. In the workshop section, long ribbons of glass, alternating with bands of stucco and broken asymmetrically to relieve monotony, furnish adequate light for the shops; in another part a great sheathing of glass with stucco borders at top and bottom is hung on cantilevered pro-

gance and, being free from clashing contrasts, contributes to that feeling of continuity which makes the house an illustration of Wright's "organic architecture."

Other European countries — Belgium, Finland, Italy, Romania, Russia, Sweden, Switzerland — were drawn into the architectural movement which the decade of the thirties saw sufficiently rooted to give it the title of the modern or international style. The latter term derives its justification from the fact that the style has encircled the globe, for it appears not only in practically all the countries of Europe and the Americas but in the Near East, as in Turkey and Palestine, and also in the Far East.

The United States has been slower than Europe to explore and carry forward the possibilities inherent in the work of Sullivan and Wright. Advance has appeared chiefly in urban industrial buildings, notably the skyscraper. The evolution of skyscraper design reached an epochal point in the international competition for the *Chicago Tribune Tower* (1922). Though the accepted design revealed a curious combination of tenacious eclectic ornament, Gothic buttresses and tracery, and the frank expression of function and material in the main shaft, the design which won the second place, submitted by Eliel Saarinen of Finland, served as a potent stimulus to the elimination of such non-functional elements. Nearly ten years later the winning artist, Raymond Hood (1881–1934), designed the almost starkly geometric *Daily News Building* of New York.

The skyscraper evolved on the one hand from concentration of industry into crowded urban centers, and on the other hand from the possibilities of steel construction and of such scientific inventions as the elevator, lighting and heating systems, and fireproof materials. From the engineering point of view, the

[A] *RCA Building. Rockefeller Center, New York. Reinhard & Hofmeister; Corbett, Harrison & McMurray; and Hood & Fouilhaux, architects. 1932.* (*Seidman Photo Service*)

builders have demonstrated that it is possible to reach any height desired with a steel framework which carries the load and hence needs no supporting walls. The framework can therefore be sheathed with thin slabs of stone, glass, or tile. From the esthetic standpoint, progress has been slower. Not until Gothic and other borrowed excrescences were eliminated did it become manifest that a lofty steel framework encased in a thin screening made up largely of in-

[A]   *Concrete Grain Elevator. Centennial Flour-
ing Mills Co., Spokane,
Washington. 1940. Henry
George & Sons, archi-
tects. (Louis Tager; Ew-
ing Galloway)*

numerable windows could, of and by itself, present to the eye so coherent a unity, so compelling a rhythm, that the total impression is one of audacious power. Highly important in attaining this unity and rhythm are the handling of fenestration, the character of the sheathing materials, and that of the necessary setbacks required by zoning laws. The *RCA Building* (Rockefeller Center, New York City; Fig. 713A), for example, shows a breath-taking upward sweep, due to the proportions of its very high, thin, rectangular volume (it is locally called "the slab") which contains a definite, boldly rhythmic movement within its mass, owing to the setbacks. Its uniform sheathing material, limestone, and its uniformly and emphatically vertical fenestration contribute to the general impression. From the

point of view of function, the thinness of the building makes possible ample light and air to every room, because the utilities are concentrated in the core of the structure, which in many skyscrapers is merely an open shaft.

The *McGraw-Hill Building* (New York City; Fig. 712A), on the other hand, with its accent upon the horizontal beams of the framework, is more reposeful, and its broad ribbons of glass, which encircle the building with but little break at the corners, produce an effect of lightness and airiness. (Contrast, in these two respects, the *RCA Building*.) In addition, the use of blue-green tiles in the sheathing enhances the light effect.

The *Philadelphia Savings Fund Society Building* (Fig. 715A) utilizes sheathing materials to produce an interplay of

[A] *Philadelphia Savings Fund Society Building. Philadelphia. Howe and Lescaze, architects. 1931–32. (Howe and Lescaze)*

texture and color. The lower stories are faced with dark-gray polished granite with aluminum-framed windows and stainless-steel lettering; above, oyster-white stone combines with gray mat brick; the lettering on the top is done in white painted metal and red neon tubes against a bright-blue ground. Here too is more variation within the basic unit of the form. The lower stories are grouped into a unit with rounding corners and large window openings indicating the offices of the bank, in contrast to the main shaft, with its more uniform fenestration, housing the small offices above.

Many industrial buildings besides skyscrapers exemplify the modern style. The huge grain elevators of the Middle West are cylinders of unabashed concrete thematically repeated and frequently contrasted with equally simple rectangular units (Fig. 714A). Many factories and powerhouses are as clean-cut as the machinery that they house. Their frank use of brick, concrete, steel, glass, tile, or metals, and their simple unadorned surfaces, stark lines, and large openings for light combine efficiency and beauty of form. Many small business blocks and shops are refreshing in their simple directness of design, in an almost geometric simplicity whose ornamentation often consists only of a sensitive interplay of color and texture of various materials. Cornices, moldings, projections of any kind about the windows, have largely disappeared. Sheer surfaces broken only by openings for windows profile against the sky. Again we see a reflection of a Machine Age.

[A]   *Karl Marx Hof. Vienna. Detail of central section. Karl Ehn, architect. 1926–30.*

[B]   *Schocken Department Store. Stuttgart. Eric Mendelsohn, architect. 1929.*

Nor has the American home been entirely untouched by the modern style. Some architects have made headway with a generally reluctant public, still eclectic in taste, in inducing them to build houses more in keeping with the contemporary age. Simplification seems to be the keynote, to conform to a mechanized, mass-production age and to fill the need for repose and relaxation in a high-keyed era. The houses of William Lescaze (1896–   ) in the East and of Richard Neutra (1892–   ) in California, among many excellent examples, illustrate the modern style. The *Lovell House* shows an asymmetrical plan and fenestration; long clean unbroken lines with an emphasis upon horizontality and a ribbonlike effect of contrasting materials; instead of ornament, a dependence upon color and texture of materials for contrast and accent; many terraces and the utilization of flat roofs as spaces for outdoor living, and, as a result, a unity of interior and exterior space. Thus the house has changed from a traditional introvert to an extrovert.

A similar simplicity and other similar characteristics are seen in modern interiors, the problem being so to organize a space that shape, proportions, and every detail of the furnishings are a part of a harmonious ensemble. Large unadorned surfaces of wall and window, unbroken lines, and materials used for their intrinsic qualities are basic elements of the style. The emphasis frequently lies upon the horizontal and the furniture hugs the floor, accented by colorful carpets, and leaving a compensating spaciousness above.[1] The decorative quality and necessary accents result from the interplay of the colors and textures of diverse materials — wood, stucco, tile, glass, various metals, and fabrics.

[1] It is interesting to contrast a Renaissance interior in which the strong accent is the elaborately decorated ceiling (Figs. 593A, 602A).

In other countries of the Americas there are notable examples of the international style, for it has spread as widely in the Western Hemisphere as the neoclassical of the nineteenth century. It has not always been understood and has frequently been used superficially and illogically, as in some tropical countries where the large openings suitable for a Northern climate have been retained without regard to protection from heat and glare.

Brazil, however, is a tropical country which has not only recognized this problem but has made contributions to its solution. The rise of modern architecture in Brazil and its challenge to Portuguese colonial and neoclassical was sudden. About 1930 a great building enterprise, chiefly in Rio de Janeiro and São Paolo, came under the control of a group of young architects trained in Europe, most of them in France (Brazil has always been close to France culturally). Within a few years the colonial patio urban house gave way to skyscraper apartment buildings, and the neoclassicism of civic structures to the modern style. In 1936 Le Corbusier was invited to Brazil as a consultant, but though his influence is clearly seen, the architects responsible for this transformation have not merely imitated his work. On the contrary, they have realized that the climate of Brazil is very different from that of France and that the materials which they might have used freely, such as steel, were not available in sufficient quantity. But within their own environment and in conformity to their own needs, they have erected buildings equal, both constructionally and esthetically, to those of any other country. Their work consists of a wide variety of buildings, chiefly domestic and civic — apartment houses and individual homes, schools, hospitals, and government buildings, and places of business and of amusement.

[A]   *ABI Building. Rio de Janeiro. Marcelo and Milton Roberto, architects. 1939. (Museum of Modern Art)*

The *Ministry of Education* (Fig. 719A) will illustrate a government building. It is a thin, boxlike building lifted on slender pillars which afford in the passages beneath protection against glaring sun and heavy rain and provide a wide view of surrounding areas. It is a concrete structure with its narrow sides unbroken and its broad sides, which face south and north, furnishing the fenestration. The northern side, which receives the glare and heat of the tropical sun, is broken into deep boxlike compartments, identical in size and shape, into which are fitted horizontal shutters which admit the air yet protect from the heat and glare.[1] As these shutters are set each in its own compartment and adjusted according to the needs of the individual occupants, there is never any monotony in a façade whose basic organization is rigidly regular. Instead, a wavering movement of light and dark plays over the surface, giving a vivacious lightness to the structure. On the roof are two cylindrical structures for water tanks and elevators. Materials and color play important roles in the design. The supporting columns and the unbroken thin sides of the building are sheathed in a local warm-gray granite; the walls of the entrance and auditorium (a structure on the ground story at one end of the building and not visible in the illustration) are covered with blue and white tiles designed by the Brazilian painter Portinari; the shutters are blue, and the tanks on the top of the building are of blue tile. The wide use of tile is a Portuguese inheritance, as well as a recognition of a material highly suitable for a hot climate.

The *ABI Building* (the Brazilian Associated Press; Rio de Janeiro, Fig. 718A), is a more nearly cubical volume, lifted on piers, with rectangular and cylindrical volumes and garden terraces on the roof. The building is more solid-looking than the *Ministry of Education* (it too is of concrete construction), partly because of the greater amount of unbroken surface area and partly because of the shutters, which are vertical and stationary, forming horizontal ribbons of strongly accented light and dark. Behind these shutters is a corridor on which the windows of the

[1] These compartments project from the framework of the structure by means of cantilevering, on the same constructional principle as in the *Bauhaus*, and it is interesting to note how climatic differences required glass in the one case to admit light and shutters in the other to exclude it.

[A] *Ministry of Education and Health. Rio de Janeiro. Lucio Costa, Oscar Niemeyer, Alfonso Reidy, Carlos Leão, Jorge Moreira, and Ernani Vasconcelos, architects, with Le Corbusier as consultant. 1937–43. (Museum of Modern Art)*

building open — a device which makes it impossible for the windows to be subjected to the direct rays of the sun. Notable is the dynamic use of lettering, as in the *Bauhaus* to break the regularity of the design.

Besides urban building, the modern style in Brazil has found expression in open areas. Here the tendency has been to build horizontally, to tie to the environment, and to use white or light colors to contrast with the rich green of the tropical flora.

One characteristic field of modern architecture must receive further mention. This is the housing project and town planning,[1] the need for which

[1] See Sigfried Giedion, *Space, Time, and Architecture*, Harvard University Press, 1941.

arose at the conclusion of World War I and even more insistently after World War II. The objective is to provide healthful living-quarters equipped with modern conveniences at a minimum rent — an objective which entails the utmost economy of materials and construction and hence the elimination of nonfunctional items; and also to arrange the parts which constitute a community into a unit which has due regard both for the conduct of the community and for the most healthful and pleasant living therein. We have already seen Oud's early answer to the housing project (Fig. 708A). Another example is the *Karl Marx Hof* (Vienna; Fig. 716A), which by its proportions, by the interplay of angular and curvilinear motifs, by the accents of the projecting balconies and towers, by the use of polychromy to differentiate the parts clearly, and by its garden courts impresses us with an efficiency not devoid of esthetic content.[1]

The erection of such housing projects and, perhaps even more important, the laying out of entirely new cities and the renovation and extension of old cities are found in various widely separated places of the world on an unprecedented scale. Of new cities, *Canberra*, the new capital of Australia, is an example. Another is *Goiania*, the new industrial center and capital of the inland Brazilian province of Goyaz. In *Goiania*, the general plan is based upon diagonals radiating from a center, with a minimum of traffic thoroughfares and a maximum of walks and recreation spaces, with a belt of parks surrounding the whole.

An example of modern extension of an older site is well illustrated by *Tel Aviv*, a suburb of Jaffa, Palestine. This site, whose development has been coincident with the recent industrial development of Palestine, provides noteworthy examples of modern planning and building with intelligent adaptations of modern principles to climate and function.

SUMMARY

The modern style in architecture is a response to a changing life in a chang-

[1] The huge size of this housing unit can be grasped only by a study of its entire plan. It consists of 1,400 apartments of from one to six rooms and accommodates 5,000 residents. About one-fifth of its ground area is built on, the remaining four-fifths being left as open spaces. As a social unit it contains two kindergartens, a school, a library, clinics, a health-insurance office, a post office, and over twenty business concerns — a town in itself. There are two washhouses with hot water and ample provision for the sanitary cleanliness of the entire unit.

ing world. It has spread, to a greater or less degree, to all parts of the globe and is international in scope in a world whose segments have been brought together into a total whole. With the machine, technology, and industry dominant factors, the modern architect, who is an artist-engineer, thinks in terms of new materials and new uses of old materials, of new functions, and of new advances in science. His break with eclecticism, both philosophically and formally, has been sharp. The demands made upon him are largely for civic, industrial, and domestic buildings, in all of which we see a simple directness in terms of function and of the potentialities of materials. Buildings tend toward asymmetry in plan and toward a pleasing massing of the volumes which evolve from the plan. The core problem is to relate spaces, both external and internal, and to express these relationships clearly. Modern buildings open up both to admit light and air (in relation to climatic setting) and to allow the inside to flow out into the out-of-doors. As a rule they have long clean unbroken lines with emphasis on the horizontal; flat roofs; and little or no ornament. They depend for their effect upon proportions of volumes, treatment of surfaces (as in fenestration), and color and texture of materials. Though at first the modern style produced an extremely austere type, "a machine in which to live," it has softened somewhat without abandoning its position as evidence of new directions in a new world.

BIBLIOGRAPHY

Barr, Alfred H., ed., *Modern Works of Art*, Museum of Modern Art, New York City, 1934

Bayer, Herbert, Gropius, Walter, and Gropius, Ise, eds., *Bauhaus, 1919–1928*, Museum of Modern Art, New York City, 1938

Behrendt, Walter C., *Modern Building*, Harcourt, Brace, 1937

Born, Esther, *The New Architecture in Mexico*, William Morrow, 1937

Brownell, Baker, and Wright, Frank L., *Architecture and Modern Life*, Harper, 1937

Cahill, Holger, and Barr, Alfred H., eds., *Art in America in Modern Times*, Reynal and Hitchcock, 1934

Cheney, Sheldon W., *The New World Architecture*, Tudor, 1935

Ford, James, and Ford, Katherine M., *The Modern House in America*, Architectural Book Publishing Company, 1940

Geddes, Norman B., *Horizons*, Little, Brown, 1932

Giedion, Siegfried, *Space, Time and Architecture*, Harvard University Press, 1941

Goodwin, Philip L., *Brazil Builds*, Museum of Modern Art, New York City, 1943

Gropius, Walter, *The New Architecture and the Bauhaus*, tr. by P. Morton Shand, Museum of Modern Art, New York City, 1937

Hitchcock, Henry R., *Modern Architecture*, Payson & Clarke, 1929

———, and Johnson, Philip, *The International Style: Architecture since 1922*, Norton, 1932

Le Corbusier (pseud.), Jeanneret, Charles É., *Towards a New Architecture*, tr. by Frederick Etchells, Payson & Clarke, 1927

Leyson, B. W., *Plastics in the World of Tomorrow*, Dutton, 1944

Modern Architecture in England, Museum of Modern Art, New York City, 1937

Mumford, Lewis, *The Culture of Cities*, Harcourt, Brace, 1938

——— *Technics and Civilization*, Harcourt, Brace, 1934

New Horizons in American Art, Museum of Modern Art, New York City, 1936

Park, Edwin A., *New Backgrounds for a New Age*, Harcourt, Brace, 1927

Pevsner, Nikolaus, *Pioneers of the Modern Movement*, Stokes, 1937

——— *An Outline of European Architecture*, Penguin Books, 1942

Richards, James M., *An Introduction to Modern Architecture*, Penguin Books, 1940

Roth, Alfred, ed., *La nouvelle architecture*, Zurich, 1940

What Is Modern Architecture?, Museum of Modern Art, New York City, 1942

Woltersdorf, Arthur, *Living Architecture*, Kroch, 1930

Wright, Frank L., *An Organic Architecture*, Transatlantic, 1939

——— *Modern Architecture*, Princeton University Press, 1931

——— *Frank Lloyd Wright on Architecture*, ed. by Frederick Gutheim, Duell, Sloan & Pearce, 1941

——— *An Autobiography*, rev. ed., Duell, Sloan & Pearce, 1943

——— *When Democracy Builds*, University of Chicago Press, 1945

——— "Architecture and Life in the U.S.S.R.," *Architectural Record*, Vol. 82, October 1937

44

TWENTIETH–CENTURY PAINTING

European Painting

ALTHOUGH architecture has drawn sculpture into the circle of its spirit and objectives, painting today is artificially segregated and, except for a relatively small number of murals, still consists largely of panels for exhibitions or dealers. It is prob-ably true that in proportion as the artist is excluded from functioning normally in the social and economic system, he is thrown into subjectivism, theory, and pure research. A hopeful sign, however, lies in the fact that not a few painters of first rank are putting their talents to work in other fields — in stage settings for the ballet, for example, in book illustration, and in many

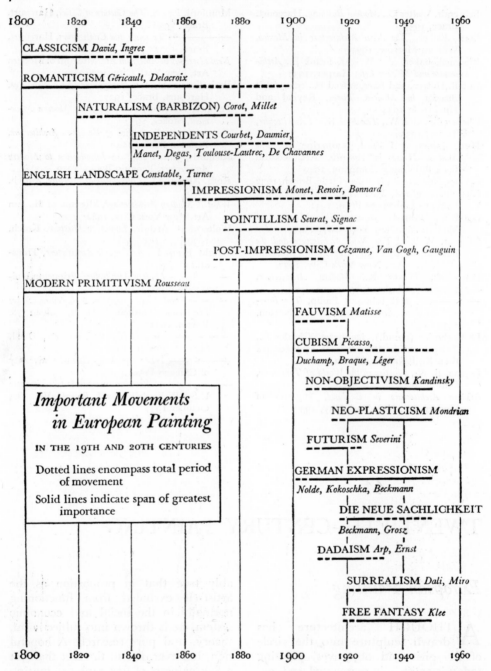

1800   1820   1840   1860   1880   1900   1920   1940   1960

CLASSICISM *David, Ingres*

ROMANTICISM *Géricault, Delacroix*

NATURALISM (BARBIZON) *Corot, Millet*

INDEPENDENTS *Courbet, Daumier,*
Manet, Degas, Toulouse-Lautrec, De Chavannes

ENGLISH LANDSCAPE *Constable, Turner*

IMPRESSIONISM *Monet, Renoir, Bonnard*

POINTILLISM *Seurat, Signac*

POST-IMPRESSIONISM *Cézanne, Van Gogh, Gauguin*

MODERN PRIMITIVISM *Rousseau*

FAUVISM *Matisse*

CUBISM *Picasso,*
Duchamp, Braque, Léger

NON-OBJECTIVISM *Kandinsky*

NEO-PLASTICISM *Mondrian*

FUTURISM *Severini*

GERMAN EXPRESSIONISM
Nolde, Kokoschka, Beckmann

DIE NEUE SACHLICHKEIT
Beckmann, Grosz

DADAISM *Arp, Ernst*

SURREALISM *Dali, Miro*

FREE FANTASY *Klee*

*Important Movements
in European Painting*

IN THE 19TH AND 20TH CENTURIES

Dotted lines encompass total period
  of movement

Solid lines indicate span of greatest
  importance

1800   1820   1840   1860   1880   1900   1920   1940   1960

of the industrial arts — and that architects, sculptors, and painters are drawing closer together in the study of formal problems and in the co-ordination of their arts.

Paris, cosmopolitan and tolerant, stimulating to adventure and experimentation, has been and until the outbreak of World War II still was the art center of the world, and its influence has penetrated far and wide. In the late nineteenth century, even before the impressionist battle was won in the show of 1886 and impressionism had become one more episode in the accumulating French tradition, several painters were striking out along new paths in order to recapture, as Renoir had already done, those qualities in the "old masters"[1] which the impressionists, too intent upon momentary realistic effects of light and air, had lost: solidity, structure, organization. These painters investigated the possibilities of art expression in various directions. The situation is not unlike that in architecture, where forward movements were carried out by individuals working in isolation. Of the group loosely called postimpressionists, four men proved so influential that they are usually considered the bases of modern painting. These are Seurat, Cézanne, Van Gogh, and Gauguin. Though all were grounded in impressionism, all early evolved out of that style into various modes, each in his individual way. Seurat has already been discussed (Chapter 42).

Paul Cézanne (1839–1906) began painting in the limited color and thick pigment of Courbet and with the baroque compositions of Tintoretto, Rubens, and Delacroix. After he had made acquaintance with the impressionists his palette broadened and lightened, and though he was drawn

into the color theories of this group, because of his long-continued studies of the "old masters" in the Louvre, he soon felt the weakness of the impressionists. "I want to make impressionism," he said, "something solid and permanent like the old masters." Thoroughly trained in the latter — "I always keep one foot in the Louvre," he said — especially by his study of Tintoretto and Poussin, who had so magnificently conquered the problem of space organization, he sought not to copy but to create equally compelling space relationships by new uses of the old means, line, light, color — an inescapable result of his own extraordinary vision. Thus he became an explorer of the painter's means of expression: line, the effect of every kind of line direction — horizontal, vertical, diagonal, curved — and the effect of line as related to line; color, the intrinsic quality of each color and the minutest detail of color relation. Through the recession of cool hues and the advance of warm hues he controlled volume and depth. Having observed that the point of saturation or highest intensity of color produces the greatest fullness of form, he painted apples, for example, in one hue only — say green — by a meticulous exactitude of value and intensity of green, so that in solidity, volume, and place in space they possess a supranatural reality. Thus he attained solidity and structure by the control of color alone[2] in place of the more usual method of light and shade; and while he made nature both his starting-point and his goal, his objective was not verisimilitude but the creation of that essential reality which is more real than a reproduction of it.

But it was not only the construction of individual forms — trees, mountains,

---

[1] It is illuminating to note how many of these painters were largely self-educated, primarily in the Louvre.

[2] See Roger E. Fry, *Transformations*, Coward-McCann, 1927, "Plastic Color." For a detailed analysis of a Cézanne still life, see Munro, *Great Pictures of Europe*, pp. 226–29.

[A]   *Cézanne. Mont Sainte-Victoire. Private Collection.*

apples, people — that engaged Cézanne, but also their organization in space. For "he saw in objective nature a chaos of disorganized movement and he set himself the task of putting it in order."[1] Every painting of Cézanne reveals an exploration of some problem connected with putting nature in order[2]; and for this purpose alone the subject matter was irrelevant — trees, landscapes, nudes, still life, portraits. Forms, their mass and solidity, their place in deep space in relation to other forms expressed according to his own visualization and method of using color

[1] W. H. Wright, *Modern Painting, Its Tendency and Meaning,* Dodd, Mead, 1915, p. 147.

[2] See the article by E. L. Johnson, "Cézanne's Country," *The Arts,* April, 1930, in which photographs and Cézanne's painting of the same subject are juxtaposed; and Erle Loran, *Cézanne's Composition,* University of California Press, 1943.

— to get upon the canvas his perception of these forms constituted his objective. As he worked over them, gradually everything inessential faded away so that the form was reduced to something nearly if not quite geometric. "Everything in nature adheres to the cone, the cylinder, and the cube." In this statement Cézanne was simply carrying but one step further — that is, into abstraction and geometry — what Giotto had already done, though his means were entirely different. Giotto was working away from a decadent abstractionism in the direction of a new naturalism; Cézanne, from a decadent naturalism into a new abstractionism; and they meet at the same stage of the evolution. As for subject matter, the fifteenth-century innovators from Giotto to Michelangelo experimented on Madonnas, biographies of the saints, or

[A]   *Cézanne. The Card-Players. 1892. Stephen C. Clark Collection, New York City.*
(*Museum of Modern Art*)

Greek mythological scenes, because their patrons commissioned these. The nineteenth- and twentieth-century innovators experimented on nudes and still life because there were no patrons to hand out commissions. When a painter is thus left entirely "free," he is most likely to concentrate upon the problems peculiarly his own — form and formal relations. Had Cézanne lived in Florence in the fourteenth century, he would probably have painted scenes from the life of Saint Francis or the Virgin Mary or Christ. Were Giotto living in twentieth-century France, he would probably be painting nudes, apples, and landscapes. Giotto's range of experience was relatively narrow and

his means were simple; Cézanne's world was broad and intricate and his means were complex.

What was of value in impressionism (color) Cézanne combined with what was of value in the whole Renaissance tradition (solidity, structure, organization in space) and then proceeded to reconstruct the fusion according to his own sensitive vision and his own use of color. In the *Mont Sainte-Victoire* (Fig. 724A), having stated clearly the plane of the canvas by the tree and the decorative branches, he carves out a space upon whose basic horizontal plane he sets each building, tree, and mountain, simply constructed as geometric units, each in its own place in space. Here we feel "Poussin made over according to nature," with a geometric simplicity that renders each object more real and solid than in visual reality. In *The Card-Players* (Fig. 725A), the figures partake of the quiet monumentality of stone sculpture, solid figures set convincingly in space (in relation to the table), each figure and each detail playing its part as inevitably as do the blocks of stone in a stone structure. In the *Large Composition with Nude Figures* (Philadelphia Museum), the figures are an inextricable part of the landscape like perfectly integrated architecture and sculpture; they unite with the trees to form the dominating arch, and carry the eye across the middle distance to unite the foreground and the background. These figures might as well have been bushes or rocks; the human figure, however, affords a more plastic means for carrying out the objective of the painter — solid organization in deep space.

Probably Cézanne was his own most discerning critic when he said that he was the primitive of the way he had opened. The highest accomplishments of this slow plodding painter have the power, the vitality, and the monumentality of great primitive art. His contribution was partly a rediscovery, at a critical time, of the fundamentals of great art, and partly the result of his prolonged independent studies over a period of thirty years, which revealed a complex relativity in color comparable, as W. H. Wright points out, to the delicate nuances and overtones in music. The discovery was a complex instrument capable of successful use only in the hands of a great master. His casual remarks have been transformed into dogmatic pronouncements by his followers. But as yet no one of his stature has appeared to carry on the "way he opened." It may be well to remember that between Giotto and Masaccio lay a century. In Cézanne's work, as in the work of other innovators who were attacking technical problems in the visual arts — Giotto, Masaccio, Uccello, Piero della Francesca, Rembrandt, Constable, Courbet, Manet — a sheer vitality results from a consuming effort. And because these men were artists as well as scientists, out of the mass of their efforts, necessarily uneven, arose indisputable masterpieces.

Van Gogh and Gauguin also moved away from the objective realism of impressionism in the direction of a subjective, spontaneous expression, in which form was the objectification of emotional reaction to actuality and imagination and often had little to do with visual perception. Vincent van Gogh (1853–1890) was a Hollander who, after tragic experiences, both physical and spiritual, in Belgium and England, found in the warmth, sunshine, and comparative peace of Provence an outlet in pigment for his emotional intensity. Almost any painting by Van Gogh proclaims its medium not only in the intensity of the color but also in the vibrating texture created by pigment manipulation. Now a thickly loaded brush moves vehemently back and forth or at right angles, giving a textilelike effect; now the palette knife or a finger rubs on or smooths the pigment; now the tube squeezes dots or streaks upon the canvas. Everywhere we feel the impetuosity with which the medium is used and which might have run wild if it had not been controlled by an innate high sensibility. Color is used in its highest intensity, color area meeting color area abruptly, thus creating an effect of emphatic line and silhouette — an influence of Japanese prints.

In the *Berceuse* (*Woman Rocking a Cradle;* Fig. 727A), large flat areas of complementary reds and greens, outlined in black, contrast with a background broken by dots, spirals, and flowers. Of this painting Van Gogh wrote: "In it I have ranged the reds from rose to orange, which rises through the yellows to lemon, with light and sombre greens. . . . A woman in green with orange hair stands out against a background of green with pink flowers. Now these discordant sharps of crude pink, crude orange, and crude green are softened by flats of red and green. I picture to myself these same canvases between those of the sunflowers, which would thus form lamp brackets or candelabras beside them. . . . Perhaps in the 'Woman Rocking' there's an attempt to get all the *music* of the color here. . . . You must realize that if you arrange them this way, say the 'Woman Rocking' in the middle and the two canvases of sunflowers to right and left, it makes a sort of triptych. And then the yellow and orange tones of the head will gain more brilliance by the proximity of the yellow wings." [1]

In the *Landscape with Cypress Trees* (Tate Gallery, London), intensity of feeling pours itself forth in a vehement brushing of pigment which creates a varied surface texture that is no mean part of the emotional effect produced by the picture. This canvas is suffused with a hot yellow into which cooler hues play to offset its warmth; in the sky the brush strokes create a textile-like pattern.

In contrast to Van Gogh, Paul Gauguin (1848–1903) presents large quiet areas of smoothish flat color, sumptuously rich, with suavely flowing lines. These color areas are clearly and sharply defined and often separated by dark contours[2] like the leads in leaded

[A] *Van Gogh. La Berceuse (Woman Rocking a Cradle). 1889. Art Institute of Chicago. (Art Institute)*

glass windows or the cloisons in cloisonné enamels, so that the effect is frankly decorative, and depth is suggested rather than presented to the eye. Though Gauguin began as an impressionist, he soon abandoned broken color with the statement: "A meter of green is greener than a centimeter if you wish to express greenness. . . . How does that tree look to you? Green? All right, then use green, the greenest on your palette. And that shadow, a little bluish? Don't be afraid. Paint it as blue as you can!" "Gauguin," says Maurice Denis, "freed us from all the restraints which the idea of copying nature had placed upon us. For instance, if it was permissible to use vermilion in painting a tree which seemed reddish . . . why not stress even to the point of deformation the curve of a beautiful shoulder or conventionalize the symmetry of a bough unmoved by a breath of air? Now we understood everything in the Louvre,

[1] *Vincent van Gogh*, Museum of Modern Art, 1935, No. 40.

[2] For this reason Gauguin was sometimes called a cloisonnist. Robert Rey, in his *Gauguin*, Dodd, Mead, 1924, calls attention to the abrupt character of the Oceanian languages, the union of words without the polish of the inflected European tongues.

the Primitives, Rubens, Veronese."[1]

Subject matter with Gauguin was important — a primitive people of the tropics, living in a primitive, colorful civilization, whose sunshine, shadow, color, and mood are all expressed in a form that is definitely nonnaturalistic and filled with an atmosphere of meaningful calm. An almost uncanny timeless immobility permeates *The Day of the God* (Fig. 729A), as in a Byzantine mosaic, however far-removed its subject matter may be. This is a surface of intensely rich color areas whose clearly defined shapes and edges create a linear pattern with smooth rhythms. Both subject matter and mode of expression are to be explained, in part at least, by atavistic tendencies and environment. From his mother Gauguin inherited a strain of Peruvian blood, as a child he lived in Lima, and as a youth was a seaman in tropical lands. Later, in France he made sympathetic contact with medieval glass, Near Eastern textiles, Japanese prints, and various primitive arts which were just then catching the attention of Paris. So not unnaturally he betook himself to live an elemental life in the South Sea Islands, where he painted his most characteristic works.

Painting, from Cimabue to Rubens, had evolved toward complexity of design, especially design in space, and richness of palette where color melts into color until, with the impressionists, everything was dissolved into scintillating light broken up into an infinite number of color spots. While Seurat and Cézanne sought structure, solidity, and organization in depth, Van Gogh and Gauguin revived flat pattern design, the use of harmonious and contrasting areas of color and emphatic line such as one finds in Byzantine and Muhammadan, Oriental and primitive, art. Their emotional intensity served as a corrective to the intellectual, scientific approach of Seurat and Cézanne, which could be used successfully only if held under perfect control by such sensitivity as those masters possessed. Their nonnaturalistic tendencies were particularly opposed to the influence of the camera, which was inciting many painters to vie with science in producing verisimilar recordings of nature. The green horses in Gauguin find their theory and their counterpart in the green pigs of the Prodigal Son and the blue hair on the head of Christ in medieval glass.

The great diversity found in Seurat, Cézanne, Van Gogh, and Gauguin is symbolic of the "many-mindedness" of modern painting and of its challenge to a new kind of seeing. Impressionism failed to be accepted as a legitimate, not to say orthodox, method of painting until people had finally caught up with the painters' vision, as they had in the case of Courbet and the Barbizon group. Always late, "a tradition, like an old family, must constantly renew itself with the body and soul of each new age. Otherwise the end is in sight. A tradition in art simply means the heritage of qualities which deserve not only to endure but to develop. If a tradition is not also an evolution it is unworthy of the reverence which we accord to it."[2] "We cannot think in terms of an indefinite multiplicity of detail; our evidence can acquire its proper importance only if it comes before us marshalled by general ideas. These ideas we inherit — they form the tradition of our civilization. Such traditional ideas are never static. They are either fading into meaningless formulae, or are gaining power by the new lights thrown by

---

[1] *First Loan Exhibition . . . 1929*, Museum of Modern Art, 1929, p. 14, by permission of the Museum.

[2] Duncan Phillips in *Leaders of French Art Today*, Phillips Memorial Gallery, Washington, December, 1927–January, 1928.

[A] *Gauguin. The Day of the God. 1894. Art Institute of Chicago. (Art Institute)*

a more delicate apprehension. They are transformed by the urge of critical reason, by the vivid evidence of emotional experience, and by the cold certainties of scientific perception. One fact is certain, you cannot keep them still. No generation can merely reproduce its ancestors. You may preserve the life in a flux of form, or preserve the form amid an ebb of life. But you cannot permanently enclose the same life in the same mold."[1]

Most of the painters of today are working in or developing trends instigated by Seurat, Cézanne, Van Gogh, and Gauguin, after a thorough saturation in the "old masters," which includes the art of the world, with a

[1] A. N. Whitehead, *Science and the Modern World*, Macmillan, 1925, p. 269.

particular emphasis upon the primitive and Oriental arts. The leaders of the nineteenth century posed problems, suggested solutions, and started innovations so striking and so profound that their influence is still directive and history repeats itself: one class of followers copies outward appearances and produces pastiches; another attempts to assimilate and to carry on new experiments with new solutions.

In a general way, most of the modern painters belong to one of two main lines of descent, with many border-line cases: Seurat–Cézanne–Picasso–the cubists; Van Gogh–Gauguin–Matisse–the fauves –the expressionists. These families are composed of intensely individual members, though they represent two fairly coherent, contrasting points of view —

[A]   *Rousseau. The Jungle. 1908. Mrs. Patrick C. Hill Collection. (Art Institute of Chicago)*

which may be illustrated roughly, one by Matisse and the fauves and the other by Picasso and the cubists.

Before turning to the various manifestations of these groups, let us consider individuals who illustrate, again, the "many-mindedness" of the contemporary situation. Pierre Bonnard (1867–1947) might be called a divergent impressionist. For he carried the objective vision of impressionism into the realm of fantasy and infused it with a personal mood.[1] With a rather narrow but subtle range of color he drenched his canvas with warm light and converted it into a decorative "luminous tapestry" constructed of "orchestral tones as vibrant and indefinite as the troubled harmonies of Debussy."[2] Bonnard strove for beautiful surfaces rather than for objective realism, for poetic fantasies with which his structureless figures are quite in harmony.

Henri Rousseau, Le Douanier (1844–1910) is another isolated individual, a folk artist who painted because he wanted to, when he was not playing the violin. His jungle scenes (Fig. 730A)

[1] For this reason Bonnard and Jean Edouard Vuillard (1867–1940) are sometimes called intimists.

[2] Duncan Phillips in *Art and Understanding*, Phillips Memorial Gallery, Washington, 1929–1930, p. 62.

[A]   *Matisse. Still Life: Apples on a Pink Tablecloth. 1922. Chester Dale Collection, New York City. (Art Institute of Chicago)*

reveal an extraordinary gift for shapes, color, and relationships and for the organization of unit shapes into a coherent pattern of great esthetic power. Again, as with Gauguin, it is flat pattern with strong linear quality. With no theory to guide him, Rousseau very innocently put on the canvas simply and directly the symbols, created in his own imagination, for what he had seen objectively.

Returning to the two main currents, we find that Henri Matisse (1869–   ) also started with a subjective reaction to the external world. Though trained in the school of Bouguereau and the Beaux Arts, and at first quite ignorant of the ferment already taking place in

French painting, he finally became aware of the new movements and, through study in the Louvre and travel, came under the influences of the color of the East, of primitive textiles, Persian miniatures and pottery, medieval glass, and Japanese prints. Although at one time early in his career — and again under an influence, that of early cubism — Matisse used sober hues, his characteristic color is as stimulating in its intensity as it is in its sharp opposition of hues, now surprising, now quietly harmonious, and showing the artist's inventiveness in producing rhythm largely by color alone. While living on the Riviera he produced some of his most characteristic work: the *White*

[A] *Picasso. La Table. 1920. Smith College Museum of Art, Northampton, Mass. (Smith College Museum)*

Plumes (Stephen C. Clark Collection), and many still lifes, odalisques, and interiors. It is an art which accents the surface, aims at surface enrichment by means of calligraphic line and flat color areas. Depth is often suggested by subtle changes in value, with a curious but not unpleasant combination of a two- and three-dimensional organization but with the main accent on animation of surface. In the *Still Life: Apples on a Pink Tablecloth* (Fig. 731A), the warm-hued, rather solid foreground group, with its combination of broad quiet curves and angles, acts as a foil to the cool blues and the exciting movement of the jagged motifs above. The two parts are united

by the pitcher and by the line, the motif, and the color of the vertical bands and circular disks.

Matisse belonged to a group known as *les fauves* (the wild beasts),[1] so named in derision at the Salon d'Automne of 1905. As a group, under the stimulation of the newly discovered exotic arts, they were motivated by a need for free expression which led them, each individually, into various paths of free invention. Deft, spirited painters, they produced canvases with no little spontaneity and verve, now with rich surface texture, now with lively linear or boldly clashing color effects, or sometimes with a limited range of hues. Their subject matter was as varied as their modes, with landscape and genre predominating. To realize the revolutionary character of the work of the fauves, we should compare it with that of the contemporary "official" academic painters of Paris — those, for example, who were working in the style of Bouguereau.

Thus the fauves carried on and expanded the trends instigated by Van Gogh and Gauguin and integrated them into the growing twentieth-century tradition. Their contribution — to repeat — consisted of the value of surface richness and emotionally exciting or subtly limited color. Of those who employed a limited palette, Rouault is unique in his use of heavy lines around each unit of the composition, within which each color area vibrates with various tones of one hue, producing much the effect of medieval glass, a craft which Rouault had pursued. In harmony with this technique, he created forms of Byzantine-like simplicity and austerity, and in them expressed a

[1] Henri Matisse; André Derain (1880–   ); Maurice de Vlaminck (1876–   ); Georges Braque (1881–   ); Georges Rouault (1871–   ); Raoul Dufy (1877–   ); Emile Othon Friesz (1879–   ); Charles Dufresne (1876–1938); André de Segonzac (1884–   ).

[A]   *Picasso. Still Life: "Vive la . . .". 1914–15. Sidney Janis Collection, New York City. (Museum of Modern Art) Note the play upon textures, both of surface and of pattern.*

religious content. In comparison with the hearty earthiness of his contemporaries, his feeling is that of a mystic.

The other line of descent from the post-impressionists — that from Cézanne — is found in Picasso and the cubists. Pablo Picasso (1881–   ) is a Spaniard, endowed with Spanish intensity and with the fervor as well as with the forms of Spanish medieval miniatures, frescoes, and sculpture. At the same time he has thrown himself into the formal problems which were paramount issues when he settled in Paris.

In some respects Picasso is characteristic of the age in his constant experimentation, in his startling shifts from one kind of painting to another and from one kind of visualization to another. Like Leonardo in somewhat similar circumstances, he seems to be motivated by curiosity and research. The great difference, however, is that strong traditions and a narrower outlook limited Leonardo; cosmopolitanism and a highly developed individualism delimit Picasso, who in the cosmopolitan world of today is probably the leading figure in the field of painting. When he finally settled in Paris in 1905, he had evolved from the sober realistic painting of Spain, through a brightening of color in an impressionistic mode, into the "blue period," in which he painted pathetic figures of his native Spain with a blue tonality. There followed a series of acrobats, harlequins, and other figures in which color, though subdued, vibrated subtly, as in *The Woman with a Fan* (W. A. Harriman Collection); and then the "rose period," in which he constructed in pinkish hues sculptural forms obviously bearing an influence from Greek sculpture, as in the *Woman with Loaves* (Philadelphia Museum). The *Gertrude Stein* (Museum of Modern Art), with its masklike face and solidity of mass, reveals an acquaintance with Negro sculpture and a more definite focus upon abstract formal problems, which led Picasso together with a group of associates[1] to a dissection of the figure into its essential volumes and planes, as a challenge to the structureless verisimilitude of the camera and the scintillating surfaces of the impressionists. They accomplished this at first without complete loss of representational content; and often included several aspects — a succession of points of view, such as front, profile, and back, known to the mind but not seen by the eye simultaneously.[2] Color was reduced to neutrals so as to eliminate any disturbing emotionalism (Fig. 732A).

Thus arose cubism, a term used originally in ridicule of Picasso and his associates. Its early phase, known as analytical cubism, was completely and coldly objective, as disciplinary as science in its investigations into form. In his *Nude Descending the Stairs*, Marcel

[1] Other members of the group were Georges Braque (1881–   ), Albert Léon Gleizes (1881–   ), Jean Metzinger (1883–   ), Marcel Duchamp (1887–   ), Francis Picabia (1879–   ), Fernand Léger (1881–   ), and Juan Gris (1887–1927).

[2] Simultaneity — the practice of combining various views or parts of an object into a design — was not original with Picasso, but is found in Egyptian painting, in Nazca pottery, in the designs of the Northwest Indians, in African Negro and Oceanian sculpture, and in Chinese bronzes, to mention but a few of many possible examples.

Duchamp, by showing the different aspects of an already analyzed figure as it walked down a stairway, added the fourth dimension, movement. So highly ascetic and disciplinary was cubism, however, that it was almost destined to develop into something which could give the painter more freedom for personal reaction and inventiveness. This Picasso found in taking the parts into which he had separated the figure and combining them freely into compositions which may or may not give clues to the object represented. In this mode, known as synthetic cubism, he used brilliant color freely and boldly and seemed intent upon producing surfaces with rich textures. Probably the climax of this style is found in *The Three Musicians* and some exquisite still lifes, such as the *Green Still Life* (Museum of Modern Art) and the *Still Life: "Vive la . . ."* (Fig. 733A). What strikes us most forcibly about these still lifes is the richly textured quality of the surface, in the attainment of which Picasso, Braque, and others had experimented with the introduction into their compositions of bits of paper, cloth, playing-cards, and other materials, and with mixing sand into the pigment to secure a very rough surface in certain parts of the painting. Such compositions, known as *papiers collés* or collages, provide the painter with more and more elastic mediums.

While still painting synthetic cubist pictures, Picasso made a sudden turn toward realistic Ingres-like drawings and colossal figures in a Greco-Roman style, such as the *Woman in White* (Museum of Modern Art). After another sudden change, about 1925 he began to produce highly simplified contorted figures, now in one mode, now in another — evidence of his extraordinary versatility. Many of these paintings are organized with heavy swirling lines and rich color. Yet when Picasso painted his *Guernica* (1937), he used white, black, and gray only, colors in tune with the grim horror of the destruction of this town in the Spanish Civil War. Also, appropriately for the stark subject matter, he composed with largely angular thematic material, areas with sharp darting angles, and so related them in violent oppositions of line, value, and shape that the panel presents the paradoxical effect of orderly confusion.

Though most of the painters in the cubist movement, like Picasso, have evolved from its hard disciplinary requirements, Georges Braque has retained his personal version of constructing fragments, both representational and nonrepresentational, into a flat pattern, on the theory that a painting is a flat surface and should remain a flat surface, animated by line, color, and texture. He works within a narrow range of restrained but subtly related color areas, with strong reliance upon related and contrasted textures. "The aim of painting," says Braque, ". . . is not to reconstruct an anecdotic fact, but to constitute a pictorial fact. . . . We must not imitate what we want to create. The aspect of things is not to be imitated, for the aspect of things is the result of them."[1]

Fernand Léger has continued to paint synthetic cubist pictures strongly in contrast to the delicately sensitive paintings of Braque. Léger's paintings have the sharp, hard precision of the machine. Even his figures have the same quality, as is seen in the *Three Women* (Museum of Modern Art). In fact, he may take parts of a factory and parts of its machinery as thematic material, and use a restricted color scheme such as reds, blacks, and grays. Or he may use a brilliant palette, as in *The City* (Fig.

661A), in which all the stress of a metropolis is suggested by strong color, violent contrasts, and sharp interplay of line and color areas.

Abstraction in painting carried to its logical conclusion becomes purely nonobjective; that is, it has no representational content and hence no associational appeal. Its aim is to stimulate emotional reactions to formal elements only: to relationships of line, light and dark, color, texture, space. Form itself, pure form, is the subject matter.

Nonobjectivity appeared, contemporary with cubism, in the paintings of the Russian Wassily Kandinsky (1866-1944), who, with a thorough understanding of the psychological effect of each element, and of the interrelationship of elements, composed paintings devoid of representational content which convey, like music, certain moods or "soul states"[2] (Fig. 737A). Completely nonobjective painting is found also in the work of the Russians Kasimir Malevich (1878-1935) and Alexander Rodchenko (1891-   ), and of the neoplasticists of the Netherlands, of whom Piet Cornelis Mondrian (1872-1944) is perhaps the best known. Figure 736A is organized into so perfect an asymmetrical balance of lines, areas, and colors that no change, even infinitesimal, is possible without disturbing that balance. The colors used are black, white, and a small amount of red; and the lines are a balance of verticals and horizontals, with no curve and no diagonal.

This art, which is concerned with one thing, form, provides a least common denominator for all the arts and has influenced them widely. This influence appears in the simple directness and the frequent asymmetry noticeable in the plans, masses, and surfaces of modern

[1] See Maurice Raynal, *Modern French Painters*, Brentano's, 1928, pp. 51-52, for this and other excerpts from the writings and sayings of many modern painters.

[2] Kandinsky's *On the Spiritual in Art*, Solomon R. Guggenheim Foundation, 1946, is an excellent exposition of abstract and nonobjective art by an artist who practiced it.

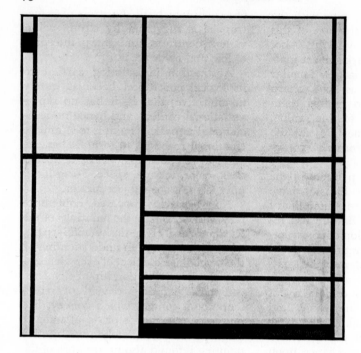

[A] *Mondrian. Composition in White, Black, and Red. 1936. Museum of Modern Art, New York City. (Museum of Modern Art)*

architecture; in posters, advertising, book design, and other industrial arts.

For many people, abstract and nonobjective art is not easy to understand and enjoy. "It is not possible to explain the pleasure or satisfaction we derive from the formal elements in art until we have laid bare the physiology of instinctive responses, explained the part played by pattern in the stimulation of visual acuteness, the relation of rhythm to bodily and perhaps (as the Chinese would have us believe) to cosmic movements, the unconscious appeal of concrete and abstract symbolism, the emotive effect of pure colours and tones, and so on."[1]

Protest against cubism and nonobjective art as something static and overintellectual arose in several quarters, notably in Italy and Germany. In Italy, the futurists sought a more elastic type of expression, one that would

[1] Herbert Read, *Art Now*, Harcourt, Brace, 1937, p. 48.

involve movement, space, and time, not only for itself alone but as an expression of life rhythms — a concept that was both scientific and mystical.[2] Severini's *Au Bal Tabarin* is neither an analysis of form into its inherent related elements nor a synthesis of such elements, but rather a synthesis of fragments of reality so combined as to convey an impression of the movement of a dancer. Thus, though not nonobjective, it is closer in aim to Kandinsky than to the cubists.

In Germany too there was less concentration than with the French on purely formal problems. German expressionism was a manifestation of subjective feeling toward objective reality or the world of imagination. The more Germanic among the Germans had

[2] Giacomo Balla (1871–   ), Luigi Russolo (1885–   ), Umberto Boccioni (1882–1916), and Gino Severini (1883–   ) are important in the group. The poet Marinetti was a spokesman. Their name implies scorn for the past.

[A] *Kandinsky. Improvisation No. 30. 1913. Art Institute of Chicago. (Art Institute)*

been averse to impressionism, as something unsuited to the truculent Northern temperament which led them to bold, vigorous brush work, to strong lines, contrasting values, and intense color. Thus they produced splendid, almost savagely powerful canvases, concisely organized and particularly expressive of intense human feeling. German expressionism[1] was an art in direct line of descent from earlier German painting and engraving, especially in its bold intense color and its linealism, its emphasis on subject matter, and its frequent transcendental overtones. Its rise was contemporary with that of the

[1] Important in the entire movement were the Scandinavian Edvard Munch (1863–1944), Ernst Ludwig Kirchner (1880–1938), Max Pechstein (1881–   ), Emil Nolde (1867–   ), the Russian Wassily Kandinsky (1866–1944), the Swiss Paul Klee (1879–1940), the Austro-Czech Oskar Kokoschka (1886–   ), Karl Hofer (1878–   ), and Max Beckmann (1884–   ). Rouault, though French, is close to this group.

fauves in Paris; it passed through several phases, though some of its painters worked independently of the group. Emil Nolde is perhaps the most sensitive of the German expressionists. Much of his work is somber in tone and mystical in feeling. Kokoschka, on the other hand, finds an outlet for his intensely emotional nature in loading the canvas with areas of brilliant color brushed on with bold strokes, Beckmann is dramatically decorative, with his intense colors, heavy lines, and strong opposition of lines and color areas (Fig. 738A). His canvases are surcharged with a bold and almost savage energy.

In the 1920's occurred a revival of realism in Germany, known as *die neue Sachlichkeit* (the new objectivity). The group included Max Beckmann, who had earlier figured among the expressionists, Otto Dix (1891–   ), and George Grosz (1893–   ). Grosz, in particular, has used his great ability toward social ends, and is as powerful

[A] *Beckmann. Departure. Triptych. 1937. Museum of Modern Art, New York City.*
(*Museum of Modern Art*)

in satire as Goya or Daumier — "everywhere his sensitive technique has its fine surgical beauty."[1]

About the same time there started in Switzerland, and spread to Germany, France, and elsewhere, a movement known as dadaism,[2] which grew out of a contempt for contemporary society and out of the bitter disillusionments which followed World War I. It also marked another trend away from the reasoned, formal aim and the cool, disciplinary requirements of cubism, and toward a spontaneous, intuitive expression of the whimsical, fantastic, humorous, sardonic, or absurd. Though Arp has produced extremely austere, non-objective, relieflike paintings based on an interplay of geometric, frequently amoeboid shapes, probably the most characteristic work of the group were the collages of Arp and Ernst.

It was but one step further from the painting of the dadaists to the subconscious and dream world of the surrealists,[3] who sought in these areas of life the actual reality or the superreality. In 1924 the poet André Breton (note that many of these twentieth-century movements have a literary counterpart) formulated their philosophy in his *Manifeste du surréalisme.* The cold dry tool of logic on the one hand, says Breton, and

[1] Herbert Read, *op. cit.*, p. 93.
[2] Important members in the group were the French Hans Arp (1888–   ), the German Max Ernst (1891–   ), and the American Man Ray (1890–   ). Dadaism lasted from about 1916 to 1922.

[3] Important surrealist painters include the dadaists Arp and Ernst; the Spaniards Salvador Dali (1904–   ) and Joan Miró (1893–   ); the Italian Giorgio de Chirico (1888–   ); the Russian Marc Chagall (1887–   ); the French André Masson (1896–   ) and Yves Tanguy (1900–   ); the Chilean Roberto Matta Echaurren (1911–   ).

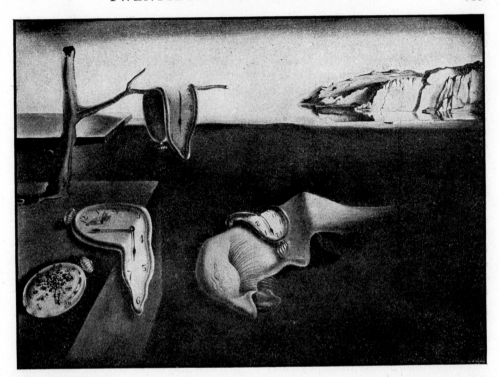

[A]   *Dali. The Persistence of Memory. 1931. Museum of Modern Art, New York City.* (*Museum of Modern Art*) *Note the effective contrast in the highly realistic rendering of highly unrealistic subject matter.*

the magic of the subconscious and the dream world (an influence from Freud) on the other — to resolve these "two seemingly contradictory states, dream and reality, into a sort of absolute reality, a *surréalité*,"[1] was the aim of the surrealists. And this motivation dominates their paintings, in which they bring together into a composition fragments of that "reality" in much the same way that seemingly unrelated fragments of life combine in the vague world of dreams. While subject matter is important, "with them it was not objects, but the images they provoke in the individual, that are the material of art."[2]

[1] Quoted in J. J. Sweeney, *Plastic Redirections in 20th Century Painting,* University of Chicago Press, 1934, p. 87.
[2] *Ibid.*

Surrealist paintings are usually puzzling and surprising, if not fantastically shocking. People who like to see pictures repeat with more or less exactitude what they see in their everyday lives find it difficult to grasp the highly imaginative quality in such painting, or let themselves go in a world of fantasy. They can find here, nevertheless, painting-as-painting of a high order. In Dali's *The Persistence of Memory* (Fig. 739A), for example, meticulous brush work produces a hard surface of jewel-like quality that is a joy in itself. Spontaneous, irrational evocations from the subconscious have been organized into an arresting form. In a darkly foreboding foreground, blue-faced watches are draped over an embryonic figure, a block, and a tree, which help carry the

eye into the deep space of a sunlit distance with its cool blues relieved by
blue-greens and yellow.

Joan Miro, by contrast, does not share
the dark brooding of Dali, perhaps because of his Catalan heritage with its
vivacious spirit and gay color. Like
other painters of fantasy, he was stoutly
antagonistic to the logical, intellectual
abstractions of the formalists: "I am
attaching more and more importance
to the subject matter of my work. To
me it seems vital that a rich and robust
theme should be present to give the
spectator an immediate blow between
the eyes before a second thought can
interpose. In this way poetry pictorially
expressed speaks its own language."[1]
In his early *Harlequin's Festival* (Albright
Gallery, Buffalo) shapes suggested by
people, animals, and objects associated
with a carnival are painted in bright,
gay color, chiefly in the primaries, black,
and white, against a neutral ground,
and are so distributed that they carry
the eye with the vivacious movement
of a festival. Intensive work in making
collages in various mediums as a study
in shapes and textures led Miro to a
greater simplification of shapes, with
stress on the curved line and amoeboid
shapes which produce a floating quality. His color became deep and muted
and his rhythms broader. In the *Composition* (Fig. 741A), against a deeply
brooding ground composed of four
areas of rather dark, closely related reds,
blues, and greens, black shapes float,
some linear, some solid areas with dramatic touches of white and vermilion.
These elements give the panel, which
is large, a highly decorative quality.
Several figures are recognizable, such
as a dog and an ox. But as Miro works
automatically, according to his biog-
raphers, and as his brush moves over
the surface without the direction of the

conscious mind — as in automatic writing or doodling at the telephone — he
himself cannot always explain the
meaning of his pictures. They are
simply a spontaneous expression of the
little-understood, submerged subconscious life.

Perhaps the freest, most intuitive expression of pure fantasy is found in the
work of the Swiss Paul Klee (1879–
1940), who, like the German expressionists, is the heir to Gothic linealism
as well as Gothic fantasy. But in his
contempt for all illusionistic art, he
turned to that of children and primitive
peoples, and sought to put upon the
canvas or paper, in terms of line, color,
and texture, a graph, as it were, of his
emotional reactions to his material. His
paintings take one who is possessed of
imagination into a world of vivid fantasy as well as into the enjoyment of a
surface sensitively organized.[2]

Though they are charged with being
psychologists or poets rather than painters, one can hardly avoid finding in the
work of the best surrealists high esthetic
quality; that is, organic structure. However, if the observer does not learn to
see organic structure in the work of the
"old masters," where representational
content is the chief cause of his satisfaction, he cannot be blamed for not
seeing it when it lies naked before his
eyes in abstract, nonobjective, and surrealist art. Whether consciously or sub-
consciously, these painters show a command over the elements of the painter
— line, light and dark, color, texture,
and space — each according to his personal bent, and a technical ability to
translate mental images, conscious and
subconscious, into skillfully organized
designs in which details are frequently
painted realistically.

[1] Quoted by J. J. Sweeney, *Joan Miro*,
Museum of Modern Art, 1941, p. 13.

[2] See Herbert Read, *op. cit.*, p. 141, for a translation of "Going for a walk with a line," a description by Klee of the way his imagination
works.

[A]   *Miro. Composition. 1933. Museum of Modern Art, New York. (Museum of Modern Art)*

This avant-garde of the twentieth century is too numerous and too influential to be cast aside lightly. Nor can its members be pigeonholed neatly into the numerous "isms" of the century. In their adventurous search for new forms and new meanings they reach out now in one direction, now in another. One over-all statement can be made; namely, that they have all in varying degrees turned from the perceptual to the conceptual approach to actuality, to subjective reaction, and to the world of the imagination and the subconscious, a trend which is in direct opposition to the main trend of European painting from Giotto to impressionism. It may well be that in this kind of painting we are witnessing the beginning of a new cycle, with a new kind of visualization as revolutionary as the Byzantine was compared to the Greco-Roman; or as Giotto's was compared to the Byzantine.

BIBLIOGRAPHY

Apollinaire, Guillaume, *The Cubist Painters; Aesthetic Meditations, 1913*, tr. by Lionel Abel, Wittenborn, 1944

Art in Our Time, Museum of Modern Art, New York City, 1939

Art in Progress, Museum of Modern Art, New York City, 1944

Barnes, Albert C., *The Art in Painting*, 3d ed. rev., Harcourt, Brace, 1937

——— and De Mazia, Violette, *The Art of Cézanne*, Harcourt, Brace, 1939

——— and De Mazia, Violette, *The Art of Henri Matisse*, Scribner, 1933

Barr, Alfred H., Jr., ed., *Fantastic Art, Dada, Surrealism*, Museum of Modern Art, New York City, 1936

——— ed., *Modern Works of Art*, Museum of Modern Art, New York City, c. 1934

——— *Picasso: Fifty Years of His Art*, Museum of Modern Art, New York City, 1946

——— ed., *Picasso; Forty Years of His Art*, 2d ed. rev., Museum of Modern Art, New York City, c. 1939

——— ed., *Vincent van Gogh*, Museum of Modern Art, New York City, c. 1935

Bell, Clive, *Since Cézanne*, Harcourt, Brace, 1922

Beskin, Osip, *The Place of Art in the Soviet Union*, American Russian Institute, 1936

Brinton, Christian, *The Art of Soviet Russia*, foreword by Fiske Kimball, American Russian Institute, 1936

Cassou, Jean, *Picasso*, tr. by Mary Chamot, Hyperion Press, 1940

Chen, Jack, *Soviet Art and Artists*, Transatlantic, 1945

Cheney, Sheldon W., *A Primer of Modern Art*, rev. ed., Tudor, 1939

——— *The Story of Modern Art*, Viking, 1941

Cubism and Abstract Art, Museum of Modern Art, New York City, 1936

Dali, Salvador, *Conquest of the Irrational*, Julien Levy, 1935

Eddy, Arthur J., *Cubists and Post-Impressionism*, McClurg, 1919

Einstein, Carl, *Die Kunst des 20. Jahrhunderts*, Berlin, 1926

——— *Georges Braque*, Paris, 1934

First Loan Exhibition, New York, November, 1929; Cézanne, Gauguin, Seurat, Van Gogh, Museum of Modern Art, New York City, 1929

Fry, Roger E., *Cézanne: A Study of His Development*, Macmillan, 1927

——— ed., *Henri Matisse*, Weyhe, 1930

——— *Transformations*, Brentano's, 1927

Gauguin, Paul, *Noa-Noa*, tr. by O. F. Theis, Greenberg, 1927

German Painting and Sculpture, Museum of Modern Art, New York City, 1931

Gogh, Vincent van, *The Letters of Vincent van Gogh to His Brother, 1872-1886*, 3 vols., Houghton Mifflin, 1927-29

Goldwater, Robert J., *Primitivism in Modern Painting*, Harper, 1938

Gómez de la Serna, Ramón, *Completa e verídica istoria di Picasso e del cubismo*, Torino, 1944

Gordon, Jan, *Modern French Painters*, rev. ed., London, 1940

Guggenheim, Peggy, ed., *Art of This Century*, Art of This Century, 1942

Janis, Sidney, *Abstract & Surrealist Art in America*, Reynal and Hitchcock, 1944

Katz, Alexander R., *Prelude to a New Art for an Old Religion*, L. M. Stein, 1945

Levy, Julien, *Surrealism*, Black Sun Press, 1936

Loran, Erle, *Cézanne's Composition*, University of California Press, 1943

Loukomski, George K., *History of Modern Russian Painting*, Hutchinson, 1945

Mackenzie, Helen F., *Understanding Picasso*, University of Chicago Press, 1940

Martin, J. L., Nicholson, Ben, and Gabo, N., eds., *Circle: International Survey of Constructive Art*, London, 1937

Meier-Graefe, Julius, *Vincent van Gogh*, tr. by John Holroyd-Reece, Blue Ribbon Books, 1936

Merin, Peter (Thoene, Peter, pseud.), *Modern German Art*, tr. by Charles Fullman, Penguin Books, 1938

Miliukov, Paul, *Outlines of Russian Culture*, ed. by Michael Karpovich, tr. by Valentine Ughet and Eleanor Davis, 3 pts.; Part III, "Architecture, Painting, and Music," University of Pennsylvania Press, 1942

Moholy-Nagy, László, *The New Vision*, Norton, 1938

——— *The New Vision and Abstract of an Artist*, 3d ed. rev., Wittenborn, 1946

Mondrian, Piet, *Plastic Art and Pure Plastic Art*, Wittenborn, 1945

Nierendorf, Karl, ed., *Paul Klee: Paintings, Watercolors, 1913 to 1939*, intro. by James J. Sweeney, Oxford University Press, 1941

Novotny, Fritz, *Cézanne*, Phaidon ed., Oxford University Press, 1937

Paalen, Wolfgang, R., *Form and Sense*, Wittenborn, 1945

Pach, Walter, *The Masters of Modern Art*, Huebsch, 1924

Phillips, Duncan and others, *Art and Understanding*, Phillips Memorial Gallery, Washington, D.C., 1929-30

Raynal, Maurice, *Modern French Painters*, tr. by Ralph Roeder, Brentano's, 1928

Read, Herbert E., *Art Now*, rev. ed., Harcourt, Brace, 1937

——— ed., *Surrealism*, Harcourt, Brace, 1937

——— *Unit 1 — The Modern Movement in English Architecture, Painting, and Sculpture*, Toronto, 1934

Rebay, Hilla, *Fourth Catalogue of the Solomon R. Guggenheim Collection of Non-Objective Paint-*

ing, Solomon R. Guggenheim Foundation, New York City, 1939

———— ed., *In Memory of Wassily Kandinsky*, Solomon R. Guggenheim Foundation, New York City, 1945

———— ed., *Kandinsky*, Solomon R. Guggenheim Foundation, New York City, c. 1945

Rey, Robert, *Gauguin*, tr. by F. C. de Sumichrast, Dodd, Mead, 1924

Rutter, Frank V. P., *Evolution in Modern Art*, rev. ed., London, 1932

Soby, James T., *The Early Chirico*, Dodd, Mead, 1941

———— *Georges Rouault*, Museum of Modern Art, New York City, 1945

Soviet Painting; 32 Reproductions of Paintings by Soviet Masters, Moscow and Leningrad, 1939

Sweeney, James J., *Joan Miro*, Museum of Modern Art, New York City, c. 1941

———— *Plastic Redirections in 20th Century Painting*, University of Chicago Press, 1934

Uhde, Wilhelm, *Henri Rousseau*, Berlin, 1923

———— *Picasso and the French Tradition*, tr. by F. M. Loving, Weyhe, c. 1929

———— *Vincent van Gogh*, Phaidon ed., Oxford University Press, 1936

Venturi, Lionello, *Georges Rouault*, Weyhe, 1940

———— *Marc Chagall*, Pierre Matisse Editions, 1945

Vollard, Ambroise, *Paul Cézanne, His Life and Art*, tr. by Harold L. Van Doren, Crown, 1937

Wheeler, Monroe, *20th Century Portraits*, Museum of Modern Art, New York City, c. 1942

Wilenski, Reginald H., *Modern French Painters*, 2d ed., London, 1944

———— *The Modern Movement in Art*, rev. ed., Toronto, 1945

Wright, Willard H., *Modern Painting, Its Tendency and Meaning*, Dodd, Mead, 1915

Zervos, Christian, *Histoire de l'art contemporain*, Paris, 1938

Painting in the United States

REVOLUTIONARY French painting has had an enormous and widespread influence. Hardly a nation in Europe or the Americas has been untouched. In the nineteenth century, the United States looked to Paris in art matters, as did the Middle, Central, and South American nations after they had severed political ties with Spain and Portugal. Officially, the advanced French painting broke upon the American public at the Armory Show in 1913. Before this, however, some painters, quietly but wholeheartedly, had absorbed lessons learned from the French and had rallied to the objective expressed by Arthur B. Davies, "Let us be emancipated." The nineteenth century "solitaries" had begun this emancipation from Europeanism, just as Sullivan and Wright had that from eclecticism in architecture. The Ten and The Eight carried on and brought painting out of stuffy studios, rooting it in American soil, and giving it formal quality.

An over-all glance at the United States from the time of the Armory Show to the present may prove helpful in attempting to get a picture of painting for those three decades. In that period occurred World War I; the boom of the 20's, the heyday of the dealer who strove to build up collections of European art; the Great Depression; World War II; and the shrinking of the world to so small a size that every nation is neighbor to every other. The youthful nation of the United States is still unformed. It is an unassimilated complex of diverse nationalities from Europe, Africa, the Near East and the Far East, each with its own traditions and ideologies, which have not as yet coalesced to form coherent traditions. This embryonic culture, in addition to its own restless ferment, is suddenly brought into contact with exotic cultures, many of them the source of certain of its ingredients of which it has hitherto been unaware. Such are the African; the forgotten or unknown American Indian; and the Far Eastern with the lofty accomplishments of its long past, formerly either unknown or disregarded by the Western world. In addition, many of our painters are foreign-born and a number of eminent European artists have found refuge here from the tyrannies of Europe and are participating creatively and educationally in art activities. Furthermore, the place of the painter in our energetic, mechanistic life is uncertain. He is largely segregated, and his paintings are looked upon merely as luxuries by an audience that still holds the nineteenth-century concept of a painting as an item for a museum or private collection — something quite foreign and inessential to everyday man. We may ask, Why has painting survived? It is chiefly because of the faith and the courage of the painter in the face of isolation and economic distress.

Notwithstanding this complex, shifting, discouraging background, an astonishing amount of competent painting has been produced, no small part of it undoubtedly of lasting quality. In general it tends to be highly individualistic, with no few dominating personalities, as in France; to be an experimental growth, motivated by a desire to attain an authentic American expression. It is experimenting in medium, subject matter, and form, and as yet reveals no consistent trends.

The Armory Show, to return to 1913, probably caused the greatest art furor the United States has ever experienced, and was followed by the formation of the Society of Independent Artists in 1917, also sponsored by The Eight. The result? The public laughed and scorned. So did many of the artists. For others, however, the show forcibly underscored the formal qualities of painting which had been the chief concern of the French painters; opened their eyes to new uses of color and to abstract painting; vitalized and broadened the painter's viewpoint by guiding him to exotic arts as well as to a more intensive study of the "old masters," from which he had been kept by the all-too-frequently heard prejudice that a study of these would

destroy his originality. Unfortunately, it stimulated a considerable number, exhilarated by their new discoveries, to paint in this exciting French style. The result was too often superficial copying devoid of real understanding — a practice which is still going on.

From 1913, American painting has followed, in a general way, the trends of late nineteenth- and twentieth-century painting in France, and, to a lesser degree, that of Germany. The highly individual character of the painters, however, militates against classifying them except into loosely connected groups, with many individuals unclassifiable.

One small group has continued in the tradition of nineteenth-century academic painting; a much larger group, in that of impressionism.[1] Another large and more independent group consists of figure, portrait, and genre painters who have kept partly within traditional lines somewhat modified by the influence of Renoir and the postimpressionists in the direction of greater insistence on structure, more brilliant color, and freer brushwork. Theirs is objective painting of a high order, sometimes imbued with social implications.[2] Eugene Speicher may be taken to illustrate the group. In his paintings we discern, above a command over the figure itself, a feeling for color and for pigment both for their emotive and their textural qualities. In contrast to the objectivity of these painters is the

[1] Important impressionist painters are Gifford Beal (1879–   ), Frederick Frieseke (1874–1939), William James Glackens (1870–1938), Childe Hassam (1859–1935), Ernest Lawson (1873–1939), and Jonas Lie (1880–1940).

[2] Illustrative of this group are Bernard Karfiol (1886–   ), Leon Kroll (1884–   ), Guy Pène du Bois (1884–   ), Kenneth Hayes Miller (1876–   ), Alexander Brook (1898–   ), and Eugene Edward Speicher (1883–   ). The first four are skillful figure-painters. Pène du Bois and Miller tend toward social implications.

[A] *Marin. Maine Islands. 1922. Phillips Memorial Gallery, Washington. (Phillips Memorial Gallery)*

work of Walt Kuhn (1880–), who looks upon the figure more abstractly and attempts to condense it; that is, to simplify it into a few essential related planes.

Perhaps Kuhn should be associated with another group, one of individual artists who illustrate what might be called the trend toward abstraction.[1] So diverse, however, are their modes of expression that no one or two can

[1] Max Weber (1881–), Marsden Hartley (1877–1943), John Marin (1870–), Charles Sheeler (1883–), Charles Demuth (1883–1935), Georgia O'Keeffe (1887–), and Yasuo Kuniyoshi (1893–) are important members of the group.

be singled out as typical of the group. Even before the Armory Show these artists had known and assimilated the objectives of Cézanne and the postimpressionists, the fauves, and the German expressionists; and in addition they had experienced a broadening acquaintance with exotic arts. Like the French, they made a direct break with the Renaissance tradition; they tended toward abstraction in form while retaining subject matter that was entirely American. Marsden Hartley looked at the mountains of Maine, where he was long resident, with the scientific objectivity of Cézanne, searching for structural solidity and expressing it by means of

[A]   *O'Keeffe. Church at Ranchos de Taos. 1929. Phillips Memorial Gallery, Washington.*
(Phillips Memorial Gallery)

scientific color relationship in pigment brushed on in bold strokes. John Marin developed a highly personal style in water color, in the technical handling of which he was one of America's great masters. With Marin, objectivity and subjectivity are co-ordinated. Though reminiscent of the ultimate conciseness of the water colors of Cézanne and also of the fresh spontaneity of Matisse, yet his attitude seems closer to the Chinese Sung painters, in that through contemplation and absorption of the scene he reached its essence, and then with a few spontaneous strokes succeeded in translating his impression to the paper. Manhattan, with its intense vitality, and the Maine coast, peacefully quiet, were favorite themes. A very personal trait was his habit of marking out an area within the frame with three or four broad strokes, as if to state forcibly — all Marin's statements are intensely

forceful, often explosive — the picture plane and through the opening to lead the onlooker directly into space by means of converging lines, or dark areas made emphatic by surrounding lights (Fig. 745A). His color is reserved, in comparison with Matisse's for example, with considerable use of neutrals combined with warm areas and lightened by the white paper.

Georgia O'Keeffe is another original painter, always an exquisite craftsman and a sensitive colorist. Her palette is subtly limited and her paintings frequently have a tonality of vibrating grays. Her subject matter is taken from her own surroundings: Lake George, Canada, New Mexico. Except for flowers painted on a large scale reminiscent of a movie close-up, her usual themes are landscape, houses, barns (*White Canadian Barn No. 2* is an excellent example), still lifes of the desert, and the

[A]   *Sheeler. Totems in Steel. 1935. Downtown Gallery, New York. (Downtown Gallery)*

adobe churches of the Southwest, such as the well-known *Church at Ranchos de Taos* (Fig. 746A). Whatever the theme, her paintings tend away from objectivity toward abstraction or at least toward a highly economic statement that does not preclude an emotional element. Sheeler, on the contrary, under the influence of cubism, is cold in his abstraction. His scenes of factories (Fig. 747A) are as concisely calculated as the machine itself. The same precise calculation appears in his *Yachts and Yachting*, which is an original version of futurism in its vivid, terse expression of the essence of wind-driven ships.

Though the painters of this group have been influenced by cubism in the direction of abstraction, they have not abandoned the representational element, as have a small group of which Stuart Davis (1894–   ) is representa-

tive. Complete or almost complete abstraction characterizes their paintings. Davis's landscapes are gay and vivid in color. Sometimes they are linear, Matisse-like, with a certain amount of representational content. Again they are flat vivacious patterns of color areas, as in the *Summer Landscape* (Fig. 748A); or again they are extremely abstract, like those of the synthetic cubists.

The last group to illustrate the reflection in America of French dominance is the surrealist group. Fantastic and surrealist painting has penetrated the United States, as it has, in greater or less degree, most of the American republics. A great impetus to its spread has been the residence here of European surrealists who fled from Europe in the thirties — Chagall, for example, Dali, and Ernst. Its influence has been felt not only in the pictorial arts but also

[A]   *Davis. Summer Landscape. 1930. Museum of Modern Art, New York City. (Museum of Modern Art)*

in advertising design similar to that of the nonobjective painting of Mondrian.[1]

Thus in the course of American painting we can trace the influence of French styles from impressionism to surrealism. Sometimes the impact was too evident, too overpowering; sometimes a French style acted as a guiding hand to individual accomplishment. To say this does not imply that there were no other elements in the accumulating American tradition. There were.

One was regional painting. All through the life of American painting has run a thread of "the American scene." In the nineteenth century this theme appears in the Currier and Ives prints; in the popular magazine illustrators, many of whom were first-rate painters, such as Winslow Homer; in the anonymous folk painters; and in Eakins, Henri, and Bellows — a clear line of descent. Its continuity was given impetus by John Sloan and others, in protest to what they considered the overintellectualism and artificiality of the abstractionists. A number of painters,[2] not a few of them pupils of Henri, Bellows, and Sloan, have given vigorous interpretations — in painting and in the graphic arts, and in varying personal modes of expression — of city

[1] Among a considerable group of surrealists may be mentioned John Atherton (1900–   ), Peter Blume (1906–   ), Arshile Gorky (1904–   ), Morris Graves (1910–   ), and O. Louis Guglielmi (1906–   ).

[2] Glenn Coleman (1887–1932), Ernest Fiene (1894–   ), Edward Hopper (1882–   ), Charles Ephraim Burchfield (1893–   ), Reginald Marsh (1898–   ), Guy Pène du Bois and William Gropper (1897–   ) are important members of this group. They select themes from town and cities, largely in the East.

[A]   *Burchfield. Civic Improvement. 1927–28. International Business Machines Corporation Collection, New York City.* (*Frank K. M. Rehn*)

crowds, back yards and alleys, shops, old houses, harbor scenes — everything in fact that is common in American life. Many of these painters comment on this life — Marsh and Burchfield (Fig. 749A), for example — and Gropper adds a bitingly satiric element. As a result, we find a kind of painting strongly tinged with social significance, partly as an expression of the social unrest in the texture of American culture and partly an influence from contemporary Mexican painting, which has been wholeheartedly devoted to the social revolution sweeping that country. In the Midwest themes were more rural[1] —

[1] Thomas Hart Benton (1889–   ), Grant Wood (1892–1942), John Steuart Curry (1897–1946), and Doris Lee (1905–   ) represent this group.

cotton-pickers, small-town and country life on the prairies and the plains. All these regional painters are very dissimilar in their modes of painting and are grouped together only because they are motivated by one desire: to make their own environment the raw material of their expression. It is a movement that seems to parallel that of contemporary regional literature and regional folk songs.

Another event in the story of the accumulating American tradition, equal in importance, though not in kind, to the Armory Show, was the formation of the Federal Art Project and the Section of Fine Arts of the Treasury Department, set up in 1935 in the midst of the depression. These projects were vital for two reasons: first, because they brought economic salvation to thousands of artists; and second, because the nature of the projects brought the artist and the people nearer to each other than they had ever been before. The projects consisted of murals in schools, libraries, and other public buildings; easel paintings, sculpture, and ceramics loaned to public institutions or placed there permanently; the establishment of community art centers which not only brought the artist and the community together but provided means and assistance for creative activity on the part of the people. In this way the American people began to realize that the artist could be not only a desirable but an essential factor in community life. At long last, there seemed to be hope that the integration of art in the cultural fabric, long lost in Europe and the United States, though never in Mexico and in the Indian cultures, might eventually become an actuality. A flowering must have roots, and roots feed on an understanding audience.

An invaluable activity of the Federal Art Project was the *Index of American Design*, in which hundreds of artists were put to work making careful copies of all kinds of objects, large and small, and in all parts of the country — making a corpus of our heritage which will lead to better understanding and appreciation of that heritage.

Another movement of considerable importance is the rise of contemporary Indian painting — partly because of its own worth; partly because, like the *Index*, it brings to attention the incalculable value of authentically American Indian art; and partly because in its abstract form it finds common ground with the abstract tendency in modern painting.

This renascent Indian painting consists of water colors, and murals in public buildings. In style it is flat, linear,

and decorative, strictly in the tradition of the kiva and sand paintings (Fig. 422A), with no accessory background and no linear perspective. In content it is an Indian regional art, consisting largely of ceremonial costumes and dances (Fig. 751A), also of hunting and other everyday scenes. Awa Tsireh, of the San Ildefonso pueblo, a village that has witnessed a revival of pottery also, was one of the founders of this school.

An important movement is a growing versatility on the part of the painters, a breaking-down of specialism as they become active in photography, stage design, graphic arts, ceramics, glass, design for the arts of the machine — to mention but a few fields.

Thus many painters, working in diverse, individual modes, some rooted deeply in the Americas, some in Europe, some in both, are striving toward what may be called a truly American style — truly American not in the narrow nationalistic sense, but in the sense of an America that, under the impact of close relationship with all its neighbors, is developing its own characteristic idiom of the world pictorial language.

BIBLIOGRAPHY

American Artists Series, Whitney Museum of American Art, New York City, 1931, 1932

American Folk Art, Museum of Modern Art, New York City, 1932

American Painting & Sculpture, 1862–1932, Museum of Modern Art, New York City, 1932

Americans, 1942, Museum of Modern Art, New York City, 1942

Boswell, Peyton, Jr., *Modern American Painting*, Dodd, Mead, 1939

Bruce, Edward, and Watson, Forbes, *Art in Federal Buildings*, Vol. I, *Mural Designs*, Art in Federal Buildings, Inc., Washington, D.C., 1936

Cahill, Holger, and Barr, Alfred H., Jr., *Art in America*, Halcyon House, 1939

————— and Barr, Alfred H., Jr., eds., *Art*

[A] *Tonita Peña (Quah Ah). Eagle Dance. (Exposition of Indian Tribal Arts, New York)*

in America in Modern Times, Reynal and Hitchcock, 1934

Cheney, Martha C., *Modern Art in America*, McGraw-Hill, 1939

Contemporary Art of the Western Hemisphere, International Business Machines Corporation, 1941

Gallery of American Art, New York World's Fair, *American Art Today*, National Art Society, 1939

Garwood, Darrell, *Artist in Iowa: A Life of Grant Wood*, Norton, 1944

Hall, William S., *Eyes on America*, Studio Publications, 1939

Janis, Sidney, *Abstract & Surrealist Art in America*, Reynal & Hitchcock, 1944

——————— *They Taught Themselves*, Dial Press, 1942

John Marin, Museum of Modern Art, New York City, 1936

Kootz, Samuel M., *Modern American Painters*, Brewer & Warren, 1930

——————— *New Frontiers in American Painting*, Hastings House, 1943

Mellquist, Jerome, *The Emergence of an American Art*, Scribner, 1942

Pagano, Grace, *Contemporary American Painting*, (Encyclopædia Britannica collection), Duell, Sloan & Pearce, 1945

Painters and Sculptors of Modern America, introduction by Monroe Wheeler, Thomas Y. Crowell, 1942

Pearson, Ralph M., *Experiencing American Pictures*, Harper, 1943

Pueblo Indian Painting, 50 Reproductions of Watercolor Paintings by Indian Artists of the New Mexico Pueblos of San Ildefonso and Sia, Nice, France, 1932

Schmeckebier, Laurence E., *John Steuart Curry's Pageant of America*, American Artists Group, 1943

Walker, John, and James, Macgill, *Great American Paintings from Smibert to Bellows, 1729–1924*, Oxford University Press, 1943

Watson, Forbes, *American Painting Today*, American Federation of Arts, 1939

Zigrosser, Carl, *The Artist in America*, Knopf, 1942

Canadian Painting

THE most northerly nation of the Western Hemisphere reveals a situation somewhat analogous, in its conservatism and close ties with academic Europe, to some of the South American republics, especially to those in whose art there is no indigenous ingredient. For, as in the United States, in Canada Indian elements were not assimilated in the evolving culture. Like the United States, Canada is very youthful, is in a ferment of assimilating many nationalities who have migrated thither and are scattered sparsely over a vast area. Thus there is a lack of coherency in which traditions can develop.

One province, however, does present a coherent unity — the French Canadian Quebec, where the intensely nationalistic population, even after the cession of 1763, continued in its traditional manner of building neat houses and churches, of carving fittingly simple furniture and ecclesiastical furnishings and ornament at a time when in Montreal and Ontario the English Georgian style supplanted the French. The traditional French Canadian arts have survived to the present or are being revived, notably weaving — rugs, blankets, and lace — and wood-carving. The abundant native timber — birch, oak, walnut, and other woods — has stimulated the continuity of wood-carving, which has flourished since its introduction in early colonial days, and has imbued the carvers with a feeling for the medium, for they rub and polish it by hand to bring out all its qualities of color, graining, and texture.

What little painting was done in Canada in the eighteenth century consisted of ecclesiastical paintings and portraits, and was executed largely by visiting artists from Europe and the United States. The nineteenth-century artists either went to Europe for training or to live there permanently, and limited themselves to the academic styles quite untouched by the French revolutionary movements which were shaping modern painting. At home the most refreshing note was found in the pictorial chroniclers of life in Canada and the folk painters who correspond to Currier and Ives and the folk artists in the United States and to the *costumbrista* painters of South America. The best known of these were Paul Kane (1810–1871), who in connection with his work for the Hudson's Bay Company traversed the vast West to the Pacific and used both this wild country and the Indians who inhabited it as his subject matter; and Cornelius Krieghoff (1812–1872), who confined his subject matter to Lower Canada, with a preference for Quebec, whose city scenes and countrysides he painted with realistic detail but with spirit and gay color.

The early twentieth century witnessed a new spirit in Canadian painting with the issuance of a manifesto by a group of young artists who painted as an avocation while they pursued teaching or commercial designing as a vocation, for no audience existed sympathetic enough to their work to support them monetarily — a situation by no means limited to Canada but perhaps more acute there than elsewhere in the hemisphere. In 1915 they formed The Seven, whose motivation, like that of The Eight in the United States, was emancipation from Europeanism and freedom to interpret the Canadian land — northern Canada, the prairies, and the Rocky Mountains — and Canadian life in their own individual ways, and to build the tradition of a truly national art. Illustrative of the group was Tom Thomson (1877–1917), who had learned the fundamentals of design as a commercial designer in an engraving house.

[A]   *Thomson. West Wind. 1917. Art Gallery of Toronto. (Art Gallery of Toronto)*

For his material he went into the wild, rugged country of northern Ontario. In his *West Wind* (Fig. 753A), we see a definite break with the traditional schools, under the impact of hints from the postimpressionists. The bold brushwork points to Van Gogh, and the flat linear quality to Gauguin. But all has been assimilated into a form that is not a description but a vigorous expression of the artist's reaction to the wild landscape that it portrays. The Seven disbanded in 1932, and merged into the Canadian Group of Painters.

Thus we find on the one hand a forward-looking group who have become emancipated from the academic, realistic tradition and have been benefited and stimulated in varying degrees, both technically and formally, by lessons learned abroad; on the other hand, a conservative group which holds fast to the academic tradition — a situation which of course is duplicated in almost every country of the Americas. In the former group are found many elements, among them a number of "primitives," and though the Canadians are shy of abstraction, a few are evolving in that direction.

Thus slowly the Canadian painters, in the face of conservatism and indifference, are working toward an expression that is both modern and Canadian.

BIBLIOGRAPHY

Abell, Walter, "Neighbors to the North," *Magazine of Art*, October 1942

Art Association of Montreal, *Loan Exhibition of Masterpieces of Painting*, Montreal, 1942

Canadian National Exhibition, Arts Catalogue, 1938, *Canadian Painting and Sculpture*, Toronto, 1938

Colgate, William G., *Canadian Art*, Toronto, 1943

Contemporary Painting in Canada, Addison Gallery of American Art, Phillips Academy, Andover, Mass., 1942

The Development of Painting in Canada, 1665–1945, Toronto, 1945

Hughes, Margaret E., comp., "A Guide to Canadian Painters," *Ontario Library Review*, May, August 1940

International Business Machines Corporation, *Contemporary Art of Canada and Newfoundland*, Toronto, 1940

McInnes, Graham, *A Short History of Canadian Art*, Toronto, 1939

MacTavish, Newton, *Fine Arts in Canada*, Macmillan, 1925

National Gallery of Canada, *Exhibition of Contemporary Canadian Painting*, Ottawa, 1936

————— *Retrospective Exhibition of Painting by Members of the Group of Seven, 1919–1933*, Ottawa, 1936

Robson, Albert H., *Tom Thomson*, Toronto, 1937

Tate Gallery, *A Century of Canadian Art*, London, 1938

Mexican Painting

NOWHERE in the Americas has modern painting been so vital as in Mexico. Mexico is a complex land, difficult to understand — a land of contrasts and contradictions, of space and of scale. It is still a land where articles of daily use are made by hand and are of an exceptionally high quality; where the people as a whole, with their high esthetic aptitudes and appreciation, provide a fertile ground for a great florescence of art. Several other elements contributed to the flowering of Mexican art. There was the recognition on the part of the artists of their rich cultural heritage, the indigenous Indian and the Hispanic American, and hence a rebellion against subservience to the Academy with its neo-European bias. In addition there was an awareness of, and participation in, the revolution, both ideologically and actively, on the part of artists who found here vital material and who received assistance from the government for their enterprises. Finally, European training had provided many of them with technical and professional proficiency to carry out their ideas.

Modern painting in Mexico cannot be understood apart from the Mexican Revolution in all its phases, political, social, economic, religious, and artistic. Although Mexico had broken with Spain (1821) and had become a republic, at least in name, the old evils continued; the laws which were passed for their alleviation could not be enforced. It was not until 1910, following a climax of greed and exploitation by the Díaz regime and of suffering and slavery on the part of the Indian and the mestizo, that the revolution burst forth with the cry *"Tierra y Libertad!"* Why *"Tierra,"* the land? The Indian is unthinkable apart from the soil. Except for the four or five large cities where industrialization has infiltrated, Mexico — and this is the real Mexico — consists of thousands of villages, chiefly remote from the capital, with intercommunication difficult; and organized, as in the time of the Aztecs, on a communal system.[1] Most of Mexico had been carved up by the small ruling class and the Church into enormous feudal estates (haciendas) which held the Indians as peons, if not as something worse. Against this system of injustice and exploitation the revolution burst forth. Its objectives were to free the oppressed classes and to restore

[1] See Stuart Chase, *Mexico: A Study of Two Americas*, Macmillan, 1935.

them to the land; to recognize their dignity as human beings and their right to their own habits of life and thinking; and to grant them their right to contribute to the evolution of a nation of whose population they constituted probably more than one-half.

A prelude and a voice of prophecy, speaking for and to the people, was found in the work of José Guadalupe Posada (1851–1913), an engraver who supplied illustrations for a publishing house during the Díaz regime. His work was prolific and covered a wide range — songs, ballads, stories, romances, murders, current news items — usually with caustic satire (Fig. 755A). Contemporary society came under his lash, often in the form of skulls and skeletons — quite comprehensible to the Mexican, for the macabre is firmly fixed in his life, as can be seen, for example, in connection with the Feast of the Dead. Posada's work constituted a dynamic commentary on life which appealed directly to an illiterate audience — first because it was

grounded in native soil, and second because of its forceful expression through the use of strong pattern, bold, economic line, and dramatic action.

The modern movement in painting began about 1910 with the fall of Díaz and with a revolt of students against the Academy. In the following turbulent decade some of the artists, notably Siqueiros, joined the revolutionaries. Orozco, in isolation, painted both caustic caricatures and poignant scenes of suffering in hues as somber as their content. Other painters, especially Rivera, were in Europe acquiring technical proficiency and assimilating ideas from French painting. Carlos Mérida had arrived in Mexico City from Guatemala with his paintings, which were based on Guatemalan Indian themes used, not to illustrate the picturesque peoples and costumes of that country, but to provide a starting-point for the creation of abstract forms. Dr. Atl (pseudonym of Gerardo Murillo, 1884–   ), Roberto Montenegro (1885–   ) and

[A] *Posada. Calavera: Don Quixote. Relief engraving on metal. L. 10¾ in. Art Institute of Chicago. (Art Institute)*

[A] *Siqueiros. Proletarian Victim. Duco on burlap. 1933. Museum of Modern Art, New York City. (Museum of Modern Art)*

Adolfo Best-Maugard (1891–) were concerned with the folk arts and with educational methods. Miguel Covarrubias (1904–), another satirist, belonged to this last group, which was bound together by a common motivation.

The welding of these forces came about in 1922, with the formation of the Syndicate of Painters and Sculptors, whose double aim was: first and negatively, to have no more of outmoded neo-European art; second and positively, to create an art that was vital because rooted in truly Mexican traditions and Mexican life. Opportunity for expression came from a revolutionary government, which commis-

sioned the painters to cover the walls of public buildings with murals whose content should be of their own choosing. More than a decade of feverish activity followed, during which Rivera, Roberto Montenegro, Siqueiros, Orozco, Jean Charlot, and others painted murals which depicted scenes of the revolutionary struggle and expressed its ideologies. These artists did not paint without opposition, however, for their work was frequently mutilated by antirevolutionists. A very important result of this decade of painting was the revival of the fresco technique. This was one of the group's greatest contributions to the art of the Americas, and has stimulated mural painting in other American countries.

Though these painters were united in motivation, they were highly individual in their mode of expression. Alfaro Siqueiros (1898–), who perhaps more than any other painter has participated actively in the revolution and in workers' revolutionary movements, in his painting reveals an intensity of feeling that may stem from these experiences. In his *Proletarian Victim* (Fig. 756A), we see a figure as compactly sculpturesque as preconquest sculpture itself. This mass consists of a succession of volumes dramatized by high lights and stressed by the coiling ropes. The figure is painted on burlap in duco, with which Siqueiros has experimented as a vehicle for pigment. Notably successful in this medium is the very sensitive portrait of *María Asúnsolo*.[1] He has recently painted murals at Chillán, Chile, and in the Electricians' Union, Mexico City.

Francisco Goitia (1884–), another painter who participated actively in the revolution, succeeds in expressing poignancy or utter despair in his paint-

[1] See the color reproduction in *Twenty Centuries of Mexican Art*, Museum of Modern Art, 1940.

[A] *Rivera. Earth and the Elements. Fresco. 1927. Chapel of the National School of Agriculture, Chapingo.*

ings, as in the *Tata Jesucristo*, an Indian wake.[1]

Diego Rivera (1886–   ) had gone to Europe in 1907 and, except for a brief return to Mexico, had remained there until 1921, assimilating the work of the cubists as well as the mosaics and frescoes of Italy. On his return to Mexico he immediately became involved in the revolutionary movement and for nearly a decade executed murals[2] which on the one hand were social and po-

[1] See the color reproduction in *Twenty Centuries of Mexican Art.*

[2] In the National Preparatory School and the Ministry of Education in Mexico City; in the Chapel of the National Agricultural College at Chapingo; in the Palace of Cortes at Cuernavaca; and in the National Palace in Mexico City.

litical propaganda, and on the other, were directed toward the evolution of a truly Mexican art.

While some of the earlier of these paintings were in encaustic, most of them were true frescoes. This technique limited his palette to the earth colors, to which he added green, blue, and black. At Chapingo, a pervading warm tonality results from the earth reds obtained from *tezontle*, a native red volcanic stone used widely in Mexican building. This tonality is an important element of unity in a decorative scheme that covers walls and ceiling. Massive figures of Earth and the Elements are symbols of the revolution (Fig. 757A). "Here we teach to exploit the soil and not man."

[A]   *Rivera. Sugar Cane. Fresco. Palace of Cortés. Cuernavaca. 1929-30.*

Rivera's ability to organize his material into a decorative mural unit, one to be seen satisfactorily from any part of the room, is apparent in all his work. In the *Flower Festival* (Fig. 759A), for example, the foreground figures, as compact as if carved from blocks of stone with the austere simplicity of Aztec sculpture, stand out against a wavering ground from which masklike faces emerge in the half-light beneath a mass of sharply pointed lilies. There is a sharp linear quality, and a tendency to flatten the forms as if to suppress space and maintain the integrity of the wall. Triangular motifs oppose curvilinear. The motif of the basket is repeated in the garments and the hands. Line, color, area shapes, light and dark — all are interrelated with clarity and precision.

In his frescoes in the open loggia of the Palace of Cortés at Cuernavaca, Rivera has chosen local history as his subject matter (Fig. 758A). Here again he reveals his command over mural design in the deft unification of several incidents to fill the space; in the diminution of scale and color at the top of the panel to allow the larger-scale figures to form a solid base; in the fine interplay of motives such as the bundles of cane, the shapes of the bending figures, the circles of hats and cart wheel; in the color scheme which integrates the cold blue-green of the cane with warm yellows and red-browns.

Rivera's influence upon mural painting in the United States in particular upon the revival of fresco, has been due in no small degree to the fact that he has executed frescoes in San Francisco (1930-31), Detroit (1932), and New York City (1933-34). Those in New York have been destroyed, but they exist in replica in the Palace of Fine Arts in Mexico City.

José Clemente Orozco (1883-   ), though imbued with the same ideology as the other members of the Syndicate, presents an entirely different personality and manner of expression. Known as the "lone wolf" of Mexican painting, he is a reticent, passionate humanitarian and a caustic satirist. While we look in vain for the mural quality found in Rivera's frescoes, we find in Orozco an intense energy, a violence of feeling, that seems to pour forth in highly dramatic designs: a frequent use of diagonals, violent clashes of line direction and of color, light and dark strongly opposed with the light areas built up to a high intensity by white. Edges tend to be blurred. The pigment is put on in broad sweeps. All this is seen in *The Barricade* (Fig. 760A). His recent frescoes at Guadalajara (Orozco forswears easel painting in favor of fresco, in the tradition of Michelangelo) cover two Renaissance domes and the walls beneath.

[A] *Rivera. A Flower Festival. Encaustic. 1931. Variant of a fresco in the Ministry of Education, Mexico. Museum of Modern Art, New York City. (Museum of Modern Art)*

In the *Chapel of the Orphanage*, figures representing Earth, Air, Sea, and Fire swirl around in one great rhythm that follows, with many minor contrasting movements, the surface of the dome, and then burst forth at its apex into infinite space in truly baroque style. In the *Assembly Hall* (University of Guadalajara), in a lunette beneath the dome, hordes of emaciated starving people, against a background of fire, rush with angry gestures toward a cowering group of their oppressors. Violent chaotic movement, vivid color and value contrasts, create an impressive passionate feeling which slows down somewhat as the gestures and the flames carry the eye to the brilliantly colored dome, which is filled with four figures, gigantic in size relative to those below, repre-

senting Man in four aspects: Scientist, Worker, Philosopher, and Skeptic (Fig. 761A). The figures are boldly constructed of sharply contrasted planes and areas of light and dark in a manner reminiscent of the Byzantines and El Greco. Although in these paintings Orozco rises in wrath against the suffering of the Mexican people in designs that are surcharged with his violent feeling, he seems to imply a more universal, more abstract protest against injustice and exploitation as such, more in the tradition, again, of Michelangelo. However, his passion for his theme overshadows feeling for the wall, which, like the baroque painters, he tends to annul. Like Rivera, Orozco has painted murals in the United States: in Pomona College, Claremont, California (1930); in the

[A]   *Orozco. The Barricade. 1931. Variant of a fresco (1924) in the National Preparatory School, Mexico. Museum of Modern Art, New York City. (Museum of Modern Art)*

New School for Social Research, New York City (1931); in the Library of Dartmouth College (1932–34).

Although these masters are still painting, the fervor of the revolution in painting has waned and a new generation has turned from the social implications of their predecessors. Some are still painting murals in schools, market places, and other public buildings. Many are turning to easel painting and are looking toward Picasso and the surrealists. Though their emphasis, as a consequence, is upon formal problems, their motivation, like that of the preceding generation, is the creation of an authentically Mexican art. Most are experimenting in technique — fresco, water color, gouache, oil, duco, lithography, etching, woodcuts — and many work in several mediums.

South American and Caribbean Painting

MEXICO, because more than any other country in the Americas it has attained a vital, authentic art, has stimulated painting not only north of the Rio Grande but also in the republics of Central and South America — especially in those of the western highlands, where, as in Mexico, the indigenous culture was high and the native traditions continuous and tenacious. The eastern coastal countries and Chile, which contain most of the large wealthy cities of South America and which have far less of an Indian component than the western highlands, are still closely allied with Europe, with

[A]   *Orozco. Man in Four Aspects. Fresco in the dome of the University of Guadalajara. 1935.* (*Frances Toor*) *At the top Man the Worker stands erect grasping the lever of a machine; at the right Man the Scientist, holding a ruler and a compass and surrounded by charts and a partly dissected cadaver, gazes intently with his five faces in as many directions; at the bottom Man the Philosopher raises his right hand and extends his left in an attitude of exposition; at the left Man the Skeptic or Rebel lies with a rope around his neck, his fists clenched, his face and body contorted with suffering.*

French influence predominant. No one of the Central and South American countries has passed through such a social revolution as has Mexico. On the contrary, they are still largely feudal in organization. Yet the influence of Mexico has been widespread and is stimulating latent capacities in the direction of a break from neo-Europeanism and toward a more authentic national expression.

Foremost in this movement is Peru, where 65 per cent of the population are descendants of the Incas. Here has

recognition to the majority Indian element in the Peruvian culture that has
been held in eclipse since the Spanish
conquest.

The leader of this group and perhaps
its most noteworthy figure is José Sabogal (1888–   ). Sabogal's forms, in
both his paintings and his woodcuts,
are direct expressions of Indian life.
His figures are commanding in scale,
filling the space, as in the *Varáyoc of
Chincheros* (Fig. 762A); and they convey
an impression of repose and dignity, as
befits his themes. His later *Landscape at
Caima, Arequipa* shows still further simplification of form, in the direction of abstraction and feeling for space relations.
Many artists hint at a feeling for mural
painting, the opportunity for which
has been meager. For no sympathetic
government involved in social revolution
has provided Peruvian painters with
walls to cover, as in Mexico. Julia
Codesido (1892–   ) paints figures
that are striking in their linear character and strong contrasts of bold, flat
color areas and that are large in scale,
like Sabogal's. Frequently her work
hints at the *costumbrista* painters of the
nineteenth century, as in her *Lima* (Museum of Fine Arts, San Francisco). In
her *Indian Women before a Chapel* (Fig.
763A), on the other hand, the figures are
strongly sculptural and in their austere
monumentality contrast strikingly with
the gold elegance of the baroque interior.[1]

Neighboring Bolivia is also rooted in
the Inca culture, and today has a very
large percentage of still submerged Indians in its population. A recognition
of these facts, together with instigation
from Mexico and Peru, especially from

[A]   *Sabogal. Varáyoc (Indian Mayor) of
Chincheros. 1925. (San Francisco Museum
of Art)*

arisen a group known as the "indigenist" school, whose aim is to produce
not an archaistic, illustrative art, but
an interpretation of twentieth-century
Peru in a mode that is rooted in its
entire cultural heritage. The ingredients of this school are the indigenous
arts, the Spanish and French contacts,
and technical proficiency gained by
European training — all of which have
been assimilated, as in Mexico, and
turned in the direction of a truly national art. Content is largely Indian
types, plaza and street scenes, and the
land itself. The individual artists vary
in style but are all motivated by one
aim: to interpret the real Peru, sometimes with indirect if not direct social
implications, and to give proportional

[1] Other members of the "indigenist" school
are Camilo Blas (1903–   ), Enrique Camino-
Brent (1909–   ), Teresa Carvallo (1903–   ),
Ricardo Florez (1893–   ), and Mario Urteaga
(1875–   ). The last, though associated with
the "indigenists," is a contemporary Peruvian
folk artist.

[A] *Codesido. Indian Women before a Chapel. 1932. (San Francisco Museum of Art)*

Sabogal, has stirred a group of painters to pursue the same path as the latter countries, though the urge for expression may not be so strong. Indian themes and the land itself provide their subject matter. Cecilio Guzmán de Rojas of Potosí (1900–   ), perhaps best known of the group, has used the brilliantly colored costumes of the Bolivians and their vivacious dances as material for paintings which tend more toward flat pattern than toward the three-dimensional expressions of the Mexicans and the Peruvians. One Bolivian painter, Roberto Guardia Berdecio (1910–   ), under the personal influence of Alfaro Siqueiros of Mexico, has not only entered the field of abstract art but has also participated in Siqueiros' experiments in duco as a painting medium.

Ecuador, Colombia, and Venezuela are still largely neo-European. Colombia, quite untouched, strangely enough, by the rich Chibcha culture, has always kept close to Spain, to the San Fernando Academy, and to the Spaniards Sorolla and Zuloaga. Venezuela tends toward the French rather than the Spanish. Ecuador, despite its great accomplishment in earlier centuries, is still weakly European. In all these countries, however, are individuals or groups among the younger artists who, usually under the influence of Mexico, are searching for a more authentically national expression not only in painting but also in the field of the folk arts and the various crafts. This is notably true in Colombia and Venezuela.

Chile, with its large bustling cities, is more akin, in this respect and also

in its lack of a strong indigenous element, to the opulent cities of the eastern
coast; and like them it remains close to
Europe — to France in particular —
and retains almost intact its Spanish
social structure. The painters hold true
to this pattern, following in general the
conservative academic French modes,
with competent craftsmanship but with
little evidence of modern Paris, despite
a considerable amount of modern architecture in Santiago. An exception is
found in the abstract paintings of Roberto Matta Echaurren, the architect
already noted, who became associated
in Paris with the surrealists. His influence, together with that of Siqueiros of
Mexico, who has recently executed murals at Chillán in Chile, may cause a
break in the general conservatism. A
promising movement appears in the
field of the industrial arts, under the
stimulating leadership of José Perotti,
director of the School of Applied Arts,
in which the native folk arts are assert-
ing their influence in weaving, pottery,
and silverwork. In the last field, one
sees an infiltration of the great accomplishment of the one Indian group to
remain intact and unconquerable by
the Spaniard, the Araucanian.

In Argentina, which is as conservative, on the whole, as Chile and even
more closely allied with Europe, we
find the painters concentrated chiefly
in animated Buenos Aires. With no indigenous stylistic element and with particularly close ties with France and
Italy, some painters follow preimpres-
sionist and impressionist styles; some,
the Spanish style of Sorolla or Zuloaga;
a few, the cubist or surrealist styles.
While their themes are local, such as
the gaucho, they tend to be illustrative
rather than interpretative. Though conservative as a whole, Argentinian paint-

[A] *Figari. Creole Dance. Museum of Modern Art, New York City. (Museum of Modern Art) Compare this static organization with the movement in Fig. 768A.*

ing is experiencing a ferment under the leadership of Alfredo Guido (1892–   ), sculptor, painter, and etcher. His impressive *Stevedores Resting* (Fig. 764A) in its simply blocked-out forms is a long step from the illustrations of local themes in the impressionist manner. Even more so are the sculpturesque portraits of Lino Enea Spilimbergo (1896–   ) and the cubist work of Emilio Pettoruti (1895–   ), which shows a direct impress of the synthetic cubist paintings of Picasso and Braque.

Across the La Plata, Uruguay also has received some degree of abstractionism into its traditions in the work of Joaquín Torres-García of Montevideo (1874–   ), who in Europe came under the influence of Piet Mondrian, Paul Klee, and Ozenfant but on his return developed a highly individual style that is reminiscent of hieroglyphics. Pedro Figari (1861–1938), on the other hand,

probably the most eminent painter of Uruguay, an attorney by profession, produced a prodigious number of pictures of the life of Uruguayan people of all classes, festivals, dances, gauchos — hardly any aspect of life has been left untouched in these small pictures, which have the clear directness of folk art, like the *retablos* of Mexico, vivid color in strong contrasts, and luscious surface texture (Fig. 765A).

In Brazil, judging from the brilliant accomplishments in architecture, we might expect an equal emergence from the nineteenth century in painting. On the contrary, there have prevailed in general the conservative academic modes set by the Fine Arts Academy in 1816 when it placed Brazilian painting in line with the French tradition. Exceptions there are, however, which appear to be laying the ground for the evolution of a more truly original Brazilian art. The center of activity is the energetic city of São Paulo, center of the coffee industry, where, after an awakening through the influence of Brazilian artists who had become impressed in Europe with modern movements, modern art burst upon Brazil in the Week of Modern Art held in São Paulo in 1922. This occasion involved not only painting but also music, the dance, folklore, and literature. It stressed particularly the place of the Negro in the culture of Brazil, his contributions to folklore and to the dance and music as seen in the work of Villa-Lobos. For while the Indian has contributed but little to the cultural fabric of Brazil, the Negro has played an important role. Frans Post pictured him in his early colonial paintings. The Week of Modern Art was an outburst affecting the whole cultural fabric and has been followed by exhibitions of the work of Picasso and other modern French painters. Probably the chief figure in this movement in painting is Cândido Portinari (1903–   ) of São Paulo, residing in Rio de Janeiro, and well known in the United States because he has exhibited here and executed murals at the New York World's Fair and in the Library of Congress. With somewhat the same motivation as the Peruvian painters, Portinari has sought to interpret the colorful life of the common folk of Brazil, their industries, and their festivals. In general his style tends to be direct and vivid, with dramatic contrasts of color and value. In the *Morro* (*Hill*) (Fig. 767A), for example, against a lusciously rich red hill stand forth the awkward, angular figures of people in vivid blues and greens highlighted with white; on the high horizon in the distance is the blue bay of Rio de Janeiro and the skyscrapers of the city, which repeat the rectangular motifs of the cabins on the hill.

In the richly tropical Caribbean area, including the Central American na-

tions, painting in general tends to be illustrative and to follow French modes. One exciting development has taken place within the last five years, in Cuba. This island has no indigenous element in its culture, as the Indians were early exterminated by the Spaniards. It does, however, have a large Negro ingredient, which has contributed vitally, especially in music and dancing. Negro, Spanish baroque, contemporary Mexico, and contemporary Paris, especially Picasso, together have converged upon a group of painters and have stirred them to an expression in painting which, though immature, is filled with fresh vitality and exuberance, and shows a complete break with traditional academism. This painting reveals no social implications, despite the presence in Cuba of the Mexican Siqueiros, one of the most social-minded of the Mexican painters. All members of the group are highly individual. Ponce de León (1895–   ), for example, works in a ghostly palette of white and pale neutrals, with heavy impasto. His subjects are largely figures and portraits, into which he often infuses an ironic vein. Markedly in contrast is the startling color of Amelia Peláez (1897–   ) who in Paris came under the influence of the synthetic cubist painters. In her paintings we feel also the late linear style of Picasso in the heavy dark lines, the sharp contrasts of color, frequently of complementary red and green. In Mario Carreño (1913–   ) too, we are perhaps first struck by the "intoxicating color," brilliant complementaries juxtaposed boldly with little gradation. In his *Sugar-Cane Cutters* is the same intensity of energy and movement as in his *Afro-Cuban Dance* (Fig. 768A), in which the bold color, and the squat bulbous figures with large feet, full of movement compressed within the canvas, create an uncanny impression of witchery. Part of this effect results from equally

[A] *Portinari. Morro. 1933. Museum of Modern Art, New York City. (Museum of Modern Art) The scene shows village life in the outskirts of Rio de Janeiro.*

bold textures created by the addition of cloth, rope, and strings of heavy pigment to the glossy effect of the duco technique.

SUMMARY

A bird's-eye view of twentieth-century painting sees Paris the magnetic focal point, which not only has drawn painters to itself but also has decentralized its influence far and wide. As a whole, the painters of Paris have broken, like the architects in their break with eclecticism, with the Renaissance tradition of visual perception which began with Giotto and culminated in impressionism. For it they substituted a conceptual subjective attitude toward na-

ture. They "analyzed forms to simplified but related elements, then reshaped them into new and subtle entities."[1] Sometimes these entities were representational, sometimes nonrepresentational, or nonobjective, or completely geometric. The painter's problem was frequently the same as that of the architect and the sculptor — space relationships; and not a few twentieth-century painters have been accomplished architects and sculptors as well. Seurat and Cézanne pointed the way; the cubists took a long stride; Kandinsky, Mondrian, and the Russians attained complete nonobjectivity; the Germans, shunning the formalism of the French, revitalized earlier traditional styles with

[1] Sweeney, *op. cit.*, p. 47.

[A] *Carreño. Afro-Cuban Dance. Duco on composition board. 1943. Perls Galleries, New York City. (Museum of Modern Art) Compare with Fig. 765A.*

a tendency both to transcendentalism and to realism; the futurists, protesting against the past vitriolically, and with eyes intent upon the present and the future, attempted to express time and space in the normally static art of painting; the realists and the surrealists in their ideology probed the subconscious and the world of pure fantasy, and often expressed it through a painstaking realism.

In the Americas, the traditional styles to a greater or less degree dominate — less in the United States, where an authentic art seems to be in the making; more in Canada and the South American countries, where academism and impressionism are still largely dominant, though in several of these countries two trends are observable: an infiltration here and there of twentieth-century French painting, and a renascence of

the indigenous cultures which is producing an art rooted in long-lived traditions. Mexican painting is the most exciting painting in the Americas. Here an authentic national art has arisen, born of the Mexican Revolution, strong in social significance, and of the highest esthetic quality, notably in its frescoes, by which it has given great impetus to the revival of mural painting in all the Americas. We are struck, first of all, with the extraordinary variety of this modern painting — which, after all, is to be expected when we consider the restless incoherence of our century. The general trend is toward a break with the past and an intent search for new directions. Probably abstract art — to use the term broadly — is one of the chief phenomena of twentieth-century painting. Whether it is the pioneer of a new style, or whether it will cleanse traditional styles of their too great emphasis on verisimilitude and revitalize them, only the future can tell. Yet in this pioneering stage, undoubted masterpieces have been created of a quality to take their places beside any of the "old masters." Another characteristic is its international overtones. Nationalism within the framework of internationalism, analogous to what we have seen in architecture and to the present political concept of national sovereignty within the framework of an international organization has by no means been attained, but a trend in that direction is clear.

Still, unfortunately, painting is concerned primarily with itself, with formal problems as ends in themselves; is devoid of function in contemporary culture, lacks an understanding audience. A healthy sign is the breaking-down of lines of specialization. Painters are putting their talents to work in many fields new to them and thus coming closer to their audience. On the whole they are responding, often prophetically, to a new age in the making, and are giving concrete expression to what they feel are the vital forces at work in our contemporary age.

BIBLIOGRAPHY

American Artists Group Monograph Series, American Artists Group, 1945–

Argentina, National Committee New York World's Fair and Golden Gate Exposition, *Fine Arts in Argentina*, Buenos Aires, 1939

Brenner, Anita, *Idols behind Altars*, Payson & Clarke, 1929

Chilean Contemporary Art, Toledo Museum of Art, Toledo, Ohio, 1942

A Comprehensive Exhibition of the Contemporary Art of Argentina, Virginia Museum of Fine Arts, Richmond, Va., 1940

Fernández, Justino, *El arte moderno en México*, Mexico City, 1937

———— *José Clemente Orozco*, Mexico City, 1944

Frescoes of Diego Rivera, Museum of Modern Art, New York City, 1933

Gamboa, Fernando, Schniewind, Carl O., and Edwards, Hugh L., *Posada, Printmaker to the Mexican People*, Art Institute of Chicago, 1944

Gómez Sicre, José, *Cuban Painting of Today*, English version by Harold T. Riddle, Havana, 1944

Grant, Frances R., *Brazilian Art*, Bulletin of the Pan American Union, Washington, D.C., January 1931

Hanson, Earl P., ed., *The New World Guides to the Latin American Republics*, 2 vols., Duell, Sloan & Pearce, 1943

Helm, MacKinley, *Modern Mexican Painters*, Harper, 1941

James, Concha R., "Spanish American Literature and Art," in *Concerning Latin American Culture*, ed. by Charles C. Griffin, Columbia University Press, 1940

Kirstein, Lincoln, *The Latin-American Collection of the Museum of Modern Art*, Museum of Modern Art, New York City, 1943

Landgren, Marchal E., "Contemporary Painting in Latin America," Studio, November 1939, p. 193

Llerena, José A., *La Pintura ecuatoriana del siglo XX*, and Chaves, A., *Primer registro bibliográfico sobre artes plásticas en el Ecuador*, Quito, Ecuador, 1942

Merida, Carlos, *Modern Mexican Artists*, Crown, 1938

———— *Orozco's Frescoes in Guadalajara*, Mexico City, 1940

Mexican Art Today, Philadelphia Museum of Art, 1943

Modern Cuban Painters, Bulletin of the Museum of Modern Art, New York City, Vol. XI, no. 5, April 1944

Oglesby, Catharine, *Modern Primitive Arts of Mexico, Guatemala and the Southwest*, McGraw-Hill, 1939

Orozco, José C., *José Clemente Orozco*, introduction by Alma Reed, Delphic Studios, 1932

Payro, Julio E., *Veintidos pintores, facetas del arte Argentino*, Buenos Aires, 1944

Portinari, Candido, *Portinari, His Life and Art*, University of Chicago Press, 1940

Portinari of Brazil, Museum of Modern Art, New York City, 1940

Rivera, Diego, *The Frescoes of Diego Rivera*, introduction by Ernestine Evans, Harcourt, Brace, 1929

Schmeckebier, Laurence E., *Modern Mexican Art*, University of Minnesota Press, 1939

Smith, Robert C., "Brazilian Art," in *Concerning Latin American Culture*, ed. by Charles C. Griffin, Columbia University Press, 1940

———— *Brazilian Painting in New York*, Bulletin of the Pan American Union, Washington, D.C., September 1939

———— "Latin American Painting Comes into Its Own," *Inter-American Quarterly*, July 1940

Toor, Frances, *Mexican Art Series — Frescoes*, Nos. 1–10, Mexico City, 1937

———— *Mexican Popular Arts*, Crown, 1939

Twenty Centuries of Mexican Art, Museum of Modern Art, New York City, 1940

Velásquez Cháves, Agustín, *Contemporary Mexican Artists*, Covici Friede, 1937

———— *Tres siglos de pintura colonial mexicana*, Mexico City, 1939

Ward, Constance A., *The Guatemalan Art Renaissance*, Bulletin of the Pan American Union, Washington, D.C., May 1941

Wolfe, Bertram D., *Diego Rivera, His Life and Times*, Knopf, 1939

Zalamea, Jorge, *Nueve artistas colombianos*, Bogotá, Colombia, 1941

[A] *Manship. Dancer
and Gazelles. Bronze.
H. 33 in. 1916. Art Institute of Chicago. (Art
Institute)*

45

TWENTIETH–CENTURY SCULPTURE

SCULPTURE, after playing a minor
role since the sixteenth century, is
now beginning to resume importance.
Despite this lag, its evolution parallels,
to a remarkable degree, that of architecture and painting, with which it has
common aims: simplification; study of
the potentials of various materials, old
and new; and concentration on formal
problems, those of organization in space
in particular. It is reaffirming the meaning of sculpture, in contrast to the conception of a statue as a copy of a model,
and is regaining its long-lost affinity
with architecture. In style it is almost
more international than architecture,
with necessarily some national diver-

gencies. As with the painters, Paris has
been the center of activity for sculptors
of most of the European countries, the
United States, and the Latin American
nations. But even before the outbreak
of World War II, many accomplished
sculptors became residents of the United
States, and now many are working here.
Thus any attempt to classify sculptors
nationally immediately breaks down.
It seems wiser to try to follow a general
line of evolution from realism, through
a modified naturalism, to abstraction
and nonobjectivity — which, to repeat,
parallels the evolution found in painting. In fact many of the greater artists
practice both arts.

This evolution has been recent, for no series of dynamic revolts occurred in sculpture in the nineteenth century, as happened in painting. It is true that some sculptors, François Rude (1784–1855) and Antoine Louis Barye (1796–1875), for example, had turned from the popular neoclassicism toward a new realism, often romantically dramatic. Auguste Rodin (1840–1917), the leading sculptor of the nineteenth century, produced work in stone, bronze, and terra cotta that was primarily literary and psychological rather than formal in its content. His concern was with surface modulation and realistic detail rather than upon mass, volume, and space, though at times his work seems to give us the impression of a solid mass beneath.

In the Americas of the nineteenth century, we observe the same kind of sculptural expression as in Europe, because the few who practiced the art studied or lived in France or Italy and worked in a weak Italianate or neoclassical style. Formal structure was almost completely lost; stonecutting had long since disappeared in favor of the clay model translated into stone by mechanical means. Probably the leading sculptor in the United States was Augustus Saint-Gaudens (1848–1907), who, in a long series of portraits and monuments, seemed to pioneer in the direction of monumentality in such figures as the *Lincoln* (Lincoln Park, Chicago) and in the *Adams Memorial* (Rock Creek Cemetery, Washington). Although in the latter the nineteenth-century literary quality is present, we observe a suppression of irritating, unorganized detail in favor of broad simplification and unbroken contours. Another pioneer was George Grey Barnard (1863–1938), whose conceptions were forceful and monumental, and whose realism was an assertive force rather than a description of facts, as seen in his

[A] *Faggi. Station of the Cross: Jesus Counsels the Daughters of Jerusalem. Bronze. 1924. Church of St. Thomas the Apostle, Chicago.*

Two Natures of Man (Metropolitan Museum, New York). Another contribution of Barnard was his plea for a return to direct stonecutting.

With this nineteenth-century background, sculpture was ill-prepared for the abrupt bursting upon the scene of primitive, archaic, and Far Eastern arts, whose influence has been as stimulating as the general ferment of new ideas and new directions found in all the arts; for these types of sculpture awakened artists to the intrinsic meaning of sculptural form. These two influences, the acquaintance with various truly sculptural arts and the forward movements in architecture and painting, served to outmode the eclectic and imitative type which had spread over all Europe and the Americas. The latter did not cease to exist. In fact it is still practiced today as "academic" art. But

[A] *Meštrović. Mounted Indian. Bronze. 1928. Chicago. (Art Institute of Chicago)*

the new ideas have infiltrated widely throughout both halves of the Western Hemisphere. In the Americas, an awakening to the powerfully sculptural quality in pre-Columbian art has had a profound effect.

In this permeation there was no sudden break with the older traditions, which at first seemed revivified by some of the pioneers who were struggling to cast off the shackles of romanticism, eclecticism, and formlessness. One of these was Paul Manship (1885–   ), who, notwithstanding a servile dependence upon early Greek art, exhibits in his small bronzes both superb crafts-

manship and an effective decorative quality, as in the *Dancer and Gazelles* (Fig. 770A), with its suave movement based on a design of curves. Decorative sculpture began to find a more harmonious relation with buildings which were breaking from the Renaissance tradition in style, as is illustrated in the reliefs of Antoine Bourdelle (1861–1929) on the Théâtre des Champs-Elysées (Paris), with their insistence on clearly cut planes. The English Eric Gill (1882–1940), engraver, draftsman, illustrator, and pre-eminently a stonecutter, contributed to the evolution and the meaning of sculpture by his writings as well as by his carvings. He cut directly, in native British stone, highly decorative reliefs and figures which were conventional in treatment and almost abstract in form. The Italo-American Alfeo Faggi (1885–   ) also, by means of symbols, conventions, and distortions, expressed profoundly religious moods, as is seen in his *Stations of the Cross* (Fig. 771A) and in his poignant presentations of the *Pietà*, in which a spiritual unity is enhanced by the close formal unity of the figures. The Yugoslav Ivan Meštrović (1883–   ), worker in stone, wood, and bronze, uses similar means both in his stone reliefs, as in the *Račić Mausoleum* (Cavtat, Yugoslavia) and his bronze *Indians* (Fig. 772A), in which mass, contours, and line combine (note the strong diagonals) to create a dynamic effect. Carl Milles (1875–   ) of Sweden, now resident in America, attains forthright strength in his work through simplification and clarity of relationships. He has made many fountains, all with an architectural quality, usually of bronze and boldly modeled in strong simple planes with emphatic repeated motifs in order to carry in the out-of-door light. Water he has treated effectively as an integral element in the design. His equestrian statue *Folke Filbyter* (Fig. 773A), with its powerful countermovement in the man and the horse, again illustrates how a forceful relationship of mass and contour achieves a forceful statement of an idea.

Rugged strength appears also in the bold, massive forms in wood and bronze of the German Ernst Barlach (1870–1938), which are permeated with passion, in tune with the intense spirit of the German expressionist painters, and also in the tradition of German woodcarving. Strongly in contrast are the bronze portraits of the French Charles Despiau (1874–1946; Fig. 774A), the surfaces of which are sensitively modu-

[A] *Milles. Folke Filbyter. Bronze. 1927. Replica of the original on a fountain in Linköping, Sweden. City Art Museum, St. Louis. (St. Louis Museum)*

lated and the forms permeated with a gentle charm and an exquisite taste that seem partly French and partly personal. Contrastingly, again, the portraits of Jacob Epstein (1880–   ), an American living in England, reveal a nervous energy, an intensity of life, due to a highly individual, emotive manner of handling clay and bronze. These portraits, though solidly constructed, receive special surface emphasis, partly in an attempt to indicate all the minute planes which exist in a head, partly for

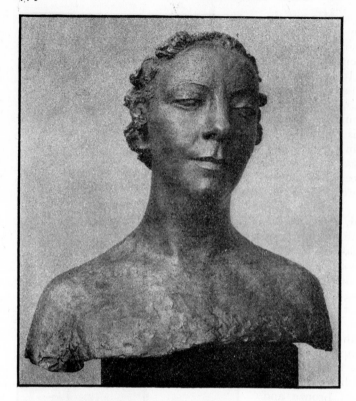

[A]   *Despiau. Antoinette Schulte. Bronze. H. 20 in. 1934. Antoinette Schulte Collection, New York City. (Antoinette Schulte)*

interpretation, and partly for the purely esthetic pleasure derived from the manner of handling the clay, as the painter depends for certain effects upon his mode of manipulating pigment. The Epstein Figure 775A, for example, shows a powerfully bold, massive intellect, while the *Oriel Ross* is feminine, with a liveliness due to a delicate playing-off of contrasting textures. Epstein's stone-carving can be illustrated by the *Day* and *Night* of the London Underground. In the latter, the decorative quality is equaled by a brooding spirit consonant with the theme.[1]

In individuals like these, sculpture regained a truly sculptural quality and a command over materials, however divergent their personal modes. If an

[1] For Epstein's own exposition of his purposes, see his *The Sculptor Speaks*, Doubleday, Doran, 1932.

over-all statement of style can be made, we might say that it was a modified naturalism, in which frequent use of conventions contributed a decorative and architectural quality.

A stronger trend toward abstract forms, toward the use of the figure for its purely esthetic possibilities, with little or no ulterior content, appears in a rather large group of sculptors working in various mediums. Aristide Maillol (1861–1944) worked in terra cotta, stone, and bronze, and was equally accomplished in drawing, lithography, and woodcutting. His *Seated Woman* (Fig. 776A) is conceived as an abstract organization constructed out of the volumes provided by the human figure. It has all the weight and solidity inherent in the material, and the largely unbroken surfaces of the simply carved masses take the light evenly and quietly.

This treatment of the figure bears a strong similarity to that of the Greek sculptors of the late archaic age, those of Olympia, for example (Fig. 136B). Yet Maillol is not archaistic, like Manship. The German Wilhelm Lehmbruck (1881–1919), in contrast to Maillol, used attenuated figures, with elongated proportions to attain an impression of lyric grace. But his motivation is the same: to use the figure as a vehicle for formal expression, usually with abstract content — if form itself is not the only meaning. Lehmbruck's *Kneeling Woman* (Fig. 778A) consists of interplaying cylindrical volumes which move suavely about a strong vertical axis and are unified and stabilized by the drapery.

The American Gaston Lachaise (1882–1935) was a sculptor expert in the use of bronze. In the *Figure of a Woman* (Fig. 777A), the strongly felt movement swells from the lightly poised feet to a climax in the large rounding hips; thence, after a sharp accent in the angle of the waist, it again swells into the broad shoulders and the bent arms. It is this abstract rhythm, symbolic of some profound power rising to a climax, that is the content of the statue. Bronze is peculiarly suitable for objectifying this upward movement. Contrast the weight and solidity, the feeling of the play of gravity, in the stone-carving of Maillol or of William Zorach (1887–   ), an American who, like Maillol, is primarily a carver in stone and seeks to compose complex arrangements of spherical and cylindrical volumes afforded by one or more figures into clearly and firmly integrated, compact structures filled with movement and enlivened by contrasts of texture. Another American, Robert Laurent (1890–   ), is also a direct stonecutter and is extremely versatile in the matter of medium. Out of the difficult translucent, striated alabaster he has created small-scale figures with

[A]   *Epstein. Albert Einstein. Bronze. H. 17¼ in. 1933. Hiram J. Halle Collection, New York City.*

sensitively related masses and suavely flowing planes. In wood he has experimented in the use of plant forms as suitable raw material for the sculptor; and in bronze he has employed bird forms for garden sculpture.

Wood-carving in a simplified manner, tending strongly toward abstraction, appears in the work of some of the Latin American artists. The abundance and variety of wood in the tropical areas naturally led sculptors to its use. The *Christ* (Fig. 778B) of Maria Martins of Brazil (1900–   ) is a commanding figure because of the almost geometric simplicity of its cylindrical form. Marina Núñez del Prado of Bolivia (1910–   ) has succeeded in infusing solid masses of wood with the vivacious rhythms of the Bolivian Indian dancers.

[A]   *Maillol. Seated Woman. c. 1901.*

An impetus toward complete abstraction, and finally to nonobjectivity — that is, to nonrepresentational sculpture — came through a wider acquaintance with Negro, primitive, and archaic sculpture, and cubism. Matisse and the Italian Amedeo Modigliani (1884–1920) show the Negro influence. Picasso applied the theories of cubism to sculpture as well as to painting. The Romanian Constantin Brancusi (1876–   ) carried abstraction as far as possible without entirely losing the representational content, and at the same time extracted from the material its maximum potentiality: from stone, in his portrait of *Madame Pogany;* from brass, in the *Bird in Flight* (Fig. 779A). In the latter everything accidental has been eliminated or compressed into the most direct and economical expression possible, and representational content has been reduced to a minimum. "In flight" is the important part of the title, the

sheer essence of movement. This the sculptor has attained by meticulous attention to proportions, contours, and surface treatment. Note the exquisite quality of the proportions and unbroken contours, and the highly polished surface. The means which Brancusi has used to stress the concept of flight esthetically are the same which the modern engineer uses in designing his "streamlined" airplanes, locomotives, and automobiles.

England — strangely enough, since the English have long been lacking in sculptural expression — has produced some sculptors of the highest creative ability who have made an important contribution to abstract and nonobjective sculpture. Of these Henry Spencer Moore (1898–   ) is the best known. His carvings in wood and stone are surcharged with a feeling for mass on a grand scale — mountains of mass alternating with valleys of empty space;

lighted solids, with deeply shadowed voids — and always show a strong tactile feeling (Fig. 780A). Sometimes the human figure is the starting-point for these constructions; sometimes non-representational shapes, repeated in subtle variation, constitute his raw material.[1]

The profound rhythms and the imperturbability in Moore's carvings contrast with the more spirited movement in the work of the Ukranian Alexander Archipenko (1887–   ) and the French Jacques Lipchitz (1891–   ), both now resident in the United States. These sculptors are versatile in the handling of various mediums and daring in their experimentations and innovations in sculptural form. Archipenko, like so many modern artists, is an accomplished draftsman, painter, and ceramist as well as a sculptor. He works deftly in many mediums — marble, brass, aluminum, wood — with a feeling for the distinctive quality of each. His abstract conceptions are based on the human figure, from which he extracts only those parts that serve his purpose. The *White Torso* is as abstract as Brancusi's *Bird in Flight*. The figure is controlled by a single suave vertical movement punctuated by the sharp angles at the waist and knee. One of his innovations is the use of concavities sunk into the mass like intaglio, which in certain lights appear as convexities.

Ossip Zadkine (1890–   ), a Pole now living in the United States, also experimented in the use of concavities. We may think of this practice as a prelude to the actual piercing of the mass,

[1] For further examples of nonobjectivity, see the work of the painter Hans Arp, who uses in his reliefs the same amoeboid shapes as in his painting; of Ben Nicholson of England, whose reliefs seem the sculptural counterpart of Mondrian's paintings; and of the Russian Antoine Pevsner, who concentrates upon the problems of the interpenetration of volumes and planes as applied to sculpture.

[A] *Lachaise. Figure of a Woman. Bronze. 1927. J. A. Dunbar Collection, New York City. (Museum of Modern Art)*

of creating open space within the space determined by the material. This Lipchitz accomplished. In the second decade of the century, when he was under the influence of primitive and cubist art, he created figures in clay, stone, cement, or bronze which consist of interpenetrating volumes and planes. Then he lightened the weight by piercing the mass (Fig. 779B), and eventually eliminated so much of the matrix that only

[A] *Lehmbruck. Kneeling Woman. Cast Stone. 1911. H. c. 6 ft. Museum of Modern Art, New York City. (Figs. 778A and B, Museum of Modern Art) A strong vertical axis stabilizes the movements of diagonals.*

[B] *Martins. Christ. Jacaranda wood. H. c. 8 ft. 1941. Museum of Modern Art, New York City.*

light strands remain which carry interwoven rhythms. These, however, are in bronze, the only suitable medium for such compositions.[1]

This piercing of the mass, with the consequent creation of interior space, seems but a step toward the attempt to create actual movement, the fourth dimension, within that space. That has

[1] It is illuminating to trace Lipchitz's treatment of the *Woman and Guitar* — a favorite subject — from his cubist period to the present.

been the accomplishment of Alexander Calder (1898–   ), whose mobiles, as they are appropriately called, made of pipe, wire, metal, and other materials are so scientifically constructed and balanced that their parts move with the slightest currents of air within the confines of a carefully calculated space — like the movements of a dancer, provided the dancer remains within a fixed space. The futurists had attempted to bring into sculpture the movement

[A] *Brancusi. Bird in Flight. Brass. 1919. Museum of Modern Art, New York City.*

[B] *Lipchitz. Pegasus. Bronze. H. 14½ in. 1929. Mrs. T. Catesby Jones Collection, New York City. (Figs. 779A and B, Museum of Modern Art) Compare with Fig. 169B. Both designs are suitable only to metal.*

which the painters had attempted to bring into painting. But while their work suggests the fourth dimension, they seem heavy and static in comparison with the light, truly moving mobiles of Calder. In *Horizontal Spines* (Fig. 781A) the delicate grace and precision of pure line in the fine steel wires contrasts and combines in constantly changing relationships with the bold dash and vigor of the sheet aluminum shapes.

SUMMARY

An outstanding event of the twentieth century was the revival of sculpture; the re-establishment of its former close relation with architecture; and its alliance with the other arts in motivation and in following the swiftly changing pattern of modern civilization. Tremendous strides were made in an exploration of the true nature of the sculptural art and of the mediums and processes,

[A] *Moore. Reclining Figure. Elm wood. L. 6 ft. 1945–46. Bucholz Gallery, New York City.*
(*Bucholz Gallery*)

notably direct stonecutting, suitable for its expression; and in this adventure fundamentals long lost sight of were rediscovered. Briefly, sculpture followed two lines: one the continuity of the old tradition, which was vivified by the revolutionary movements in all the arts; and the other, a break with traditional forms, a concentration upon formal problems which eventuated in abstract and completely nonobjective work. As in painting, form itself became the theme. In a remarkably short time sculpture has evolved from the status of a weak imitation of nature and eclecticism to that of a robust, truly sculptural conception. "The artistic fruit of man," says Hans Arp, "shows, for the most part, ridiculous ambition to imitate the appearance of other things. I like nature but not its substitutes." [1]

BIBLIOGRAPHY

Agard, Walter R., *The New Architectural Sculpture*, Oxford University Press, 1935
Art in Our Time, Museum of Modern Art, New York City, 1939
Aumonier, William, ed., *Modern Architectural Sculpture*, Scribner, 1930
Casson, Stanley, *Sculpture of Today*, Studio Publications, 1939
———— *Some Modern Sculptors*, Oxford University Press, 1928

[1] Quoted by Alfred H. Barr, ed., *Cubism and Abstract Art*, Museum of Modern Art, 1936, p. 13.

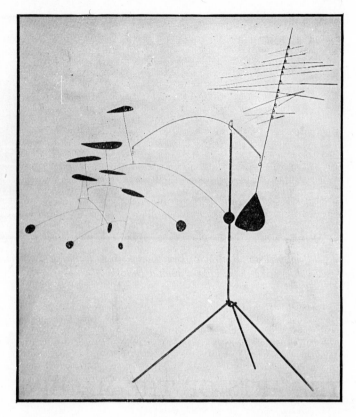

[A] *Calder. Horizontal Spines. Mobile. Aluminum and steel. H. c. 4½ ft. 1942. Addison Gallery of American Art, Phillips Academy, Andover, Mass. (Addison Gallery)*

Casson, Stanley, *XXth Century Sculptors*, Oxford University Press, 1930

Cubism and Abstract Art, Museum of Modern Art, New York City, 1936

Edgerton, Harold E., and Killian, James R., Jr., *Flash! Seeing the Unseen by Ultra High-speed Photography*, Hale, Cushman & Flint, 1939

Epstein, Jacob, *The Sculptor Speaks*, Doubleday, Doran, 1932

Giedion-Welcker, C., *Modern Plastic Art*, English version by P. Morton Shand, Zurich, 1937

Grigson, Geoffrey, *Henry Moore*, Penguin Books, 1943

Martel, Jan, and Martel, Joel, *Sculpture*, Paris, 1928

Martin, J. L., Nicholson, Ben, and Gabo, N., eds., *Circle: International Survey of Constructive Art*, London, 1937

Meštrović, Ivan, *Meštrović*, Zagreb, 1938

Moholy-Nagy, László, *The New Vision*, Norton, 1938
———— *Vision in Motion*, Paul Theobald, 1947

Moore, Henry S., *Henry Moore: Sculpture and Drawings*, introd. by Herbert Read, London, 1944

Painting and Sculpture from 16 American Cities, Museum of Modern Art, New York City, 1933

Pound, Ezra, *Gaudier-Brzeska*, John Lane, 1916

Read, Herbert E., *Unit 1 — The Modern Movement in English Architecture, Painting and Sculpture*, Toronto, 1934

Rewald, John, *Maillol*, Hyperion Press, 1939

Ritchie, Andrew C., ed., *Aristide Maillol*, Albright Art Gallery, Buffalo, N.Y., 1945

Rogers, Meyric R., *Carl Milles*, Yale University Press, 1940

Sculpture of the Western Hemisphere, International Business Machines Corp., 1942

Valentiner, W. R., *Origins of Modern Sculpture*, Wittenborn, 1946

Wilenski, Reginald H., *The Meaning of Modern Sculpture*, Frederick A. Stokes, 1933

Wilhelm Lehmbruck, Aristide Maillol, Museum of Modern Art, New York City, 1930

[A] *Pennsylvania Railroad T–1 Locomotive. Baldwin Locomotive Works and Raymond Loewy, designers. 1942. (Pennsylvania Railroad)*

46

THE ARTS OF THE MACHINE

ANOTHER aspect of the contemporary situation that in its distinctive character is consistent with the trends seen in modern architecture, painting, and sculpture is found in the world of the industrial arts. We cannot help observing the enormous advance, in appearance and in efficiency, in the everyday things of our present world — in "five-and-ten" products, clothing, jewelry, furnishings, silver, glass, tools, automobiles — the list is endless. And it may well be that the twentieth century is witnessing the truth of the prophecy of James Jackson Jarvis in 1864, which bears repetition, in part: "His [the American's] clipper-ships, fire engines, locomotives, and some of his machinery and tools combine that equilibrium of lines, proportions, and masses, which are among the fundamental causes of abstract beauty . . . and is an indication of what may happen to the rest of his work when he puts into it an equal amount of heart and knowledge." [1] That time appears to have arrived and to have provided a healthy situation, because here art and the people meet as they do not meet in the seclusion of studios, museums, and collections. And it may well be that future generations will look upon the utilitarian, machine-made products of modern industry as the most forthright expression of the twentieth century, in the first place, because they express "the felt necessities of the time" (Justice Oliver Wendell Holmes), and in the second place, because they display high esthetic quality.

[1] For the full quotation see pages 668–69.

Consider for a moment what is perhaps the dominating factor of this century — the machine. We who have become so accustomed to the machine find it difficult to realize that for thousands of years man had been making what he needed for daily living by hand; and that only in the last century has he opened the door upon the new world of technology, with its unbelievable potentialities, which is already initiating not only vast social and economic changes but is originating new trends and traditions in the arts. Already we have seen that the machine, with the co-operation of the artist, can produce objects which not only function effectively, but which are as satisfying in their own way as the handmade objects of premachine days. "Whenever the final product of the machine is designed or determined by anyone sensitive to formal values, that product can and does become an abstract work of art in the subtler sense of the term."[1] Even mass production is not an unmitigated evil, for it gives the creative faculty wide scope for combining shapes, textures, and colors, which individually might seem commonplace, into novel arrangements.

In its early days, the machine was looked upon merely as a laborsaving device to reproduce quickly and in quantity handmade articles. Unfortunately that conception has not been entirely outgrown. For we are still making electric candles and machine-made hand-wrought silver and iron. The true product of the machine, on the other hand, has an entirely different character from the product made by hand. There can be no translation of the one into the other. In the handmade object appear the warmth of personality, the marks of tools, irregularity of shape, and subtle variations of hue or texture. The

machine, by contrast, is cold and precise, and in its products requires of the observer a response to the beauty of geometry. To be sure, geometry is basically present in all art of all times, though it may not be discernible to the untrained eye.

Just what, then, is the character of machine art, and what is the function of the artist in its creation? Machine art we meet at every turn. Almost imperceptibly this new art has permeated our everyday world from chain-store products to B-29s — our advertising, window displays, automobiles, kitchens, packaging, household furnishings, and utensils, to mention but a few. The materials of machine art include not only the old materials, often used in new ways — glass, for example — but an ever increasing number of new ones, notably plastics. Each has its own potentiality for color and texture and, technologically, for machine production. The forms of machine-made articles seem to bear a relation to the machine itself in their clean lines, often long and unbroken; in their unbroken surfaces made effective by texture; and in their lack of ornament. This form, however, is dependent upon the "equilibrium of lines, proportions, masses," in fact upon all the elements used in the construction of any organic structure; and also upon function — to do efficiently what it is made to do. The word "streamlined" is frequently used in connection with machine art. The term has two connotations, one technological, the other esthetic. As applied technologically to airplanes, locomotives and trains, automobiles, and ships, where movement is in question, the term is based upon the fact that smooth unbroken surfaces and rounding corners offer least resistance to air currents and thus assure the greatest potentiality for power and speed. By extension of meaning, the term is being applied to static

[1] Herbert Read, *Art and Industry*, Harcourt, Brace, 1935, p. 37.

articles which have similar characteristics and in whose simplicity, clean unbroken lines, and smooth surfaces we
take intuitive delight.

This machine art, though made in
mass production, originates, after all,
with the artist who collaborates with
business and with the consumer. He
must be a technologist, just as the
Gothic and the modern builders were
and are engineers. For he must know
the potentialities of his materials. Does
this or that material lend itself to manufacture by a machine? Does the product
function adequately? Will it sell? How
will people react to it? It is at this point
that artist and people come into closest
contact. And where the artist can win
popular acceptance — and to a large
extent he has done so — he is breaking
down that present segregation of the
arts from life that has plagued the world
for at least a hundred and fifty years.
Most people thrill at the sight of our
airplanes (Fig. 785A) and "streamliners"
(Fig. 782A), the superlative curves of
our highways, and the sweep of our
bridges, which seem to spring so lightly
across rivers and canyons. All these
combine scientific skill and esthetic
quality. Yet people seldom consider
them in the same category as buildings,
paintings, and sculpture. The reason for
their delight, however, is essentially the
same.

Basically, the machine arts are in
total harmony with modern buildings
and abstract or nonobjective painting
and sculpture. And to bring them into
conformity with all buildings, painting,
and sculpture of all ages, which are as
fundamentally geometric as they, may
not be too difficult a step to take.
Above and beyond the character of the
form, however, lies its *quality*. And just
as a painting, a building, a statue, or a
textile is judged in the last analysis by
a *quality* that is as indefinable as the
nature of art itself and yet is felt in-

tuitively by the artist and the spectator,
just so any machine-made article is to
be judged on the basis of whether the
artist, after he has met all the demands
of the machine, of function, and of economics, has been able to infuse his
original design with that *quality* which
distinguishes art. It is the same problem that faced the Paleolithic maker of
flints. That many of our designers have
met this test seems inescapable. They
have produced a dynamic art, definitely
expressive of contemporary living.

It is in the United States, probably,
that machine art has advanced farthest,
for here technological development and
industrialization have made greatest
progress. Some of its roots, however,
are found in Europe — in the William
Morris movement in England, for example, which pointed a direction though
it still clung to making by hand rather
than by machine. In some European
countries traditions have been strong
and have given way to the machine
reluctantly, as in the Scandinavian
countries, where handmade and machine-made objects are produced side
by side. In fact, contemporary industrial
arts are by no means all machine-made.
Handcrafts are still pursued in probably
much more than half the world: in the
Far East, Africa, the South American
countries outside the large cities, French
Canada, Mexico, and among the Indians. Even in mechanized countries
there is still a luxury demand for handmade objects, as well as a revival of the
folk arts. In many, but by no means
all, of the traditional handcrafts is discernible an affinity with machine art in
their simplicity, their suppression or
elimination of ornament, their sensitive
feeling for materials, with a disciplined
regard for the idiom of each. A good
illustration is found in Swedish arts.

Furnishings exemplify excellently the
modern style. Kitchens, bathrooms, and
utility rooms reveal striking and satis-

[A]   *Constellation. Built by Lockheed Aircraft Corp. from Trans World Airline specifications.*
1945. (Trans World Airline)

fying innovations in the directions noted. Furniture has become more functional in order to meet, in a direct way, the needs of human living, the need for comfort and relaxation in an age of great stress and strain. It has become simplified, bereft of dust-collecting ornament; it has utilized new materials such as glass, plastics, and tubular metal; and in the use of the old, it has shown a regard for intrinsic qualities — in wood, for example, where the artists have sought to make the most of textures, color, and graining, perhaps as a result of lessons from the Japanese and the Scandinavians. In furnishings in general there is evident a desire to attain a consistent whole, through an integration of the house itself, its interior space organization, and of the furniture, textiles, and other contributing articles; to select and relate all the elements involved so as to bring about a unity with variety of spaces, shapes, colors, and textures.

Textiles, so important in furnishings, are using such new materials as the synthetic and glass fibers, and new weaving techniques, as well as reviving older or exotic processes, such as the batik and block printing of the Far East. Traditionalism and modernism often find common ground. Swedish textiles are an example. For traditional Swedish hangings and rugs, in the austere simplicity of their conventionalized forms and color patterns — often in several tones of one hue — are strikingly modern in style. Indeed the forms of this revived art are so in harmony in spirit and in form with the modern that the transition, the transformation, from the former to the latter, almost seems accomplished without a realization that the transformation is taking place.

In ceramics, the increased use of terra cotta and glazed tiles in the building art has created a demand for fabrics, both molded and painted, of a thoroughly architectural design. With pottery in the round there is a tendency away from realistically painted decoration — pictures of landscapes or university buildings — toward forms that depend upon shape, proportions, color, and texture for their effects and are architectural in their simplicity, and toward true clay shapes, often with a one-color glaze filled with subtle modulations. Experiments are producing high-fired products, porcelain and stoneware, of unusually simple shapes and textures. Wherever painted decoration is used the work tends toward a decorative pattern following constructional lines and the same decorative fitness that is found in Persian and Chinese wares. At the same time a considerable amount of small ceramic sculpture is being produced that is imaginative, freely naturalistic, or abstract, and which provides needed accents of color and texture.

The field of the metalworkers has been greatly enlarged by the introduction of new materials and by new technical processes for working them: silver, pewter, inlaid and patined brass and copper, iron, aluminum, lead, bronze, zinc, and stainless steel. Here are wide possibilities for selection of a material suitable to the project in hand, for treatment to secure surface variations, and for combinations of materials to produce contrasts of color and texture.

An enormous expansion in the use of glass marks the twentieth century, partly because of new demands for it in building and furnishings and partly because of a wider use for small everyday objects. Huge quantities of both opaque and transparent glass are to be used for industrial and also for domestic buildings, and modern technical processes have enabled builders to secure an infinite variety of effects of color and texture for decorative purposes. According to its function, glass can be made delicately thin or massively thick, of meticulously uniform texture or bubbled, streaked, sand-blasted, acid-engraved, or colored within an infinite range of hues. True window-making, as distinguished from pictures painted on glass and inserted in window openings, has returned since its eclipse of more than three centuries because of its unfortunate attempt to transmute itself into the painting medium. The best windows now are built on the practices of the window-makers of Chartres: a mosaic made by leading together pieces of glass, generally colored through and through or so treated by mechanical processes that the desired effect of color and texture can be secured. This art still finds a wide use in church-building, and at times clings to the representative, symbolic design of the medieval windows, as in the windows at *Princeton Chapel* and in the rose of *St. John the Divine* (New York City) by Charles J. Connick. Or at times it takes on a purely abstract form, as in the windows of the church at *Le Raincy*, and in its uses in secular buildings. In both uses, however, the ultimate effect results from the manipulation of the material according to its own capacities and limitations. In industrial buildings such windows or panels are in increasing demand both for decoration and for advertising, for lettering is in perfect harmony with its principles of design.

In making small objects of glass there is a similar variety of processes for working the medium. It can be blown; molded or pressed; and cut with grinding and polishing for a finish. Preeminent work consists of individual pieces whose form is inherent in the medium and in a suitable process of working it. A bottle or a jar by Marinot of France, for example, is likely to be an austere massive geometric shape with a bubbly texture and intense color accent, or possibly a bit of severely restrained conventional incising. This glass, however, is made for a limited few, is a luxury item, as is the Steuben glass for which eminent artists (painters and sculptors included) have cre-

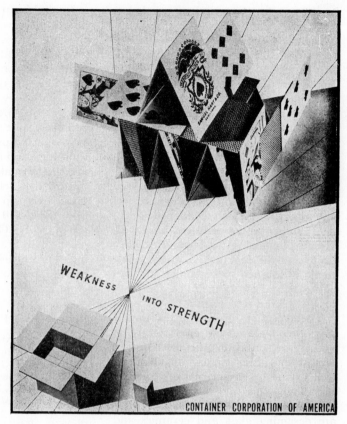

[A] *Herbert Bayer. Weakness Into Strength. Advertising design. Photomontage, water color, and air brush. 1941. (Container Corporation of America)*

ated designs — an indication of the breakdown of specialization.

Mention at least should be made of bookmaking, of the art that sees the entire book as a unit. Typography, illustration, format, binding — each exists not as a separate unit but as one element of a complete design. The woodcut is again finding wider use as the kind of illustration that harmonizes best with the printed page. Experimentation is going on in cutting new type faces in which a severe simplicity is evident.

An art that has evolved from the exigencies of the modern industrial world is advertising design, a new graphic art that under the stimulation of a definite function is reaching in our best advertising a high quality of forceful pattern which contributes as much

to the driving power as the content of the words used — perhaps even more (Fig. 787A).

SUMMARY

The pattern of modern art seen in architecture, sculpture, and painting appears equally in those arts which have changed from hand to machine technique. Strikingly noticeable in this pattern is the effort to get down to fundamentals; an insistence upon adequate functioning; a keen regard for materials and the idiom of each; a forthright directness of approach which results in clear, concise forms — all of which bears a direct or indirect relation to science and the machine. Thus all the arts are moving on a wide front, each faithful to its own function and material, but with a unity that predicates the emergence of a twentieth-century modern style. Two elements in the contemporary situation bear a large responsibility. In the first place, we are living in an age of science and technology, and consequently an age of the machine, to whose swift advances of only a century and a half we have not yet made complete adjustment. In the second place, through scientific advances in transportation and communication, the world has been so interknit that it has become in reality one world, in which advanced, decadent, and primitive cultures, highly diversified in ideology and art forms, have been brought together, head on. The result is destined to be confusion, with old ways and old forms in conflict with new ways and new forms.

The evolution of a culture is slow; it progresses by trial and error. Thus we find experimentation on every hand; in literature, music, drama, and dance as well as in the visual arts. Artists are broadening their scope, breaking down the barriers of specialization; painters are designing glass and ceramics and stage settings; and all are designing for the machine arts. Experiments in abstract space design are applicable equally to architecture, painting, sculpture, and the machine arts. Specialism is giving way to broader outlooks; and the attitude toward the past and to hitherto unknown or neglected styles has changed radically. Never have these arts been studied so intensively, but now with a shift of emphasis from archaeology, eclecticism, and matters of fact to esthetic worth and the power of the arts to teach invaluable lessons in the creation of form. Thus, the artist has profited greatly and has come to realize that what he has hitherto considered quaint and exotic is great art, only in a different dialect, frequently a more powerful dialect, than his own.

In all this confusion and experimentation, we are witnessing the slow death of the Renaissance and the birth of a new age. What form it will eventually assume, we do not know. We only know that it is on the way, and is moving at a pace never before equaled. The alert artist, so often prophetic, and the onlooker alike have eyed the past and looked at the present and have come to the realization that tremendous changes are in the making; and their attitude toward these changes might well be expressed by a prophetic attitude of Dr. Oliver Wendell Holmes of a century ago (1835): "To Oliver, his father's news meant merely that the world was moving. Oliver desired not to censure or impede, but to move with it."[1]

BIBLIOGRAPHY

Art in Progress, Museum of Modern Art, New York City, 1944

Bayer, Herbert, Gropius, Walter, and Gropius, Ise, eds., *Bauhaus, 1919–1928*, Museum of Modern Art, New York City, 1938

Chase, Stuart, *Men and Machines*, Macmillan, 1937

Faulkner, Ray, Ziegfeld, Edwin, and Hill, Gerald, *Art Today*, Holt, 1941

Forsyth, Gordon M., *20th Century Ceramics*, Studio Publications, 1936

Geddes, Norman B., *Horizons*, Little, Brown, 1932

Giedion, Siegfried, *Mechanization Takes Command*, Oxford University Press, 1948

Holme, Geoffrey, *Industrial Design and the Future*, Studio Publications, 1934

Janneau, Guillaume, *Modern Glass*, Studio Publications, 1931

Johnson, Philip, *Machine Art*, foreword by Alfred H. Barr, Jr., Museum of Modern Art, New York City, and Norton, 1934

Kahn, Ely J., *Design in Art and Industry*, Scribner, 1935

Kiesler, Frederick, *Contemporary Art Applied to the Store and Its Display*, Brentano's, 1930

Langdon, William C., *Everyday Things in American Life*, Scribner, 1941

[1] Catherine D. Bowen, *Yankee from Olympus: Justice Holmes and His Family*, Little, Brown, 1944, p. 69.

Leyson, Burr W., *Plastics in the World of Tomorrow*, Dutton, 1944

Mansperger, Dale E., and Pepper, Carson W., *Plastics; Problems and Processes*, International Textbook Press, 1938

Moholy-Nagy, László, *The New Vision*, Norton, 1938

——————— *Vision in Motion*, Paul Theobald, 1947

Mumford, Lewis, *Technics and Civilization*, Harcourt, Brace, 1934

Plastes (pseud.), *Plastics in Industry*, Chemical Publishing Co., 1941

Read, Herbert E., *Art and Industry*, Harcourt, Brace, 1935

Richards, Charles R., *Art in Industry*, Macmillan, 1929

Schoen, Max, ed., *The Enjoyment of the Arts*, Philosophical Library, 1944

Skelley, Mrs. Leloise D., *Modern Fine Glass*, Richard R. Smith, 1937

Stiles, Helen E., *Pottery in the United States*, Dutton, 1941

Teague, Walter D., *Design This Day*, Harcourt, Brace, 1940

Train, Arthur K., *The Story of Everyday Things*, Harper, 1941

Waugh, Sidney, *Modern Glass*, Steuben Glass, 1939

See also the General Bibliography, pp. 791–92.

APPENDIX

General Bibliography

General Histories

Abbot, E. R., *The Great Painters*, Harcourt, Brace, 1927

Ackerman, Phyllis, *Tapestry, the Mirror of Civilization*, Oxford University Press, 1933

American Institute of Architects, *The Significance of the Fine Arts*, new ed., Marshall Jones, 1923

Buckley, Wilfred, Rackham, Bernard, and Hudig, Ferrand, *European Glass*, London, 1926

Chase, G. H., and Post, C. R., *History of Sculpture*, Harper, 1924

Dillon, Edward, *Glass*, Putnam, 1907

Faure, Élie, *History of Art*, tr. by Walter Pach, 5 vols., Harper, 1921–30

Fletcher, Sir B. F., *History of Architecture on the Comparative Method*, 9th ed., Scribner, 1931

Gardner, J. S., *Ironwork*, rev. by W. W. Watts, 4th ed., 2 vols., Victoria and Albert Museum, London, 1927–30

Gilman, Roger, *Great Styles of Interior Architecture*, Harper, 1924

Glazier, Richard, *A Manual of Historic Ornament*, 4th ed. rev., Scribner, 1926

Hamlin, A. D. F., *History of Ornament*, 2 vols., Century, 1923

Herbert, J. A., *Illuminated Manuscripts*, Putnam, 1911

Hind, A. M., *History of Engraving and Etching*, Houghton Mifflin, 1923

————— *An Introduction to a History of Woodcuts*, 2 vols., Houghton Mifflin, 1935

Jones, E. A., *Old Silver of Europe & America from Early Times to the Nineteenth Century*, Lippincott, 1928

Kimball, S. F., and Edgell, G. H., *History of Architecture*, Harper, 1918

Magonigle, H. V. B., *The Nature, Practice, and History of Art*, Scribner, 1924

Maskell, Alfred, *Ivories*, Putnam, 1905

————— *Wood Sculpture*, Putnam, 1911

Moore, N. H., *Old Glass, European and American*, Stokes, 1924

Mumford, Lewis, *Technics and Civilization*, Harcourt, Brace, 1934

Pijoan José, *History of Art*, tr. by Ralph L. Roys, 3 vols., Harper, 1927

Pollard, A. W., *Fine Books*, Putnam, 1912

Post, C. R., *History of European and American Sculpture*, 2 vols., Harvard University Press, 1921

Rindge, A. M., *Sculpture*, Harcourt, Brace, 1929

Robb, David M., and Garrison, J. J., *Art in the Western World*, rev. ed., Harper, 1942

Statham, H. H., *A Short Critical History of Architecture*, Scribner, 1912

Stites, Raymond S., *The Arts and Man*, McGraw-Hill, 1940

Triggs, H. I., *Garden Craft in Europe*, Scribner, 1913

Technique and Design

Batchelder, E. A., *Design in Theory and Practice*, Macmillan, 1910

Best-Maugard, Adolfo, *A Method for Creative Design*, Knopf, 1926

Birren, Faber, *Functional Color*, Crimson Press, 1937

Blake, Vernon, *The Art and Craft of Drawing*, Oxford University Press, 1927

Casson, Stanley, *The Technique of Early Greek Sculpture*, Oxford University Press, 1933

Doerner, Max, *The Materials of the Artist and Their Use in Painting*, Harcourt, Brace, 1934

Franklin, Christine (Ladd), *Colour and Colour Theories*, Harcourt, Brace, 1929

Ghyka, Matila, *The Geometry of Art and Life*, Sheed & Ward, 1946

Gill, Eric, *Sculpture*, Ditchling, Sussex, England, 1925

Holmes, Sir C. J., *A Grammar of the Arts*, Macmillan, 1932

————— *Notes on the Science of Picture-Making*, new ed., Stokes, 1928

Laurie, A. P., *The Materials of the Painter's Craft*, Lippincott, 1911

————— *The Painter's Methods and Materials*, Lippincott, 1926

Moreau-Vauthier, Charles, *The Technique of Painting*, Putnam, 1912

Petrina, John, *Art Work; How Produced, How Reproduced*, Pitman, 1934

Phillipps, L. M., *Form and Colour*, Scribner, 1915

Pope, Arthur, *An Introduction to the Language of Drawing and Painting*, 2 vols., Harvard University Press, 1929

Reath, N. A., *The Weaves of Hand-Loom Fabrics*, Pennsylvania Museum, 1927

Robins, W. P., *The Etching Craft*, Dodd, Mead, 1923

Ross, D. W., *On Drawing and Painting*, Houghton Mifflin, 1912

———— *A Theory of Pure Design*, Houghton Mifflin, 1907

Sargent, Walter, *The Enjoyment and Use of Color*, Scribner, 1923

Weitenkampf, Frank, *How to Appreciate Prints*, new ed. rev., Scribner, 1932

Esthetics and Criticism

Barnes, Albert C., *The Art in Painting*, 3d ed. rev., Harcourt, Brace, 1937

Bell, Clive, *Art*, Stokes, 1924

Blake, Vernon, *Relation in Art*, Oxford University Press, 1925

Brown, G. B., *The Fine Arts*, 4th ed., London, 1920

Buermeyer, Laurence, *The Aesthetic Experience*, Barnes Foundation, 1924

Croce, Benedetto, *The Essence of Aesthetic*, London, 1921

Dewey, John, *Art as Experience*, Minton Balch, 1934

Dudley, Louise, and Faricy, Austin, *The Humanities*, McGraw-Hill, 1940

Edman, Irwin, *The World, the Arts and the Artist*, Norton, 1928

Ellis, Havelock, *The Dance of Life*, Houghton Mifflin, 1923

Flaccus, L. W., *The Spirit and Substance of Art*, Crofts, 1926

Fry, Roger E., *Vision and Design*, Brentano's, 1924

———— *Transformations*, Brentano's, 1927

Gill, Eric, *Beauty Looks after Herself*, Sheed & Ward, 1933

Goldwater, Robert, and Treves, Marco, eds., *Artists on Art*, Pantheon Books, 1945

Hamlin, T. F., *The Enjoyment of Architecture*, Scribner, 1921

Hildebrand, Adolf, *The Problem of Form in Painting and Sculpture*, Stechert, 1907

Huneker, J. G., *Promenades of an Impressionist*, Scribner, 1910

Kandinsky, Wassily, *The Art of Spiritual Harmony*, tr. by M. T. H. Sadler, Houghton Mifflin, 1914

Langfield, H. S., *The Aesthetic Attitude*, Harcourt, Brace, 1920

Lethaby, W. R., *Form in Civilization*, Oxford University Press, 1922

Lewisohn, Ludwig, ed., *A Modern Book of Criticism*, Modern Library, Boni & Liveright, 1919

McMahon, A. P., *The Meaning of Art*, Norton, 1930

Maritain, Jacques, *Art and Scholasticism*, Scribner, 1930

Mather, Frank J., Jr., *Estimates in Art*, Scribner, 1916

———— *Estimates in Art; Series II*, Holt, 1931

Munro, Thomas, *Scientific Method in Aesthetics*, Norton, 1928

Neuhaus, Eugen, *The Appreciation of Art*, Ginn, 1924

Ogden, C. K., Richards, I. A., and Wood, J. E. H., *The Foundations of Aesthetics*, London, 1922

Opdyke, H. G., *Art and Nature Appreciation*, Macmillan, 1933

Parker, De W. H., *Analysis of Art*, Yale University Press, 1926

Pearson, R. M., *Experiencing Pictures*, Harcourt, Brace, 1932

Phillips, Duncan, *The Artist Sees Differently*, 2 vols., Weyhe, 1931

Santayana, George, *The Life of Reason*, 2d ed., Scribner, 1922

———— *The Sense of Beauty*, Scribner, 1896

Scott, Geoffrey, *The Architecture of Humanism*, 2d ed. rev., Scribner, 1924

Sirén, Osvald, *Essentials in Art*, Lane, 1920

Smith, S. C. K., *Art and Common Sense*, London, 1932

Wölfflin, Heinrich, *Principles of Art History*, Holt, 1932

Worringer, Wilhelm, *Form in Gothic*, tr. by Herbert Read, London, 1927

Glossary of Technical Terms

(The references to figure numbers are not exhaustive.)

Abacus. A flat block forming the upper member of the capital of a column. Fig. 125Aa.

Ambulatory. A passageway. It may be outside, as in a cloister (*see* Cloister) or inside; used especially of the passageway around the chevet. Fig. 338A4 (p. 339).

Amphora. A jar with two handles for general storage purposes. Figs. 146A, 150A.

Apse. The recess, usually semicircular, at the end of a Roman basilica, or of a Christian church. Figs. 178A, 251A, 338A1. In a Gothic cathedral, the semicircular or polygonal projecting end of the choir. Figs. 338A4, 335A.

Aqueduct. A channel for conducting water; frequently supported by arches. Fig. 174D.

Arabesque. Literally, like the Arabian. Strictly, a Muhammadan decorative motif "composed of gracefully curving scrolls, crossed or interlaced, and bearing stylized motifs suggesting a leaf or flower" (Dimand). Figs. 288B, 292A, 293A. By extension, any kind of fanciful ornament with flowing lines, foliage, fruit, flowers, or figures combined or interwoven.

Arcade. A series of arches supported on piers or columns. Figs. 180A, 255A.

Arch. A constructional device to span an opening; a true arch is curved in shape, and made of wedge-shaped blocks (voussoirs). Figs. 9A, 91A, 180A, 336A, 438A.

Architrave. The lintel or lowest division of the entablature. Fig. 125Aa.

Atrium. The court of a Roman house, near the entrance and partly open to the sky. Fig. 185A. The open court in front of a Christian basilica. Figs. 251A, 316A.

Aureole. A frame or halo around the figure of a sacred personage. Fig. 321A.

Baldacchino (baldachin). In Italy, a canopy on four columns frequently built over an altar. Fig. 433A.

Barrel vault. See Vault.

Basilica. In Roman architecture, a public building for assemblies, especially tribunals, rectangular in plan, with a central nave terminating in an apse. Fig. 178A. In Christian architecture, an early church somewhat resembling the Roman basilica; usually entered through an atrium. Figs. 251A–255A.

Batter. The inward slope of a wall, often almost imperceptible. Fig. 62A.

Bay. A compartment that serves as a unit of division in a building. In a Gothic cathedral the transverse arches and adjacent piers of the arcade divide the building into bays, the design of which is an architectural unit repeated in each bay. Fig. 338A.

Blind arcade (wall arcade). An arcade, applied to a wall surface, with no actual openings, to serve as a decoration. Fig. 318A.

Bottega. A shop. The studio-shop of an Italian artist. Pp. 432, 520.

Brocaded textile. A fabric in which additional weft threads are used to enrich the surface, frequently by the introduction of gold and silver. Fig. 523A.

Broken color. See Divisionism.

Broken pediment. A pediment in which the cornice is broken at the apex. Figs. 529A, 590A.

Buttress. A masonry support to counterbalance the lateral thrust of an arch or vault. A pier buttress is a solid mass of masonry. A flying buttress is an arch or series of arches that carry the thrust over the aisles to the solid buttresses. Figs. 335A, 340A, 350A.

Cabriole. In furniture, a curved leg ending in an ornamental foot, frequent in Queen Anne and Chippendale styles.

Campanile. Italian word for a bell tower. Sometimes it is free-standing; sometimes it is a part of the building. Figs. 254A, 439A.

Capital. The upper member of a column, usually decorated, that serves as a transition from the shaft to the lintel. Fig. 125Aa.

Cartoon. A preliminary drawing for a painting.

Caryatid. A draped female figure that serves, like a column, as a support. Fig. 127A.

Cassone. A large chest. An important piece of Italian furniture. P. 440, note 1.

Cella. The inclosed chamber, the essential feature of a classical temple, in which usually stood the cult statue. Fig. 123A.

Centering. A wooden framework to hold an arch, or vault, during its construction until, when complete, it becomes self-supporting.

Ceramics (keramics). A general term for the art of pottery.

Chalice. A cup or goblet, especially that used in the sacraments of the Church. Figs. 271B, 330A.

Chamfer. To cut off a square angle; to bevel.

Champlevé enamel. A process of enameling in which the design is cut out of a metal plate, leaving thin raised lines that correspond to the cloisons in the cloisonné process, to hold the enamel. P. 23; Fig. 359A.

Chasing. Ornamentation of a metal surface by embossing or cutting away parts. Fig. 521A.

Chevet. The term applied to the apse of a cathedral, together with its ambulatories and apsidal chapels. Fig. 338A4.

Chevron. A zigzag or V-shaped motif of decoration.

Chiaroscuro. Literally, clear-obscure. The treatment of light and dark in a work of art.

Chiton. A Greek tunic, the essential and often only garment of both men and women, the other being the mantle (*see* Himation). There were two kinds of tunics, the Doric and Ionic. The Doric was a rectangular piece of woolen stuff, usually folded over at the top, wrapped about the body and left open at the left side, sleeveless, fastened on the shoulders with buckles, and girdled. Fig. 141A. The Ionic was longer, more voluminous, of soft goods such as cotton or linen, and often caught at intervals by fastenings to form sleeves. Fig. 143B.

Choir. The space separated from the rest of the church by a screen and reserved for the clergy and choir. In the Gothic cathedral it occupies the nave between the crossing and the apse. Fig. 338A.

Choir stalls. Seats for the clergy and choristers, usually ranged along the sides of the choir.

Ciborium. A canopy, usually standing free and supported on four columns, erected over an altar (*see* Baldacchino). Fig. 433A. Also a covered cup used in the sacraments of the Church.

Cire-perdue process. Literally the "wax-lost" process. A method of bronze casting by which the wax in which the figure is modeled is melted away and the space thus left filled with molten bronze. Pp. 12; 521, note 1.

Clerestory. That part of a building which rises above the roofs of the other parts and whose walls contain openings for lighting. Figs. 52c, 64A, 178A, 251A, 340A, 345A.

Cloison. Literally, a partition. A metal wire or narrow strip, usually gold, soldered to a metal base to form cells for holding enamel. P. 23.

Cloisonné enamel. A process of enameling in which strips of metal (cloisons) are soldered to a base, forming cells into which the enamel is poured and fused. P. 23; Figs. 271A, 329A.

Cloister. A court, usually with covered ambulatories on the sides. Figs. 318B, 352A.

Clustered pier. See Compound pier.

Codex. A manuscript in the form of a volume with pages bound together. P. 266, note 1.

Coffer. A sunken ornamental panel in a soffit, vault, or ceiling. Fig. 176A, 253A.

Coin type. The pattern or design used to decorate a coin.

Collage. A composition made by pasting together various materials, such as newspaper, wallpaper, printed text and illustrations, photographs, cloth, etc. Sometimes used interchangeably with "montage," which refers specifically to combinations of photographs. P. 734.

Colonnade. A series or range of columns, usually spanned by lintels. Fig. 118A.

Colonnette. A small column. Fig. 449B.

Colophon. An inscription at the end of a book or manuscript which gives the title, possibly the name of the writer or illustrator, the place of writing, and the date — information now placed on the title page.

Column. A circular weight-carrying member, consisting of a base (sometimes omitted), a shaft, and a capital. Fig. 125A.

Compound or *clustered pier.* A pier composed of a group or cluster of members from each of which springs one or more ribs of the vaulting. Especially characteristic of Gothic architecture. Figs. 317A, 337A.

Console. A bracket, or corbel, usually S-shaped. Fig. 603B.

Cool color. Blue and the hues that approach blue, blue-green, and blue violet.

Corbel. A projecting stone used as a support.

Corbel table. A projecting course of masonry supported by corbels, frequently connected by arches. Fig. 316A.

Corbeled arch. A constructional device for spanning an opening by projecting successive courses of masonry inward until the opening is closed. Figs. 9A, 110A and B, 232A. Not a true arch (*see* Arch).

Cornice. The projecting crowning member of the entablature. Also used for any crowning projection. Fig. 125A.

Cramp. A device, usually metal, to hold together blocks of stone. Fig. 122A.

Crater (krater). A large bowl for mixing wine and water, the usual beverage of the Greeks. Figs. 147c, 149B.

Crocket. A projecting foliate ornament that decorates a pinnacle, gable, buttress, or spire. Its purpose is to break a long line against the sky. Fig. 346ab.

Cromlech. A circle of monoliths. Fig. 41A.

Crossing. The space in a cruciform church where the nave and transept intersect. Fig. 338A.

Crown of an arch or vault. The topmost part of an arch or vault.

Cuneiform. Literally, wedge-shaped. A system of writing, used in Babylonia-Assyria, in which the characters were wedge-shaped. Figs. 86A, 88A.

Custodia. An elaborate tabernacle, usually architectural in design, for the host. Fig. 559A.

Cylix (kylix). A Greek drinking cup. Figs. 146B, 151A.

Dado. A horizontal band, often decorated, at the base of a wall or pedestal.

Damascene. To inlay metal with another kind of metal or other material for decorative purposes. Fig. 306A.

Dentils. Small toothlike projecting blocks in the molding of a cornice. Figs. 125A, 440A, 445B.

Diptych. Consisting of two leaves. A Roman two-hinged writing tablet; used also for commemorative purposes by the Christian Church.

Divisionism or *broken color.* The method of juxtaposing small strokes of pure color directly upon the canvas for the eye to mix at a distance rather than mixing the colors first upon the palette. A method practiced by Constable, Turner, and Delacroix, and perfected by the French impressionists. The principle was used also by the twelfth-century glassworkers.

Dolmen. Several large stones capped with a covering slab.

Donjon. A massive tower forming the stronghold of a medieval castle.

Dowel. A wooden or metallic pin to hold together two pieces of stone or other material. Fig. 122Aa.

Drum. The circular wall which supports a dome. Figs. 177A, 265A, 277A. The circular stones of which a built shaft is made. Fig. 122Ab.

Echinus. Literally a sea urchin. The convex member of a capital, somewhat resembling a sea urchin, that supports the abacus. Fig. 125Aa.

Emboss. To ornament a surface with raised work.

Enamel. See Champlevé, Cloisonné.

Encaustic. Painting by means of wax with which colors are combined, and which is afterwards fused with hot irons, thus fixing the colors. Fig. 759A.

Engaged column. A columnlike member forming part of the wall and projecting more or less from it. Figs. 175A, 180A, 181A.

Engraving. The process of incising a design upon a substance with a sharp instrument (*see* Incising). The process of incising a design upon a copper plate from which a printed impression can be made. Also the impression made from such a plate. Fig. 550A.

Entablature. The part of a building of lintel construction between the capitals of the columns and the roof or upper story. Fig. 125A.

Entasis. A slight, almost imperceptible, curvature in the shaft of a column. Fig. 125Aa.

Etching. The process of engraving a design upon a copper plate, by means of an acid or mordant, from which a printed impression can be taken. Also the impression from a plate so made. Fig. 580A.

Façade. The front of a building, usually the principal front but also applied to the other sides when they are given emphasis by architectural treatment.

Faïence. From Faenza, in Italy, a center for the manufacture of majolica; restricted in meaning by some authors to tin-glazed pottery except porcelain; used by others as a general term for all kinds of glazed earthenware.

Fan vaulting. A development of lierne vaulting, found in English Perpendicular Gothic, in which the ribs radiate from the impost in such a way that they form an inverted cone. Fig. 355A.

Fenestration. Strictly, the arrangement of the windows in a building; by extension, the arrangement of all the openings (windows, doors, arcades) in architectural design.

Ferro-concrete. See Reinforced concrete.

Filigree. Delicate and intricate metallic ornament made of fine wire. Fig. 330A.

Finial. A knoblike ornament, usually with a foliate design, in which a pinnacle terminates. Fig. 346AC.

Flamboyant. Meaning flamelike, applied to the late Gothic style in which the restless type of decoration is based upon wavy lines and the ogee arch. Figs. 350B, 351A.

Flush. On the same level or plane as the adjoining surfaces.

Flute (fluting). Vertical channeling, usually semicircular. Used principally on columns and pilasters. Figs. 118A, 126A, 159A, 175A, 454A.

Flying buttress. See Buttress.

Fresco. Painting on freshly spread moist plaster. The pigments are mixed with water and become chemically incorporated with the plaster. Also a painting so executed. Figs. 473A–477A, 757A, 758A.

Fret or *meander.* An ornament consisting of interlocking angular motifs. Frequently in bands but also covering surfaces. Figs. 148B, 211A and B.

Gargoyle. A waterspout, usually carved or in the form of a grotesque, to throw the water from the gutters away from the walls. Figs. 346Af, 347A.

Genre. Style or subject matter dealing realistically with scenes from everyday life. Figs. 163A and B, 581A and B, 607A, 694A.

Gesso. Prepared plaster mixed with a binding material, used as a ground for painting or for relief. Fig. 635A.

Glaze. A vitreous coating applied to the surface of pottery to make it impervious and for decorative purposes.

Gopura. In Hindu architecture, the high elaborate gateway of the southern Indian temples. Figs. 365A, 366C.

Gouache. Opaque watercolor, or a picture painted in this medium. Figs. 304A, 358A.

Granulation. In jewelry a method of ornamenting, in which small grains of metal, usually gold, are soldered to a flat surface.

Greek cross. A cross consisting of two equal bars meeting at right angles.

Grille. A grating, usually of iron, for protection with visibility. Fig. 440B.

Groin. The edge formed by the intersection of two vaults. Fig. 174A.

Groin vault. See Vault.

Guilloche. An ornament consisting of interlacing curving bands.

Hammer-beam ceiling. An English Gothic open timber ceiling. Fig. 586A.

Haunch. The part of an arch, from a third to two-thirds the distance from the spring to the crown, where the lateral thrust is most strongly exerted.

Hieroglyphs or *hieroglyphics.* A system of writing derived from picture writing, but also phonetic, used by the ancient Egyptians. By extension, applied to other writings also, such as the Mayan. Figs. 48A, 60B, 68A, 69A, 72A, 74A, 236B, 237A and B.

Himation. A Greek mantle worn by men and women over the tunic and draped in various ways. Figs. 144A, 156A.

Historiated. Ornamented with figures that have a representational or narrative element, such as plants, animals, or human figures, in distinction from purely decorative elements. Historiated initial letters were a popular form of manuscript decoration in the Middle Ages. Fig. 523B.

Hue. The name of a color. The primary hues are blue, red, and yellow, which, together with green, orange, and violet, form the chief colors of the spectrum. Between these lie the intermediates which partake of the qualifications of both adjacent hues: red-orange, yellow-orange, yellow-green, blue-green, blue-violet, and red-violet. Fig. 7A.

Hypostyle hall. A hall whose roof is supported by columns. Applied to the colonnaded hall of the Egyptian pylon temple. Figs. 61A, 64A.

Icon. Literally, a portrait or image. Used especially in the Greek Church for the panels containing representations of sacred personages. Fig. 283A.

Iconostasis. In East Christian churches, a screen or partition, with doors and many tiers of icons, that separates the sanctuary from the main body of the church. Fig. 275A.

Illumination. To decorate with gold, silver, and bright color, especially the initial letters of a manuscript. An illuminated manuscript may or may not contain miniatures. Fig. 328A.

Impost. The architectural member from which an arch springs.

Incising. To cut into a surface with a sharp instrument. A method of decoration, especially on metal and pottery. Figs. 89B, 383A.

Intaglio. A design sunk below the surface so that an impression made from it is in relief. Used especially on gems, seals, and dies for coins. Also applied to an object so decorated. Figs. 87A, 155A.

Intercolumniation. The space between the columns in a colonnade.

Isocephaly. Literally, heads equal or on a level. A principle by which natural proportion is distorted so as to bring all the objects in a composition to an equal height for the purpose of design. Figs. 142A, 476A.

Kakemono. A Chinese or Japanese painting in the form of a hanging, not framed, but mounted on brocade.

Keystone. The uppermost voussoir in an arch (*see* Voussoir). Fig. 9AC.

Kiln. An oven in which pottery is baked to harden it and to fuse the glazes.

Lacquer. A varnish containing lac; or a hard varnish obtained from the sap of the lacquer tree, *Rhus vernicifera*, by making incisions in the bark. The latter is the Chinese and Japanese lacquer. Pp. 395–96.

Lantern. A small structure that crowns a dome, turret, or roof with openings for lighting, though frequently the purpose of the lantern is design only. Figs. 439A, 441B, 461A, 588A.

Latin cross. A cross consisting of two bars meeting at right angles, the lower arm longer than the others.

Lierne. A short cross rib inserted between the main ribs of a vaulting. Fig. 354A.

Lintel. A horizontal beam of any material to span an opening. Fig. 9AA.

Lithograph. The impression of a design made on a certain kind of stone by means of a greasy pencil or crayon. P. 21; Fig. 678A.

Loggia. A gallery that has an open arcade or colonnade on one side. Fig. 442A.

Lunette. Literally, little or half moon. Having the shape of a crescent or half-moon; especially a wall space over an arched door or window. Figs. 258A, 454A.

Luster. A thin glaze, usually metallic, sometimes used on pottery to produce a rich, often iridescent, color when it catches the light. Found especially in Persian wares, and in Spanish and Italian majolica. Fig. 307B.

Majolica. Specifically, a kind of Italian pottery coated with a whitish tin enamel, brilliantly painted and often lustered. Fig. 520A.

Makimono. A Chinese or Japanese painting in the form of a long scroll. Fig. 380A.

Mandapam. In Hindu architecture, an assembly hall attached to a temple. Figs. 364A, 366A.

Mastaba. Literally, a bench. A bench-shaped Egyptian tomb. Fig. 46A.

Medallion. A decorative, medal-shaped panel, usually enclosing a figure, portrait, or ornament. Figs. 273A, 301C, 308A, 520A, 555A.

Medium. The vehicle or liquid with which pigment is mixed, such as water, egg, oil, wax. In a more general sense, the substance, material, or agency through which an artist expresses his idea, such as stone, pigment, metal, wood, enamel, words, tones, movements.

Megaron. The large central hall of an Aegean house.

Menhir. Monoliths, uncut or roughly cut, standing singly or in rows or circles. Fig. 41A.

Metope. The space between two triglyphs in a Doric frieze. Fig. 125Aa.

Mihrab. The niche in a mosque which indicates the direction of Mecca. Figs. 287A, 291A.

Minaret. A tall slender tower belonging to a mosque, with one or more balconies from which the summons to prayer is chanted. Figs. 288A, 290A, 371B.

Miniature. A small picture illustrating a manuscript. Derived from the Latin verb *miniare*, to decorate with vermilion. By extension, any small portrait, usually on ivory or porcelain, or anything small. Figs. 304A, 357A, 358A.

Molding. An architectural term for a continuous narrow surface, either projecting or recessed, plain or ornamented, whose purpose is to break up a surface, to accent, or to decorate by means of the light and shade it produces.

Monolith. A single stone block, large in size.

Montage. A composition made by fitting together parts of various photographs. Also motion picture effects produced by superimposing images (*see* Collage).

Mosaic. A surface or decoration made of small pieces of stone or glass (tesserae) set in cement. Figs. 255A and B, 256A, 257A, 258A.

Mosque (masjid). A Muslim place of worship. Figs. 285A, 287A, 288A, 290A, 302A.

Mudéjar. A Muslim who, though subject to a Christian ruler, still retains his religion, laws, and customs. By extension, the Moorish-influenced art of Spain and the Spanish colonies. Figs. 561A, 623A.

Mullion. A vertical bar that separates a window into more than one light. Figs. 354A, 443A.

Narthex. A porch, generally colonnaded or arcaded, forming the vestibule of a church. Fig. 251Ae.

Nave. From *navis*, ship, an early symbol of the Church. The main part of a church, between the chief entrance and the chancel, and separated from the aisles, if present, by piers. Figs. 251Aa, 252A, 338Aa, 345A.

Obverse of a coin or medal. The side of a coin or medal that bears the principal type or inscription. The opposite side is the reverse.

Ogee. A molding having a double or S-shaped curve. An arch of this form. Figs. 350B, 351A.

Order. In classical architecture, the unit of design of the column and entablature. Fig. 125A. *See also* Superimposed order.

Oriel. A window projecting from the face of the wall. Fig. 549A.

Pagoda. In China and Japan, a tower of several stories, usually associated with a temple or monastery. Fig. 214A.

Patina. An incrustation that forms on bronze through chemical action. The term is also applied to incrustation on other materials. P. 212, note 1.

Patio. In Spanish architecture, a court open to the sky.

Pediment. The triangular space (gable) at the end of a building, formed by the sloping roof. Fig. 175A. Also an ornamental feature of this character. Figs. 177A, 458B.

Pendentive. A concave, triangular piece of masonry (a triangular section of a hemisphere). By means of pendentives a dome can be erected over a square area, and the pendentives carry its load to the isolated supports at the four corners. Figs. 9Ae, 260Aa, 261A.

Peripteral. Surrounded by a colonnade. Fig. 118A, 123Ae, f, and g.

Peristyle. A continuous range of columns surrounding a building or a court. Fig. 118A, 123Ae, f, and g.

Perspective. The science of representing, on one plane, distance and distant objects as they appear to the eye. Fig. 527A.

Photomontage. A combination of several photographs or parts of photographs into one composition. Fig. 787A. *See* Montage.

Pier. A vertical masonry support to carry the load of a superstructure.

Pilaster. A flat rectangular member projecting from the wall, of which it forms a part. It usually carries a base and a capital and is often fluted. Figs. 459A, 461A, 463A, 600A, **643A**.

Pile fabric. A textile in which extra warps or wefts, looped above the surface and then cut, form a pile or nap, as in velvets and carpets. Figs. 308A, 309A, 523A.

Pillar. A general inclusive term used for a weight-carrying member of any kind. It may be a pier or a column. Also an isolated structure used for a commemorative purpose.

Pinnacle. An upright architectural member generally ending in a small spire, often ornamental, but used functionally in Gothic architecture to give additional weight to a buttress or an angle pier. Figs. 341A5, 346A, 350A.

Porcelain. Strictly speaking, pottery made on a base of kaolin that is translucent, impervious, and resonant. By extension the term is sometimes applied to pottery that is translucent, whether made of kaolin or not. Fig. 383A.

Pottery. Objects of any kind that are made of clay and hardened by firing.

Predella. Literally, a footstool. In Italian art the narrow panel, at the back of the altar, on which the altarpiece rests. P. 502, note 1.

Putto (pl. putti). A young boy. A favorite subject in Italian painting and sculpture. Figs. 444B, 449B.

Pylon. The monumental entrance of an Egyptian temple. Figs. 62A, 63B, 68A.

Quoins. Large, slightly projecting stones at the angle of a building, sometimes rusticated. Fig. 458B.

Raking cornice. The cornice on the sloping sides of a pediment. Fig. 125Aa.

Ramp. An inclined plane that takes the place of steps in the ascent of a structure. Figs. 83A, 90A.

Reinforced concrete (ferro-concrete). Concrete strengthened by iron or steel network or bars imbedded before the concrete hardens.

Reja. A Spanish wrought-iron grille to inclose a shrine or chapel. Fig. 559B.

Relief. In sculpture, figures projecting from a background to which they are attached. They may be high (high relief), low (low or bas relief), or sunk into the surface (hollow relief or intaglio).

Reliquary. A small receptacle for holding a sacred relic. Usually of precious material richly decorated. Fig. 359A.

Repoussé. The process of decorating metal by beating it into relief from the back, leaving the impression on the face. The metal plate is hammered into a hollow mold of wood or some pliable material with hammer and punch and finished with the graver. Figs. 89B, 117A, 190A, 244A, 420A.

Retable. Shortened form of *retrotabulum*, behind the altar. An architectural screen or wall-facing set up behind an altar, usually containing painting, sculpture, carving, or other decorations. Especially elaborate is the Spanish retable. Fig. 557A.

Reverse of a coin or medal. The side opposite the obverse. *See* Obverse.

Rib. A masonry arch, usually projecting from the surface and molded. In Gothic architecture the ribs form the framework of the vaulting. Figs. 317A, 324B, 336A, 337A, 345A, 354A.

Rococo. A style of ornament particularly popular about the time of Louis XV. It consists of a profusion of rockwork, wheels, scrolls, and the like. P. 602, note 1; Fig. 602A.

Roof crest. A pierced wall rising above the roof. Found in Mayan architecture. Figs. 232A, 233A.

Rose or wheel window. The round window with tracery frequently found on the façade of Romanesque and Gothic churches. Figs. 333A, 348A and B, 349A and B, 350A.

Rusticated stone. Stone masonry with beveled joints and roughened surface. Figs. 438A, 458B, 665A.

Sculpture in the round. Free-standing figures, carved or modeled in three dimensions.

Sgraffito. Decoration produced by scratching through a surface layer of plaster, glazing, etc., revealing a differently colored ground. Also pottery or other ware so decorated.

Shaft. The part of a column between the capital and base. Fig. 125Aa.

Shikara. In Hindu architecture the high tower that rises over the shrine of the temples of Vishnu. Figs. 364A, 366A.

Soffit. The underside of an architectural member, such as an arch, lintel, cornice, or stairway.

Spandrel. The triangular space between the curve of an arch and the rectangle formed by inclosing moldings. It is frequently decorated. Fig. 263A.

Splayed opening. A splay (a shortened form of "display") is a large chamfer. In splayed openings the wall is cut away diagonally so that the outer opening is wider than the inner. Figs. 348A and B, 349A and B.

Squinch. An architectural device to make a transition from a square to a polygonal base for a dome. It may be composed of lintels, corbels, or arches. Figs. 9Af, 260Ab, 290A.

Stalactite. A pendant architectural ornament common in Muhammadan architecture. P. 290, note 1; Figs. 290A, 303A.

Stele. A stone slab or pillar used commemoratively, as a gravestone, or to mark a site. Fig. 215A.

Stilted arch or dome. An arch or dome having its

springing higher than the level of the impost. Fig. 277A.

Stone mosaic. A kind of decoration made with small pieces of cut stone embedded in cement. Used most effectively by the Maya. Fig. 410A.

Stoneware. A kind of pottery of the nature of porcelain but with a coarser base.

Stringcourse. A horizontal molding to indicate a division in the architectural design. Figs. 345A, 348A.

Stucco. Fine plaster or cement used as a coating for walls or for decorations. Fig. 587A.

Stupa. In the Buddhist architecture of India, a domelike structure which marks a sacred site. Fig. 198A.

Stylobate. The upper member of the base of a building that serves as a continuous base of the columns. Fig. 125Aa.

Superimposed order. The placing of one order of architecture above another in an arcaded or colonnaded building; usually Doric on the first story, Ionic on the second, and Corinthian on the third. Found in the Greek *stoas*, used widely by the Romans, and thence by the Renaissance builders. Figs. 180A, 465A.

Tempera. A technical method of painting upon an especially prepared panel with pigment mixed with egg or glue, or milk, etc. P. 18; Figs. 468A–472A, 484A.

Terra cotta. Hard baked clay. Used for sculpture and building material. It may or may not be glazed or painted. Figs. 163B, 168A, 169A, 456B.

Tesserae. Small pieces of glass or stone used in making mosaics.

Textile. A fabric made by interlacing or weaving threads.

Thrust. The outward force exerted by an arch or vault that must be counterbalanced by abutments.

Tracery. Stone ornament that decorates a window and holds the glass; particularly characteristic of Gothic. In plate tracery, the stone is pierced with geometric designs. In bar tracery the design is built up of stone bars or moldings fitted together on the principle of the arch. Bar tracery has greater possibilities for design than plate, and soon replaced the latter. Most of the great rose, lancet, and Perpendicular windows are bar tracery. Fig. 354A. The western rose of Chartres, Fig. 333A, is plate; those at Amiens and Reims, Figs. 348B, 349A, bar. Tracery is also used in woodwork. Fig. 586A. In India entire windows were filled with elaborate marble tracery. Fig. 372A.

Transept. The arm of a cruciform church at right angles with the nave. Fig. 338Ad.

Triforium. In a Gothic cathedral, the space between the vault of the aisle and the sloping roof over it; it is represented in the nave wall by the story that lies between the ground-story arcade and the clerestory. Figs. 337A, 340A, 345A.

Triglyph. The projecting grooved member of the Doric frieze separating the metopes. Figs. 118A, 125Aa.

Tympanum. The space over a doorway inclosed by the lintel and the arch. Figs. 312A, 321A.

Uraeus. The serpent used as a symbol of royalty in Egyptian art. Figs. 60B, 79A.

Value of a color. The amount of light and dark in a color. The greater the amount of light, the higher its value; the greater amount of dark, the lower its value.

Vault. A stone, brick, or concrete roof constructed on the arch principle. A barrel vault is semicylindrical in shape. Figs. 174A, 459A. A groin vault consists of two barrel vaults intersecting at right angles. Figs. 174B and c, 179A. A ribbed vault is one in which a framework of ribs supports light masonry. Figs. 324B, 336A, 337A, 345A. A dome is a hemispherical vault. Fig. 176A.

Volute. A spiral scroll, especially characteristic of the Greek Ionic capital. Figs. 125Ab, 126A, 149B.

Voussoir. A wedge-shaped block used in the construction of a true arch. The central voussoir, which sets the arch, is called the keystone. *See* Arch. Fig. 9AC.

Wainscot. A wooden facing for an interior wall, usually paneled. Fig. 587A.

Wall arcade. See Blind arcade.

Warm color. Red and the hues that approach red, orange, yellow, and possibly yellow-green.

Warp. The lengthwise threads with which a loom is strung.

Weft (woof). The thread which is inserted in the warp at right angles in the process of weaving.

Woodcut. A design engraved upon a block of wood in such a way that all the wood is cut away to a slight depth except the lines forming the design. Also the printed impression made from the wood block. Figs. 394A, 395A, 524A, 550B, 552A.

Ziggurat. In Babylonia-Assyria, a staged tower with ramps for ascent. Fig. 83A.

NOTE ON PRONUNCIATION

The problem of the pronunciation of foreign names is a very real problem because of (1) the lack of any one exhaustive, authoritative source; (2) the differences among authorities on points of pronunciation, frequently due to dialect; (3) the inherent difficulties and varying systems of transliteration of non-Latin alphabets; (4) the fact that English vowels do not coincide in sound with foreign and that there are no English equivalents for some foreign consonants; (5) the tendency to anglicize in the case of well known names; (6) the difficulty in finding authority in the case of modern artists.

The key and pronunciation here given represent a simplified cross section of the following sources, in addition to assistance from individual specialists, and at times an arbitrary choice of one source in preference to another:

The Century Dictionary and Cyclopedia, Century Company, 1911, vol. XI, "The Century Cyclopedia of Names"
The Columbia Encyclopedia, Columbia University Press, 1946
Lippincott's New Gazetteer, Philadelphia, Lippincott, 1931
Dictionary of Pronunciation of Artists' Names, by G. E. Kaltenbach, Art Institute of Chicago
The Standard Dictionary, Funk and Wagnalls, 1913
Webster's New International Dictionary, Second edition, Merriam, 1945
The standard foreign dictionaries

While the accent has been used in most cases it may be well to point out that stress is equally distributed in Far Eastern languages.

KEY TO PRONUNCIATION

ă as in făt	ĕ as in mĕt	ŏ as in tŏp	ŭ as in tŭb
ā as in fāte	ē as in mēte	ō as in ōde	ū as in blūe
å as in senåte	ê as in sociêty, bêgin	ô as in ôbey	ú as in cúrve, French un, le
ä as in fär	ĭ as in pĭn	ô as in ôff	ü as in French mur, German über
	ī as in nīne	ōō as in tōō	ø as in French feu, fleur, German Goethe
		ou as in house	

Two dots after a vowel (ā:) indicates the lengthening of that same vowel sound. A tilde over a vowel (ã) indicates nasalization of the same sound, as in French Amiens, Redon, champlevé.

ch as in church	ng as in singer
dz as in adze	ŗ as in French metre
g as in guest	s as in sing
h as in ham	th as in thin
kh as in Scotch loch, German koch	z as in zebra
ļ approximates l as in William	zh as in azure
ñ as in canyon	

INDEX

Abacus (ăb′-ŭ-kŭs), 126, 128, 158, 263, *illus.*, 125; definition, 793
Abbas I, Shah (1587–1628), 302
Abbaye-aux-Dames (ä-bĕ[y]ē′ô-dâm), Caen, France, plan, *diag.*, 338–39
Abbaye-aux-Hommes (ô-zôm) (St. Etienne), Caen, France, 323–24, *illus.*, 324; buttresses, 341, *illus.*, 340; vaulting, *illus.*, 340
Abbey, Edwin A. (1852–1911), 688
Abbey churches, 313, 314, 325
ABI building, Rio de Janeiro, 718–19, *illus.*, 718
Absolute monarchy, 531, 613–15
Absolute reality, 739
Abstraction and abstractionism: African Negro use, 401; Brancusi, 776; Canada, 753; Cézanne, 724; Giotto, 724; machine arts, 784; Manet, 678; painting, 473, 735; Picasso, 734; Ryder, 692; sculpture, 776; Uruguay, 765; wood-carving, 775
Abusir (ä-bōō-sēr′), Egypt, *map*, 43. *See also* Sahure, pyramid of
Abydos (ŭ-bī′-dŏs), Egypt, *map*, 43. *See also* Seti I, temple of
Academic school (Renaissance), 464–65
Academicians (Paris c. 1850), 677, 678
Académie Française, 664; Latin America, influence in, 697, 698
Academy, Venice: *Feast in the House of Levi* (Veronese), 513, *illus.*, 515; *Miracle of St. Mark* (Tintoretto), 512–13, *illus.*, 513
Academy of Arts (Russia), 614
Acanthus, 158, 180, 181, 440; Santa Sophia, 260, 262, *illus.*, 263
Achaeans (ŭ-kē′-ŭnz), 106
Achaemenian Persian art (ăk-ê-mĕn′-ĭ-ŭn), 98–103; architecture, 99–100; bibliography, 103; metalwork, 100–03; sculpture, 99–100
Achaemenidae (people), 98 fn., 99
Acolman convent, Mexico, 618
Acropolis (ŭ-krŏp′-ŭ-lĭs), Athens, 120, *illus.*, 26; *Athena Lemnia* (Phidias), 139–40, *illus.*, 141; Athens votive figures, 132–33, *illus.*, 132. *See also* Parthenon
Acropolis Museum, Athens, Erechtheum, carving from, *illus.*, 128; Jar-Carriers (Parthenon), 143–44, *illus.*, 144; *Nike Fixing Her Sandal*, *illus.*, 145
Actopán, fortress-church, Mexico, 618; frescoes, 634
Adam, Robert (1728–1792), 591–92; dining-room, St. James Square, London, 591, *illus.*, 593
Adams Memorial, Rock Creek Cemetery, Washington, 771
Addison Gallery of American Art, Phillips Academy, Andover, Mass., *Horizontal Spines* (Calder), 779, *illus.*, 781
Adobe (a·dō′bĭ), 240, 633

Adoration of the Lamb (J. and H. van Eyck), 534–37, 538, 540, *illus.*, 536
Adoration of the Magi (da Vinci), 491 (*illus.*)
Adoration of the Shepherds (Ghirlandaio), 540 fn.
Adoration of the Trinity (Dürer), 551
Advertising design, 787 (*illus.*)
Aegean art (ê·jē′ăn), 104–17; architecture, 106–12; bibliography, 117; metalwork, 114–17; painting, 106–12; pottery, 114–17; sculpture, 113–14
Aegean Sea, *map*, 43
Aegina (ē-jĭ′-nŭ), Greece, *map*, 121; Temple of Aphia, *Archer*, 135, *illus.*, 133; eastern pediment, 135, 136, *illus.*, 133
Aeolus (ē′-ô-lŭs) (Liberale da Verona), *illus.*, 523
Aeschylus (ĕs′-kĭ-lŭs), 120
African art, 399–404; bibliography, 408; carving, 399–400, 402; human figure, 400–01; Negro art, 399–404; painting, 403–04; prehistoric, 40; sculpture, 399–400, *map*, 400; tribes, 400; west-central, 399, *map*, 400
Afro-Cuban Dance (Carreño), 766–67, *illus.*, 768
Agora (ăg′ô-rŭ) (market place), 119
Agra (ä′-grä). *See* Taj Mahall
Ahmadabad (ä-mŭd-ä-bäd′), carved marble window (15th cent.), 372–73, *illus.*, 372
Ahriman (ä′-rĭ-mŭn), 98
Ahuramazda (ä-hŭ-rä-măz′-dŭ), 98
Airplanes, 784, *illus.*, 785
Aisle, Gothic use of, *diags.*, 338, 339
Ajanta (ŭ-jŭn′-tŭ), caves, India, 203–05, *illus.*, 205; frescoes, 229
Akhetaton (äkh′-ĕ-tä-tôm), Egypt, 57. *See also* Amarna
Akhnaton (Egyptian king), 57–58, 68; naturalism, 75; Nofretete, 70; palace, *illus.*, 75, 76; portrait, 70 (*illus.*); religious revolution, 80
Akkad (city), Sumeria, 82; *map*, 43
Ala (wing), 184, *diag.*, 185
Alaska: Indians, 651–52; map, 231
Albert Einstein (Epstein), *illus.*, 775
Alberti (äl-bĕr′-tê) (1404–1472), 438, 439
Alcalá (äl-kä-lä′), Spain, Archiepiscopal palace, 556; ceiling, 561 (*illus.*)
Aldobrandini Villa (äl-dô-brän-dē′-nê), Frascati, Italy, 528
Aleijadinho, O. (ä-lä-zhä-dê′nyō, ô) (Lisboa, Antonio Francisco), 630, 632
Aleppo, Syria, mosques, 286 fn.
Alexander, the Great, 99, 160, 201 fn.
Alexander VII (pope), tomb, St. Peter's, Rome, 529
Alexander I, Russian czar (1801–1825), 613–14
Alexander, John W. (1856–1915), 687 fn.
Alexander Mosaic, 164–65 (*illus.*)
Alexandria, Egypt, 286
Alhambra (äl·hăm′brä), 294–95

INDEX

INDEX

JOHN ASKLING: Indexer